National Trust

Handbook 2010

The complete guide for
members and visitors.
1 January to 31 December 2010

For much more about
National Trust places, visit
www.nationaltrust.org.uk

Everything you can do with the National Trust

Contents

Visit

Membership

People and places, clockwise from top left: **farm produce at Chirk Castle in Wrexham, Wales; the Brecon Beacons in Powys, Wales; Arlington Court and the National Trust Carriage Museum, Devon; Farne Islands, Northumberland; Cornish Mines and Engines, Cornwall; Petworth House and Park, West Sussex; Osterley Park and House, Middlesex; Ickworth House, Park and Gardens, Suffolk.** *Previous page, clockwise from top left:* **Scobbiscombe in Devon; Lode Mill at Anglesey Abbey, Cambridgeshire; red squirrel on Brownsea Island, Dorset; the Butler's Pantry at Uppark House and Garden, West Sussex; Brimham Rocks, Yorkshire.**

Enjoy your free time in

2010

Spring awakening
Banish those winter blues and give your spirits a lift by experiencing nature's re-awakening at first hand. Join your friends for a stroll and spot spring flowers breaking through frosty landscapes, rise and shine with a 'dawn chorus' walk and listen out for the songbirds – they like to put on a good show – or tickle your taste buds and be inspired by the fresh, new dishes in our cafés and restaurants.

Before your very eyes
Several National Trust places offer stunning displays of bluebells:
186
Blickling Hall, Gardens and Park, Norfolk. Enjoy time with friends and explore the delights of the secret garden, woodland dell and 18th-century orangery.
338
Dinefwr Park and Castle, Carmarthenshire. You will be spoilt for choice; there are several bluebell walks to choose from throughout this wooded estate, with its ancient trees.
363
Mount Stewart House, Garden and Temple of the Winds, County Down, Northern Ireland. Immerse yourself in the exotic; this luxuriant garden is set in a unique microclimate.

Blickling

Hidcote

Summer treats
Long evenings and, hopefully, sun-filled days mark the arrival of summer. Make the most of these by spending as much time as possible in the fresh air. Go adventuring and enjoy real family time – there are hundreds of family events to choose from during the summer holidays. Take a walk on the wild side and get back to nature, 'roll up, roll up' and be transported to faraway lands through open-air theatre, or try something completely different – from archery lessons to fancy dress. Alternatively, lovers of tranquillity can seek out the perfect picnic spot.

Bring me sunshine
For the perfect summer's day treat head to:
66
Hidcote Manor Garden, Gloucestershire. There is always something to delight in this garden, one of England's finest. Its exquisite garden 'rooms' offer surprises all year round.
161
The Vyne, Hampshire. The charming gardens and grounds showcase an ornamental lake and one of England's first summerhouses.
200
Oxburgh Hall, Norfolk. As well as the mysterious and intriguing house, with its children's trails and quizzes, there is an orchard, captivating kitchen garden and woodland walks to explore.

Buy prints of images in this *Handbook* from www.ntprints.com

Autumn flavour

Enjoy autumn's offerings. Relish the simple pleasure of crunching leaves underfoot and the priceless satisfaction of easing conkers from their prickly cases. Visit ancient orchards and wander among trees laden with ripe fruit, then celebrate and champion local, seasonal varieties at food festivals and farmers' markets. Or head to the woods and wonder at the technicolor display, as leaves turn a variety of fiery hues. Finally, treat yourself to a spot of pure 'me-time' by indulging in some of our mouth-watering autumnal puddings.

Setting the tone

To find stunning autumn colour visit:

94
Stourhead, Wiltshire. With a magnificent lake as its centrepiece, and temples and follies galore, this world-famous iconic garden is alive with vivid autumn colour.
151
Scotney Castle, Kent. Bright oranges and reds light up the garden, and there are numerous walks to explore on the wider estate and through the woodland, as well as wonderful views.
334
Bodnant Garden, Conwy, Wales. Discover a seasonal beauty, with stunning displays throughout its upper gardens, lower wooded valley and wild garden.

Giant's Causeway

Stourhead

Winter respite

Find yourself in a world far away from the frenetic high street. Explore houses dressed for the festive season, alive with carol singing and the comforting aroma of mulled spices and log fires. Take tea in one of our Historic House Hotels (see overleaf), then wrap up against the chill and brave the elements to discover the calming stillness of our gardens in winter. Delight in the variety of treats on offer at Christmas markets and pick up some last-minute gifts. Or create unforgettable memories for your children, by taking them to visit Father Christmas in his magical grotto.

The great escape

For winter adventures don't miss:

44
Castle Drogo, Devon. Explore the last castle to be built in England. Its garden stands in stark contrast to Dartmoor's ancient woodland.
159
Stowe Landscape Gardens, Buckinghamshire. More than 40 monuments and temples nestle among the wintry open spaces – the most perfectly tranquil place.
362
Giant's Causeway, County Antrim, Northern Ireland. Steeped in history and legend, this iconic World Heritage Site is just the thing to revive the spirits midwinter. It is a magical place, and we are determined that it shall remain so, which is why we have launched our appeal, 'A Giant Cause', which aims to raise £2.25 million to spend on protecting and enhancing this special place for future generations. Find out more at www.agiantcause.com

The Historic House Hotels of the National Trust

Bodysgallen Hall in North Wales, Hartwell House near Aylesbury (long leasehold), and Middlethorpe Hall in York make up the three properties of Historic House Hotels. These very special places became the inalienable property of the National Trust by donation in September 2008. All three are already accessible to the public as hotels, and all warmly welcome guests to stay, to dine in the restaurants and to enjoy afternoon tea. All paying guests to the hotels are welcome to walk in the gardens and parks.

Below: **Middlethorpe Hall Hotel, Restaurant and Spa (page 304). Built in 1699, this quintessentially William and Mary house was once the home of the 18th-century diarist Lady Mary Wortley Montagu. Furnished with antiques and fine paintings and set in manicured gardens with parkland beyond, Middlethorpe Hall's country-house character remains unspoilt.**

Above: **Bodysgallen Hall Hotel, Restaurant and Spa (page 335). This Grade I listed 17th-century house has the most spectacular views towards Conwy Castle and Snowdonia. The romantic gardens, which have won awards for their restoration, include a rare parterre – filled with sweet-smelling herbs – as well as several follies, a cascade, walled garden and formal rose gardens. Beyond, the hotel's parkland offers miles of stunning walks.**

Left: **Hartwell House Hotel, Restaurant and Spa (page 131). The most famous resident of this elegant stately home was Louis XVIII, the exiled King of France, who lived here with his Queen and members of his court for five years from 1809. Only one hour from central London, the magnificent grounds include a romantic ruined church, lake and bridge.**

Top ten properties without a car

Aberconwy House (page 333)
Only a few minutes' walk from Conwy station is this medieval merchant's house, the only one to survive in the walled town and well interpreted by an audio-visual presentation.

Birmingham Back to Backs (page 242)
Only a short walk from New Street station, this court of working-class houses represents the way millions of people lived in the country's industrial cities.

Brownsea Island (page 42)
A pleasant boat ride from Poole Quay, Sandbanks, Bournemouth or Swanage, this oasis of peace for red squirrels and visitors also has a rich history.

Greenway (page 62)
What better way to reach the summer home of crime writer Agatha Christie than steam train to Kingswear and ferry to Dartmouth for a cruise up the glorious Dart Estuary?

Hadrian's Wall and Housesteads Fort (page 321)
The AD122 bus links the key sites along the wall with several railway stations, making it an ideal way to explore the most extensive Roman site in Britain.

Ham House (page 174)
The walk along the River Thames from Richmond is one of the finest stretches of waterway in the vicinity of London. Ham House and garden is a late 17th-century jewel.

Lanhydrock (page 75)
The carriage drive from Bodmin Parkway station is the perfect approach to the magnificent gatehouse and country house remarkable for its extensive servants' quarters.

Mount Stewart House, Garden and Temple of the Winds (page 363)
A bus from Belfast drops you at the gates of this opulent Neo-classical house and the celebrated gardens created by Lady Londonderry. The Temple of the Winds is one of the most romantically sited buildings in the UK.

Ormesby Hall (page 307)
Easily reached by bus, this 18th-century mansion has a fine Victorian laundry, game larder and a welcoming tea-room – as well as model railway layouts to delight the young and not so young.

Quarry Bank Mill and Styal Estate (page 284)
A half-mile walk from well-served Styal station brings visitors to this exceptionally complete water- and steam-powered textile mill within an estate that encompasses the owner's house and garden and the Apprentice House.

Benefits of membership

Join the National Trust and enjoy:

- free entry and parking at more than 300 historic houses and gardens;

- free parking at our many countryside and coastline locations;

- the members' *Handbook* – the complete guide to all the places you can visit;

- regional newsletters packed with details of special events at locations near you;

- three editions of our magazine exclusively for members – featuring news, views, gardening and letters;

- information on your local supporter groups and details on how you can get involved;

- membership also entitles you to free admission to properties cared for by the National Trust for Scotland.

Best of all, you will know that you are helping to protect the places you enjoy for ever, for everyone.

Using the Handbook

This *Handbook* gives details of the many National Trust places you can visit, including opening arrangements for 2010 from the start of January to the end of December, and available facilities. Property entries are arranged by area (see map on page 11) and are ordered alphabetically. Maps for each area appear on pages 12 to 24, and these show properties with a charge for entry, together with a selection of coast and countryside places. Maps also show main population centres.

To find places within a particular county/administrative area, please refer to the index on page 390. County names are included in the postal address of individual entries.

Date at which the place (or first part of the place) was acquired by the National Trust.

A simple grid reference is given in each entry. These refer first to the number of the appropriate map in this Handbook, then to the grid square, for example ④ K6.

Property features are indicated by symbols. The key to the symbols is on the inside front cover.

Ordnance Survey (Landranger series or OSNI for Northern Ireland) grid references are given at the beginning of the 'Getting here' section.

Information regarding access is shown using symbols. For the key to the Access symbols, please see the inside front cover.

Baddesley Clinton

Rising Lane, Baddesley Clinton, Warwickshire B93 0DQ

Map ④ K6   🏛️ ✝️ ✿ 🔔 ⛲ 🍵 | 1980 |

Getting here: 139:SP199723. **Foot**: Heart of England Way passes close by. **Train**: Lapworth, 2 miles; Birmingham International 9 miles. **Road**: ¾ miles west of A4141 Warwick–Birmingham road, at Chadwick End, 7½ miles north west of Warwick, 6 miles south of M42 exit 5; 15 miles south east of central Birmingham. **Parking**: free, 100 yards.

Finding out more: 01564 783294 or baddesleyclinton@nationaltrust.org.uk

Access for all: ♿ 🚻 📷 🖥️ 🚶 👁️
Building 🔼 ♿ ⬇️ Grounds 🔼 ♿ ➡️ ⬇️

For information on prices please telephone 0844 800 1895 or visit **www.nationaltrust.org.uk**

Opening arrangements

The information is given in table format, intended to show at a glance when places or parts of places are open and when they are closed.

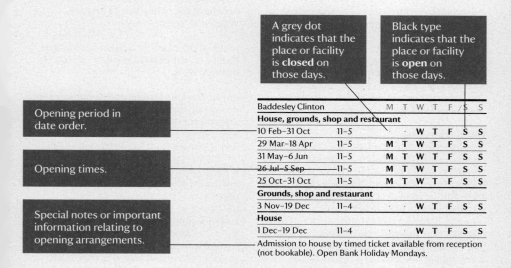

A grey dot indicates that the place or facility is **closed** on those days.

Black type indicates that the place or facility is **open** on those days.

Opening period in date order.

Opening times.

Special notes or important information relating to opening arrangements.

Baddesley Clinton		M	T	W	T	F	S	S
House, grounds, shop and restaurant								
10 Feb–31 Oct	11–5	·	·	W	T	F	S	S
29 Mar–18 Apr	11–5	M	T	W	T	F	S	S
31 May–6 Jun	11–5	M	T	W	T	F	S	S
26 Jul–5 Sep	11–5	M	T	W	T	F	S	S
25 Oct–31 Oct	11–5	M	T	W	T	F	S	S
Grounds, shop and restaurant								
3 Nov–19 Dec	11–4	·	·	W	T	F	S	S
House								
1 Dec–19 Dec	11–4	·	·	W	T	F	S	S

Admission to house by timed ticket available from reception (not bookable). Open Bank Holiday Mondays.

Please note the following points about this year's *Handbook*:

- areas are shown in hectares (1 hectare = 2.47 acres) with the acres equivalent in brackets. Short distances are shown in yards (1 yard = 0.91 metre); longer distances are measured in miles. Heights are shown in metres.

- although opening times and arrangements vary considerably from place to place and from year to year, most houses will be open during the period 1 March to 31 October inclusive, usually on three or more days per week between about noon and 5pm.

Please note that, unless otherwise stated in the property entry, last admission is 30 minutes before the stated closing time.

- we make every effort to ensure that property opening times and available facilities are as published, but very occasionally it is essential to change these at short notice. Always check the current *Handbook* for details and, if making a special journey, please telephone in advance for confirmation. You can also check our website **www.nationaltrust.org.uk**

- when telephoning a property, please remember that we can provide a better service if you call on a weekday morning, on a day when the property is open. Alternatively, call our Membership Department on 0844 800 1895, seven days a week (9 to 5:30 Monday to Friday, 9 to 4 at weekends and bank holidays).

Extra copies of the National Trust *Handbook* are available, while stocks last.

Introductory notes

Car parking sticker
This year your car parking sticker can be found between pages 384 and 385 of this *Handbook*, lightly glued to a bookmark which can also be easily removed.

If you need a replacement or additional car sticker just ask at your next property visit (see bookmark page 385).

Do please also remember that the parking sticker is not in any way a substitute for your valid membership card, which should continue to be shown to staff on request whenever you enter Trust places and pay and display car parks.

Gift Aid on Entry
This year, most National Trust places will again be operating the Gift Aid on Entry scheme at their admission points. Where the scheme is operating, non-members are offered a choice between paying the standard admission price or paying the Gift Aid Admission, which includes a 10 per cent voluntary donation. Gift Aid Admissions enable the National Trust to reclaim tax on the whole amount paid* – currently an extra 25 per cent – potentially a very significant boost to property funds.

The admission prices shown on the National Trust's website, or which are available on request from the Trust's Membership Department, are inclusive of the 10 per cent voluntary donation where places are operating the Gift Aid on Entry scheme, but both the standard admission price and the Gift Aid Admission will be displayed at the place and on our website.

Most National Trust members already pay their subscriptions using Gift Aid, helping the Trust to the tune of many millions of pounds every year at no extra cost to themselves. If you would like to know more about Gift Aid please contact the Membership Department on 0844 800 1895.

* Gift Aid donations must be supported by a valid Gift Aid declaration, and a Gift Aid declaration can only cover donations made by an individual for him/herself or for him/herself and members of his/her family.

The National Trust
– looks after special places for ever, for everyone.

– is a registered charity, founded in 1895, to look after places of historic interest or natural beauty permanently for the benefit of the nation across England, Wales and Northern Ireland.

– is independent of the Government and we receive no direct state grant or subsidy for our core work.

– one of Europe's leading conservation bodies, protecting through ownership, management and covenants 250,000 hectares (617,763 acres) of land of outstanding natural beauty and 709 miles (1,141 kilometres) of coastline.

– is dependent on the support of its 3.8 million members and its visitors, volunteers, partners and benefactors.

– is responsible for historic buildings dating from the Middle Ages to modern times, ancient monuments, gardens, landscape parks and farmland leased to over 1,000 tenant farmers.

– has the unique statutory power to declare land inalienable. Such land cannot be voluntarily sold, mortgaged or compulsorily purchased against the Trust's wishes without special parliamentary procedure. This special power means that protection by the Trust is for ever.

– spends all its income on the care and maintenance of the land and buildings in its protection, but cannot meet the cost of all its obligations and so is always in need of financial support.

Our strategic aims are:

– engaging supporters;
– improving our conservation and environmental performance;
– investing in our people;
– financing our future.

Area maps

This key shows how England, Wales and Northern Ireland are divided into eleven areas for the purposes of this *Handbook*, and displayed on seven maps. The maps show those places which have individual entries as well as many additional coast and countryside sites in the care of the National Trust.

In order to help with general orientation, the maps show main roads and population centres. However, the plotting of each site serves only as a guide to its location. (Full-scale maps can be purchased from National Trust shops.) Please note that some countryside places, for example those in the Lake District, cover many thousands of hectares. In such cases the symbol is placed centrally as an indication of general location.

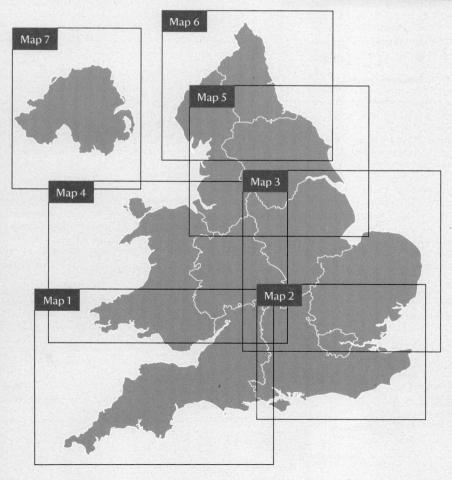

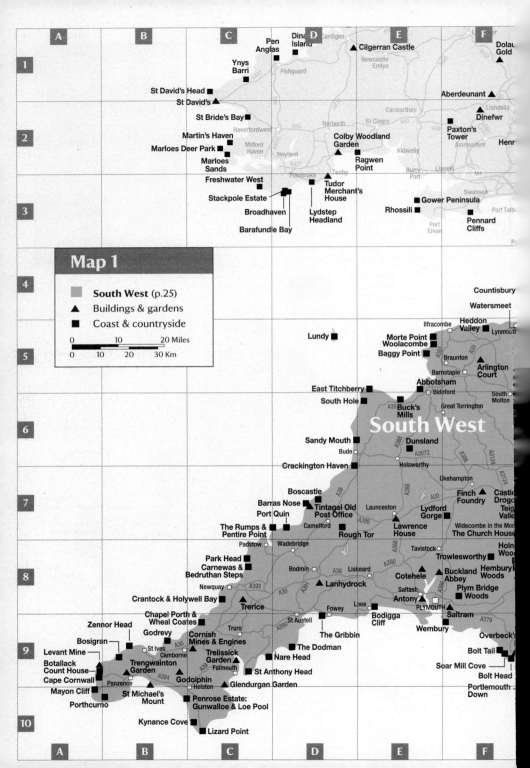

Map 1

South West (p.25)

▲ Buildings & gardens

■ Coast & countryside

0 — 10 — 20 Miles
0 — 10 — 20 — 30 Km

South West

Row 1 (top):
Pen Anglas ■
Dinas Island ■
Cardigan
Cilgerran Castle ▲
Dolau Gold ▲

Ynys Barri ■
Fishguard
Newcastle Emlyn

St David's Head ▲
St David's ▲

Aberdeunant ▲

St Bride's Bay ■
Carmarthen
Llandeilo
Dinefwr ■

Martin's Haven ■
Narberth
St Clears
Paxton's Tower ■
Henr

Marloes Deer Park ■
Haverfordwest
Milford Haven
Neyland
Colby Woodland Garden ▲
Kidwelly
Ammanford

Marloes Sands ■
Pembroke
Ragwen Point ■
Burry Port

Freshwater West ■
Tenby
Tudor Merchant's House ▲
Swansea

Stackpole Estate ■
Rhossili ■
Gower Peninsula ■
Port Talb

Broadhaven ■
Lydstep Headland ■
Port Einon
Pennard Cliffs ■

Barafundle Bay ■

Lower section:
Lundy ■
Ilfracombe
Heddon Valley ■
Countisbury
Watersmeet
Lynmouth

Morte Point ■
Woolacombe ■
Baggy Point ■
Braunton
Arlington Court ▲

Barnstaple
Abbotsham ■

East Titchberry ■
Bideford
South Molton

South Hole ■
Buck's Mills ■
Great Torrington

South West

Sandy Mouth ■
Bude
Dunsland ■

Crackington Haven ■
Holsworthy

Okehampton

Boscastle ■
Finch Foundry ▲
Castle Drogo ▲

Barras Nose ■
Tintagel Old Post Office ▲
Launceston
Lydford Gorge ■
Teign Valley

Port Quin ■
Camelford
Lawrence House ▲
Widecombe in the Moor

The Rumps & Pentire Point ■
Rough Tor ■
The Church House

Padstow
Wadebridge

Park Head ■
Tavistock
Holn Woo

Carnewas & Bedruthan Steps ■
Bodmin
Trowlesworthy ■

Newquay
Liskeard
Cotehele ▲
Buckland Abbey ▲
Hembury Woods ■

Crantock & Holywell Bay ■
Lanhydrock ▲
Saltash
Plym Bridge Woods ■

Chapel Porth & Wheal Coates ■
Trerice ▲
Antony ▲
PLYMOUTH

Zennor Head ■
Truro
Fowey
Looe
Saltram ▲

Godrevy ■
St Austell
Bodigga Cliff ■
Wembury ■

Bosigran ■
St Ives
Cornish Mines & Engines ▲
The Gribbin ■
Overbeck's ▲

Levant Mine ■
Camborne
Trelissick Garden ▲
The Dodman ■
Bolt Tail ■

Botallack Count House ▲
Trengwainton Garden ▲
Nare Head ■
Soar Mill Cove ■

Cape Cornwall ▲
Penzance
Godolphin ▲
Falmouth
St Anthony Head ■
Bolt Head ■

Mayon Cliff ■
Helston
Glendurgan Garden ▲
Portlemouth Down

Porthcurno ■
St Michael's Mount ▲

Penrose Estate: Gunwalloe & Loe Pool ■

Kynance Cove ■

Lizard Point ■

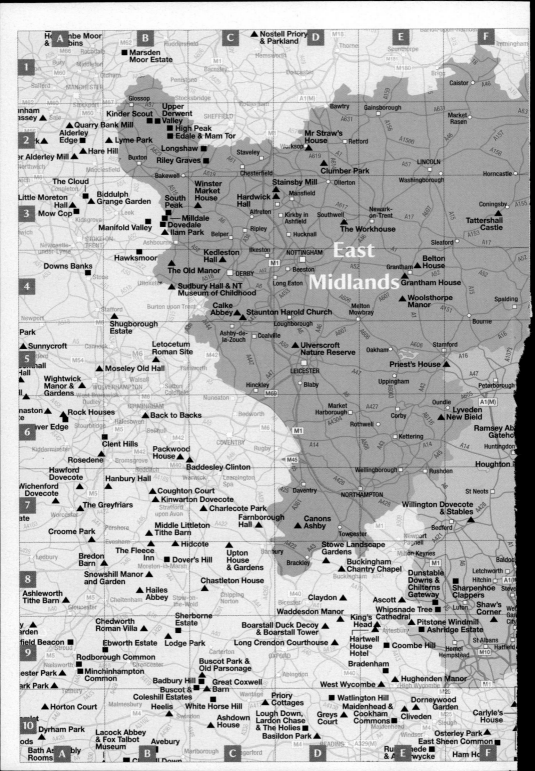

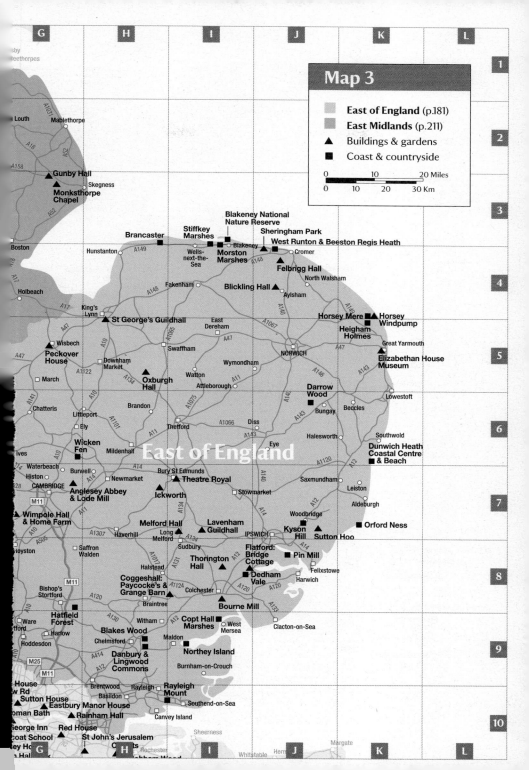

Map 3

■ East of England (p.181)
■ East Midlands (p.211)
▲ Buildings & gardens
■ Coast & countryside

0   10   20 Miles
0 10   20 30 Km

East of England

Grimsby
Cleethorpes
Mablethorpe
Louth
A1031
A16
A52
A158
▲ Gunby Hall
Skegness
Monksthorpe Chapel
A52
Boston
A17
Holbeach
A16
A17
King's Lynn
Hunstanton
A149
Brancaster
Stiffkey Marshes
Wells-next-the-Sea
Blakeney National Nature Reserve
Blakeney
Morston Marshes
A148
Sheringham Park
West Runton & Beeston Regis Heath
Cromer
Felbrigg Hall
North Walsham
▲ St George's Guildhall
A47
A10
East Dereham
A1065
A47
Fakenham
A148
Blickling Hall
Aylsham
A140
Horsey Mere
Horsey Windpump
Heigham Holmes
A1067
A47
NORWICH
A143
Great Yarmouth
Elizabethan House Museum
□ Wisbech
Peckover House
A47
A1122
Downham Market
Swaffham
A134
A10
Watton
Wymondham
A11
A140
A146
Lowestoft
□ March
Chatteris
A1075
Attleborough
Oxburgh Hall
Brandon
Thetford
A1066
Diss
A143
Darrow Wood
Bungay
Beccles
Littleport
A1101
Ely
Eye
Halesworth
Southwold
Wicken Fen
Mildenhall
A1120
Dunwich Heath Coastal Centre & Beach
Ives
Waterbeach
Burwell
Bury St Edmunds
A14
Saxmundham
Leiston
Histon
Newmarket
Theatre Royal
Aldeburgh
CAMBRIDGE
M11
Anglesey Abbey & Lode Mill
Ickworth
A134
Stowmarket
A12
Woodbridge
Wimpole Hall & Home Farm
A10
Melford Hall
Lavenham Guildhall
A14
Kyson Hill
Sutton Hoo
Orford Ness
A1307
Haverhill
Long Melford
A134
IPSWICH
A505
Saffron Walden
Sudbury
Flatford: Bridge Cottage
Pin Mill
Royston
A131
Thorington Hall
Felixstowe
M11
Halstead
A1124
Dedham Vale
Harwich
Bishop's Stortford
Coggeshall: Paycocke's & Grange Barn
Colchester
A120
A133
Braintree
Bourne Mill
Hatfield Forest
A120
A130
Witham
A12
Copt Hall Marshes
West Mersea
Ware
Harlow
Blakes Wood
Chelmsford
Maldon
Clacton-on-Sea
Hoddesdon
M25
Danbury & Lingwood Commons
Northey Island
M11
A414
A12
Burnham-on-Crouch
House
Brentwood
Rayleigh
Rayleigh Mount
Sutton House
Basildon
Southend-on-Sea
Eastbury Manor House
Canvey Island
Roman Bath
Rainham Hall
Sheerness
George Inn
Red House
Margate
School
St John's Jerusalem
Rochester
Whitstable
Herne

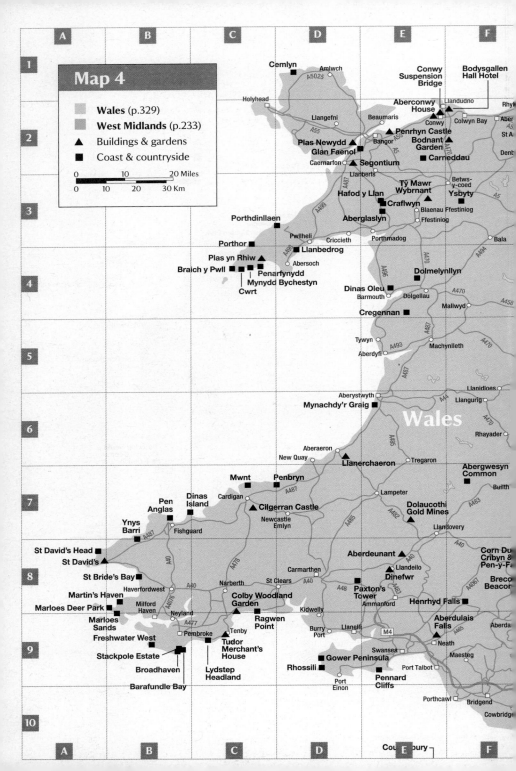

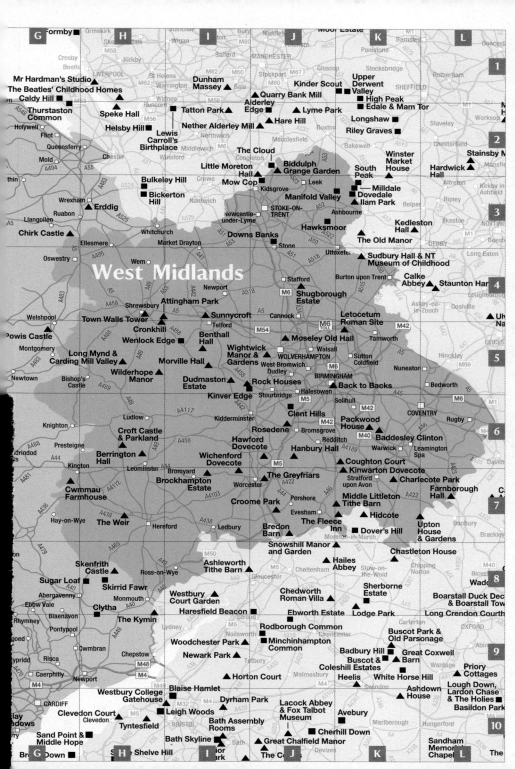

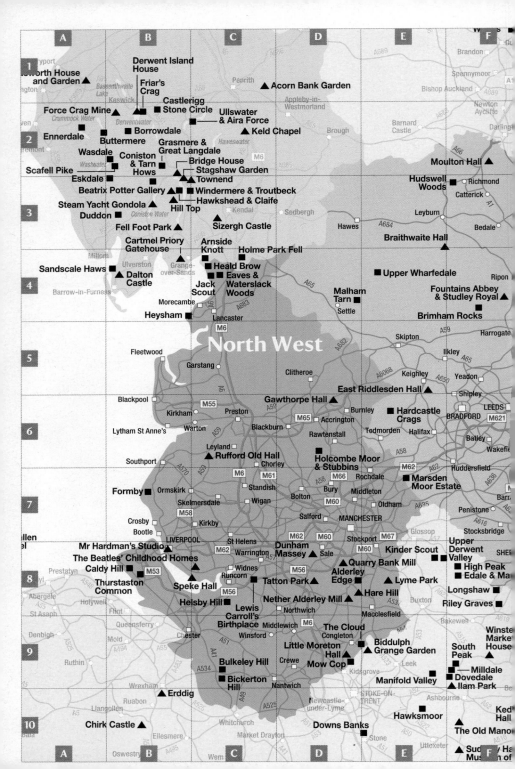

North West

Grid labels (top): A B C D E F

Row labels (left): 1 2 3 4 5 6 7 8 9 10

Seaworth House and Garden ▲
Derwent Island House
Friar's Crag
Acorn Bank Garden ▲
Bassenthwaite Lake
Keswick
Penrith
Brandon
Spannymoor
Bishop Auckland
Newton Aycliffe
Darling...

Castlerigg Stone Circle ■
Force Crag Mine ▲
Crummock Water
Derwentwater
Borrowdale ■
Ullswater & Aira Force ■
Keld Chapel ▲
Appleby-in-Westmorland
Brough
Barnard Castle

Ennerdale ■
Buttermere ■
Grasmere & Great Langdale
Hawes Water
Moulton Hall ▲

Wasdale ■
Coniston & Tarn Hows
Bridge House ▲
Stagshaw Garden ▲
Hudswell Woods ■
Richmond
Catterick

Scafell Pike ▲
Wastwater
Townend ▲
Windermere & Troubeck ■
Leyburn
Bedale

Eskdale ■
Beatrix Potter Gallery ▲ ■
Hawkshead & Claife ■
Sedbergh
Braithwaite Hall ▲

Steam Yacht Gondola ▲
Hill Top
Coniston Water
Kendal
Hawes
A684

Duddon ■
Sizergh Castle ▲
Fell Foot Park ▲

Cartmel Priory Gatehouse ■
Arnside Knott ▲
Holme Park Fell ■
Upper Wharfedale ■
Ripon

Sandscale Haws ■
Dalton Castle ■
Ulverston
Grange-over-Sands
Heald Brow ■
Eaves & Waterslack Woods ■
Fountains Abbey & Studley Royal ▲

Millom
Jack Scout ■
Malham Tarn ■
Brimham Rocks ■

Morecambe
Lancaster
Settle
Barrow-in-Furness

Heysham ■

North West

Fleetwood
Garstang
Clitheroe
Skipton
Harrogate
Ilkley
Yeadon

Blackpool
Kirkham
Preston
Keighley
Shipley

East Riddlesden Hall ■
Lytham St Anne's
Warton
Blackburn
Burnley
Hardcastle Crags ■
LEEDS
BRADFORD

Gawthorpe Hall ▲
Accrington
Todmorden
Halifax
Batley
Wakefi...

Leyland
Rawtenstall
Marsden Moor Estate ■
Huddersfield

Southport
Rufford Old Hall ▲
Chorley
Holcombe Moor & Stubbins ■
Rochdale
Penistone

Formby ■
Ormskirk
Standish
Bury
Middleton
Oldham
Stocksbridge

Skelmersdale
Wigan
Bolton
Salford
MANCHESTER
Glossop

Crosby
Kirkby
Stockport
Upper Derwent Valley ■

Bootle
LIVERPOOL
St Helens
Warrington
Dunham Massey ▲
Sale
Kinder Scout ▲
High Peak ■
Edale & Ma...

Mr Hardman's Studio ▲
Widnes
Quarry Bank Mill ▲
Alderley Edge ■
Lyme Park ▲
Longshaw ■

The Beatles' Childhood Homes ▲
Runcorn
Tatton Park ▲
Hare Hill ▲
Riley Graves ■

Caldy Hill ■
Thurstaston Common
Speke Hall ▲
Nether Alderley Mill ▲
Buxton

Helsby Hill ▲
Northwich
Macclesfield

Lewis Carroll's Birthplace ▲
Middlewich
Winster Market House ■

Chester
Winsford
The Cloud ▲
Congleton
South Peak ■

Bulkeley Hill ■
Little Moreton Hall ■
Biddulph Grange Garden ▲
Milldale ■

Bickerton Hill ■
Crewe
Mow Cop ▲
Manifold Valley ■
Dovedale ■
Ilam Park ▲

Nantwich
Newcastle-under-Lyme
STOKE-ON-TRENT
Ashbourne
Ked... Hall

Erddig ▲
Hawksmoor ▲
The Old Manor

Chirk Castle ▲
Whitchurch
Downs Banks ■
Stone
Uttoxeter
Sud... Mus...

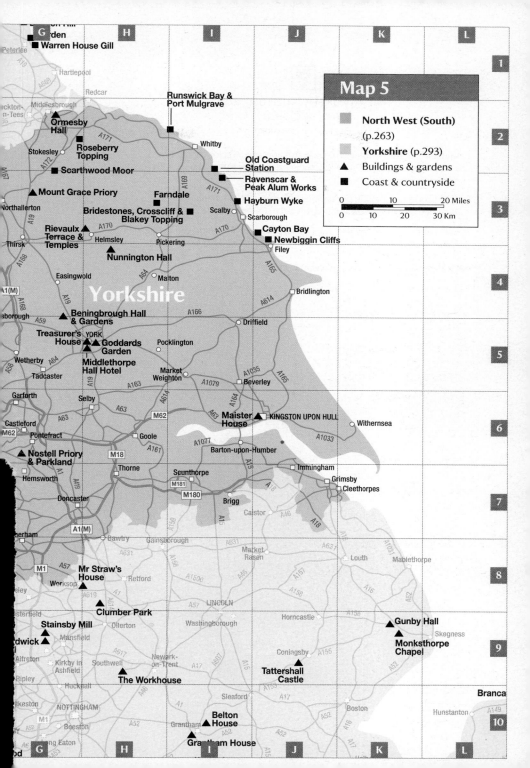

Map 5

■ North West (South) (p.263)

□ Yorkshire (p.293)

▲ Buildings & gardens

■ Coast & countryside

0   10   20 Miles
0   10   20   30 Km

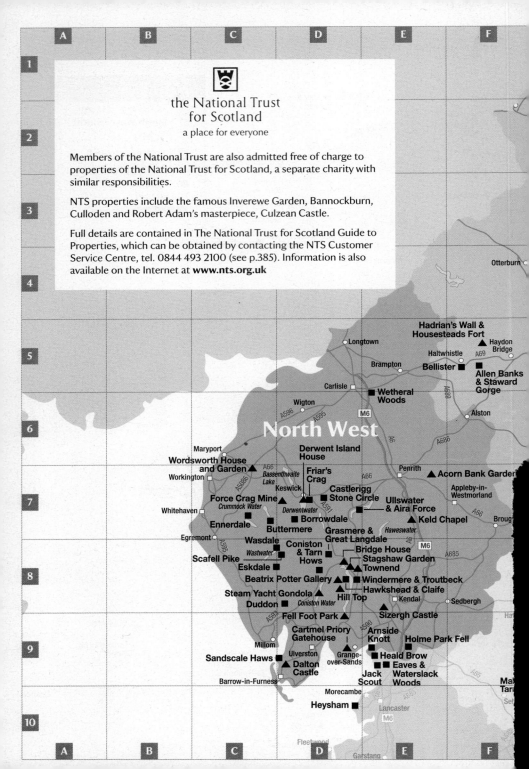

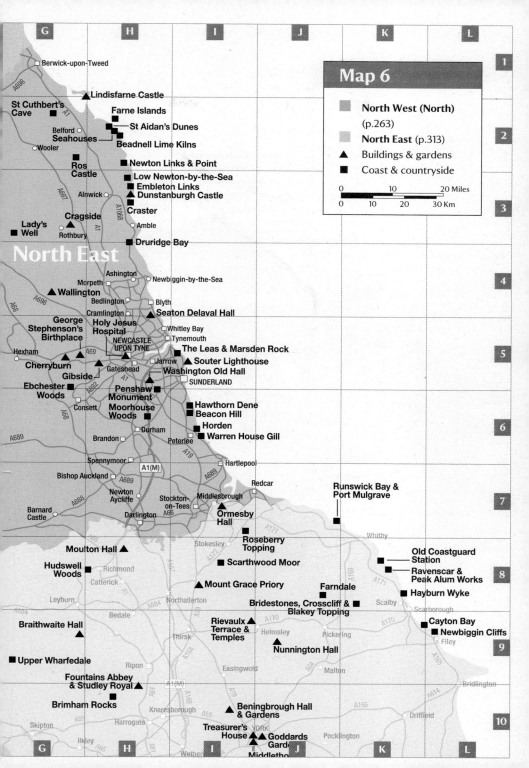

South West

Early-morning mist drifts away revealing the silver-grey stone of the dreamily beautiful Antony

Outdoors in the South West

Miles of coastline, expanses of woodland, moors, farmland and downland – it is no wonder the glorious South West exudes a powerful magnetism. The distinctive landscape, so unspoilt and so beautiful, offers a huge variety of places to visit and activities to enjoy.

Right:
the wildly beautiful Heddon Valley in Devon

What makes it so special?

Most people will say that what they love best about the South West is the coast. The Trust protects 370 miles (36 per cent) of the coastline in Devon and Cornwall, and wherever you are in the two far western counties you are never more than 25 miles from the sea: from the great sandy surfing beaches of the north coast to the high rocky headlands, rock pools, coves and tidal inlets of the south coast. Around all this runs the incomparable South West Coast Path, linking everywhere and providing unparalleled access on foot to all the lonely shores and soaring cliffs. Totalling 630 miles, it is the longest national trail in the country.

The Trust cares for more than 50,000 hectares (123,550 acres) of countryside in the South West. As well as the peninsula of Devon and Cornwall, there is Gloucestershire in the north, Somerset and Wiltshire, then Dorset further south, with spectacular stretches of coastline, chalk downland, high moorland, historic landscapes and beautiful rolling countryside. The northern Cotswolds boasts many lovely villages, some of which, such as Sherborne, are partly owned by the Trust – which also owns uplands, farmland and ancient woodland.

Go pool-dipping or fossil hunting

Devon and Cornwall are rightly famous for their surfing beaches, such as Godrevy and Chapel Porth. But there are many other attractions. In Cornwall, the Lizard's Kynance Cove has been famous since Victorian times for its fantastic rocks and botanical rarities; Wembury, close to Plymouth Sound, has fabulous rock pools and many popular children's events; and Carnewas overlooks the famous beauty spot of Bedruthan Steps.

In Devon and Cornwall glorious beaches such as Woolacombe Sands, Holywell Bay and Crantock, Sandy Mouth and Duckpool on the north coast, and South Milton Sands, Porthcurno and Gunwalloe on the south coast are rightly popular with families. While in Dorset anyone with an interest in nature and prehistory will be drawn to the Purbeck Estate, which boasts one of Britain's best beaches at Studland, two National Nature Reserves, and is home to the richest ten square miles of wild flowers in the country.

The Jurassic Coast, stretching all the way along the Dorset and East Devon coast, is a World Heritage Site and covers Purbeck, Burton Bradstock and Golden Cap, and Branscombe. The landscape is wonderfully varied, ranging from heathland, dunes and a mile-long stretch of sand, to shingle and sandstone cliffs – perfect for picnics, walking and fossil hunting.

History at every turn

There is so much to explore in the old mining areas of Cornwall and West Devon, now a World Heritage Site. Visit the many ruined engine houses protected and preserved by the Trust. Some of them, such as those at Botallack near St Just, seem to defy gravity, clinging to the cliff edge just above the sea. In Botallack's Count House Workshop, you can while away hours examining the fascinating displays on St Just coast's mining history.

There are many curious structures to be discovered around the coasts of Devon and Cornwall, each of which has a story to tell relating to this peninsula's colourful past. There are the military fortifications at Froward Point near Brixham and St Anthony Head near St Mawes, Parson Hawker's driftwood hut high on the cliffs at Morwenstow, the castellated coastguard lookout at Mayon Cliff above Sennen Cove and the candy-striped 25.6-metre-high Gribbin daymark near Fowey.

Above:
Bedruthan Steps in Cornwall, seen from Carnewas in the south, looking north to Park Head promontory

In West Dorset the historic landscape includes magnificent Iron Age hill forts, such as Hod Hill, Eggardon and Lambert's Castle. Make sure you don't miss North Somerset's Cheddar cliffs. Cheddar, Britain's largest gorge, was carved by melt-water from the last Ice Age and has been forming and changing over the past two million years. Not far away is dramatic Brean Down. This extends a mile and a half into the Bristol Channel and has truly breathtaking views, as well as abundant wildlife and fascinating history – including a Roman Temple, Napoleonic era fort and Second World War gun battery.

If you would like to delve a bit more deeply into this rich history, see page 31 for details of how to obtain one of the many leaflets available covering the Trust's coast and countryside.

Outdoors in the South West

Below:

children sitting against the breakwater on the beach at Brownsea Island, Poole Harbour, Dorset

Wildlife in abundance

We have spent many years on pioneering nature conservation work, and all the hard work has paid off, for our coast and countryside sites in Devon and Cornwall now boast an abundance of wildlife. Walk along the Rosemergy and Bosigran cliffs near Zennor in West Penwith, between Bolt Head and Bolt Tail in South Devon, or from Kynance to Mullion on the Lizard, and appreciate the swathes of wild flowers which carpet the grazed clifftops in spring and summer.

The Cornish chough – a truly emblematic bird – has returned to breed in Cornwall at last. It has made its home on the grazed cliffs of the Lizard, so if you visit Lizard Point, be sure to stop by the Chough Watchpoint next door to the café, particularly at fledging time in the summer. Or if you are near Plym Bridge Woods (close to Plymouth) do go to the observation post of the successful Peregrine Falcon Watch. Positioned on an old viaduct, this was set up to protect nearby breeding falcons (www.plym-peregrines.co.uk).

On the Exmoor coast of North Devon and Somerset, in West Penwith and around Chapel Porth in Cornwall the glorious rolling heathland provides a rich habitat for birds and insects. Ashclyst Forest on the Killerton Estate and Lydford Gorge are great spots for bats and butterflies (as are the Lanhydrock and Arlington estates), and there are numerous other sites, including areas of Dartmoor, such as Hembury, where the Trust's protective grazing regimes have encoraged rare butterflies to flourish.

One high-summer sight not to be missed in the fields of West Pentire, near Crantock in North Cornwall, is the astonishing display of vivid arable flowers, such as poppies and corn marigolds, along with Venus's looking glass and weasel's snout.

While over in Wiltshire, some of the most important areas of chalk grassland in the country can be found at Calstone Coombes, Cherhill Down and Whitesheet Hill. Calstone and Cherhill Down also have a wide range of wildlife, including 25 varieties of breeding butterfly, while Fontmell and Melbury Downs in North Dorset are rich in flora.

As well as Studland, one of the richest areas for flora and fauna in Dorset is Brownsea Island in Poole Harbour. It boasts an immensely diverse range of wildlife and habitats, and is one of the few places in the country where there are red squirrels.

Two of Dorset's largest remaining expanses of heathland are near Corfe Castle and at Holt Heath, near Kingston Lacy. These are important breeding sites for heathland birds, as well as being home to sand lizards, snakes, dragonflies, grasshoppers, crickets, moths, beetles and butterflies.

At Minchinhampton and Rodborough Commons in Gloucestershire there are rare butterflies and wild flowers, including thirteen recorded species of orchid, while Holnicote Estate in Somerset boasts sixteen species of bat, and Collard Hill in the same county is home to the rare large blue butterfly.

Above:
Glastonbury Tor, Somerset, with the 15th-century tower of St Michael at its summit

Below:
Sand lizards, a European protected species, can be seen at Studland, Dorset

Open to everyone
The Trust has provided many specially adapted or graded paths and viewpoints, such as those at Glebe Cliff by Tintagel, Loe Pool near Helston, Snapes Point and Bolberry Down near Salcombe, Cadsonbury on the River Lynher near Callington, and Branscombe and Salcombe Hill in East Devon.

Further east, Burrow Mump in Somerset has stunning views across the Levels and Moors to the River Parrett and Glastonbury Tor. There are also 87 miles of footpaths, bridleways and cycle paths running across the beautiful Holnicote Estate – perfect for exploring the open moors and deep-sided valleys in the heart of Exmoor National Park. Take a picnic to Horner Wood, with its magnificent pollarded oaks and heathland grazed by red deer, or climb to Exmoor's highest point on Dunkery Beacon and enjoy the views along the coast. The Sherborne Estate, in the Cotswolds, has stunning water meadows, as does Eyebridge on the Kingston Lacy Estate in Dorset.

One walk not to be missed is the Bath Skyline. Skirting the city, this six-mile walk passes through woodlands and wildflower meadows. There are many excellent kite-flying and picnic spots, as well as quiet corners for those after some peace. Leigh Woods, on Bristol's doorstep, is another unique experience (see 'My favourite walk', overleaf). A National Nature Reserve with numerous waymarked trails and paths, it even has an all-ability orienteering trail.

Outdoors in the South West

My favourite walk
My favourite walk has to be through Leigh Woods near Bristol, with its constant seasonal changes and the fascinating hints it offers to the site's history.

An ancient Holloway leads from the North Road entrance to the Plain. Crossing this clearing, glimpses of Bristol remind you of the proximity of the city. Following the top of Nightingale Valley the path is flat until it arrives at the ramparts of Stokeleigh Camp, an Iron Age hill fort. Stunning views from the camp of the Avon Gorge help you appreciate why it was an ideal place for a hill fort. It's also a good spot to look for rare whitebeams, including the endemic Bristol whitebeam, or for a peregrine falcon swooping over the gorge.

My favourite beach
For some people it could be white sand or a donkey ride, for others, pebbles or the view. For me it has to be the solitude the beach can bring; the solitude from within the water, on top of an Atlantic roller which has travelled half an ocean to be met by the same stunning coastline it has always crashed upon... and me.

Below:
Leigh Woods,
Bristol, Somerset

I've walked the coast path numerous times and never seen the same view twice: that's why this is a tricky question for me to answer. If I were pushed, I would have to say Godrevy: a sweep of sand held tight by dunes alive with grasses, birds and insects, with a nature trail winding its way through them ending on the thrift-covered clifftop, overlooking the seal-encrusted lighthouse rock and surf-soaked bay.

For all of its solitude, Godrevy is under careful conservation management, as it is a place which offers and means so much to so many people. There are also two of Cornwall's best surf schools here, which cater for everyone whatever your ability or disability... so, jump in – the water's lovely!

Robyn Davies
National Trust Surf Project
Co-ordinator,
Devon and Cornwall

Passing through the other end of the ramparts you pass veteran pollards, evidence of past wood pasture. Another legacy of past grazing is the Parish Wall, built by the neighbouring estate to exclude stock. Further along the wall the 600-year-old yew shows this was a boundary long before the wall itself was built. Follow the Blue trail, one of several waymarked routes, and you will find yourself back at the start.

Bill Morris
Head Warden, Leigh Woods, Bristol

Coast and countryside guides

To help you make the most of your time and to discover more about the places you visit, there are nearly 40 in-depth guide leaflets available covering the coast and countryside owned by the Trust in Devon and Cornwall. For a full list, please contact either the Cornwall or the Devon office. To buy specific Cornwall leaflets, contact the shop at Lanhydrock (01208 265952); for Devon leaflets contact the shop at Arlington Court (01271 851116).

Coastal car parks in the West Country

The Trust owns numerous coastal car parks in Dorset, Devon and Cornwall, most of which are simply inconspicuous parking spots providing access to lovely remote coves, cliffs and headlands, undisturbed homes to a host of birds, bugs and butterflies. Some of the Trust's car parks are the gateways to more popular destinations, where you will find facilities such as beach cafés and WCs.

Dorset

Cogden, West Dorset	SY 503 883
Stonebarrow Hill	SY 383 933
Langdon Hill	SY 413 931
Burton Bradstock	SY 491 888
Ringstead Bay	SY 760 822
Spyway	SY 996 785
Studland	SZ 036 835

Devon

Barna Barrow, Countisbury	SS 753 497
Countisbury	SS 747 497
Combe Park, Hillsford Bridge	SS 740 477
Woody Bay	SS 676 486
Hunter's Inn, Heddon Valley	SS 655 481
Trentishoe Down	SS 635 480
Trentishoe Down	SS 628 479
Torrs Walk, Ilfracombe	SS 511 475
Baggy Point, Croyde	SS 433 397
Brownsham, Hartland	SS 285 259
East Titchberry, Hartland	SS 244 270
Wembury Beach	SX 517 484
Stoke	SX 556 465
Ringmore	SX 649 457
South Milton Sands	SX 677 415
Bolberry Down	SX 689 384
East Soar	SX 713 376
Snapes Point	SX 739 404
Prawle Point	SX 775 354
Little Dartmouth	SX 874 492
Higher Brownstone	SX 905 510
Coleton Camp	SX 909 513
Scabbacombe	SX 912 523
Man Sands	SX 913 531
Salcombe Hill	SY 139 882
Branscombe	SY 197 887

Cornwall

Morwenstow	SS 205 154
Duckpool	SS 202 117
Sandy Mouth	SS 203 100
Northcott Mouth	SS 204 084
Strangles Beach	SX 134 952
Glebe Cliff, Tintagel	SX 050 884
Port Quin	SW 972 805
Lundy Bay	SW 953 796
Lead Mines, Pentireglaze	SW 942 799
Pentire Farm	SW 935 803
Park Head	SW 853 707
Carnewas (for Bedruthan Steps)	SW850 690
Crantock	SW 789 607
Treago Mill (for Polly Joke)	SW 778 601
Holywell Bay	SW 767 586
St Agnes Beacon	SW 704 503
Wheal Coates	SW703 500
Chapel Porth	SW 697 495
Basset's Cove	SW638 440
Reskajeage Downs	SW623 430
Deadman's Cove	SW 625 432
Derrick Cove	SW620 429
Hudder Down	SW 612 428
Hell's Mouth	SW 599 427
Godrevy	SW 582 432
Carn Galver	SW 422 364
Levant	SW 368 345
Botallack	SW 366 334
Cape Cornwall	SW 353 318
Bollowall	SW 354 314
Porth Nanven (Cot Valley)	SW 358 308
Highburrow (Loe Bar west)	SW 635 249
Penrose (Loe Pool west)	SW 639 259
Degibna Chapel (Loe Pool east)	SW 653 252
Chyvarloe (Loe Bar east)	SW 653 235
Gunwalloe Church Cove	SW 660 207
Predannack	SW 669 162
Kynance Cove	SW 688 132
Lizard Point	SW 703 116
Poltesco	SW 726 156
Bosveal (for Durgan)	SW 775 276
Trelissick	SW 836 397
St Anthony Head	SW 847 313
Porth Farm (Towan Beach)	SW 867 329
Pendower Beach	SW 897 384
Carne Beach	SW 905 384
Nare Head	SW 922 380
Penare (Dodman Point)	SW 998 404
Lamledra (Vault Beach)	SW 011 411
Coombe Farm	SX 110 512
Pencarrow Head	SX 150 513
Frogmore	SX 157 517
Lansallos	SX 174 518
Hendersick	SX 236 520
Bodigga	SX 273 543
Cotehele Quay	SX 424 682

A la Ronde

Summer Lane, Exmouth, Devon EX8 5BD

Map ① G7   1991

This unique sixteen-sided house, described by Lucinda Lambton as having 'a magical strangeness that one might dream of only as a child', was built for two spinster cousins, Jane and Mary Parminter, on their return from a grand tour of Europe in the late 18th century. It contains many objects and mementoes of their travels. The extraordinary interior decoration includes a feather frieze, gathered from native game birds and chickens, laboriously stuck down with isinglass, and a fragile shell-encrusted gallery, said to contain nearly 25,000 shells, which can be viewed in its entirety on closed-circuit television. **Note**: small and fragile rooms. Large/bulky bags/cameras to be left in lockers at house.

Exploring
– Be amazed and inspired by the decorative wow factor!
– Dress up as a Regency lady or Victorian gentleman.
– Discovery Room with silhouette and shell activities.
– Wildlife brass rubbing and spotter sheets in the grounds.
– Enjoy free garden games – croquet, snakes and ladders and more.
– New art exhibition and sale of work every two weeks.

Eating and shopping: buy local and regional products in the shop. Home-cooked lunches and afternoon teas using local, regional produce. Get a drink or an ice-cream in the shop.

You may also enjoy: Overbeck's, near Salcombe, another house with amazing collections of curios and glorious coastal views.

Making the most of your day: full programme of events and exhibitions, school holiday craft activities. Self-guided themed tours and family trail in house. Stunning views over Exe estuary and panorama showing places of interest. Dogs welcome, on leads, in car park and orchard picnic area.

Access for all: ⬛⬛⬛⬛⬛⬛⬛⬛⬛⬛
House ⬛⬛ Tea-room ⬛ Grounds ➡

Getting here: 192:SY004834. **Foot**: East Devon Way borders property. South West Coast Path within ¾ mile. **Bus**: Stagecoach in Devon 57/58 Exeter–Exmouth/Budleigh Salterton to within ½ mile. **Train**: Lympstone Village 1¼ miles; Exmouth 2 miles. **Road**: 2 miles north of Exmouth on A376. **Parking**: free. Coaches must be booked. Caravans/trailers telephone ahead.

Finding out more: 01395 265514 (property office). 01395 255918 (shop). 01395 255912 (tea-room) or alaronde@nationaltrust.org.uk

A La Ronde		M	T	W	T	F	S	S
27 Feb–7 Mar	11–5	·	·	·	·	·	S	S
13 Mar–30 Jun	11–5	M	T	W	·	·	S	S
2 Jul–3 Sep	11–5	M	T	W	·	F	S	S
4 Sep–31 Oct	11–5	M	T	W	·	·	S	S

Also open Good Friday. Shop, tea-room and grounds open as house, but shop and grounds 10:30 to 5:30, tea-room 10:30 to 5. Due to the size and nature of the house, small delays may occur at busy times. Last admission to house one hour before closing.

The intriguing A la Ronde, Devon

Antony

Torpoint, Cornwall PL11 2QA

Map ① E8   🏚️🏠🟦🌳⛵ 1961

'**Because Antony is still a family home, the experience of visiting is unique. We love coming back again and again.**'
Helen Munzer, York

Faced in silver-grey Pentewan stone and flanked by colonnaded wings of mellow brick, this classically beautiful house is a beguiling mixture of the formal and informal. Still the home of the Carew Pole family, it contains fine collections of paintings, furniture and textiles. The grounds bordering the Lynher estuary, landscaped by Repton, include a formal garden with topiary, a knot garden, modern sculptures and the National Collection of Daylilies. The Woodland Garden has outstanding rhododendrons, azaleas, magnolias and camellias. Antony was used as the film set for Walt Disney's *Alice in Wonderland*, directed by Tim Burton. **Note**: members free to Woodland Garden (not National Trust) only when house is open.

Antony, Cornwall: very much a family home

Access for all: 🖭🚻♿️🛗🔄📷🔦📖 :•:
Building 🖭🔄♿️ Grounds 🔄▶️

Exploring
— Enjoy a unique and quirky *Alice in Wonderland* Experience.
— Discover Alice's bedroom.
— Visit the exhibition and amazing installations in the garden.
— Join in an *Alice in Wonderland* tea party.
— Sit on the terrace and enjoy breathtaking river views.
— Hear amazing stories about the Carew Pole ancestors.

Eating and shopping: enjoy traditional lunches and light snacks in our tea-room. Shop with a good range of souvenirs and gifts.

You may also enjoy: Saltram, a beautiful Georgian mansion, is only a short distance away in Plymouth.

Making the most of your day: following the recent filming of Walt Disney's *Alice in Wonderland*, this year the garden will be transformed. Discover your own Wonderland and join in Alice-related events and activities.

Getting here: 201:SX418564. **Cycle**: NCN27, 2 miles. **Ferry**: Torpoint 2 miles. **Bus**: First 81 from Plymouth (passing close Plymouth 🚉) alight Great Park Estate, ¼ mile. **Train**: Plymouth 6 miles via vehicle ferry. **Road**: 6 miles west of Plymouth via Torpoint car ferry, 2 miles north west of Torpoint, north of A374, 16 miles south east of Liskeard, 15 miles east of Looe. **Parking**: free, 120 yards.

Finding out more: 01752 812191 or antony@nationaltrust.org.uk

Antony		M	T	W	T	F	S	S
Garden, shop and tea-room								
6 Mar–31 Oct	11–5	M	T	W	T	·	S	S
House								
16 Mar–31 Oct	12–5	·	T	W	T	·	·	S
Woodland Garden								
1 Mar–31 Oct	11–5	M	T	W	T	·	S	S

Open Bank Holiday Mondays and Good Friday. Above opening arrangements are for 2010 only. Bath Pond House interior can only be seen by written application to the Property Manager, on days house is open.

Visit

Arlington Court and the National Trust Carriage Museum

Arlington, near Barnstaple, Devon EX31 4LP

Map (1) F5

'**Arlington Court Gardener's Relish is delicious – please could we have a larger jar? Lovely walks.'**
Mrs A. C. Otter, Ilfracombe

Arlington Court is an unexpected jewel: a complete family estate. The intimate Regency house contains treasures for all tastes, from model ships to shells, all collected by the Chichesters. Offering incident and contrast, the 19th-century picturesque garden is a perfect place to explore, picnic or play. The walled kitchen garden provides fruit and vegetables for the tea-room and flowers for the house. The tranquil estate, abundant with wildlife, includes an ancient heronry. The Carriage Museum in the stables, has a vehicle for every occasion from cradle to grave. Our working horses and carriage rides keep the story alive.

Exploring
- Delve into a house full of treasures and secrets.
- Discover the romance of carriage travel in a bygone age.
- Explore three gardens in one: productive, flower and pleasure grounds.
- Take a ride in a horse-drawn carriage (01271 851117).
- Spy on our lesser horseshoe bats with the bat-cam.
- Stretch your legs searching for rare breeds on the estate.

Eating and shopping: buy jams and preserves made locally from Arlington-grown produce. Taste local, seasonal fruit and vegetables in our tea-room. Eat in the original Victorian kitchen: our tea-room! Stay longer in one of the estate's holiday cottages.

You may also enjoy: Dunster Castle, near Minehead. For carriages, try Charlecote Park in Warwickshire.

Making the most of your day: daily harnessing demonstration, family quizzes and Tracker Packs. Range of events, from children's crafts to living history costumed tours. Variety of waymarked walks around the estate. Dogs, on leads, in garden, Carriage Museum and the wider estate.

Access for all: House Carriage Museum Grounds

Getting here: 180:SS611405. **Bus**: TW Coaches 309 Barnstaple–Lynton, infrequent. **Train**: Barnstaple 8 miles (1 mile from bus station). **Road**: 8 miles north of Barnstaple on A39. Use A399 from South Molton if travelling from the east. **Parking**: free, 150 yards. Coaches access car park at second entrance. An area will be marked off if prior warning is given.

Finding out more: 01271 850296 or arlingtoncourt@nationaltrust.org.uk

A tranquil spot at Arlington Court, Devon

View from the coachman's seat on the carriage ride up to the house at Arlington Court, Devon

Arlington Court		M	T	W	T	F	S	S
House, Carriage Museum and bat-cam								
13 Feb–21 Feb	11–3	M	T	W	T	F	S	S
27 Feb–7 Mar	11–3	·	·	·	·	·	S	S
13 Mar–31 Oct	11–5	M	T	W	T	F	S	S
Shop								
1 Jan–3 Jan	11–3	·	·	·	·	F	S	S
Shop, tea-room and garden								
13 Feb–21 Feb	11–3	M	T	W	T	F	S	S
27 Feb–7 Mar	11–3	·	·	·	·	·	S	S
13 Mar–31 Oct	10:30–5	M	T	W	T	F	S	S
6 Nov–19 Dec	11–3	·	·	·	·	·	S	S
20 Dec–28 Dec	11–3	M	T	W	T	·	·	S

Access to house by guided tour only from 13 February to 7 March, last tour starts 2. House and Carriage Museum open for special events on weekends in November and December. Grounds open dawn to dusk, 1 January to 31 December.

Ashleworth Tithe Barn

Ashleworth, Gloucestershire GL19 4JA

Map ① J2 🐘 1956

The barn, with its immense stone-tiled roof, is picturesquely situated close to the banks of the River Severn. **Note**: no WC.

Getting here: 162:SO818252. 6 miles north of Gloucester, south east of Ashleworth.

Finding out more: 01452 814213 or ashleworth@nationaltrust.org.uk

Ashleworth Tithe Barn		M	T	W	T	F	S	S
Open all year	Dawn–dusk	M	T	W	T	F	S	S

Other times by appointment.

Avebury

near Marlborough, Wiltshire SN8 1RF

Map ① K4 🐘✝🏛🐾🏠 1943

In the 1930s, the pretty village of Avebury, partially encompassed by the stone circle of this World Heritage site, was witness to the excavations of archaeologist Alexander Keiller. In re-erecting many of the stones, Keiller uncovered the true wonder of one of the most important megalithic monuments in Europe. The fascinating finds from his excavations are on display in the 17th-century threshing barn and stables galleries of the Alexander Keiller Museum, where interactive displays and activities for children bring the landscape to life. The 16th-century dovecote also displays a variety of alternating interpretations throughout the year.

Note: English Heritage holds guardianship of Avebury stone circle, which is managed by the National Trust.

Exploring — Walk to the Bronze Age burial mounds at Windmill Hill.
— Visit the Lansdowne Monument and Iron Age earthwork of Oldbury.
— Discover Avebury's buried past secrets in the museum.
— Enjoy a picnic among the stones of the neolithic circle.
— Take a guided tour across this fascinating World Heritage site.
— Explore the mysteries of the neolithic, inside West Kennet Longbarrow.

Avebury, Wiltshire: a World Heritage site

Eating and shopping: local, seasonal food at Circles, the only Trust vegetarian restaurant! Children's meals, homemade cakes and picnic food are also available. Buy a memento of your visit at the shop. Don't miss the Wessex range of locally sourced giftware.

You may also enjoy: Dyrham Park and Lacock Abbey.

Making the most of your day: with world-renowned experts in archaeology on the Trust team at Avebury, be sure to look out for forthcoming lectures and events of archaeological interest on the Avebury calendar. Dogs on leads are welcome.

Access for all: [icons] **Building** [icon] **Grounds** [icon]

Getting here: 173:SU102699. **Foot**: Ridgeway National Trail. **Cycle**: NCN4 and 45.
Bus: Stagecoach in Swindon 49 Swindon–Trowbridge; Wiltshire and Dorset 96 Swindon–Pewsey. Both pass close Swindon ≋. **Train**: Pewsey 10 miles; Swindon 11 miles.
Road: 6 miles west of Marlborough, 1 mile north of the Bath road (A4) on A4361 and B4003.
Parking: pay and display, 500 yard (off A4361). National Trust and English Heritage members free. Parking during the Summer Solstice in late June may be limited. Telephone estate office before travelling. Overnight parking prohibited.

Finding out more: 01672 539250 or avebury@nationaltrust.org.uk.
National Trust Estate Office, High Street, Avebury, Wiltshire SN8 1RF

Avebury		M	T	W	T	F	S	S
Stone Circle								
Open all year		M	T	W	T	F	S	S
Museum and galleries								
1 Jan–31 Mar	10–4:30	M	T	W	T	F	S	S
1 Apr–31 Oct	10–6	M	T	W	T	F	S	S
1 Nov–31 Dec	10–4:30	M	T	W	T	F	S	S
Shop and Circle restaurant								
1 Jan–31 Mar	10:30–4	M	T	W	T	F	S	S
1 Apr–31 Oct	10–5:30	M	T	W	T	F	S	S
1 Nov–31 Dec	10:30–4	M	T	W	T	F	S	S

Museum, galleries, shop and restaurant closed two Mondays, Tuesdays and Wednesdays in January; also closed 24 to 26 December.

Avebury Manor and Garden

near Marlborough, Wiltshire SN8 1RF

Map (1) K4   1991

With notable Queen Anne alterations and Edwardian renovation, the present buildings of the house date from the early 16th century. Ancient walls and clipped box hedges contain the 'rooms' of the garden, where splendid topiary and tranquil space provided inspiration for Vita Sackville-West, a frequent visitor in the 1920s. **Note**: prolonged wet weather may necessitate the closure of the house and garden.

Exploring
- Take a guided tour of the rooms of the garden.
- Book tea and a tour of Avebury Manor.
- Enjoy a picnic in the tranquil garden.
- Look out for the special events at Avebury Manor.

Eating and shopping: picnics and hot food available from The Circle vegetarian restaurant. 'Wessex' artisan confectionery and drinks available from the shop. **New**: colour Avebury guidebook available from shop, restaurant and museum.

Making the most of your day: from costumed role-play to high tea and a tour, interpretation at Avebury Manor is never the same experience twice. Visit the website for the latest on forthcoming events.

Access for all: ⬚⬚⬚⬚⬚⬚
Building ⬚⬚ **Grounds** ⬚▶

Getting here: 173:SU100699. **Foot**: Ridgeway National Trail. **Cycle**: NCN4 and 45.
Bus: Stagecoach in Swindon 49 Swindon–Trowbridge; Wiltshire and Dorset 96 Swindon–Pewsey. Both pass close Swindon ⬚. **Train**: Pewsey 10 miles; Swindon 11 miles.
Road: 6 miles west of Marlborough, 1 mile north of the Bath road (A4) on A4361 and B4003. **Parking**: in main Avebury car park, 600 yards (pay and display). Located off A4361. National Trust and English Heritage members free. Parking during the Summer Solstice in late June will be very limited. Telephone estate office before travelling. Parking charge may vary.

Finding out more: 01672 539250 or avebury@nationaltrust.org.uk

Avebury Manor and Garden		M	T	W	T	F	S	S
Manor*								
2 Apr–31 Oct	12–5	M	T	·	·	F	S	S
Gardens								
2 Apr–31 Oct	11–5	M	T	·	·	F	S	S

Manor opening arrangements subject to change. *Friday and Saturday opening dependent on number of volunteers. Booking may be necessary at peak times (visit website for details). Manor Garden opening is subject to weather restrictions.

Barrington Court

Barrington, near Ilminster, Somerset TA19 0NQ

Map ① I6

'**It is great to have access to more at Barrington Court... perfect as it is. I have fallen in love.**'
T. H. Wellington, Somerset

The echoes of the past haunt this now empty Tudor manor house, so beautifully restored in the 1920s by the Lyle family. They lived in style, installing a sprung dance floor; the winding mechanism can still be seen under the sweeping main staircase. What were once cow yards, pens and fields became delightful flower gardens, their design influenced by Gertrude Jekyll. The working stone-walled kitchen garden produces a variety of wonderful fruit and vegetables, which can be enjoyed in the restaurant, while the arboretum delights visitors with vivid autumn hues. Overall a place to relax and refresh the senses.

Exploring
- Discover the new exhibition in the Court House.
- Play hide and seek in the apple orchards.
- Gain inspiration for your own vegetable garden.
- Smell the scent of the flowers in the garden.
- Watch a game of cricket on the village pitch.
- Take a longer walk and explore the rolling parkland.

Eating and shopping: eat freshly cooked vegetables straight from the gardens. Drink our own south Somerset-produced cider or apple juice. Sit outside and have a pasty and cup of tea. Browse in the shop – buy a present for someone special.

You may also enjoy: slightly newer (Elizabethan) but much larger in size – Montacute House, just eight miles away.

Barrington Court, Somerset, the plant sales area

Making the most of your day: we are well known for our annual Wassail (17 January) and for our jazz music on the lawn event. Interesting and practical one-and-a-half day vegetable gardening courses.

Access for all: 🅿️ 🚻 🚻 🚻 🚻 🚻 ⓐ
Building 🦽 Grounds 🦽 ➡️ 🦽 🦽

Getting here: 193:ST396182. **Cycle**: NCN30. **Bus**: First 632/3 Ilminster–Martock, with connections on 30A from Taunton. **Train**: Crewkerne 7 miles. **Road**: in Barrington village, 5 miles north east of Ilminster, on B3168. Signposted from A358 (Ilminster–Taunton) or A303 (Hayes End roundabout). **Sat Nav**: incorrectly directs visitors to a rear entrance – please follow the brown tourist signs. **Parking**: free, 30 yards.

Finding out more: 01460 242614 (Infoline). 01460 241938 or barringtoncourt@nationaltrust.org.uk

Barrington Court		M	T	W	T	F	S	S
House, gardens and shop								
27 Feb–31 Oct	11–5	M	T	·	T	F	S	S
6 Nov–28 Nov	11–4	·	·	·	·	·	S	S
Strode House Restaurant								
27 Feb–30 Mar	11–5	M	T	·	T	F	S	S
1 Apr–30 Sep	12–3	M	T	·	T	F	·	·
3 Apr–26 Sep	12–5	·	·	·	·	·	S	S
1 Oct–31 Oct	11–5	M	T	·	T	F	S	S
6 Nov–28 Nov	11–4	·	·	·	·	·	S	S
Beagles Café								
1 Apr–3 Oct	11–5	M	T	·	T	F	S	S

1 April to 30 September: restaurant open for lunches only weekdays, for lunches and teas weekends. Café may close in poor weather (October). Bookings for Strode House Restaurant accepted up to 24 hours prior to visit. On Bank Holiday weekends we operate on a first-come, first-served basis (not bookable).

Bath Assembly Rooms

Bennett Street, Bath, Somerset BA1 2QH

Map ① J4   🏠 🔔 🍸 1931

The Assembly Rooms were at the heart of fashionable Georgian society, the perfect venue for entertainment. When completed in 1771, they were described as 'the most noble and elegant of any in the kingdom'. The Fashion Museum (Bath & North East Somerset Council) is on lower ground floor. **Note**: limited visitor access during functions. Charge for the Fashion Museum includes members.

Exploring
- Holiday activities for families, on a fashion theme.
- Enjoy the summer exhibition in the Ball Room.
- New museum displays and exhibitions, visit www.fashionmuseum.co.uk
- For concerts and music festivals, visit www.bathfestivals.org.uk

Eating and shopping: café open nearly every day: coffee, light lunch or tea. Browse the extensive gift shop and renowned fashion bookshop. Savour an ice-cream in the garden café this summer.

Making the most of your day: stop for coffee, browse the bookshop and enjoy the latest fashion exhibition.

Access for all: 🚻 🚻 🚻 🚻 🚻 🚻
Building 🦽 🦽 ⬆️ 🦽 Grounds 🦽

Getting here: 156:ST749653. **Cycle**: NCN4, ¼ mile. **Bus**: from Bath Spa 🚆 and surrounding areas. **Train**: Bath Spa ¾ mile. **Road**: north of Milsom Street, east of the Circus. **Parking**: city centre car parks (pay and display), nearest Charlotte Street (not National Trust), charge including members. Very little on-street parking, park and ride recommended.

Finding out more: 01225 477173 or bathassemblyrooms@nationaltrust.org.uk

Bath Assembly Rooms		M	T	W	T	F	S	S
1 Jan–28 Feb	10:30–4	M	T	W	T	F	S	S
1 Mar–31 Oct	10:30–5	M	T	W	T	F	S	S
1 Nov–31 Dec	10:30–4	M	T	W	T	F	S	S

Last admission one hour before closing. Closed when in use for booked functions and on 25 and 26 December.
*Access to all rooms guaranteed in August until 4:30, at other times some rooms may be closed (visitors should telephone in advance).

Blaise Hamlet

Henbury, Bristol BS10 7QY

Map (1) I3

A delightful hamlet of nine picturesque cottages. Designed by John Nash in 1809 to accommodate Blaise Estate pensioners. **Note**: access to green only; cottages not open. No WC.

Getting here: 172:ST559789. 4 miles north of central Bristol.

Finding out more: 01934 844518 or blaisehamlet@nationaltrust.org.uk

Blaise Hamlet	M	T	W	T	F	S	S
Open all year	M	T	W	T	F	S	S

Boscastle

Cornwall

Map (1) D7

Much of the land in and around Boscastle is owned by the Trust. This includes the cliffs of Penally Point and Willapark, which guard the sinuous harbour entrance, Forrabury Stitches, high above the village and divided into ancient 'stitchmeal' cultivation plots, as well as the lovely Valency Valley. **Note**: WC by main car park (neither National Trust).

Exploring
- Wander through the village and down to the picturesque harbour.
- Stroll along the peaceful Valency Valley to Minster church.
- Follow the coast path and discover Forrabury church.

Eating and shopping: browse in the Trust shop by the lower harbour. Visit the adjoining café and enjoy the courtyard seating area.

Making the most of your day: children's quiz/trail. Look out for family events in school holidays. Dogs welcome in café courtyard.

Access for all: 🚻♿🏠 Grounds 🏞

Getting here: 190:SX097914. **Bus**: Western Greyhound 595 from Bude, 594 from Wadebridge (connections with 555 at Wadebridge for Bodmin Parkway ☰). **Road**: 5 miles north of Camelford, 3 miles north east of Tintagel on B3263. **Parking**: pay and display, 100 yards (not National Trust). Charge including members.

Finding out more: 01840 250353 or boscastle@nationaltrust.org.uk

Boscastle		M	T	W	T	F	S	S
Open all year		M	T	W	T	F	S	S
Shop, café and NT info								
13 Feb–28 Mar	11–4	M	T	W	T	F	S	S
29 Mar–31 Oct	10–5	M	T	W	T	F	S	S
1 Nov–14 Nov	11–4	M	T	W	T	F	S	S
19 Nov–5 Dec	11–4	·	·	·	·	F	S	S
11 Dec–19 Dec	11–4	·	·	·	·	·	S	S
27 Dec–31 Dec	11–4	M	T	W	T	F	·	·

Shop sometimes open later than 5 in high season.

Boscastle Harbour, on the north Cornish coast

Bradley

Newton Abbot, Devon TQ12 6BN

Map (1) G8 1938

Unspoilt and fascinating medieval manor house, still a relaxed family home, in a green haven of riverside meadows and woodland. **Note**: no WC or refreshments.

Getting here: 202:SX848709. ½ mile from Newton Abbot town centre.

Finding out more: 01803 661907 or bradley@nationaltrust.org.uk

Bradley Manor, Devon: still a relaxed family home

Bradley		M	T	W	T	F	S	S
1 Apr–30 Sep	2–5		**T**	**W**	**T**	·	·	·

5 to 29 October open weekdays by prior appointment. Telephone at least one day in advance.

Branscombe: the Old Bakery, Manor Mill and Forge

Branscombe, Seaton, Devon EX12 3DB

Map (1) H7  1965

Charming settlement of 'chocolate box' thatched buildings dating back more than 200 years, located in one of the most beautiful coastal villages in Devon. Visit the working mill and forge, enjoy a traditional cream tea in the Old Bakery. A perfect start or finishing point for coastal and countryside walks. **Note**: WCs at bakery and village hall.

Exploring
- Visit the old Forge and watch the blacksmith in action.
- Enjoy open fires and a bit of baking history.
- Discover the restored water-powered Manor Mill along the millstream.

Eating and shopping: quality ironwork on sale – candlestick holders to log burners. Delicious homemade soups, ploughman's and sandwiches served all day.

Making the most of your day: cycling along bridleways or walking along an extensive network of paths is the perfect way to enjoy this area. Dogs on leads and only in garden and Old Bakery information room.

Access for all: 🚻 Building 🦽♿ Manor Mill 🚶 Grounds 🦽

Getting here: 192:SY198887. **Foot**: South West Coast Path within ¾ mile. **Cycle**: public bridleway from Great Seaside to Beer gives shared access for cyclists. **Bus**: Axe Valley 899 Sidmouth–Seaton (connections from Axminster ≋ or Honiton ≋). **Train**: Honiton 8 miles. **Road**: in Branscombe village, off A3052. **Parking**: free. Small National Trust car park adjacent to Forge, also car park adjacent to village hall; donations in well.

Finding out more: 01752 346585 or branscombe@nationaltrust.org.uk. South and East Devon Countryside Office, The Stables, Saltram House, Plymouth, Devon PL7 1UH

Branscombe		M	T	W	T	F	S	S
Old Bakery								
1 Apr–30 Jun	10:30–5	·	·	**W**	**T**	**F**	**S**	**S**
1 Jul–31 Aug	10:30–5	**M**	**T**	**W**	**T**	**F**	**S**	**S**
1 Sep–31 Oct	10:30–5	·	·	**W**	**T**	**F**	**S**	**S**
Manor Mill								
28 Mar–27 Jun	2–5	·	·	·	·	·	·	**S**
4 Jul–1 Sep	2–5	·	·	**W**	·	·	·	**S**
5 Sep–31 Oct	2–5	·	·	·	·	·	·	**S**
Old Forge								
Open all year	Times vary	**M**	**T**	**W**	**T**	**F**	**S**	**S**

Old Forge: telephone for details of opening times.

Brean Down

Brean, North Somerset

Map (1) H4 1954

One of the most striking landmarks of the Somerset coastline, Brean Down projects dramatically into the Bristol Channel. Offering magnificent views for miles around, it is rich in wildlife and history; an ideal place to explore. The Palmerston Fort, built 1865, provides a unique insight into Brean's past. **Note**: steep climbs and cliffs; please stay on main paths. Dangerous beach (not National Trust).

Exploring
— Enjoy the bracing steep climb to the Fort.
— See the gun magazines on most Saturday and Sunday afternoons.
— Learn at the Fort and Down exhibition.

Eating and shopping: treat yourself at Brean Down Cove Café (not National Trust). Settle down for a long, lazy picnic.

Making the most of your day: there are circular walks for all abilities. Dogs on leads only.

Access for all: 🚾 **Building** ♿

Getting here: 182:ST290590. **Bus**: First 112 Highbridge–Weston-super-Mare (passing close Highbridge 🚉 and close Weston-super-Mare 🚉), alight Brean, 1¾ miles. **Train**: Highbridge 8½ miles. **Road**: between Weston-super-Mare and Burnham-on-Sea, 8 miles from exit 22 of M5. **Parking**: 200 yards, at Brean Down Cove Café at the bottom of Brean Down. The higher Down is a steep climb from the car park and the Fort is approximately 1½ miles further.

Finding out more: 01934 844518 or breandown@nationaltrust.org.uk

Brean Down	M	T	W	T	F	S	S
Open all year	**M**	**T**	**W**	**T**	**F**	**S**	**S**

Bredon Barn

Bredon, near Tewkesbury, Worcestershire GL20 7EG

Map (1) K1 1951

Beautifully constructed 14th-century barn made from local Cotswold stone. Dramatic aisled interior and unusual stone chimney cowling are notable. **Note**: no WC.

Getting here: 150:SO919369. 3 miles north-east of Tewkesbury.

Finding out more: 01451 844257 or bredonbarn@nationaltrust.org.uk

Bredon Barn		M	T	W	T	F	S	S
10 Mar–31 Oct	10–6	·	·	**W**	**T**	·	**S**	**S**

Closes dusk if earlier. All other times by appointment only.

Stunning views from Brean Down, Somerset

Brownsea Island

Poole Harbour, Poole, Dorset BH13 7EE

Map ① K7 ⊞ ⬆️🚻♨️🎣🏠 1962

'**William Morris wrote of his "Earthly Paradise", Brownsea Island is mine. It never fails to bring inspiration and contentment**.'
Berni Conolly, Sutton Coldfield

Brownsea Island is dramatically located in Poole Harbour, with spectacular views across to the Purbeck Hills. Thriving natural habitats – including woodland, heathland and a lagoon – create a haven for wildlife, such as the rare red squirrel and a wide variety of birds. Visitors will be fascinated by the island's rich history, for as well as boasting daffodil farming and pottery works, it was the birthplace of the Scouting and Guiding movement. So whether you love wildlife or just want to escape from the stresses of modern life, Brownsea is the perfect place to explore and enjoy throughout the year. **Note**: part of island leased to Dorset Wildlife Trust, 01202 709445. No public access to castle.

Exploring
- Get wild about wildlife with a family Tracker Pack.
- Visit the Baden Powell Outdoor Centre and scout stone.
- Look out for pottery remains on the seashore.
- Enjoy peace, tranquillity and breathtaking coastal views.
- Watch avocets, terns and godwits on the lagoon.
- Find out more about Brownsea Island in the Visitor Centre.

Eating and shopping: enjoy stunning views and delicious food in the Villano Café. Browse in the shop for Brownsea Island gifts. Take home a Brownsea Island Red Squirrel souvenir.

You may also enjoy: Corfe Castle and Studland Beach.

Making the most of your day: seasonal family activities and trails. Wildlife walks and talks.

Brownsea open-air theatre. Daily introductory walks and guided tractor trailer tours for less mobile visitors (bookable). Brownsea Island is a nature reserve, so dogs are not permitted.

Access for all: 🅿️♿🚻🅿️:•🄰
Building 🅰️🅰️♿ Grounds ♿➡️♿

Getting here: 195:SZ032878. In Poole Harbour, access by ferry. **Foot**: close to start/ end of South West Coast Path at Shell Bay. **Ferry**: half-hourly boat service from 10 (not National Trust) from Poole Quay (01202 631828 or 01929 462383) and Sandbanks (01929 462383). Boat trips available from Bournemouth (01202 558550 for details). Wheelchair users are advised to contact ferry operators. **Bus**: Wiltshire and Dorset 50 Bournemouth–Swanage, alight Sandbanks; 52 Poole–Sandbanks. Buses from surrounding areas to Poole Bridge, few minutes' walk from Poole ferry. **Train**: Poole ½ mile to Poole Quay; Branksome or Parkstone, both 3½ miles to Sandbanks.

Finding out more: 01202 707744 or brownseaisland@nationaltrust.org.uk

Brownsea Island		M	T	W	T	F	S	S
Boat service from Sandbanks only								
13 Mar–26 Mar	10–5	M	T	W	T	F	S	S
Full boat service from Poole Quay and Sandbanks								
27 Mar–31 Oct	10–5	M	T	W	T	F	S	S
Limited opening for booked groups only*								
1 Nov–31 Dec	10–5	M	T	W	T	F	S	S

Shop and Villano Café close 15 minutes before the island.
*1st November to 31 December: limited opening for booked adult organisations, school and youth groups only (01202 492161).

The magical Brownsea Island, Dorset

Buckland Abbey

Yelverton, Devon PL20 6EY

Map ① E8 🏛🐘✝♣⚓☂ 1948

In the 13th century, Buckland Abbey was home to the Cistercian monks who built the Abbey and the incredible Great Barn and farmed the then vast estate. The Abbey, now a house with a combination of furnished rooms and interactive museum galleries, tells the story of how two seafaring adventurers – Sir Richard Grenville and Sir Francis Drake – changed the shape of the house and the fate of the country. Discover the Buckland estate, the meadows, the orchards and the late spring bluebells. Enjoy the peace and tranquillity of the Tavy Valley and the far-reaching views. **Note**: the Abbey is presented in association with Plymouth City Museum.

Exploring
- Witness 700 years of history and change in the Abbey.
- Escape on one of our four woodland walks.
- Try on a Tudor costume.
- Take the challenge of our letterbox trail!
- See the famous Drake's Drum and learn the legend.
- Full programme of events, from concerts to living history.

Eating and shopping: 14th-century Refectory Restaurant serving freshly cooked local produce. Enjoy your picnic in the beautiful grounds. Browse for that special gift or plant in our shop. Restaurant available for private function hire.

You may also enjoy: Saltram, Cotehele, Lydford Gorge.

Making the most of your day: spring brings Sheep Day, guided walks and Easter trails. Concerts, craft fairs (small entrance charge, including members) and living history during summer, followed by a large living history Christmas event.

The south front of Buckland Abbey, Devon

Access for all: 🅿♿🦽🚻🔊🅰🎧💻🛗👁♿
Abbey 🦽♿🛗 Reception, shop, restaurant ♿🛗
Grounds 🦽♿➡

Getting here: 201:SX487667. **Cycle**: Drake's Trail, NCN27, 2 miles. **Bus**: DAC 55 from Yelverton (with connections from Plymouth ➤) Monday–Saturday; First 48 from Plymouth Sundays. **Train**: Plymouth 11 miles.
Road: 6 miles south of Tavistock, 11 miles north of Plymouth: turn off A386 ¼ mile south of Yelverton. **Parking**: free, 164 yards.

Finding out more: 01822 853607 or bucklandabbey@nationaltrust.org.uk

Buckland Abbey		M	T	W	T	F	S	S
12 Feb–21 Feb	11–4:30	M	T	W	T	F	S	S
26 Feb–7 Mar	11–4:30					F	S	S
13 Mar–31 Oct	10:30–5:30	M	T	W	T	F	S	S
5 Nov–12 Dec	11–4:30					F	S	S
17 Dec–23 Dec	11–4:30	M	T	W	T	F	S	S

Last admission 45 minutes before closing. Some areas may occasionally be closed to visitors due to private functions.

Carnewas and Bedruthan Steps

Bedruthan, St Eval, Wadebridge, Cornwall PL27 7UW

Map ① C8   1930

This is one of the most popular destinations on the Cornish coast. Spectacular clifftop views stretch across Bedruthan beach (not Trust-owned). The Trust has rebuilt the cliff staircase to the beach, but visitors need to be aware of the risk of being cut off by the tide. **Note**: it is unsafe to bathe at any time. WC not always available.

Exploring
- Enjoy magnificent walks along the coast path towards Park Head.
- Discover more in *Coast of Cornwall* leaflet, number six.

Eating and shopping: browse in the National Trust shop. Treat yourself in the popular café (National Trust-approved concession). Relax in the clifftop tea garden, adjoining the café.

Making the most of your day: children's quiz/trail, walks leaflet and information panel. Occasional family events, including treasure hunts and rock pooling. Dogs allowed.

Access for all: �♿♿♿♿♿

Getting here: 200:SW849692.
Foot: ¾ mile of South West Coast Path on property. **Bus**: Western Greyhound 556, Newquay–Padstow ➡. **Train**: Newquay 7 miles. **Road**: just off B3276 from Newquay to Padstow, 6 miles south west of Padstow. **Parking**: free.

Finding out more: 01637 860563 or carnewas@nationaltrust.org.uk

Carnewas and Bedruthan Steps		M	T	W	T	F	S	S
Clifftop walks								
Open all year		M	T	W	T	F	S	S
Shop								
12 Feb–28 Feb	10:30–3:30	M	T	W	T	F	S	S
6 Mar–7 Mar	10:30–3:30						S	S
13 Mar–31 Oct	10:30–5	M	T	W	T	F	S	S
Café								
12 Feb–21 May	11–4	M	T	W	T	F	S	S
22 May–30 Sep	10:30–5	M	T	W	T	F	S	S
1 Oct–19 Dec	11–4	M	T	W	T	F	S	S

Cliff staircase closed throughout winter from 1 November. For café enquiries telephone 01637 860701.

Castle Drogo

Drewsteignton, near Exeter, Devon EX6 6PB

Map ① F7   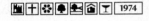 1974

Inside this remarkable granite building, set above the Teign Gorge, is a surprisingly warm and comfortable family home. Commissioned by retail tycoon Julius Drewe, and designed by Sir Edwin Lutyens, the castle harks back to a romantic past, while its brilliant design heralds the modern era. Behind the imposing façade, poignant family keepsakes sit alongside 17th-century tapestries. The dramatic Dartmoor setting can be appreciated from the delightful formal garden and walks into a rhododendron valley. Tours and fun activities are arranged throughout the year. Our visitor centre and café specialising in local produce have been enlarged and improved. **Note**: approach lane is narrow with tight corners. Extreme moorland weather may be experienced.

Exploring
- Within the austere granite castle, discover unexpected family comforts.
- Explore the Arts & Crafts-inspired garden.
- Enjoy the estate's changing landscapes, from moorland to woodland.
- Visit the woodchip boiler and discover Drogo's green initiatives.
- Follow in Mr Drewe's footsteps along the gorge edge.

Castle Drogo, set high above the Teign Gorge in Devon

Exploring — **New**: improved and 'greener' visitor centre open throughout the year.

Eating and shopping: new café: local produce, open-air seating and play area. Try the delicious Drogo breakfasts from 8:30 every morning. Shop sells local products and plants inspired by Drogo garden. Café available for corporate and private functions and parties.

You may also enjoy: Finch Foundry, Lydford Gorge and Coleton Fishacre.

Making the most of your day: events throughout the year. Enjoy a guided tour or activity, available most days. Waymarked walks through estate and garden. Quizzes and trails. Play croquet on dry summer days. Dogs on leads welcome throughout estate and informal garden areas.

Access for all: 🅿 🄳 🄳♿ 🖼 🚻 🕶♿ 👐 🖼 🎞 ♫ ∴ 🅰
Building 🚶♿♿ Grounds 🚶♿♿ ➡

Getting here: 191:SX721900. **Foot**: Two Moors Way. **Bus**: Dartline Service 173 Exeter–Moretonhampstead (passing Exeter Central ➿), Monday to Saturday. Country Bus 274 from Okehampton ➿, Sundays and Bank Holiday Mondays, May to September. **Train**: Yeoford 8 miles. **Road**: 5 miles south of A30 Exeter–Okehampton. Take A382 Whiddon Down–Moretonhampstead road; turn off at Sandy Park. **Parking**: free, 400 yards. Tight corners and narrow lanes.

Finding out more: 01647 433306 or castledrogo@nationaltrust.org.uk

Castle Drogo		M	T	W	T	F	S	S
Castle								
13 Feb–21 Feb	11–5	M	T	W	T	F	S	S
27 Feb–7 Mar	11–5	·	·	·	·	·	S	S
13 Mar–31 Mar	11–5	M	·	W	T	F	S	S
1 Apr–5 Sep	11–5	M	T	W	T	F	S	S
6 Sep–31 Oct	11–5	M	·	W	T	F	S	S
27 Nov–12 Dec	11–4:30	·	·	·	·	·	S	S
18 Dec–23 Dec	11–4:30	M	T	W	T	·	S	S
Visitor centre and garden*								
13 Mar–31 Oct	8:30–5:30	M	T	W	T	F	S	S
18 Dec–23 Dec	8:30–5	M	T	W	T	·	S	S
27 Dec–31 Dec	8:30–5	M	T	W	T	F	S	S

*Visitor centre and garden also open weekends in January, February, early March, November and early December, plus every day 13 to 21 February. Garden opens 9:30.

Chedworth Roman Villa

Yanworth, near Cheltenham, Gloucestershire GL54 3LJ

Map ① K2   🏛 | 1924

'It was fantastic, very interesting, very well documented. Extremely kind and helpful staff, and amazing activities for children.'
The Carré family, London

Mosaic at Chedworth Roman Villa, Gloucestershire

The remains of one of the largest Roman villas in the country provide a fascinating insight into 4th-century Roman Britain. The site was discovered in 1864 on the Earl of Eldon's estate by a local gamekeeper, and subsequently excavated by his estate workers. More than a mile of walls survives, along with beautiful mosaics, two bathhouses, hypocausts, a water shrine and latrine. Visitors to the museum will discover artefacts from the villa, and an audio-visual presentation brings history to life. The ruins nestle in a wooded combe in the heart of the Cotswolds, with beautiful woodland walks. **Note**: property opening later due to building works. Access to mosaics may be restricted occasionally.

Exploring
- Discover Roman mosaics, underfloor heating, bathhouses and latrines.
- Find out about life in 4th-century Roman Britain.
- Enjoy stunning Cotswold scenery and wonderful wildlife.
- Experience Roman life at our living history events.
- Have a picnic in the romantic Roman ruins.
- Explore the villa with our family Tracker Packs.

Eating and shopping: our shop is *the* Roman retail experience! Wide range of Roman-themed gifts and plants. Large selection of Roman/archaeological books and classic Roman novels. Light snacks and drinks available in shop or tea tent.

You may also enjoy: Lodge Park, Sherborne Park Estate, Snowshill Manor and Hidcote.

Making the most of your day: Romano-British costumed interpretation and Living History events throughout the season, including Gladiators and Roman soldiers. Children's drop-in mosaic-making sessions, trails and quizzes during school holidays.

Access for all: 🅿🚻♿🔁🚻📷🚗 ▪▪
Building 🏛♿ Grounds 🚶

Getting here: 163:SP053135.
Train: Cheltenham Spa 14 miles. **Road**: 3 miles north west of Fossebridge on Cirencester–Northleach road (A429); approach from A429 via Yanworth or from A436 via Withington (coaches must approach from Fossebridge).
Parking: two car parks. Villa car park, 15 yards from entrance; overflow car park (April to September), 250 yards from entrance.

Finding out more: 01242 890256 or chedworth@nationaltrust.org.uk

Chedworth Roman Villa		M	T	W	T	F	S	S
13 Mar–27 Mar	10–4	·	T	W	T	F	S	S
28 Mar–31 Oct	10–5	·	T	W	T	F	S	S
2 Nov–14 Nov	10–4	·	T	W	T	F	S	S

Open Bank Holiday Mondays. Tea tent open weekends and school holidays.

Trying on a reproduction Roman helmet at Chedworth Roman Villa, Gloucestershire

The Church House

Widecombe-in-the-Moor, Newton Abbot,
Devon TQ13 7TA

Map ① F7   1933

One of the finest examples of a 16th-century Church House, originally used for parish festivities or 'ales'. **Note**: no WC, nearest in public car park. Adjoining National Trust shop (walks leaflets available).

Getting here: 191:SX718768. In centre of Widecombe, north of Ashburton, west of Bovey Tracey. On B3387 about 12 miles from A38, Bovey Tracey. 270 bus runs daily in August.

Finding out more: 01364 621321 or churchhouse@nationaltrust.org.uk

Clevedon Court

Tickenham Road, Clevedon,
North Somerset BS21 6QU

Map ① I4   🏛 ❀ 1961

Home to the lords of the manor of Clevedon for centuries, the core of the house is a remarkable survival from the medieval period. The house was purchased by Abraham Elton in 1709 and it is still the much-loved family home of his descendants today. **Note**: the Elton family opens and manages the property for the National Trust.

Exploring   – Be delighted by the fascinating collection of Nailsea glass.
– Look at striking examples of Eltonware pottery.
– Explore the delightful terraced garden.

Eating and shopping: quench your thirst at the tea kiosk (not National Trust).

Making the most of your day: new family guide. Children's quiz/trail.

Access for all: 🅿🅳🅳🦽🏠♿🚻 🔵🔵🅰
Building 🔼 Grounds 🔼

Getting here: 172:ST423716. **Bus**: First X7 (direct) Bristol–Clevedon or 364 (passing Nailsea and Blackwell ≋). **Train**: Yatton 3 miles. **Road**: 1½ miles east of Clevedon, on Bristol road (B3130), signposted from M5 exit 20. **Parking**: free onsite parking, 50 yards. Unsuitable for trailer caravans or motor caravans. Alternative parking 100 yards east of entrance in cul-de-sac.

Finding out more: 01275 872257 or clevedoncourt@nationaltrust.org.uk

The Church House		M	T	W	T	F	S	S
12 Feb–24 Dec	10:30–*	**M**	**T**	**W**	**T**	**F**	**S**	**S**

Church House: open to visitors when not in use as a village hall; telephone shop to check opening times. *Shop/ information centre closing time dependent on weather, but never before 4.

Clevedon Court		M	T	W	T	F	S	S
1 Apr–30 Sep	2–5	·	·	**W**	**T**	·	·	**S**

Open Bank Holiday Mondays. Car park opens at 1:15. Entry to house by timed ticket, on a first-come, first-served basis. Tea kiosk: telephone for opening arrangements.

Clouds Hill

Wareham, Dorset BH20 7NQ

Map ① J7   1937

This tiny isolated brick and tile cottage in the heart of Dorset was the peaceful retreat of T. E. Lawrence ('Lawrence of Arabia'). The austere rooms are much as he left them and reflect his complex personality and close links with the Middle East, as detailed in a fascinating exhibition. **Note**: no WC.

Exploring
- 'Lawrence Trail', three-mile circular walk, organised by Purbeck Council.
- Visit www.purbeck.gov.uk for information on 'Lawrence Trail'.
- Follow the trail to a perfect hill-top picnic spot.

Eating and shopping: the small shop features Lawrence memorabilia and books.

Access for all: ⦂• Building 🏞 Grounds 🏠

Getting here: 194:SY824909. **Train**: Wool 3½ miles; Moreton 3½ miles. **Road**: 1 mile north of Bovington Tank Museum, 9 miles east of Dorchester, 1½ miles east of Waddock crossroads (B3390), 4 miles south of A35 Poole–Dorchester. **Parking**: free in small car park, 30 yards. No coaches (only minibuses) or trailer caravans.

Finding out more: 01929 405616 or cloudshill@nationaltrust.org.uk

Clouds Hill		M	T	W	T	F	S	S
18 Mar–31 Oct	12–5	·	·	·	T	F	S	S

Open Bank Holiday Mondays. Closes at dusk if earlier: no electric light.

Coleridge Cottage

35 Lime Street, Nether Stowey, Bridgwater, Somerset TA5 1NQ

Map ① H5   1909

Discover the former home of Samuel Taylor Coleridge, who lived in the cottage for three years from 1797. It was here that he wrote *The Rime of the Ancient Mariner*, *Frost at Midnight* and *Kubla Khan*. Mementoes of the poet can be seen here. **Note**: nearest WC at village library, 500 yards. Property is managed by Dunster Castle.

Exploring
- See the cottage of this great Romantic poet.
- Enjoy a walk on the nearby Quantock Hills.

Eating and shopping: visit the pubs in Nether Stowey village (not National Trust).

Making the most of your day: children's trail for cottage. Displays and poetry books in reading room.

Access for all: ⦂• ⓐ Building 🏠

Getting here: 181:ST191399. **Bus**: First 14 Bridgwater–Williton (passing close Bridgwater ⧩). **Train**: Bridgwater 8 miles. **Road**: at west end of Lime Street, opposite Ancient Mariner pub, 8 miles west of Bridgwater. **Parking**: 500 yards (not National Trust). Coach parking available by arrangement.

Finding out more: 01278 732662 or dunstercastle@nationaltrust.org.uk

Coleridge Cottage		M	T	W	T	F	S	S
1 Apr–26 Sep	2–5	·	·	·	T	F	S	S

Open Bank Holiday Mondays and Easter.

Clouds Hill, Dorset:
T. E. Lawrence's retreat

Coleton Fishacre

Brownstone Road, Kingswear, Devon TQ6 0EQ

Map (1) G9   1982

Travel back in time to the Jazz Age at the holiday home of the D'Oyly Carte family. You can lose yourself in the magical 12-hectare (30-acre) garden: viewpoints give enticing glimpses out to sea, paths weave through glades past tranquil ponds, and tender plants from the Mediterranean, South Africa and New Zealand thrive in the moist and sheltered valley. This most evocative of holiday homes, built in the Arts & Crafts style, is imbued with 1920s' elegance. A light, joyful atmosphere fills the rooms and music plays, echoing the family's Gilbert and Sullivan connections. **Note**: narrow busy approach lane, reversing required – especially around busiest time (1 to 2:30).

An inviting path through the woodland garden at Coleton Fishacre, Devon

Exploring
- Soak up the gorgeous Art Deco style in the house.
- Play the Blüthner piano in the Saloon.
- Explore the network of pathways through the valley garden.
- Relax by the ponds or in the gazebo.
- Walk the coast path, parking at Coleton Camp or Brownstone.
- Seemly Hut open, with garden and Pudcombe Cove information.

Eating and shopping: fabulous 'Taste of the West' award-winning licensed tea-room. Try Peter and Colleen's famous Coleton cream tea. Shop features items with an Art Deco/Jazz Age influence. Unusual shrubs and garden furniture in the plant centre.

You may also enjoy: Greenway, the holiday home of Agatha Christie, on the River Dart.

Making the most of your day: guided garden walks every day at 2:15. Family activity packs, quizzes and trails. Exhibitions by local artists in the house. Music and theatre events in house

and garden. Dogs on leads only on surrounding National Trust land. Dog crèche. Magnificent coastal footpaths.

Access for all: 🅿️🚻♿🅱️🔾🖐️📷🎫🔔 ••
Building 🔾🔾🔾 Grounds 🔾➡️

Getting here: 202:SX910508. **Foot**: South West Coast Path within ¾ mile.
Bus: Stagecoach in Devon 120 Paignton–Kingswear; otherwise Stagecoach in Devon 22/4 Brixham–Kingswear (with connections from Paignton). On all, alight ¾ mile south west of Hillhead, 1½ miles walk to garden.
Train: Paignton 8 miles; Kingswear (Paignton & Dartmouth Steam Railway) 2¼ miles by footpath, 2¾ miles by road. **Road**: 3 miles from Kingswear; take Lower Ferry road, turn off at toll house (take care in narrow lanes). 6 miles from Brixham, take A3022 to Kingwear, turn left at toll house. Narrow entrance and drive.
Parking: free, 20 yards. For visitors to house and garden only. Coaches must book.

Finding out more: 01803 752466 or coletonfishacre@nationaltrust.org.uk

Coleton Fishacre		M	T	W	T	F	S	S
1 Mar–31 Oct	10:30–5	M	T	W	·	·	S	S
Open Good Friday.								

Compton Castle

Marldon, Paignton, Devon TQ3 1TA

Map (1) G8 1951

A rare survivor, this medieval fortress with high curtain walls, towers and a portcullis, set in a landscape of rolling hills and orchards, is a bewitching mixture of romance and history. Home for nearly 600 years to the Gilbert family, including Sir Humphrey Gilbert, half-brother to Sir Walter Ralegh. **Note**: credit cards not accepted. Few rooms open. Restricted access for those with limited mobility.

Exploring	– Feed your imagination among machicolations, spiral staircases and squints.
	– Discover Humphrey Gilbert, Elizabethan adventurer and explorer, and his family.
	– Enjoy the lovely rose, knot and herb gardens.

Eating and shopping: refreshments available at Castle Barton restaurant (not National Trust). Table-top shop selling souvenirs, guidebooks and postcards.

Making the most of your day: house, squirrel and garden trails. Guided castle tours at 2. Walks with the gardener on National Gardens Scheme garden day.

Access for all: ⊠⊠⊡⊡⊡⊡⊡
Building ⊡⊡ Grounds ⊡⊡➡

Getting here: 202:SX865648. **Bus**: Country Bus 7 Paignton–Marldon ➡; 111 Dartmouth–Torquay (passing Totnes ➡), on both alight Marldon, 1½ miles. **Train**: Torquay 3 miles. Newton Abbot 6 miles. **Road**: at Compton, 5 miles west of Torquay, 1½ miles north of Marldon. Signposted off A380 to Marldon (not suitable for coaches) or turn south from A381 Totnes road at Ipplepen – 2 miles to Compton. **Parking**: free, 30 yards. Additional parking at Castle Barton opposite entrance, 100 yards. Access for coaches via Ipplepen, not Marldon. Coaches may park at bus turning area opposite, 125 yards.

Finding out more: 01803 661906 or comptoncastle@nationaltrust.org.uk

Compton Castle		M	T	W	T	F	S	S
1 Apr–28 Oct	10:30–4:30	**M**	·	**W**	**T**	·	·	·

Corfe Castle

The Square, Corfe Castle, Wareham, Dorset BH20 5EZ

Map (1) K7 1982

'**A favourite haunt from my childhood, which I now share with my grandchild – and it is still as exciting!'**
Mary Rooker, Sherborne

One of Britain's most majestic ruins and once a controlling gateway through the Purbeck Hills, the castle boasts breathtaking views and several waymarked walks. The demolition of the castle in 1646 by the Parliamentarians marked the end of a rich history as both fortress and royal residence. With its fallen walls and secret places, it is a place to explore, a giant playground for children of all ages. The crumbling ruins and subtle invasion by plants and animals, along with its almost ethereal quality as light and weather change, all contribute to the unique atmosphere of Corfe Castle. **Note**: steep, uneven slopes, steps and sudden drops.

Exploring	– Uncover the secrets of Dorset's iconic medieval monument.
	– Discover how royalty, warfare and nature has shaped the castle.
	– Spot the 'murder holes' and count the arrow loops.
	– Guided tours are often available through the main season.
	– Try a self-guided walk around the surrounding Purbeck countryside.
	– Visit the pretty village, with its medieval church tower.

Eating and shopping: delightful licensed 18th-century tea-room, with tea garden. Enjoy a traditional Dorset cream tea with local clotted cream. Treat yourself to a light lunch and homemade pudding. Locally made gifts in our shop in the village square.

You may also enjoy: Kingston Lacy, built by the Bankes family after the castle was destroyed.

Making the most of your day: open-air theatre and cinema. Enid Blyton's birthday celebration (11 August). Family and general tours. Castle Quests during school holidays. Living history events and jester fun days. Dogs welcome on a short lead.

Access for all: 🅿🐕♿🚻🚼📷👓📖🅰

Grounds 🚶🚶

Getting here: 195:SY959824. **Bus**: Wiltshire and Dorset 40 Poole–Swanage (passing Wareham ≷). **Train**: Wareham 4½ miles.

Corfe Castle (Swanage Steam Railway) a few minutes walk (park and ride from Norden station). **Road**: on A351 Wareham–Swanage road. **Parking**: pay and display at Castle View, off A351 (800 yards walk uphill to castle). Members free. Norden park and ride (all-day parking, ½ mile walk to castle) and West Street in village (pay and display, neither National Trust).

Finding out more: 01929 481294 (Infoline). 01929 480921 (shop). 01929 480609 (Learning) or corfecastle@nationaltrust.org.uk

Corfe Castle		M	T	W	T	F	S	S
1 Jan–28 Feb	10–4	M	T	W	T	F	S	S
1 Mar–31 Mar	10–5	M	T	W	T	F	S	S
1 Apr–30 Sep	10–6	M	T	W	T	F	S	S
1 Oct–31 Oct	10–5	M	T	W	T	F	S	S
1 Nov–31 Dec	10–4	M	T	W	T	F	S	S

Tea-room: closed for refurbishment 4 to 29 January (01929 481332). Shop and tea-room close 5:30 April to September. Property completely closed 25 and 26 December. High winds can cause closure of all or parts of castle.

Corfe Castle, Dorset: one of Britain's most majestic ruins

Cornish Mines and Engines

Pool, near Redruth, Cornwall TR15 3ED

Map ① C9   🔧T 1967

At the very heart of the Cornish Mining World Heritage Site sit these two great beam engines, originally powered by high-pressure steam boilers introduced by local hero Richard Trevithick. Preserved in their towering engine houses, they are a reminder of Cornwall's days as a world-famous centre of industry, engineering and innovation. Our pumping engine is one of the largest surviving Cornish beam engines in the world, and our restored winding engine can be seen in action daily. So come and enjoy our film, displays, models and knowledgeable guides, and discover the whole dramatic story of Cornish mining. **Note**: Trevithick Cottage is nearby at Penponds (open April to October, Wednesday 2 to 5).

Exploring
- Discover the massive 52-ton beam in Taylor's engine house.
- See the 1887 Michell's winding engine in action every day.
- Experience the dizzying view inside a 36-metre-high chimney.
- Watch the atmospheric film about the history of Cornish mining.
- Enjoy a peaceful moment in our secluded grounds.
- Find out more about the Cornish Mining World Heritage Site.

Eating and shopping: comprehensive selection of mining and local history books for sale. Spoil yourself with local fudge and chocolate from the Lizard. Local rocks, minerals and Cornish tin available from our shop.

You may also enjoy: the cliff-top Levant Mine and Beam Engine in nearby West Penwith.

Making the most of your day: guided tours of the whole site. Regular films about the history of the mine and the Cornish World Heritage Site. Lots of specialist events and family days throughout the year.

Access for all: 🅿️♿🚾👶📷♿🔊

Taylor's engine house ⬆️ Michell's engine house ♿

Visitor centre and shop ♿♿➡️

Getting here: 203:SW672415. at Pool, 2 miles west of Redruth on either side of A3047 midway between Redruth and Camborne. **Cycle**: NCN3, ½ mile. **Bus**: First 14/18 Penzance/St Ives–Truro (passing Camborne and Redruth ≋). **Train**: Redruth 2 miles; Camborne 2 miles. **Road**: site is signposted from A30 'Camborne East' and 'Redruth' junctions. Industrial Discovery Centre and Taylor's engine house reached through Morrisons' car park. **Parking**: free at Morrisons' superstore, 27 yards from site entrance. Secondary car park (not National Trust) outside Michell's engine house off A3047.

Finding out more: 01209 315027 or cornishmines@nationaltrust.org.uk. Trevithick Road, Pool, Cornwall TR15 3NP

Cornish Mines and Engines		M	T	W	T	F	S	S
21 Mar–30 Jun	11–5	M	·	W	T	F	·	S
1 Jul–30 Aug	11–5	M	·	W	T	F	S	S
1 Sep–31 Oct	11–5	M	·	W	T	F	·	S

November to end February by arrangement only.

A quiet moment at Cotehele, Cornwall

Cotehele

St Dominick, near Saltash, Cornwall PL12 6TA

Map (1) E8

| 1947

'**We ran out of time. This magical place has so much to see we almost needed two days.**'
Pearn family, Ilchester, Somerset

A Tudor house with many stories and legends, festooned with tapestries and adorned with textiles, arms and armour, pewter, brass and old oak furniture; a magical experience as little has changed over the years. Outside, explore the formally planted terraces, or lose yourself in the Valley Garden, which includes a medieval stewpond and dovecote. Seek tranquillity in the Upper Garden or visit the two orchards planted with local apples and cherries. Cotehele Quay is the home of the restored Tamar sailing barge 'Shamrock' and gateway to a wider estate. The Discovery Centre tells the story of the Tamar Valley.

Exploring
- Climb the 18th-century Prospect Tower folly, with fantastic views.
- Explore the quay's Discovery Centre, open daily.
- Relax in the Mother Orchard.
- Discover the woodland trails.
- Walk miles of footpaths exploring wildlife and industrial ruins.
- Discover England's oldest domestic clock, still in its original position.

Eating and shopping: buy Cornish food, gifts and local plants in our shop. Enjoy local produce in the Barn Restaurant and Edgcumbe Arms. Browse the exquisite work in Cotehele Gallery. Stay in one of the nine holiday cottages at Cotehele.

You may also enjoy: Cotehele Mill, Buckland Abbey, Lydford Gorge and Antony.

Making the most of your day: meet our housekeeping team and learn how they look after the house. Join in with our gardeners. Lots of family events. 'The lost art of improvisation': a new exhibition. Dogs welcome on the estate (not the formal garden).

Access for all: Building Grounds

Getting here: 201:SX422685. **Cycle**: NCN27, 8 miles. Hilly route from Tavistock to Cotehele. **Ferry**: Calstock can be reached from Plymouth by water (contact Plymouth Boat Cruises Ltd, 01752 822797) and from Calstock local river passenger ferry operates during summer subject to tides (01822 833331). **Bus**: First 190 Plymouth–Gunnislake–Cotehele–Gunnislake (Sundays, June to September only); DAC 79 Tavistock–Callington (passes Gunnislake ⭍) to Calstock within 1½ miles. **Train**: Calstock, 1½ miles (signposted from station). **Road**: on west bank of the Tamar, 1 mile west of Calstock by steep footpath (6 mile by road), 8 mile south west of Tavistock, 14 miles from Plymouth via Saltash Bridge; 2 miles east of St Dominick, 4 miles from Gunnislake (turn at St Ann's Chapel). Coaches only by prior arrangement. **Parking**: free. Parking charge on quay.

Finding out more: 01579 351346. 01579 352711 (restaurant). 01579 352717 (tea-room) or cotehele@nationaltrust.org.uk

Cotehele		M	T	W	T	F	S	S
House								
13 Mar–31 Oct	11–4:30	M	T	W	T	·	S	S
Hall of House and garland								
8 Nov–24 Dec	11–4	M	T	W	T	F	S	S
Garden and estate								
Open all year	10–dusk	M	T	W	T	F	S	S
Barn Restaurant, shop, plant sales and gallery								
13 Feb–12 Mar	11–4	M	T	W	T	F	S	S
13 Mar–31 Oct	11–5	M	T	W	T	F	S	S
1 Nov–24 Dec	11–4	M	T	W	T	F	S	S
Edgcumbe Arms								
13 Feb–12 Mar	11–4	M	T	W	T	F	S	S
13 Mar–31 Oct	11–5	M	T	W	T	F	S	S
6 Nov–19 Dec	11–4	·	·	·	·	·	S	S

House open Good Friday. Barn Restaurant opens 10:30 from 13 March to 31 October.

Cotehele Mill

St Dominick, near Saltash, Cornwall PL12 6TA

Map ① E8 🏠❌🗼🍴🏠 1947

This working mill is an atmospheric reminder of the recent past when corn was ground here for the local community. A range of outbuildings includes a traditional furniture maker and a potter, along with re-creations of wheelwright's, saddler's and blacksmith's workshops. **Note**: no WCs or parking (park at the Quay).

Exploring
- Watch the mill grinding (Tuesdays and Thursdays) and buy flour.
- Find out more about the hydro-power scheme.
- Jump on the shuttle bus to Cotehele House and Quay.
- Stay in one of the mill's two holiday cottages.

Eating and shopping: buy Cotehele flour here or at the main shop. Walk to the quay for a pasty or ice-cream. Enjoy local produce in the Edgcumbe Arms.

Making the most of your day: tours every day at 3. Family trails. Dogs welcome, but not in the workshops.

Access for all: 🇩♨🚻📖♿
Building 🦽 Grounds ♿

Getting here: 201:SX417682. **Cycle**: NCN27, 8 miles. Hilly route from Tavistock to Cotehele. **Ferry**: Calstock can be reached from Plymouth by water (contact Plymouth Boat Cruises Ltd, 01752 822797) and from Calstock local river passenger ferry operates during summer subject to tides (01822 833331). **Bus**: First 190 Plymouth– Gunnislake-Cotehele-Gunnislake (Sundays, June to September only); DAC 79 Tavistock-Callington (passes Gunnislake 🚃) to Calstock within 1½ miles. **Train**: Calstock, 1½ miles (signposted from station). **Road**: on west bank of the Tamar, 1 mile west of Calstock by steep footpath (6 miles by road), 8 miles south west of Tavistock, 14 miles from Plymouth via Saltash Bridge; 2 miles east of St Dominick, 4 miles from Gunnislake (turn at St Ann's Chapel). Coaches by prior arrangement only. **Parking**: no parking, except by prior arrangement for visitors with disabilities. All other visitors must park at Cotehele Quay and walk ½ mile through the woods.

Finding out more: 01579 350606. 01579 351346 (property office) or cotehele@nationaltrust.org.uk

Cotehele Mill		M	T	W	T	F	S	S
13 Mar–30 Sep	11–5	**M**	**T**	**W**	**T**	**F**	**S**	**S**
1 Oct–31 Oct	11–4:30	**M**	**T**	**W**	**T**	**F**	**S**	**S**

Cotehele Quay, Cornwall, a short walk from the Mill

The peaceful lily pond in The Courts Garden, Wiltshire

The Courts Garden

Holt, near Bradford-on-Avon,
Wiltshire BA14 6RR

Map ① J4   ✿ 1943

Full of variety, this charming garden shows the English country style at its best. Peaceful water gardens and herbaceous borders, with organically shaped topiary, demonstrate an imaginative use of colour and planting, creating unexpected vistas. Stroll through the arboretum with its wonderful species of trees and naturally planted spring bulbs.

Exploring
— Relax in our tranquil garden with topiary and colourful borders.
— Productive small vegetable garden and orchard.
— Arboretum with naturalised bulbs.
— Orchard room display area.

Eating and shopping: tea-room serving coffee, lunches, afternoon tea (not National Trust). Plants for sale grown on the property.

Making the most of your day: events programme including Orchard Room exhibitions by local artists, guided tours and children's trail. Cross-country walk to Great Chalfield Manor (National Trust).

Access for all: ⬚⬚⬚⬚⬚⬚ Garden ⬚⬚⬚

Getting here: 173:ST861618. **Cycle**: NCN4, 1¼ miles. **Bus**: Faresaver 237 Trowbridge–Melksham (passing close Trowbridge ≋). **Train**: Bradford-on-Avon 2½ miles; Trowbridge 3 miles. **Road**: 3 miles south west of Melksham, 2½ miles east of Bradford-on-Avon, on south side of B3107. Follow signs to Holt. **Parking**: free (not National Trust), 80 yards, in village hall car park opposite, on north side of B3107. Additional parking, when signed, at Tollgate Inn and at Manor Farm (for coaches and cars), both on the B3107 towards Bath. No visitor parking on village streets.

Finding out more: 01225 782875 or courtsgarden@nationaltrust.org.uk

The Courts Garden		M	T	W	T	F	S	S
13 Feb–31 Oct	11–5:30	M	T	·	T	F	S	S

Out of season by appointment only.

Dunster Castle

Dunster, near Minehead, Somerset TA24 6SL

Map ① G5  1976

Dramatically sited on a wooded hill, a castle has existed here since at least Norman times, with an impressive medieval gatehouse and ruined tower giving a reminder of its turbulent history. Home of the Luttrell family for more than 600 years, the present building was remodelled in 1868–72 by Antony Salvin. The fine oak staircase and plasterwork ceiling he adapted can still be seen. Visitors can relax on the sunny sheltered terrace, which is home to a variety of subtropical plants and the National Collection of Strawberry Trees. Magnificent views over the surrounding countryside add to the ambience.

The Stair Hall at Dunster Castle, Somerset

Exploring
- Enjoy breathtaking views across Exmoor and the Bristol Channel.
- Spy on the bats of Tenants Hall using our batcam.
- Discover the beautiful plasterwork ceilings and carved staircase.
- Uncover Antony and Cleopatra's story in 17th-century leather hangings.
- Look out for spooks on the Ghostbusters Trail.
- Visit medieval Dunster village.

Eating and shopping: our 17th-century stables shop has local and original gifts. Visit Dunster village for more shops and places to eat.

You may also enjoy: a carriage ride at Arlington Court, home of the National Trust's Carriage Collection.

Making the most of your day: range of family trails to help you explore the castle and gardens. Costumed guided tours and basement tours through the season. Dogs in park only on lead.

Access for all:
Castle 🔆🔆🔆 Stables 🔆 Grounds 🔆➡🔆

Getting here: 181:SS995435. **Bus**: First 398 Tiverton–Minehead; also 28 Taunton–Minehead (passing Taunton ≋), alight Dunster Steep, ½ mile. **Train**: Dunster (West Somerset Railway) 1 mile. **Road**: in Dunster, 3 miles south east of Minehead. National Trust car park approached direct from A39. **Parking**: 300 yards.

Finding out more: 01643 823004 (Infoline). 01643 821314 or dunstercastle@nationaltrust.org.uk

Dunster Castle		M	T	W	T	F	S	S
Castle*								
13 Mar–21 Jul	11–5	M	T	W	·	F	S	S
23 Jul–1 Sep	11–5	M	T	W	·	F	S	S
3 Sep–31 Oct	11–5	M	T	W	·	F	S	S
Garden and park								
1 Jan–12 Mar	11–4	M	T	W	T	F	S	S
13 Mar–31 Oct	11–5	M	T	W	T	F	S	S
1 Nov–31 Dec	11–4	M	T	W	T	F	S	S
Shop**								
2 Feb–12 Mar	11–4	M	T	W	T	F	S	S
13 Mar–31 Oct	10–5	M	T	W	T	F	S	S
1 Nov–31 Dec	11–4	M	T	W	T	F	S	S

Garden, park and shop closed 25 and 26 December. *Last entry 4, 13 March to 21 July and 3 September to 31 October. **Shop may open weekends during January, subject to essential repairs.

Dunster Working Watermill

Mill Lane, Dunster, near Minehead, Somerset TA24 6SW

Map ① G5   🗙 1976

A restored 18th-century watermill built on the site of a mill mentioned in the Domesday Survey of 1086. **Note**: the mill is a private business and members pay the admission charge.

Getting here: 181:SS995435. On River Avill, beneath Castle Tor.

Finding out more: 01643 821759 or dunstercastle@nationaltrust.org.uk

Dunster Working Watermill		M	T	W	T	F	S	S
Mill								
1 Apr–31 Oct	11–4:30	**M**	**T**	**W**	**T**	**F**	**S**	**S**
Tea-room*								
1 Apr–31 Oct	10:30–4:45	**M**	**T**	**W**	**T**	**F**	**S**	**S**

*Tea-room hours may vary (01643 821759). Mill open Good Friday.

Dyrham Park

Dyrham, near Bath, Gloucestershire SN14 8ER

Map ① J4   🏯✝🌸♣🔔 1961

'Delightful gardens, so well maintained. Good gardening advice. House interesting and staff so helpful. Tea-room so welcoming, excellent lunch.'
Janet van Rensburg, Sheepscombe

Set in a beautiful Gloucestershire valley and surrounded by 110 hectares (272 acres) of garden and rolling parkland, this grand baroque house with spectacular sweeping views towards Bristol was designed by Talman for William Blathwayt, Secretary at War during the reign of William III. Lavish 17th-century collections reflect the fashion for all things Dutch, including paintings and furniture. Later 18th-century additions include furniture by Gillow and Linnell, and the Victorian domestic quarters provide visitors with an intriguing insight into life below stairs. **Note**: some rooms have very low light levels to protect contents.

Exploring
– Follow the park trails.
– Let off steam in the Old Lodge play area.
– Have fun with the park and garden Tracker Packs.
– Join one of the special introductory tours of the house.
– Step out on a guided park and garden walk.
– Look out for the historic deer.

Eating and shopping: local venison and perry pear are used in recipes. Quench your thirst in the tea garden, with snack kiosk. Look out for the plant sales in the shop. The shop offers a selection of local produce.

You may also enjoy: if you are visiting Bath, don't miss Prior Park Landscape Garden.

Making the most of your day: Open-air theatre in the summer, children's workshops, guided tours of the house, park and garden. Dogs in dog walking area close to main car park only.

Access for all:
Building 🏛🔧 Grounds ♿➡

The west front of Dyrham Park, Gloucestershire

Getting here: 172:ST743757. **Foot**: Cotswold Way passes property. **Cycle**: Avon and Wiltshire cycleways. **Bus**: special link from Queen's Square, ½ mile Bath Spa ⬛ (0117 937 2501 for times). **Train**: Bath Spa 8 miles. **Road**: 8 miles north of Bath, 12 miles east of Bristol; approached from Bath–Stroud road (A46), 2 miles south of Tormarton interchange with M4, exit 18. **Sat Nav**: SN14 8HY. **Parking**: free, 500 yards.

Finding out more: 0117 937 2501 or dyrhampark@nationaltrust.org.uk

Dyrham Park		M	T	W	T	F	S	S
House*								
13 Mar–31 Oct	11–5	M	T	·	·	F	S	S
Garden, shop and tea-rooms								
27 Feb–7 Mar	11–5	·	·	·	·	·	S	S
13 Mar–4 Jul	11–5	M	T	·	·	F	S	S
5 Jul–29 Aug	11–5	M	T	W	T	F	S	S
30 Aug–31 Oct	11–5	M	T	·	·	F	S	S
6 Nov–19 Dec	11–4	·	·	·	·	·	S	S
Park**								
Open all year	11–5:30	M	T	W	T	F	S	S

Open Bank Holiday Mondays and Good Friday, 11 to 5. Last admission one hour before closing. *Between 11 and 12 access to the house will be by introductory tour only (limited numbers, allocated on arrival). **Park: closes dusk if earlier, closed 25 December.

Finch Foundry

Sticklepath, Okehampton, Devon EX20 2NW

Map ① F7   🏠 🔧T 1994

Set amid beautiful Dartmoor countryside in the village of Sticklepath, this last remaining water-powered forge in England gives a unique insight into village life in the 19th century. In its heyday the foundry made 400 tools a day, including sickles, scythes and shovels for West Country farmers and miners.

Exploring
- Demonstrations and tours of the machinery every hour.
- Watch the large waterwheels driving the tilt hammer and grindstone.
- Learn about the lives of the foundry owners and workers.

Exploring — See Tom Pearse's summerhouse, of Widecombe Fair fame.

Eating and shopping: local blacksmiths' items and plants on sale in the shop. Try delicious local ice-cream at the tea-room. Stay in the lovely Foundry House holiday cottage next door.

Making the most of your day: family activities, vintage vehicle rallies. Dogs welcome in all areas except tea-room, shop and foundry during demonstrations.

Access for all: 🅳♿ 🚻 ♿ 👁
Foundry ♿ Upstairs Gallery ♿ Grounds

Getting here: 191:SX641940. In the centre of Sticklepath village. **Foot**: on the 180-mile Tarka Trail. **Cycle**: on West Devon Cycle Route. **Bus**: Western Greyhound 510 Exeter–Okehampton (passing Exeter Central ⬛), First X9, Carmel Coaches 179 Okehampton–Moretonhampstead. **Train**: Okehampton (Sunday, June–September only) 4½ miles. **Road**: 4 miles east of Okehampton off A30. **Parking**: free. Not suitable for coaches and high vehicles. Access is narrow and low.

Finding out more: 01837 840046 or finchfoundry@nationaltrust.org.uk

Finch Foundry		M	T	W	T	F	S	S
20 Mar–31 Oct	11–5	M	·	W	T	F	S	S

Foundry and shop open for St Clement's Day (patron saint of blacksmiths) on 20 November.

The forge at Finch Foundry, Devon

Fyne Court

Broomfield, Bridgwater, Somerset TA5 2EQ

Map ① H5 1967

A real hidden Somerset gem, back under Trust management. Originally designed as the pleasure grounds of the Crosse family and the pioneer 19th-century electrician Andrew Crosse. Spend a magical day walking through the woodland garden, before meandering through bluebell-filled copses and the delightful meadows on the wider estate.

Exploring
   – Walk through an enchanting landscape with folly and boathouse.
   – Learn about the scientist Andrew Crosse, 'thunder and lightning man'.
   – Visit our nature reserve and follow our nature trails.
   – Headquarters of the Quantock Hills Area of Outstanding Natural Beauty.

Eating and shopping: a small catering outlet is due to open at Easter.

Making the most of your day: exciting seasonal events programme. Listen to birdsong in spring, go wild in the woods and take part in our family activities. Dogs under close control on estate only.

Access for all: ⬚⬚⬚ Grounds ⬚⬚

Getting here: 182:ST222321. 6 miles north of Taunton; 6 miles south west of Bridgwater. **Train**: Taunton 6 miles, Bridgwater 6 miles. **Parking**: 150 yards.

Finding out more: 01823 451873 or fynecourt@nationaltrust.org.uk

Fyne Court		M	T	W	T	F	S	S
Open all year	9–5	**M**	**T**	**W**	**T**	**F**	**S**	**S**

Gates close at 5. Closed 24 to 31 December.

Glastonbury Tor

near Glastonbury, Somerset

Map ① I5 1933

The dramatic and evocative Tor dominates the surrounding countryside and offers spectacular views over Somerset, Dorset and Wiltshire. At the summit of this very steep hill an excavation has revealed the plans of two superimposed churches of St Michael, of which only a 15th-century tower remains. **Note**: no WC.

Tower of St Michael, Glastonbury Tor, Somerset

Exploring
   – Climb the Tor for spectacular views over three counties.
   – Walk the public footpaths across the Tor.

Eating and shopping: enjoy the perfect picnic.

Access for all: ⬚⬚ Grounds ⬚⬚

Getting here: 182/183:ST512386. **Foot**: short walk from the town centre, eastwards along A361. **Cycle**: NCN3. **Bus**: First 377 Wells–Yeovil within ½ mile. **Road**: signposted from Glastonbury town centre, from where seasonal park and ride (not National Trust) operates. **Parking**: no parking (except for orange or blue badge holders). Use council-run park and ride from centre of Glastonbury from April to September, or park in free car park at Somerset Rural Life Museum, Abbey Farm, Glastonbury. Telephone 01458 831197 to confirm times available. Lower entrance to the Tor is approximately ¼ mile from museum car park.

Finding out more: 01934 844518 or glastonburytor@nationaltrust.org.uk

Glastonbury Tor	M	T	W	T	F	S	S
Open all year	**M**	**T**	**W**	**T**	**F**	**S**	**S**

Glendurgan Garden

Mawnan Smith, near Falmouth,
Cornwall TR11 5JZ

Map (1) C9 1962

'What a lovely environment to learn about all these incredible plants the world has to offer.'
Keith Swinton, Evesham

Lose yourself in the three valleys of Glendurgan Garden – full of fun, natural beauty and amazing plants. Discover giant rhubarb plants in the jungle-like lower valley and spiky arid plants basking in the sunny upper slopes. Wander through the garden down to the beautiful hamlet of Durgan on the Helford River: a place to watch birds and boats, skim stones and build sand-castles. Find a boat-seat, gigantic tulip-trees and ponds teeming with wildlife. Learn about the Fox family who created this 'small peace [sic] of heaven on earth'.

Exploring
- Get lost in the 176-year-old cherry laurel maze.
- Become airborne on the 'Giant's Stride' swing.
- Explore three beautiful valleys leading to the Helford River.
- Discover weird and wonderful plants from all around the world.
- Find tranquillity among the many native wild flowers and wildlife.
- Challenge yourselves to a stone-skimming competition on Durgan beach.

Eating and shopping: treat yourself to delicious home-cooked locally sourced food. Indulge in an irresistible cream tea or slice of cake. Sample the best of Cornish produce from our shop. Find a living souvenir of Glendurgan from the plant sales.

You may also enjoy: Trelissick, with its stunning views over the sea and river, plus its fantastic plant collection.

Glendurgan, Cornwall: the maze in mid summer

Making the most of your day: a variety of special events for families and keen gardeners takes place throughout the year. Information Room in Durgan village with stories about the Helford River and its wildlife.

Access for all:

Getting here: 204:SW772277. **Foot**: South West Coast Path within ¾ mile. **Ferry**: link between Helford Passage (1½ mile walk from Durgan) and Helford Village on south side of Helford River. **Bus**: First 35 Falmouth–Helston. **Train**: Penmere 4 miles. **Road**: 4 miles south west of Falmouth, ½ mile south west of Mawnan Smith, on road to Helford Passage. **Parking**: free. Car park gates locked at 5:30.

Finding out more: 01326 252020 (during opening hours). 01872 862090 (out of hours). 01326 250247 (tea-house) or glendurgan@nationaltrust.org.uk

Glendurgan Garden		M	T	W	T	F	S	S
13 Feb–31 Jul	10:30–5:30	·	T	W	T	F	S	·
2 Aug–4 Sep	10:30–5:30	M	T	W	T	F	S	·
7 Sep–30 Oct	10:30–5:30	·	T	W	T	F	S	·

Open Bank Holiday Mondays. Closed Good Friday.

Godolphin

Godolphin Cross, Helston, Cornwall TR13 9RE

Map ① B9 〔🎫🏠🏛⚓🎡❋⚑〕 〔2000〕

Beautiful romantic old house and outbuildings. Centuries of benign neglect have given the house, garden and surrounding estate buildings a haunting air of antiquity and peace. The garden is unchanged since the 16th century and is considered to be one of the most important in Europe. Archaeologically rich estate walks. **Note:** major conservation work underway. House will not be open except for hard-hat tours.

The haunting garden at Godolphin, Cornwall

Exploring
– Enjoy the peace and tranquillity of the ancient garden.
– Hard-hat tours of building conservation work in action.
– Explore surrounding countryside with lots of archaeological features.

Eating and shopping: enjoy tea, coffee and biscuits. Small souvenirs, postcards, walks booklets on sale.

Making the most of your day: food fairs, family activities, special tours with 'Jack', our 700-year-old Godolphin handyman. Guided walks, virtual tour of inaccessible places. Dogs on estate only.

Access for all: Garden 〔♿〕

Getting here: 203:SW599321. **Bus:** First 39* Camborne–Helston (passing close Camborne ≋). **Train:** Camborne 9 miles. **Road:** from Helston take A394 to Sithney Common, turn right on to B3302 to Leedstown, turn left and follow signs. From Hayle take B3302 to Leedstown, turn right and follow signs. From west, take B3280 through Goldsithney and turn right at Townshend. **Parking:** free. Coach access from Townshend.

Finding out more: 01736 763194 or godolphin@nationaltrust.org.uk

Godolphin	M	T	W	T	F	S	S
Garden							
13 Mar–31 Oct 10–4	**M**	**T**	**W**	·	·	**S**	**S**
Estate							
Open all year	**M**	**T**	**W**	**T**	**F**	**S**	**S**

'Hard-hat' tours of the house will be available on a regular basis through the season.

Godrevy

Gwithian, near Hayle, Cornwall TR27 5ED

Map ① B9 〔🚻〕 〔1939〕

Awe-inspiring expanse of sandy beaches around St Ives Bay. Wild cliffs, rich in wildlife and archaeology, with popular café. **Note:** beware of cliff edges, unstable cliffs and incoming tides. WC not always available.

Getting here: 203:SW582430. Hayle 5 miles. Just off the B3301 north of Gwithian village.

Finding out more: 01872 552412 (Area Warden) or godrevy@nationaltrust.org.uk

Godrevy	M	T	W	T	F	S	S
Open all year	**M**	**T**	**W**	**T**	**F**	**S**	**S**

Sunset as seen from Godrevy, Cornwall

Great Chalfield Manor and Garden

near Melksham, Wiltshire SN12 8NH

Map ① J4    1943

This beautiful medieval manor sits in peaceful countryside. Cross the upper moat, passing barns, gatehouse and delightful parish church to enjoy fine oriel windows and the soldiers, griffons and monkey adorning the rooftops. Romantic gardens offer terraces, topiary houses, gazebo, lily pond, roses and views across the spring-fed fishpond. **Note:** home to donor family tenants who manage it for the National Trust.

Exploring
- Explore gardens designed by Alfred Parsons, replanted by the family.
- Elegant architecture and Edwardian restoration completed for the donor.
- Enjoy stone looking-masks, furniture, tapestries and Tropnell's Cartulary.
- Beautiful adjacent parish church (not National Trust), donations welcome.

Eating and shopping: enjoy tea/coffee in the Motor House (not National Trust). Buy plants grown on site from the gardens and orchards. Pick up a guidebook and postcards of the manor.

Making the most of your day: spot woodpeckers or nesting swallows. Enjoy history posters and slide show of the garden in the Edwardian Motor House. Walk to the nearby Courts Garden for lunch or tea.

Access for all: 🅿️ ♿ 🚻 📷 🖼️ ♿ •••
Manor ♿ ♿ Garden ♿ ➡️

Getting here: 173:ST860631. **Foot:** 1-mile walk by public footpath from The Courts Garden (National Trust), Holt. **Cycle:** NCN4. On the Wiltshire Cycleway. **Bus:** Faresaver 237 Trowbridge–Melksham (passing close Trowbridge 🚉), alight Holt, 1 mile. **Train:** Bradford-on-Avon, 3 miles. **Road:** 3 miles south west of Melksham off B3107 via Broughton Gifford Common (follow sign for Broughton Gifford, take care in narrow lane). Coaches must approach from north (via Broughton Gifford); lanes from south too narrow. **Parking:** free, 100 yards, on grass verge outside manor gates.

Finding out more: 01225 782239 or greatchalfieldmanor@nationaltrust.org.uk

Great Chalfield Manor		M	T	W	T	F	S	S
Manor House								
1 Apr–31 Oct	*			T	W	T			S
Garden								
1 Apr–28 Oct	11–5			T	W	T			
1 Apr–31 Oct	2–5								S

*Admission to manor house by guided tour only (not bookable). Tuesday to Thursday: tours at 11, 12, 2, 3 and 4. Sunday: tours at 2, 3 and 4. Tours take 45 minutes and numbers are limited. Visitors arriving during a tour can visit the adjoining parish church and garden first. Group visits welcome on Friday and Saturday (not Bank Holidays) by written arrangement with the donor family tenant, Mrs Robert Floyd (charge applies).

Greenway

Greenway Road, Galmpton, near Brixham, Devon TQ5 0ES

Map ① G8   🏛️🏠❄️♿🏠🍴 2000

This is an extraordinary glimpse into the private holiday home of the famous and much-loved author Agatha Christie and her family. The relaxed and atmospheric house is set in the 1950s, and contains many of the family's collections, including archaeology, Tunbridgeware, silver, botanical china and books. Outside you can explore the large and romantic woodland garden, with a restored vinery, wild edges and rare plantings, which drifts down the hillside towards the sparkling Dart estuary. Please consider 'green ways' to get here, to relieve pressure on congested lanes: eg cycling, walking or ferries from Dartmouth, Torquay and Brixham. **Note:** timed entry system: tickets cannot be booked and sell out quickly. Cars must be booked.

Exploring
- Enjoy the adventure of arriving by ferry at Greenway Quay.
- Use our touch screens to learn about writing and archaeology.
- Explore the garden and estate on a network of walks.
- Discover 'Ralegh's Boathouse' on the Dart.
- Stay in the Lodge or holiday apartment in the house.
- Theatre, literary and garden events and The Great Create Festival.

Eating and shopping: licensed Barn Café specialising in local produce and vegetarian food. Greenway Kitchen serving award-winning lunch and afternoon tea. Shop specialising in Agatha Christie's books and memorabilia. Local products, works of art and plant sales.

You may also enjoy: Coleton Fishacre close by: magnificent garden with sea views and Arts & Crafts-style house.

Making the most of your day: regular events include gallery exhibitions, guided tours of the house, holiday apartment and garden. Children's trails and quizzes, family Tracker Packs. Dogs on leads on main drive. Watering and tethering in courtyard. Great estate walks.

Access for all: ⊞ ♿ ♿ ⌂ ♿ ♿ ♿ ♿ ⌂ ⊞ ♿
Greenway House ♿ Boathouse ♿ Garden ♿ ➡

Getting here: 202:SX876548. **Foot**: walk the Dart Valley Trail from Kingswear or Dartmouth. Greenway walk from Brixham. Parking Bascombe Road pay & display.
Ferry: catch a ferry from Dartmouth (use Dartmouth park and ride only), Totnes (tidal, Steamer Quay) Brixham and Torquay. Contact Greenway Ferry service on 0845 489 0418 or www.greenwayferry.co.uk for all information (individuals and groups), or visit the ticket office in Dartmouth opposite National Trust shop. Please allow at least 6 hours parking, from whichever destination you travel. Please note there is a steep uphill 800-yd walk from Greenway Quay to visitor reception.
Train: Paignton 4½ miles, Churston 2 miles. Catch a steam train or bus: contact Paignton & Dartmouth Steam Railway on 01803 834488/555872 or www.paignton-steamrailway.co.uk. **Parking**: limited booked parking only, early sell-outs possible, especially on Wednesdays and in the school holidays (book at least three days in advance on 01803 842382 or on www.nationaltrust.org.uk/greenway). Unbooked cars will be turned away. No parking on Greenway Road or in Galmpton village. Groups by road: midi-coaches only, limited to one per day (booked only).

Finding out more: 01803 842382 or greenway@nationaltrust.org.uk

Greenway		M	T	W	T	F	S	S
3 Mar–18 Jul	10:30–5	·	·	**W**	**T**	**F**	**S**	**S**
20 Jul–31 Aug	10:30–5	·	**T**	**W**	**T**	**F**	**S**	**S**
1 Sep–31 Oct	10:30–5	·	·	**W**	**T**	**F**	**S**	**S**

Limited timed tickets to the house allocated on arrival only, and early sell-outs are possible; on busy days there will be a delay during which time you can enjoy the garden, café, gallery and shop.

The River Dart seen from Greenway, Devon

Hailes Abbey

near Winchcombe, Cheltenham, Gloucestershire GL54 5PB

Map (1) K1 ✚ 🏛 1937

Once a Cistercian abbey, founded in 1246 by Richard of Cornwall and dissolved Christmas Eve 1539, Hailes never housed large numbers of monks but had extensive and elaborate buildings. It was financed by pilgrims visiting its renowned relic, 'the Holy Blood of Hailes' – allegedly a phial of Christ's blood. **Note**: financed, managed and maintained by English Heritage (0117 9750700, www.english-heritage.org.uk/hailes).

Exploring — Explore the ruins of this 13th-century Cistercian Abbey.
— New interpretation panels guide you around the abbey buildings.
— Sculptures, stonework and other finds are displayed in the museum.
— The adjacent parish church has medieval wall-paintings.

Eating and shopping: browse in the shop. Choose a treat from the refreshments. Settle down for a picnic in the grounds.

Access for all: ⠿ Building 🚻

Getting here: 150:SP050300. **Foot**: Cotswold Way within ¾ mile. **Bus**: Castleways 606 Cheltenham–Willersey, alight Greet, 1¾ miles by footpath. **Train**: Cheltenham 10 miles. **Road**: 2 miles north east of Winchcombe, 1 mile east of Broadway road (B4632, originally A46). **Parking**: free (not National Trust).

Finding out more: 01242 602398 or hailesabbey@nationaltrust.org.uk

Hailes Abbey		M	T	W	T	F	S	S
1 Apr–30 Jun	10–5	M	T	W	T	F	S	S
1 Jul–31 Aug	10–6	M	T	W	T	F	S	S
1 Sep–30 Sep	10–5	M	T	W	T	F	S	S
1 Oct–31 Oct	10–4	M	T	W	T	F	S	S

Opening times subject to change. Please confirm with the property.

Hardy Monument

Black Down, Portesham, Dorset

Closed in 2010 due to refurbishment.

Hardy's Cottage

Higher Bockhampton, near Dorchester, Dorset DT2 8QJ

Map (1) J7   1948

Thomas Hardy was born in 1840 in this small cob and thatch cottage, which was built by his great-grandfather and is little altered since the family left. His early novels *Under the Greenwood Tree* and *Far from the Madding Crowd* were written here. **Note**: no WC.

Exploring — Be delighted by the charming cottage garden.

Eating and shopping: Thomas Hardy's books for sale.

Making the most of your day: programme of events throughout the season.

Access for all: 🅳 ♿ ⠿ ⊘
Building 🚻 Grounds 🚻 ➡

Getting here: 194:SY728925. **Train**: Dorchester South 4 miles; Dorchester West 4 miles. **Road**: 3 miles north east of Dorchester, ½ mile south of A35. From Kingston Maurward roundabout follow signs to Stinsford and Higher Bockhampton. **Parking**: free (not National Trust), 600 yards. Drop-off point by prior arrangement with property.

Finding out more: 01297 561900 or hardyscottage@nationaltrust.org.uk

Hardy's Cottage

For further information of opening times for Hardy's Cottage please contact the West Dorset Office on 01297 561900.

Hardy's Cottage, Dorchester, Dorset, dates from 1800. Thomas Hardy was born here in 1840

Access for all: 🔲🔲🔲

Getting here: 180:SS655481. **Foot**: South West Coast Path within ¾ mile. **Bus**: TW Coaches 309, 310 Barnstaple–Lynton (passing close Barnstaple ≡), alight just north of Parracombe, then 2 miles. **Road**: halfway between Combe Martin and Lynton, off A39 at Hunters Inn. **Parking**: 50 yards.

Finding out more: 01598 763402 or heddonvalley@nationaltrust.org.uk

Heddon Valley		M	T	W	T	F	S	S
Heddon Valley								
Open all year		M	T	W	T	F	S	S
Shop								
13 Feb–21 Feb	11–3	M	T	W	T	F	S	S
27 Feb–7 Mar	11–3	·	·	·	·	·	S	S
13 Mar–30 Apr	10:30–4	M	T	W	T	F	S	S
1 May–30 Sep	10:30–5	M	T	W	T	F	S	S
1 Oct–31 Oct	10:30–4	M	T	W	T	F	S	S

Heddon Valley

Heddon Valley, Parracombe, Barnstaple, Devon EX31 4PY

Map ① F5   🔲🔲🔲 1963

The West Exmoor Coast, favourite landscape of the Romantic poets and smugglers, offers not only the Heddon Valley, but also Woody Bay and Hangman Hills to explore. There are spectacular coastal and woodland walks, as well as an information centre, car park and gift shop in Heddon Valley itself.

Exploring
- Enjoy the South West Coast Path and dramatic sea cliffs.
- Download circular walks in the area from our website.
- Discover the fantastic birdlife of Woody Bay.
- Don't miss the majestic Hangman Hills.

Eating and shopping: outdoor wear, Exmoor products and great gifts in the shop. Delicious local ice-creams with flavours to suit all tastes.

Making the most of your day: free family activity packs and all-terrain buggies to borrow at Heddon. The whole family can learn about and enjoy the nature and history of the Heddon Valley. Dogs welcome.

Heelis

Kemble Drive, Swindon, Wiltshire SN2 2NA

Map ① K3   🔲🔲🔲 2005

The National Trust's award-winning central office is a remarkable example of innovative and sustainable building construction. Designed by Feilden Clegg Bradley Architects in 2005, this architectural gem uses timber from our woodlands and wool from Herdwick sheep grazed on Trust farmlands, to help make Heelis a unique working environment.

Exploring
- Tours every Friday, except Bank Holidays.

Eating and shopping: Heelis café serves a range of delicious local food. There is plenty of choice in our spacious, airy shop.

Making the most of your day: a virtual tour of Heelis is available at reception every day during normal opening hours.

Access for all:

Building 🚻

Getting here: 173:SU141850. **Bus**: Thamesdown Transport and Stagecoach, 13 and 14, alight Rodbourne Road, then 200 yards. **Train**: Swindon, ¾ mile, from station, turn right along Station Road,follow signs to Designer Outlet through second tunnel under railway line. **Road**: off B4289. Follow signs for Swindon Designer Outlet Centre. Park and ride from Wroughton. **Parking**: parking (not National Trust), 100 yards (pay and display). Additional car and coach parking at Outlet Centre North car park. Heelis operates a green travel policy, visitor parking facilities are limited and must be booked with reception.

Finding out more: 01793 817400 or heelisreception@nationaltrust.org.uk

---

Heelis

Admission to offices by booked guided tour only. Heelis, shop and café open daily throughout the year, with the exception of Christmas Day, Boxing Day, New Year's Day and Easter Sunday. Please contact Heelis for further information.

Heelis, the central office of the National Trust in Swindon, Wiltshire

Hidcote Manor Garden

Hidcote Bartrim, near Chipping Campden, Gloucestershire GL55 6LR

Map ①L1   🌼 1947

Hidcote is one of England's great gardens. Designed and created by the horticulturist Major Lawrence Johnston in the Arts & Crafts style, it is made up of exquisite garden rooms, each possessing its own special character. Visitors will discover rare shrubs and trees, outstanding herbaceous borders and unusual plant species. The garden changes in harmony with the seasons, from vibrant spring bulbs to autumn's glorious Red Border. Nestled in the Cotswolds with sweeping views across the Vale of Evesham, Hidcote is appealing all year round.

Exploring
- Challenge family and friends to a game of tennis.
- See the transformation of the new Kitchen Garden.
- Learn about Lawrence Johnston through one of our free talks.
- Discover great views on one of the many public footpaths.
- Be inspired by breathtaking garden design and planting.
- Enjoy a game of croquet on the Theatre Lawn.

Eating and shopping: enjoy a delicious meal in our Garden Restaurant. Browse the largest plant centre in the National Trust. Seasonal menus inspired by our fresh Kitchen Garden produce. Buy exclusive Hidcote souvenirs in the shop.

You may also enjoy: the small organic garden at Snowshill Manor.

Making the most of your day: daily introductory talks, programme of private evening Head Gardener tours, open-air theatre, themed family trails and workshops.

The long walk at Hidcote Manor Garden, Gloucestershire

Access for all: [icons]
Visitor Reception [icons] **Grounds** [icons]

Getting here: 151:SP176429. **Foot**: 1½ miles by public footpath from Mickleton (route is uphill and steep). **Cycle**: NCN5, 1¼ miles. **Train**: Honeybourne 4½ miles. **Road**: close to village of Mickleton, 4 miles north east of Chipping Campden, 1 mile east of B4632 (originally A46), off B4081. Coaches are not permitted through Chipping Campden High Street. **Parking**: free, 100 yards. Coaches must book – space limited.

Finding out more: 01386 438333 or hidcote@nationaltrust.org.uk

Hidcote Manor Garden		M	T	W	T	F	S	S
Garden, shop, restaurant, plant sales and Barn Café								
27 Feb–7 Mar	11–4	·	·	·	·	·	S	S
13 Mar–27 Jun	10–6	M	T	W	·	·	S	S
28 Jun–29 Aug	10–6	M	T	W	T	F	S	S
30 Aug–29 Sep	10–6	M	T	W	·	·	S	S
2 Oct–31 Oct	10–5	M	T	W	·	·	S	S
6 Nov–19 Dec	12–4	·	·	·	·	·	S	S
Barn Café and plants sales additional opening								
8 Apr–25 Jun	11–4	·	·	·	T	F	·	·

Open Good Friday. All facilities close at the same time as last admission (one hour before closing). Restaurant closed November and December for refurbishment.

Holnicote Estate

Selworthy, Minehead, Somerset TA24 8TJ

Map ① G5 [icons] 1944

This stunning estate, within Exmoor National Park, offers breathtaking panoramic views. Spectacular coastline and more than 100 miles of footpaths lead through enchanting rural landscapes, woods, moors, farmland and villages. Noted for its diversity of wildlife, many rare species can be discovered in the Horner and Dunkery National Nature Reserve. **Note**: WCs at Bossington, Allerford, Selworthy and Horner.

Exploring
– Climb to the highest point on Exmoor.
– Discover the walks, including easy access trails.
– Look out for the enchanting cottages in pretty villages.

Eating and shopping: refuel at the tea-rooms at Horner, Bossington and Selworthy.

Making the most of your day: visit Exmoor Falconry Centre and the West Somerset Rural Life Museum. Dogs on leads only.

Access for all: [icon] **Grounds** [icons]

Getting here: 181:SS920469. **Foot**: 3¾ miles of South West Coast Path on property; Coleridge Way; Macmillan Way. **Bus**: Quantock 39 Minehead–Porlock, 300 Minehead–Lynmouth, alight Holnicote, then ½ mile. **Train**: Minehead (West Somerset Railway) 5 miles. **Road**: off A39 Minehead–Porlock, 3 miles west of Minehead. **Parking**: free at Allerford, North Hill, Dunkery, Webbers Post and Selworthy. Parking (pay and display) at Horner and Bossington. Only Horner car park is suitable for coaches.

Finding out more: 01643 862452 or holnicote@nationaltrust.org.uk

Holnicote Estate	M	T	W	T	F	S	S
Open all year	M	T	W	T	F	S	S

Estate office: open Monday to Friday, 8:30 to 5; closed Bank Holidays and public holidays.

Horton Court

Horton, near Chipping Sodbury, South
Gloucestershire BS37 6QR

Closed in 2010 due to refurbishment.

Killerton

Broadclyst, Exeter, Devon EX5 3LE

Map ① G6 🏛️🏕️✝️🏚️❄️🌳
🖼️🏠🍸 1944

'**Stunning gardens and house, utterly
beautiful. Hard to leave as it feels like you've
gone back in time**.'
Hayley Fernandes, Toronto

Would you give away your family home for
your political beliefs? Sir Richard Acland did
with his estate, one of the largest the National
Trust has acquired at 2,590 hectares (6,400
acres) with 20 farms and 200-plus cottages.
Killerton House, built in 1778–9, brings to life
generations of the Aclands, one of Devon's
oldest families. The historic fashion exhibition,
'Elegance', explores the fabulous and luxurious
dress of the past 200 years. The gem of
Killerton, beautiful year round, is the garden
created by John Veitch, with rhododendrons,
magnolias and rare trees surrounded by rolling
Devon countryside.

Exploring
— Feel at home in the relaxed
atmosphere of the house.
— Escape into the garden
with majestic trees and
sloping lawns.
— Discover the rustic
summerhouse – the
Bear's Hut.
— Have fun or discover more
at one of our events.
— Meander through the ancient
parkland, woods and
Devon countryside.
— Enjoy 'Elegance', an exhibition
of glamorous fashion over
two centuries.

Eating and shopping: buy Killerton cider,
chutney, flour or honey in the shop. Plant
centre with peat-free plants. Two tea-rooms
using local produce and Killerton estate flour.
Stay in one of Killerton's four thatched
holiday cottages.

Killerton, Devon, sits in gardens with majestic trees and sloping lawns

You may also enjoy: Knightshayes Court. On the Killerton estate: Broadclyst village, Marker's Cottage, Clyston Mill, Ashclyst Forest.

Making the most of your day: discover 'Killerton's Characters'. Try on replica costumes. Browse in the second-hand bookshop. For families: Tracker Packs, play area, Discovery Centre (school holidays), trails. Waymarked walks and orienteering routes. Dogs welcome on leads in park and estate walks only. Dog bowls and posts available.

Access for all: ⬚⬚⬚⬚⬚⬚⬚⬚⬚⬚⬚
House ⬚⬚⬚ shop ⬚⬚ Grounds ⬚➡⬚

Getting here: 192:SS973001. **Cycle**: NCN52.
Bus: Stagecoach in Devon 1/A/B Exeter–Tiverton Parkway ⬚ (passing close Exeter Central ⬚), alight Killerton Turn ¾ mile.
Train: Pinhoe, not Sunday, 4½ miles; Whimple, 6 miles; Exeter Central and St David's, both 7 miles. **Road**: off Exeter–Cullompton road (B3181); from M5 northbound, exit 30 via Pinhoe and Broadclyst; from M5 southbound, exit 28. **Parking**: free, 280 yards.

Finding out more: 01392 881345 or killerton@nationaltrust.org.uk

Killerton		M	T	W	T	F	S	S
Park and garden								
Open all year	10:30–7	M	T	W	T	F	S	S
House								
13 Feb–21 Feb	2–4	·	·	W	T	F	S	S
10 Mar–31 Oct	11–5	M	T	W	T	F	S	S
4 Dec–23 Dec	2–4	M	T	W	T	F	S	S
Shop and tea-room								
2 Jan–7 Feb	11–4	·	·	·	·	·	S	S
Shop, plant sales and tea-room								
13 Feb–31 Oct	11–5:30	M	T	W	T	F	S	S
Shop and plant sales								
1 Nov–31 Dec	11–5:30	M	T	W	T	F	S	S
Tea-room								
1 Nov–31 Dec	11–4	M	T	W	T	F	S	S

Orchard tea-room and shop close at 3 on Christmas Eve and all day Christmas Day and Boxing Day. In winter, shop and Orchard tea-room may not open in bad weather. Garden tea-room usually open when house open (variable opening times) and open on selected dates in December for Christmas lunches.

Killerton: Budlake Old Post Office

Broadclyst, Killerton, Exeter, Devon EX5 3LW

Map ① G7

Close to Killerton, this small thatched cottage was the village post office, serving Killerton House and the local community, until the 1950s. The cottage has a delightful cottage garden including rose borders, herb and vegetable plots. **Note**: nearest WCs at Killerton.

Exploring
- Discover the privvy and pigsty.
- Listen to reminiscences of life in the post office.
- Step back in time amid the 1950s memorabilia.
- Imagine doing the washing in the Victorian wash-house.

Eating and shopping: visit nearby Killerton for tea-rooms, shop and plants.

Making the most of your day: footpath to Killerton along old carriage drive. Dogs on leads in garden only.

Access for all: ⬚ Building ⬚ Grounds ⬚

Getting here: 192:SS973001. **Cycle**: NCN52.
Bus: Stagecoach in Devon 1/A/B Exeter–Tiverton Parkway ⬚ (passing close Exeter Central ⬚), alight Killerton Turn ¾ mile.
Train: Pinhoe, not Sunday, 4½ miles; Whimple, 6 miles; Exeter Central and St David's, both 7 miles. **Road**: off Exeter–Cullompton road (B3181); from M5 northbound, exit 30 via Pinhoe and Broadclyst; from M5 southbound, exit 28. **Parking**: limited parking. Ample parking for cars and coaches at Killerton, 800 yards.

Finding out more: 01392 881690 or budlakepostoffice@nationaltrust.org.uk

Budlake Old Post Office		M	T	W	T	F	S	S
4 Apr–31 Oct	2–5	M	T	·	·	·	S	

Last admission 10 minutes before closing.

Killerton: Clyston Mill

Broadclyst, Exeter, Devon EX5 3EW

Map (1) G7   1944

Historic water-powered corn mill in a picturesque setting by the River Clyst surrounded by farmland and orchards. Corn is still ground here to make flour, keeping alive traditional skills. Discover more about what life would have been like for the miller, with hands-on activities and interpretation. **Note**: nearest parking and WCs in Broadclyst.

Exploring – Wander through Broadclyst's old churchyard to visit the mill.
– Watch the mill grinding flour (Sundays and Bank Holidays).
– See where the mill boy slept.
– Picnic by the river and listen to the birds.

Eating and shopping: buy a bag of Clyston Mill flour. Visit Killerton for cakes made from Clyston Mill flour.

Making the most of your day: children's trail and hands-on activities.

Access for all: Building 🦽 Grounds 🚶

Getting here: 192:SX981973. **Cycle**: NCN52.
Bus: Stagecoach in Devon 1/A/B Exeter–Tiverton Parkway 🚃 (passing close Exeter Central 🚃), alight Killerton Turn ¾ miles.
Train: Pinhoe, not Sunday, 4½ miles; Whimple, 6 miles; Exeter Central and St David's, both 7 miles. **Road**: off Exeter–Cullompton Road (B3181) in village of Broadclyst. Park in village car park, walk towards church and follow signs through churchyard. **Parking**: free (not National Trust), 450 yards.

Finding out more: 01392 462425 (Mill) or clystonmill@nationaltrust.org.uk

Killerton: Clyston Mill		M	T	W	T	F	S	S
4 Apr–31 Oct	2–5	**M**	**T**	·	·	·	·	**S**

Killerton: Marker's Cottage

Townend, Broadclyst, Exeter, Devon EX5 3HX

Map (1) G7   1944

An intriguing medieval cob cottage with a thatched roof and smoke-blackened timbers. Discover the fascinating history of the cottage including the unusual painted decorative screen showing St Andrew. A cross passage opens out onto a garden with a contemporary cob summerhouse and blacksmith's workshop. **Note**: nearest parking and WCs in Broadclyst.

Exploring – Find the painting of St Andrew and his boat.
– Be a history detective and follow the cottage's timeline.
– Discover the art of pargetting.
– Spot the dead rat.

Eating and shopping: visit nearby Killerton for tea-rooms, shop and plant centre.

Making the most of your day: handling collection and trail. Follow the Broadclyst village trail.

Access for all: 🅿 Building 🚶 Grounds 🚶

Getting here: 192:SX985973. **Cycle**: NCN52.
Bus: Stagecoach in Devon 1/A/B Exeter–Tiverton Parkway 🚃 (passing close Exeter Central 🚃). **Train**: Pinhoe, not Sunday, 2½ miles; Whimple, 4½ miles; Exeter Central and St David's, both 6 miles. **Road**: in village of Broadclyst. Park in village car park. Leaving car park by vehicle entrance, turn left, then right and turn right on to Townend.

The medieval Marker's Cottage, Killerton in Devon

Marker's Cottage is second cottage on left.
Parking: free (not National Trust), 250 yards.

Finding out more: 01392 461546 or
markerscottage@nationaltrust.org.uk

Killerton: Marker's Cottage		M	T	W	T	F	S	S
4 Apr–31 Oct	2–5	M	T	·	·	·	·	S

King John's Hunting Lodge

The Square, Axbridge, Somerset BS26 2AP

Map (1) I4   1968

This early Tudor timber-framed wool merchant's house (*circa* 1500) provides a fascinating insight into local history. Its strong medieval character is enhanced by the appearance of arcaded stalls opening onto the street on the ground floor (recreated by the National Trust during the building's restoration). **Note**: run as a local history museum by Axbridge and District Museum Trust.

Exploring — Find out local history in the museum.

Eating and shopping: visit the shop in museum (not National Trust).

Making the most of your day: occasional tours of historic Axbridge start from the museum.

Access for all: [🏛] Building [♿]

Getting here: 182:ST431545. In the Square, on corner of High Street. **Bus**: First 126 Weston-super-Mare–Wells (passing close Weston-super-Mare ≥). **Train**: Worle 8 miles. **Parking**: 100 yards (not National Trust).

Finding out more: 01934 732012 or kingjohns@nationaltrust.org.uk

King John's Hunting Lodge		M	T	W	T	F	S	S
2 Apr–30 Sep	1–4	M	T	W	T	F	S	S

1 October to 31 December: open first Saturday of month, 10 to 4, to coincide with farmers' market.

Kingston Lacy

Wimborne Minster, Dorset BH21 4EA

Map (1) K7    1982

'**What a superb house! Room after room was presented in stunning perfection.**'
Mrs Sansom, Huddersfield

The Japanese Garden at Kingston Lacy, Dorset

Home of the Bankes family for more than 300 years, this striking 17th-century house is noted for its lavish interiors. The outstanding art collection includes paintings by Rubens, Van Dyck, Titian and Brueghel, with the largest private collection of Egyptian artefacts in the UK. Outside, stroll across the beautiful lawns towards the restored Japanese tea garden. There are several waymarked walks through the surrounding parkland, with its fine herd of North Devon cattle, and the 3,443-hectare (8,500-acre) estate is dominated by the Iron Age hill fort of Badbury Rings, home to fourteen varieties of orchid.

Exploring — Outstanding art collection, including works by Rubens and Titian.
— View the restored Guido Reni fresco in Library.
— Explore the Edwardian Japanese Gardens.

Visit

Exploring
- Stroll through the Cedar Walk, Lime Walk and Nursery Wood.
- Seek out the Egyptian obelisk and sarcophagus.
- Enjoy Eyebridge riverside walk (hard, level surface) and Badbury Rings.

Eating and shopping: be sure to sample our prize-winning scones. Try our beef, from the Kingston Lacy North Devon herd. Treat yourself to regional and local foods and wines. Take home some National Trust-grown plants.

You may also enjoy: White Mill, Corfe Castle, Hardy's Cottage, Max Gate and Studland.

Making the most of your day: 'Putting the House to Bed' tours in November, bookings only. Throughout the year: farmers' markets, open-air theatre, tractor trailer tours, children's Victorian craft and 'Above and Below Stairs'. Dogs on leads in restaurant courtyard, park and woodlands only.

Access for all: ⬛⬛⬛⬛⬛⬛⬛⬛⬛⬛
⬛⬛⬛ Building ⬛ Grounds ⬛⬛⬛⬛

Getting here: 195:ST980019. **Bus**: Wilts & Dorset 13 from Bournemouth, 3 from Poole (passing Bournemouth ≋ and close Poole ≋), alight Wimborne Square, change on to Nordcat Service 88 Wimborne Minster–QE School. **Train**: Poole 8½ miles. **Road**: on B3082 Blandford–Wimborne road, 1½ miles west of Wimborne Minster. Sat Nav data unreliable, follow B3082. **Parking**: free. Charge at Badbury Rings on point-to-point race days.

Finding out more: 01202 883402 (Infoline) or kingstonlacy@nationaltrust.org.uk

Kingston Lacy		M	T	W	T	F	S	S
House								
13 Mar–31 Oct	11–5	·	·	**W**	**T**	**F**	**S**	**S**
Garden, park, shop and restaurant*								
5 Feb–7 Mar	10:30–4	·	·	·	·	**F**	**S**	**S**
13 Mar–31 Oct	10:30–6	**M**	**T**	**W**	**T**	**F**	**S**	**S**
1 Nov–23 Dec	10:30–4	**M**	**T**	**W**	**T**	**F**	**S**	**S**

Open Bank Holiday Mondays. Admission by timed ticket may operate on Bank Holiday Sundays and Mondays. Last admission to house one hour before closing. Garden, park, shop and restaurant closed 24 to 31 December. *Shop and restaurant close 30 minutes earlier.

Knightshayes Court

Bolham, Tiverton, Devon EX16 7RQ

Map ① G6  1973

One of the finest surviving Gothic Revival houses, built in the lush landscape of mid Devon, Knightshayes Court is a rare example of the work of the eccentric and inspiring architect William Burges. Built for the grandson of pioneer lace-maker John Heathcoat in 1869, the house is an exciting architectural experience, with extraordinary 'medieval' romantic interiors, rich decoration and ceramics. The vast garden, which was the Heathcoat Amory family's great passion, is renowned for its rare trees, shrubs and seasonal colours. The restored and fully productive organic kitchen garden is a treat for everyone who enjoys local produce. **Note**: access may be restricted during early spring and winter.

Exploring
- Enjoy the wonderfully re-created 'Burges Bedroom'.
- Relax in the peaceful and glorious garden.
- Discover the Seven Deadly Sins in the Billiard Room.
- Search for the Talbot dogs in the house and garden.
- Explore the celebrated 'Garden in the Wood'.
- See the chickens and geese in the kitchen garden.

Eating and shopping: gluten-free and dairy-free menu options available daily. Enjoy organic kitchen garden produce in the restaurant. Exceptionally well-stocked plant centre. Produce for sale in kitchen garden.

You may also enjoy: Killerton.

Making the most of your day: daily introductory talks in the house, special 'Conservation in Action' sessions Wednesdays, circular and introductory garden walks. Programme of open-air, family, Christmas, gardening and restaurant events. Picnics in parkland. Dogs on leads in woodland and park.

Knightshayes Court, Devon, designed by William Burgess

Access for all: 🅿 🅓 ♿ 🚾 ⬆ 🦽 📷 📖 🎧 📱 **Building** 🦽 ♿ 🚶 **Grounds** 🏞 ➡

Getting here: 181:SS960151. **Cycle:** NCN3.
Bus: First 398 Tiverton–Minehead, alight
Bolham, then ¾ mile. Otherwise Stagecoach
in Devon 1 from Tiverton Parkway ≋; 55/A/B
Exeter–Tiverton (passing close Exeter Central
≋), alighting Tiverton 1¾ miles. **Train:** Tiverton
Parkway 8 miles. **Road:** 7 miles from M5 exit 27
(A361); 2 miles north of Tiverton; turn right off
Tiverton to Bampton road (A396) at Bolham.
Sat Nav: turn off on reaching Tiverton and
follow signs. **Parking:** free.

Finding out more: 01884 254665. 01884
257381 (reception). 01884 259010 (shop) or
knightshayes@nationaltrust.org.uk

Knightshayes Court		M	T	W	T	F	S	S
House								
13 Feb–21 Feb	11–4	M	T	W	T	·	S	S
27 Feb–7 Mar	11–4	·	·	·	·	·	S	S
13 Mar–31 Oct	11–5	M	T	W	T	·	S	S
4 Dec–19 Dec	11–3	·	·	·	·	·	S	S
Garden, shop, plant centre and restaurant								
13 Feb–21 Feb	11–4	M	T	W	T	F	S	S
25 Feb–7 Mar	11–4	·	·	·	T	F	S	S
13 Mar–31 Oct	11–5	M	T	W	T	F	S	S
4 Nov–19 Dec	11–4	·	·	·	T	F	S	S
20 Dec–26 Dec	11–3	M	T	W	·	·	·	S
27 Dec–31 Dec	11–3	M	T	W	T	F	S	S

Open Good Friday. Access to house in December is limited
(reduced admission prices). House closed 12 December.

Lacock Abbey, Fox Talbot Museum and Village

Lacock, near Chippenham, Wiltshire SN15 2LG

Map ① K4   🏚 🏠 ✝ ♿ 🏊 ≋ 🍽 🏠 1944

Set in rural Wiltshire, Lacock village is famous
for its picturesque streets, historic buildings
and more recently as a TV and film location.
The Abbey, located at the heart of the village
within its own woodland grounds, is a quirky
country house of various architectural
styles, built upon the foundations of a
former nunnery. Visitors can experience the
atmosphere of the medieval rooms and cloister
court, giving a sense of the Abbey's monastic
past. The museum celebrates the achievements
of former Lacock resident, William Henry Fox
Talbot, famous for his contributions to the
invention of photography.

Exploring
- See newly opened parts of the Abbey.
- Enjoy the colourful spring bulbs in the Abbey grounds.
- Summer borders and newly completed greenhouse in the botanic garden.
- Wonderful changing exhibitions in the Upper Gallery of the museum.
- Enjoy the wider countryside on circular walks from the village.
- Visit the location of films like *Harry Potter* and *Cranford*.

Eating and shopping: find locally made
products in the National Trust shop.
Browse the museum shop or take home a
plant. Enjoy shopping, lunch or a drink in the
village. Experience Lacock with a stay in our
holiday cottage.

You may also enjoy: Courts Garden at Holt –
a mere six miles from Lacock.

Making the most of your day: full programme of events runs throughout the year, including family fun days, themed activities, open-air theatre, exhibitions and walks.

Access for all:

Abbey ▫▫ Museum ▫▫▫

Grounds ▫▫▫▫

Getting here: 173:ST919684. **Foot**: surrounding network of footpaths including route beside Wiltshire & Berkshire Canal. **Cycle**: NCN4, 1 mile. **Bus**: Faresaver X34/First 234 Chippenham–Frome (passing Melksham ≋, close Chippenham ≋ and close Trowbridge ≋). **Train**: Melksham 3 miles; Chippenham 3½ miles. **Road**: 3 miles south of Chippenham. M4 exit 17, signposted to Chippenham (A350). Follow A350 (signposted Poole/Warminster) until you reach Lacock, following signs leading to main car park. **Parking**: 220 yards (pay and display). No visitor parking on village streets.

Finding out more: 01249 730459 or lacockabbey@nationaltrust.org.uk

Lacock		M	T	W	T	F	S	S
Village*								
Open all year		M	T	W	T	F	S	S
Abbey and grounds**								
2 Jan–7 Feb	11–4	·	·	·	·	·	S	S
13 Feb–31 Oct	11–5	M	T	W	T	F	S	S
6 Nov–19 Dec	11–4	·	·	·	·	·	S	S
Museum, exhibition and bookshop								
2 Jan–7 Feb	11–4	·	·	·	·	·	S	S
13 Feb–31 Oct	11–5:30	M	T	W	T	F	S	S
6 Nov–19 Dec	11–4	·	·	·	·	·	S	S
High Street shop***								
2 Jan–12 Feb	11–4	M	T	W	T	F	S	S
13 Feb–31 Oct	10–5:30	M	T	W	T	F	S	S
1 Nov–31 Dec	11–4	M	T	W	T	F	S	S

*Businesses in village open at various times. **Access to Abbey on Tuesdays and winter weekends limited to cloisters only. Closed Good Friday (excluding village and High Street shop), ***High Street shop closed 1 January plus 25 and 26 December.

The fine medieval cloisters of Lacock Abbey, Wiltshire

Always remember your membership card

Lanhydrock

Bodmin, Cornwall PL30 5AD

Map (1) D8 1953

'What an insight into Victorian life! A place with everything – gorgeous gardens and parkland and a home people have loved.'
Liz Finlayson, Edinburgh

Lanhydrock is the perfect country house and estate, with the feel of a wealthy but unpretentious family home. Follow in the footsteps of generations of the Robartes family, walking in the 17th-century Long Gallery among the rare book collection under the remarkable plasterwork ceiling. After a devastating fire in 1881 the house was refurbished in the high-Victorian style, with the latest mod cons. Boasting the best in country-house design and planning, the kitchens, nurseries and servants' quarters offer a thrilling glimpse into life 'below stairs', while the spacious dining room and bedrooms are truly and deeply elegant.

Exploring
- There are 50 rooms to explore – allow plenty of time!
- Don't miss Tommy Agar-Robartes's poignant wartime suitcase.
- Play the Steinway piano in the Long Gallery.
- Explore the extensive garden and estate, colourful all the year.
- Discover the network of woodland, park and riverside paths.
- Don't miss our picnic area and adventure playground.

Eating and shopping: we serve local seasonal food in our friendly licensed restaurants. Go Cornish and have an Oggie pasty and cream tea. Local food and gifts available in the shop. Plant centre in car park outside the tariff area.

You may also enjoy: Trerice and Cotehele.

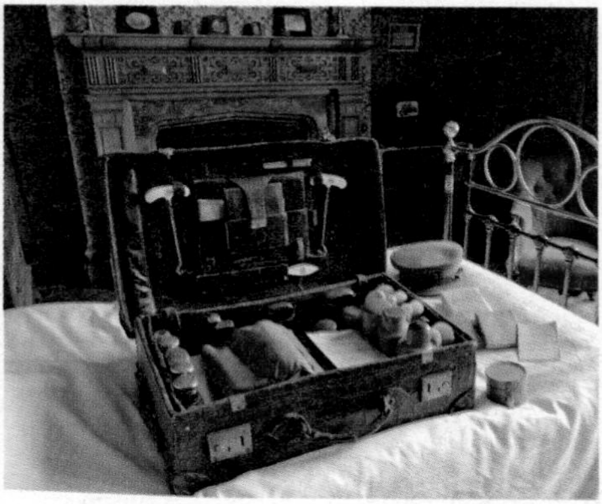

Tommy Agar Robartes's room in Lanhydrock, Cornwall

Making the most of your day: open-air theatre, garden tours and children's activities throughout the year. Dogs welcome on leads in park and woods.

Access for all: **Building** **Grounds**

Getting here: 200:SX088636. **Cycle**: NCN3, runs past entrance. **Train**: Bodmin Parkway 1¾ miles via original carriage-drive to house, signposted in station car park; 3 miles by road. **Road**: 2½ miles south east of Bodmin. Follow signposts from either A30, A38 Bodmin–Liskeard or take B3268 off A390 at Lostwithiel. **Parking**: free, 600 yards.

Finding out more: 01208 265950 or lanhydrock@nationaltrust.org.uk

Lanhydrock		M	T	W	T	F	S	S
House								
13 Mar–30 Sep	11–5:30	·	**T**	**W**	**T**	**F**	**S**	**S**
1 Oct–31 Oct	11–5	·	**T**	**W**	**T**	**F**	**S**	**S**
Garden								
Open all year	10–6	**M**	**T**	**W**	**T**	**F**	**S**	**S**
Shop and refreshments								
2 Jan–7 Feb	11–4	·	·	·	·	·	**S**	**S**
13 Feb–12 Mar	11–4	**M**	**T**	**W**	**T**	**F**	**S**	**S**
13 Mar–30 Sep	11–5:30	**M**	**T**	**W**	**T**	**F**	**S**	**S**
1 Oct–31 Oct	11–5	**M**	**T**	**W**	**T**	**F**	**S**	**S**
1 Nov–31 Dec	11–4	**M**	**T**	**W**	**T**	**F**	**S**	**S**

House open Bank Holiday Mondays and Mondays during school holidays. Plant centre open as house. Refreshments open 10:30, 13 March to 31 October. Closed 25 and 26 December. Shop and refreshments are inside the tariff area.

Lawrence House

9 Castle Street, Launceston, Cornwall PL15 8BA

Map ① E7   1964

Built in 1753, Lawrence House is leased to Launceston Town Council and used as a local museum and civic centre.

Getting here: 201:SX330848. 1 mile approximately north of the A30 in the oldest part of Launceston.

Finding out more: 01566 773277 or lawrencehouse@nationaltrust.org.uk

The Engine House at Levant Mine, Cornwall

Lawrence House		M	T	W	T	F	S	S
29 Mar–29 Oct	10:30–4:30	**M**	**T**	**W**	**T**	**F**	·	·

Open by appointment at other times for groups or individuals for study.

Levant Mine and Beam Engine

Trewellard, Pendeen, nr St Just, Cornwall TR19 7SX

Map ① A9   1967

Part of Cornwall and West Devon Mining World Heritage Site, this is the only Cornish beam engine anywhere in the world that is still in steam on its original mine site. The famous Levant engine is housed in a small engine house perched on the edge of the cliffs. Restored after 60 idle years by a group of volunteers known as the 'Greasy Gang', it is a thrilling experience for young and old alike to see this old engine in action, with its evocative sounds and smells.

Exploring
– A film tells the story of Levant Mine.
– Take a short underground tour through the miners' dry tunnel.

Exploring
– A cliff walk takes you to Botallack Mine.
– View historical displays at the Botallack Count House Workshop.
– Close by is Geevor Mine and museum (not National Trust).

Eating and shopping: vending machine available for drinks. Small shop with mining-related goods and books.

You may also enjoy: Industrial Discovery Centre at Cornish Mines and Engines. Botallack Count House.

Making the most of your day: experience Levant through a guided tour or a self-guided family trail. Follow a biodiversity trail along the cliffs to Geevor (Tracker Packs available for children). Associated buildings also open. Dogs welcome.

Access for all: ♿ 🧏 ⠿ 🖼 Building 🏛

Getting here: 203:SW368346. **Foot**: South West Coast Path passes entrance. **Bus**: First 17/A from Penzance ⮕. **Train**: Penzance 7 miles. **Road**: 1 mile west of Pendeen, on B3306 St Just–St Ives road. **Parking**: free, 100 yards. Not suitable for coaches. Limited parking for coaches at Geevor Mine, ½ mile walk to Levant mine.

Finding out more: 01736 786156 or levant@nationaltrust.org.uk

Levant Mine and Beam Engine		M	T	W	T	F	S	S
Steaming								
2 Apr–28 May	11–5	·	·	W	·	F	·	·
2 Jun–30 Jun	11–5	·	·	W	T	F	·	S
1 Jul–30 Sep	11–5	·	T	W	T	F	·	S
6 Oct–29 Oct	11–5	·	·	W	·	F	·	·
Not steaming								
8 Jan–26 Mar	11–4	·	·	·	·	F	·	·
5 Nov–17 Dec	11–4	·	·	·	·	F	·	·

Open Bank Holiday Sundays and Mondays.

Little Clarendon

Dinton, Salisbury, Wiltshire SP3 5DZ

Map ① K5   🏠 ✚ 1940

Late 15th-century stone house and curious chapel adjoining. **Note**: no WC.

Getting here: 184:SU015316. ¼ mile east of Dinton church, close to post office; take B3089 from Salisbury to Dinton.

Finding out more: 01985 843600 or littleclarendon@nationaltrust.org.uk

Little Clarendon		M	T	W	T	F	S	S
5 Apr	2–5	M	·	·	·	·	·	·
3 May	2–5	M	·	·	·	·	·	·
31 May	2–5	M	·	·	·	·	·	·
30 Aug	2–5	M	·	·	·	·	·	·

The Lizard and Kynance Cove

The Lizard, near Helston, Cornwall

Map ① C10   🏠 ⬆ ♨ 🏞 ➤ 🏠 1935

Lizard Point, Britain's most southerly point, offers dramatic cliff walks, wild flowers and geological features. Marconi's historic wireless experiments are celebrated at The Lizard Wireless Station and the Marconi Centre at Poldhu. Two miles north lies Kynance Cove, considered one of the most beautiful beaches in the world. **Note**: Kynance car park WCs closed in winter (Cove WCs open all year). Some sheer cliffs.

Exploring
- At the Point, watch Cornish choughs fledge and fly.
- Learn about the fascinating history of wireless technology.
- Walk the coast path to hidden beaches around the peninsula.
- Savour a Cornish cream tea above white sands at Kynance.

Eating and shopping: café (Trust-approved concession) at Kynance Cove (March to October). Café (Trust-approved concession) at Lizard Point (March to October).

Making the most of your day: visit in May and June to see the wild flowers at their best – you may even spot basking sharks. For guided walks, see our What's On guide or website. Seasonal dog bans on some beaches, including Kynance.

Access for all: 🚻 Grounds 🅿

Enjoy dramatic clifftop walks at The Lizard, Cornwall

Getting here: 203:SW688133.
Foot: 3¾ miles of South West Coast Path on property. **Bus**: First T34 Redruth–Helston–Lizard ≋, then to Kynance Cove 1½ miles; to Lizard Point 1 mile. **Road**: from Helston, A3083 to Lizard town. **Parking**: National Trust car parks at Kynance and Lizard Point (charge Easter to November). Free parking in Lizard town, from where a footpath leads to Lizard Point. No caravans or trailers.

Finding out more: 01326 561407 or lizard@nationaltrust.org.uk

The Lizard and Kynance Cove	M	T	W	T	F	S	S
Open all year	**M**	**T**	**W**	**T**	**F**	**S**	**S**

Telephone for opening times of both The Lizard Wireless Station at Bass Point and the Marconi Centre at Poldhu.

Lodge Park and Sherborne Estate

Lodge Park, Aldsworth, near Cheltenham, Gloucestershire GL54 3PP

Map ① K2/L 🏠🌳♿🏚🔔⚓⛵ 1983

17th-century grandstand created in 1634 by John 'Crump' Dutton inspired by his passion for gambling, banqueting and entertaining. The National Trust's first restoration project relying on archaeological evidence. Impressive views of the deer course and park (designed by Charles Bridgeman in the 1720s). **Note**: WC at Lodge Park only. May close for weddings.

Exploring
- England's only surviving 17th-century deer course and grandstand.
- Dramatic views from the grandstand of Charles Bridgeman's landscape.
- Explore the windswept and romantic countryside.
- Plenty of space for picnics and ball games.

Eating and shopping: small National Trust shop. Hot and cold drinks available (local apple juice). Ice-cream and sandwiches.

Making the most of your day: annual Deerhound Day recreates a 17th-century 'day at the races'. Open-air theatre during the summer. Walks around the surrounding Sherborne Estate. Christmas at Lodge Park. Dogs under close control welcome.

Access for all: 🅿️ 🇩 ♿ 🚻 📷 ∴ Building 🔼♿

Getting here: 163:SP146123. **Bus**: Swanbrook 853 Oxford–Gloucester (passing Gloucester ≋ and close Oxford ≋). 1½ miles walk to Lodge Park from bus stop or 1 mile Sherborne; also 833 Cheltenham–Northleach. **Road**: 3 miles east of Northleach; approach from A40 only. **Parking**: estate walks, parking at Ewe Pen Barn car park, 163:SP158143, and water meadows, 163:SP175154. Donation of £1 welcome.

Finding out more: 01451 844130 or lodgepark@nationaltrust.org.uk

Lodge Park and Sherborne	M	T	W	T	F	S	S
12 Mar–31 Oct	11–4	·	·	·	·	**F**	**S**	**S**
11 Dec–12 Dec	11–4	·	·	·	·	·	**S**	**S**

Open Bank Holiday Mondays. Property occasionally closes for weddings (telephone to confirm opening times). Sherborne Park Estate open all year (access from Ewe Pen car park). Essential repairs at end of 2010 may require scaffolding.

Lodge Park on the Sherborne Estate in Gloucestershire. Spectators watched deer coursing from the balcony

Loughwood Meeting House

Dalwood, Axminster, Devon EX13 7DU

Map (1) H7　†| 1969 |

Set in the beautiful East Devon countryside, this atmospheric 17th-century thatched Baptist meeting house is dug into the hillside.
Note: no WC.

Getting here: 192/193:SY253993. 4 miles west of Axminster, 1 mile south of Dalwood, 1 mile north west of Kilmington.

Finding out more: 01752 346585 or loughwood@nationaltrust.org.uk.
South and East Devon Countryside Office, The Stables, Saltram House, Plymouth, Devon PL7 1UH

Loughwood Meeting House	M	T	W	T	F	S	S
Open all year	**M**	**T**	**W**	**T**	**F**	**S**	**S**

Services held twice yearly. Details at Meeting House.

Lundy

Bristol Channel, Devon EX39 2LY

Map (1) D5　 1969

Undisturbed by cars, the island encompasses a small village with an inn and Victorian church, and the 13th-century Marisco Castle. For nature-lovers there are the variety of seabirds, wildlife, flora and fauna. Designated the first Marine Conservation Area, Lundy offers opportunities for diving and seal watching.
Note: Lundy is financed, administered and maintained by the Landmark Trust. Holiday cottages available to rent.

Lundy, in the Bristol Channel, is a haven for wildlife

Exploring
– A unique island experience.
– Sail from Ilfracombe or Bideford onboard 'MS Oldenburg'.
– Peaceful and remote – a world apart.

Eating and shopping: Marisco Tavern serves hot and cold food and drinks. Island shop sells souvenirs, Lundy stamps, snacks and ice-creams.

Making the most of your day: there is a wealth of things to do, including walking, letterboxing, birdwatching and discovering the varied wildlife.

Access for all: 🏷️ 🏷️ 🏷️ 🏷️
Building 🏷️ Grounds 🏷️

Getting here: 180:SS130450. In the Bristol Channel 11 miles north of Hartland Point, 25 miles west of Ilfracombe, 30 miles south of Tenby. **Cycle**: NCN31 (Bideford). **Ferry**: sea passages from Bideford or Ilfracombe according to tides up to four days a week, March to end October. Small landing charge, including members. **Bus**: First 3 Barnstaple–Ilfracombe, First 1, 2 Barnstaple–Bideford ▣. **Train**: Barnstaple: 8½ miles to Bideford, 12 miles to Ilfracombe. **Parking**: at Bideford or Ilfracombe for ferries (pay and display).

Finding out more: 01271 863636 or lundy@nationaltrust.org.uk. The Lundy Shore Office, The Quay, Bideford, Devon EX39 2LY

Lundy
'MS Oldenburg' sails from Bideford or Ilfracombe up to four times a week from the end of March until the end of October carrying both day and staying passengers. Small landing charge, including members. A helicopter service operates from Hartland Point from November to mid March, Mondays and Fridays only, for staying visitors.

The Devil's Cauldron at Lydford Gorge, Devon

Lydford Gorge

Lydford, near Tavistock, Devon EX20 4BH

Map ① F7   1947

This lush oak-wooded steep-sided river gorge (the deepest in the South West), with its natural beauty, fascinating history and many legends, can be explored through a variety of exhilarating short or long walks. Around every corner the river Lyd plunges, tumbles, swirls and gently meanders as it travels through the gorge. Throughout the seasons there is an abundance of wildlife and plants to see, from woodland birds to wild garlic (you can smell it too) in the spring and fungi in the autumn. **Note**: strenuous walking, rugged terrain, vertical drops. Unsuitable for visitors with heart complaints or walking difficultes.

Exploring
- Discover the magical 30-metre-high Whitelady Waterfall.
- Walk out over the bubbling Devil's Cauldron.
- Watch woodland birds from the bird hide.

Exploring
- See the water tumble through Tunnel Falls.
- Learn about the myths of the Gubbins and Whitelady Waterfall.
- Keep a look out for the woodland sculptures.

Eating and shopping: browse in the shop and plant centre. Wildlife books and related products in the shop. Enjoy Devon cream teas at one of two tea-rooms. Add to your picnic with takeaway drinks and food.

You may also enjoy: the last working water-powered forge: Finch Foundry in Sticklepath near Okehampton.

Making the most of your day: school holiday and family events, wildlife-themed activities, warden's rambles, children's play area, bird hide. Dogs welcome on leads.

Access for all: 🅿️♿🚻♿♿📷♿♿·♿
Buildings ♿ Gorge ♿

Getting here: 191/201:SX509845. **Foot**: as road directions or via Blackdown Moor from Mary Tavy. **Cycle**: NCN27 and 31. Property is close to three cycle routes: Devon Coast to Coast, West

Devon Way and Plym Valley. **Bus**: Holsworthy 118 Tavistock–Barnstaple, bus stop at main entrance and waterfall entrance to gorge. **Road**: 7 miles south of A30. Halfway between Okehampton and Tavistock, 1 mile west off A386 opposite Dartmoor Inn; main entrance at west end of Lydford village; waterfall entrance near Manor Farm. **Parking**: free.

Finding out more: 01822 820320 or lydfordgorge@nationaltrust.org.uk

Lydford Gorge		M	T	W	T	F	S	S
Gorge, shop and tea-rooms								
13 Feb–21 Feb	11–3:30	M	T	W	T	F	S	S
13 Mar–3 Oct	10–5	M	T	W	T	F	S	S
4 Oct–31 Oct	10–4	M	T	W	T	F	S	S
Gorge (partially open) and tea-rooms								
6 Nov–19 Dec	11–3:30	·	·	·	·	·	S	S
Shop								
6 Nov–28 Nov	11–3:30	·	·	·	·	·	S	S
2 Dec–19 Dec	11–3:30	·	·	·	·	T	F	S	S
20 Dec–23 Dec	11–3:30	M	T	W	T	·	·	·

Parts of the gorge are closed in February, November and December due to weather conditions, higher river levels, reduced daylight hours and maintainance work. Please check by telephone or on website. The short walk from the waterfall entrance to the base of the Whitelady Waterfall is open throughout the year.

Lytes Cary Manor

near Charlton Mackrell, Somerton, Somerset TA11 7HU

Map ① 15    1949

'First visit since mid 1970s. Wonderfully thrilled by the house and the gardens – fabulous surprise.'
M. R. and S. C. Adams, Radstock, near Bath

This intimate manor house was the former home of medieval herbalist Henry Lyte; here visitors can learn about his famous 16th-century plant directory, *Lytes Herbal*. The manor spans many years with its 14th-century chapel and 15th-century Great Hall. In the 20th century it was rescued from dereliction by Sir Walter Jenner. Its Arts & Crafts-style garden is a combination of outdoor rooms, topiary, statues and herbaceous borders. Explore the walks through the wider estate and riverside and discover many features typical of farmed lowland England, including ancient hedges, rare arable weeds and farmland birds.

Looking through the gate towards the Apostles topiary at Lytes Cary Manor, Somerset

Exploring
- Explore the intimate manor house and chapel.
- Stroll around the Arts & Crafts garden.
- Admire the topiary, statues and herbaceous borders of the garden.
- Walk the wider estate with waymarked tracks.
- Discover the estate with children's Tracker Packs and trails.
- Play croquet on the lawn – equipment is available to hire.

Eating and shopping: enjoy light refreshments at our 'Simple Foods' kiosk. Be inspired by our large range of plants for sale. Visit our well-stocked garden sundries and gift shop.

You may also enjoy: Montacute House, Tintinhull Garden, Barrington Court, Stourhead House and Gardens.

Making the most of your day: many events, including dawn chorus walks and croquet days. Family-themed events throughout the summer, visit website for details. Dogs on leads on estate walks only.

Access for all: 🅿️♿🚻⌷∴
Building ♿♿ Grounds ♿

Getting here: 183:ST529269. **Bus**: First 377 Wells–Yeovil, 54/A/B/C Taunton–Yeovil (passing close Taunton ☰). Both pass within ¾ mile Yeovil Pen Mill ☰. Alight Kingsdon, 1 mile. **Train**: Yeovil Pen Mill 8½ miles; Castle Cary 9 miles; Yeovil Junction 10 miles. **Road**: near village of Kingsdon, off A372. Signposted from Podimore roundabout where A303 meets A37. **Parking**: free, 40 yards. Coaches by prior arrangement only.

Finding out more: 01458 224471 or lytescarymanor@nationaltrust.org.uk

Lytes Cary Manor		M	T	W	T	F	S	S
House, garden, shop and catering								
13 Mar–31 Oct	11–5	**M**	**T**	**W**	·	**F**	**S**	**S**
Estate walks								
Open all year	Dawn–dusk	**M**	**T**	**W**	**T**	**F**	**S**	**S**

Open Good Friday and Bank Holiday Mondays. Closes dusk if earlier.

Max Gate

Alington Avenue, Dorchester, Dorset DT1 2AB

Map ①J7   🏠❄ 1940

Thomas Hardy designed this house and lived here from 1885 until his death in 1928. This is where he wrote *Tess of the d'Urbervilles, Jude the Obscure* and *The Mayor of Casterbridge*, as well as much of his poetry. **Note**: no WC.

Exploring   – Visit Thomas Hardy's home.

Making the most of your day: guided tours of house available on request.

Access for all: ⌷∴🅰 Building ♿

Getting here: 194:SY704899. **Bus**: Coach House Travel 4 from town centre. **Train**: Dorchester South 1 mile; Dorchester West 1 mile. **Road**: 1 mile east of Dorchester. From Dorchester follow A352 Wareham road to roundabout named Max Gate (at junction of A35 Dorchester bypass). Turn left and left again into cul-de-sac outside the house. **Parking**: free (not National Trust), 50 yards.

Finding out more: 01297 561900 or maxgate@nationaltrust.org.uk

Max Gate		M	T	W	T	F	S	S
28 Mar–29 Sep	2–5	**M**	·	**W**	·	·	·	**S**

Only hall, dining and drawing rooms, and garden open. Private visits, tours and seminars for schools, colleges and literary societies at other times, by appointment with the tenants, Mr and Mrs Andrew Leah.

Max Gate, Dorset: the house that Thomas Hardy designed and lived in from 1885 until his death in 1928

Mompesson House

The Close, Salisbury, Wiltshire SP1 2EL

Map (1) K5   [⌂][❀][T][1952]

'**A beautiful house and garden, with wonderful furniture, ceramics and glass – so well displayed and with such helpful stewards.**'
Mrs A. McGraw, Berkshire

The chimneypiece in the Library at Mompesson House, Salisbury, Wiltshire

When walking into the celebrated Cathedral Close in Salisbury, visitors step back into a past world, and on entering Mompesson House, featured in the award-winning film *Sense and Sensibility*, the feeling of leaving the modern world behind is deepened. The tranquil atmosphere is enhanced by the magnificent plasterwork, fine period furniture and graceful oak staircase, which are the main features of this perfectly proportioned Queen Anne house. In addition, the Turnbull collection of 18th-century drinking glasses is of national importance. The delightful walled garden has a pergola and traditionally planted herbaceous borders.

Exploring
– Perch on the window seats to admire the fine plasterwork.
– Children, seek out all the human faces in the mouldings.
– In cooler weather, sit in the Library by the fire.
– Treat yourself to a delicious cream tea in the garden.
– View the exceptional Turnbull Collection of 18th-century drinking glasses.
– Fantasise about living in this townhouse in the 18th century.

Eating and shopping: locally baked scones and cakes served in the tea-room. Light lunches and teas can be eaten in the garden. Salisbury National Trust shop is only 60 yards. Recently published catalogue of Turnbull Glass Collection available for sale.

You may also enjoy: Mottisfont Abbey.

Making the most of your day: regular croquet sessions on the lawn for people of all ages and ability. Hands-on craft sessions. Music includes pianists playing our 1790s Broadwood square piano and Northumbrian Pipers sessions.

Access for all: [♿][WC][♨][▣][♿][∷][⊘]
Building [♿][♿] Grounds [♿][♿]

Getting here: 184:SU142297. On north side of Choristers' Green in the Cathedral Close, near High Street Gate. **Bus**: Wilts & Dorset buses from surrounding area. **Train**: Salisbury ½ mile. **Road**: park and ride on all main routes into city. **Parking**: 260 yards in city centre (not National Trust, pay and display). Coach parking in Central Car Park. Coach drop-off point 100 yards at St Ann's Gate.

Finding out more: 01722 420980 (Infoline). 01722 335659 or mompessonhouse@nationaltrust.org.uk

Mompesson House			M	T	W	T	F	S	S
13 Mar–31 Oct	11–5		**M**	**T**	**W**	·	·	**S**	**S**
Open Good Friday.									

Montacute House

Montacute, Somerset TA15 6XP

Map ① I6  1931

Montacute House is a magnificent, glittering mansion, built in the late 16th century for Sir Edward Phelips. There are many renaissance features, and the Long Gallery, the longest of its kind in England, displays over 60 of the finest Tudor and Elizabethan portraits from the National Portrait Gallery collection. The state rooms display a fine range of period furniture and textiles, including samplers from the Goodhart collection. Montacute's formal gardens are perfect for a stroll and include a collection of roses, mixed borders and famous wobbly hedges. Waymarked walks lead around the wider estate, which encompasses St Michael's Hill.

Exploring — Trails and Tracker Packs available to enhance family visits.

Exploring
- Varied and exciting events programme, including farmers' markets.
- Parkland with walks for countryside and nature lovers.
- Many seating areas around the property to relax in.
- Excellent printed information easily accessible in each room.
- Stroll the famous West Drive, used in many feature films.

Eating and shopping: tasty local home-cooked food available in the Courtyard Café. Large, well-stocked gift shop and plant sales. Children's menu and lunch boxes available. A whole range of delicious fresh coffee and hot chocolate.

You may also enjoy: Barrington Court, Lytes Cary Manor, Tintinhull Garden and Stourhead.

Making the most of your day: many events, including farmers' markets, open-air theatre and craft fairs, also many free family activity days. Licensed for weddings and private functions. Dogs under control in parkland only.

Access for all:

Building Grounds

Montacute House, Somerset: a magnificent, glittering mansion

Why not visit us by public transport? See page 376

Getting here: 183/193:ST499172. **Foot**: Leyland Trail and Monarch Trail both pass through Montacute Park. **Cycle**: NCN30, passes Montacute village. **Bus**: South West Coaches 81 Yeovil Bus Station–South Petherton (passing within ¾ mile Yeovil Pen Mill 🚆). **Train**: Yeovil Pen Mill 5½ miles; Yeovil Junction 7 miles (bus to Yeovil Bus Station); Crewkerne 7 miles. **Road**: in Montacute village, 4 miles west of Yeovil, on south side of A3088, 3 miles east of A303; signposted. **Parking**: free. Limited parking for coaches.

Finding out more: 01935 823289 or montacute@nationaltrust.org.uk

Montacute House		M	T	W	T	F	S	S
House								
13 Mar–31 Oct	11–5	M	·	W	T	F	S	S
Gardens								
1 Jan–12 Mar	11–4	·	·	W	T	F	S	S
13 Mar–31 Oct	11–5:30	M	·	W	T	F	S	S
3 Nov–31 Dec	11–4	·	·	W	T	F	S	S
Shop								
2 Jan–7 Mar	11–4	·	·	·	·	·	S	S
13 Mar–31 Oct	11–5:30	M	·	W	T	F	S	S
3 Nov–19 Dec	11–4	·	·	W	T	F	S	S
Café								
13 Mar–31 Oct	11–5:30	M	·	W	T	F	S	S
6 Nov–19 Dec	11–4	·	·	·	·	·	S	S
Parkland								
Open all year	Dawn–dusk	M	T	W	T	F	S	S

House and all facilities open the first four Tuesdays in August. Gardens, shop and café open 13 to 21 February, except Monday and Tuesday. Half-term: last entry to house 4:30.

Newark Park

Ozleworth, Wotton-under-Edge, Gloucestershire GL12 7PZ

Map ① J3 🏠✿♣♟🏠 1949

From its Tudor origins to today, Newark Park contains elements reflecting 450 years of history. The atmospheric house is lived in and is furnished with an eclectic mix of old and modern. Outside, the wild romantic garden and landscape, with fantastic views to the distant Mendips, are breathtaking.

Newark Park, Gloucestershire

Exploring
- Discover fascinating stories about those who lived in the house.
- Enjoy spectacular unspoilt countryside.
- Marvel at the view.
- Relax in the wild, romantic garden.

Eating and shopping: browse in the intimate shop. Be tempted by the plant stall. Enjoy a cup of tea.

Making the most of your day: waymarked countryside walks and footpath link to the Cotswold Way. Family events and children's house and garden quiz. Croquet set for hire. Picnics welcome in garden (rugs for hire). Dogs on leads in grounds only.

Access for all: 🅿️🔲📷🚻 ❙❙ 🅰️
Building 🔲🔲 **Grounds** 🔲

Getting here: 172:ST786934. **Foot**: Cotswold Way passes property. **Bus**: First 309, 310 Bristol–Dursley, alight Wotton-under-Edge, 1¾ miles. Frequent services link Bristol Temple Meads 🚆 with the bus station. **Train**: Stroud 10 miles. **Road**: 1½ miles east of Wotton-under-Edge, 1¾ miles south of junction of A4135 and B4058, follow signs for Ozleworth. House signposted from main road. **Parking**: free, 100 yards. Coaches by prior arrangement only.

Finding out more: 01793 817666 (Infoline). 01453 842644 or newarkpark@nationaltrust.org.uk

Newark Park		M	T	W	T	F	S	S
3 Mar–27 May	11–5	·	·	W	T	·	·	·
2 Jun–31 Oct	11–5	·	·	W	T	·	S	S

Open Bank Holiday Mondays and Good Friday, 11 to 5. Closes dusk if earlier. Open Easter Saturday and Sunday, 11 to 5.

Visit

Overbeck's, Devon: looking down towards Salcombe estuary

Overbeck's

Sharpitor, Salcombe, Devon TQ8 8LW

Map ① F9   1937

**'What a fabulous place,
so beautiful and tranquil.'**
Mrs R. Coxs, Braughing

One of the most fascinating and exotic gardens in the South West; explore the banana garden, meander through the towering purple echiums or just relax beneath palms and soak up the spectacular panorama across miles of beautiful coastline and estuary. Continue your journey of discovery into the Edwardian house of Otto Overbeck to see his amazing invention – the rejuvenator, hear the giant (1890s) music box and prepare to be intrigued by his collections. The perfect day out for families who enjoy exploring, or the keen gardener who wants to be inspired and excited. **Note**: the grounds are very steep in places.

Exploring
- Find out more by enjoying one of our family trails.
- Join our garden tours and discover how we garden organically.
- Discover the abundance of rare and exotic plants.
- Hunt for Fred the friendly ghost in the house.
- Listen to the melodious sounds of the Victorian music box.

Eating and shopping: enjoy local crab in a freshly prepared sandwich. Kick off those boots and relax by a warming fire. Book a luxury picnic hamper to make the day complete. Take home a bar of South Devon chilli chocolate.

You may also enjoy: A La Ronde, Coleton Fishacre, Greenway, Saltram, Salcombe: Thurlestone to Torcross.

Making the most of your day: garden tours: learn more about our organic exotic garden. Listen to the rare polyphon play its melodies. Find Fred the friendly ghost. Children's trails available all season.

Access for all: 🅿️ 🅿️ 🚻 ♿ 🔄 🖥️ 🎵 ⠿ Ⓐ
Building 🏛️♿ Grounds 🏞️♿

Getting here: 202:SX728374. **Foot**: South West Coast Path within ⅔ mile. **Ferry**: from Salcombe to South Sands, then ½ mile strenuous walk (uphill). **Bus**: Stagecoach in Devon X64, Sunday and Bank Holidays only; Tally Ho! 164, 606 from Totnes ⬚. From all alight Salcombe, 1½ miles. **Road**: 1½ miles south west of Salcombe, signposted from Malborough and Salcombe (narrow approach road). Roads leading to Overbeck's are steep and single track and not suitable for coaches over 25 seats or large vehicles. **Sat Nav** warning: continue towards Salcombe ignoring Sat Nav in Malborough and follow the brown signs thereafter. **Parking**: small car park reserved for visitors to Overbeck's, 150 yards. Charge for non-members (refundable on paid admission). Limited parking on driveway. Care must be taken on steep narrow ascent to entrance. Not suitable for motorhomes/large vehicles (telephone for advice).

Finding out more: 01548 842893. 01548 845013 (shop). 01548 845014 (tea-room) or overbecks@nationaltrust.org.uk

Overbeck's		M	T	W	T	F	S	S
Garden only								
1 Feb–11 Mar	11–4	M	T	W	T	·	·	·
1 Nov–30 Dec	11–4	M	T	W	T	·	·	·
Garden, house and shop								
13 Mar–15 Jul	11–5	M	T	W	T	·	S	S
17 Jul–5 Sep	11–5	M	T	W	T	F	S	S
6 Sep–31 Oct	11–5	M	T	W	T	·	S	S

Open every day during Devon school holidays, February to October. Tea-room open as house, but closes 4:15.

Penrose Estate: Gunwalloe and Loe Pool

near Helston, Cornwall TR13 0RD

Map ① B10  1974

Loe Bar separates Cornwall's largest freshwater pool, The Loe, from the sea. At Gunwalloe, beautiful beaches frame a medieval church. **Note**: cliff edges and coast path subject to erosion. Seasonal dog ban on Gunwalloe church cove.

Loe Pool, Cornwall, looking inland

Getting here: 203:SW639259. 2 miles south west of Helston.

Finding out more: 01326 561407 or southwestcornwall@nationaltrust.org.uk

Penrose Estate	M	T	W	T	F	S	S
Open all year	M	T	W	T	F	S	S

Beach refreshments kiosk (not National Trust) at Gunwalloe open during season.

Philipps House and Dinton Park

Dinton, Salisbury, Wiltshire SP3 5HH

Map ① K5   1943

Neo-Grecian house with fine Regency furniture, designed by Jeffry Wyatville for William Wyndham, 1820. Excellent parkland walks throughout year. **Note**: no WC.

Getting here: 184:SU004319. 9 miles west of Salisbury, on north side of B3089; Tisbury 5 miles.

Finding out more: 01722 716663 or philippshouse@nationaltrust.org.uk

Philipps House and Dinton Park		M	T	W	T	F	S	S
House								
27 Mar–30 Oct	10–1	·	·	·	·	·	S	·
29 Mar–25 Oct	1–5	M	·	·	·	·	·	·
Park								
Open all year		M	T	W	T	F	S	S

Priest's House

Muchelney, Langport, Somerset TA10 0DQ

Map ① I6 ⊞ 1911

This medieval hall-house, built in 1308 for the parish priest, has been little altered since the early 17th century. **Note**: house is tenanted. No WC.

Getting here: 193:ST429250. 1 mile south of Langport.

Finding out more: 01458 253771 or priestshouse@nationaltrust.org.uk

Priest's House		M	T	W	T	F	S	S
14 Mar–26 Sep	2–5	**M**	·	·	·	·		**S**

Admission by guided tour, last tour 4:30.

Prior Park, Somerset, was created by Ralph Allen

Prior Park Landscape Garden

Ralph Allen Drive, Bath, Somerset BA2 5AH

Map ① J4 ❖ 1993

'Recent developments here have made this an excellent landscape refuge. Well done!'
Ms F. Hills, Bath

One of only four Palladian bridges of this design in the world can be crossed at Prior Park, which was created in the 18th century by local entrepreneur Ralph Allen, with advice from 'Capability' Brown and the poet Alexander Pope. The garden is set in a sweeping valley where visitors can enjoy magnificent views of Bath. Restoration of the 'Wilderness' has reinstated the Serpentine Lake, Cascade and Cabinet. A five-minute walk leads to the Bath Skyline, a six-mile circular route encompassing beautiful woodlands and meadows, an Iron Age hill fort, Roman settlements, 18th-century follies and spectacular views. **Note**: mansion not accessible. There are steep slopes, steps and uneven paths in the garden.

Exploring
– A green tourism site with disabled parking only.
– Beautiful and intimate 18th-century garden.
– Fabulous views of the City of Bath.
– Restored Wilderness area.
– One of only four Palladian bridges in the world.
– Free family activity packs.

Eating and shopping: refresh yourself at our tea kiosk by the lakes.

You may also enjoy: the Bath Skyline, Dyrham Park, The Courts, Lacock and Stourhead.

Making the most of your day: free family activity packs throughout the year. Open-air events programme. Guided tours of the Wilderness. Dogs on leads allowed November to end February.

Access for all: ⬛⬛⬛⬛⬛⬛⬛
Grounds ⬛⬛

Getting here: 172:ST760633. Prior Park is a green tourism site; there is only disabled car parking (please telephone to book), but public transport runs regularly (every 30 minutes) to and from the park. Please telephone for leaflet or download from the website. **Foot**: 1 mile very steep uphill walk from railway station. To rear of railway station cross river, pass Widcombe shopping parade, turn right on to

Prior Park Road at White Hart PH, proceed up steep hill, garden on left. Kennet & Avon canal path ¾ mile. **Cycle**: NCN4, ¾ mile. **Bus**: First 2, Bath–Combe Down. Pick up on Dorchester Street by the bus station. City Sightseeing Skyline Tour open-top tour bus runs to the garden (last stop on tour) every 20 minutes in summer, every hour in winter (11 to 5). Pick up from railway station and Abbey. £1 off for members. Ticket valid for 24 hours. **Train**: Bath Spa 1 mile. **Road**: no brown signs. **Parking**: no on-site parking – Prior Park is a Green Tourism Site. Please park in the city and follow the directions above.

Finding out more: 01225 833422 or priorpark@nationaltrust.org.uk

Prior Park Landscape Garden		M	T	W	T	F	S	S
Garden								
2 Jan–7 Feb	11–5:30	·	·	·	·	·	S	S
13 Feb–31 Oct	11–5:30	M	·	W	T	F	S	S
6 Nov–26 Dec	11–5:30	·	·	·	·	·	S	S
Tea kiosk								
13 Feb–31 Oct	11:30–4:30	·	·	·	·	·	S	S

Last admission one hour before closing. Closed 25 December. Closes dusk if earlier than 5:30. Kiosk also open school holidays, events and Bank Holidays.

St Anthony Head

Portscatho, Cornwall TR2 5EY

Map ① C9   1959

Overlooking the spectacular entrance to the Fal Estuary. Excellent coastal and sheltered creekside walks. Newly revealed remains of defensive fortifications. **Note**: WCs adjacent to main car park.

Getting here: 204:SW847313. South of St Mawes.

Finding out more: 01872 862945 or stanthonyhead@nationaltrust.org.uk

St Anthony Head	M	T	W	T	F	S	S
Open all year	**M**	**T**	**W**	**T**	**F**	**S**	**S**

St Michael's Mount

Marazion, Cornwall TR17 0HT

Map ① B9    1954

Still home to the St Aubyn family as well as a small community, this iconic rocky island is crowned by a medieval church and castle – with the oldest buildings dating from the 12th century. Immerse yourself in history, wonder at the architecture and discover the legend of Jack the Giant Killer. Look down on the subtropical terraced garden and enjoy the breathtaking views of spectacular Mount's Bay. If the weather is favourable, take a short evocative boat trip to the island, or at low tide enjoy the walk across the causeway. **Note**: run and maintained in partnership with the St Aubyn family. Uneven, steep paths. Narrow passageways.

Exploring
- Enjoy the adventure of getting here – by foot or ferry.
- Find the giant's heart in the path to castle.
- Discover the amazing plaster frieze showing medieval hunting scenes.
- See the model of the Mount made from champagne corks!
- Explore the exotic subtropical garden.
- Guided tours of the castle in the winter months.

Eating and shopping: Island café: enjoy a cream tea or a Cornish pasty. Sail Loft Restaurant (licensed): hearty dishes, finest Cornish ingredients. The island shop offers local gifts and artwork.

You may also enjoy: Godolphin, Trengwainton Garden and Levant Mine.

Making the most of your day: children's quiz for castle and garden. Live music most Sundays during summer. Garden tours (by arrangement). Special garden evenings. Sunday church services: Whitsun to end September. Winter guided tours.

Access for all: ⚏🚻 🔊 💻 ⚐ Castle 🔗 Grounds ♿

St Michael's Mount, Cornwall: this iconic island is accessible at low tide via a causeway and at high tide by ferry

Getting here: 203:SW515298. **Foot**: South West Coast Path within ¾ mile. **Cycle**: NCN3, ¾ mile. **Bus**: First 2/A/B Penzance–Helston; 17B Penzance–St Ives. All pass Penzance ≉. **Train**: Penzance 3 miles. **Road**: ½ mile south of A394 at Marazion, from where there is access on foot over the causeway at low tide or, during summer months only, by ferry at high tide, if weather conditions favourable. **Parking**: on mainland at Marazion opposite St Michael's Mount, 400 and 800 yards (not National Trust, fee payable).

Finding out more: 01736 710507/710265 (general enquiries/tide information). 01736 711067 (shop). 01736 710748 (restaurant) or stmichaelsmount@nationaltrust.org.uk

St Michael's Mount		M	T	W	T	F	S	S
28 Mar–30 Jun	10:30–5	M	T	W	T	F	·	S
1 Jul–31 Aug	10:30–5:30	M	T	W	T	F	·	S
1 Sep–31 Oct	10:30–5	M	T	W	T	F	·	S

Last admission 45 minutes before castle closing time (enough time should be allowed for travel from the mainland). Castle winter opening: Tuesday and Friday, entry by guided tour only, 11 and 2 (subject to weather conditions). Telephone in advance. Garden: open weekdays in May and June; Thursday and Friday in July to October. Special garden tours some evenings – see local information or website.

Saltram

Plympton, Plymouth, Devon PL7 1UH

Map ① F8    1957

'We enjoyed the walk along the estuary and the kids loved feeding the ducks on the pond.'
Julie Alderton, Plymouth

Still a largely undiscovered treasure, and the result of centuries of sophistication and extravagance, Saltram is the perfect family day out: close to Plymouth and yet in a world of its own. Home to the Parker family for nearly 300 years, the house with its original contents provides a fascinating insight into country-estate life throughout the centuries. Fine Robert Adam interiors and beautiful collections bring the 'age of elegance' to life at Saltram. Learn about some of the fascinating characters and family stories, including the correspondence between Frances, the first Countess, and Jane Austen.

Exploring

- Escape the Plymouth hustle and bustle in this green haven.
- Be blown away by the grandeur of the impressive Saloon.
- Visit the Western Apartments, newly opened to visitors.
- Transform yourself into a Georgian with the dressing-up clothes.
- Hunt out the romantic follies in the magnificent garden.
- Ride your bike or fly a kite in the parkland.

Eating and shopping: enjoy the local and seasonal food in the Park Restaurant. Park Restaurant is available for special occasions and private functions. Browse the gift and garden shops. Visit the Chapel Gallery for local arts and crafts.

You may also enjoy: Antony, still home to the Carew Pole family.

Making the most of your day: varied year-round events programme, open-air theatre, craft fairs, costumed Georgian evenings. Special events for families include Wizard School, held in the cellars, and Pirates and Princesses Day. Dogs on leads on designated paths only.

Access for all: ♿ ♿ ♿ WC ♿ ♿ ♿ ♿ ••
Building ♿ ♿ ♿ Grounds ♿ ➡

Getting here: 201:SX520557. **Foot**: South West Coast Path within 4 miles. **Cycle**: NCN27. **Bus**: Plymouth Citybus 22 from Plymouth, alight Merafield Road, ½ mile. **Train**: Plymouth 3½ miles. **Road**: 3½ miles east of Plymouth city centre. Travelling south (from Exeter): leave A38, 3 miles north of Plymouth. Exit is signed Plymouth City Centre/Plympton/Kingsbridge. At roundabout take centre lane, then 3rd exit for Plympton. Take right-hand lane and follow brown signs. Travelling north (from Liskeard): leave A38 at Plympton exit. At roundabout take first exit for Plympton, then as before. **Sat Nav**: please add Merafield Road to the address. **Parking**: free, 50 yards.

Finding out more: 01752 333503 or saltram@nationaltrust.org.uk

Saltram		M	T	W	T	F	S	S
Park								
Open all year	Dawn–dusk	M	T	W	T	F	S	S
House								
20 Feb–28 Feb	12–4:30	·	·	·	·	·	S	S
13 Mar–31 Oct	12–4:30	M	T	W	T	·	S	S
Catering								
2 Jan–11 Mar	10:30–4	M	T	W	T	·	S	S
13 Mar–31 Oct	10:30–5	M	T	W	T	F	S	S
1 Nov–30 Dec	10:30–4	M	T	W	T	·	S	S
Garden, shops and gallery								
2 Jan–11 Mar	11–4	M	T	W	T	·	S	S
13 Mar–31 Oct	11–5	M	T	W	T	·	S	S
1 Nov–30 Dec	11–4	M	T	W	T	·	S	S

Open Good Friday. Last admission to house 45 minutes before closing. Parts of house open for special Christmas events, visit website for details. Garden, shops and gallery closed 24 to 26 December. Catering closed 25 and 26 December but open Fridays 1 January and 31 December.

Saltram, Devon: in a world of its own

Shute Barton

Shute, near Axminster, Devon EX13 7PT

Map ① H7 1959

A fascinating medieval manor house, with a later Tudor gatehouse and battlemented turrets, set in pretty grounds.

Note: Shute is in the process of being converted into National Trust holiday apartments.

Getting here: 177/193:SY253974. 3 miles south west of Axminster, 2 miles north of Colyton on Honiton to Colyton road (B3161).

Finding out more: 01752 346585 or shutebarton@nationaltrust.org.uk. South and East Devon Countryside Office, The Stables, Saltram House, Plymouth, Devon PL7 1UH

Shute Barton		M	T	W	T	F	S	S
15 May–16 May	11–5						S	S
19 Jun–20 Jun	11–5						S	S
18 Sep–19 Sep	11–5						S	S
16 Oct–17 Oct	11–5						S	S

Snowshill Manor and Garden

Snowshill, near Broadway, Gloucestershire WR12 7JU

Map ① K1 1951

'**Absolutely fascinating – what a find! The whole place is just mind-boggling.**'
Ms S. Mellenchip, Stoke-on-Trent

Charles Wade embodied his family motto 'Let nothing perish', spending his life and inherited wealth amassing a spectacular collection of everyday and extraordinary objects from across the globe. He bought objects because of their colour, craftsmanship and design, restoring the ancient, golden-yellow Cotswold manor house to display them. Laid out theatrically according to Mr Wade's wishes, the Manor is literally packed to the rafters with 22,000 or so unusual objects – from tiny toys to splendid suits of Samurai armour. The Manor is surrounded by an intriguing terraced hillside garden designed in the Arts & Crafts style.

Exploring
- Be fascinated by the story of collector Charles Wade.
- Be amazed by his vast and astonishing collection.

Charles Wade's astrological clock, the nychthemeron, in the garden at Snowshill Manor and Garden, Gloucestershire

Exploring
- Be intrigued by stunning examples of craftsmanship.
- Relax in the 'outdoor rooms' of the peaceful hillside garden.
- Have a go at one of our children's trails.

Eating and shopping: enjoy a delicious home-cooked lunch in the restaurant. Try one of our legendary cream teas on the terrace. Treat yourself to local produce in our gift shop. Pick up a bargain in the second-hand bookshop.

You may also enjoy: the Wade Costume Collection at Berrington Hall in Herefordshire (by prior appointment only).

Making the most of your day: monthly Snowshill Secrets Explorer Tours. Children's trails indoors and around garden. Apple Weekend 23 and 24 October. Winter weekend events in November and December.

Access for all: ⛰🏰♿🚻👶📷📖🖥⛳📱🅿

Manor ♿ Grounds ♿♿

Getting here: 150:SP096339. **Foot**: Cotswold Way within ¾ mile. **Bus**: Castleways 559, Evesham–Broadway, then 2½ miles uphill. **Train**: Moreton-in-Marsh 7 miles, Evesham 8 miles. **Road**: 2½ miles south west of Broadway; turn from A44 Broadway bypass into Broadway village; at green turn right uphill to Snowshill. **Parking**: free, 500 yards. Walk from car park to manor and garden along undulating country path. Transfer available.

Finding out more: 01386 852410 or snowshillmanor@nationaltrust.org.uk

Snowshill Manor and Garden		M	T	W	T	F	S	S
Manor								
13 Mar–31 Oct	12–5	·	·	W	T	F	S	S
Priest's House								
13 Mar–31 Oct	11–5	·	·	W	T	F	S	S
Garden								
13 Mar–31 Oct	11–5:30	·	·	W	T	F	S	S
Shop, restaurant and grounds								
13 Mar–31 Oct	11–5:30	·	·	W	T	F	S	S
6 Nov–12 Dec	12–4	·	·	·	·	·	S	S

Admission by timed ticket. Tickets issued at reception on a first-come, first-served basis and cannot be booked in advance. Tickets often run out at peak times; please arrive early. Last admission: manor 4:10; garden 5. Open Bank Holidays.

Stembridge Tower Mill

High Ham, Somerset TA10 9DJ

Map ① I5   1969

Built in 1822, this is the last remaining thatched windmill in England – the last survivor of five in the area. **Note**: holiday cottage on site, please respect the tenants' privacy. No WC. Parking limited.

Getting here: 182:ST432305. 2 miles north of Langport, ½ mile east of High Ham.

Finding out more: 01935 823289 or stembridgemill@nationaltrust.org.uk

Stembridge Tower Mill		M	T	W	T	F	S	S
13 Mar–31 Oct	11–5	**M**	**T**	**W**	**T**	**F**	**S**	**S**

Interior open 25 April, 27 June and 22 August, 12 to 5.

Stoke-sub-Hamdon Priory

North Street, Stoke-sub-Hamdon, Somerset TA4 6QP

Map ① I6   1946

The priests who lived here served the Chapel of St Nicholas (now destroyed). The Great Hall is open to visitors. **Note**: no WC.

Getting here: 193:ST473175. 2 miles west of Montacute between Yeovil and Ilminster.

Finding out more: 01935 823289 or stokehamdonpriory@nationaltrust.org.uk

Stoke-sub-Hamdon Priory		M	T	W	T	F	S	S
14 Mar–26 Sep	11–5	**M**	**T**	**W**	**T**	**F**	**S**	**S**

Closes dusk if earlier. Only Great Hall open.

Stonehenge Landscape

3 Stonehenge Cottages, King Barrows, Amesbury, Wiltshire SP4 7DD

Map ① K5 1927

Within the Stonehenge World Heritage Site, the Trust manages 827 hectares (2,100 acres) of downland surrounding the famous stone circle. Walking across the grassland visitors can discover other prehistoric monuments, including the Avenue, the King Barrows, Winterbourne Stoke Barrows, the great henge of Durrington Walls and the Cursus. **Note**: stone circle managed by English Heritage (National Trust members admitted free).

Exploring
– Monuments among open access grassland can be explored on foot.
– Book ahead for a guided walk to reveal hidden histories.

Eating and shopping: catering kiosk at the stone circle (not National Trust).

Making the most of your day: book ahead for a guided walk to reveal hidden histories. Dogs welcome under close control.

Access for all: 🅿♿ 🚾

Getting here: 184:SU120420. **Bus**: Stonehenge Tour bus Salisbury ➡–Stonehenge.
Train: Salisbury 9½ miles. **Road**: Stonehenge car park 2 miles west of Amesbury, on A344.
Parking: 50 yards (not National Trust). Charge may apply between June and October (National Trust members free).

Finding out more: 01980 664780 or stonehenge@nationaltrust.org.uk

Stonehenge Landscape	M	T	W	T	F	S	S
Open all year	**M**	**T**	**W**	**T**	**F**	**S**	**S**

Stourhead

Stourhead Estate Office, Stourton, Warminster, Wiltshire BA12 6QD

Map ① J5  1946

Lying in secluded privacy in its own valley, Stourhead features one of the world's finest 18th-century landscape gardens. A magnificent lake is central to the design, and there are classical temples, enchanting grottos and rare and exotic trees. The Hoare family history can be uncovered at Stourhead House, a majestic Palladian mansion housing a unique Regency library with fabulous collections of Chippendale furniture and paintings, all set amid delightful lawns and parkland. Stourhead is at the heart of a 1,072-hectare (2,650-acre) estate where chalk downs, ancient woods and farmland are managed for nature conservation.

Exploring
– Step back in time with our Richard Colt Hoare exhibition.
– Climb 205 steps to the top of King Alfred's Tower.
– Families can become nature detectives with our Tracker Packs.
– Discover garden secrets on a fascinating free tour.
– Enjoy the woods and chalk downs on waymarked walks.
– Learn about the rarities and champions with our tree list.

Eating and shopping: browse one of the largest National Trust shops/plant centre. Taste local, seasonal dishes in our assisted-service restaurant. Drink or dine in the 18th-century Spread Eagle Inn. Enjoy real dairy ice-cream from the ice-cream parlour.

You may also enjoy: Montacute House: a glittering Elizabethan mansion with National Portrait Gallery exhibition, delightful gardens and parkland.

The magnificent lake and one of the temples at Stourhead, Wiltshire

Finding out more: 01747 841152 or stourhead@nationaltrust.org.uk

Stourhead		M	T	W	T	F	S	S
Garden								
Open all year	9–6	M	T	W	T	F	S	S
House and King Alfred's Tower								
13 Mar–31 Oct	11–5	M	T	·	·	F	S	S
Restaurant*								
Open all year	10–4:30	M	T	W	T	F	S	S
Shop**								
1 Jan–28 Feb	10–4	M	T	W	T	F	S	S
1 Mar–31 Oct	10–5	M	T	W	T	F	S	S
1 Nov–31 Dec	10–4	M	T	W	T	F	S	S
Farm Shop***								
2 Jan–26 Mar	10–4	M	T	W	T	F	S	S
27 Mar–23 Dec	10–5	M	T	W	T	F	S	S

Garden and tower close dusk if earlier. Farm shop closed 24 to 31 December. Garden, house, tower, shop and restaurant closed 25 December. *Resturant open until 5:30, 1 March to 31 October. **Shop open until 6, 1 April to 30 September. ***Farm shop open until 6, 27 March to 22 October.

Making the most of your day: our exciting events programme has something for everyone, with open-air music and drama, free garden and estate tours, family fun activities and free quizzes and trails. Dogs in garden, November to February, on short leads; on estate all year, close control.

Access for all: 🅿️♿🚽♿♿🔄📷 Building 🏛️♿ Grounds ♿➡️🚬♿

Getting here: 183:ST780340. **Cycle**: Wiltshire Cycle Way runs through estate. **Bus**: First 58 Shaftesbury–Wincanton (passing Gillingham ≊), alight Zeals, 1¼ miles. **Train**: Gillingham 6½ miles; Bruton 7 miles. **Road**: at Stourton, off B3092, 3 miles north west of Mere (A303), 8 miles south of Frome (A361). King Alfred's Tower: 3½ miles by road from main car park. **Parking**: 400 yards. Shuttle transfer (main season only), to house and garden entrances. King Alfred's Tower: designated parking 50 yards.

Studland Beach and Nature Reserve

Purbeck Estate Office, Studland, Swanage, Dorset BH19 3AX

Map ① K7 🏊🏖️🐾🏠 1982

'**Purbeck is amazing, better than abroad. The outdoors is made so much easier to enjoy with the National Trust.**'
The Jones family

A glorious slice of natural coastline in Purbeck featuring a four-mile stretch of golden, sandy beach, with gently shelving bathing waters and views of Old Harry Rocks and the Isle of Wight. Ideal for water sports and includes the most popular naturist beach in Britain. The heathland behind the beach is a haven for native wildlife and features all six British reptiles. Designated trails through the sand dunes and woodlands, allow for exploration and spotting of deer, insects and bird life as well as a wealth of wild flowers. Studland was the inspiration for Toytown in Enid Blyton's *Noddy*. **Note**: WCs at Knoll Beach and Middle Beach. Shell Bay WCs are low-water flush.

Enjoying a day out at Studland Beach, Dorset

Exploring
- The start of the South West Coast Path.
- Try the summer watersports, including boat hire, kayaking and windsurfing.
- Picnic in the dunes watching the activities in Poole Bay.
- Discover the bird life on Little Sea in the winter.
- Rent a wooden beach hut.
- Enjoy a BBQ in the designated beach areas.

Eating and shopping: bucket and spades, fishing nets and wet suits to buy. Indoor and open-air seating with a spectacular sea view. Local Purbeck ice-creams and daily seasonal specials. Serving local meat dishes from the wider estate.

You may also enjoy: Corfe Castle and Brownsea Island.

Making the most of your day: wide range of events year round, including children's trails, guided walks, food events and wildlife discovery walks. Coastal change interpretation hut open all year. Dog restrictions apply 1 May to 30 September.

Access for all: [icons] Grounds [icons]

Getting here: 195:SZ036835. **Foot**: 5 miles of South West Coast Path on property. **Ferry**: car ferry from Sandbanks, Poole, to Shell Bay. **Bus**: Wiltshire and Dorset 50 Bournemouth–Swanage to Shell Bay and Studland.
Train: Branksome or Parkstone, both 3½ miles to Shell Bay or 6 miles to Studland via vehicle ferry. **Parking**: at Shell Bay and South Beach, 9 to 11; Knoll Beach and Middle Beach, 9 to 8. Prices vary through season. Members must show cards on entry. Some car parks are pay and display.

Finding out more: 01929 450259 or studlandbeach@nationaltrust.org.uk

Studland Beach		M	T	W	T	F	S	S
Beach								
Open all year		M	T	W	T	F	S	S
Shop/café								
1 Jan–20 Mar	10–4	M	T	W	T	F	S	S
21 Mar–2 Jul	9:30–5*	M	T	W	T	F	S	S
3 Jul–1 Sep	9:30–6	M	T	W	T	F	S	S
2 Sep–31 Oct	9:30–5	M	T	W	T	F	S	S
1 Nov–31 Dec	10–4	M	T	W	T	F	S	S

*Shop and café open one hour later at weekends. Shop and café open hours may be longer in fine weather and shorter in poor weather. Visitor Centre, shop and café closed 25 December. **Car parks can be very full in peak season.**

Tintagel Old Post Office

Fore Street, Tintagel, Cornwall PL34 0DB

Map ① D7   1903

Nestling among the modern buildings of Tintagel high street, this unusual and atmospheric 14th-century yeoman's farmhouse, with a famously wavy roof, beckons the curious to explore. The name dates from the Victorian period when it briefly held a licence to be the letter receiving station for the district. **Note**: nearest WC in Trevena Square (not National Trust).

Exploring
– Discover Victorian postal memorabilia and 19th-century samplers.
– A tranquil cottage garden offers respite from the busy street.
– Enjoy the traditionally made rag rugs and quilts.

Eating and shopping: visit our small shop.

Making the most of your day: children's trail.

Access for all: 🏷️🔲🎦🎦👓📷
Building 🦽🦽 Grounds 🦽🦽

Getting here: 200:SX056884. In centre of village.
Foot: South West Coast Path within ¾ mile.
Bus: Western Greyhound 594 St Columb Major–Boscastle via Wadebridge (connections with 555 at Wadebridge from Bodmin Parkway ⧖).
Parking: no parking on site. Numerous pay and display car parks in village (not National Trust).

Finding out more: 01840 770024 or tintageloldpo@nationaltrust.org.uk

Tintagel Old Post Office		M	T	W	T	F	S	S
13 Feb–21 Feb	11–4		M	T	W	T	F	S	S
13 Mar–2 Apr	11–4		M	T	W	T	F	S	S
3 Apr–28 May	10:30–5		M	T	W	T	F	S	S
29 May–1 Oct	10:30–5:30		M	T	W	T	F	S	S
2 Oct–31 Oct	11–4		M	T	W	T	F	S	S

Tintinhull Garden

Farm Street, Tintinhull, Yeovil, Somerset BA22 8PZ

Map ① I6   1953

Created last century around an attractive 17th-century manor house (available as a holiday let), this is one of the most harmonious small gardens in Britain. It features secluded lawns, small pools and colourful borders. There is also an attractive kitchen garden, woodland walk and orchard to explore. Even the car park is set among picturesque orchards and you won't fail to miss the geese grazing in the paddock.

Tintinhull Garden, Somerset

Exploring
– Sit by the tranquil pools and just enjoy.
– Discover interesting facts about Tintinhull in the Village Exhibition.
– Be enchanted by the bird feeding area.
– Relax on the newly upholstered sofa in the garden room.
– Tintinhull House is a beautiful holiday let that sleeps eight.

Eating and shopping: small, pretty tea-room serving delicious cakes and cream teas. Sit outside and enjoy your food in the sunshine. Take home a plant or a postcard, available in reception.

You may also enjoy: Montacute House, Lytes Cary, Barrington Court and Stourhead.

Making the most of your day: summer family activities. Pick up an explorer sheet from the exhibition and explore the beautiful villlage of Tintinhull.

Access for all: ⯑⯑⯑⯑
Building ⯑⯑ Gardens ⯑➡⯑

Getting here: 183:ST503198. **Bus**: First 52 Yeovil Bus Station–Martock (passing within ¾ mile Yeovil Pen Mill ⯑). **Train**: Yeovil Pen Mill 5½ miles; Yeovil Junction 7 miles (bus to Yeovil Bus Station). **Road**: 5 miles north west of Yeovil, ½ mile south of A303, on east outskirts of Tintinhull. Follow road signs to Tintinhull village. **Parking**: free, 150 yards.

Finding out more: 01935 823289 or tintinhull@nationaltrust.org.uk

Tintinhull Garden		M	T	W	T	F	S	S
14 Mar–31 Oct	11–5	·	·	**W**	**T**	**F**	**S**	**S**

Closes dusk if earlier. Open Bank Holiday Mondays.

Treasurer's House

Martock, Somerset TA12 6JL

Map ① I6 1971

Medieval house with Great Hall, completed 1293 – with kitchen added 15th century. Solar Block contains an unusual wall-painting.
Note: no WC.

Getting here: 193:ST462191. 1 mile north west of A303, between Ilminster and Ilchester.

Finding out more: 01935 825015 or treasurersmartock@nationaltrust.org.uk

Treasurer's House		M	T	W	T	F	S	S
14 Mar–26 Sep	2–5	**M**	**T**	·	·	·	·	**S**

Trelissick Garden

Feock, near Truro, Cornwall TR3 6QL

Map ① C9 ⯑⯑⯑⯑⯑⯑⯑ 1955

'**My daughter looked at the Water Tower and decided that Trelissick is magic before we even got into the garden!**'
Lisa Richardson, Midhurst

This modern garden was created within shelter belts planted 200 years ago. It is constantly evolving, with new planting and fresh ideas. Trelissick has seen trees grow to maturity, the tide ebbing and flowing, but has become a dynamic, forward-looking estate. The iconic Water Tower was built for irrigation and fire-control; now the lavatories are flushed with rainwater stored underground in modern reservoirs. Heat is extracted from kitchen appliances and the sun to provide hot water and heating. The River Fal is now more than just a beautiful setting for Trelissick; many visitors arrive by boat each summer.

Exploring
- Discover not one but four summerhouses dotted around the garden.
- Turn cartwheels on the tennis lawn (avoiding the ha-ha)!
- Find the perfect place to picnic in the sheltered garden.
- Explore the magical Cryptomeria tree in the main lawn.
- Get close to nature on the riverside woodland walks.
- Relax in the spacious parkland overlooking the River Fal.

Eating and shopping: taste Cornish produce indoors or out at Crofters Restaurant. Find the perfect souvenir in our shop and plant sales. Discover work from Cornish artists and craftspeople in the gallery. Stay! Trelissick's five holiday cottages include the Water Tower.

You may also enjoy: Glendurgan – a valley garden of natural beauty leading down to the Helford River.

Trelissick Garden, Cornwall, is constantly evolving

Making the most of your day: open-air theatre in summer, exhibitions and shows held in the stables by local groups, monthly guided walks around the garden, extensive calendar of events for all the family. Dogs on leads welcome in the park and woodland walks.

Access for all: ♿🏠🔔♿🚶🎧👁👁🅿
Grounds 🚶🏠➡🚶

Getting here: 204:SW837396. **Cycle**: NCN3. **Ferry**: link from Falmouth, Truro and St Mawes: Enterprise boats 01326 374241, K&S Cruisers 01326 211056, Newman's Cruises/Tolverne Ferries 01872 580309. **Bus**: First 93 Truro–Feock. **Train**: Truro 5 miles; Perranwell, 4 miles. **Road**: 4 miles south of Truro, on B3289 above King Harry Ferry. **Parking**: 50 yards, £3.50 (refunded on admission to garden).

Finding out more: 01872 862090 or trelissick@nationaltrust.org.uk

Trelissick Garden		M	T	W	T	F	S	S
2 Jan–12 Feb	11–4	M	T	W	T	F	S	S
13 Feb–31 Oct	10:30–5:30	M	T	W	T	F	S	S
1 Nov–23 Dec	11–4	M	T	W	T	F	S	S
27 Dec–31 Dec	11–4	M	T	W	T	F	·	·

Garden closes dusk if earlier. Garden, gallery, shop and restaurant closed Friday 5 February. Copeland China Collection open Thursdays, May and September, 2 to 4. Please note: property open all year.

Trengwainton Garden

Madron, near Penzance, Cornwall TR20 8RZ

Map ① B9   🦋🏠 1961

'**As near to paradise as you can imagine**.'
Mr and Mrs Gibson, Leeds

With plants from around the globe scattered throughout this 10-hectare (25-acre) garden, there is something to inspire around every corner. Champion magnolias and vibrant rhododendrons make way for lush banana plants and soaring echiums. Unusually, the restored walled kitchen garden was built to the dimensions of Noah's Ark, and is today used to demonstrate contemporary varieties of fruit and vegetables. A colourfully bordered stream leads up to a shady pond and sunny terrace, with stunning views across Mount's Bay.

Exploring
— Be inspired by some great kitchen garden ideas.
— Imagine dinosaurs as you explore the giant tree fern glades.
— Enthuse the children with our family trail.
— Find your bearings in the amazing view from the toposcope.
— Wander along wooded paths or picnic on grassy spaces.

Eating and shopping: enjoy some retail therapy in the shop and plant centre. Indulge yourself with our range of Cornish products. Sample mouth-watering cakes in the tea-room. Enjoy light meals with ingredients sourced from the kitchen garden.

You may also enjoy: Levant Beam Engine, Glendurgan Garden.

Making the most of your day: programme of events and activities for all the family throughout the year. Dogs on leads welcome, except in the tea-room and its garden.

The sloping beds in Trengwainton's kitchen garden, Cornwall

Trerice

Kestle Mill, near Newquay, Cornwall TR8 4PG

Map ① C8   🏰 ✤ 🏠 ⊤   1953

'Very helpful and friendly staff and volunteers. Great children's activities and great to have touchable replica artefacts.'
Jane Bartholomew, Bristol

An intimate Elizabethan manor and a Cornish gem, Trerice remains little changed by the advances in building fashions over the centuries, thanks to long periods under absentee owners. Today the renowned stillness and tranquillity of Trerice, much prized by visitors, is occasionally pierced by the curious lilts of Tudor music or shouts of excitement from the Bowling Green (surely you will want to try a game of Kayling or Slapcock?), bringing back some of the bustle and noise that must have typified its time as a busy manor house.

Exploring
- Handle replica artefacts and armour and make a brass rubbing.
- Discover the beautiful architecture and fine plaster ceilings.
- Enjoy the tranquillity of the informal garden and Cornish orchard.
- Try the Tudor open-air games of Kayling and Slapcock.
- Find out about the Elizabethan Great Squirt.

Eating and shopping: relax in the Barn Kitchen tea-room or tea-garden. Try some Tudor recipes or our famous lemon meringue pie. Browse the shop and buy some local produce.

You may also enjoy: Godolphin and Cotehele.

Making the most of your day: look out for Tudor-themed family and adult workshops, family trails, special Living History days and don't miss your chance to get wet trying the replica Elizabethan Great Squirt.

Access for all: 🅿️♿ Dⓙ 🖼️ 👶🍴 🚾 🎧 :: 🅰️
Tea-room ♿ Shop/Reception ♿ Grounds ♿➡️♿

Getting here: 203:SW445315. **Foot**: footpath to the property from Penzance via Heamoor.
Cycle: NCN3, 2½ miles. **Bus**: First 17/A/B St Ives–St Just (passing Penzance ≋).
Train: Penzance 2 miles. **Road**: 2 miles north west of Penzance, ½ mile west of Heamoor off Penzance–Morvah road (B3312), ½ mile off St Just road (A3071). **Parking**: free, 150 yards.

Finding out more: 01736 363148 or trengwainton@nationaltrust.org.uk

Trengwainton Garden		M	T	W	T	F	S	S
14 Feb–31 Oct	10:30–5	**M**	**T**	**W**	**T**	·	·	**S**

Open Good Friday. Tea-room opens 10. Last admission 15 minutes before closing.

Access for all: ⬚⬚⬚⬚⬚⬚⬚⬚⬚⬚
House ⬚⬚ Garden ⬚⬚➡⬚

Getting here: 200:SW841585. **Cycle**: NCN32.
Bus: Western Greyhound 527 Newquay
🚃–St Austell 🚃, alight Kestle Mill, ¾ mile.
Train: Quintrell Downs, 1½ miles.
Road: 3 miles south east of Newquay via A392
and A3058 signed from Quintrell Downs (turn
right at Kestle Mill), or signed from A30 at
Summercourt via A3058. **Sat Nav**: instructions
via Kestle Mill A3058. **Parking**: free, 300 yards.
Coach access only via Kestle Mill 1 mile.

Finding out more: 01637 875404 or
trerice@nationaltrust.org.uk

Trerice		M	T	W	T	F	S	S
House								
1 Mar–31 Oct	11–5	M	T	W	T	·	S	S
Great Hall only								
3 Dec–19 Dec	11–4	·	·	·	·	F	S	S
Garden, shop and tea-room								
1 Mar–31 Oct	10:30–5	M	T	W	T	·	S	S
3 Dec–19 Dec	11–4	·	·	·	·	F	S	S

Open on Good Friday.

Trerice, Cornwall: playing a game of Kayling

Tyntesfield

Wraxall, Bristol, Somerset BS48 1NX

Map ① I4  2002

Whether you're visiting for the first time, or
coming back to see the progress, you'll be
amazed by this unique conservation project.
Saved for the nation in 2002, this spectacular
Victorian house and gardens were created by the
Gibbs family. As work continues to conserve the
estate for the future, you can learn from specialist
craftsmen, climb the viewing tower to see the
roof repairs or explore the beautiful gardens and
woodland. From re-roofing to rolling carpets,
your visit to Tyntesfield offers you the chance to
be up close with the restoration of this unique
Victorian estate.

Exploring
- Climb the roof viewing
  tower and experience a
  different perspective.
- Explore the estate with
  woodland walks and
  environmental
  discovery activities.
- Take home fresh produce
  from the working
  kitchen garden.
- Handle items from
  the collection at our
  Discovery Tables.
- Visit the stables for the
  interactive batcam and
  virtual tour.
- Explore the gardens with
  family activity packs.

Eating and shopping: pick up Tyntesfield
souvenirs and local Somerset produce.
Look out for kiosk serving hot and cold
light refreshments. Plant centre with garden
furniture and ornaments. Courtyard area with
picnic benches and heated undercover seating.

You may also enjoy: Clevedon Court, Dyrham
Park and Prior Park Landscape Garden.

Stained glass window with sun design in the Chapel at Tyntesfield, Somerset

Making the most of your day: glimpse some family bedrooms on the first floor, open for the first time. Relax in the arboretum, play croquet on the lawn or track down the eight champion trees. Dogs welcome on the estate walks.

Access for all: [symbols]
Building [symbols] Grounds [symbols]

Getting here: ST502724. 7 miles south west of Bristol. **Bus**: First X7 Bristol–Clevedon (stops on B3130 at bottom of driveway), and First 354 Bristol–Nailsea (drops on B3130 at Wraxall, 1,000 yards' walk including steep steps). **Train**: Nailsea and Backwell 1½ miles. **Road**: on B3128. 7 miles south west of Bristol; M5 southbound exit 19 via A369 (towards Bristol), B3129, B3128. M5 northbound exit 20, B3130 (towards Bristol), B3128. Brown signs from exit 19 and 20 of M5. For a Tyntesfield Travel Map, please contact the property. **Parking**: free. Car park 500 to 1,000 yards to house depending on route taken (transfer available).

Finding out more: 0844 800 4966 (Infoline). 01275 461900 or tyntesfield@nationaltrust.org.uk

Tyntesfield		M	T	W	T	F	S	S
House and chapel								
20 Mar–31 Oct	11–5	M	T	W	·	·	S	S
Gardens, visitor reception, shop and kiosk								
20 Mar–31 Oct	10:30–5:30	M	T	W	·	·	S	S
4 Dec–19 Dec	10–4	·	·	·	·	·	S	S

Open Good Friday. Last admission to house one hour before closing. Entry cannot be guaranteed on busy days. Free-flow entry to the house is by ticket only (issued at visitor reception on arrival).

Watersmeet

Watersmeet Road, Lynmouth, Devon EX35 6NT

Map ① F5 [symbols]

A haven for wildlife, with waterfalls and excellent walking, where the lush valleys of the East Lyn and Hoar Oak Water tumble together. At the heart of this area sits Watersmeet House, a 19th-century fishing lodge, which is a tea-room and tea-garden, shop and information point. **Note**: deep gorge with steep walk down to house.

Exploring
 − Download a circular walk of the area from our website.
 − Enjoy fishing the best salmon river in England.
 − Walk the nearby highest seacliffs, from Countisbury to Foreland Point.

Eating and shopping: enjoy local and seasonal food in Watersmeet's riverside setting. Local produce, walking gear and gifts available in the shop.

Making the most of your day: nature and family-themed events such as bats and moths evenings, Teddy Bears' Picnic. Walks for all ages and abilities. Dogs allowed, including in the tea-garden.

Access for all: [symbols] Building [symbols] Grounds [symbols]

Getting here: 180:SS744487. **Foot**: South West Coast Path within ¾ mile. **Bus**: TW Coaches 309, 310 from Barnstaple (passing close Barnstaple [symbol]), Quantock 300 from Minehead; Filers 300 from Ilfracombe. On all, alight Lynmouth, then walk through National Trust gorge.
Road: 1½ miles east of Lynmouth, in valley on east side of Lynmouth–Barnstaple road (A39). **Parking**: pay and display (not National Trust), 500 yards. Free National Trust car parks at Combepark, Hillsford Bridge and Countisbury.

Finding out more: 01598 753348 or watersmeet@nationaltrust.org.uk

The tea garden at Watersmeet House, Devon

Wembury

Wembury Beach, Wembury, Devon PL9 0HP

Map (1) F9   1939

A coastal village with a small, pretty beach and a charming 19th-century mill, which is now a tea-room. With beautiful views, excellent rock pooling and a great starting point for coastal and inland walks, Wembury, near the Yealm estuary, is a popular place to visit.

Exploring
- Join a rock pool ramble discovering life under the sea.
- Enjoy miles of coastal trails.
- Simply relax and enjoy the beautiful sunsets.
- Treat yourself to a cream tea at the Old Mill.

Eating and shopping: morning coffees, homemade cakes, soups, pasties and ice-creams. Beach shop sells everything from spades and wetsuits to windbreaks.

Making the most of your day: discover a wide variety of activities at Wembury including rock pooling (01752 862538), sailing, surfing, kayaking, walking and horse-riding. Dogs allowed on beach, 1 October to 31 March only.

Getting here: 201:SX517484. **Foot**: South West Coast Path from Plymouth City to Heybrook Bay, then on to Warren Point, where you can take the seasonal ferry across to Noss Mayo and rejoin the path through to the River Erme (low tide only). Path continues at Wonwell and towards Bigbury-on-Sea, where there are seasonal ferries to Bantham. **Bus**: First 48 Plymouth–Wembury, twice-hourly, Monday to Saturday. Limited Sunday service. For Wembury Point: City Bus 49 Plymouth–Heybrook Bay, via Wembury Point, Monday to Saturday. **Train**: Plymouth 10 miles. **Road**: For Wembury Point and beach follow the A379 from Plymouth, then turn right at Elburton, signposted Wembury. **Parking**: charge, including members.

Finding out more: 01752 346585. 01752 862314 (Old Mill Café) or wembury@nationaltrust. org.uk. South and East Devon Countryside Office, The Stables, Saltram House, Plymouth, Devon PL7 1UH

Wembury		M	T	W	T	F	S	S
Open all year		M	T	W	T	F	S	S

The Old Mill Café is open in the main season and holidays all year.

The view from Wembury Point, Devon, with the Great Mew Stone in the distance

West Pennard Court Barn

West Pennard, near Glastonbury, Somerset BA6 8LR

Map ① I5 🏠 1938

15th-century barn with an unusual roof and an upper floor of compacted earth. **Note**: access by key only – see opening arrangements. Ground slippery in winter. No WC.

Getting here: 182/183:ST547370. 3 miles east of Glastonbury, 7 miles south of Wells, 1½ miles south of West Pennard (A361).

Finding out more: 01985 843600 (Regional office). 01458 850212 or westpennardcourtbarn@nationaltrust.org.uk

West Pennard Court Barn

Admission by appointment. Access by key, to be collected by arrangement with Mr P. H. Green, Court Barn Farm, West Bradley, Somerset BA6 8LR.

Westbury College Gatehouse

College Road, Westbury-on-Trym, Bristol BS9 3EH

Map ① I3 🏠 1907

15th-century gatehouse to the 13th-century College of Priests – where the 14th-century theological reformer, John Wyclif, lived. **Note**: access by key. No WC.

Getting here: 172:ST572775. 3 miles north of the centre of Bristol.

Finding out more: 01934 844518 or westburycollege@nationaltrust.org.uk

Westbury College Gatehouse

Access (Monday to Friday) by key to be collected by appointment from the Parish Office, Church Road, Westbury-on-Trym, Bristol BS9 4AG. 0117 950 8644 (afternoons only).

Westbury Court Garden

Westbury-on-Severn, Gloucestershire GL14 1PD

Map ① J2 1967

'**Very important garden, which enables us to see how gardening trends have changed over time.**'
Mrs Williams, Dorking

Originally laid out between 1696 and 1705, this is the only restored Dutch water garden in the country. Visitors can explore canals, clipped hedges and working 17th-century vegetable plots and discover many old varieties of fruit trees.

Exploring
– See the gardening style of the late 18th century.
– The huge tulip tree flowers at the end of June.
– One of the oldest Holm oaks in the country.
– Historic fruit and vegetables grown and sold throughout the year.
– Footpath access to the River Severn.
– Lovely picnicing spot.

You may also enjoy: Ashleworth Tithe Barn, The Kymin, May Hill and The Weir.

Making the most of your day: evening garden tours, Easter Egg trails, Apple Day.

Access for all: 🅿️🚾🔵 Grounds 🔵🔵

Getting here: 162:SO718138. **Foot**: River Severn footpath runs from garden to river. **Bus**: Stagecoach in South Wales 73 Gloucester ⑆–Chepstow; Stagecoach in Wye and Dean 30/31 Gloucester ⑆–Coleford. **Train**: Gloucester 9 miles. **Road**: 9 miles south west of Gloucester on A48. **Parking**: free, 300 yards.

Finding out more: 01452 760461 or
westburycourt@nationaltrust.org.uk

Westbury Court Garden		M	T	W	T	F	S	S
10 Mar–30 Jun	10–5	·	·	W	T	F	S	S
1 Jul–29 Aug	10–5	M	T	W	T	F	S	S
1 Sep–31 Oct	10–5	·	·	W	T	F	S	S

Open Bank Holiday Mondays. Open other times of year
by appointment.

**The parterre at Westbury Court Garden, Gloucestershire:
England's only restored Dutch water garden**

Westwood Manor

Bradford-on-Avon, Wiltshire BA15 2AF

Map (1) J4   1960

This beautiful small manor house, built over
three centuries, has late Gothic and Jacobean
windows, decorative plasterwork and two
important keyboard instruments. There is
some fine period furniture, 17th- and 18th-
century tapestries and a modern topiary
garden. **Note**: administered for the National
Trust by the tenant. No WC.

Exploring
- Enjoy an elegant manor house with a friendly, domestic atmosphere.
- The country's earliest Italian keyboard instrument in playing order.
- A variety of woods, colours and textiles in the furniture.
- Sit in the peaceful garden surrounded by yew topiary.

Making the most of your day: atmospheric
musical recordings of recently restored virginal
and spinet. Children's quizzes for five to
eight year olds, plus eight and aboves. House
unsuitable for under fives.

Access for all: ⬚🔳⬚🅰 Manor 🔳🔳 Garden 🔳

Getting here: 173:ST812590. **Cycle**: NCN4,
¾ mile. **Bus**: Libra 94, Bodmans 96 Bath ≋–
Trowbridge (passing close Trowbridge ≋).
Train: Avoncliff, 1 mile; Bradford-on-Avon
1½ miles. **Road**: 1½ miles south west of
Bradford-on-Avon, in Westwood village, beside
the church; Westwood village is signposted off
Bradford-on-Avon to Rode road (B3109) and
turn left opposite the New Inn pub towards the
church. **Parking**: free, 90 yards.

Finding out more: 01225 863374 or
westwoodmanor@nationaltrust.org.uk

Westwood Manor		M	T	W	T	F	S	S
4 Apr–29 Sep	2–5	·	T	W	·	·	·	S

Small groups at other times by written application with sae.

White Mill

Sturminster Marshall, near Wimborne Minster, Dorset BH21 4BX

Map ① K6   1982

Corn mill with original wooden machinery in a peaceful riverside setting. **Note**: nearest WC at the Mill House.

Getting here: 195:ST958006. On the River Stour in the parish of Shapwick, close to Sturminster Marshall.

Finding out more: 01258 858051 or whitemill@nationaltrust.org.uk

White Mill		M	T	W	T	F	S	S
27 Mar–31 Oct	12–5	·	·	·	·	·	**S**	**S**

Admission by guided tour. Open Bank Holiday Mondays: 12 to 5, last tour 4.

Woodchester Park

Nympsfield, near Stonehouse, Gloucestershire GL10 3TS

Map ① J3 1994

The tranquil wooded valley contains a 'lost landscape'; remains of an 18th- and 19th-century landscape park with a chain of five lakes. The restoration of this landscape is an ongoing project. Waymarked trails (steep in places) lead through picturesque scenery, passing an unfinished Victorian mansion (not National Trust). **Note**: WC not always available.

Exploring — Don't miss Woodchester Mansion Open Days (01453 861541).

Making the most of your day: follow the waymarked trails through the valley. Dogs under close control, on leads where requested.

Access for all: Grounds

Getting here: 162:SO797012. 4 miles south west of Stroud. **Foot**: Cotswold Way within ¾ mile. **Bus**: Cotswold Green 35 Stroud–Nympsfield (passing close Stroud ≑). **Train**: Stroud 5 miles. **Road**: off B4066 Stroud–Dursley road. **Parking**: £2 (pay and display). Accessible from Nympsfield road, 300 yards from junction with B4066. Last admission to car park one hour before dusk.

Finding out more: 01452 814213 or woodchesterpark@nationaltrust.org.uk. The Ebworth Centre, The Camp, Stroud, Gloucestershire GL6 7ES

Woodchester Park		M	T	W	T	F	S	S
Open all year	Dawn–dusk	**M**	**T**	**W**	**T**	**F**	**S**	**S**

Woodchester Park, Gloucestershire

South & South East

Looking for fairies among the temples and follies of Stowe Landscape Gardens

by Deneille Lee,
member since 2008

Outdoors in the South and South East

The South and South East of England is one of the country's most densely populated areas, however thanks to organisations such as the National Trust, it still boasts extensive and beautiful green spaces and miles of dramatic coastline – perfect places to enjoy some outdoor fun.

When you visit Surrey set yourself the challenge of cycling up the steep slopes of Box Hill. If you succeed in reaching the top, treat yourself to a visit to the new Discovery Zone, where you can test your senses. If you prefer something a little less demanding, then hire a boat and take in the delights of the River Wey. The county also boasts some of the region's best views. Follow the footpaths up Leith Hill and climb to the top of the Gothic tower, and it is possible to see St Paul's Cathedral to the north, while to the south is a panorama stretching from the Weald to the English Channel. Amazingly, on a clear day, thirteen counties are visible!

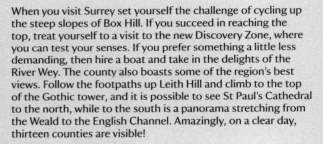

If a day at the beach is your idea of heaven then East Head, at the mouth of Chichester Harbour in West Sussex, is ideal. Take an opportunity to relax and soak up the sun or get a group together for a friendly game of cricket. West Sussex also boasts the perfect site for a favourite English pastime: the vast open space of Devil's Dyke attracts people from far and wide to fly kites.

Kent is well known for its woodlands which were devastated by the great storm of 1987; however more than 20 years on, places such as Toys Hill, near Westerham, are thriving as a result; with more types of flora and fauna than before. The county also offers pockets of beautiful green space, or 'green lungs', in urban areas, such as Petts Wood and the Hawkwood Estate near Bromley and Cobham Wood near Gravesend, all teeming with wild flowers and ancient trees.

Above: **the Seven Sisters, East Sussex**
Right: **having fun at Polesden Lacey, Surrey**
Far right: **Compton Down, Isle of Wight**

Secret bays and rock pools

The inspiring coastline of East Sussex is a magnificent sight. The guardians of the South Downs, the Seven Sisters, stretch between Birling Gap and Cuckmere Haven, and all the way along them there are glistening rock pools and secret bays carved out by the sea just waiting to be explored.

The most southerly point of the region is the Isle of Wight, where much of the finest countryside and coastline of the island is owned by the National Trust, including the fine chalk downs of Ventnor, Tennyson Down and the Needles Headland. This means that the natural beauty and rich wildlife of this popular holiday island, including its famous red squirrels, will continue to survive and thrive for future generations to enjoy.

Walk, picnic or cycle

In Hampshire, local residents and visitors alike enjoy many of the areas of countryside cared for by the Trust, including Selborne Hill, Ludshott Common, Waggoners Wells and The Chase – all great places for walking and enjoying the flora and fauna.

To the north of the region there are many popular beauty spots in the Chilterns, including Watlington Hill, West Wycombe Hill, Coombe Hill and Ivinghoe Beacon along the Chiltern escarpment. If you are looking for an action-packed day the Ashridge Estate, which covers more than 2,000 hectares (5,000 acres) of outstanding Chilterns countryside, attracts tens of thousands of visitors who flock to enjoy its fine walks, picnic areas and cycling routes. There is also a lively Discovery Room in the Bridgewater Monument Visitor Centre, with updates on wildlife, events and activities. In Oxfordshire don't miss the famous White Horse at Uffington – the oldest chalk figure in the country. It is set amid a landscape that is peppered with ancient sites and monuments, including Dragon's Hill where St George was reputed to have slain the dragon, and the famous Neolithic burial chamber known, somewhat enigmatically, as Wayland's Smithy. The nearby villages and agricultural estates of Buscot and Coleshill are well worth exploring, with a range of pleasant circular walks.

Following the old methods

Around the region the National Trust relies on livestock to help look after our amazing landscapes. Hindhead Common in Surrey is home to Exmoor ponies, while pigs are a favourite of visitors to Woolbeding in West Sussex, and cows stroll leisurely all along the Surrey Hills. In the wild heaths of the New Forest the historic method of grazing animals on common land continues into the 21st century, ensuring that it remains a unique landscape.

Wild wonders

If wildlife spotting is your passion, then the summer spectacle of the Adonis blue butterflies on Cissbury Ring, West Sussex, or Denbies Hillside, Surrey, is not to be missed. Or see if you can spot the seals off the beach at East Head. As well as all these treats, the successful reintroduction of red kites to the Chilterns means that these magnificent birds are now a common sight across an ever-widening area.

Outdoors in the South and South East

'My favourite time of year is autumn, when the woodlands across the Surrey Hills come alive with colour and the beech trees turn a magnificent gold.'

David Kennington
Property Manager, Surrey Hills

Tales of times past

There is also an array of unique places with fascinating stories of times past and our ancestors. Saddlescombe Farm near Devil's Dyke in West Sussex is just one. This ancient farmstead was once home to the Knights Templar, and visitors can find out about its fascinating 1,000 years of history during public open days in spring and autumn – alternatively it is possible to arrange special guided tours. Another place full of historical interest is Runnymede on the banks of the River Thames. The Magna Carta was signed here in 1215, and now you can enjoy occasional guided walks by the warden. Or why not book a guided tour of Reigate Fort in Surrey, once used to defend us from invasion?

Challenge yourself

As well as numerous places to visit and explore there is also an extensive programme of open-air events to take advantage of – from bug hunts to rock-pooling, and hurdle making to bat watching. Of particular interest to those with children, is the thriving programme of family events and activities the National Trust runs across its countryside properties – from the Newtown Nature Reserve in the Isle of Wight all the way across the Surrey Hills.

Don't miss...
Saddlescombe Farm Open Days, Sussex: telephone 01273 857712 or see the What's On section of the regional newsletter for details.

Guided tours of Reigate Fort, Surrey: discover this fascinating building, which was once used to defend us from invasion. To book special guided tours or study days telephone 01342 843225.

My favourite walk

I believe the walk from Hughenden to West Wycombe and on to Bradenham is unbeatable.

There is a choice of paths you can take, so there is plenty of variety. But whichever route you choose you will find yourself passing through very different central Chilterns' landscapes. The paths meander across ancient wooded commons, over grazed parkland and through cathedral-like beechwoods and pretty small villages.

Along the way you pass by chalk streams, veteran trees and historic houses, all interspersed with a farmed landscape.

You are never very far from the motorway and busy conurbations, however these wonderful places seem a million miles away from the hubbub of everyday life.

Neil Harris
Gardens and Countryside Manager for Hughenden, West Wycombe and Chilterns Countryside

Alfriston Clergy House

The Tye, Alfriston, Polegate,
East Sussex BN26 5TL

Map (2) H8   🏠 ❄ 1896

This rare 14th-century Wealden 'hall house' was
the first building to be acquired by the National
Trust, in 1896. The thatched, timber-framed
house is in an idyllic setting, with views across
the River Cuckmere, and surrounded by a
delightful, tranquil cottage garden featuring a
magnificent Judas tree. **Note**: no WC, nearest
in village car park.

Exploring
- Admire the first house the National Trust saved.
- Enjoy the tranquillity of our English cottage garden.
- Discover the chalk and sour milk floor in the hall.
- Soak up the atmosphere of this 600-year-old house.

Eating and shopping: browse in the shop for a
souvenir of your visit.

Making the most of your day: children's
quizzes and trails. Varied events programme all
year. Short circular walks and longer distance
hikes over South Downs. Situated in the
interesting and historic medieval village
of Alfriston.

Access for all: 🔲 👓 🅰
Building 🏠 **Grounds** 🏠 🏠

Getting here: 189:TQ521029. **Foot**: South
Downs Way within ¾ mile. **Cycle**: NCN2.
Bus: Countryliner 125 from Lewes, Renown
126 from Eastbourne and Seaford (pass close
Lewes ≋ and Seaford ≋). **Train**: Berwick
2½ miles. **Road**: 4 miles north east of Seaford,
just east of B2108, in Alfriston village, adjoining
The Tye and St Andrew's church.
Parking: 500 yards at other end of village
(not National Trust).

Finding out more: 01323 870001 or
alfriston@nationaltrust.org.uk

Alfriston Clergy House		M	T	W	T	F	S	S
27 Feb–1 Aug	10:30–5	M	·	W	T	·	S	S
2 Aug–29 Aug	10:30–5	M	·	W	T	F	S	S
30 Aug–31 Oct	10:30–5	M	·	W	T	·	S	S
1 Nov–19 Dec	11–4	M	·	W	T	·	S	S

Open Good Friday. Special Friday openings in August.

The cottage garden at Alfriston Clergy House, East Sussex

Ascott

Wing, near Leighton Buzzard,
Buckinghamshire LU7 0PS

Map (2) E3   🏠 ❄ 1949

This half-timbered Jacobean farmhouse,
transformed by the de Rothschilds towards
the end of the 19th century, now houses
an exceptional collection of paintings, fine
furniture and superb oriental porcelain. The
extensive gardens are an attractive mix of
formal and natural, with specimen trees and
shrubs and some unusual features.

Exploring
- See one of the best small picture collections in Britain.
- Tell the time by the unusual topiary sundial.
- Relax in the Dutch Garden admiring the Eros Fountain.

Access for all:
Building ♿♿♿ Grounds ♿♿➡

Getting here: 165:SP891230. **Bus**: Arriva
100 Aylesbury–Milton Keynes (passing close
Aylesbury ≋ and Leighton Buzzard ≋).
Train: Leighton Buzzard 2 miles. **Road**: ½ mile
east of Wing, 2 miles south west of Leighton
Buzzard, on south side of A418. **Parking**: free,
220 yards, and coach parking.

Finding out more: 01296 688242 or
ascott@nationaltrust.org.uk

Ascott		M	T	W	T	F	S	S
23 Mar–25 Apr	2–6	·	T	W	T	F	S	S
27 Apr–22 Jul	2–6	·	T	W	T	·	·	·
27 Jul–10 Sep	2–6	·	T	W	T	F	S	S

Open Bank Holiday Mondays and Good Friday. Last
admission one hour before closing. Gardens open in aid
of National Gardens Scheme on Mondays 3 May and 30
August (charge including members).

Ashdown House

Lambourn, Newbury, Berkshire RG17 8RE

Map ② C5   🏠🌼♿ 1956

This extraordinary building with a dolls'-house
appearance nestles in a beautiful valley on the
Berkshire Downs, surrounded by woodland.
Note: no WC. The house is tenanted. Access
limited to the staircase and roof (100 steps).

Getting here: 174:SU282820. 2½ miles south
of Ashbury, 3½ miles north of Lambourn, on
west side of B4000.

Finding out more: 01494 755569 (Infoline).
01793 762209 or
ashdownhouse@nationaltrust.org.uk

Ashdown House		M	T	W	T	F	S	S
3 Apr–30 Oct	2–5	·	·	W	·	·	S	·

Admission by guided tour to house at 2:15, 3:15 and 4:15
(numbers limited).

Ashridge Estate

Visitor Centre, Moneybury Hill, Ringshall,
Berkhamsted, Hertfordshire HP4 1LT

Map ② E3   1926

'**Totally amazing, a lovely walk on an autumn
afternoon enjoyed with my mum**.'
Helena Benet, Bedfordshire

Ashridge Estate, Hertfordshire

This magnificent and varied countryside estate
runs across the borders of Hertfordshire and
Buckinghamshire, along the main ridge of
the Chiltern Hills. There are 2,000 hectares
(4,942 acres) of woodlands, commons and
chalk downland supporting a rich variety of
wildlife and offering splendid walks through
outstanding scenery. The focal point is the
Monument, erected in 1832 to the Duke
of Bridgewater. Ivinghoe Beacon provides
wonderful views of the surrounding landscape,
inhabited from pre-history to the current
day. Ideas for walks and family days out can
be found at the Visitor Centre. **Note**: WC not
always available.

Exploring
– Escape to fresh air
and freedom.
– Discover more about
local wildlife at our lively
Visitor Centre.
– Acres of breathtaking scenery,
from ancient woodland to
chalk downland.
– Experience a landscape rich in
history and archaeology.
– Climb the Bridgewater
Monument for wonderful
panoramic views.

Eating and shopping: enjoy browsing for gifts in our newly refurbished shop. Local walks, maps and books available to purchase. Treat yourself to delicious homemade food (National Trust approved concession).

You may also enjoy: Waddesdon Manor, Stowe Landscape Gardens and Dunstable Downs.

Making the most of your day: the Visitor Centre provides information on local facilities, walks and events. Children will enjoy the Discovery Room and our self-guided family trails. Dogs must be under close control (deer roam freely).

Access for all: ♿🚻🚐👂📷🖊

Visitor Centre 🔄 Grounds 🚶➡🚲

Getting here: 181:SP970131. **Foot**: 2¾ miles of the Ridgeway on property. **Bus**: Visitor Centre and Monument: Arriva 30/31 from Tring ≋, alight Monument Drive or Aldbury ½ mile on foot (steep climb). Ivinghoe Beacon: Arriva 61 Aylesbury–Luton (passing close Aylesbury ≋ and Luton ≋). **Train**: Visitor Centre and Monument: Tring ≋, 1¾ miles; Ivinghoe Beacon: Cheddington ≋ 3½ miles. **Road**: Visitor Centre and Monument: between Berkhamsted and Northchurch, and Ringshall and Dagnall, just off B4506. **Sat Nav**: some Sat Nav's stop at Aldbury. Continue up Tom's Hill, turning left at the T-junction (B4506). **Parking**: free at the Visitor Centre, Ivinghoe Beacon and around the Estate.

Finding out more: 01494 755557 (Infoline). 01442 851227 or ashridge@nationaltrust.org.uk

Ashridge Estate		M	T	W	T	F	S	S
Estate								
Open all year		M	T	W	T	F	S	S
Visitor Centre and shop*								
13 Feb–19 Dec	10–5	M	T	W	T	F	S	S
Monument (weather dependent)								
3 Apr–31 Oct	12–4:30	·	·	·	·	·	S	S
Tea-room**								
1 Jan–1 Apr	10–4	M	T	W	T	F	S	S
2 Apr–31 Oct	8–6	M	T	W	T	F	S	S
1 Nov–31 Dec	10–4	M	T	W	T	F	S	S

*Visitor Centre, shop and tea-room may close at dusk if earlier than the published closing time. **Tea-room closed 25 December.

Basildon Park

Lower Basildon, Reading, Berkshire RG8 9NR

Map ② D5 🏛❄♣🛶🔔🍷 1978

This impressive Georgian mansion, surrounded by glorious parkland, was lovingly rescued from ruin by Lord and Lady Iliffe in the mid 1950s, when they restored the elegant interior and scoured the country salvaging 18th-century architectural fixtures and fittings. They filled their comfortable new home with fine paintings, fabrics and furniture, which can still be enjoyed by visitors today. There are waymarked trails through the historic parkland and gravel paths around the gardens. Why not visit our 'on location' exhibition and find out what goes on behind the scenes?

Exploring
- Be inspired by the remarkable restoration of Basildon Park.
- Visit the fascinating stonework conservation exhibition (closes this year).
- Discover the magic of the Shell Room.
- Relax in the gardens and on the croquet lawn.
- Burn off some energy on the parkland trails.
- Drink in the beauty of our parkland views.

Eating and shopping: enjoy traditional English fare in our tea-room. Treat yourself to afternoon tea, with homemade cakes and scones. Don't miss the plant sale area and gift shop. Browse in our second-hand bookshop.

You may also enjoy: Greys Court and The Vyne. Or, for something completely different, Sandham Memorial Chapel.

Making the most of your day: introductory talks, waymarked trails and picnic tables. Family-friendly events and activities, toys on the croquet lawn. Exciting events programme, including open-air theatre. Dogs welcome, on leads only.

The Octagon Drawing Room at Basildon Park, Berkshire

Bateman's

Bateman's Lane, Burwash,
East Sussex TN19 7DS

Map ② H7　 1940

'It feels as though Kipling might return home at any time.'
Alan Truett, Hastings

'That's She! The Only She! Make an honest woman of her – quick!' was how Rudyard Kipling and his wife, Carrie, felt the first time they saw Bateman's. Surrounded by the wooded landscape of the Sussex Weald, this 17th-century house, with its mullioned windows and oak beams, provided a much needed sanctuary to this world-famous writer. The rooms, described by him as 'untouched and unfaked', remain much as he left them, with oriental rugs and artefacts reflecting his strong association with the East. Bateman's is very much a family home, but impressive none the less. **Note**: the garden, shop and tea-room are open free of charge in November and December.

Exploring
- Soak up the atmosphere in Kipling's book-lined study.
- Enjoy the serenity of the Formal Garden.
- Walk by the river as it flows through the meadow.
- Watch the watermill grind flour most Wednesday and Saturday afternoons.
- Experience 'Kipling Country', with a walk through the valley.
- Discover Kipling's 1928 Rolls-Royce Phantom I.

Access for all:

[access icons] Building [icons] Grounds [icons]

Getting here: 175:SU611782. **Bus**: Thames Travel 133 Reading ⬛–Goring & Streatley ⬛, alight Lower Basildon (Park Wall Lane), ½ mile. **Train**: Pangbourne 2½ miles; Goring & Streatley 3 miles. **Road**: between Pangbourne and Streatley, 7 miles north west of Reading, on west side of A329; leave M4 at exit 12 and follow signs for Beale Park (not National Trust) through Pangbourne, then brown National Trust signs to Basildon Park. **Sat Nav**: please use main entrance from A329. **Parking**: free, 400 yards from mansion (buggy transfer service available).

Finding out more: 0118 984 3040 or basildonpark@nationaltrust.org.uk

Eating and shopping: buy Kipling books and souvenirs in the shop. Eat in the tea-room, with its wonderful garden setting. Relax and have fun in the picturesque Picnic Glen.

You may also enjoy: Scotney Castle, a Victorian country house and romantic garden with a 14th-century ruin.

Basildon Park		M	T	W	T	F	S	S
House (main show rooms)								
10 Mar–31 Oct	12–5	·	·	W	T	F	S	S
1 Dec–12 Dec	12–4	·	·	W	T	F	S	S
Ground floor exhibition area, tea-room, shop and grounds								
10 Feb–7 Mar	11–3	·	·	W	T	F	S	S
10 Mar–31 Oct	11–5	·	·	W	T	F	S	S
3 Nov–19 Dec	11–3	·	·	W	T	F	S	S
1 Dec–12 Dec	11–4	·	·	W	T	F	S	S

Open Bank Holiday Mondays.

Making the most of your day: programme of events, family fun days, storytelling, re-enactment weekends, garden and countryside walks. Virtual tour of watermill and first floor of house. Children's quizzes/trails. Dogs on leads and only in car park, dog crèche.

Access for all: 🅿️♿️🌮🏛️📷🚻 👓🅰️
Building 🏠♿️♿️ Grounds 🏠➡️♿️

Getting here: 199:TQ671238. Burwash, East Sussex, TN19 7DS. **Bus**: Renown 318/9 Uckfield–Etchingham ≥. **Train**: Etchingham 3 miles. **Road**: ½ mile south of Burwash. A265 west from Burwash, first turning on left. **Parking**: free, 30 yards. Coaches: tight left turn into first bay.

Finding out more: 01435 882302 or batemans@nationaltrust.org.uk

Bateman's	M	T	W	T	F	S	S
Garden, shop and tea-room							
27 Feb–7 Mar	11–4	·	·	·	·	·	S	S
1 Nov–22 Dec	11–4	M	T	W	·	·	S	S
House, garden, shop and tea-room*							
13 Mar–31 Oct	11–5	M	T	W	·	·	S	S
House							
4 Dec–19 Dec	11:30–3:30	·	·	·	·	·	S	S

Open Good Friday: 11 to 5. ***Shop and garden close 5:30 13 March to 31 October**. The mill grinds corn most Wednesdays and Saturdays at 2. House: downstairs rooms decorated for traditional Edwardian Christmas on 4 and 5, 11 and 12 and 18 and 19 December, 11:30 to 3:30.

Volunteer miller in the watermill at Bateman's, East Sussex

Bembridge Windmill

High Street, Bembridge,
Isle of Wight PO35 5SQ

Map ② D9   🗙🚽 1961

This tiny gem, the only surviving windmill on the Isle of Wight, is one of its most iconic images. Built around 1700, it last operated in 1913 but still has most of its original machinery intact. Climb to the top and follow the milling process back down its four floors.
Note: no WC.

Exploring	– See how the parts move with our working model.
	– Feel the wooden parts worn smooth by the years.
	– Enjoy the views that inspired J. W. M. Turner.

Eating and shopping: treat yourself with ice-creams or drinks in the kiosk. Buy a souvenir as a reminder of your visit.

Making the most of your day: children's I-Spy trail sheet. The start of the Culver Trail.

Access for all: 🅿️📷🏛️🚽👓 Building 🏠

Getting here: 196:SZ639874. **Cycle**: NCN67, ½ mile. **Ferry**: Ryde (Wightlink Ltd) 6 miles (0871 376 1000); East Cowes (Red Funnel) 13 miles (0844 844 9988). **Bus**: Southern Vectis 14 from Ryde Esplanade ≥ to within ½ mile; 10 Newport–Sandown to within ¼ mile. **Train**: Brading 2 miles by footpath. **Road**: ½ mile south of Bembridge on B3395. **Parking**: free (not National Trust), 100 yards in lay-by.

Finding out more: 01983 873945 or bembridgemill@nationaltrust.org.uk

Bembridge Windmill	M	T	W	T	F	S	S
13 Mar–31 Oct	11–5	M	T	W	T	F	S	S

Closes dusk if earlier. Conducted school groups and special visits March to end October (not July or August) by written appointment.

Boarstall Duck Decoy

Boarstall, near Bicester,
Buckinghamshire HP18 9UX

Map ② D3 1980

Rare survival of a 17th-century duck decoy
in working order. One of only a few left in
the country.

Getting here: 164/165:SP624151. Midway
between Bicester and Thame, 2 miles west of
Brill. Entrance through farm.

Finding out more: 01280 822850 or
boarstalldecoy@nationaltrust.org.uk

Boarstall Duck Decoy		M	T	W	T	F	S	S
3 Apr–29 Aug	10–4	·	·	·	·	·	**S**	**S**
7 Apr–25 Aug	3:30–6	·	·	**W**	·	·	·	·
Open Bank Holiday Mondays, 10 to 4.								

Boarstall Tower

Boarstall, near Bicester,
Buckinghamshire HP18 9UX

Map ② D3 1943

14th-century moated gatehouse, built by
John de Haudlo and once part of a fortified
manor house, set in gardens.
Note: property is tenanted.

Getting here: 164/165:SP624141. Midway
between Bicester and Thame, 2 miles
west of Brill.

Finding out more: 01280 822850 or
boarstalltower@nationaltrust.org.uk

Boarstall Tower

Open Wednesdays, 2 to 5, from 2 June to 25 August. Open
11 to 5 on 3 and 5 April, 3 and 31 May, 28 and 30 August.
Admission by timed ticket only (subject to availability),
including members.

Bodiam Castle

Bodiam, near Robertsbridge,
East Sussex TN32 5UA

Map ② I7 1926

'**Relived my childhood and visited Bodiam
Castle with grandchildren and family. A
beautiful castle and a stunning day out**.'
Martin Cherry, London

One of the most famous and evocative castles
in Britain, Bodiam was built in 1385, as both a
defence and a comfortable home. The exterior
is virtually complete and the ramparts rise
dramatically above the moat. Enough of the
interior survives to give an impression of castle
life. There are spiral staircases and battlements
to explore, and wonderful views of the Rother
Valley from the top of the towers. In the
impressive gatehouse is the castle's original
wooden portcullis, an extremely rare example
of its kind. **Note**: nearest WCs in car park.
Bodiam Castle is often used by educational
groups during term.

Exploring   – Explore the courtyard and
        battlements and imagine
        medieval castle life.
       – Meet real castle characters
        on selected dates throughout
        the year.
       – Discover Bodiam's story
        through a superb film
        and exhibition.
       – 'Bat pack' children's
        discovery packs available, plus
        seasonal challenges.
       – Climb the towers for
        wonderful views of the
        Rother Valley.
       – See the original portcullis,
        probably the oldest
        in England.

Eating and shopping: the shop has a range
of exciting gifts and produce. Try our Bodiam
wine and local honey, plus much more. The
Wharf tea-room serves seasonal, local food
cooked onsite. Ice-creams and drinks available
from castle kiosk (seasonal).

The dramatic ramparts of Bodiam Castle, East Sussex

Access for all: ⬚⬚⬚⬚⬚⬚⬚⬚⬚⬚⬚
Building ⬚⬚⬚ Grounds ⬚⬚⬚

Getting here: 199:TQ785256. **Foot**: on the Sussex Border path. **Ferry**: Bodiam Ferry (seasonal) from Newenden Bridge (A28). **Bus**: Stagecoach in Hastings 349 Hastings ⊠–Hawkhurst. **Train**: steam railway (seasonal) from Tenterden ¼ mile; Robertsbridge 5 miles; Battle 10 miles. **Road**: 3 miles south of Hawkhurst, 3 miles east of A21 Hurst Green midway between Tunbridge Wells and Hastings. **Parking**: 400 yards, £2. Coaches £5.

Finding out more: 01580 830196 or bodiamcastle@nationaltrust.org.uk

Bodiam Castle		M	T	W	T	F	S	S
2 Jan–7 Feb	11–4	·	·	·	·	·	**S**	**S**
13 Feb–31 Oct	10:30–5	**M**	**T**	**W**	**T**	**F**	**S**	**S**
3 Nov–23 Dec	11–4	·	·	**W**	**T**	**F**	**S**	**S**

13 February to 31 October, gift shop and tea-room close at 5 most days but at 5:30 during school summer holidays. Entrance to castle 400 yards from car park.

Box Hill

The Old Fort, Box Hill Road, Box Hill, Tadworth, Surrey KT20 7LB

Map ② F6

An outstanding area of woodland and open chalk downland. It has much to offer families, as well as ramblers and naturalists, with many beautiful walks and views towards the South Downs. On the summit there is a Discovery Zone, shop, servery, ample car parking and a magnificent view.

Exploring	– Visit the new Discovery Zone and 'Bee' amazed.
	– New mountain bike hire facilities – explore Box Hill by bike.
	– Many guided walks, including impromptu tours – see noticeboard for details.
	– Three self-guided trails reveal the heart of Box Hill.

You may also enjoy: Bateman's – the beautiful home of Rudyard Kipling.

Making the most of your day: exciting events programme – from mid February challenge to Santa's Christmas Grotto, with open-air theatre and 'The Grand Medieval weekend'. Activities for all the family daily through August. Dogs welcome on leads in grounds only.

Eating and shopping: homemade sandwiches and cakes, including famous 'Rider's Revival' flapjack. Try our gluten-free, dairy-free and fat-free options. Treat your children to a special lunch box.

Making the most of your day: children's quiz/trail. Special Christmas shopping day Friday 17 December. Suitable for school groups. Education room/centre. Dogs under close control where sheep grazing.

Access for all: ⓟ♿🚾♿♿•• Building ♿🔲 Grounds ♿

Getting here: 187:TQ171519. **Foot**: 1 mile of North Downs Way from Stepping Stones to South Scarp; 1 mile of Thames Down link footpath at Mickleham Downs; 1 mile from Dorking station (½ mile from Boxhill station). Many rights of way lead to Box Hill summit. **Bus**: Sunray Travel 516 Leatherhead ≋– Dorking to Box Hill east car park; Arriva 465 Kingston–Dorking to foot of Box Hill, 1½ miles to summit. **Train**: Boxhill & Westhumble 1½ miles. **Road**: 1 mile north of Dorking, 2½ miles south of Leatherhead on A24. **Parking**: £3 (pay and display). Coaches must **not** use zig-zag road from Burford Bridge on west side of hill as weight restriction applies, but should approach from east side of hill B2032 or B2033; car/coach parks at summit.

Finding out more: 01306 885502 (Information) or boxhill@nationaltrust.org.uk

Box Hill		M	T	W	T	F	S	S
Countryside								
Open all year		M	T	W	T	F	S	S
Servery								
1 Jan–27 Mar	10–4	M	T	W	T	F	S	S
28 Mar–30 Oct	9–5	M	T	W	T	F	S	S
31 Oct–31 Dec	10–4	M	T	W	T	F	S	S
Shop/Discovery Zone								
1 Jan–27 Mar	11–4	M	T	W	T	F	S	S
28 Mar–30 Oct	11–5	M	T	W	T	F	S	S
31 Oct–31 Dec	11–4	M	T	W	T	F	S	S

Shop, Discovery Zone and servery closed 25 December.

Bradenham Village

near High Wycombe, Buckinghamshire

Map ② E4 🏠♿ 1956

Scenic village with cottages clustered around a village green. 17th-century manor house (not open) and church provide impressive backdrop. **Note**: designated parking at the village green above the cricket pavilion.

Getting here: 165:SU825970. 4 miles north west of High Wycombe, off A4010.

Finding out more: 01494 755573 or bradenham@nationaltrust.org.uk

Bradenham Village	M	T	W	T	F	S	S
Open all year	M	T	W	T	F	S	S

Contact property for garden tours.

Bradenham Village, Buckinghamshire: quintessentially English

Brighstone Shop and Museum

North Street, Brighstone, Isle of Wight PO30 4AX

Map ② C9 1989

In a row of traditional thatched cottages by the small village museum is the National Trust shop. **Note**: nearest WC in public car park, 100 yards.

Getting here: 196:SZ428828. Next to post office, just off B3399 in Brighstone.

Finding out more: 01983 740689 or brighstone@nationaltrust.org.uk

Brighstone Shop and Museum		M	T	W	T	F	S	S
2 Jan–1 Apr	10–1	M	T	W	T	F	S	·
2 Apr–28 May	10–4	M	T	W	T	F	S	·
29 May–25 Sep	10–5	M	T	W	T	F	S	·
30 May–26 Sep	12–5	·	·	·	·	·	·	S
27 Sep–23 Dec	10–4	M	T	W	T	F	S	·
24 Dec–31 Dec	10–1	·	·	W	T	F	·	·

Buckingham Chantry Chapel

Market Hill, Buckingham, Buckinghamshire MK18 1JX

Map ② D2 🏠✝ 1912

15th-century chapel, restored by Gilbert Scott in 1875 (second-hand bookshop with refreshments).

Getting here: 152/165:SP693340. On Market Hill, opposite post office.

Finding out more: 01280 822850 or buckinghamchantry@nationaltrust.org.uk

Buckingham Chantry Chapel		M	T	W	T	F	S	S
2 Jan–28 Dec	9:30–3	·	T	·	·	·	S	·

Coffee shop open as bookshop. Property available for hire. Closed 25 December.

The Buscot and Coleshill Estates

Coleshill Estate Office, Coleshill, Swindon, Wiltshire SN6 7PT

Map ② B4  1956

These estates on the western borders of Oxfordshire include the attractive, unspoilt villages of Buscot and Coleshill, each with a thriving village shop and tea-room. There are circular walks of differing lengths and a series of footpaths criss-crossing the estates. **Note**: WCs in Coleshill estate office yard and next to Buscot village shop.

Exploring
- Enjoy countryside walks across Coleshill Park.
- From Buscot enjoy access to the River Thames.
- See the Iron Age hill fort at Badbury Hill.

Eating and shopping: Buscot tea-rooms offer lunches and afternoon tea. The Radnor Arms and Coleshill shop offer locally sourced produce.

Making the most of your day: range of guided walks throughout the year. Dogs on leads only.

Getting here: SU239973. **Cycle**: NCN45, 10 miles. Regional Route 40: Oxfordshire Cycleway. **Bus**: Stagecoach in Swindon 64 Swindon–Carterton (passing close Swindon ≷), alight Highworth, 2 miles. **Train**: Swindon 10 miles. **Road**: Coleshill village on B4019 between Faringdon and Highworth. Buscot village on A417 between Faringdon and Lechlade. **Parking**: car parks at Buscot village and Badbury Clump, parking at Coleshill is at Estate Office.

Finding out more: 01793 762209 or buscotandcoleshill@nationaltrust.org.uk

Buscot and Coleshill	M	T	W	T	F	S	S
Open all year	M	T	W	T	F	S	S

Mill open second Sunday of the month: April to October, 2 to 5.

Buscot Old Parsonage

Buscot, Faringdon, Oxfordshire SN7 8DQ

Map (2) C4   1949

Early 18th-century house with small walled garden, situated on the banks of the River Thames. **Note**: no WC.

Getting here: 163:SU231973. 2 miles from Lechlade, 4 miles from Faringdon on A417.

Finding out more: 01793 762209 or buscot@nationaltrust.org.uk

Buscot Old Parsonage		M	T	W	T	F	S	S
7 Apr–27 Oct	2–6	·	·	**W**	·	·	·	·

Admission by written appointment with the tenant. Please mark envelope 'National Trust booking'.

Buscot Park

Estate Office, Buscot Park, Faringdon, Oxfordshire SN7 8BU

Map (2) C4   1949

'**Buscot is exciting, vibrant and constantly being improved.**'
Stuart Richmond-Watson, Northamptonshire

Family home of Lord Faringdon, who continues to care for the property as well as the family art collection, the Faringdon Collection, which is displayed in the house. Consequently, despite the grandeur of their scale, both the house and grounds remain intimate and idiosyncratic and very much a family home. They also continue to change and develop – nothing is preserved in aspic here! Outside a new water feature, Faux Fall, by David Harber. Inside, contemporary glassware by Colin Reid and Sally Fawkes. **Note**: administered on behalf of the National Trust by Lord Faringdon (www.buscotpark.com).

Exploring
- Explore one of England's finest water gardens.
- Discover the Faringdon Collection of Art.
- Enjoy the scents of the Four Seasons Walled Garden.
- Marvel at Burne-Jones's *Legend of the Briar Rose*.
- Revisit your childhood in the Swinging Garden.
- **New**: decorative scheme in the Sitting Room.

Eating and shopping: savour a delicious homemade tea. Pick up some local honey, fudge and cider. Buy surplus plants and kitchen garden produce, when available. Treat yourself to an ice-cream and enjoy a picnic.

You may also enjoy: Buscot and Coleshill Estate and Buscot Parsonage.

Making the most of your day: occasional events in grounds and theatre (available for hire). Dogs allowed in the Paddock area only.

Access for all: 🅿️👁️♿🚾💺📷👓
Building 🏛️ **Grounds** 👣🧎▶️🚜

Getting here: 163:SU239973. **Foot**: 4 miles by footpath from Faringdon, 3 miles from Lechlade. **Bus**: Stagecoach 65/66 Oxford/Swindon–Faringdon. Stagecoach in Swindon 64 Swindon–Carterton (passing close Swindon ➡), alight Lechlade, 3¼ miles. **Train**: Oxford 18 miles, Swindon 10 miles. **Road**: between Faringdon and Lechlade on south side of A417. **Parking**: free.

Finding out more: 0845 345 3387 (Infoline). 01367 240786 or estbuscot@aol.com, www.buscotpark.com

Buscot Park		M	T	W	T	F	S	S
House, grounds and tea-room*								
1 Apr–30 Sep	2–6	·	·	**W**	**T**	**F**	·	·
Grounds only								
6 Apr–28 Sep	2–6	**M**	**T**	·	·	·	·	·

Open Bank Holiday Mondays. Last admission to house one hour before closing. ***House, grounds and tea-room weekend opening**: 3 and 4, 17 and 18 April; 1 and 2, 15 and 16, 29 and 30 May; 12 and 13, 26 and 27 June; 10 and 11, 24 and 25 July; 14 and 15, 28 and 29 August; 11 and 12, 25 and 26 September, 2 to 6 (tea-room 2:30 to 5:30).

Chartwell

Mapleton Road, Westerham, Kent TN16 1PS

Map ② G6   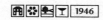 1946

Bought by Sir Winston Churchill for its
magnificent views over the Weald of Kent,
Chartwell was his home and the place from
which he drew inspiration from 1924 until the
end of his life. The rooms remain much as
they were when he lived here, with pictures,
books and personal mementoes evoking
the career and wide-ranging interests of
this great statesman. The hillside gardens
reflect Churchill's love of the landscape and
nature. They include the lakes he created,
Lady Churchill's Rose Garden and the kitchen
garden. Many of Churchill's paintings can be
seen in the studio.

Exploring
  — Explore the Churchills'
    stunning family home.
  — Enjoy wandering through the
    beautiful, tranquil garden.

Exploring
  — Discover Sir Winston's
    paintings in his
    fascinating studio.
  — Spot the black swans on
    Sir Winston's lake.
  — Take a walk around
    the surrounding
    Wealden countryside.
  — Watch the gardeners at
    work in the productive
    kitchen garden.

Eating and shopping: large, popular restaurant
with regular special events. Enjoy fresh
produce from the Chartwell kitchen garden.
Beautiful shop stocking Churchill memorabilia
and interesting local ranges. Kiosk serving light
bites, drinks and snacks on busy days.

You may also enjoy: Emmetts Garden and
Quebec House.

Making the most of your day: year-round
events programme, free talks and tours on
selected days, daily studio talks, children's trails
and activities, walk sheets available from car
park. Dogs on short leads in gardens only.

The light, airy dining room at Chartwell, Kent

Access for all:

Getting here: 188:TQ455515. **Foot**: Greensand Way passes through car park. **Bus**: Surrey Connect 236 Westerham–East Grinstead (passing Edenbridge ≅ and Edenbridge Town ≅), Monday–Friday only, to within ½ mile. SelKent 246 from Bromley North (passing Bromley South ≅); Arriva 401 from Tunbridge Wells (passing Sevenoaks ≅). Both Sundays and Bank Holidays only. Kent Passenger Services 238 Sevenoaks ≅–Edenbridge, Wednesdays only. **Train**: Edenbridge 4 miles; Edenbridge Town 4½ miles; Oxted 5 miles; Sevenoaks 6½ miles. **Road**: 2 miles south of Westerham, fork left off B2026 after 1½ miles; leave M25 at exit 5 or 6. **Parking**: 250 yards (pay and display). Year-round opening (except 25 December) for countryside access; gates locked 5:30 March to October, 4:30 November to 31 December.

Finding out more: 01732 866368 (Infoline). 01732 868381 or chartwell@nationaltrust.org.uk

Chartwell		M	T	W	T	F	S	S
House and studio								
13 Mar–31 Oct	11–5	·	·	W	T	F	S	S
7 Jul–24 Aug	11–5	·	T	W	T	F	S	S
Garden, shop and restaurant								
1 Jan–12 Mar	11–4	·	·	W	T	F	S	S
13 Mar–31 Oct	10:45–5	·	·	W	T	F	S	S
7 Jul–24 Aug	10:45–5	·	T	W	T	F	S	S
3 Nov–19 Dec	11–4	·	·	W	T	F	S	S
20 Dec–24 Dec	11–4	M	T	W	T	F	·	·
27 Dec–31 Dec	11–4	M	T	W	T	F	·	·
Catering kiosk								
1 Jul–31 Aug	11–4	M	T	W	T	F	S	S
Car park*								
Open all year	9–5:30	M	T	W	T	F	S	S

*Car park closes 4, 1 January to 12 March and 1 November to 31 December, or dusk if earlier; also closed 25 December. Admission to house by timed ticket, which should be purchased immediately on arrival (not bookable) as these can sell out on busy days. Open Bank Holiday Mondays. Last admission 45 minutes before house closing. Garden open in winter, weather and conditions permitting.

Chastleton House

Chastleton, near Moreton-in-Marsh, Oxfordshire GL56 0SU

Map ② C3 1991

'**Fantastic! A truly amazing house – like stepping back in history. And the staff are so friendly, knowledgeable and helpful**.'
Annie Coles, Finedon

A rare gem of a Jacobean country house, Chastleton House was built between 1607 and 1612 by a wealthy wool merchant as an impressive statement of wealth and power. Owned by the same increasingly impoverished family until 1991, the house remained essentially unchanged for nearly 400 years as the interiors and contents gradually succumbed to the ravages of time. With virtually no intrusion from the 21st century, this fascinating place exudes an informal and timeless atmosphere in a gloriously unspoilt setting. There is no shop or tea-room, so you can truly believe you have stepped back in time. **Note**: essential maintenance may mean published opening arrangements change; please telephone or check website before visiting.

Exploring
– Discover rooms full of rare objects without ropes or barriers.
– Enjoy the garden with Jacobean topiary and a vegetable plot.
– See a kitchen ceiling last cleaned in 1612.
– Learn family history through exhibitions of everyday items and costume.
– See rare 17th-century wall coverings still in place.

Eating and shopping: picnics welcome in car park.

You may also enjoy: Snowshill Manor and Charlecote Park.

Step back in time at Chastleton House, Oxfordshire

Making the most of your day: free family Explorer packs; seasonal concerts; garden party; family events during school holidays; private views each Wednesday and themed events on last Saturday of each month during open season. Dogs allowed (on leads) in field opposite house.

Access for all: 🅿️♿♿🚾🦯📖👁️⚙️
Building 🦽♿ Garden 🦽

Getting here: 163:SP248291. **Cycle**: cycles can be hired from Country Lanes at Moreton-in-Marsh station, Easter to 30 September (telephone 01608 650065). **Train**: Moreton-in-Marsh 4 miles. **Road**: 6 miles from Stow-on-the-Wold. Approach only from A436 between A44 (west of Chipping Norton) and Stow. **Parking**: free, 270 yards. Return walk to car park includes a short but steep hill. Sensible shoes recommended.

Finding out more: 01494 755560 (Infoline). 01608 674981 or chastleton@nationaltrust.org.uk

Chastleton House		M	T	W	T	F	S	S
24 Mar–25 Sep	1–5	·	·	**W**	**T**	**F**	**S**	·
29 Sep–30 Oct	1–4	·	·	**W**	**T**	**F**	**S**	·

Admission by timed ticket. Last admission one hour before closing. Visitor numbers are limited to conserve the fragile house (at busy times entry cannot be guaranteed). If possible visit on quieter days, such as Wednesday and Thursday. **Essential maintenance may mean changes to published opening arrangements; please telephone or check website before visiting**.

Clandon Park

West Clandon, Guildford, Surrey GU4 7RQ

Map ② F6   🏛️🦇✿🔔🍸 1956

Clandon Park was built circa 1730 for the 2nd Lord Onslow by Venetian architect Giacomo Leoni. One of the country's most complete example of a Palladian mansion, it contains a superb collection of 18th-century furniture, porcelain and textiles, much of which was acquired in the 1920s by connoisseur Mrs Gubbay. While the wider parkland is still in the hands of the Onslow family, the mansion is set in intimate gardens which are home to a Maori meeting house, brought back from New Zealand in 1892. The Onslow family is unique in providing three Speakers of the House of Commons. **Note**: the Queen's Royal Surrey Regiment Museum is based at Clandon Park.

Exploring
- Be awed by the stunning two-storey white marble hall.
- Enjoy the informal gardens, including the secluded sunken Dutch Garden.
- Take in a wealth of ceramics, tapestries and furniture.
- Discover the Maori meeting house – unique in the UK.
- Come on a Wednesday to learn more about 'Clandon Uncovered'.
- Enjoy a children's trail around the house or garden.

Eating and shopping: visit our shop in the 19th-century kitchen. Enjoy a meal in the vaulted undercroft restaurant (approved concession).

You may also enjoy: Hatchlands Park, a beautiful mansion set in stunning Repton parkland.

Making the most of your day: events include 'Waking Up Clandon' (28 February and 7 March) and 'Putting the House to Bed' (7, 14, 21 November). Re-enactments, children's activities, conservation demonstrations, behind-the-scenes tours.

Access for all: 🅿️ 🄳 🚾 ♿ 🄻 ▨ 🖥 ⠿ 🅐
Building 🄻 ◫ ♿ Grounds 🄻 🚶

Getting here: 186:TQ042512. **Foot**: follow the drive to reception. **Bus**: Countryliner 479 Guildford–Epsom (passing Leatherhead ≋, close Guildford ≋), 463 Guildford–Woking ≋, alight Park Lane roundabout, ½ mile to park west gate. **Train**: Clandon 1 mile – turn left when leaving the station. **Road**: at West Clandon on A247, 3 miles east of Guildford; if using A3 follow signposts to Ripley to join A247 via B2215. **Sat Nav**: may be incorrect – make sure you enter from A247. **Parking**: free, 300 yards.

Finding out more: 01483 222482. 01483 222502 (Clandon Park Restaurant) or clandonpark@nationaltrust.org.uk

Clandon Park		M	T	W	T	F	S	S
House and garden								
14 Mar–31 Oct	11–5	·	T	W	T	·		S
Queen's Royal Surrey Regiment Museum								
14 Mar–31 Oct	12–5	·	T	W	T	·		S
Shop and restaurant*								
28 Feb–7 Mar	12–4	·	·	·	·	·		S
14 Mar–31 Oct	11–5	·	T	W	T	·		S
2 Nov–30 Nov	12–4	·	T	W	T	·		S
1 Dec–23 Dec	12–4	M	T	W	T	·		S

Open Bank Holiday Mondays, Good Friday and Easter Saturday. *Restaurant open 12 to 10 in December (booking essential). Lift availability restricted (booking essential).

Claremont Landscape Garden

Portsmouth Road, Esher, Surrey KT10 9JG

Map ② F6 ❀ 🍴 1949

Claremont is a beautiful garden surrounding a small lake and featuring an unusual grass amphitheatre. The garden's creation and development has involved great names in garden history, including Sir John Vanbrugh, Charles Bridgeman, William Kent and 'Capability' Brown. In 1726 it was described as 'the noblest of any in Europe' and the garden today is of national importance. Visitors walking round the lake will see the island and pavilion, grotto and many viewpoints and vistas. There are hidden features to enjoy as well as wider estate walks and a new children's play area.

Exploring
- Camellia Terrace is a mass of blooms December to May.
- Don't miss the rhododendrons and azaleas flowering, late spring.
- Marvel at the stunning autumn colour.
- Enjoy the constant changing views around the lake.
- Children will love their exciting new play area.
- Special children's trails and activities during school holidays.

Eating and shopping: tea-room – morning pastries, coffee, light lunches and afternoon teas. Be tempted by the local seasonal menu. There are highchairs, play area and a menu for children. Tea-room and shop now open daily April to October.

You may also enjoy: The Homewood, a 20th-century Modernist house and garden.

Making the most of your day: open-air theatre events June to July. Children's craft workshops, storytelling and trails during school holidays. Guided walks April to October. Full yearly programme of walks, talks and activities. Dogs allowed between 1 November and 31 March only (on short leads).

Access for all: 🅿️ 🄳 🚾 ♿ 🄻 ▨ 🅐
Grounds 🄻 ➡️

Getting here: 187:TQ128634. **Bus**: Travel London 515/A Kingston–Guildford (passing close Esher ≋). **Train**: Esher 2 miles; Hersham 2 miles; Claygate 2 miles. **Road**: 1 mile south of centre of Esher, on east side of A307 (no access from Esher bypass). **Parking**: free, at entrance.

Finding out more: 01372 467806 or claremont@nationaltrust.org.uk

Claremont Landscape Garden		M	T	W	T	F	S	S
1 Jan–31 Mar	10–5	·	T	W	T	F	S	S
1 Apr–24 Oct	10–6	M	T	W	T	F	S	S
25 Oct–31 Oct	10–5	M	T	W	T	F	S	S
2 Nov–31 Dec	10–5	·	T	W	T	F	S	S

Open Monday 15 February and Bank Holiday Mondays, including 27 December. Closes dusk if earlier. Closed 25 December. Open 1 January, 10 to 4. Belvedere Tower: open 1 January, 11 to 2, and first weekend each month May to October, 2 to 5. Late night openings 5, 12, 19, 26 June until 9. Shop and tea-room close one hour before garden. Property may close early on events days in June and July and in bad weather, especially high winds (telephone before visit).

Claydon

Middle Claydon, near Buckingham, Buckinghamshire MK18 2EY

Map ② D3   🏠✝❄🌸🌱🔔🍽   1956

In the 1750s at his family seat in Buckinghamshire, Sir Ralph Verney set out to create a country house of extraordinary grandeur that would dazzle his wealthy neighbours and outdo his political rivals. Thirty years on he was facing financial ruin. Today the interiors that remain are among the most ambitious and lavish ever created in the 18th century. Claydon has been continually occupied by the Verney family for more than 550 years; the place is a testament to their fascinating fluctuating fortunes, from

Claydon, Buckinghamshire: extraordinary grandeur

their close involvement in the English Civil War to the family connection with Florence Nightingale. **Note**: the gardens are maintained by the Verney family, additional entry charges apply (including members).

Exploring
- Be amazed by the extravagant room decoration.
- Explore the rooms used by Florence Nightingale.
- Wander through the picturesque parkland and around the lakes.
- Visit the tranquil parish church of All Saints.
- Discover the restored Claydon Gardens (run by the Verney family).

Eating and shopping: browse in our second-hand bookshop. Visit the courtyard craft shops and galleries (not National Trust). Relax in the Carriagehouse restaurant/tea-room (not National Trust). Vegetables for sale from kitchen garden, when in season.

You may also enjoy: Waddesdon Manor and Stowe Landscape Gardens – also on a grand scale.

Making the most of your day: family activity worksheets. Dogs in park only on leads.

Access for all: 🅿♿🚻♿🚻🔄📷🖼🚶👓
Building 🔼♿🔽 Grounds 🔼♿➡

Getting here: 165:SP720253. **Foot**: Bernwood Jubilee Way. **Cycle**: NCN51. **Road**: in Middle Claydon 13 miles north west of Aylesbury, 4 miles south west of Winslow; signposted from A413 and A41 (M40 exit 9 12 miles); entrance by north drive only. **Parking**: free.

Finding out more: 01494 755561 (Infoline). 01296 730349 or claydon@nationaltrust.org.uk

Claydon		M	T	W	T	F	S	S
House								
20 Mar–31 Oct	1–5	M	T	W	·	·	S	S
Garden, restaurant and shops								
20 Mar–31 Oct	12–5	M	T	W	·	·	S	S
Tea-room, church and bookshop								
20 Mar–31 Oct	11–5:30	M	T	W	·	·	S	S

Open Good Friday.

Cliveden

Taplow, Maidenhead,
Buckinghamshire SL6 0JA

Map ② E5  1942

**'I never tire of Cliveden – we now have four
generations who have enjoyed it.'**
Wendy Jeffery, Woodley

This spectacular country estate overlooking the
River Thames, open daily for most of the year,
was once the glittering hub of society as the
home of Waldorf and Nancy Astor. Later in the
20th century it was infamously associated with
the Profumo Affair. The various formal gardens
include topiary and colourful seasonal planting
in the Long Garden and the celebrated parterre
with its breathtaking views. An outstanding
collection of sculpture and statues from the
ancient and modern worlds adorn the gardens.
Part of the house, now let as a private hotel, is
open to visitors at limited times. **Note**: no WC
at woodlands.

Exploring
— Relax in grand style in these
  magnificent gardens.
— Don't miss the introductory
  video Cliveden and the Astors.
— Stunning views from this
  haunt of the rich and famous.

Exploring
— See the fabulous spring
  display of 25,000 tulips.
— Find out about the long-lost
  maze we are recreating.
— Stretch your legs with a
  riverside or woodland walk.

Eating and shopping: wide selection of
plants and products in the gift shop. Enjoy
home-cooked lunches and afternoon tea at
The Orangery. Many dishes on the menu have
historic links with Cliveden. Kiosk in the car
park sells light refreshments.

You may also enjoy: Hughenden Manor, and
the elegant mansion of Basildon Park.

Making the most of your day: waymarked
walks in the woodlands. New picnic and play
areas. Full programme of events and guided
walks. Dogs under close control in specified
woodlands only.

Access for all: ⊞ ⊞ ⊞ ⊞ ⊞ ⊞ ⊞ ⊞ ⊞
Building ⊞ ⊞ ⊞ Grounds ⊞ ➡

Getting here: 175:SU915851. **Train**: Taplow (not
Sunday) 2½ miles; Burnham 3 miles. **Road**:
2 miles north of Taplow; leave M4 at exit 7 on
to A4, or M40 at exit 4 on to A404 to Marlow
and follow brown signs. Entrance by main gates
opposite Feathers Inn. **Parking**: free.

Finding out more: 01494 755562 (Infoline).
01628 605069 or cliveden@nationaltrust.org.uk

Cliveden, Buckinghamshire: the house as seen from the celebrated parterre

Cliveden		M	T	W	T	F	S	S
Estate, garden, shop and refreshment kiosk								
13 Feb–31 Mar	11–5	M	T	W	T	F	S	S
1 Apr–30 Oct	11–5:30	M	T	W	T	F	S	S
31 Oct–23 Dec	11–4	M	T	W	T	F	S	S
House (part), chapel								
1 Apr–28 Oct	3–5:30	·	·	·	T	·	·	S
The Orangery (café)								
1 Mar–30 Oct	11–5	M	T	W	T	F	S	S
31 Oct–19 Dec	11–3	·	·	·	·	·	S	S
Woodlands								
2 Jan–31 Mar	11–4	M	T	W	T	F	S	S
1 Apr–30 Oct	11–5:30	M	T	W	T	F	S	S
31 Oct–23 Dec	11–4	M	T	W	T	F	S	S

Admission to house is limited and by timed ticket only from the information kiosk. Some areas of formal garden may be roped off when ground conditions are bad.

Cobham Wood and Mausoleum

South Lodge Barn, Lodge Lane, Cobham, Kent DA12 3BS

Map (2) H5　🏠🅿️ 2010

Absorb the atmosphere at the wonderfully restored Darnley Mausoleum, designed by James Wyatt and so memorably featured in the BBC's 'Restoration' programme. Then follow in the footsteps of the Darnley family while walking through the peaceful woodland, once part of their extensive estate and recently acquired by the National Trust. **Note**: no vehicle access or parking at the property. No WCs.

Exploring
- Discover the beautifully restored Grade I listed mausoleum.
- Explore the varied habitats of Cobham Park's ancient woodland.
- Enjoy far-reaching, commanding views over the Medway and Thames.
- Learn about the people who shaped this unique landscape.

Eating and shopping: refreshments and WCs available at Shorne Wood Country Park.

Visit

Making the most of your day: guided walks (visit website for details). Dogs under control in the wood (stock grazing).

Access for all: Mausoleum 🦽

Getting here: (178:TQ694683). **Foot**: 2 miles from Shorne Wood Country Park via waymarked footpath to South Lodge and mausoleum. **Cycle**: Multi-user trail passes mausoleum. **Train**: Sole Street 1 mile. **Road**: Exit A2 at Shorne/Cobham junction and follow signs to Shorne Wood Country Park. **Sat Nav**: do not use South Lodge Barn postcode. **Parking**: at Shorne Wood Country Park. Pay and display (not National Trust).

Finding out more: 01474 816764 or cobham@nationaltrust.org.uk

Cobham Wood and Mausoleum	
Visit website for opening information.	

Dorneywood Garden

Dorneywood, Burnham, Buckinghamshire SL1 8PY

Map (2) E5　🌸 1942

1930s-style garden, with herbaceous borders, rose garden, cottage garden and lily pond. **Note**: upkeep funded by Dorneywood Trust, at no cost to National Trust or public. No photography.

Getting here: 175:SU938848. On Dorneywood Road, south west of Burnham Beeches, 1½ miles north of Burnham village, 2 miles east of Cliveden.

Finding out more:
dorneywood@nationaltrust.org.uk

Dorneywood Garden		M	T	W	T	F	S	S
In aid of National Garden Scheme*								
21 Apr	2–6	·	·	W	·	·	·	·
26 May	2–6	·	·	W	·	·	·	·
16 Jun	2–6	·	·	W	·	·	·	·
24 Jul	2–6	·	·	·	·	·	S	·
In aid of Dorneywood Trust*								
26 Jun	2–6	·	·	·	·	·	S	·

Admission by appointment only (email for tickets, giving at least two weeks' notice). *Charge including members.

Emmetts Garden

Ide Hill, Sevenoaks, Kent TN14 6AY

Map ② H6   1965

Charming Emmetts – an Edwardian estate owned by Frederick Lubbock – was a plantsman's passion and a much-loved family home. Influenced by William Robinson, the delightful garden was laid out in the late 19th century and contains many exotic and rare trees and shrubs from across the world. Explore the rose and rock gardens, take in the spectacular views and enjoy glorious shows of spring flowers and shrubs, followed by vibrant autumn colours.

Exploring
– Stunning rock garden returned to its original design.
– Charming formal rose garden.
– Unique collection of exotic shrubs.
– Beautiful woodland and spectacular views.

Eating and shopping: stable tea-room, famed for its homemade cakes. Enchanting tack room shop. Plants available to buy.

You may also enjoy: Chartwell and Quebec House nearby.

Making the most of your day: year-round events programme, guided tours on selected days, children's activities, walks sheets for surrounding countryside. Dogs on short leads only.

Access for all: [icons]
Grounds [icons]

Getting here: 188:TQ477524. **Foot**: from Ide Hill (½ mile). Weardale walk from Chartwell (3 miles) – guide leaflet available. **Bus**: New Enterprise 404 from Sevenoaks, Monday to Friday only, alight Ide Hill, 1½ miles. **Train**: Sevenoaks 4½ miles; Penshurst 5½ miles. **Road**: 1½ miles south of A25 on Sundridge to Ide Hill road, 1½ miles north of Ide Hill off B2042, leave M25 exit 5, then 4 miles. **Parking**: free, 100 yards.

The late 19th-century Emmetts Garden, Kent

Finding out more: 01732 751509 (Infoline). 01732 868381 or emmetts@nationaltrust.org.uk. Chartwell Office, Mapleton Road, Westerham, Kent TN16 1PS

Emmetts Garden		M	T	W	T	F	S	S
13 Mar–31 Oct	11–5	M	T	W	·	·	S	S

Open Bank Holiday Mondays and Good Friday. Shop and tea-room close 30 minutes earlier. Last admission 45 minutes before closing.

Great Coxwell Barn

Great Coxwell, Faringdon, Oxfordshire SN7 7LZ

Map ② C4   1956

Former monastic barn was a favourite of William Morris, who would regularly bring his guests to wonder at the structure. **Note**: no WC, narrow access lanes.

Getting here: 163:SU269940. 2 miles south west of Faringdon between A420 and B4019.

Finding out more: 01793 762209 (Coleshill Estate office) or greatcoxwellbarn@nationaltrust.org.uk

Great Coxwell Barn		M	T	W	T	F	S	S
Open all year	Dawn–dusk	M	T	W	T	F	S	S

No opening or closing times.

Greys Court

Rotherfield Greys, Henley-on-Thames,
Oxfordshire RG9 4PG

Map (2) D5 🏠🔭🌼🌳🌿🔔 1969

An intimate family home and peaceful estate
set in the rolling hills of the Chilterns. This
picturesque 16th-century mansion and tranquil
gardens were home to the Brunner family until
recent years. Reopening in 2010 after two years of
closure for conservation work, the house exudes
a welcoming atmosphere with a well-stocked
kitchen and homely living rooms. The series
of walled gardens is a colourful patchwork of
interest set amid medieval ruins. Other buildings
from earlier eras include the Great Tower from
the 12th century and a rare Tudor donkey wheel,
in use until the early 20th century.

Exploring
- Soak up the atmosphere of a real family home.
- Stroll around the enchanting gardens.
- Climb the Great Tower and watch the Red Kites soar.
- Burn off some energy in the beech woodlands.
- Find out how the donkey drew water from the well.
- Follow your food from plot to plate.

Eating and shopping: treat yourself to tea
and cake in the tea-room. Buy a memento for
your garden from the plant stall. Browse in our
unusual bookshop. Pick up seasonal organic
produce from the gardens (when available).

You may also enjoy: on a grander scale: Basildon
Park and the magnificent gardens of Cliveden.

Making the most of your day: programme of
open-air events and garden days. Wider estate
walk, taking in the interesting ice-house. Family
activities, including explorer packs and garden
and house trails. Dogs on the estate walk only.

Access for all: 🅿️♿🚻♿👓📷🅰️
House 🏠 Tea-room 🏠 Grounds 🏠

Getting here: 175:SU725834. **Cycle**: on
Oxfordshire cycleway. **Bus**: White's 145 from
Henley-on-Thames town hall (½ mile walk from
Henley-on-Thames ≋). Alight Greys Green
and follow signed footpath to Greys Court
(approx ¼ mile). **Train**: Henley-on-Thames
3 miles. **Road**: west of Henley-on-Thames.
From Nettlebed mini-roundabout on A4130
take B481 and property is signed to the left
after approx. 3 miles. There is also a direct
(unsigned) route from Henley-on-Thames town
centre. Follow signs to Badgemore Golf Club
towards Peppard, approximately 3 miles out of
Henley. **Parking**: free, 220 yards.

Finding out more: 01494 755564 (Infoline).
01491 628529 or
greyscourt@nationaltrust.org.uk

Greys Court		M	T	W	T	F	S	S
House								
1 Apr–26 Sep	2–5	·	·	**W**	**T**	**F**	**S**	**S**
Garden								
1 Apr–26 Sep	11–5	·	·	**W**	**T**	**F**	**S**	**S**
Tea-room								
1 Apr–26 Sep	11–4:30	·	·	**W**	**T**	**F**	**S**	**S**
Volunteer-run bookshop*								
1 Apr–26 Sep	1–4:30	·	·	**W**	**T**	**F**	**S**	**S**

Open Bank Holiday Mondays. Closed Good Friday. On village
fête day, 5 September, special opening arrangements apply
(charge including members), contact property for details.
*Bookshop hours may vary dependent on volunteer availability.

Greys Court, Oxfordshire: tranquil gardens

Hatchlands Park

East Clandon, Guildford, Surrey GU4 7RT

Map ② F6   🏛 🏠 ✤ 🌳 1945

'**I love the homeliness of the house, and walking around the park seeing the magnificent trees in their natural setting.**'
J. Swift, Surrey

Hatchlands Park was built in the 1750s for Admiral Boscawen, hero of the Battle of Louisburg. Robert Adam ceilings decorate the house, featuring appropriately nautical motifs. Today the mansion is a family home, containing tenant Alec Cobbe's superb collection of paintings. Six rooms also display the Cobbe Collection, Europe's largest collection of keyboard instruments associated with famous composers such as J. C. Bach, Chopin and Elgar. The mansion is set in informal grounds, with one small parterre garden designed by Gertrude Jekyll. The surrounding parkland provides a number of waymarked walks in a tranquil and beautiful setting.

Exploring
— An intimate mansion with an exemplary collection.
— Listen to the instruments with an audio guide (charge applies).
— More than 161 hectares (400 acres) of parkland to explore.
— A stunning bluebell wood in April and May.
— Trails for children both inside and out.
— Thursday guided tours of the mansion.

Eating and shopping: homely tea-room (Trust-approved concession) in the original kitchen. Visit the friendly shop for a memento of your visit.

You may also enjoy: Clandon Park, another 18th-century property.

Making the most of your day: walk in the parkland, come for a 'Conservation in Action' demonstration or a Cobbe Collection Trust

Hatchlands Park, Surrey: an intimate mansion

concert (telephone 01483 211474 or visit www.cobbecollection.co.uk). Dogs welcome under close control in designated parkland areas only.

Access for all: 🅿♿🚻🏷📷🎵 ∴ 🅰
Building ♿ ⬆♿ **Grounds** ♿ ➡

Getting here: 187:TQ063516. **Bus**: Countryliner 478/9 Guildford–Leatherhead (passing Leatherhead ≋ and close Guildford ≋). **Train**: Clandon 2 miles, Horsley 2½ miles. **Road**: entry off the A246 between Guildford and Leatherhead. **Sat Nav**: please follow brown signs to main entrance on the A246. **Parking**: free, 300 yards.

Finding out more: 01483 222482 or hatchlands@nationaltrust.org.uk

Hatchlands Park		M	T	W	T	F	S	S
House and garden								
1 Apr–29 Jul	2–5:30	·	T	W	T	·	·	S
1 Aug–31 Aug	2–5:30	·	T	W	T	F	·	S
1 Sep–31 Oct	2–5:30	·	T	W	T	·	·	S
Park walks								
1 Apr–11 Apr	11–6	M	T	W	T	F	S	S
12 Apr–9 May	10–6	M	T	W	T	F	S	S
10 May–31 Oct	11–6	M	T	W	T	F	S	S
Shop*								
1 Apr–31 Oct	12–5:30	·	T	W	T	·	·	S
Tea-room*								
1 Apr–31 Oct	11–5	·	T	W	T	·	·	S

Open Bank Holiday Mondays. *Shop and tea-room open Fridays in August. Timed tickets may be used on Bank Holidays and busy periods.

Hartwell House Hotel, Restaurant and Spa

Vale of Aylesbury, Bucks HP17 8NR

Map (2) E3

This Grade 1 listed building stands in 36 hectares (90 acres) of parkland. Its most famous resident was Louis XVIII, the exiled King of France, who lived here for five years from 1809.

The house and gardens are already accessible to the public as a hotel, and welcome guests to stay, to dine in the restaurants and to have afternoon tea (booking strongly advised). All paying guests to the hotel are welcome to walk in the garden and park.

Finding out more: 01296 747444; 01296 747450 (fax) or info@hartwell-house.com; www.hartwell-house.com

Hindhead Commons and The Devil's Punch Bowl Café

London Road, Hindhead, Surrey GU26 6AB

Map (2) E7 1906

Walk through Hindhead Commons to see why this area of open heathland is classified an Area of Outstanding Natural Beauty. Enjoy stunning scenery of the Devil's Punch Bowl from a special viewpoint 50 yards from the National Trust café, and half a mile to enjoy the view from Highcombe Edge.

Exploring
- Waymarked path from café (some steep paths).
- See north portal of new A3 tunnel from viewing platform.
- New guided walks throughout the year.

Eating and shopping: treat yourself to breakfast from 9. Enjoy hot food until 2:30. Pick up homemade cakes and sandwiches throughout the day.

Making the most of your day: maps and local walks leaflets on sale from the Devil's Punch Bowl Café. Dogs allowed (under close control during bird-nesting season, March to October).

Access for all: Café Grounds

Getting here: 133:SU895356. Beside A3, at Hindhead, near crossroads with A287. **Bus**: Stagecoach No. 18 or 19; No. 71 from Haslemere. No service Sundays or public holidays. Haslemere –Aldershot . Coach National Express 30 London to Portsmouth stops at Hindhead. **Train**: Haslemere 3 miles. **Parking**: £2 (pay and display). No lorries. Coach parties by arrangement.

Finding out more: 01428 604040 (Wardens). 01428 608771 (café) or hindhead@nationaltrust.org.uk

Hindhead Commons		M	T	W	T	F	S	S
Countryside								
Open all year		**M**	**T**	**W**	**T**	**F**	**S**	**S**
Café								
1 Jan–31 Mar	9–4	**M**	**T**	**W**	**T**	**F**	**S**	**S**
1 Apr–31 Oct	9–5	**M**	**T**	**W**	**T**	**F**	**S**	**S**
1 Nov–31 Dec	9–4	**M**	**T**	**W**	**T**	**F**	**S**	**S**

Devil's Punch Bowl Café closed 25 December.

Stunning scenery at Hindhead Commons, Surrey

Hinton Ampner

Bramdean, near Alresford,
Hampshire SO24 0LA

Map (2) D7 🏠 ❀ 🔔 ⊤ | 1986 |

The vision of one man, Hinton Ampner is best known for its magnificent garden with stunning views to the south. The elegant country house was remodelled by Ralph Dutton, the 8th and last Lord Sherborne, in 1960 after a devastating fire, and contains his collection of Georgian and Regency furniture, Italian pictures and objets d'art. The gardens were also laid out by Ralph Dutton and are widely acknowledged as a masterpiece of 20th-century design, mixing formal and informal planting, providing all year round interest.

Exploring
- Admire the elegant interiors and fine furnishings.
- Visit the upstairs rooms.
- Stroll through the different areas of the formal gardens.
- Wander through the walled garden.
- Enjoy the views of the South Downs.

Eating and shopping: produce from the walled garden used in the tea-room. Enjoy homemade cakes in the tea-room. Browse the shop and plants for sale. Property plants and produce on sale, when available.

You may also enjoy: Uppark, Winchester City Mill and Mottisfont.

Making the most of your day: our gardeners are always on hand to chat and answer your questions. Free guided walk in the garden on Tuesdays.

Access for all: P 🅿 WC ♿ ⓑ 📷 ⓙ ∴ 🅰
Building 🏠♿ 🅱 Grounds ♿ ➡

Getting here: 185:SU597275. Midway between Winchester (M3) and Petersfield (A3) on the A272. **Bus**: Stagecoach in Hampshire 67 Winchester–Petersfield (passing close Winchester 🚆 and passing Petersfield 🚆).
Train: Winchester 9 miles; Alresford (Mid-Hants Railway) 4 miles. **Road**: on A272, 1 mile west of Bramdean village, 8 miles east of Winchester, leave M3 at exit 9 and follow signs to Petersfield. **Sat Nav**: please use entrance off the A272 not via village road as directed by Sat Nav. **Parking**: free. Special entrance for coaches – map indicating where coaches can park sent with confirmation of booking.

Finding out more: 01962 771305 or hintonampner@nationaltrust.org.uk

Hinton Ampner		M	T	W	T	F	S	S
Shop, walled garden and tea-room								
27 Feb–28 Feb	11–4						S	S
6 Mar–7 Mar	11–4						S	S
6 Nov–28 Nov	11–4						S	S
Garden, shop and tea-room								
13 Mar–31 Oct	11–5	M	T	W			S	S
House, garden, shop and tea-room								
13 Mar–31 Oct	11:30–5	M	T	W			S	S
House*								
4 Dec–12 Dec	11–4	M	T	W	T	F	S	S

House and garden open Good Friday, 11 to 5. *Last entry 3:45, except Friday when property closes 7.

Spring at Hinton Ampner, Hampshire

Hughenden Manor, Buckinghamshire: from Disraeli to the Second World War, there is something to interest everyone

The Homewood

Portsmouth Road, Esher, Surrey KT10 9JL

Map ② F6   1999

20th-century house and garden designed by the architect Patrick Gwynne reflecting the style and ethos of the Modern Movement. **Note**: administered by a tenant. No WC.

Getting here: 187:TQ130635. **Access is via minibus from Claremont Landscape Garden only**.

Finding out more: 01372 476424 or thehomewood@nationaltrust.org.uk

---

The Homewood

Entrance by booked guided tours only – every Friday and the last Saturday of the month, 9 April to 30 October. Five guided tours (45 minutes approximately), 10:30, 11:30, 12.30, 2 and 3. Charge including members.

Hughenden Manor

High Wycombe, Buckinghamshire HP14 4LA

Map ② E4 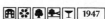 1947

Hughenden Manor offers a vivid insight into the charismatic personality and colourful private life of the most unlikely Victorian Prime Minister, Benjamin Disraeli, who lived here from 1848 to 1881. Visitors can browse among an extraordinary collection of personal memorabilia and there are hands-on activities for children. Hughenden's secret wartime past is revealed in our Second World War room in the cellars, with interactive exhibits and eye-witness accounts. The formal garden has been recreated based on the original designs of Mary Anne Disraeli and there are beautiful woodland walks surrounding this fascinating country home. **Note**: limited electric light.

Exploring

- Get to know Queen Victoria's favourite PM.
- Explore the newly flourishing walled garden.
- Stroll in the Chilterns countryside with woodlands and chalk stream.
- Discover the enduring love story of Disraeli and Mary Anne.
- Second World War exhibition: share Hughenden's 'Top Secret' past.
- Don't miss a glimpse into servants' life below stairs.

Eating and shopping: enjoy home-grown produce in many of our dishes. Browse in the glorious gift shop. Choose a plant from our volunteer-run stall.

You may also enjoy: on a grand scale: Waddesdon Manor, West Wycombe Park and Cliveden.

Making the most of your day: varied events programme, woodland trails, introductory film, morning guided tour of Manor at 11.20. Children's hands-on activities and I-Spy sheets. Dogs welcome under close control in park and woodland.

Access for all:

Building **Grounds**

Hughenden Manor, Buckinghamshire

Getting here: 165:SU866955. **Foot**: 1½ miles from High Wycombe. **Bus**: Arriva 300 High Wycombe–Aylesbury (passing close High Wycombe). Note: long and steep walk to house entrance. **Train**: High Wycombe 2 miles. **Road**: 1½ miles north of High Wycombe; on west side of the Great Missenden road (A4128). **Parking**: free, 200 yards. Some waiting possible at peak times; parking for only one coach; overflow car park, 400 yards.

Finding out more: 01494 755565 (Infoline). 01494 755573 or hughenden@nationaltrust.org.uk

Hughenden Manor		M	T	W	T	F	S	S
House, garden, shop and restaurant*								
17 Feb–2 Apr	11–5	·	·	**W**	**T**	**F**	**S**	**S**
3 Apr–18 Apr	11–5	**M**	**T**	**W**	**T**	**F**	**S**	**S**
21 Apr–28 May	11–5	·	·	**W**	**T**	**F**	**S**	**S**
29 May–6 Jun	11–5	**M**	**T**	**W**	**T**	**F**	**S**	**S**
9 Jun–23 Jul	11–5	·	·	**W**	**T**	**F**	**S**	**S**
24 Jul–30 Aug	11–5	**M**	**T**	**W**	**T**	**F**	**S**	**S**
1 Sep–31 Oct	11–5	·	·	**W**	**T**	**F**	**S**	**S**
Conservation in action month**								
3 Nov–28 Nov	11–4	·	·	**W**	**T**	**F**	**S**	**S**
Christmas opening**								
4 Dec–19 Dec	11–4	·	·	**W**	**T**	**F**	**S**	**S**
Park								
Open all year	Dawn–dusk	**M**	**T**	**W**	**T**	**F**	**S**	**S**

*House opens 12. **House closes 3. Admission by timed ticket on Bank Holidays and other busy days. Open Bank Holiday Mondays. Last entry 4:30 or dusk if earlier. Occasional early closing for special events and weddings. Conservation in action during November. Please note first floor closed during December opening.

Ightham Mote

Mote Road, Ivy Hatch, Sevenoaks, Kent TN15 0NT

Map ② H6 1985

'This house alone makes my National Trust membership worthwhile!'
Tony Bohan, Devon

Nestling in a sunken valley, Ightham Mote, dating from 1320 with important later additions and alterations, is a rare example of a moated medieval manor house. An

Entry is still possible at most places up to 30 minutes before closing

exhibition depicts the largest conservation project undertaken by the Trust, which was completed in 2004. Ightham Mote has many special features, including a Great Hall, crypt, Tudor chapel with a hand-painted ceiling and the apartments of the American donor Charles Henry Robinson. An enchanting feature is the Grade I-listed dog kennel, situated in the picturesque courtyard. Ightham Mote also offers lovely gardens and water features, with lakeside and woodland walks. **Note**: very steep slope from reception (lower drop-off point available).

Exploring
– Join an introductory talk and hear about the previous owners.
– Climb to the top of the tower – experience amazing views.
– Enjoy a garden tour, to include the South Lake.
– See the only Grade I-listed dog kennel in England.
– Don't miss the amazing hand-painted Tudor chapel ceiling.

Eating and shopping: shop for locally produced jewellery, food, wine, beauty products. Choose from a wide variety of shrubs and herbaceous plants. Enjoy a menu packed full with local food and wine. Check out the Mote Restaurant programme of events.

You may also enjoy: Knole, Chartwell, Emmetts Garden, Old Soar Manor, Quebec House and Toys Hill.

Making the most of your day: open-air theatre. Children's house and garden quizzes/trails, activity cart and memory sticks. Family events and activities. Programme of restaurant events. Walks (from one to eight miles). Dogs on estate walks only.

Access for all: ♿🅿️🅳🆆🅱️🔊🎒📷🖼️VT 🚶♿Building ♿♿♿♿Grounds♿➡️

Getting here: 188:TQ584535. Between Sevenoaks and Borough Green 1¾ miles south of A25. **Bus**: New Enterprise 404 from Sevenoaks ≋, calls Thursday and Friday only, on other days alight Ivy Hatch, ¾ mile. Autocar 222 Tonbridge–Borough Green ≋, alight Fairlawne, ½ mile by footpath. Arriva 306/8

Ightham Mote, Kent: moated medieval manor house

Sevenoaks ≋–Gravesend (passing Borough Green ≋), alight Ightham Common, 1½ miles. **Train**: Borough Green and Wrotham 3 miles; Hildenborough 4 miles; Sevenoaks 6 miles. **Road**: 6 miles north of Tonbridge on A227; 6 miles south of Sevenoaks on A25; 16 miles west of Maidstone on A20/A25. **Parking**: free, 200 yards.

Finding out more: 01732 811145 (Infoline). 01732 810378 Ext. 100 or ighthammote@nationaltrust.org.uk

Ightham Mote		M	T	W	T	F	S	S
House*								
13 Mar–31 Oct	11–5	M	·	·	T	F	S	S
4 Nov–19 Dec	11–3	·	·	·	T	F	S	S
Shop, restaurant and garden**								
13 Mar–31 Oct	10:30–5	M	·	·	T	F	S	S
4 Nov–19 Dec	11–3	·	·	·	T	F	S	S
Restaurant**								
20 Dec–30 Dec	11–3	M	T	W	T	F	S	S
Estate								
Open all year	Dawn–dusk	M	T	W	T	F	S	S

Restaurant open for occasional themed evenings and booked functions. Telephone 01732 811314 for opening times of Mote Restaurant and 01732 811203 for shop opening times outside normal property hours. Booking at Mote Restaurant advised winter and evenings. *Partial gardens, courtyard and ground floor access November and December, 11 to 3. **Except when function ongoing. Closed January 2011. ***Not 24 and 25 December. Great Hall dressed for Christmas during November and December.

King's Head

King's Head Passage, Market Square, Aylesbury,
Buckinghamshire HP20 2RW

Map ② E3   🏠 🍴 🍷 1925

Set in the heart of this historic market town,
the King's Head is one of England's best
preserved coaching inns. Dating back to 1455,
the building has many fascinating architectural
features, including rare stained-glass windows,
exposed wattle and daub and the original
stabling for the inn.

Exploring
- Visit the small retail outlets in the cobbled courtyard.
- Don't miss the King's Head Festival in July.
- Browse for the perfect book in the second-hand bookshop.

Eating and shopping: have a read while
enjoying a freshly made coffee. Award-winning
Farmers' Bar run by local Chiltern Brewery.

Making the most of your day: around the
courtyard is Aylesbury Tourist Information
Centre, a second-hand bookshop/coffee shop
and small retail outlets. Tours on Wednesday,
Friday and Saturday. Meeting and function
facilities available.

Access for all: 🚾♿♿ Building 🪜 Grounds ♿

Getting here: 165:SP818137. At top of
Market Square in the centre of Aylesbury.
Access through cobbled lane near the War
Memorial. **Bus**: from surrounding areas.
Train: Aylesbury 400 yards. **Sat Nav**: will bring
you into Aylesbury, but not the King's Head.
Parking: no onsite parking. Car parks in town
centre (not National Trust).

Finding out more: 01296 381501 or
kingshead@nationaltrust.org.uk

King's Head	M	T	W	T	F	S	S
Open all year 10:30–4		T	W	T	F	S	

Closed Bank Holiday Mondays. Tours available Wednesday,
Friday and Saturday at 2 (telephone to check availability).

Knole, Kent, is one of England's greatest show houses

Knole

Sevenoaks, Kent TN15 0RP

Map ② H6   🏠 ♣ ♣ 1946

Set at the heart of a timeless deer park, Knole
has fascinating links with kings, queens and
nobility, as well as literary connections with
the novelists Vita Sackville-West and Virginia
Woolf. Knole was the birthplace and childhood
home of Vita Sackville-West, who went on to
create the gardens at Sissinghurst. Thirteen
magnificent state rooms are laid out much
as they were in the 18th century to impress
visitors with the wealth of the Sackville family,
who still live at Knole today. The house
includes world-renowned rare furniture,
important paintings and the prototype of the
famous Knole settee. **Note**: wheelchair access
not possible beyond Great Hall (virtual reality
tour available).

Exploring
- New: visitor centre with audio-visual display due to open May/June.
- New: Orangery due to open in May/June.
- New: discover more with the family courtyard guide 'Speaking Stones'.
- Witness the important conservation project on the James II bed.
- Explore the deer park, a Site of Special Scientific Interest.
- Explore Lord Sackville's private garden (Tuesdays, April to September).

Eating and shopping: treat yourself to some local produce in the Knole shop. Browse through a large selection of books for sale. Enjoy a cream tea in the original 'Brew House'. Get a drink or an ice-cream in the kiosk.

You may also enjoy: Sissinghurst Castle Garden, the creation of Vita Sackville-West and Harold Nicolson.

Making the most of your day: guided park walks and school holiday family trails and activities. Housekeeping days, evening candlelit tours, Christmas workshops and carol concerts. Annual plant and book stall. Dogs welcome on leads and in the park only.

Access for all: [symbols] Building [symbols] Grounds [symbols]

Getting here: 188:TQ532543. **Foot**: park entrance at south end of Sevenoaks town centre, opposite St Nicholas's church. **Bus**: from surrounding area to Sevenoaks, ¾-mile walk. **Train**: Sevenoaks 1½ miles. **Road**: leave M25 at exit 5 (A21). Park entrance in Sevenoaks town centre off A225 Tonbridge Road (opposite St Nicholas's church). **Sat Nav**: some Sat Nav systems may not direct you to Knole. **Parking**: 60 yards, £2.50. Park only open to vehicles from 10:30 when house open, otherwise parking is available in nearby town centre. Park open to vehicles in winter when shop and tea-room open. Park gates locked at 6.

Finding out more: 01732 450608 (Infoline). 01732 462100 or knole@nationaltrust.org.uk

Knole		M	T	W	T	F	S	S
House								
13 Mar–31 Oct	12–4	·	·	W	T	F	S	S
Shop, tea-room and courtyards								
13 Mar–5 Apr	10:30–5	·	·	W	T	F	S	S
6 Apr–3 Oct	10:30–5	·	T	W	T	F	S	S
6 Oct–31 Oct	10:30–5	·	·	W	T	F	S	S
Christmas shop, tea-room and courtyards								
3 Nov–19 Dec	11–4	·	·	W	T	F	S	S
Garden								
6 Apr–28 Sep	11–4	·	T	·	·	·	·	·

Open Bank Holiday Mondays. Park open daily for pedestrians. Vehicles admitted only when house open. Garden (open courtesy of Lord Sackville): note limited opening. As this is a private garden, seating is limited and plants are not labelled.

Lamb House

West Street, Rye, East Sussex TN31 7ES

Map ②J8   [symbols] 1950

Fine brick-fronted house with literary associations – both Henry James and E. F. Benson lived here. Surprisingly large town garden. **Note**: administered and largely maintained on the National Trust's behalf by a tenant. No WC.

Getting here: 198:TQ920202. In West Street, facing west end of church.

Finding out more: 01580 762334 or lambhouse@nationaltrust.org.uk

Lamb House		M	T	W	T	F	S	S
18 Mar–23 Oct	2–6	·	·	·	T	·	S	·

Lamb House, East Sussex: literary associations

Enjoy exhilarating walks through the woods at Leith Hill, Surrey

Leith Hill

Leith Hill, 1 mile west of Coldharbour village, near Dorking, Surrey

Map ② F7    1923

The highest point in south-east England, crowned by an 18th-century Gothic tower, with panoramic views north to London and south to the English Channel. There are colourful displays of rhododendrons and bluebells in May and June. Rugged countryside provides exhilarating walking in woodland and over heathland and farmland. **Note**: no WC. Henman basecamp (for recreational, corporate, conservation working groups). Etherley Farm Campsite 01306 621423.

Exploring
— New 360 degree panoramic leaflet/quiz available from tower.
— Child entry includes panoramic leaflet/quiz, pencil and telescope token.
— New guide to Rhododendron Wood available from car park noticeboard.

Eating and shopping: light refreshments sold from tower (opening hours only).

Making the most of your day: programme of guided walks and activities, including children's fun afternoons throughout the year. Two circular waymarked nature trails, with accompanying leaflet available from tower and Rhododendron Wood. Dogs under close control in Rhododendron Woods.

Access for all: Tower 🏞 Grounds 🦽

Getting here: 187:TQ139432.
Foot: comprehensive network of rights of way including the Greensand Way National Trail. **Cycle**: many rights of way. **Bus**: Arriva 21 Guildford–Dorking (passing close Guildford ≋ and passing Chilworth ≋ and Dorking), alight Holmbury St Mary, 2½ miles, not on Sunday or Public Holidays. **Train**: Holmwood, not Sunday, 2½ miles; Dorking 5½ miles. **Road**: 1 mile south west of Coldharbour A29/B2126. **Parking**: free in designated areas along road at foot of the hill (some steep gradients to tower). No direct vehicle access to summit. Rhododendron Wood £2 per car.

Finding out more: 01306 712711 or leithhill@nationaltrust.org.uk

Leith Hill		M	T	W	T	F	S	S
1 Jan–27 Mar	10–3:30	·	·	·	·	·	**S**	**S**
28 Mar–30 Oct	10–5	·	·	**W**	·	**F**	**S**	**S**
31 Oct–31 Dec	10–3:30	·	·	·	·	·	**S**	**S**

Open Bank Holidays, except 25 December (tower). Last ticket sold 30 minutes before closing.

Long Crendon Courthouse

Long Crendon, Aylesbury,
Buckinghamshire HP18 9AN

Map (2) D4   1900

Building is a fine example of early timber-frame construction. The ground floor (now tenanted) was the village poor house. **Note**: stairs are extremely steep. Village exhibition on display. No WC.

Getting here: 165:SP698091. Next to the parish church at the end of High Street.

Finding out more: 01280 822850 or longcrendon@nationaltrust.org.uk

Long Crendon Courthouse		M	T	W	T	F	S	S
3 Apr–26 Sep	11–6	·	·	·	·	·	S	S
7 Apr–29 Sep	2–6	·	·	W	·	·	·	·
Open Bank Holiday Mondays, 11 to 6.								

Monk's House

Rodmell, Lewes, East Sussex BN7 3HF

Map (2) G8   1980

18th-century weatherboarded cottage, novelist Virginia Woolf's country retreat – featuring the room where she created her best-known works. **Note**: administered and largely maintained on the National Trust's behalf by a tenant.

Getting here: 198:TQ421063. In Rodmell village, near church, 4 miles south of Lewes.

Finding out more: 01323 870001 (c/o Alfriston Clergy House) or monkshouse@nationaltrust.org.uk

Monk's House		M	T	W	T	F	S	S
3 Apr–30 Oct	2–5:30	·	·	W	·	·	S	·

Mottisfont

Mottisfont, near Romsey, Hampshire SO51 0LP

Map (2) C7    1957

At the heart of this tranquil rural estate is Mottisfont Abbey, set in glorious grounds alongside the fast-flowing River Test. There are many layers of history for the visitor to explore, including the Gothic remains of the original 13th-century Augustinian priory. In the mid 20th century the final private owner, society hostess and patron of the arts Maud Russell, used the Abbey as a base for her racy and intriguing life. The River Test is one of the finest chalk steams in the world and the walled gardens house the National Collection of old-fashioned roses. **Note**: during the rose season in June weekday and/or evening visits are recommended.

Exploring
- View the fine collection of 20th-century art.
- Don't miss the spectacular *trompe-l'oeil* Drawing Room.
- Picnic on the lawn, under our majestic plane trees.
- Discover the enchanting walled gardens.
- Explore the wider estate on our six-mile walk.
- Spot brown trout in the crystal-clear stream.

The south front of Mottisfont, Hampshire

Eating and shopping: taste Mottisfont's home-cooked, locally sourced food. Sample our popular cake of the month. Browse and buy in our new Coach House shop. Find a bargain in the thriving second-hand bookshop.

You may also enjoy: a visit to The Vyne.

Making the most of your day: a comprehensive events programme runs throughout the year. Enjoy our popular open-air theatre, guided walks and talks, and throughout the school holidays take part in activity days and trails. Dogs on estate walk only.

Access for all:
Building Grounds

Getting here: 185:SU327270. In Test Valley between Romsey and Stockbridge. **Foot**: situated on Hampshire's long-distance path, Testway. Clarendon Way passes 2 miles to the north. **Cycle**: on Testway. **Train**: Dunbridge ¾ mile. **Road**: signposted off A3057 Romsey to Stockbridge, 4½ miles north of Romsey. Also signposted off B3087 Romsey to Broughton. **Parking**: free.

Finding out more: 01794 340757 or mottisfont@nationaltrust.org.uk

Mottisfont		M	T	W	T	F	S	S
Garden, shop and Kitchen Café								
6 Feb–28 Feb	11–4	·	·	·	·	·	S	S
15 Feb–21 Feb	11–4	M	T	W	T	F	S	S
Garden, shop, Kitchen Café and house*								
1 Mar–25 Mar	11–5	M	T	W	T	·	S	S
27 Mar–18 Apr	11–5	M	T	W	T	F	S	S
19 Apr–30 May	11–5	M	T	W	T	·	S	S
31 May–6 Jun	11–5	M	T	W	T	F	S	S
7 Jun–20 Jun	11–8	M	T	W	T	F	S	S
21 Jun–24 Oct	11–5	M	T	W	T	·	S	S
25 Oct–31 Oct	11–5	M	T	W	T	F	S	S
Garden, shop and Kitchen Café								
6 Nov–19 Dec	11–4	·	·	·	·	·	S	S

*1 to 21 March timed tours of the house only at 12 and 2. 7 to 20 June house closes at 4:30. House and garden open Friday 25 June. Weekends in December open until 5. Last orders in café 4:45. Car park gates close at 6, except 7 to 20 June when close at 8. Open weekends until 5 in December. Access to some show rooms in house may occasionally be restricted due to functions.

Mottistone Manor Garden

Mottistone, Isle of Wight PO30 4EA

Map ② C9   1965

'**An absolute treat – such a shame we live on the mainland or we'd be here all the time**.'
Mr and Mrs Boon, Kent

Set in a sheltered valley this magical garden is full of surprises, with shrub-filled banks, hidden pathways and colourful herbaceous borders. Surrounding an attractive Elizabethan manor house this 20th-century garden is experimenting with a Mediterranean-style planting scheme to take advantage of its southerly location. Other surprises include a young olive grove, a small organic kitchen garden and a traditional tea garden set alongside The Shack, a unique cabin retreat designed as their summer drawing office by architects John Seely (2nd Lord Mottistone) and Paul Paget. There are also delightful walks across the adjoining Mottistone Estate. **Note**: manor house is only open one day a year.

Exploring
– Enjoy this hillside garden throughout the seasons.
– Relish the informality – a bit on the wild side.
– Discover our resident flowerpot people.
– Explore the garden with a family discovery pack.
– Extend your visit with a walk to the Long Stone.
– Venture inside The Shack, a unique 1930s garden cabin.

Eating and shopping: browse in our gift shop. Take home a plant from the plant stall. Snap up a second-hand book bargain. Relax in the tea garden (not National Trust).

You may also enjoy: The Needles Old Battery, Newtown Old Town Hall, Bembridge Windmill and Brighstone Shop and Museum.

Making the most of your day: programme of family events and activity packs. Flowerpot trail and estate walks. Dogs welcome on leads only.

Access for all: ⬚⬚⬚⬚⬚⬚⬚⬚⬚
Grounds ⬚⬚⬚

Getting here: 196:SZ406838. **Foot**: 1 mile north of coastal path; 1 mile south of Tennyson Trail. **Cycle**: NCN67. On the 'Round the Island' cycle route. **Ferry**: Yarmouth (Wightlink Ltd) 5 miles (0871 376 1000); East Cowes (Red Funnel) 16 miles (0844 844 9988). **Bus**: Southern Vectis 7 Newport–Alum Bay. **Road**: at Mottistone, between Brighstone and Brook on B3399. **Parking**: free, 50 yards.

Finding out more: 01983 741302 or mottistonemanor@nationaltrust.org.uk

Mottistone Manor Garden		M	T	W	T	F	S	S
14 Mar–28 Oct	11–5		M	T	W	T		S

Closes dusk if earlier. House open Bank Holiday Monday 31 May only, 2 to 5. Additional charges apply. Guided tours for members on that day 9:30 to 12 by timed ticket (available on the day). Late night opening: Wednesday 23 June, garden open until 9.

The Needles Old Battery and New Battery

West High Down, Alum Bay, Isle of Wight PO39 0JH

Map ② C9   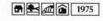 1975

Perched high above the Needles, amid acres of unspoilt countryside, is the Needles Old Battery, a Victorian fort built in 1862 and used throughout both world wars. The Parade Ground has two original guns and the Fort's fascinating military history is brought to life with a series of vivid cartoons by acclaimed comic book artist Geoff Campion. An underground tunnel leads to a searchlight emplacement with dramatic views over the Needles rocks. The New Battery, further up

Mottistone Manor Garden, Isle of Wight

the headland, has an exhibition on the secret British rocket tests carried out there during the Cold War. **Note**: steep paths and uneven surfaces. Spiral staircase to tunnel. WC at Old Battery only.

Exploring
- Enjoy dramatic sea views from the cliff-top walk.
- Discover the rooms where soldiers worked with gunpowder.
- Explore the site with a family activity pack.
- See the Needles from our wheelchair-friendly viewing platform.
- Don't miss one of our most unusual tea-rooms.
- Discover recently revealed secrets of Britain's rocket test programme.

Eating and shopping: enjoy homemade food in our cliff-top tea-room. Treat yourself to a souvenir in the guardroom shop. Drinks and ice-creams available at the New Battery kiosk.

You may also enjoy: Mottistone Manor Garden, Newtown Old Town Hall, Bembridge Windmill and Brighstone Shop and Museum.

Making the most of your day: programme of family events. Family activity packs, children's quiz and soldier trail. Cliff-top walks to Tennyson Monument and beyond. Dogs welcome on leads only.

Access for all: ⬚⬚⬚⬚⬚⬚
Building ⬚⬚⬚ **Grounds** ⬚⬚

The Needles Headland and Tennyson Down, Isle of Wight

Getting here: 196:SZ300848. **Foot**: access is on foot only from Alum Bay ¾ mile along a well-surfaced private road, Highdown National Trust car park 2 miles, Freshwater Bay 3½ miles. **Cycle**: NCN67, ½ miles. 'Round the Island' route. **Ferry**: Yarmouth (Wightlink Ltd) 5 miles (0871 376 1000); East Cowes (Red Funnel) 16 miles (0844 844 9988). **Bus**: Southern Vectis 7 Newport–Alum Bay, then ¾ mile. Southern Vectis 'Needles Tour' from Yarmouth and Alum Bay (March–November). Half-price fare for members. **Road**: Alum Bay west of Freshwater Bay (B3322). **Parking**: no onsite parking. Limited disabled parking by prior arrangement with property. Car park at Alum Bay (not National Trust; minimum charge £4), or in Freshwater Bay (Isle of Wight Council) or Highdown car park SZ325856 (National Trust) and walk over Downs.

Finding out more: 01983 754772 or needlesoldbattery@nationaltrust.org.uk

The Needles Batteries		M	T	W	T	F	S	S
Tea-room								
9 Jan–28 Feb	11–3	·	·	·	·	·	S	S
Old Battery and tea-room								
13 Mar–31 Oct	10:30–5	M	T	W	T	F	S	S
New Battery*								
13 Mar–31 Oct	11–4	·	T	·	·	·	S	S
Tea-room								
6 Nov–19 Dec	11–3	·	·	·	·	·	S	S

Closes dusk if earlier. Property closes in high winds: telephone on day of visit to check. *Open other days where possible: please telephone to check.

Newtown Old Town Hall

Newtown, Newport, Isle of Wight PO30 4PA

Map ② C9   1933

Tucked away in a tiny hamlet adjoining the National Nature Reserve, the 17th-century Old Town Hall is the only remaining evidence of Newtown's former importance. It's hard to believe that this tranquil corner of the island once held often turbulent elections before sending two Members to Parliament. **Note**: nearest WC in car park.

Exploring
 — Discover the surprising local and political history.
 — Learn about the mysterious Ferguson Gang who saved the Hall.
 — Enjoy regular art and photographic exhibitions.
 — Take a delightful estuary walk.

Eating and shopping: treat yourself to a small memento of your visit.

Making the most of your day: children's quiz sheet. Programme of countryside family activities (bookable) run by the Newtown Warden from a nearby Visitor Point. Nature Reserve information, 01983 531622.

Access for all: ♿🗝️🏠👓📷 Building 🏃

Getting here: 196:SZ424905. **Cycle**: NCN67, ½ mile. **Ferry**: Yarmouth (Wightlink Ltd) 5 miles (0871 376 1000); East Cowes (Red Funnel) 11 miles (0844 844 9988). **Bus**: Wightbus 35 from Newport; otherwise Southern Vectis 7 Newport–Yarmouth, alight Shalfleet, Barton's Corner, 1 mile. **Road**: Newtown is between Newport and Yarmouth, 1 mile north of A3054. **Parking**: free, 15 yards. Not suitable for coaches.

Finding out more: 01983 531785 or oldtownhall@nationaltrust.org.uk

Newtown Old Town Hall		M	T	W	T	F	S	S
14 Mar–30 Jun	2–5	M	·	W	·	·	·	S
4 Jul–31 Aug	2–5	M	T	W	T	·	·	S
1 Sep–27 Oct	2–5	M	·	W	·	·	·	S

Last admission 15 minutes before closing. Open Good Friday and Easter Saturday. Closes dusk if earlier than 5.

Nymans

Handcross, Haywards Heath,
West Sussex RH17 6EB

Map ② G7    1954

'The garden is a triumph of hope – full of experiments, giving endless pleasure, with careful thought bestowed on each plant.'
Muriel Messel, Nymans

Set in the High Weald with splendid views, the garden is a series of experimental designs with spectacular planting and beauty all year. Both a horticulturalist's dream and a peaceful country garden, it is easy to lose yourself in its intimate and surprising corners. The house, transformed into a Gothic mansion in the 1920s, burnt down shortly after, leaving romantic ruins. The remaining rooms are unexpectedly charming, filled with flowers from the garden as Anne Messel, Countess of Rosse had them. Ancient woods beyond the garden dip into the valley, with walks among avenues, wild flowers, lake and cascades.

Exploring
- Beauty and interest every season, with spectacular colours and perfumes.
- Rediscovery project, including Lily Pond and Sunken Rock Garden restoration.
- Anne Messel's rooms – 17th-century furniture and Flemish tapestries.
- Discover the intriguing ruins, summerhouses and statues.
- Walk through the woodland, with wild flowers, lake and cascades.
- Enjoy the splendid views across the Sussex countryside.

Eating and shopping: large shop supporting local products. Garden centre and nursery sells plants propagated from the garden. New-look restaurant: open-air covered seating, serving homecooked food. Refresh yourself at the garden catering buggy.

You may also enjoy: Standen's Arts & Crafts, landscape garden at Sheffield Park and Devil's Dyke's countryside.

Making the most of your day: information point, trails and MP3 guides. Mobility buggy tours of garden. Bamboo jungle. Touchscreen tour: different seasons. Events include family activities, open-air theatre, horticulture and compost workshops, bat walks. Dogs welcome in the woodland only.

Access for all: 🅿️ 🅿️ 🚻 ♿ 🔄 📷 🎦 📱 ♿
Building ♿ ♿ ♿ Grounds ♿ ➡️ ♿ ♿

Getting here: 187:TQ265294. 5 miles south of Crawley. **Foot**: 5 miles by footpath from Balcombe. **Cycle**: on the National Cycle Network route 20. **Bus**: Metrobus 273 Brighton to Crawley, 271 Haywards Heath to Crawley. Both stop outside Nymans. Both pass Crawley ⊕. **Train**: Balcombe 4 miles; Crawley 5 miles. **Road**: on B2114 at Handcross, just off London to Brighton M23/A23. **Parking**: free. Designated coach bays.

Finding out more: 01444 405250 or nymans@nationaltrust.org.uk

Nymans		M	T	W	T	F	S	S
Garden, woods, restaurant*, shop and garden centre								
Open all year	10–5	·	·	W	T	F	S	S
House								
10 Mar–31 Oct	11–4	·	·	W	T	F	S	S

Open Bank Holiday Mondays. November to February Nymans closes at 4. Closed 25 to 31 December. *Restaurant closes at 4:30.

Nymans, West Sussex

Oakhurst Cottage

Hambledon, near Godalming, Surrey GU8 4HF

Map ② E7   1952

A restored and furnished simple labourer's dwelling, containing artefacts reflecting four centuries of continual occupation, with delightful cottage garden. **Note**: no WC.

Getting here: 186:SU965380. Off A283 between Wormley and Chiddingfold.

Finding out more: 01798 342207 or oakhurstcottage@nationaltrust.org.uk

Oakhurst Cottage		M	T	W	T	F	S	S
24 Mar–24 Oct	2–5			**W**	**T**		**S**	**S**

Admission by guided tour and appointment only. Open Bank Holiday Mondays, 2 to 5. Please book at least three days in advance.

Old Soar Manor

Plaxtol, Borough Green, Kent TN15 0QX

Map ② H6   1947

Rare remaining structure of a late 13th-century knights dwelling, including solar chamber, barrel-vaulted undercroft, chapel and garderobe. **Note**: no WC.

Getting here: 188:TQ619541. 2 miles south of Borough Green (A25); approached via A227 and Plaxtol.

Finding out more: 01732 810378 Ext. 100 or oldsoarmanor@nationaltrust.org.uk

Old Soar Manor		M	T	W	T	F	S	S
1 Apr–30 Sep	10–6	**M**	**T**	**W**			**S**	**S**

Owletts

The Street, Cobham, Gravesend, Kent DA12 3AP

Map ② H5   1938

An interesting red-brick Charles II house and garden, home of the architect Sir Herbert Baker. **Note**: occupied and administered on the National Trust's behalf by descendant of the donor. No WC.

Getting here: 177:TQ665687. 1 mile south of A2 at west end of village, at junction of roads from Dartford and Sole Street.

Finding out more: 01304 207326 or owletts@nationaltrust.org.uk

Owletts		M	T	W	T	F	S	S
25 Mar–23 Oct	2–5:30				**T**		**S**	

Petworth House, West Sussex: stunning collections

Petworth House and Park

Petworth, West Sussex GU28 0AE

Map (2) E7 1947

The vast late 17th-century mansion is set in a beautiful 283-hectare (700-acre) deer park, landscaped by 'Capability' Brown and immortalised in Turner's paintings. The house contains the National Trust's finest collection of pictures, with numerous works by Turner, Van Dyck, Reynolds and Blake, ancient and Neo-classical sculpture, fine furniture and carvings by Grinling Gibbons. The servants' quarters contain fascinating kitchens (including a copper *batterie de cuisine* of more than 1,000 pieces) and other service rooms. On weekdays additional rooms in the house are open by kind permission of Lord and Lady Egremont.

Exploring
- Discover the National Trust's largest painting and sculpture collection.
- See the 'Leconfield Aphrodite', a sculpture from 4th century BC.
- Year-round horticultural interest in the Pleasure Ground.
- Explore the magnificent park, landscaped by 'Capability' Brown.
- Magnificent historic kitchens with 1,000 copper pots and moulds.
- Find the largest herd of fallow deer in England.

Eating and shopping: Audit Room Restaurant offers local and seasonal home-cooked food. Visit the National Trust shop with its extensive gift selection. Look out for the plants and garden products for sale. Also, hand-turned Petworth wood gifts.

You may also enjoy: 18th-century Uppark House and Garden.

Deer at Petworth Park, West Sussex

Making the most of your day: extensive and varied event and exhibition programme, including open-air opera, tours and guided walks. Dogs under close control in park only.

Access for all: 🅿️ 🄳 ♿ 🚾 ♿ ♿ 🎨 🖥️ 🆅🆃 ♿ ⣿ 🅰️ **Building** ♿ 🏛️ ♿

Getting here: 197:SU976218. **Bus**: Stagecoach in the South Downs 1 Worthing–Midhurst (passing Pulborough ≋); Compass 76 Horsham–Petworth (passing Horsham ≋). **Train**: Pulborough 5¼ miles. **Road**: in centre of Petworth (A272/A283); both house and park car parks on A283; pedestrian access from Petworth town and A272. No vehicles in park. **Parking**: 700 yards. Coaches can drop off at Church Lodge entrance and park in house car park. Petworth Park car park: £2 charge for non-members.

Finding out more: 01798 343929 (Infoline). 01798 342207 or petworth@nationaltrust.org.uk

Petworth House and Park		M	T	W	T	F	S	S
House								
13 Mar–3 Nov	11–5	M	T	W	·	·	S	S
Shop and restaurant								
27 Feb–10 Mar	10:30–3:30	M	T	W	·	·	S	S
13 Mar–3 Nov	11–5	M	T	W	·	·	S	S
10 Nov–19 Dec	10:30–3:30	·	·	W	T	F	S	S
Pleasure ground								
27 Feb–10 Mar	10:30–3:30	M	T	W	·	·	S	S
13 Mar–3 Nov	11–6	M	T	W	·	·	S	S
10 Nov–19 Dec	10:30–3:30	·	·	W	T	F	S	S

Open Good Friday. **Extra rooms shown weekdays from 1**: Monday (not Bank Holiday Mondays), White and Gold Room and White Library; Tuesday and Wednesday, three bedrooms on first floor.

Pitstone Windmill

Ivinghoe, Buckinghamshire

Map ② E3   ⊠ 1937

A rare and striking example of an early form of windmill. **Note**: no WC. Located at the end of a rough track.

Getting here: 181:SP945157. ½ mile south of Ivinghoe, 3 miles north east of Tring, just west of the B488.

Finding out more: 01442 851227 or pitstonemill@nationaltrust.org.uk

Pitstone Windmill			M	T	W	T	F	S	S
6 Jun–29 Aug	2:30–6			·	·	·	·	·	**S**

Open Bank Holiday Monday 30 August. Due to staffing restrictions, property may not open as publicised (telephone to check).

Polesden Lacey

Great Bookham, near Dorking, Surrey RH5 6BD

Map ② F6   🏛 ❄ ♣ 🍴 🏠 ▼ 1942

'We loved every minute of it! Everyone was very helpful and smiley – felt like we were Mrs Greville's guests.'
Karen Gerrard, Reigate

Beautiful 566-hectare (1,400-acre) estate located in an exceptional setting and enjoying stunning views across the Surrey Hills. The house was remodelled in 1906–9 by the Hon. Mrs Ronald Greville, a well-known Edwardian hostess, and was the venue for the honeymoon of the future King George VI and Queen Elizabeth. Enjoy Mrs Greville's collections, displayed in the reception rooms and galleries as they were at the time of her celebrated house parties. Explore the beautiful walled rose garden, with its variety of scented plants, before strolling through the extensive grounds, lawns and landscape walks.

Polesden Lacey, Surrey: remodelled in 1906–9

Exploring
- Enjoy the stunning formal gardens, including the famous Rose Garden.
- Feel like one of Mrs Greville's house-party guests.
- Take in the stunning countryside on a landscape walk.
- Discover nature and history with family activities and play area.
- Discover the secrets behind Polesden Lacey at a themed event.
- Enjoy the music and drama festival, 2 to 4 July.

Eating and shopping: take home local, seasonal produce from our farm shop. Savour home-cooked seasonal menus at our restaurant. Unique shopping experience, including items from Surrey artists. Live the Polesden Lacey life in our holiday cottage.

You may also enjoy: Clandon Park, Hatchlands Park and Box Hill.

Making the most of your day: welcome talks and guided tours, extensive events programme, including specialist tours and opening of the House in February, November and December. Shops and restaurant located outside the pay perimeter. Dogs on leads in designated areas, under close control on landscape walks, estate and farmland.

Access for all: 🅿️ 🅳 ♿ ⬛ ⬛ ⬛ ⬛ 🖊 ▣ 🎵 ⬛ Ⓐ **Building** ⬛ ⬛ ♿ **Grounds** ⬛ ➡ ⬛ ♿

Getting here: 187:TQ136522. **Foot**: North Downs Way within ¾ mile. **Bus**: Countryliner 479 Leatherhead ≢–Little Bookham, alight Great

Bookham 1½ miles. **Train**: Boxhill & Westhumble 2 miles; Dorking 4 miles. **Road**: 5 miles north west of Dorking, 2 miles south of Great Bookham, off A246 Leatherhead–Guildford road. **Parking**: 200 yards (pay and display), 7:30 to dusk. £2.50 charge for non-members, redeemable against purchases over £10 in shops or restaurant or membership taken out at Polesden Lacey. No charges 1 to 23 December.

Finding out more: 01372 458203 (Infoline). 01372 452048 or polesdenlacey@nationaltrust.org.uk

Polesden Lacey		M	T	W	T	F	S	S
House*								
3 Mar–31 Oct	11–5			·	·	**W**	**T**	**F**	**S**	**S**
Garden, restaurant, gift shop and farm shop**								
1 Jan–12 Feb	10–4	**M**	**T**	**W**	**T**	**F**	**S**	**S**
13 Feb–31 Oct	10–5	**M**	**T**	**W**	**T**	**F**	**S**	**S**
1 Nov–31 Dec	10–4	**M**	**T**	**W**	**T**	**F**	**S**	**S**
Car Park								
Open all year	7:30–dusk	**M**	**T**	**W**	**T**	**F**	**S**	**S**

Open Bank Holiday Mondays. Admission to house by timed ticket at busy times. Tickets issued at reception on a first-come, first-served basis and cannot be booked in advance. Tickets may run out at peak times, please arrive early. *Weekends in February, house open by guided tour, spaces limited. **Closed 16 March. Closed 24 and 25 December. Gift shop closed 24 to 26 December.

Priory Cottages

1 Mill Street, Steventon, Abingdon, Oxfordshire OX13 6SP

Map (2) C5   1939

Former monastic buildings, now converted into two houses. Properties were gifted by the famous Ferguson's Gang. **Note**: Priory Cottage South only open. No WC.

Getting here: 164:SU466914. 4 miles south of Abingdon.

Finding out more: 01793 762209 or priorycottages@nationaltrust.org.uk

Priory Cottages		M	T	W	T	F	S	S
1 Apr–30 Sep	2–6	·	·	·	**T**	·	·

Admission by written appointment with the tenant.

Quebec House

Quebec Square, Westerham, Kent TN16 1TD

Map (2) G6   1918

This Grade I-listed gabled house in the beautiful village of Westerham has features of significant architectural and historical interest. Quebec House was the childhood home of General James Wolfe, and is full of family and military memorabilia. The coach house contains an exhibition about the 1759 Battle of Quebec.

Exploring
- Charming 16th-century family home.
- Pretty garden with newly created vegetable plot and herb beds.
- Detailed exhibition telling the story of the Battle of Quebec.
- Look out for the fascinating architectural features.

Quebec House, Kent: charming family home

Eating and shopping: enjoy tea, coffee and homemade cakes and biscuits. Delightful shop in the old coach house.

Making the most of your day: exciting events programme, including special talks, children's activities and family trails.

Access for all: ⬚⬚⬚⬚⬚⬚
Building ⬚⬚⬚⬚ Grounds ⬚

Getting here: 187:TQ449541. **Bus**: SelKent 246 from Bromley North ⬛ (passing Bromley South ⬛); Arriva 401 from Sevenoaks ⬛ (also Tunbridge Wells ⬛ Sundays). **Train**: Sevenoaks 4 miles; Oxted 4 miles. **Road**: at east end of village, on north side of A25, facing junction with B2026 Edenbridge road. M25 exit 5 or 6. **Parking**: 200 yards east of Quebec House on A25 (not National Trust). Visitors should follow footpath beside A25 to house.

Finding out more: 01732 866368 (Infoline). 01732 868381 or quebechouse@nationaltrust.org.uk. Chartwell Office, Mapleton Road, Westerham, Kent TN16 1PS

Quebec House		M	T	W	T	F	S	S
House								
13 Mar–31 Oct	1–5	·	·	**W**	**T**	**F**	**S**	**S**
Garden and exhibition								
13 Mar–31 Oct	12–5	·	·	**W**	**T**	**F**	**S**	**S**

Open Bank Holiday Mondays.

River Wey and Godalming Navigations and Dapdune Wharf

Navigations Office and Dapdune Wharf, Wharf Road, Guildford, Surrey GU1 4RR

Map ② F6 ⬚⬚⬚⬚ 1964

'**What a little gem of a waterway! So much here of interest, well-presented and lovingly maintained!**'
John Land, British Colombia, Canada

The Wey was one of the first British rivers to be made navigable, and opened to barge traffic in 1653. This 15½-mile waterway linked Guildford to Weybridge on the Thames, and then to London. The Godalming Navigation, opened in 1764, enabled barges to work a further four miles upriver. The award-winning visitor centre at Dapdune Wharf in Guildford tells the story of the Navigations and the people who lived and worked on them. Visitors can see where the huge Wey barges were built and climb aboard 'Reliance', one of three surviving barges. **Note**: mooring and fishing fees payable by all, including members.

River Wey, Surrey: one of the first British rivers to be made navigable

Exploring
- Take a boat trip on our electric launch.
- Climb aboard 'Reliance', one of the last surviving Wey barges.
- Enjoy the peace and tranquillity of a towpath walk.
- Have a go at pond dipping in the creek.
- For schools: our river studies workshop.

Eating and shopping: small tea-room serves sandwiches, ice-cream and drinks. Small shop with plant sales. Picnic areas at Dapdune Wharf.

You may also enjoy: Shalford Mill, an evocative example of an earlier industrial age.

Making the most of your day: year-round events programme, with children-focused events at Dapdune and programme of guided walks along the towpath and beyond. Guildford Festival Boat Gathering annually in July. Overnight moorings available. Dogs on leads at Dapdune Wharf and lock areas; elsewhere under control.

Access for all: ⓟ♿🚽♿♿⠿◎♿

Grounds ♿

Getting here: 186:SU993502. **River**: visiting craft can enter from the Thames at Shepperton or slipways at Guildford or Pyrford. Visitor moorings available at Dapdune Wharf and along towpath side of Navigations. **Foot**: North Downs Way crosses Navigations south of Guildford. Easy access from town centre on foot via towpath. **Bus**: Arriva 28 Guildford–Woking, Stagecoach Hants and Surrey 20 Guildford–Aldershot, Arriva 4 Guildford–Park Barn (cricket ground, 100 yards). **Train**: Addlestone ≋, Byfleet and New Haw, Guildford, Farncombe and Godalming all close to the Navigations. **Road**: Dapdune Wharf is on Wharf Road to rear of Surrey County Cricket Ground, off Woodbridge Rd (A322), Guildford. Access to rest of Navigations from A3 and M25. **Parking**: free, 10 yards at Dapdune Wharf. Parking for the Navigations in Godalming town centre, Catteshall Road bridge. Dapdune Wharf: Bowers Lane (Guildford), Send village, Newark Lane (B367) and New Haw Lock.

Finding out more: 01483 561389 or riverwey@nationaltrust.org.uk

River Wey and Dapdune Wharf		M	T	W	T	F	S	S
13 Mar–31 Oct	11–5	M	·	·	T	F	S	S

River trips 11 to 4 (conditions permitting). Access to towpath during daylight hours all year.

Runnymede

Runnymede Estate Office, North Lodge, Windsor Road, Old Windsor, Berkshire SL4 2JL

Map ② F5

Runnymede is a famous historical site which witnessed, in 1215, King John's sealing of Magna Carta. Set within the beautiful natural landscape are various memorials by Maufe, Jellicoe and Lutyens. The memorials commemorate moments in world history and provide the perfect countryside setting in which to remember and reflect. **Note**: WC only available when tea-room is open. Mooring/fishing fees payable, including members.

Exploring
- Reflect on world history at the Memorials.
- Stroll along the River Thames.
- Explore the ancient woodlands.
- Wander through the historic meadows.

Eating and shopping: tea-room (not National Trust). Art gallery in summer at North Lodge. See events on website for forthcoming artists/exhibitions.

Making the most of your day: guided walks throughout the year and Easter Trail event on Easter Monday. Dogs on leads near livestock.

Access for all: 🚽⠿◎

Building ♿ Grounds ♿♿

Getting here: 176:TQ007720.
Foot: 1¼ miles of Thames Path, National Trail.
Cycle: 1¼ miles of Thames Path.
Bus: First 71 Windsor ≋–Heathrow, alight 'Bells of Ouzeley'. **Train**: Egham ≋ 1¼ miles from Memorials. **Road**: by the River Thames, 2 miles west of Runnymede Bridge, on south side of A308 (M25, exit 13), 6 miles east of Windsor.
Parking: pay and display. Limited space for coaches on hard-standing. Riverside grass/seasonal car park closed when wet.

Finding out more: 01784 432891 or runnymede@nationaltrust.org.uk

Runnymede		M	T	W	T	F	S	S
Open all year	Dawn–dusk	M	T	W	T	F	S	S
Memorials car park (hard-standing)								
1 Jan–14 Apr	9–5	M	T	W	T	F	S	S
15 Apr–15 Sep	8:30–7	M	T	W	T	F	S	S
16 Sep–31 Dec	9–5	M	T	W	T	F	S	S
Riverside car park (grass/seasonal)								
15 Apr–15 Sep	10–7	M	T	W	T	F	S	S

Car parks may close at dusk if earlier. Car parks closed 25 and 26 December. Riverside grass car park open when ground and weather conditions permit.

St John's Jerusalem

Sutton-at-Hone, Dartford, Kent DA4 9HQ

Map ② H5   ✚ ❀ 1943

This 13th-century chapel, surrounded by a tranquil moated garden, was part of the former Commandery of the Knights Hospitallers.
Note: occupied as a private residence, maintained and managed by a tenant on National Trust's behalf.

Getting here: 177:TQ558703. 3 miles south of Dartford at Sutton-at-Hone.

Finding out more: 01732 810378 (c/o Ightham Mote) or stjohnsjerusalem@nationaltrust.org.uk

St John's Jerusalem		M	T	W	T	F	S	S
7 Apr–29 Sep	2–6	·	·	W	·	·	·	·
6 Oct–27 Oct	2–4	·	·	W	·	·	·	·

Sandham Memorial Chapel, Hampshire

Sandham Memorial Chapel

Harts Lane, Burghclere, near Newbury, Hampshire RG20 9JT

Map ② C6   ✚ ❀ 1947

Modest red-brick building housing an unexpected treasure – an outstanding series of large-scale paintings by acclaimed artist Stanley Spencer. Inspired by his experiences as a First World War medical orderly and soldier, and peppered with personal and unexpected details, these paintings are considered to be among his finest achievements. **Note**: no WC. No credit card facilities on site.

Exploring
   – Revel in the details of this extraordinary work of art.
   – Wander through the orchard to spot wild flowers.
   – Enjoy the surroundings, with walks and views to Watership Down.

Eating and shopping: a selection of books and postcards are available for purchase.

Making the most of your day: bring a picnic and enjoy the garden. Reference folders, children's quiz and handling kit available. No artificial lighting so bright days are best for viewing. Dogs in grounds only on leads.

Access for all: 🗐🗓⭐📷
Building 🗓🗓 Grounds 🗓🗓

Getting here: 174:SU463608. **Bus**: Cango C21/2 'demand-responsive' service from Newbury. Book on 0845 602 4135. **Train**: Newbury approx 4 miles. **Road**: 4 miles south of Newbury, ½ mile east of A34. From M4, follow A34, then brown signs. From A339 (Basingstoke to Newbury) follow brown signs and white National Trust signs. Exit A34 at Tothill services. **Parking**: no onsite parking. Parking in public lay-by opposite chapel, or village car park ¼ mile.

Finding out more: 01635 278394 or sandham@nationaltrust.org.uk

Sandham Memorial Chapel		M	T	W	T	F	S	S
6 Mar–28 Mar	11–3	·	·	·	·	·	**S**	**S**
31 Mar–3 Oct	11–5	·	·	**W**	**T**	**F**	**S**	**S**
6 Oct–31 Oct	11–3	·	·	**W**	**T**	**F**	**S**	**S**
6 Nov–19 Dec	11–3	·	·	·	·	·	**S**	**S**

Open Bank Holiday Mondays, 11 to 5. Open other times by appointment. Groups of more than ten people must book to avoid queuing.

Scotney Castle

Lamberhurst, Tunbridge Wells, Kent TN3 8JN

Map ② I7   🏠🏰🔭✿🌳🏊  1970

Scotney is not one but two houses. At the top of the hill is the new house, designed by Anthony Salvin in Elizabethan style and built in 1837 for Edward Hussey III, who took the 'Picturesque' style as his inspiration. At the bottom of the valley are the romantic ruins of a medieval castle and moat. This is the focal point of the celebrated gardens featuring spectacular displays of rhododendrons, azaleas and kalmia in May/June with trees and shrubs providing autumnal colour. The estate is open all year, offering a variety of walks through beautiful parkland, woodland and farmland.

Exploring
 – One of England's most romantic gardens.
 – Superb display of rhododendrons and azaleas.
 – Large, beautiful estate, with woodland and parkland to explore.
 – The only National Trust-owned working hop farm.
 – Garden and estate designated a Site of Special Scientific Interest.

Scotney Castle, Kent: the romantic ruins of a medieval castle and moat

Eating and shopping: Coach House tea-room serves sandwiches, hot and cold lunches. Buy an ice-cream from the shop or tea-room. Seek out Scotney ale and plant sales in the shop. Estate 'Explorer' map available from the shop and visitor reception.

You may also enjoy: Bateman's, Bodiam Castle and Sissinghurst Castle Garden.

Making the most of your day: a wide range of activities throughout the year, including open-air theatre and opera, lecture lunches, family activities and estate and wildlife walks. Events programme available. Dogs welcome on leads around estate but not permitted in the garden.

Access for all: ⓟ♿🚪♿🚻♿🍴♿📷🎨 ⓥⓣ 👓 ♿
House ♿♿ Grounds ♿➡♿

Getting here: 188:TQ688353. **Foot**: links to local footpath network. **Cycle**: NCN18, 3 miles. **Bus**: telephone for details of Trust/East Sussex County Council-run Tunbridge Wells service. **Train**: Wadhurst 5½ miles. **Road**: Signposted from A21 at Lamberhurst. **Parking**: 130 yards. Limited parking, cannot be guaranteed at busy times. Grass car park may be closed when wet.

Finding out more: 01892 893820 (Infoline). 01892 893868 or scotneycastle@nationaltrust.org.uk

Scotney Castle		M	T	W	T	F	S	S
House								
13 Mar–31 Oct	11–5	·	·	W	T	F	S	S
4 Dec–19 Dec	11–4	·	·	·	·	·	S	S
Shop and tea-room								
27 Feb–31 Oct	11–5:30	·	·	W	T	F	·	·
27 Feb–31 Oct	10–5:30	·	·	·	·	·	S	S
6 Nov–19 Dec	11–4:30	·	·	W	T	F	S	S
Old Castle*								
31 Mar–26 Sep	11–3	·	·	W	T	F	S	S
Garden*								
27 Feb–31 Oct	11–5:30	·	·	W	T	F	·	·
27 Feb–31 Oct	10–5:30	·	·	·	·	·	S	S
6 Nov–19 Dec	11–4	·	·	W	T	F	S	S
Estate walks								
Open all year		M	T	W	T	F	S	S

Open Bank Holiday Mondays and Good Friday. Last admission one hour before closing. *Closes dusk if earlier. Timed tickets for the house are limited and may sell out on busy days.

Sheffield Park Garden, East Sussex

Shalford Mill

Shalford, near Guildford, Surrey GU4 8BS

Map ② E6   🎫 ♿ 1932

Large timber-framed watermill on the River Tillingbourne with well-preserved machinery – almost unaltered since ceasing operations in 1914. **Note**: no WC. No parking. Regular guided tours.

Getting here: 186:TQ001476. 1½ miles south of Guildford on A281 opposite Seahorse Inn.

Finding out more: 01483 561389 or shalfordmill@nationaltrust.org.uk

Shalford Mill		M	T	W	T	F	S	S
28 Mar–31 Oct	11–5	·	·	W	·	·	·	S

Guided tours for groups by arrangement, except Wednesday and Sunday.

Sheffield Park Garden

Sheffield Park, East Sussex TN22 3QX

Map (2) G7 1954

This magnificent informal landscape garden was laid out in the 18th century by 'Capability' Brown and further developed in the early years of the 20th century by its owner, Arthur G. Soames. The original four lakes form the centrepiece. There are dramatic shows of daffodils and bluebells in spring, and the rhododendrons and azaleas are spectacular in early summer. Autumn brings stunning colours from the many rare trees and shrubs, and winter walks can be enjoyed in this garden for all seasons. Visitors can now also explore South Park, 107 hectares (265 acres) of historic parkland, with stunning views.

Exploring
- Don't miss 'What's in the garden' board.
- Take a walk to our historic cricket pitch.
- Enjoy the mirror-like reflections in the lakes.
- Explore our parkland – stunning countryside views.
- Go on a tour, Tuesdays and Thursdays in May/October.

Eating and shopping: enjoy a drink or a snack from the catering buggy. Local products available in our shop. Browse our plants for sale, sourced from National Trust properties.

You may also enjoy: Standen, Alfriston Clergy House, Bateman's or Nyman's garden.

Making the most of your day: special events throughout the year (telephone or visit website for details). Family activities available to pick up in reception. Dogs on leads in parkland only (restrictions apply when livestock grazing).

Access for all: 🅿️ 🚻 ♿ 📷 🎦 👓 Ⓐ
Reception ♿ 👓 Grounds ♿ ➡️ 🚶 👓

Getting here: 198:TQ415240. **Bus**: Bluebell Railway link (Metrobus 473) from near East Grinstead ≋–Kingscote ≋, Countryliner 121 from close Lewes ≋ (Saturday only), 246 from Uckfield (Monday, Wednesday, Friday only). **Train**: Sheffield Park (Bluebell Railway) ¾ mile; Uckfield 6 miles; Haywards Heath 7 miles. **Road**: midway between East Grinstead and Lewes, 5 miles north west of Uckfield, on east side of A275 (between A272 and A22). **Parking**: Free parking.

Finding out more: 01825 790231 or sheffieldpark@nationaltrust.org.uk

Sheffield Park Garden		M	T	W	T	F	S	S
Garden								
1 Jan–14 Feb	10:30–4	·	·	·	·	·	S	S
15 Feb–31 Oct	10:30–5:30	M	T	W	T	F	S	S
1 Nov–31 Dec	10:30–4	M	T	W	T	F	S	S
Parkland								
Open all year	Dawn–dusk	M	T	W	T	F	S	S

Closed 24 to 27 December. Autumn: open 9:30 weekends only, 9 October to 7 November. Closes at dusk if earlier (see board on entry). Last admission one hour before closing time.

Sissinghurst Castle Garden

Sissinghurst, Biddenden Road, near Cranbrook, Kent TN17 2AB

Map (2) I7  1967

This internationally renowned garden was developed by Vita Sackville-West and Sir Harold Nicolson around the surviving parts of an Elizabethan mansion. It comprises small enclosed compartments, with colour throughout the season, resulting in an intimate and romantic atmosphere (the garden is more peaceful after 4). The new vegetable garden, now fully productive, supplies fresh vegetables and fruit to the licensed restaurant. The surrounding Wealden landscape, along with the property's accompanying farm, were central to Vita and Harold's love and overall vision for Sissinghurst.

Sissinghurst Castle Garden, Kent: internationally renowned

Exploring
- Meander around our intimate, romantic garden.
- Stroll through our estate, a haven for Wealden wildlife.
- Visit our working vegetable garden between May and September.
- Shop at the farmers' market – second Monday of every month.
- Climb the steps of the tower and enjoy the view.

Eating and shopping: enjoy hot and cold fresh, local seasonal food. Fresh vegetables from our own vegetable garden. Taste homemade cakes and scones. Waitress service November to December.

You may also enjoy: Bateman's, Bodiam Castle, Stoneacre, Smallhythe Place, Knole and Scotney Castle.

Making the most of your day: special summer garden evenings, walks and talks, lecture lunches and lots more. Dogs on leads welcome on estate only.

Access for all: 🅿️🦽♿👂🔊🐕📷📖🔆
Building 🦽♿ **Grounds** 🦽♿➡️

Getting here: 188:TQ810380. **Foot**: from Sissinghurst village, past church to footpath on left, signposted to garden. Path can get muddy. **Cycle**: NCN18, 8 miles. **Bus**: special link from Staplehurst to Garden, Tuesday, Sunday and Bank Holidays only (telephone property for times) otherwise Arriva 5 Maidstone–Hawkhurst (passing Staplehurst ☒). Alight Sissinghurst 1¼ miles (20-minute walk). **Train**: Staplehurst 5½ miles.
Road: 2 miles north east of Cranbrook, 1 mile east of Sissinghurst village on Biddenden Road, off A262. **Parking**: 315 yards, £2.

Finding out more: 01580 710701 (Infoline). 01580 710700 or sissinghurst@nationaltrust.org.uk

Sissinghurst Castle Garden		M	T	W	T	F	S	S
Garden*								
13 Mar–31 Oct	11–6	M	T	·	·	F	S	S
Vegetable garden								
1 May–28 Sep	12–4	M	T	·	·	F	S	S
Shop and restaurant**								
13 Feb–7 Mar	11–4	·	·	·	·	·	S	S
13 Mar–31 Oct	10:30–5:30	M	T	·	·	F	S	S
1 Nov–21 Dec	11–4	M	T	·	·	F	S	S
Estate								
Open all year		M	T	W	T	F	S	S

*Closes half hour before dusk if earlier than 6. **Garden, shop and restaurant open Saturday, Sunday and Bank Holidays from 10. Also available: coffee shop and plant shop open from 13 March. Restrictions on entry into the garden may apply. Please note that the garden is more peaceful after 4.

Smallhythe Place

Smallhythe, Tenterden, Kent TN30 7NG

Map (2) I7   🏠 ❄ 1939

The half-timbered house, built in the early 16th century when Smallhythe was a thriving shipbuilding yard, was the home of the Victorian actress Ellen Terry from 1899 to 1928, and contains her fascinating theatre collection. The cottage grounds include her rose garden, orchard, nuttery and the working Barn Theatre.

Exploring
- Wonder at Ellen Terry's fabulous theatrical costume collection.
- Pick up an events programme for the excellent Barn Theatre.
- Discover Smallhythe's shipbuilding heritage with our fascinating exhibition.
- Ellen Terry's informal cottage garden – a tranquil retreat.

Eating and shopping: try local ale and cider at the Barn Theatre café. Look out for garden produce for sale in the autumn.

Making the most of your day: unique open-air theatre, indoor plays and music in the Barn Theatre. Family fun days, including children's theatre. Smallhythe Music and Beer Festival in September. Dogs allowed on leads in grounds.

Access for all: 🦽📖♿ ⦂🅿
Building 🦽🦽 Grounds 🦽➡

Getting here: 189:TQ893300. **Bus**: Coastal Coaches 312 Rye ➡–Tenterden. **Train**: Rye 8 miles; Appledore 8 miles; Headcorn 10 miles. **Road**: 2 miles south of Tenterden, on east side of Rye road (B2082). **Parking**: free (not National Trust), 50 yards. Coaches park at Chapel Down Winery, 500 yards.

Finding out more: 01580 762334 or smallhytheplace@nationaltrust.org.uk

Smallhythe Place			M	T	W	T	F	S	S
House									
27 Feb–31 Oct	11–5		M	T	W	·	·	S	S
Café									
27 Feb–31 Oct	12–4		M	T	W	·	·	S	S

Open Good Friday. Last admission 4:30 or dusk if earlier.

Smallhythe Place, Kent: the former home of Victorian actress Ellen Terry

South Foreland Lighthouse

The Front, St Margaret's Bay, Dover,
Kent CT15 6HP

Map ② K6  1989

A distinctive, historic landmark with unrivalled
views well worth the walk along the White
Cliffs. The building has a fascinating tale to
tell: a beacon of safety guiding ships past the
infamous Goodwin Sands; the first lighthouse
powered by electricity and the site of the first
international radio transmission. **Note**: no
access for cars. External decoration taking
place during May and June.

Exploring
  – Guided tours for all visitors.
  – Discover the challenges of
    navigating the Strait of Dover.
  – Learn about the pioneering
    scientific experiments of
    Marconi and Faraday.
  – 360-degree views of the Kent
    countryside and
    English Channel.

Eating and shopping: bottled water and
confectionery available. Small shop selling gifts
and souvenirs.

Making the most of your day: children's
events during school holidays. Guided
walks programme throughout the year, in
conjunction with The White Cliffs of Dover.
Dogs allowed in the grounds.

Access for all: 🖼️ ♿ ⠿ 🅿️
Building 🏢 Grounds ♿

Getting here: 179:TR359433. **No vehicular
access. Foot**: on public footpaths 2½ miles
from Dover, 1 mile from St Margaret's.
Cycle: NCN1, ½ mile. **Bus**: Stagecoach in East
Kent Diamond 15; Canterbury–Dover–Deal,
alight Bay Hill 1 mile (via Lighthouse Road).
Train: Martin Mill 2½ miles; Dover Priory
3½ miles by footpath.

South Foreland Lighthouse, Kent

Parking: **no onsite parking**. Parking at The
White Cliffs of Dover (National Trust), then
walk along clifftops to lighthouse (2 miles
approximately) or at St Margaret's village/bay,
Kent (1 mile approximately).

Finding out more: 01304 852463 or
southforeland@nationaltrust.org.uk

South Foreland Lighthouse		M	T	W	T	F	S	S
12 Mar–28 Mar	11–5:30	M	·	·	·	F	S	S
29 Mar–18 Apr	11–5:30	M	T	W	T	F	S	S
19 Apr–30 May	11–5:30	M	·	·	·	F	S	S
31 May–6 Jun	11–5:30	M	T	W	T	F	S	S
7 Jun–25 Jul	11–5:30	M	·	·	·	F	S	S
26 Jul–5 Sep	11–5:30	M	T	W	T	F	S	S
6 Sep–24 Oct	11–5:30	M	·	·	·	F	S	S
25 Oct–31 Oct	11–5:30	M	T	W	T	F	S	S

Admission by guided tour, last tour 5. Open by arrangement
during closed period for booked groups only.

Sprivers Garden

Horsmonden, Kent TN12 8DR

Map (2) H7 1966

Small 18th-century-style formal garden with walled and hedged compartments, herbaceous borders, a rose garden and nearby woodland walk. **Note**: occupied as private residence – administered by tenant. No access to house. No WC.

Getting here: 188:TQ693400. 3 miles north of Lamberhurst on B2162.

Finding out more: 01892 893868 or sprivers@nationaltrust.org.uk

Sprivers Garden		M	T	W	T	F	S	S
5 Jun–7 Jun	2–5	**M**	·	·	·	·	**S**	**S**

Woodland walk (outside garden) open all year.

Standen

West Hoathly Road, East Grinstead, West Sussex RH19 4NE

Map (2) G7  1973

Late Victorian family home brought vividly to life in this gem of the Arts & Crafts Movement. Standen is hidden at the end of a quiet Sussex lane with breathtaking views over the High Weald and Weirwood Reservoir. The design of the house is a monument to the combined genius of architect Philip Webb and his friend William Morris. All the big names of the Arts & Crafts period are represented, including ceramics by William De Morgan and metalwork by W. A. S. Benson. The beautiful hillside gardens provide year-round interest; the woodlands, a number of easily accessible walks.

Philip Webb, close friend of William Morris, designed Standen in West Sussex

Standen in West Sussex

Exploring
- Enjoy many designs of Morris & Co throughout the house.
- Explore the Sussex countryside through our picturesque woodland walks.
- Soak up the atmosphere of a Victorian family's home.
- Discover our lovely garden anew in every season.
- New: study and play with learning resources for all ages.
- New: learn about designers at Standen through our specialist trails.

Eating and shopping: discover our unique shop with gifts inspired by William Morris. Enjoy delicious local and seasonal food in the Barn Restaurant. Get fresh produce from the barrow in our kitchen garden. Add colour to your garden from our plant sales area.

You may also enjoy: Red House – William Morris's own home, also built by his friend, Philip Webb.

Making the most of your day: open-air theatre, guided walks, children's school holiday activity days, regular temporary exhibitions and workshops, introductory talks, conservation demonstrations, lecture lunches, special Christmas programme of festive events and activities. Dogs welcome on leads in designated areas, including the extensive woodland walks.

Access for all: 🅿️ 🐕 💧 🚻 👶 🖥️ ♿ ⦂ 🅰️
Building 🔼🔼🔼 **Grounds** 🔼🔼➡️

Getting here: 187:TQ389356. **Cycle**: NCN21, 1¼ miles. **Bus**: Metrobus 84 East Grinstead ⬛–Crawley (passing Three Bridges ⬛), alight at approach road just north of Saint Hill, ½ mile, or at Saint Hill, then ¾ mile by footpath. **Train**: East Grinstead 2 miles; Kingscote (Bluebell Railway) 2 miles. **Road**: 2 miles south of East Grinstead, signposted from town centre and B2110 (Turners Hill Road). **Parking**: free, 200 yards.

Finding out more: 01342 323029 or standen@nationaltrust.org.uk

Standen		M	T	W	T	F	S	S
27 Feb–7 Mar	11–4:30	·	·	·	·	·	**S**	**S**
13 Mar–4 Apr	11–4:30	·	·	**W**	**T**	**F**	**S**	**S**
5 Apr–18 Apr	11–4:30	**M**	·	**W**	**T**	**F**	**S**	**S**
21 Apr–25 Jul	11–4:30	·	·	**W**	**T**	**F**	**S**	**S**
26 Jul–30 Aug	11–4:30	**M**	·	**W**	**T**	**F**	**S**	**S**
1 Sep–24 Oct	11–4:30	·	·	**W**	**T**	**F**	**S**	**S**
25 Oct–31 Oct	11–4:30	**M**	·	**W**	**T**	**F**	**S**	**S**
6 Nov–19 Dec	11–3	·	·	·	·	·	**S**	**S**

Open Bank Holiday Mondays. Bank Holidays and event days: queuing on approach possible. **Shop and restaurant close at 5, garden at 5:30** (at 3, from 6 November to 19 December).

Stoneacre

Otham, Maidstone, Kent ME15 8RS

Map ② I6   🏠 ❀ 1928

15th-century half-timbered yeoman's house, featuring a great hall and surrounded by harmonious garden, orchard and meadows. **Note**: occupied as private residence and administered on the National Trust's behalf by tenants. No WC.

Getting here: 188:TQ800535. at north end of Otham village, 3 miles south east of Maidstone, 1 mile south of A20.

Finding out more: 01892 893861 or stoneacre@nationaltrust.org.uk

Stoneacre		M	T	W	T	F	S	S
20 Mar–2 Oct	11–5:30	·	·	·	·	·	**S**	·

Open Bank Holiday Mondays. Last admission one hour before closing. Coach bookings welcome.

Stowe Landscape Gardens

Buckingham, Buckinghamshire MK18 5DQ

Map ② D2 🏠🍴♠🔊☂ 1990

'I enjoyed my day – lovely sights and something new at every turn of the way.'
Hannah Gillman, Stony Stratford

The scale, grandeur and beauty of Stowe has inspired writers, philosophers, artists, politicians and members of the public from the 18th century to the present day. One of the most remarkable creations of Georgian England, Stowe was created by a family once so powerful they were richer than the king. Since the National Trust acquired the gardens in the late 1980s, an ambitious programme of restoration has ensured that over 40 temples and monuments remain, gracing an inspiring backdrop of lakes and valleys with an endless variety of walks and trails, a delight to explore at any time of year.
Note: Stowe House (not National Trust) open days: 01280 818166/818229.

Exploring
— Wander through one of the 18th-century's greatest landscapes.
— Pick your favourite temple and guess its hidden meaning.
— Enjoy the lakeside walks, wooded valleys and open vistas.
— Discover the deeper meaning of Stowe with a guided tour.

Eating and shopping: enjoy freshly produced meals in the tea-room. Find the perfect present in the gift shop. Pick the perfect picnic spot – among temples, lakes and valleys. Look for the mobile food buggy offering snacks and drinks.

You may also enjoy: intriguing Claydon and magnificent Waddesdon Manor.

Making the most of your day: guided walks most days. Tracker Packs for families. Occasional open-air theatre events. Dogs on leads only.

Access for all: 📶♿♿🚻🧑‍🦽🔉🚫📷
Building 🏠↕ **Grounds** 🧑‍🦽➡🚶

Getting here: 152:SP665366. **Foot**: 3 miles from Buckingham along Stowe Avenue and along bridleway through park. **Bus**: nearest buses serve Buckingham (3 miles), then taxi. **Train**: Bicester North 9 miles; Milton Keynes Central 14 miles. **Road**: 3 miles north west of Buckingham via Stowe Avenue, off A422 Buckingham–Banbury road. Motorway access from M40 (exits 9 to 11) and M1 (exits 13 or 15a). **Parking**: free, 200 yards.

Finding out more: 01494 755568 (Infoline). 01280 822850. 01280 818825 (Saturday and Sunday) or stowegarden@nationaltrust.org.uk

Stowe Landscape Gardens		M	T	W	T	F	S	S
Gardens, shop and tea-room*								
2 Jan–28 Feb	10:30–4						S	S
3 Mar–31 Oct	10:30–5:30			W	T	F	S	S
6 Nov–19 Dec	10:30–4						S	S
Shop only special Christmas opening								
3 Nov–17 Dec	11–3			W	T	F		
Parkland								
Open all year	Dawn–dusk	M	T	W	T	F	S	S

Open Bank Holiday Mondays and Monday and Tuesday during half terms 15 to 19 February, 31 May to 4 June, 25 to 29 October. Last admission 90 minutes before closing or dusk if earlier. **Closed Saturday 29 May.** *Tea-room closes 30 minutes before gardens and shop. Please note gardens may close early towards end of October due to shorter daylight hours. May close in severe weather conditions.

Stowe Landscape Gardens, Buckinghamshire: contains more than 40 temples and monuments

Uppark House and Garden

South Harting, Petersfield,
West Sussex GU31 5QR

Map ② E8  1954

This gem on the South Downs, rescued after a major fire in 1989, houses an elegant Georgian interior with a famous Grand Tour collection, which includes paintings, furniture and ceramics. An 18th-century dolls' house with original contents, is one of the highlights. The complete servants' quarters in the basement are shown as they were in Victorian days when H. G. Wells' mother was housekeeper. The beautiful and peaceful garden is now fully restored in the early 19th-century Picturesque style, in a downland and woodland setting.

Uppark House, West Sussex

Exploring
- Complete 18th-century dolls' house.
- Fascinating servants' tunnels to explore.
- Fabulous views across the Downs to the sea.
- House and garden trails and toy box for the children.
- Garden tours and welcome talks.
- Woodland walk with eco seat.

Eating and shopping: local honey from Paynes Southdown Bee Farm in the shop. Cheeses from Stonegate Cheese Dairy, Sussex, served in the restaurant.

You may also enjoy: Hinton Ampner.

Making the most of your day: 'Conservation in Action' week and 'A Closer Look' events enable you to make the most of your visit to the house and its collection. Dogs on leads on woodland walk only.

Access for all: 🅿️🐕♿🚾🍴♿📹 📷🅰️
House ♿♿⬆️♿ Shop and restaurant ♿♿♿
Gardens ♿♿➡️♿

Getting here: 197:SU775177. **Foot**: South Downs Way within ¾ mile. **Bus**: Countryliner 54 Petersfield ⭢–Chichester ⭢ (bus stop is 500 yards from property, via a steep hill). **Train**: Petersfield 5½ miles. **Road**: 5 miles south east of Petersfield on B2146, 1½ miles south of South Harting. **Parking**: free, 300 yards.

Finding out more: 01730 825857 (Infoline). 01730 825415 or uppark@nationaltrust.org.uk

Uppark House and Garden		M	T	W	T	F	S	S
House								
21 Mar–31 Oct	12:30–4:30	M	T	W	T	·	·	S
Part of house								
4 Dec–16 Dec	11–3	M	T	W	T	·	·	S
Garden, shop and restaurant								
21 Mar–31 Oct	11:30–5	M	T	W	T	·	·	S
4 Dec–16 Dec	11–3	M	T	W	T	·	·	S

Open Good Friday. Bank Holiday Mondays and Bank Holiday Sundays: garden, shop and restaurant open 11 to 5 and house 11:30 to 4:30. Open Saturday 4 December. Garden tours first Thursday of each month and every Thursday in July and August. Print Room open first Monday of each month (times as house).

Why not visit us by public transport? See page 376

The Vyne

Sherborne St John, Basingstoke,
Hampshire RG24 9HL

Map ② D6

Originally built as a great Tudor 'power house',
The Vyne was visited by King Henry VIII on at
least three occasions and later became a family
home, cherished by the Chute family for more
than 350 years. Dramatic improvements and
changes over the centuries have made The
Vyne a fascinating microcosm of changing
fads and fashions. The house is filled with an
eclectic mix of fine furniture, portraits, textiles
and sculpture. The attractive gardens and
grounds feature an ornamental lake, delightful
woodlands and flourishing wetlands, a haven
for wildlife and water fowl which can be
observed from the bird hide.

Exploring
– Discover 500 years of history
  in one family home.
– Stroll through the tranquil
  grounds and gardens.
– Don't miss the Tudor chapel
  visited by Henry VIII.
– Find out about the restoration
  of our Walled Garden.
– Explore our woodlands
  and wetlands, a rich haven
  for wildlife.

Eating and shopping: visit the Coach House
shop for gifts and local produce. Plants and
garden-related products in our tea-garden.
Delicious home-cooked food available in the
Tudor Brewhouse restaurant. New refreshment
kiosk in the car park.

You may also enjoy: other fine houses and
gardens: Mottisfont and Hinton Ampner.
Something completely different: Sandham
Memorial Chapel.

Making the most of your day: free quiz trails
and children's Tracker Packs. Waymarked
woodland walks. Changing displays within
house. Special events, from open-air theatre to

The Vyne, Hampshire: a great Tudor 'power house'

Orchard Day. Dogs welcome in the designated
picnic area, woods and parkland.

Access for all: 🅿♿🚻👶🧒👨‍🦽🐕🖥 🏊♿ Building ♿♿ Grounds ♿♿

Getting here: 175/186:SU639576.
Cycle: NCN23, 1 mile. **Bus**: Stagecoach in
Hampshire 45 from Basingstoke (passing
Basingstoke ➤). No Sunday service.
Train: Bramley 2½ miles; Basingstoke
4 miles. **Road**: 4 miles north of Basingstoke
between Bramley and Sherborne St John.
From Basingstoke Ring Road A339, follow
North Hampshire Hospital signs until property
signs. Follow A340 Aldermaston Road towards
Tadley. Right turn into Morgaston Road. Right
turn into car park. **Parking**: free, 40 yards.
⅓ mile walk through gardens from visitor
reception to house entrance.

Finding out more: 01256 883858 or
thevyne@nationaltrust.org.uk

The Vyne		M	T	W	T	F	S	S
House								
13 Mar–31 Oct	11–5	·	·	·	·	·	S	S
15 Mar–27 Oct	1–5	M	T	W	·	·	·	·
Gardens, shop and restaurant								
6 Feb–7 Mar	11–5	·	·	·	·	·	S	S
15 Feb–19 Feb	11–5	M	T	W	T	F	·	·
13 Mar–31 Oct	11–5	M	T	W	·	·	S	S
House, gardens, shop and restaurant								
4 Dec–19 Dec	11–3	M	T	W	·	·	S	S

House open Good Friday and Bank Holiday Mondays, 11 to 5.

Waddesdon Manor

Waddesdon, near Aylesbury,
Buckinghamshire HP18 OJH

Map ② D3 ⬛⬛⬛⬛⬛⬛⬛ 1957

Waddesdon Manor, Buckinghamshire, seen from the air

'The jewel in the National Trust's crown! We love the beautiful interior and our grandson loves the wonderful Woodland Playground.'
Mrs P. Hayes, Great Missenden

This renaissance-style château was built by Baron Ferdinand de Rothschild to display his outstanding collection of art treasures and to entertain the fashionable world. The 45 rooms on view combine the highest quality French furniture and decorative arts from the 18th century with superb English portraits and Dutch Old Masters. The Victorian garden is considered one of the finest in Britain with its parterre, seasonal displays, fountains and statuary. At its heart lies the aviary, stocked with species once part of Baron Ferdinand's collection. Visit the new contemporary art gallery in the Coach House at the Stables. **Note**: managed by a Rothschild family charitable trust. House entrance by timed tickets only.

Exploring
 — See one of the finest collections of Sèvres porcelain.
 — Marvel at Marie-Antoinette's writing desk.
 — Discover contemporary sculptures in the gardens.
 — Relax in the rose garden, aviary glade and parterre.
 — Enjoy the wildlife interpretation trail and woodland playground.
 — Visit the new contemporary art gallery at the Stables.

Eating and shopping: enjoy a meal in one of the two licensed restaurants. Have a snack or drink at the Summerhouse. Browse and buy in the shops and plant centre. Visit the old-fashioned sweet shop at the Stables.

You may also enjoy: Claydon, Cliveden, Hughenden Manor, King's Head and Stowe Landscape Gardens.

Making the most of your day: family events and free activities, children's quiz/trail and tours in school holidays. Special interest days, audio-visual presentations, wine tastings, Christmas opening and events, garden workshops, plant centre.

Access for all: ⬛⬛⬛⬛⬛⬛⬛⬛⬛⬛⬛
Building ⬛⬛⬛ Grounds ⬛➡

Getting here: 165:SP740169. **Bus**: Arriva 16 from Aylesbury (passing close Aylesbury ⬛). **Train**: Aylesbury Vale Parkway 2 miles; Aylesbury 6 miles; Haddenham & Thame Parkway 9 miles. **Road**: access via Waddesdon village, 6 miles north west of Aylesbury on A41; M40 (westbound) exit 6 or 7 via Thame and Long Crendon or M40 (eastbound) exit 9 via Bicester. **Parking**: free.

Finding out more: 01296 653211 (Infoline). 01296 653226 or waddesdonmanor@nationaltrust.org.uk

Members may have to pay on special events days

Waddesdon Manor		M	T	W	T	F	S	S
Gardens, aviary, woodland playground, shops and restaurants								
2 Jan–28 Mar	10–5	·	·	·	·	·	S	S
31 Mar–31 Dec	10–5	·	·	W	T	F	S	S
House and wine cellars								
31 Mar–29 Oct	12–4	·	·	W	T	F	·	·
3 Apr–31 Oct	11–4	·	·	·	·	·	S	S
17 Nov–23 Dec	12–4	·	·	W	T	F	·	·
20 Nov–19 Dec	11–4	·	·	·	·	·	S	S
House, wine cellars, gardens*, shops and restaurants								
27 Dec–31 Dec	12–4	M	T	W	T	F	·	·
Bachelors' Wing								
31 Mar–29 Oct	12–4	·	·	W	T	F	·	·

*Gardens include aviary and woodland playground. Open Bank Holiday Mondays. Last admission one hour before closing. Sculpture in garden uncovered week before Easter, weather permitting. Bachelors' Wing: space limited and entry cannot be guaranteed. Coffee bar and Summerhouse open weather permitting. Property closed 24 to 26 December. All visitors require a timed ticket to visit the house, including members, available from the ticket office or www.waddesdon.org.uk (limited number of tickets available for house daily – they may sell out on busy days, especially at weekends and throughout December).

Wakehurst Place

Ardingly, Haywards Heath,
West Sussex RH17 6TN

Map ② G7

'**Stunning gardens – wonderful ambitions and a credit to the nation.**'
Sue and Graham Gillion, Tasmania, Australia

The National Trust's most visited property. Open throughout the year, Wakehurst is the country estate of the Royal Botanic Gardens, Kew. The varied landscape is of international significance for its beautiful botanic gardens and tree collections, as well as for its science-based plant conservation and research. A feast for the senses, Wakehurst features natural woodland and lakes, formal gardens, an Elizabethan house and the 21st-century architecture of Kew's Millennium Seed Bank. Wakehurst marks an international conservation milestone in 2010, having conserved seeds from ten per cent of the world's plant species. **Note:** funded and managed by the Royal Botanic Gardens, Kew (www.kew.org).

Exploring
– Journey through changing landscapes of garden, wetland and woodland.
– Discover and enjoy plants from all around the world.
– Take time to visit the nature reserves.
– Watch science in action at the Millennium Seed Bank.
– Join one of the informative free guided tours.
– Be inspired as each season brings something new.

Eating and shopping: enjoy lunch of seasonal and local produce at The Stables. Fresh homemade sandwiches and cakes at the Seed Café. Take home the perfect gift from the Kew-run shop. Enhance your own garden with something from the plant centre.

You may also enjoy: the beauty of Nymans, the Arts & Crafts of Standen and Sheffield Park Garden.

Making the most of your day: year-round events. Daily tours. Children's trails and family guide. Kingfisher hide. Loder Valley nature reserve – additional woodland, wetland and meadowland – admission limited to 50 people per day.

Access for all:
Building Grounds

Kew's Millennium Seed Bank at Wakehurst Place, West Sussex

Visit

Getting here: 187:TQ339314. **Foot**: footpath from Balcombe (4 miles). **Bus**: Metrobus 81/82 Haywards Heath–Crawley (visit www.metrobus.co.uk for timetable and route). **Train**: Haywards Heath 6 miles; East Grinstead 6 miles. **Road**: on B2028, 1 mile north of Ardingly; 3 miles south of Turners Hill. From M23 exit 10, take A264 towards East Grinstead. **Parking**: not National Trust, charges may apply.

Finding out more: 01444 894066. wakehurst@kew.org; www.kew.org

Wakehurst Place		M	T	W	T	F	S	S
1 Jan–28 Feb	10–4:30	M	T	W	T	F	S	S
1 Mar–31 Oct	10–6	M	T	W	T	F	S	S
1 Nov–31 Dec	10–4:30	M	T	W	T	F	S	S

Last admission to Seed Bank and house 90 minutes before closing. Closed 24 and 25 December. Shop closed Easter Sunday. Note: reciprocal organisations do not receive free entry.

West Green House Garden

West Green, Hartley Wintney, Hampshire RG27 8JB

Map ② D6   1957

A delightful series of walled gardens surrounds the charming 18th-century house. **Note**: lessee has agreed to open on a limited basis.

Getting here: 175:SU745564. 1 mile west of Hartley Wintney, 10 miles north east of Basingstoke, 1 mile north of A30.

Finding out more: 01252 844611 or westgreenhouse@nationaltrust.org.uk

West Green House Garden		M	T	W	T	F	S	S
3 Apr–11 Sep	11–4	·	·	W	·	·	S	·

West Wycombe Park

West Wycombe, Buckinghamshire HP14 3AJ

Map ② E4   1943

The fine landscape garden was created in the mid 18th century by Sir Francis Dashwood, founder of the Dilettanti Society and Hellfire Club. The mansion is among the most theatrical and Italianate in England. Lavishly decorated, it has featured in films and television series, including, *Little Dorrit* and *The Duchess*. **Note**: Hellfire Caves and café privately owned.

Exploring
- Stroll round the beautiful lake.
- Discover the temples and follies created by Sir Francis.
- Imagine living in an aristocratic family home.

Eating and shopping: refreshments at garden centre and village pubs (not National Trust). Browse among the quaint high street shops (not National Trust).

Making the most of your day: fabulous guided tours of house on open weekdays. Hire an audio guide of park or try a family trail.

Access for all: 🅿️♿🔊📷
Building 🔽♿ Grounds ♿

Getting here: 175:SU828947. **Foot**: circular walk links West Wycombe with Bradenham and Hughenden Manor. **Bus**: Arriva 40 High Wycombe–Thame, Red Rose 275 High Wycombe–Oxford; Magpie Travel 321 High Wycombe–Princes Risborough. **Train**: High Wycombe 2½ miles. **Road**: 2 miles west of High Wycombe. At west end of West Wycombe, south of the Oxford road (A40). **Parking**: 250 yards. Disabled parking adjacent to house.

Finding out more: 01494 755571 (Infoline). 01494 513569 or westwycombe@nationaltrust.org.uk

The theatrical West Wycombe Park in Buckinghamshire

West Wycombe Park		M	T	W	T	F	S	S
Grounds only								
1 Apr–31 May	2–6	M	T	W	T	·	·	S
House and grounds								
1 Jun–31 Aug	2–6	M	T	W	T	·	·	S

Admission by guided tour only on weekdays, tours every 20 minutes (approximately). Last admission 45 minutes before closing.

West Wycombe Village and Hill

West Wycombe, Buckinghamshire

Map ② E4  1934

Historic village with cottages and inns of architectural interest dating from 16th century. Far-reaching views from West Wycombe Hill. **Note**: church, mausoleum and caves are not National Trust. Nearest WCs in village.

Getting here: 175:SU828946. 2 miles west of High Wycombe, on both sides of A40.

Finding out more: 01494 755573 or westwycombe@nationaltrust.org.uk

West Wycombe Village and Hill	M	T	W	T	F	S	S
Open all year	M	T	W	T	F	S	S

The White Cliffs of Dover

Langdon Cliffs, Upper Road, Dover, Kent CT16 1HJ

Map ② K7  1968

'**It's so beautiful. There is tons of wildlife. I wish all this was in my back yard.**' Alex Miller, aged nine, Carlisle

There can be no doubt that the White Cliffs of Dover are one of this country's most spectacular natural features. They are an official Icon of Britain and have been a sign of hope and freedom for centuries. Millions of people now wonder at them every year when crossing the English Channel. Thousands more now enjoy their special appeal through the seasons by taking one of the clifftop paths, offering views of the French coast and savouring the rare flora and fauna that can only be found across this chalk grassland. **Note**: WC only available when Visitor Centre open.

Exploring
- Spectacular cross Channel panorama to France.
- View the world's busiest shipping lanes.
- Dramatic clifftop countryside walks.

- Search out rare chalk grassland flora and fauna.
- Explore the hidden wartime heritage of Hellfire Corner.
- Discover the challenges of English Channel navigation at the lighthouse.

Eating and shopping: browse in the shop for gifts to suit all ages. White Cliffs souvenirs and items of local interest. Seasonal light lunches in the coffee shop. A unique view to accompany your afternoon tea.

You may also enjoy: a visit to the South Foreland Lighthouse.

Making the most of your day: self-guided walks and Tracker Packs. Events and guided walks throughout the year, including spring plant fair and Christmas walks. Dogs under close control at all times (stock grazing).

Access for all: 🅿 ♿ 🚻 🏢 📷 🎵 ⦿ 📷
Visitor Centre ♿♿ **Grounds** ♿

Getting here: 138:TR336422. **Foot**: signed pathways from the port, station and town centre. Located on the Saxon Shore Way

path. **Cycle**: NCN1. **Bus**: Stagecoach in East Kent Diamond 15 Canterbury–Dover–Deal, alight Castle Hill then 1 mile (via Upper Road – no footpath). Also 15a, alight Dover Docks. **Train**: Dover Priory 2½ miles. **Road**: from A2/A258 Duke of York roundabout, take A258 towards Dover town centre. After 1 mile turn left into Upper Road. Entrance on right after 1 mile. From A20 go straight ahead at first four roundabouts. Turn left at second set of lights into Woolcomber Street. Turn right onto Castle Street at next lights. After ½ mile turn right into Upper Road. Entrance on right after 1 mile. **Sat Nav**: may direct you to Eastern Docks.

Finding out more: 01304 202756 or whitecliffs@nationaltrust.org.uk

The White Cliffs of Dover		M	T	W	T	F	S	S
Visitor Centre								
1 Jan–28 Feb	11–4	M	T	W	T	F	S	S
1 Mar–31 Oct	10–5	M	T	W	T	F	S	S
1 Nov–31 Dec	11–4	M	T	W	T	F	S	S
Car park								
1 Jan–28 Feb	8–5	M	T	W	T	F	S	S
1 Mar–31 Oct	8–6	M	T	W	T	F	S	S
1 Nov–31 Dec	8–5	M	T	W	T	F	S	S

Visitor Centre closed 24, 25 and 26 December. Car park closed 24 and 25 December.

The White Cliffs of Dover, Kent: a sign of hope and freedom for centuries

Winchester City Mill, Hampshire

Winchester City Mill

Bridge Street, Winchester,
Hampshire SO23 0EJ

Map ②D7

The City Mill is a rare surviving example of an urban working corn mill, powered by the fast-flowing River Itchen, which can be seen passing under the mill, thrilling our visitors. Rebuilt in 1743 on a medieval mill site, it remained in use until the early 20th century. The National Trust recently undertook an ambitious restoration project, and the mill resumed grinding flour in March 2004. With hands-on activities for families and audio-visual displays about milling and the rich wildlife in the area, the City Mill is a lively and informative place for all ages to enjoy. **Note**: no WC.

Exploring
- Discover a millennium of milling history.
- Enjoy our weekend milling demonstrations.
- Have a go at milling flour using hand querns.
- Watch CCTV footage of Winchester's resident otters.
- Escape to the nearby Winnall Moors Nature Reserve.
- Watch our new video about the beautiful River Itchen.

Eating and shopping: browse in our shop for gifts, books and local produce. Buy a bag of freshly milled wholemeal flour.

You may also enjoy: Hinton Ampner, The Vyne, Sandham Memorial Chapel and Mottisfont.

Making the most of your day: wide ranging programme of events. Family activities and children's activities during school holidays. Regular milling demonstrations.

Access for all: 🚹♿🅿️🎧🖼️🚻👓📷 Building ♿

White Horse Hill

Uffington, Oxfordshire

Map ②C4   1979

The oldest chalk figure in the country and an Iron age hill fort, two of many local ancient sites. **Note**: archaeological monuments under English Heritage guardianship. No WC.

Getting here: SU299863. Southwest Oxfordshire, on the Ridgeway between Swindon and Wantage.

Finding out more: 01793 762209 (Buscot and Coleshill Estate Office) or whitehorsehill@nationaltrust.org.uk

White Horse Hill	M	T	W	T	F	S	S
Countryside							
Open all year	M	T	W	T	F	S	S
National Trust information trailer*							
3 Apr–26 Sep 10–4						S	S

*Information trailer may be closed at short notice.

Getting here: 185:SU487294. At foot of High Street, beside City Bridge. **Foot**: South Downs Way, King's Way, Itchen Way, Three Castles Path, Clarendon Way – all pass through or terminate at Winchester. **Bus**: from surrounding areas. **Train**: Winchester 1 mile. **Road**: junction 9 from north M3. Junction 10 from south M3. **Sat Nav**: postcode not appropriate. **Parking**: no onsite parking. Parking at Chesil car park. Park and Ride, St Catherines to Winchester from M3, exit 10.

Finding out more: 01962 870057 or winchestercitymill@nationaltrust.org.uk

Winchester City Mill		M	T	W	T	F	S	S
13 Feb–21 Feb	10:30–4	**M**	**T**	**W**	**T**	**F**	**S**	**S**
6 Mar–7 Mar	10:30–5	·	·	·	·	·	**S**	**S**
13 Mar–4 Apr	10:30–5	·	·	**W**	**T**	**F**	**S**	**S**
5 Apr–18 Apr	10:30–5	**M**	**T**	**W**	**T**	**F**	**S**	**S**
21 Apr–30 May	10:30–5	·	·	**W**	**T**	**F**	**S**	**S**
31 May–6 Jun	10:30–5	**M**	**T**	**W**	**T**	**F**	**S**	**S**
9 Jun–11 Jul	10:30–5	·	·	**W**	**T**	**F**	**S**	**S**
12 Jul–12 Sep	10:30–5	**M**	**T**	**W**	**T**	**F**	**S**	**S**
15 Sep–24 Oct	10:30–5	·	·	**W**	**T**	**F**	**S**	**S**
25 Oct–24 Dec	10:30–5	**M**	**T**	**W**	**T**	**F**	**S**	**S**

Open Bank Holiday Mondays including 1 January, 10 to 4.

Winkworth Arboretum

Hascombe Road, Godalming, Surrey GU8 4AD

Map (2) F7 1952

Established in the 20th century, this hillside arboretum now contains more than 1,000 different shrubs and trees, many of them rare. The most impressive displays are in spring, with magnolias, bluebells and azaleas, and autumn, when the colour of the foliage is stunning. In the summer it is an ideal place for family days out and picnics. **Note**: steep slopes and banks of lake are only partially fenced.

Exploring
- Woodlands offer peace and tranquillity.
- Superb display of old English bluebells in springtime.
- Magnolias, cherry blossom and azaleas.
- Famed for stunning autumn colour.
- Many unusual and rare trees.
- Award-winning collection: over 1,000 different shrubs and trees.

Eating and shopping: delicious home-prepared light lunches. Afternoon teas with homemade cakes and biscuits. Visit our small, friendly tea-room.

You may also enjoy: Sheffield Park Garden.

Making the most of your day: programme of events of walks and talks throughout the year (send sae for details). Dogs on leads only welcome throughout the year.

Access for all: Grounds

Getting here: 169/170/186:SU990412. **Bus**: Arriva 42/44 Guildford–Cranleigh (passing close Godalming). **Train**: Godalming 2 miles. **Road**: near Hascombe, 2 miles south east of Godalming on east side of B2130. **Parking**: free, 100 yards.

Finding out more: 01483 208477 or winkwortharboretum@nationaltrust.org.uk

Winkworth Arboretum		M	T	W	T	F	S	S
Arboretum								
Open all year	Dawn–dusk	**M**	**T**	**W**	**T**	**F**	**S**	**S**
Tea-room								
9 Jan–28 Feb	11–4	·	·	·	·	·	**S**	**S**
3 Mar–28 Mar	11–4	·	·	**W**	**T**	**F**	**S**	**S**
31 Mar–24 Oct	11–5	·	·	**W**	**T**	**F**	**S**	**S**
27 Oct–28 Nov	11–4	·	·	**W**	**T**	**F**	**S**	**S**
4 Dec–19 Dec	11–4	·	·	·	·	·	**S**	**S**

Tea-room open Bank Holiday Mondays. Arboretum may be closed in bad weather (especially in high winds).

Winkworth Arboretum, Surrey: famed for stunning colour

London

A particularly lavish corner of the rich interiors at Osterley Park and House, a feast for the senses

Outdoors in London

Despite being one of the world's major conurbations, London still contains numerous green and relatively tranquil areas. Many are fragments of the city's once extensive common land and have been saved thanks, in part, to the efforts of the National Trust.

The phenomenal growth of the capital over the centuries has meant that several Trust properties, which once stood in open countryside, now fall within the Greater London area. Sutton House in Hackney, for example, was once part of a small village, yet has long since been surrounded by encroaching development. It is now in the heart of a densely populated area, making it ideally placed for carrying out the Trust's work with local communities and inner-city schools.

A green haven

The large estate of Osterley Park is another property which has been subsumed by the city. It was originally created as a retreat, where wealthy guests could be entertained away from the hustle and bustle of urban life. Since then, of course, the city has crept up on it, and instead of being a countryside property it now sits in the midst of suburbia – providing a welcome green haven for local residents and visitors.

Valuable tranquil places

Osterley House was designed in 1761 by Robert Adam, the leading architect and interior designer of his day, and the interiors are dazzling and impressive. The land surrounding the mansion stretches to 145 hectares (359 acres) of park and farmland and is a much-loved local amenity. At present the Trust is in the midst of a major project which will gradually restore the gardens to their former 18th-century splendour.

An unexpected oasis

There is another unexpected oasis in South West London. Morden Hall Park is a picturesque and historic park with meadows, waterways and lovely old buildings. It also has an impressive rose garden with more than 2,000 rose bushes, and is the perfect safe haven, whether you want to take the family for a picnic or a pleasant day out or go for a stroll or a jog.

Accessible to all

A trip to Morden Hall Park or Osterley Park is particularly rewarding for all visitors with walking difficulties. Both properties have extremely accessible paths: Osterley Park boasts numerous routes suitable for wheelchair users – encircling the lake as well as through the wider parkland – while Morden Hall Park's routes run through the rose garden and along the River Wandle.

Above:
Morden Hall Park in South West London

Blewcoat School Gift Shop

23 Caxton Street, Westminster,
London SW1H OPY

Map (2) G5   🏠 | 1954

Built in 1709 as a school for poor children, this architectural gem now houses a shop selling attractive gifts. **Note:** no WC.

Getting here: 176:TQ295794. Near the junction of Caxton Street and Buckingham Gate.

Finding out more: 020 7222 2877 or blewcoat@nationaltrust.org.uk

Blewcoat School Gift Shop		M	T	W	T	F	S	S
Open all year	10–5:30	**M**	**T**	**W**	**T**	**F**	·	·
6 Nov–18 Dec	10–4	·	·	·	·	·	**S**	·

Closed Bank Holiday Mondays and Good Friday.

Carlyle's House

24 Cheyne Row, Chelsea, London SW3 5HL

Map (2) F5   🏛 ❖ | 1936

Preserved since 1895 this writer's house in the heart of one of London's most famous creative quarters tells the story of Thomas and Jane Carlyle. The couple moved here from their native Scotland in 1834 and became an unusual but much-loved celebrity couple of the 19th-century literary world.

Exploring
- Discover the writer who inspired Charles Dickens.
- Learn about the Carlyles' many other illustrious friends.
- Enjoy the evocative atmosphere in this Victorian literary shrine.

Making the most of your day: guided tours of Carlyle's House for booked groups (maximum 20), on Wednesday, Thursday and Friday at 11 till 12:30. Learn more about the area's literary and artistic heritage.

Access for all: 🔲 🔲 :: Building 🔲 Grounds 🔲

Getting here: 176:TQ272777. Off Oakley Street (between the King's Road and Albert Bridge), National Trust sign on corner of Upper Cheyne Row. Or off Cheyne Walk, National Trust sign on corner of Cheyne Row. **Foot:** Thames Path within ¾ mile. **Cycle:** NCN4. **Bus:** 11, 19, 22, 49, 319 to Carlyle Square then walk down Bramerton Street. 170 to Albert Bridge. **Train:** Victoria 2 miles. **Underground:** Sloane Square (District and Circle lines) 1 mile; South Kensington (Piccadilly, District and Circle lines) 1 mile. **Parking:** no parking. Very limited street parking at nearby meters (pay and display).

Finding out more: 020 7352 7087 or carlyleshouse@nationaltrust.org.uk

Carlyle's House		M	T	W	T	F	S	S
10 Mar–29 Oct	2–5	·	·	**W**	**T**	**F**	·	·
13 Mar–31 Oct	11–5	·	·	·	·	·	**S**	**S**

Open Bank Holiday Mondays, 11 to 5.

Ralph Waldo Emerson frequented Carlyle's House, Chelsea

Eastbury Manor House

Eastbury Square, Barking, London IG11 9SN

Map ② G5   1918

Important brick-built Tudor gentry house, completed about 1573, little altered since. Early 17th-century wall-paintings showing fishing scenes and a cityscape grace the former Great Chamber. Evocative exposed timbers in attic, fine original spiral oak staircase in turret, soaring chimneys, cobbled courtyard, peaceful walled garden with bee boles. **Note:** managed by the London Borough of Barking and Dagenham (www.barking-dagenham.gov.uk).

Exploring
– New: discover Eastbury through attic displays and fresh interpretation.
– Consider intriguing Gunpowder Plot connections (especially Saturday 6 November).
– Marvel at the skills of the Tudor builders and craftsmen.

Eating and shopping: relax in our garden tea-room, or at tables outside. Enjoy hot and cold drinks, sandwiches and snacks. Drop in to our Old Buttery gift shop.

Eastbury Manor House in Barking

Making the most of your day: volunteer-led guided tours. Themed Family Days every first Saturday of the month – tour guides in costume and homemade cakes. School holiday activities. Candlelit tours (last Tuesday of the month). Dogs in grounds only on leads.

Access for all:
Building   Courtyard   Grounds

Getting here: 177:TQ457838. In Eastbury Square, 750 yards walk south from Upney (District Line, follow brown signs). **Cycle:** LCN15 ¾ mile and local link. **Bus:** TfL 62, 287, 368. **Train:** Barking, 1½ miles, then Underground to Upney. **Road:** ½ mile north of A13, signposted from A123 Ripple Road. **Parking:** free parking on street adjacent to property.

Finding out more: 020 8724 1002 or eastburymanor@nationaltrust.org.uk

Eastbury Manor House		M	T	W	T	F	S	S
House and grounds								
Open all year	10–4	**M**	**T**	·	·	·	·	·
Tea-room and shop								
Open all year	10–3:30	**M**	**T**	·	·	·	·	·

Closed Bank Holiday Mondays and 27 and 28 December.
Also open every first and second Saturday of month.

Fenton House

Hampstead Grove, Hampstead, London NW3 6SP

Map ② G4   1952

'A treasure house full of charm and atmosphere. We were lucky enough to hear instruments played – the house came alive.'
Penny West, Highgate, London

This charming 17th-century merchant's house has remained architecturally little altered during more than 300 years of continuous occupation, while the large garden is also remarkably unchanged since it was described in 1756 as 'pleasant... well planted with fruit-trees, and a kitchen garden, all inclos'd

Fenton House, Hampstead: a charming 17th-century merchant's mansion

with a substantial brick wall'. Lady Katherine Binning bought the house in 1936 and filled it with her highly decorative collections of porcelain, Georgian furniture and 17th-century needlework. The sound of early keyboard instruments and the colours of early 20th-century drawings and paintings add to a captivating experience.

Exploring
– 'London's most enchanting country house' (*Country Life*).
– World-class collections of Oriental, European and English porcelain.
– Benton Fletcher Collection of early keyboard instruments, in playing condition.
– Delightful decorative schemes by John Fowler.
– Extensive walled garden with topiary hedges and fine mixed borders.
– Apple orchard and abundant displays of spring flowers.

Eating and shopping: range of property-related cards, books and CDs to buy.

You may also enjoy: 2 Willow Road, Sutton House and Carlyle's House.

Making the most of your day: Easter Trail and Apple Day. Summer lunchtime and evening concerts, demonstration tours of instruments. To audition to play the early keyboard instruments, email property.

Access for all: 🔲🏠📻📷📃
Building 🔲🏠 Grounds 🔲🏠

Getting here: 176:TQ262860. Visitors' entrance on west side of Hampstead Grove. **Bus**: frequent local services (020 7222 1234). **Train**: Hampstead Heath or Finchley Road & Frognal (Overground) 1 mile. **Underground**: Hampstead (Northern Line), 328 yards. **Parking**: no onsite parking.

Finding out more: 01494 755563 (Infoline). 020 7435 3471 or fentonhouse@nationaltrust.org.uk. Fenton House, Windmill Hill, Hampstead, London NW3 6RT

Fenton House		M	T	W	T	F	S	S
20 Mar–31 Oct	11–5						**S**	**S**
24 Mar–29 Oct	2–5			**W**	**T**	**F**		

Open Bank Holiday Mondays and Good Friday, 11 to 5.

Topiary at Ham House and Garden, Richmond-upon-Thames, Surrey: 400-year-old treasure trove

George Inn

The George Inn Yard, 77 Borough High Street, Southwark, London SE1 1NH

Map ② G5 1937

Dating from the 17th century this public house, leased to a private company, is London's last remaining galleried inn. **Note**: telephone to book a table.

Getting here: 176:TQ326801. On east side of Borough High Street, near London Bridge ≋.

Finding out more: 020 7407 2056 or georgeinn@nationaltrust.org.uk

George Inn			M	T	W	T	F	S	S
Open all year		*		M	T	W	T	F	S	S

*Open daily during normal licensing hours.

Ham House and Garden

Ham Street, Ham, Richmond-upon-Thames, Surrey TW10 7RS

Map ② F5  1948

A 400-year-old treasure trove waiting to be discovered and one of a series of grand houses and palaces alongside the River Thames. Ham House and Garden is an unusually complete survival of the 17th century that impressed in its day and continues to do so today. Rich in history and atmosphere, Ham is largely the vision of Elizabeth Murray, Countess of Dysart, who was deeply embroiled in the politics of the English Civil War and subsequent restoration of the monarchy. The fine interiors and historic gardens make this an unusual and fascinating place to visit.

Exploring
- Help us celebrate Ham's 400th anniversary throughout 2010.
- Discover an outstanding collection of furniture and textiles.
- Play with our interactive model of Ham House.
- Learn about 17th-century global trade.
- Relax in our historic gardens, including a kitchen garden.
- Enjoy home-grown produce in the Orangery Café.

Eating and shopping: try our home-cooked menus. Taste a delicious home-baked cake. Find an unusual gift in our shop.

You may also enjoy: Osterley Park and House – an extravagant 18th-century mansion.

Making the most of your day: free garden tours on some days, please check with property. Discovery room with interactive family activites. Family garden trails and explorer pack. Wide-ranging programme of events throughout the year.

Access for all: [access icons]
Building [icons] Grounds [icons]

Getting here: 176:TQ172732. On south bank of Thames, west of A307, between Richmond and Kingston; Ham gate exit of Richmond Park. **Foot**: Thames Path passes main entrance. 1½ miles from Richmond, 3 miles from Kingston. **Cycle**: NCN4. Ferry access from Twickenham. **Ferry**: Seasonal foot/bike ferry across River Thames from Twickenham towpath (by Marble Hill House–English Heritage) to Ham House. **Bus**: TfL 371 Richmond–Kingston, alight Ham Street by Royal Oak pub, then ½ mile walk. 65 Ealing Broadway–Kingston, alight Petersham Road by Ham Polo Ground, ¾ mile walk along historic avenues (both pass Richmond [rail] and Kingston) – 020 7222 1234. **Train**: Richmond 1½ miles by footpath, 2 miles by road. **Road**: on south bank of the Thames, west of A307, between Richmond and Kingston; Ham gate exit of Richmond Park, readily accessible from M3, M4 and M25. **Parking**: free, 400 yards (not National Trust).

Finding out more: 020 8940 1950 or hamhouse@nationaltrust.org.uk

Ham House and Garden		M	T	W	T	F	S	S
House 'sneak preview' tours*								
13 Feb–28 Feb	12–4	M	T	W		·	S	S
6 Mar–7 Mar	12–4	·	·	·	·	·	S	S
House								
13 Mar–31 Oct	12–4	M	T	W		·	S	S
Garden, shop and café								
2 Jan–7 Feb	11–4	·	·	·	·	·	S	S
13 Feb–31 Oct	11–5	M	T	W		·	S	S
6 Nov–19 Dec	11–5	·	·	·	·	·	S	S

Closed 1 January. Open Good Friday. *'Sneak preview' tours of selected rooms (30 minutes' duration). Tours start every half hour from 12 to 3:30. Places on tours are limited and available on a first-come, first-served basis on the day (20 tickets maximum per tour), normal admission charges apply (members free). Special Christmas openings: 4 and 5, 11 and 12, 18 and 19 December.

Lindsey House

99/100 Cheyne Walk, Chelsea, London SW10 0DQ

Map (2) G5   1951

Elegant 17th-century town house. Only the ground-floor entrance hall with staircase and the garden are accessible to visitors. **Note**: occupied by a tenant.

Getting here: 176:TQ268775. On Cheyne Walk, west of Battersea Bridge near junction with Milman Street on Chelsea Embankment.

Finding out more: 020 7799 4553 or lindseyhouse@nationaltrust.org.uk

Lindsey House

Only open on Saturday of London Open House weekend.

Morden Hall Park

Morden Hall Road, Morden, London SM4 5JD

Map ②G5 🏠🚽🍴🌣♣🚣🚶 1942

'The industrial heritage of the Wandle Valley echoes through this suburban oasis.'
Leo Hanmer, New Malden, Surrey

A green oasis in suburbia, giving visitors a glimpse back in time to Victorian London. This tranquil former deer park is one of the few remaining estates that lined the River Wandle during its industrial heyday. The river meanders through the park, creating a haven for wildlife, while the snuff mills, which generated the park's fortunes, still survive – with the western mill having been renovated into an Environmental Education Centre. The park is a much-loved rural idyll in a built-up area, and some of the surviving estate buildings are used as workshops by local craftspeople and artisans.

Exploring
- Enjoy the two miles of paths around the park.
- Discover the wetland wildlife and wildflower meadows.
- Relax in the fragrant rose garden from June to October.
- Look out for our colony of herons.
- Pick up a Family Explorer Pack for fun and discovery.
- Follow the Wandle Trail to Deen City Farm.

Eating and shopping: eat in the café with a delightful riverside setting. Browse in the shop for our extensive range of gifts. Visit our second-hand bookshop for a variety of books. Explore the garden centre (not National Trust) for your gardening.

You may also enjoy: on a grander scale – Ham House and Garden and Polesden Lacey.

Making the most of your day: selection of trails. Extensive events programme including walks, talks and open-air theatre. Snuff Mill open first and third Sunday from April to October. Thursday family activities in school holidays. Dogs on leads around buildings and rose garden; under close control elsewhere.

Access for all: 🅿🚻♿👶🔄📷♿ 📷
Building ♿♿♿ Grounds ♿➡

Getting here: 176:TQ261684. Near Morden town centre. **Foot**: Wandle Trail from Croydon or Carshalton to Wandsworth. **Cycle**: Sustrans route 20 passes through park. **Bus**: frequent from surrounding areas (020 7222 1234). **Train**: Tramlink to Phipps Bridge stop, on park boundary ½ mile. **Road**: off A24, and A297 south of Wimbledon, north of Sutton. **Parking**: free, 25 yards.

Finding out more: 020 8545 6850 or mordenhallpark@nationaltrust.org.uk

Morden Hall Park		M	T	W	T	F	S	S
Park								
Open all year	8–6	M	T	W	T	F	S	S
Shop and café								
Open all year	10–5	M	T	W	T	F	S	S
Bookshop								
Open all year	11–3	M	T	W	T	F	·	·
Open all year	12–4	·	·	·	·	·	S	S

Car park by café, shop and garden centre closes 6. Shop and café closed 1 January, 25 February and 25, 26 December. Rose garden and estate buildings area open 8 to 6. Snuff Mill Environmental Education Centre open first Sunday of April to October, 12 to 4.

Morden Hall Park, London

Osterley Park and House

Jersey Road, Isleworth, Middlesex TW7 4RB

Map ② F5  1949

With a spectacular mansion surrounded by gardens, park and farmland, Osterley is one of the last surviving country estates in London. Once described as 'the palace of palaces', Osterley was created in the late 18th century by architect and designer Robert Adam for the Child family to entertain and impress their friends and clients. Today you can explore the dazzling interior with handheld audio-visual guides, which bring the house to life in a completely new way. Outside the gardens are a delightful retreat from urban life and the park is perfect for picnics and leisurely strolls.

Exploring
- Atmospheric film in the Tudor stables brings Osterley to life.
- Extravagant show rooms created by the great designer Robert Adam.
- Explore servants' lives in the fascinating 'below stairs' area.
- Dressing up and hands-on activities for children.
- Beautiful gardens currently being restored to their 18th-century glory.
- Varied events programme, including walks, tours and themed weeks.

Eating and shopping: enjoy homecooked lunches and afternoon teas in the Stables Café. Browse in the National Trust gift shop. Farm shop with fresh vegetables and flowers.

You may also enjoy: Ham House and Garden near Richmond-upon-Thames, and Cliveden near Maidenhead.

Making the most of your day: family activities and trails for the house and garden. Walks around park and lake; free leaflet available. Cycling in park on shared paths. Dogs allowed in park only (on leads unless indicated).

Osterley Park and House, Middlesex

Access for all: 🅿️♿♿♿♿🚻♿♿🔖📷🖼️ 📺♿♿🖊️ House ♿♿ Café and shop ♿♿ Garden ♿➡️♿♿

Getting here: 176:TQ146780. **Cycle**: links to London cycle network. **Bus**: TfL H28 Hayes–Hounslow–Osterley, H91 Hounslow–Hammersmith to within 1 mile. **Train**: Isleworth 1½ miles. **Underground**: Osterley (Piccadilly Line) 1 mile. **Road**: on A4 between Hammersmith and Hounslow. Follow brown tourist signs on A4 between Gillette Corner and Osterley underground station; from west M4, exit 3 then follow A312/A4 towards central London. Main gates at junction with Thornbury and Jersey Roads. **Sat Nav**: enter 'Jersey Road' and 'TW7 4RB'. **Parking**: 400 yards. Booked coach parking free.

Finding out more: 020 8232 5050 or osterley@nationaltrust.org.uk

Osterley Park and House		M	T	W	T	F	S	S
House								
3 Mar–31 Oct	12–4:30	·	·	W	T	F	S	S
4 Dec–19 Dec	12–3:30	·	·	·	·	·	S	S
Garden								
3 Mar–31 Oct	11–5	·	·	W	T	F	S	S
Park and car park*								
1 Jan–27 Mar	8–6	M	T	W	T	F	S	S
28 Mar–30 Oct	8–7:30	M	T	W	T	F	S	S
31 Oct–31 Dec	8–6	M	T	W	T	F	S	S
Café and shop**								
3 Mar–31 Oct	11–5	·	·	W	T	F	S	S
3 Nov–19 Dec	12–4	·	·	W	T	F	S	S

Open Good Friday and Bank Holiday Mondays. *Car park closed 1 January, 25 and 26 December. **Shop opens at 12.

Rainham Hall

The Broadway, Rainham, Havering, London RM13 9YN

Map ② H5 🏠🏠❄ 1949

Charming Georgian house set in a peaceful, simple garden, with some surprising features, quality materials and fine craftmanship. Awaiting conservation. **Note**: no WC.

Getting here: 177:TQ521821. 5 miles east of Barking. Just south of the church.

Finding out more: 020 7799 4552 or rainhamhall@nationaltrust.org.uk

Rainham Hall		M	T	W	T	F	S	S
3 Apr–30 Oct	2–5						S	

Open Bank Holiday Mondays, April to October, 2 to 5. Open for Rainham Christmas Fair and May Day event.

Stained-glass with William Morris's motto at Red House, Bexleyheath

Red House

Red House Lane, Bexleyheath, London DA6 8JF

Map ② H5 🏠🏠❄ 2003

'**A great treat to explore a charming garden and atmospheric house. Friendly people and delicious teacakes made our day. Thanks!**' Mr and Mrs Fletcher, Barnstaple

The only house commissioned, created and lived in by William Morris, founder of the Arts & Crafts movement, Red House is a building of extraordinary architectural and social significance. When it was completed in 1860, it was described by Edward Burne-Jones as 'the beautifullest place on earth'. Only recently acquired by the Trust, the house is not fully furnished, but the original features and furniture by Morris and Philip Webb, stained glass and paintings by Burne-Jones, the bold architecture and a garden designed to 'clothe the house', add up to a fascinating and rewarding place to visit.

Exploring
- Enjoy this unique place at your own leisure.
- Book a guided tour to discover more.
- Relax in the garden and play croquet on the lawn.
- Follow the leafy garden trail, perfect for children.
- Discover the original stables.

Eating and shopping: Morris-related gifts – textiles, books, china, homeware. Second-hand bookshop in the old stables. Delicious light refreshments – all served with a smile.

You may also enjoy: Standen.

Making the most of your day: Easter Fun, 150th Anniversary Arts & Crafts Fair, Open Day, Apple Day in the orchard and carols at Christmas. Garden games, nature trail and picnicking in the orchard always available.

Access for all:
Building 🔧 Grounds

Getting here: 177:TQ481750. **Bus**: frequent local services. **Train**: Bexleyheath ⊠, ¾ mile. **Road**: M25 Jct 2 to A2 for Bexleyheath. Exit at Danson interchange and follow A221 Bexleyheath. **Parking**: no onsite parking (except disabled parking space, which must be booked). Parking at Danson Park (approximately 1 mile). Charge at weekends and Bank Holidays.

Finding out more: 020 8304 9878 or redhouse@nationaltrust.org.uk

Red House		M	T	W	T	F	S	S
3 Mar–28 Nov	11–5	·	·	**W**	**T**	**F**	**S**	**S**
3 Dec–19 Dec	11–5	·	·	·	·	**F**	**S**	**S**

Open Bank Holiday Mondays. Guided tours at 11, 11:30, 12, 12:30 and 1. Free-flow self-guided viewing from 1:30 until last entry at 4:15.

The Tudor Sutton House, Hackney

'Roman' Bath

5 Strand Lane, London WC2

Map ② G5 🏛 1948

Remains of a bath – possibly Roman. Viewed through a grille all year, appointments required to see interior. **Note**: administered and maintained by Westminster City Council. No WC.

Getting here: 176:TQ309809. Just west of Aldwych station (now closed), approach via Surrey Street.

Finding out more: 020 7641 5264 (bookings). 020 8232 5050 or romanbath@nationaltrust.org.uk

'Roman' Bath		M	T	W	T	F	S	S
1 Apr–30 Sep	1–5	·	·	**W**	·	·	·	·

Admission by appointment only with Westminster County Council during office hours (020 7641 5264, 24-hours' notice). Bath visible through grille from pathway all year, 9 to dusk.

Sutton House

2 and 4 Homerton High Street, Hackney, London E9 6JQ

Map ② G4 🏠 🔔 1938

Built in 1535 by prominent courtier of Henry VIII, Sir Ralph Sadleir, Sutton House retains much of the atmosphere of a Tudor home despite some alterations by later occupants, including a succession of merchants, Huguenot silkweavers, and squatters. Discover oak-panelled rooms, original carved fireplaces and a charming courtyard.

Exploring
– Experience the sights and smells of a real Tudor kitchen.
– Relax in our tranquil and stunning courtyard.
– Enjoy interactive treasure chests representing our unusual residents.
– Discover a hidden gem in the heart of East London.

Eating and shopping: charming, fully licensed tea-room. Browse in the second-hand bookshop. Small shop, stocking limited range of local and Trust goods.

Making the most of your day: lively and varied programme of events for all tastes and ages. Craft fairs, fantastic themed family days. Monthly Sunday guided tours, February to November.

Access for all: ⬛⬛⬛⬛⬛⬛⬛⬛⬛⬛
Building ⬛⬛⬛⬛

Getting here: 176:TQ352851. At the corner of Isabella Road and Homerton High Street. **Cycle**: NCN1, 1¼ miles. **Bus**: frequent local services (020 7222 1234). **Train**: Hackney Central ¼ mile; Hackney Downs ½ mile. **Parking**: no onsite parking. Limited metered parking on adjacent streets.

Finding out more: 020 8986 2264 or suttonhouse@nationaltrust.org.uk

Sutton House	M	T	W	T	F	S	S
Historic rooms							
4 Feb–19 Dec 12:30–4:30	·	·	·	**T**	**F**	**S**	**S**
Café, gallery and shops							
4 Feb–19 Dec 12–4:30	·	·	·	**T**	**F**	**S**	**S**

Open Bank Holiday Mondays. Closed Good Friday. Sutton House is a lively property in regular use by local community groups. The rooms will always be open as advertised, but please telephone in advance if you would like to visit the property during a quiet time.

2 Willow Road

Hampstead, London NW3 1TH

Map ② G5   🏠 | 1994 |

This unique Modernist home was designed by architect Ernö Goldfinger in 1939 for himself and his family. With surprising design details that were ground-breaking at the time and still feel fresh today, the house also contains the Goldfingers' impressive collection of modern art, intriguing personal possessions and innovative furniture. **Note**: nearest WC at local pub.

Exploring
– Join a tour.
– Or explore on your own between 3 and 5.

Exploring
– See a special display about Goldfinger's designs for children.

Making the most of your day: evening events, London guided walks programme. Local attractions, including Fenton House. Children's quiz/trail.

Access for all: ⬛⬛⬛⬛⬛⬛ **Building** ⬛⬛

Getting here: 176:TQ270858. On corner of Willow Road and Downshire Hill. **Foot**: from Hampstead Underground, left down High Street and first left down Flask Walk (pedestrianised). Turn right at the end into Willow Road and walk down the hill almost to end of road. **Bus**: frequent local services (020 7222 1234). **Train**: Hampstead Heath ¼ mile. **Underground**: Hampstead (Northern Line) ¼ mile. **Parking**: no onsite parking. Limited onstreet parking. East Heath Road municipal car park, 100 yards, open intermittently (usually closed Bank Holiday weekends, due to local fair).

Finding out more: 01494 755570 (Infoline). 020 7435 6166 or 2willowroad@nationaltrust.org.uk

2 Willow Road	M	T	W	T	F	S	S
13 Mar–31 Oct 12–5	·	·	·	**T**	**F**	**S**	**S**
6 Nov–28 Nov 12–5	·	·	·	·	·	**S**	**S**

Entry by guided tour only at 12, 1 and 2. Places on tours limited and available on a first-come first-served basis on the day. Non-guided viewing 3 to 5, with timed entry when busy. Introductory film shown at regular intervals. Thursdays and Fridays are generally less busy.

The Top Landing at 2 Willow Road, Hampstead

East of England

A windmill stands proud against the sometimes bright, sometimes moody, skies at Wicken Fen

by Charles Taylor, supporter

Outdoors in the East of England

The East of England is a region of surprising contrasts. Dramatic seascapes, breathtaking views over sweeping scenery, acres of parkland to explore, gardens in which to sit and watch life pass by – whatever mood you are in you'll find somewhere to match it.

Dotted along the roads of the region you will spot brown signs with a white acorn logo and a place name. Those that follow the signs already know what pleasures are to be found: whether it's a stately home set in beautiful parkland, a wild stretch of coast, a tree cathedral or an ancient fen abundant with wildlife.

The Trust cares for 11,000 hectares (27,000 acres) of land, of which almost half supports such a rich biological diversity that they are designated Sites of Special Scientific Interest. Whether you are a serious 'twitcher' or just enjoy getting out into the countryside, regular visitors know that time spent in these wonderful places is time well spent.

Wicken Fen National Nature Reserve in Cambridgeshire is a haven for rare wildlife and virtually the last remnant of the extensive wild fenland that once covered much of the East of England. Now in its tenth year, the 'Wicken Fen Vision' aims to create the largest nature reserve in the region, offering access to people and wildlife in an area increasingly under pressure from surrounding development.

If you are a member you can explore more than 49 miles of coastline in the East of England.

The North Norfolk coast, as well as being home to several major colonies of common and grey seals, hosts more than 3,000 pairs

Below: **Wicken Fen National Nature Reserve, Cambridgeshire**

of breeding Sandwich terns in the summer, while in the autumn and winter thousands of waders and waterfowl descend upon the marshes of Blakeney Freshes.

The Trust maintains this delicate mecca for people and wildlife for the benefit of future generations, successfully balancing access with conservation.

Above:
family fun week at Brancaster Millennium Activity Centre, Norfolk

Further down the coast in Suffolk is Orford Ness, the once-secret military test site which is now an internationally important nature reserve and vital habitat for rare species. Unique is a term often overused, however Orford Ness is something special: with it's rare flora and fauna, and unusual military architecture.

Natural habitats nearby include Dunwich Heath, a surviving fragment of the sandy heaths locally known as the Sandlings. The heath is where the rare Dartford warbler returned to this part of the country, and is now home to a strong breeding population. When the heather and gorse are in full bloom you will struggle to find a more colourful breath of fresh air!

Ascending above the rhododendron canopy at Sheringham Park, visitors are treated to a magnificent sight; stretching away from you to the sea is a riot of colour and scents guaranteed to lift the tiredest of spirits (see 'My favourite place', overleaf).

History alive

Ever thought you'd like to take a step back in time and experience life as it may have been in the past? Well, at various properties throughout the East of England this year you'll have the opportunity to time travel with us back to the dramatic periods that shaped our country, and us.

At Sutton Hoo you could find yourself in the royal presence of King Raedwald himself as he tells you of the battles he fought to shape our nation, or get your hands dirty with a 1930s archaeologist, one of the amateur band who discovered Raedwald's ship burial.

Life above and below stairs before the Second World War is brought vividly to life at Blickling Hall. See if you would have preferred to shine shoes or clean a fire grate as one of the army of staff; or perhaps you would have liked to accompany the famous garden designer Norah Lindsay as she sketched out plans for the fashionably new double borders?

The dramatic years of the Second World War were a time of sacrifice and hardship, but it was an age of unprecedented community spirit. Join in at Wimpole Hall or Anglesey Abbey and whisk yourself back to a time of powdered egg and rationing. Take a turn with the Home Guard or learn how to make do and mend – or even take the opportunity to taste what many people lived on in the blackout.

With a multitude of historical events throughout the season at places like Ickworth, Hatfield Forest, Shaw's Corner, Melford Hall and Oxburgh, you'll be able to fly through the centuries like a Time Lord!

The start of an adventure

A visit to a National Trust property is an ideal place to start your exploration of an area. Most of the places you'll visit with the Trust are set in, or near, historic, beautiful, bustling, tranquil or picturesque towns and villages.

On the Essex/Suffolk border, at the heart of 'Constable Country', Bridge Cottage is the perfect starting point for a breathtaking walk into the beautiful Dedham Vale.

My favourite place

It is the middle of May as I stroll along the main driveway of Sheringham Park through acres of rhododendrons, admiring the billows of pink and purple flower heads sparkling in the sunshine.

The cultivated species provide a wonderful show, but wild rhododendrons in the surrounding woodland are weeds and swamp the native trees. Fortunately, there is a merry band of volunteers (me among them) happy to take on, under the expert leadership and guidance of the National Trust staff, the never-ending job of rhododendron clearing and other woodland management tasks.

I like to pause at the thatched shelter and look to the right through the trees, across fields and meadows to the coastguard lookout and the sea. As I follow the curved path, I can see the beautiful proportions of Sheringham Hall. Here, I either turn right, past the farm and grazing cows into the flint-walled village of Upper Sheringham, or turn left and follow the path along the edge of the woods to Weybourne Station.

For a real sense of escapism, I like to climb the gazebo tower behind Sheringham Hall and look out across the canopy of oak trees and enjoy the stunning view along the North Norfolk coast. The steam train on the Poppy Line often puffs into view on its way through the fields of oilseed rape, and on a clear day you can see Weybourne Mill and the shingle spit to Blakeney Point. A perfect panorama!

Humphry Repton, originator of the term 'landscape gardener', designed Sheringham Park and described it as his 'most favourite work'. It is certainly my favourite place.

David Tottman
National Trust volunteer

Many other excellent walks are to be had on Dunstable Downs in Bedfordshire, which command outstanding views over the Vale of Aylesbury and along the Chiltern Ridge. A great starting point is the new Gateway Centre sitting atop the Downs and offering wonderful views.

If you take the opportunity to stay in one of the Trust's many holiday cottages, you'll find them a perfect base to explore the surrounding property, countryside or towns.

Burnham Overy in North Norfolk is one of the prettiest spots you'll see, and the nearby coastal villages of Brancaster and Stiffkey offer the chance to potter about the galleries and shops. Or if you are feeling more energetic then take a trip out to sea to see the seals. And if the weather is kind, why not just kick off your shoes and feel the sand between your toes as you wander along some of Britain's finest beaches?

Above:
fabulous views at Sheringham Park, Norfolk

Anglesey Abbey, Gardens and Lode Mill

Quy Road, Lode, Cambridge, Cambridgeshire CB25 9EJ

Map ③ G7　🏠 ✕ ❄ 🍴　1966

'**Just like home, sinking into a chair with a newspaper – bliss!**'
The Rodgers family, Yorkshire

A passion for tradition and impressing guests inspired one man to transform a run-down country house and desolate landscape. At the age of 30, the future Lord Fairhaven began to create his first home. Wanting to inspire and surprise visitors, he created a spectacular garden with planting for all seasons, and a cosy house in which to entertain. Life revolved around horse racing and shooting, and guests enjoyed 1930s luxury. Inside, fine furnishings, books, paintings, silver and rare clocks give a feeling of opulence. Outside, 46 hectares (114 acres) offer vibrant colour, delicious scent, and the simple pleasures of nature.

Exploring
– Imagine yourself a guest stepping into the elegant dining room.
– Catch the chime of one of the 37 rare clocks.
– Peek at the dapper outfits in Lord Fairhaven's wardrobe.
– Feel the wow factor of the Himalayan silver birches.
– Look and listen to discover all kinds of amazing creatures.
– Unwind with a peaceful stroll through the gardens.

Eating and shopping: visit the plant centre and recreate the look. Dip into the shop for locally sourced gifts. Try delicious home-cooked food, made with fresh local ingredients. Feel revitalised in the tranquil setting of Redwoods Restaurant.

You may also enjoy: learn about 1930s life below stairs at Blickling Hall.

Making the most of your day: exhibitions, activities and events all year around. Family trails and activity packs. Experience 1930s living and discover fascinating facts with the help of room cards and volunteer room guides.

Access for all: 🅿♿🚻🚹🔍📷📖🖥 VI
🔼⠿Ⓐ **Building** ♿♿ **Grounds** 🚶➡🚸♿

Lode Mill at Anglesey Abbey, Cambridgeshire

Getting here: 154:TL533622. **Foot**: Harcamlow Way from Cambridge. **Cycle**: NCN51, 1¼ miles. **Bus**: Stagecoach in Cambridge 10 from Cambridge (frequent services link Cambridge ➔ and bus station). **Train**: Cambridge 6 miles. **Road**: 6 miles north east of Cambridge on B1102. Signposted from A14, junction 35. **Sat Nav**: systems may give incorrect directions owing to recent postcode change. **Parking**: free, 50 yards.

Finding out more: 01223 810080 or angleseyabbey@nationaltrust.org.uk

Anglesey Abbey		M	T	W	T	F	S	S
Garden, restaurant, shop and plant centre								
1 Jan–28 Feb	10:30–4:30	M	T	W	T	F	S	S
1 Mar–31 Oct	10:30–5:30	M	T	W	T	F	S	S
1 Nov–31 Dec	10:30–4:30	M	T	W	T	F	S	S
House								
3 Mar–31 Oct	11–5			W	T	F	S	S
Lode Mill								
1 Jan–28 Feb	11–3:30	M	T	W	T	F	S	S
1 Mar–31 Oct	11–5	M	T	W	T	F	S	S
1 Nov–31 Dec	11–3:30	M	T	W	T	F	S	S

House open Bank Holiday Mondays. Closed Christmas Eve, Christmas Day and Boxing Day. Areas of garden open according to season. Snowdrop season 18 January to 21 February. Picture galleries and dining room only also open 1 to 17 January and 17 November to 31 December, 11 to 3:30.

Blakeney National Nature Reserve

Morston Quay, Quay Road, Morston, Norfolk NR25 7BH

Map ③ I3

Wide open spaces and uninterrupted views of the natural and dynamic coastline make for an inspiring visit to Blakeney, at any time of the year. The moving tides, covering pristine saltmarsh or exposing the harbour, combined with the varying light of Norfolk's big skies, create an ever-changing scene. **Note**: nearest WC at Morston Quay and Blakeney Quay (not National Trust).

Exploring
- Blakeney Point – internationally important for seabirds and seals.
- Follow the Norfolk Coast Path for great views and wildlife.
- Learn about marine life at Stiffkey, Morston and Blakeney.
- Guided walks (small charge) for schools and groups by arrangement.

Eating and shopping: refreshments and seafood stall (not National Trust) at Morston Quay. Seafood, including Morston Mussels from local suppliers (not National Trust). Nearby pubs and hotels offering locally themed menus.

Making the most of your day: learn more about this dynamic coastal environment – Information Centres at Morston Quay and Blakeney Point. Dogs welcome, some restrictions apply (particularly Blakeney Point) from 1 April to mid August.

Access for all: 🖵 Morston Quay Information Centre 🏔 Lifeboat House and WCs 🚻

Getting here: 133:TG000460. **Foot**: Norfolk Coast Path passes property. **Cycle**: Regional route 30 runs along ridge above the coast. **Ferry**: to Blakeney Point (not National Trust).

Blakeney National Nature Reserve, Norfolk

Bus: Norfolk Green 'Coast Hopper' Cromer–Hunstanton 🚂. **Train**: Sheringham 8 miles. **Road**: Morston Quay, Blakeney and Cley are all off A149 Cromer–Hunstanton road. **Parking**: Pay and display at Morston Quay. Sat Nav NR25 7BH. Car £3 all day (50p after 6), car with trailer £4, coach £10. Parking also at Blakeney Quay (administered by Blakeney Parish Council), Sat Nav NR25 7NE. Quayside car parks are liable to tidal flooding.

Finding out more: 01263 740241 or blakeneypoint@nationaltrust.org.uk. Norfolk Coast Office, Friary Farm, Cley Road, Blakeney, Norfolk NR25 7NW

Blakeney	M	T	W	T	F	S	S
Blakeney National Nature Reserve							
Open all year	M	T	W	T	F	S	S
Lifeboat House (Blakeney Point)*							
5 Apr–30 Sep	M	T	W	T	F	S	S

*Lifeboat House and WCs (Blakeney Point) open dawn to dusk. Refreshment kiosk (not National Trust) and Information Centre at Morston Quay open according to tides and weather.

Blickling Hall, Gardens and Park

Blickling, Norwich, Norfolk NR11 6NF

Map ③ J4

At Blickling, you can go on a journey of discovery and follow four centuries of history. Imagine yourself a guest at one of Lord Lothian's house parties just before the outbreak of war, discussing the latest politics and religious matters.

Learn what life was like as a servant and hear the stories of the real people who kept Blickling going. The estate is a treasure trove of romantic buildings, beautiful and extensive gardens and landscaped park. From herbaceous formal gardens to the stunning parterre and woodland wilderness, there is something for everyone at any time of the year.

Exploring — Experience the four seasons through the spectacular garden.
— Discover the splendour of a country house through four centuries.
— See the interiors inspired by the people in the portraits.
— Listen to the actual voices of Blickling's servants.
— Enjoy the tranquillity of the lake (coarse fishing available).
— Follow Blickling's wartime history in the RAF Museum.

Eating and shopping: browse for that special gift in our East Wing shop. Enjoy local seasonal food in the restaurant and Courtyard Café. Plant Centre and Garden Shop for the green fingered. Second-hand bookshop with bargains from 50p to £150.

You may also enjoy: Experience the luxurious 1930s' lifestyle of Lord Fairhaven at Anglesey Abbey.

Making the most of your day: highlight tour of house most mornings, afternoon garden tours, RAF Museum, croquet in garden, cycle hire. Events and exhibitions throughout the year. Dogs welcome in park and woods, on leads at all times.

Access for all: 🅿️ 🚻 ♿ 🔊 🎧 📷 ♿ 👁️ Ⓐ

Building 🏠♿⬆️♿ **Grounds** ♿➡️♿♿

Getting here: 133:TG178286. **Foot**: Weavers' Way from Great Yarmouth and Cromer (Aylsham, 2 miles). **Cycle**: permitted path alongside Bure Valley Railway, Wroxham 🚉– Aylsham. **Bus**: Sanders 4, 41/43/44, First 50, Norfolk Green X5 Norwich–Holt/Sheringham (passing close Norwich 🚉), alight Aylsham 1½ miles. **Train**: Aylsham (Bure Valley Railway from Hoveton & Wroxham 🚉) 1¾ miles; North Walsham 8 miles. **Road**: 1½ miles north west of Aylsham on B1354. Signposted off A140 Norwich (15 miles north) to Cromer (10 miles south) road. **Parking**: 400 yards, £2.50.

Finding out more: 01263 738030 or blickling@nationaltrust.org.uk

Blickling Hall		M	T	W	T	F	S	S
House								
27 Feb–18 Jul	11–5	·	·	W	T	F	S	S
21 Jul–5 Sep	11–5	M	·	W	T	F	S	S
8 Sep–31 Oct	11–5		·	W	T	F	S	S
Garden, shop, restaurant and bookshop								
2 Jan–26 Feb	11–4	·	·	·	T	F	S	S
27 Feb–31 Oct	10:15–5:15	M	T	W	T	F	S	S
4 Nov–31 Dec	11–4	·	·	·	T	F	S	S
Plant centre								
13 Mar–31 Oct	10:15–5:15	M	T	W	T	F	S	S
Cycle hire								
3 Apr–31 Oct	10:15–5	·	·	·	·	·	S	S
Park								
Open all year		M	T	W	T	F	S	S

House also open Monday 5, 12, 19 April, 3 and 31 May. Cycle hire available daily during Norfolk County Council school holidays. Property closed 1 January, plus 25 and 26 December.

Blickling Hall, Gardens and Park, Norfolk: discover four centuries of history

Bourne Mill

Bourne Road, Colchester, Essex CO2 8RT

Map ③ I8   1936

A delightful piece of late Elizabethan playfulness. Built for banquets and converted into a mill, still with working waterwheel.
Note: no WC. Limited parking in mill grounds.

Bourne Mill, Essex

Getting here: 168:TM006238. 1 mile south of centre of Colchester, in Bourne Road, off the Mersea Road (B1025).

Finding out more: 01206 572422 or bournemill@nationaltrust.org.uk

Bourne Mill		M	T	W	T	F	S	S
6 Jun–27 Jun	2–5							S
1 Jul–29 Aug	2–5				T			S

Open Easter, May and August Bank Holidays, Sundays and Mondays.

Brancaster

Brancaster Millennium Activity Centre, The Dial House, Harbour Way, Brancaster Staithe, Norfolk PE31 8BW

Map ③ H3    1923

Famous for its mussels, the fishing village of Brancaster Staithe lies on the shores of the beautiful north Norfolk coast. Follow the history of the fishing industry at Brancaster Quay, enjoy one of the many courses available at the flagship Brancaster Millennium Activity Centre or be inspired at Brancaster beach.
Note: nearest WC at Brancaster beach (not Trust). Scolt Head Island NNR managed by Natural England.

Exploring
- Enjoy the harbour or spectacular views from nearby Brancaster beach.
- Follow the Norfolk Coast Path for great views and wildlife.
- Fun courses for adults, families and school groups.
- Step back in time at the Roman fort of Branodunum.

Eating and shopping: try the fabulous Brancaster mussels or locally caught fresh fish. Quench your thirst at Brancaster Staithe's pubs.

Making the most of your day: explore the creeks at high tide during one of Brancaster Millennium Activity Centre's Family Fun Weeks (booking essential). Learn about the innovative 'Energy Busters' outreach programme for Norfolk schools. Dog restrictions (April to mid August) at Brancaster Beach and Scolt Head (not National Trust).

Access for all: Brancaster Millennium Activity Centre 🚾🚻 Grounds 🚾

Getting here: 132:TF800450. **Foot**: Norfolk Coast Path passes property. **Cycle**: NCN1, runs along ridge above the coast.
Bus: Norfolk Green Coast Hopper 36 Sheringham ≅–Hunstanton. **Road**: Brancaster Staithe is halfway between Wells and Hunstanton on A149 coast road. **Parking**: at Beach Road, Brancaster (not National Trust). Charge including members. Limited parking at the quay, Brancaster Staithe.

Finding out more: 01485 210719 or brancaster@nationaltrust.org.uk

Brancaster	M	T	W	T	F	S	S
Open all year	M	T	W	T	F	S	S

Kite flying at Dunstable Downs, Bedfordshire

Coggeshall Grange Barn

Grange Hill, Coggeshall, Colchester,
Essex CO6 1RE

Map ③ I8 1989

One of Europe's oldest timber-framed
buildings, it has a cathedral-like interior.
Exhibition of local woodcarving and tools.

Getting here: 168:TL848223. Off A120
Coggeshall bypass; ¼ mile south from centre
of Coggeshall, on B1024.

Finding out more: 01376 562226 or
coggeshall@nationaltrust.org.uk

Coggeshall Grange Barn	M	T	W	T	F	S	S
1 Apr–10 Oct	1–5		·	·	**T**	**F**	**S**	**S**

Open Bank Holiday Mondays. May be closed some
Saturdays for private functions.

Dunstable Downs, Chilterns Gateway Centre and Whipsnade Estate

Dunstable Road, Whipsnade,
Bedfordshire LU6 2GY

Map ③ E8  1928

Acres of space to enjoy with fabulous views
over the Vale of Aylesbury and along the
Chiltern Ridge. Dunstable Downs is an Area
of Outstanding Natural Beauty and a kite-
flying hotspot. Chalk grassland, rich in wildlife,
provides prime walking country – spot the
gliders soaring over the glorious landscape!
Note: Chilterns Gateway Centre is owned by
Central Bedfordshire Council and managed by
the National Trust.

Exploring
   – Enjoy the views from the
     comfort of our Visitor Centre.
   – Have fun flying kites from the
     top of Dunstable Downs.

Exploring – Walk across chalk grassland habitats and explore fascinating archaeological features.

Eating and shopping: try local foods, like the Bedfordshire Clanger, in the café. Explore the shop, which sells an excellent range of kites. Downs-based circular walks leaflets available from the Centre.

Making the most of your day: kite-flying all year round and annual kite festival. Waymarked routes, multi-user trail to Five Knolls and regular guided walks. Monthly farmers' market and wide programme of events. Dogs under close control, on leads near livestock.

Access for all: 🅿️♿👣♿🚻

Chilterns Gateway Centre 🏛 Dunstable Downs ➡

Getting here: 165/166:TL002189. **Foot**: from West Street and Tring Road, Dunstable. **Cycle**: bridleway from West Street, Dunstable, and Whipsnade. **Bus**: Arriva 60 from Luton, Centrebus 327 from Hemel Hempstead 🚉 and Red Rose 343 from St Albans 🚉, all Sundays only; otherwise Arriva 61 Aylesbury–Luton 🚉 to within 1½ miles. **Train**: Luton 7 miles. Luton Airport Parkway 7 miles. **Road**: on B4541 west of Dunstable. **Sat Nav**: use LU6 2GY (or LU6 2TA for older equipment). **Parking**: Dunstable Downs, off B4541 (£1.50); Bison Hill, off B4540; Whipsnade Tree Cathedral, B4540 (off village green); Whipsnade crossroads (Whipsnade Heath), junction of B4541 and B4540. Space for three coaches only at Dunstable, booking essential (no other coach facilities).

Finding out more: 01582 500920 or dunstabledowns@nationaltrust.org.uk

Dunstable Downs		M	T	W	T	F	S	S
Downs								
Open all year		M	T	W	T	F	S	S
Chilterns Gateway Centre								
1 Jan–12 Mar	10–4	M	T	W	T	F	S	S
13 Mar–30 Oct	10–5	M	T	W	T	F	S	S
31 Oct–31 Dec	10–4	M	T	W	T	F	S	S

Chilterns Gateway Centre closed 24 and 25 December. Centre closes dusk if earlier. Car park adjacent to Centre locked dusk in winter and 6 in summer.

Dunwich Heath: Coastal Centre and Beach

Dunwich, Saxmundham, Suffolk IP17 3DJ

Map ③ K6  1968

Tucked away on the Suffolk coast, Dunwich Heath offers you peace and quiet and a true sense of being at one with nature. A rare and precious habitat, the Heath is home to special species such as the Dartford warbler, nightjar, woodlark, ant-lion, adders and much more. Quiet and serene, wild and dramatic, this is an inspiring visit, whatever the time of year. From July to September, the Heath is alive with colour; a patchwork of pink and purple heather and coconut-scented yellow gorse is an unmissable experience. **Note**: parking restrictions may operate at times of extreme fire risk.

Exploring – Follow a waymarked nature trail.
– Inspiring walks linking beach and heath.
– SeaWatch lookout – spot porpoise, seals and birds.
– New smugglers and history trails.
– See the scarce Dartford warbler.
– Self-drive and chauffeured mobility vehicles.

Eating and shopping: award-winning tea-room, local produce, children's menu. Coastal-themed gifts in the shop. Holiday in our three clifftop flats or a village cottage. Eat outside and enjoy beautiful coastal views.

You may also enjoy: the wild and remote former 'secret site' of Orford Ness offers a unique experience.

Making the most of your day: guided walks, family nature trails, Tracker Packs, smugglers and history trails, tea-room events, wildlife identification charts and telescopes. Dogs allowed, although restrictions apply (see notices).

Dunwich Heath, Suffolk: immerse yourself in the magnificent display of purple heather and yellow gorse in summer

Access for all: 🅿♿🅳♿⚒♿🛗♿📷🖼🖌🖼

Tea-room and gift shop ♿🔽

SeaWatch building ♿🔽 Grounds ➡🔽

Getting here: 156:TM476685. **Foot**: Suffolk Coast and Heaths Path and Sandlings Walk. **Cycle**: On Suffolk coastal cycle route. **Bus**: Coastlink from Darsham 🚉 and Saxmundham. Book only on 01728 833526. **Train**: Darsham 6 miles. **Road**: 1 mile south of Dunwich, signposted from A12. From Westleton/Dunwich road, 1 mile before Dunwich village turn right into Minsmere road. Then 1 mile to Dunwich Heath. **Parking**: 150 yards (pay and display). Cars £4.20, caravans/motorhomes £12, motorcycles £3.20, coaches £32 (unless booked to use tea-room), limited to three coaches.

Finding out more: 01728 648501 or dunwichheath@nationaltrust.org.uk

Dunwich Heath		M	T	W	T	F	S	S
Tea-room and shop*								
3 Mar–31 Mar	10–4	·	·	**W**	**T**	**F**	**S**	**S**
1 Apr–11 Apr	10–5	**M**	**T**	**W**	**T**	**F**	**S**	**S**
14 Apr–11 Jul	10–5	·	·	**W**	**T**	**F**	**S**	**S**
12 Jul–12 Sep	10–5	**M**	**T**	**W**	**T**	**F**	**S**	**S**
15 Sep–19 Dec	10–4	·	·	**W**	**T**	**F**	**S**	**S**
27 Dec–31 Dec	10–4	**M**	**T**	**W**	**T**	**F**	**S**	**S**

Open Bank Holiday Mondays. Open Monday to Sunday during local half-term holidays. *Shop and tea-room closing times vary.

Elizabethan House Museum

4 South Quay, Great Yarmouth, Norfolk NR30 2QH

Map ③ K5   🏠

An amazing 'hands on' museum to enthral all ages. This 16th-century quayside building reflects the life and times of the families who lived here from Tudor to Victorian times. Decide for yourself if the death of Charles I was plotted in the Conspiracy Room! **Note**: house is leased to Norfolk Museums and Archaeology Service.

Exploring
- See how the Tudors lived in the 16th century.
- Discover Victorian life 'upstairs and downstairs'.
- Enjoy a stroll along Great Yarmouth's historic South Quay.

Making the most of your day: Tudor costumes to try on; activity-packed toy room for children and hands-on activities.

Access for all: 🅿🖼🖥🖌👓 Building ♿♿

Elizabethan House Museum, Norfolk

Felbrigg Hall, Garden and Park

Felbrigg, Norwich, Norfolk NR11 8PR

Map ③ J4 🏛️🐾✝️❄️🌳 💪🏠🍴 1969

Getting here: 134:TG523073. On Great Yarmouth's historic South Quay. **Foot**: level walk from railway station along North Quay on to South Quay. **Cycle**: Regional Route 30 Great Yarmouth–Cromer. **Bus**: local services, plus services from surrounding areas. **Train**: Great Yarmouth ½ miles. **Road**: From A47 take town centre signs, then follow brown Historic South Quay signs. From A12 follow brown signs. **Parking**: at the rear of the museum, operated by Borough Council (pay and display). Other parking available near to the museum, town centre and historic quayside.

Finding out more: 01493 855746 or elizabethanhouse@nationaltrust.org.uk

Truly a hidden gem, the Hall is a place of surprises and delights, a mixture of opulence and homeliness where each room has something to feed the imagination. Outside, the decorative and productive walled garden is a gardener's delight, providing fruit and vegetables for the restaurant, flowers for the hall and inspiration to visitors. The rolling landscape park with a lake, 211 hectares (520 acres) of woods and waymarked trails is a great place to explore the nature and wildlife on this bountiful estate.

Exploring	– Admire the sumptuous interiors, full of original contents.
	– Enjoy a 'Grand Tour' of the Cabinet.
	– See Dr Johnson's famous dictionary in the Gothic Library.
	– Take inspiration from the walled garden.

Elizabethan House Museum		M	T	W	T	F	S	S
1 Apr–29 Oct	10–4	**M**	**T**	**W**	**T**	**F**	·	·
3 Apr–31 Oct	12–4	·	·	·	·	·	**S**	**S**

Felbrigg Hall, Norfolk: a surprising mixture of opulence and homeliness

Help the Trust with Gift Aid on Entry for non-members

Exploring
- Enjoy miles of walks around the estate and woodlands.
- Find the 300-year-old fire engine.

Eating and shopping: Carriages Brasserie, using seasonal produce from the walled garden. Tea-room serving cakes and snacks. Gift shop and plant sales. Second-hand bookshop.

You may also enjoy: Blickling Hall, built at the same time and by some of the same craftsmen.

Making the most of your day: Easter and summer children's trails. Chilli Fiesta on 4 August, harvest events in October and 'The Hall at Christmas'. Dogs on leads in parkland when stock grazing, under close control in woodland.

Access for all: 🅿️ 🅳 ♿ 🚻 🔛 🔍 🎧 📖 📺 ⠿ Ⓐ
Hall 🔍 ♿ 🔍 **Shop and catering** 🔍
Grounds ♿ 🔍 ➡️ 🔍

Getting here: 133:TG193394. **Foot**: Weavers' Way runs through property. **Cycle**: Regional Route 30, Great Yarmouth–Wells. **Train**: Cromer or Roughton Road, both 2½ miles. **Road**: near Felbrigg village, 2 miles south west of Cromer; entrance off B1436, signposted from A148 and A140. **Sat Navs**: give poor directions, please follow 'brown signs'. **Parking**: 100 yards, £2 non members.

Finding out more: 01263 837444 or felbrigg@nationaltrust.org.uk

Felbrigg Hall, Garden and Park		M	T	W	T	F	S	S
House								
1 Mar–31 Oct	11–5	M	T	W	·	·	S	S
Gardens, refreshments and shop								
1 Mar–31 Oct	11–5	M	T	W	T	F	S	S
4 Nov–19 Dec	11–4	·	·	·	T	F	S	S
27 Dec–31 Dec	11–3	M	T	W	T	F	S	S
Refreshments and shop								
2 Jan–28 Feb	11–3	·	·	·	·	·	S	S
Park								
Open all year	Dawn–dusk	M	T	W	T	F	S	S

Open Good Friday 11 to 5. Bookshop open as house and winter weekends 2 January to 28 February, 4 November to 19 December, 11 to 3.

Flatford: Bridge Cottage

Flatford, East Bergholt, Suffolk CO7 6UL

Map ③ I8   🏠 🔧 1943

In the heart of the beautiful Dedham Vale, the charming hamlet of Flatford is the location for some of John Constable's most famous pastoral paintings. Find out more about Constable at the exhibition in Bridge Cottage. Next door is the riverside tea-room and gift shop. **Note**: no public access to Flatford Mill.

Exploring
- Visit the sites of Constable's famous paintings.
- Discover more about Constable in Bridge Cottage.
- Escape on foot and explore the peaceful Dedham Vale.
- Take a boat or just relax beside the River Stour.

Eating and shopping: enjoy homemade food in the lovely riverside tea-room. Local gifts and Constable souvenirs in the thatched shop.

Making the most of your day: guided tours of Constable's painting locations, programme of longer rambles in the Dedham Vale, special tours of Flatford Mill buildings. Family activity trail.

Access for all: 🅿️ 🚻 🔛 🔍 🎧 🔍 ⠿ Ⓐ
Building ♿ 🔍 **Grounds** ♿ 🔍 🔍

Getting here: 168:TM075333. ½ mile south of East Bergholt. **Foot**: accessible from East Bergholt, Dedham and Manningtree. **Bus**: Network Colchester 93 Ipswich–Colchester (passing Ipswich 🚉 and close Colchester Town 🚉), Monday–Saturday alight East Bergholt, ¾ mile. **Train**: Manningtree 1¾ miles by footpath, 3½ miles by road. **Road**: Flatford is south of East Bergholt off the B1070. **Parking**: 200 yards, pay and display (not National Trust), charge including members.

Finding out more: 01206 298260 or
flatfordbridgecottage@nationaltrust.org.uk

Flatford: Bridge Cottage		M	T	W	T	F	S	S
2 Jan–28 Feb	11–3:30						S	S
3 Mar–31 Mar	11–4			W	T	F	S	S
1 Apr–30 Apr	11–5	M	T	W	T	F	S	S
1 May–30 Sep	10:30–5:30	M	T	W	T	F	S	S
1 Oct–31 Oct	11–4:30	M	T	W	T	F	S	S
3 Nov–23 Dec	11–3:30			W	T	F	S	S

Open Bank Holiday Mondays. Property may close early in
winter if weather is bad (October to March).

Hatfield Forest

near Bishop's Stortford, Essex

Map ③ G8 | 1924 |

An ancient tree in Hatfield Forest, Essex

No other forest on earth evokes the
atmosphere of a medieval hunting forest so
completely. The ancient trees of the forest
are like magnificent living sculptures, peaceful
giants worn and fragile from centuries of
seasons and use. Some of our extraordinary
ancient trees are 1,200 years old! Just imagine
what these trees have lived through and
the stories they could tell. Whether you
want somewhere for the children to run off
energy, somewhere you can run to keep fit,
or somewhere to walk where you can quietly
reflect, you will find your own special place
somewhere in Hatfield Forest.

Exploring
- Explore the hidden depths of the woods.
- See the conservation team at work in the forest.
- Relax in beautiful surroundings.
- Be inspired by the intricacies of the Shell House.
- Space for children to run off energy.
- Marvel at the half a billion buttercups in spring.

Eating and shopping: delight in finding
beautiful locally produced gifts in our shop.
Discover the healthy option of Hatfield Forest
venison. Enjoy seasonal, local food from the
Forest Café. Buy our sustainable woodland
products, from firewood to beanpoles.

You may also enjoy: explore Wimpole Hall's
Adventure Woodland and meet the animals at
Home Farm.

Making the most of your day: full programme
of family events. Tracker Packs and trail guides,
Batricar and all-terrain pushchair available to
help you explore the site. Dogs on leads near
livestock and lake (please note; lakeside
dog-free area).

Access for all: 🅿️ 🚻 🔍 🅰️
Grounds 🦽 ➡️ ♿ 👇

Getting here: 167:TL547203. 4 miles east
of Bishop's Stortford. **Foot**: Flitch Way from
Braintree. Three Forests Way and Forest Way
pass through the forest. **Cycle**: Flitch Way.
Bus: Excel Coaches 7 Stansted–Mountfitchet,
alight Takeley Street (Green Man), ½ mile.
Train: Stansted Airport 3 miles. **Road**: from M11
exit 8, take B1256 towards Takeley. Signposted
from B1256. **Parking**: Cars £4.60, minibuses
£6.50, coaches £25, school coaches £10.

Finding out more: 01279 874040 (Infoline).
01279 870678 or
hatfieldforest@nationaltrust.org.uk.
Hatfield Forest Estate Office, Takeley, Bishop's
Stortford, Hertfordshire CM22 6NE

Hatfield Forest		M	T	W	T	F	S	S
Hatfield Forest								
Open all year	Dawn–dusk	M	T	W	T	F	S	S
Elgins and Shell House car parks								
3 Jan–7 Mar	10–3:30	·	·	·	·	·	·	S
13 Mar–31 Oct	10–5	M	T	W	T	F	S	S
7 Nov–26 Dec	10–3:30	·	·	·	·	·	·	S
Refreshments								
1 Jan–12 Mar	10–3:30	·	·	W	T	F	S	S
13 Mar–31 Oct	10–5	M	T	W	T	F	S	S
3 Nov–31 Dec	10–3:30	·	·	W	T	F	S	S
Shop								
2 Jan–7 Mar	10–3:30	·	·	·	·	·	S	S
13 Mar–31 Oct	10–5	M	T	W	T	F	S	S
1 Nov–19 Dec	10–3:30	·	·	·	·	·	S	S

Elgins and Shell House car parks, refreshments and shop open daily during February and December school holidays, 10 to 3:30. Elgins and Shell House car park exits close 8.

Horsey Windpump

Horsey Staithe Stores, Horsey,
Great Yarmouth, Norfolk NR29 4EF

Map (3) K4  1948

The striking windpump provides stunning views of the coast and broadland landscape, internationally important for wildlife. Small shop and refreshments.

Note: Horsey Estate is managed by the Buxton family, from whom it was acquired.

Getting here: 134:TG457223. 15 miles north of Great Yarmouth on B1159; 4 miles north east of Martham. **Sat Nav**: NR29 4EF.

Finding out more: 01263 740241 or horseywindpump@nationaltrust.org.uk. Norfolk Coast Office, Friary Farm, Cley Road, Blakeney, Norfolk NR25 7NW

Horsey Windpump		M	T	W	T	F	S	S
6 Mar–28 Mar	10–5	·	·	·	·	·	S	S
31 Mar–5 Sep	10–5	M	T	W	T	F	S	S
8 Sep–24 Oct	10–5	·	·	W	T	F	S	S
25 Oct–31 Oct	10–5	M	T	W	T	F	S	S

Open all Bank Holidays between 6 March and 31 October. Car park open all year, dawn to dusk.

Houghton Mill

Houghton, near Huntingdon,
Cambridgeshire PE28 2AZ

Map (3) F6 1939

Situated in a stunning riverside setting and full of excellent hands-on activities for all the family, this five-storey historic building is the last working watermill on the Great Ouse. Flour is for sale, ground in the traditional way by water-powered mill stones. **Note**: milling demonstrations subject to river levels.

Houghton Mill, Cambridgeshire

Exploring
– Milling demonstrations: Sundays and Bank Holiday Mondays, 1 to 5.
– Wander or cycle through the neighbouring water meadows.
– New conservation room – discover more about the local wildlife.

Eating and shopping: have a snack in our delightful riverside tea-room. Spend some time browsing in the second-hand bookshop. Buy some of our freshly ground Houghton Mill wholemeal flour.

Making the most of your day: family events programme including open-air theatre and hands-on baking days. Dogs on leads in grounds only.

Access for all: [symbols]
Building [symbols] Grounds [symbol]

Getting here: 153:TL282720. **Foot**: Ouse Valley Way from Huntingdon and St Ives. **Cycle**: NCN51 from Huntingdon. **Bus**: Stagecoach in Huntingdon 55, Whippet 1A, Cambridge–Huntingdon (passing close Huntingdon ⊒). **Train**: Huntingdon 3½ miles. **Road**: in village of Houghton, signposted off A1123 Huntingdon to St Ives. **Parking**: 20 yards, £2 (pay and display). No access for large coaches (drop off in village square).

Finding out more: 01480 301494 or houghtonmill@nationaltrust.org.uk

Houghton Mill		M	T	W	T	F	S	S
Mill								
20 Mar–31 Oct	11–5	·	·	·	·	·	S	S
3 May–29 Sept	1–5	M	T	W	·	·	·	·
Tea-room								
As Mill	11–5							

Open Bank Holiday Mondays and Good Friday 11 to 5. Caravan and campsite (managed by the Caravan Club) open March to October. Groups and school parties at other times by arrangement. Car park closes at 8 or dusk if earlier.

Ickworth House, Park and Gardens

The Rotunda, Horringer, Bury St Edmunds, Suffolk IP29 5QE

Map ③ H7      1956

'**Exploring acres of woodland, losing myself in the sweeping beauty of the valley, then stunned by this incredible house.**'
Mr Wallis, Shimpling, Suffolk

Explore acres of space, woodland, wildlife, and a stunning architectural oddity, all with a story to match. See how one eccentric man's passion for art, Italy and for having a party led to the creation of this remarkable house and its renowned collection of paintings, portraits, furniture and other treasures. Let your imagination run riot as you stroll in one of England's finest, and possibly earliest, Italianate gardens, and explore the wonderfully intimate Spring and Silver Gardens or the intriguing Stumpery. Go wild, amble or ramble in miles of beautiful woodland walks or even bring a bike.

Note: conference, banqueting, wedding facilities (01284 735957); family hotel (01284 735350).

Exploring
- Marvel at Ickworth's grand entrance hall and State Rooms.
- Stare at a family portrait close up, eyeball to eyeball!
- Find the interesting Silverfish collection in the Museum Room upstairs.
- Explore delightful gardens, terraces, the Orangery, parkland and woodland.
- Stroll to the summerhouse and swan around the lake.
- Try out the cycle route, trim trail and play area.

Eating and shopping: contemporary menu in our friendly, modern West Wing restaurant. Sweets and treats, toys and gifts and books and things. Vineyard tours and Ickworth's very own label wine. Plant and garden furniture centre conveniently near the car park.

You may also enjoy: Wimpole Hall – Georgian architecture and sumptuous interiors on a grand scale.

Making the most of your day: friendly staff and volunteers will greet you at West Wing reception. Relax in the restaurant and pick up a Tracker Pack or Family Guide to help you throughout your day. Dogs on leads in grounds only.

Access for all: �P♿ D♿ ♿wc ♿ ▢ ⌕ :: ⊘
House ♿ ♿ ♿ ♿ West Wing ♿ ♿
Grounds ♿ ♿ ➡ ♿

Getting here: 155:TL810610. **Foot**: 4½ miles via footpaths from Bury St Edmunds. **Bus**: Burtons 344/5 Bury St Edmunds–Haverhill (passing close Bury St Edmunds ⊒). **Train**: Bury St Edmunds 3 miles. **Road**: in Horringer, 3 miles south west of Bury St Edmunds on west side of A143. **Parking**: free, 200 yards.

Finding out more: 01284 735270 or ickworth@nationaltrust.org.uk

Ickworth House, Park and Gardens in Suffolk, offers so much to discover

Ickworth House		M	T	W	T	F	S	S
House								
1 Mar–31 Oct	11–5	M	T	·	·	F	S	S
Park								
Open all year	8–8	M	T	W	T	F	S	S
Gardens								
1 Jan–28 Feb	11–4	M	T	W	T	F	S	S
1 Mar–1 Nov	10–5	M	T	W	T	F	S	S
2 Nov–31 Dec	11–4	M	T	W	T	F	S	S
Shop and restaurant								
1 Jan–28 Feb	11–4	M	T	·	·	F	S	S
1 Mar–1 Nov	10–5	M	T	·	·	F	S	S
2 Nov–31 Dec	11–4	M	T	·	·	F	S	S

Open all Bank Holiday Mondays, Good Friday and 1 January. Property closed 24, 25 and 26 December. Park closes 8 or dusk if earlier.

Lavenham Guildhall

Market Place, Lavenham, Sudbury, Suffolk CO10 9QZ

Map ③ I7 1951

During the boom years of the cloth trade in the 15th and 16th centuries, the residents of Lavenham paid even more in tax than the city of York. The village today is famed for its wealth of surviving timber-framed buildings, which make it one of the best-preserved medieval villages in England. One of the finest of these buildings is the Guildhall of Corpus Christi. Inside, you can follow the changing fortunes of Lavenham through exhibits on the local cloth industry, farming and agriculture before exploring the unique streets that have changed little in five centuries.

Exploring
- Learn about timber-framed construction and medieval guilds.
- Exhibits on cloth working, local railways and agriculture.
- See Ramesses, the mummified cat, discovered in a nearby roof.
- Tranquil walled garden with traditional dye plants.
- Summer programme of guided walks and talks.
- Don't miss Lavenham church, one of Suffolk's finest.

Eating and shopping: ploughman's lunches with local bread, regional cheeses and Norfolk ham. Mouthwatering cream teas, with the famous Guildhall scones. Local gifts, souvenirs, books and plants in the shop.

You may also enjoy: Tudor architecture on a grander scale at Melford Hall.

Making the most of your day: children's trails around the house, Tudor dressing-up costumes and 'Discovery Days'.

Visit

Lavenham Guildhall, Suffolk

Access for all: 🅿♿🔊📷📋🚶👆🅰

Building ♿♿♿ **Grounds** ♿♿

Getting here: 155:TL916493. **Foot**: 4-mile 'railway walk' links Lavenham with Long Melford. **Cycle**: South Suffolk Cycle Route A1. **Bus**: Chambers 753 Bury St Edmunds–Colchester (passes close Bury St Edmunds ☒ and Sudbury ☒). **Train**: Sudbury 7 miles. **Road**: A1141 and B1071. **Parking**: free (not National Trust) in front of the Guildhall.

Finding out more: 01787 247646 or lavenhamguildhall@nationaltrust.org.uk

Lavenham Guildhall		M	T	W	T	F	S	S
Shop								
9 Jan–28 Feb	11–4	·	·	·	·	·	S	S
6 Nov–19 Dec	11–4	·	·	·	T	F	S	S
Guildhall, tea-room and shop								
6 Mar–28 Mar	11–4	·	·	W	T	F	S	S
29 Mar–31 Oct	11–5	M	T	W	T	F	S	S
6 Nov–28 Nov	11–4	·	·	·	·	·	S	S
Tea-room								
6 Nov–19 Dec	11–4	·	·	·	·	·	S	S

Closed Good Friday. Parts of the Guildhall may be closed occasionally for community use.

Melford Hall

Long Melford, Sudbury, Suffolk CO10 9AA

Map ③ I7   🏠 ❁ ♠ | 1960

'**A real sense of a family home – as welcoming, informal and friendly as it is impressive.**'
Giles Dixon, Bishop Stortford

For almost five centuries the picturesque turrets of Melford Hall have dominated Long Melford's village green. Devastated by fire in 1942, the house was nurtured back to life by the Hyde Parker family and it remains their much-loved family home to this day. Their interior decoration and furnishings chart changing tastes and fashions over two centuries, but it is the stories of family life at Melford – from visits by their relation Beatrix Potter with her menagerie of animals, through to children sliding down the grand staircase on trays – that make this house more than just bricks and mortar.

Exploring
– Chat to our friendly volunteers and uncover Melford's stories.
– Discover 250 years of naval service and ancient captured treasure.
– See Beatrix Potter's Jemima Puddleduck toy and her bedroom.
– View the gardens from the 17th-century Banqueting House.
– Selection of traditional garden games available in the summer holidays.
– New: relax on the family sofas in the Great Hall!

Eating and shopping: delve deeper into Melford's history with our souvenir guidebook. Refurbished refreshment room for cream teas, cakes, tea and coffee. Gatehouse shop for souvenirs, gifts, second-hand books and plants.

You may also enjoy: nearby Lavenham Guildhall: see Tudor wealth on a smaller scale.

Making the most of your day: wide programme of walks, talks and family events April to October. Children's treasure hunt in the house and garden trails. Some annual events in the park are non-National Trust.

Access for all:
Building 🏠🏠🏠♿ Grounds 🏠🏠

Getting here: 155:TL867462. **Foot**: Railway Walk linking Long Melford with Lavenham, 4 miles. **Bus**: Beestons/Chambers/Felix various services, Monday–Saturday from Sudbury; Chambers 753, Monday–Saturday Bury St Edmunds–Colchester; Network Colchester 90C, Sunday Haverhill–Ipswich (passes Ipswich ≥). All pass close Sudbury ≥. **Train**: Sudbury 4 miles. **Road**: in Long Melford off A134, 14 miles south of Bury St Edmunds, 3 miles north of Sudbury. **Parking**: free at Gatehouse car park, 200 yards. Access for coaches and other large vehicles by gated entrance 100 yards north of main gatehouse entrance. Further free parking in nearby Long Melford.

Finding out more: 01787 376395 (Infoline). 01787 379228 or melford@nationaltrust.org.uk

Melford Hall		M	T	W	T	F	S	S
3 Apr–11 Apr	1:30–5	M	·	W	T	F	S	S
17 Apr–25 Apr	1:30–5	·	·	·	·	·	S	S
1 May–3 Oct	1:30–5	·	·	W	T	F	S	S
9 Oct–31 Oct	1:30–5	·	·	·	·	·	S	S

Also open on Bank Holiday Monday afternoons. Closed Good Friday.

Orford Ness National Nature Reserve

Quay Office, Orford Quay, Orford, Woodbridge, Suffolk IP12 2NU

Map ③ K7   🏠🚻🦞🎨🏆 1993

Take a short boat trip to this wild and remote shingle spit, the largest in Europe. Follow trails through a stunning landscape and a history that will both delight and intrigue. Discover an internationally important nature reserve littered with debris and unusual, often forbidding, buildings from a sometimes disturbing past. **Note**: charge for ferry (including members). Steep, slippery steps. 'Pagodas' accessible on guided events only.

Exploring
- Explore this 'top-secret site' with our self-guiding booklet.
- Experience the wild, wide open spaces and the big skies.
- Children's trail – become a spy for the day!
- Come face to face with a nuclear bomb.

Eating and shopping: try some freshly caught fish for sale from the quay. Take home a flavour of the coast from local smokehouses.

Melford Hall, Suffolk: a much-loved family home

Making the most of your day: guided tours and events (booked only). Crossings limited, arrive early to avoid disappointment. Bring own food and drink (and suitable clothing). No dogs or cycles allowed.

Access for all: [icons]
All buildings [icons] Grounds [icons]

Getting here: 169:TM425495. **Foot**: Suffolk Coast Path runs nearby on mainland via Orford Quay. **Cycle**: NCN1, 1 mile. No cycle parking. **Ferry**: only access to Ness via National Trust ferry *Octavia*. See 'opening arrangements'. **Bus**: Far East Travel 71 from Woodbridge (passing Melton ≥). **Train**: Wickham Market 8 miles. **Road**: access from Orford Quay, Orford town 10 miles east of A12 (B1094/1095), 12 miles north east of Woodbridge B1152/1084. **Parking**: in Quay Street, 150 yards, not National Trust (pay and display). Charge including members.

Finding out more: 01728 648024 (Infoline). 01394 450900 or orfordness@nationaltrust.org.uk

Orford Ness		M	T	W	T	F	S	S
3 Apr–26 Jun	10–2						S	
29 Jun–2 Oct	10–2		T	W	T	F	S	
9 Oct–30 Oct	10–2						S	

The only access is by National Trust ferry from Orford Quay, with boats crossing regularly to the Ness between 10 and 2 only, the last ferry leaving the Ness at 5.

Military Pagodas at Orford Ness, Suffolk

Oxburgh Hall

Oxborough, near King's Lynn, Norfolk PE33 9PS

Map ③ H5 1952

No one ever forgets their first sight of Oxburgh. A romantic, moated manor house, it was built by the Bedingfeld family in the 15th century and they have lived here ever since. Inside, the family's Catholic history is revealed, complete with a secret priest's hole which you can crawl inside. See the astonishing needlework by Mary, Queen of Scots, and the private chapel, built with reclaimed materials. Outside, you can enjoy panoramic views from the gatehouse roof and follow the woodcarving trails in the gardens and woodlands. The late winter drifts of snowdrops are not to be missed.

Exploring
– Wonder at the wealth of heraldry.
– Walk through the secret door in the library.
– Marvel at the needlework by Mary, Queen of Scots.
– Climb the original spiral stairs to the gatehouse roof.
– Be inspired in the kitchen garden.
– Wander through the woodlands and meadow.

Eating and shopping: Old Kitchen tea-room, open-air kiosk and picnic tables. Well-stocked gift shop, including local Norfolk products. Browse in the second-hand bookshop. Plant sales for the green-fingered.

You may also enjoy: another moated Catholic manor house, Baddesley Clinton in Warwickshire.

Making the most of your day: free garden tours every open day. Free children's trails in the house and garden, plus dressing-up clothes. Year-round events programme. Woodland walks and nature trails.

Oxburgh Hall, Norfolk: a romantic, moated manor house

Access for all: [icons]
Hall [icons] **Chapel** [icons] **Garden** [icons]

Getting here: 143:TF742012. **Train**: Downham Market 10 miles. **Road**: at Oxborough, 7 miles south west of Swaffham on south side of Stoke Ferry road; 3 miles from A134 at Stoke Ferry. **Parking**: free.

Finding out more: 01366 328258 or oxburghhall@nationaltrust.org.uk

Oxburgh Hall		M	T	W	T	F	S	S
Garden, shop and tea-room								
2 Jan–21 Feb	11–4	·	·	·	·	·	S	S
27 Feb–31 Jul	11–5	M	T	W	·	·	S	S
1 Aug–31 Aug	11–5	M	T	W	T	F	S	S
1 Sep–31 Oct	11–5	M	T	W	·	J	S	S
6 Nov–19 Dec	11–4	·	·	·	·	·	S	S
House and chapel								
27 Feb–31 Jul	11–5	M	T	W	·	·	S	S
1 Aug–31 Aug	11–5	M	T	W	T	F	S	S
1 Sep–29 Sep	11–5	M	T	W	·	·	S	S
2 Oct–31 Oct	11–4	M	T	W	·	·	S	S

House and Garden open during Easter week from Good Friday, 2 to 11 April, 11 to 5. Chapel closes at 4:30 (4 in October).

Paycocke's

25 West Street, Coggeshall, Colchester, Essex CO6 1NS

Map ③ I8   [icons] 1924

Marvel at the stunning woodcarving and elaborate panelling inside this merchant's house. Built around 1500 for Thomas Paycocke, the house is a grand example of the wealth generated by the cloth trade in the 16th century. Outside, there is a beautiful and tranquil cottage garden. **Note**: nearest WC at Grange Barn.

Exploring
- Examine the fine examples of the famous Coggeshall Lace.
- Explore the sights and smells of the garden.
- Discover the intriguing history of the house and past residents.
- Experience the atmosphere of this remarkable 500-year-old building.

Making the most of your day: children's activities. Guided tours on request. Dogs in the garden only.

Access for all: [icons]
Building [icons] **Grounds** [icons]

Getting here: 168:TL848225. **Foot**: close to Essex Way. **Bus**: First 70 Colchester–Braintree (passing Marks Tey ≥). **Train**: Kelvedon 2½ miles. **Road**: 5½ miles east of Braintree. Signposted off A120. On south side of West Street, 400 yards from centre of Coggeshall, on road to Braintree next to the Fleece Inn. **Parking**: Grange Barn (½ mile) until 5. Very limited roadside parking.

Finding out more: 01376 561305 or paycockes@nationaltrust.org.uk

Paycocke's		M	T	W	T	F	S	S
6 Mar–28 Mar	1–5	·	·	·	·	·	S	S
1 Apr–31 Oct	11–5	·	·	W	T	F	S	S

Open Bank Holiday Mondays.

Peckover House and Garden

North Brink, Wisbech, Cambridgeshire PE13 1JR

Map ③ G5 🏛🔭❄🏠🔔☂ 1943

Peckover House is a secret gem, an oasis hidden away in an urban environment. A classic Georgian merchant's townhouse, it was lived in by the Peckover family for 150 years. The Peckovers were staunch Quakers, which meant they had a very simple lifestyle; yet at the same time they ran a successful private bank. Both facets of their life can be seen as you wander through the house and gardens. The gardens themselves are outstanding – 0.8 hectare (two acres) of sensory delight, complete with orangery, summerhouses, croquet lawn and rose garden with more than 60 species of rose. **Note**: no vehicular access due to essential flood defence works (pedestrian access and parking unchanged).

Exploring	
	– Admire the Rococo plasterwork in the Drawing Room and Landing.
	– Examine the Cabinet of Curiosities – both old and new.
	– Take a peek inside the unrestored Butler's Pantry.
	– Learn about the Quaker history of the Peckover family.

Exploring	
	– See oranges growing in the Orangery – where else!
	– Poignant pets' graveyard, plus two live property cats!

Eating and shopping: tea-room in the thatched 17th-century barn. Gift shop in the old Banking wing. Pick up a bargain in the second-hand bookshop. Plant sales for the green-fingered.

You may also enjoy: another Georgian gem, Fenton House, in the heart of Hampstead, London.

Making the most of your day: play our Bechstein piano, free garden tours most days and croquet in summer. Children's handling collection and trails. Behind the Scenes tours on selected days. Special events.

Access for all: 🄳🔣🚾♿🅿💻VT 🎫
Main house 🚶♿ Tea-room ♿ Garden ♿➡♿

Getting here: 143:TF458097. **Foot**: from Chapel Road car park walk up passageway to left of W Four Restaurant, turn right by river. Peckover House is 150 yards on right. **Cycle**: NCN1, ¼ mile. **Bus**: First X1 Peterborough ≋–Lowestoft; X1 and Norfolk Green 46 from King's Lynn (passing close King's Lynn ≋). **Train**: March 9½ miles. **Road**: west of Wisbech town centre on north bank of River Nene (B1441). **Parking**: Chapel Road, 250 yards. Free (not National Trust).

Finding out more: 01945 583463 or peckover@nationaltrust.org.uk

There is a hidden oasis to explore at Peckover House and Garden, Cambridgeshire

Peckover House and Garden		M	T	W	T	F	S	S
Garden and tea-room								
13 Feb–7 Mar	12–4	·	·	·	·	·	S	S
13 Mar–31 Oct	12–5	M	T	W	·	·	S	S
House								
13 Mar–31 Oct	1–4:30	M	T	W	·	·	S	S
Shop and bookshop								
13 Mar–31 Oct	12:30–4:30	M	T	W	·	·	S	S

Open during Easter week (including Good Friday), 2 to 11 April, 12 to 5, and for Wisbech Rose Fair, 1 and 2 July (garden open at 11). We recommend visitors with disabilities telephone ahead of their visit to discuss specific access needs.

Ramsey Abbey Gatehouse

Abbey School, Ramsey, Huntingdon, Cambridgeshire PE17 1DH

Map (3) F6 1952

This charming former gatehouse is all that remains of the once great Benedictine abbey at Ramsey. **Note**: on school grounds please respect school security. Exterior can be seen all year.

Getting here: 142:TL291851. At south-east edge of Ramsey, at point where Chatteris road leaves B1096, 10 miles south east of Peterborough.

Finding out more: 01480 301494 or ramseyabbey@nationaltrust.org.uk

---

Ramsey Abbey Gatehouse

Open 1 to 5 first Sunday of month, April to September, including group visits by appointment on other weekends.

Rayleigh Mount

Rayleigh, Essex

Map (3) I10 1923

Early medieval motte and bailey castle site, now an urban wildlife haven affording sweeping views. Adjacent windmill houses historical exhibition.

Note: exhibition in windmill operated by Rochford District Council.

Getting here: 178:TQ805909. 100 yards from High Street, next to Mill Hall car park.

Finding out more: 01284 747500 or rayleighmount@nationaltrust.org.uk

---

Rayleigh Mount		M	T	W	T	F	S	S
Open all year	7–6	M	T	W	T	F	S	S

Mount closes at 2 on Saturdays and 5 in winter, other opening times may vary. For windmill exhibition opening times telephone 01702 318120.

St George's Guildhall

29 King Street, King's Lynn, Norfolk PE30 1HA

Map (3) H5 1951

The largest surviving medieval guildhall in England, with many original features. The guildhall is now a theatre and arthouse cinema.

Getting here: 132:TF616202. On west side of King Street close to the Tuesday Market Place.

Finding out more: 01553 765565 or stgeorgesguildhall@nationaltrust.org.uk

---

St George's Guildhall		M	T	W	T	F	S	S
Guildhall								
Open all year	10–2	M	T	W	T	F	·	·
Crofters coffee shop								
Open all year	9:30–5	M	T	W	T	F	S	·
Riverside Restaurant								
Open all year	12–2	M	T	W	T	F	S	·
Open all year	6:30–9:30	M	T	W	T	F	S	·

Closed first Monday in January, Good Friday, Bank Holiday Mondays and 24 December. Not usually open on days when there are theatre performances. Telephone box office on 01553 764864 for details (Monday to Saturday, 10 to 6).

Shaw's Corner

Ayot St Lawrence, near Welwyn,
Hertfordshire AL6 9BX

Map ③ F9 🏠⚜ 1944

Home to George Bernard Shaw for over
40 years, Shaw's Corner is a 1902 Arts &
Crafts house set in a quintessentially English
garden. It feels like Shaw has just left the
room, from the clothes in his wardrobe to the
typewriter and glasses on the desk in his study.
Note: access roads very narrow.

Shaw's Corner, Hertfordshire

Exploring
– Discover Shaw's revolving
   writing hut in the garden.
– See the 1938 Oscar
   for *Pygmalion*.
– Enjoy a picnic in the garden
   or the orchard.
– Get up close to some of
   Shaw's personal belongings.

Eating and shopping: pre-1950s varieties of
plants for sale. Ice-creams and soft drinks for
enjoying in the garden. Take time to browse in
the second-hand bookshop.

Making the most of your day: open-air
performances of George Bernard Shaw's plays
each summer in the garden. Regular events
including poetry and conservation days, music
evenings and family activity days.

Access for all: 🅿♿📷🔊👁️🅰️
Building 🔵🔵🔵 **Grounds** 🔵

Getting here: 166:TL194167. **Cycle**: NCN12,
1 mile. **Bus**: Centrebus 304/Harpenden Taxis
904 from St Albans ≥, Sundays April–October
only; Arriva 304 St Albans ≥-Hitchin, alight
Gustardwood, 1¼ miles. **Train**: Welwyn North
4½ miles; Harpenden 5 miles. **Road**: in the
village of Ayot St Lawrence. A1(M) exit 4 or M1
exit 10. Signposted from B653 Welwyn Garden
City–Luton road near Wheathampstead. Also
from B656 at Codicote. **Parking**: free,
30 yards. Small car park, not suitable for
very large vehicles.

Finding out more: 01438 829221 (Infoline).
01438 820307 or
shawscorner@nationaltrust.org.uk

Shaw's Corner		M	T	W	T	F	S	S
House								
12 Mar–30 Oct	1–5		·	·	**W**	**T**	**F**	**S**	**S**
Garden								
12 Mar–30 Oct	12–5:30		·	·	**W**	**T**	**F**	**S**	**S**

Open Bank Holiday Mondays and Good Friday. May close
earlier when evening events occur.

Sheringham Park

Visitor Centre, Wood Farm, Upper Sheringham,
Norfolk NR26 8TL

Map ③ J4  1987

'**Its natural beauty makes Sheringham Park
the sparkle in the gem of the Norfolk coast.**'
Gary Fowkes, Cromer

Wander through Sheringham Park and you'll
discover why it became the personal favourite
of its designer, Humphry Repton. You can still
see Repton's 'Red Book' showing his designs
for the Park. Famous for its vast collection of
rhododendrons and azaleas, the last owner,
Tom Upcher, would hold rhododendron
champagne parties in the 1950s to show them
off. Ladies would arrive in their fine gowns,
some wearing Wellington boots to walk down
the main carriageway, sipping champagne
and admiring the colours! Today, you can
climb to the top of the towers to experience
breathtaking views of this beautiful landscape.

Note: Sheringham Hall is privately occupied. April to September: limited access by written appointment with leaseholder.

Exploring
- Enjoy the wild garden designed by landscape gardener Humphry Repton.
- Relax by the pond in the new Sheringham Bower.
- Climb the gazebo viewing tower to enjoy stunning coastal views.
- Look out for gorgeous white admiral butterflies in the woodland.
- Discover exciting wildlife facts with our children's Tracker Packs.
- Hear the wonderful sound of skylarks down by the cliffs.

Eating and shopping: purchase a rhododendron to remind you of your visit. Enjoy a cream tea from our refreshment kiosk. Visit our shop for a souvenir of Sheringham Park. Relax after a walk with a drink in the courtyard.

You may also enjoy: a walk around the Great Wood and lake at Felbrigg Hall.

Making the most of your day: guided walks and events all year round. Wildlife trails for children during school holidays. Discover the history of the Park in the exhibtion barn. North Norfolk Railway nearby. Dogs on leads near livestock and visitor facilities.

Access for all: ♿🅿️🚻♿🔊 🖼️🎦⬇️ 🔵
Building 🔵♿ Grounds 🔵➡️🚶

Getting here: 133:TG135420. **Foot**: Norfolk Coast Path passes through property. **Cycle**: Regional Route 30 1½ miles south of property. **Bus**: First 50 from Norwich, Norfolk Green X6 from Cromer (passing close Cromer ☒), alight main entrance (both passing Sheringham ☒). Saunders Coaches (services 4 and 5) will stop on request at main entrance to Park. **Train**: Sheringham 2 miles. **Road**: 2 miles south west of Sheringham, 5 miles west of Cromer, 6 miles east of Holt. Main entrance at junction A148/B1157. **Parking**: 60 yards, £4.50 (pay and display). Coaches free (book in advance).

Finding out more: 01263 820550 or sheringhampark@nationaltrust.org.uk

Sheringham Park		M	T	W	T	F	S	S
Park								
Open all year		M	T	W	T	F	S	S
Visitor Centre								
2 Jan–14 Mar	11–4	.	.	.	.	.	S	S
15 Mar–30 Sep	10–5	M	T	W	T	F	S	S
1 Oct–31 Oct	10–5	.	.	W	T	F	S	S
6 Nov–31 Dec	11–4	.	.	.	.	.	S	S
Refreshment kiosk								
15 Mar–30 Sep	11–5	M	T	W	T	F	S	S
1 Oct–31 Oct	11–5	.	.	W	T	F	S	S

Visitor Centre and kiosk open 10 to 6 at weekends, 15 May to 13 June. Visitor Centre open every day during local school holidays except Christmas Day and Boxing Day. Refreshments available when kiosk is closed.

Sutton Hoo

Tranmer House, Sutton Hoo, Woodbridge, Suffolk IP12 3DJ

Map ③ J7  1998

At Sutton Hoo, on the eve of the Second World War, archaeologists discovered one of the greatest treasures ever found in Britain. It had lain undisturbed for 1,300 years and changed the way we thought about our ancestors. It was the ulimate discovery, the ship burial of an Anglo-Saxon king and his most treasured possessions. Today, you can walk in the footsteps of royalty around the atmospheric burial mounds and visit our award-winning exhibition with its full-size reconstruction of the burial chamber. The exhibition also displays original Anglo-Saxon treasure on loan from the British Museum.

The burial mounds at Sutton Hoo, Suffolk

Exploring
- Meet a 1930s archaeologist and help them unearth the past.
- Take a guided tour of the royal burial mounds.
- Hear an 'amazing artefact' mini-talk in the exhibition.
- View the illustrations of *Time Team* artist Victor Ambrus.
- Explore the beautiful walks with fine estuary views.
- Stay for longer in one of our Edwardian holiday flats.

Eating and shopping: enjoy local, seasonal food in our licensed café. Discover exclusive ceramics and jewellery in our gift shop. Browse in our extensive second-hand bookshop.

You may also enjoy: lovely walks and views at Flatford that inspired artist John Constable.

Making the most of your day: family events, living history, exclusive behind-the-scenes tours and changing exhibitions. Wildlife/nature walks. Children's play area, quiz/trails, Tracker Packs and dressing-up box. Dogs welcome on leads in park and café terrace area only.

Access for all: 🅿🚻♿🔖📷✏👜
Building ♿🔖 Grounds ♿▶🔖🔖

Getting here: 169:TM288487. **Foot**: 1¼ miles from Melton station. **Bus**: First 63/4/5 Ipswich–Framlingham (passing Melton ≥). **Train**: Melton 1¼ miles, Woodbridge 3 miles. **Road**: on B1083 Melton–Bawdsey. Follow signs from A12 north of Woodbridge. **Parking**: 30 yards (pay and display when exhibition closed). Motorcycle parking area, cycle racks and free pannier lockers.

Finding out more: 01394 389700 or suttonhoo@nationaltrust.org.uk

Sutton Hoo		M	T	W	T	F	S	S
1 Jan–14 Feb	11–4	·	·	·	·	F	S	S
15 Feb–21 Feb	11–4	M	T	W	T	F	S	S
27 Feb–7 Mar	11–4	·	·	·	·	·	S	S
13 Mar–4 Apr	10:30–5	‑	·	W	T	F	S	S
5 Apr–31 Oct	10:30–5	M	T	W	T	F	S	S
6 Nov–19 Dec	11–4	·	·	·	·	·	S	S
27 Dec–31 Dec	11–4	M	T	W	T	F	S	S

Open Bank Holiday Mondays. Estate walks open daily all year, 9 to 6 (except for some Thursdays, November to end December).

Theatre Royal, Bury St Edmunds

Westgate Street, Bury St Edmunds, Suffolk IP33 1QR

Map ③ I7   1974

One of the country's most significant theatre buildings and the only surviving Regency playhouse in Britain, the recently restored Grade I listed Theatre Royal in Bury St Edmunds offers visitors a unique and authentic experience of theatre-going in the early 19th century.

Exploring
- Unique year-round programme of professional period and contemporary productions.
- Highly entertaining guided tours provide a fascinating and lively introduction.
- Admire the beautiful interior, including the painted sky ceiling.

Eating and shopping: enjoy delicious food and drinks in spacious, modern surroundings. Browse in the theatre shop for gifts and souvenirs. Short walk to historic town centre and modern shopping arcade.

Making the most of your day: combine a guided tour with lunch, a matinée performance or one of our special heritage-themed events.

Access for all: ♿🚻 Building ♿♿

Getting here: 155:TL856637. **Bus**: from surrounding areas. **Train**: Bury St Edmunds ¾ mile. **Road**: on Westgate Street on south side of A134 from Sudbury (one-way system). **Parking**: nearest in Swan Lane, 546 yards. Limited parking in Westgate Street.

Finding out more: 01284 769505 or theatreroyal@nationaltrust.org.uk

The exquisite Theatre Royal, Suffolk

This incredible Tree Cathedral was created after the First World War in a spirit of 'faith, hope and reconciliation'. **Note**: owned by the National Trust and administered by the Trustees of Whipsnade Tree Cathedral Fund.

Getting here: 165/166:TL008180. 4 miles south of Dunstable, off B4540. Free parking (spaces limited). Signposted off B4540.

Finding out more: 01582 872406 or whipsnadetc@nationaltrust.org.uk. Trustees c/o Chapel Farm, Whipsnade, Dunstable, Bedfordshire LU6 2LL

Theatre Royal, Bury St Edmunds	M	T	W	T	F	S	S
2 Feb–30 Nov	2–4	·	**T**	·	**T**	·	·
2 Feb–30 Nov	10:30–1	·	·	·	·	·	**S**	**S**

Closed during performances. Please telephone in advance for changes in the schedule before you visit.

Whipsnade Tree Cathedral	M	T	W	T	F	S	S
Open all year	**M**	**T**	**W**	**T**	**F**	**S**	**S**

Car park: 1 January to 27 March, locked at 5; 28 March to 31 October, locked at 7; 1 November to 31 December, locked at 5.

Thorington Hall

Stoke by Nayland, Suffolk CO6 4SS

Map (3) I8 1940

Rambling Suffolk farmhouse built around 1600.

Getting here: 155:TM013355. 2 miles south east of Stoke by Nayland.

Finding out more: 01284 747500 or thoringtonhall@nationaltrust.org.uk

Thorington Hall

Open on Saturday during Heritage Open Day in September. Telephone for other opening arrangements.

Whipsnade Tree Cathedral

Whipsnade Tree Cathedral, Whipsnade, Dunstable, Bedfordshire LU6 2LL

Map (3) E8 1960

Wicken Fen National Nature Reserve

Lode Lane, Wicken, Ely, Cambridgeshire CB7 5XP

Map (3) G6  1899

Wicken Fen, one of Europe's most important wetlands, supports an abundance of wildlife. There are more than 8,000 species, including a spectacular array of plants, birds and dragonflies. The raised boardwalk and lush grass droves allow easy access to a lost landscape of flowering meadows, sedge and reedbeds, where you can encounter rarities such as hen harriers, water voles and bitterns. The Wicken Fen Vision, an ambitious landscape-scale conservation project, is opening up new areas of land to explore. Our grazing herds of Highland cattle and Konik ponies are helping to create a diverse range of new habitats.

Visit

East of England

Wicken Fen, Cambridgeshire

Exploring — Step back in time to experience fenland as it was.
— Listen to the reeds as you enjoy a boat ride.
— Dip and discover the underwater world of pond creatures.
— See spectacular harriers hunting over the sedge fields at dusk.
— Imagine living as a fen worker in the Fen Cottage.
— Refresh your soul under huge inspiring skies.

Eating and shopping: remember your visit with craft made especially for Wicken Fen. Find your perfect book from our range of wildlife titles. Try delicious home-cooked soup made with seasonal produce. Cake – the perfect reward after your walk!

You may also enjoy: discover the wildlife at a completely different historic landscape at Hatfield Forest.

Making the most of your day: packed family events programme, all year round. Trails for all, with nine wildlife observation hides. Summer boat trips on Wicken Lode. See the last working fenland windpump. Dogs on leads only.

Access for all: ♿🚻♿🔊📷🎁👁️🐕

Building ♿🦽 Grounds ♿🦽

Getting here: 154:TL563705. **Cycle**: NCN11 from Ely. **Bus**: Stagecoach in Cambridge 12 from Cambridge, Ely and Newmarket, alight Soham High Street, 3 miles, or X9, 9 Cambridge–Ely, alight Stretham, 6 miles. All pass Ely ☒. **Train**: Ely 9 miles. **Road**: south of Wicken (A1123), 3 miles west of Soham (A142), 9 miles south of Ely, 17 miles north east of Cambridge via A10. **Parking**: 120 yards, £2 (pay and display).

Finding out more: 01353 720274 or wickenfen@nationaltrust.org.uk

Wicken Fen		M	T	W	T	F	S	S
Reserve, Visitor Centre and shop								
Open all year	10–5	**M**	**T**	**W**	**T**	**F**	**S**	**S**
Café								
1 Jan–28 Feb	10–4:30	·	·	**W**	**T**	**F**	**S**	**S**
1 Mar–31 Oct	10–5	**M**	**T**	**W**	**T**	**F**	**S**	**S**
3 Nov–31 Dec	10–4:30	·	·	**W**	**T**	**F**	**S**	**S**
Fen Cottage								
27 Mar–31 Oct	2–5	·	·	·	·	·	**S**	**S**

Closed 25 December. Reserve closes at dusk during winter months. Some paths may be closed in very wet conditions. Fen Cottage also open Bank Holiday Mondays.

Willington Dovecote and Stables

Willington, near Bedford, Bedfordshire

Map ③ F7   🏠 1914

Enjoy the tranquil setting of this outstanding 16th-century stone-built dovecote and stable buildings alongside Willington church. **Note**: no WC.

Getting here: 153:TL107499. 4 miles east of Bedford, just north of the Sandy road (A603).

Finding out more: 01480 301494 or willingtondovecote@nationaltrust.org.uk

---

Willington Dovecote

Open on the last Sunday afternoon of the month (April to September), 1 to 5, **otherwise** admission by appointment with the Voluntary Custodian, Mrs J. Endersby, 21 Chapel Lane, Willington MK44 3QG. Telephone 01234 838278.

Wimpole Hall

Arrington, Royston, Cambridgeshire SG8 0BW

Map ③ G7

'**Fantastic opportunity to visit many more times and still find something new to discover**.'
Mr M. Woodhams, St Albans

The impressive mansion, at the heart of this estate, is evidence of Rudyard Kipling's daughter, Elsie Bambridge's success in creating a home. Intimate rooms contrast with beautiful and unexpected Georgian interiors, including Soane's breathtaking Yellow Drawing Room and wonderful plunge bath. The fascinating basement corridor offers a glimpse into life below stairs. Stroll around the colourful parterre garden and wander through the Pleasure Grounds to the walled garden, abundant with fruit, vegetables and herbaceous borders. Stride out across the landscape park, among the rare-breed cattle, and imagine the previous owners planning their visions of grand avenues and spectacular vistas.

Exploring
- Imagine dining in the opulence of the Dining Room.
- See the 70 plus tomato varieties we grow each year.
- Meet the servants on certain days throughout the year.
- Walk to the lakes or through the shaded woods.
- Look up! Can you see the gasolier?

Eating and shopping: taste delicious dishes made with produce from our walled garden. Buy local pottery, plants, gifts, rare-breeds meat and more! Pick up a bargain in the second-hand bookshop. Plenty of gifts for children in the shop.

You may also enjoy: Tatton Park, a country estate with a house, kitchen garden and rare-breeds farm.

Making the most of your day: open-air theatre and film, talks and Living History days, school holiday activities, family trails and activity packs. Dogs on leads in the park only.

Access for all: ⬚⬚⬚⬚⬚⬚⬚⬚⬚ ⬚⬚ Mansion ⬚⬚ Gardens ⬚⬚⬚⬚

Getting here: 154:TL336510. **Foot**: Wimpole Way from Cambridge, Harcamlow Way. **Cycle**: National Trust-permitted cycle path to entrance from Orwell (A603). **Bus**: Whippet 75 from Cambridge. Alight Arrington, then a 1-mile walk; return bus from Orwell, a 2-mile walk. **Train**: Shepreth 5 miles. Royston station with taxi service 8 miles. **Road**: 8 miles south west of Cambridge (A603), 6 miles north of Royston (A1198). **Parking**: 275 yards, £2.

Finding out more: 01223 206000 or wimpolehall@nationaltrust.org.uk

Wimpole Hall		M	T	W	T	F	S	S
Park								
Open all year		M	T	W	T	F	S	S
Hall								
27 Feb–21 Jul	11–5	M	T	W	·	·	S	S
24 Jul–26 Aug	11–5	M	T	W	T	·	S	S
28 Aug–31 Oct	11–5	M	T	W	·	·	S	S
Garden, restaurant, shop and bookshop*								
2 Jan–24 Feb	11–4	M	T	W	·	·	S	S
27 Feb–31 Oct	10:30–5	M	T	W	T	F	S	S
1 Nov–22 Dec	11–4	M	T	W	·	·	S	S
27 Dec–30 Dec	11–4	M	T	W	T	·	S	S

Whole property closed Friday 9 July. Hall, farm and gardens open Bank Holidays including Good Friday. *Also Saturday to Thursday during local February half-term. Refreshments and shop in Stable Block open Boxing Day 11 to 4. Bookshop open weekends only in January and early February.

Wimpole Hall, Cambridgeshire

Wimpole Home Farm

Wimpole Estate, Arrington, Royston,
Cambridgeshire SG8 0BW

Map (3) G7 1976

Arriving at this part of the Estate you are in awe of the Great Barn, set within the traditional farmyard, contrasting with the modern piggery and cattle sheds. Discover rare breeds of cattle, sheep, pigs, poultry, goats and horses and see how we care for them. Learn about food and farming with daily activities: try our 'milking buckets', watch the Jersey cow on the milking machine and join in grooming the donkeys. See the Farm Manager's office and find out how he manages a modern arable and livestock farm, day by day, and takes it forward into the future. **Note**: members pay half price entry to support the rare breeds conservation programme.

Exploring
- Spot the tiny piglets escaping their sty.
- Take a Shire horse wagon ride to the farm.
- Learn about growing and harvesting barley and wheat.
- Let off steam in the Adventure Woodland.
- Meet our Victorian farmers every Saturday during the summer.
- Join in with feeding the goats.

Eating and shopping: taste our award-winning rare-breed sausages. Toy shop is full of cuddly friends to take home. Wimpole Estate meat – buy it to take home for dinner!

You may also enjoy: go wild at Wicken Fen.

Making the most of your day: daily farm activities, talks and Living History days. School holiday activities, family trails and activity packs. Dogs on leads in the park only.

Access for all: ♿ ♿ ♿ ♿ ♿ ♿ ♿ ♿
Barns and sheds ♿ ♿ ♿ **Farm Café** ♿ ♿

Getting here: 154:TL336510. **Foot**: Wimpole Way from Cambridge, Harcamlow Way. **Cycle**: National Trust-permitted cycle path to entrance from Orwell (A603). **Bus**: Whippet 75 from Cambridge. Alight Arrington, then a 1-mile walk; return bus from Orwell, a 2-mile walk. **Train**: Shepreth 5 miles. Royston station with taxi service 8 miles. **Road**: 8 miles south west of Cambridge (A603), 6 miles north of Royston (A1198). **Parking**: 500 yards, £2.

Finding out more: 01223 206000 or wimpolefarm@nationaltrust.org.uk

Wimpole Home Farm		M	T	W	T	F	S	S
2 Jan–21 Feb	11–4	·	·	·	·	·	S	S
27 Feb–31 Oct	10:30–5	M	T	W	T	F	S	S
6 Nov–19 Dec	11–4	·	·	·	·	·	S	S
27 Dec–30 Dec	11–4	M	T	W	T	·	S	S

Closed Friday 9 July. Open Bank Holiday Mondays and Good Friday. Open Saturday to Thursday during local February half-term.

Having fun at Wimpole Home Farm, Cambridgeshire

East Midlands

Immerse yourself in Robert Adam's magnificent creation of Kedleston Hall. A mansion built to impress and entertain

Outdoors in the East Midlands

The East Midlands is an area of breathtakingly diverse scenery, ranging from the heather-clad moors of the Peak District to the peaceful woods of Clumber Park in Nottinghamshire and the rolling parklands of its many historic properties in Derbyshire.

Drama abounds in this landscape, with soaring limestone cliffs, deep grassland gorges and tumbling streams. There are fantastic walking routes suitable for all abilities – with Dovedale, the Manifold Valley in the South Peak and Winnats Pass in the High Peak being rightly popular.

Perfect peaks

The National Trust cares for around 14,970 hectares (37,000 acres) of land within the Peak District National Park, so there is plenty to explore in this iconic landscape. Enjoy a leisurely stroll around picturesque Ilam Park, or challenge yourself with a brisk walk to the top of Mam Tor, where you will be rewarded with amazing views.

The wild and dramatic heather moorlands of High Peak, incised by deep wooded valleys such as Edale, offer important breeding grounds for birds, including the golden plover and short-eared owl. At the Longshaw Estate enjoy a paddle in the tumbling stream at Padley Gorge and look out for the millstones scattered around offering clues to Longshaw's industrial past. Alternatively, why not follow one of our guided walks and find out more about the area from an expert guide?

Wonderful wildlife

We care for two National Nature Reserves at Dovedale in the South Peak and Calke Park in Derbyshire, both hosting a wide variety of flora and fauna.

Calke Park is home to some of the oldest trees in Europe, and the decaying wood of these trees provides a habitat for several endangered beetles. At Dovedale flower-rich grasslands support rare plants, including Jacob's ladder, and the large areas of woodland are home to many invertebrates, including at least seven nationally scarce beetles, as well as breeding woodland birds.

Something to see all year round

Whatever the time of year there is always something to do in the East Midlands countryside. Pick up a copy of the 'Discover Your Peak District' leaflet to find out just how many walks there are on offer and events you can get involved in. There is also so much for children to do, from pond dipping to butterfly hunting, all allowing them to have fun while learning about wildlife.

In the autumn and winter, when many National Trust properties close their doors, the parks and countryside are still open. So why not enjoy a winter walk and then warm up with a well-deserved hot drink at one of our cafés at Longshaw, Edale and South Peak?

Right:
two children with their terrier sitting on a slope admiring the view of Dovedale and Thorpe Cloud

Stately parkland

Our historic houses offer great activities and lots to see indoors and out.

At Belton House in Lincolnshire visitors can enjoy the beautiful landscaped park with its attractive herd of deer, while those looking for an oasis of tranquility can visit the restored boathouse. Calke Abbey offers great opportunities for a family adventure, including wildlife-themed Tracker Packs for children and suggested walking trails.

With picturesque parkland, peaceful woodland, open heath and a serpentine lake, Clumber Park has more than enough space to relax in and explore. There are more than 20 miles of open tracks, and whether you are keen on a gentle stroll around the lake or a more vigorous hike, Clumber is ideal. There are even bicycles available to hire, including those suitable for children, and there are many accessible pathways perfect for wheelchair users.

My favourite view

One of my favourite views is from the Fisherman's car park at Calke Park. In the months when the trees have lost their leaves there is a super view from here over Betty's Pond to the south, looking towards Deer Cote Spinney. It is easy to appreciate why the ancient trees are called 'stag headed'. The bare, white, hardened tops of branches shine against the browns and greens of the bark on the living areas of trunk and the wood pastures in between.

The view goes beyond the old park boundary to the furthest point of the estate, the ridge at Pistern Hills one and a half miles away. The valley between is a good area to spot buzzards and, more recently, red kites and ravens – all of which are especially worth watching through a pair of binoculars.

Close by there is a large oak that has collapsed over the years. If you have children with you, challenge them to find the 'dragon' that has been created within the fallen branches! It can be busy here at times, but it is easy to plan your visit to avoid crowds and just sit and enjoy the view.

Bill Cove
Head Warden, Calke Abbey

Below:
**Calke Park,
Derbyshire**

Belton House

Grantham, Lincolnshire NG32 2LS

Map ③ E4  1984

'Magnificent house and gardens! So much to explore, from basements to boat house, adventure playground to family fun trails!'
Trina Redfern, Lincoln

The perfect English country house, set in its own extensive deer park, Belton was designed to impress. Built in the late 17th century for 'Young' Sir John Brownlow, with family fortunes founded in law, it is one of the finest examples of Restoration architecture and was, for centuries, the scene of lavish hospitality. Opulent décor, stunning silverware, imposing paintings and personal mementos convey wealth while retaining a family atmosphere. Delightful gardens, luxuriantly planted orangery and lakeside walks ensure Belton is a pleasure to explore all year round. Featured in the BBC's TV adaptation of *Pride and Prejudice* starring Colin Firth. **Note**: building work on Visitor Reception is planned for 2010.

Exploring
— Discover the ornate ormolu table centrepiece in the Dining Room.
— Explore tranquil lakeshore, with newly restored boat house.
— Burn off energy in Lincolnshire's largest adventure playground.
— Enjoy family actitivites: Discovery Centre open weekends, April to October.
— Step 'below stairs' – basements open 11 to 12 (main season).
— Enjoy seasonal 'I Spy' trails in the park and garden.

Eating and shopping: find year-round inspiration in our plant and garden shop. Try Belton venison casserole and local dishes in our restaurant. Visit the gift shop for tasty treats and perfect presents. Enjoy local food and craft showcases on selected weekends.

You may also enjoy: on a smaller scale: Woolsthorpe Manor, Isaac Newton's birthplace, and Tattershall Castle.

Belton House, Lincolnshire: designed to impress, this is the perfect English country house

Making the most of your day: varied events programme, Easter and Hallowe'en trails, 'Paint the Garden', open-air theatre, family fun weekends, garden tours, Christmas craft market, Wildlife Explorers' Club. Dogs on leads in parkland and stable yard only.

Access for all: House ⬚⬚⬚⬚ Grounds ⬚➡⬚⬚

Getting here: 130:SK930395. **Bus**: Stagecoach in Lincolnshire 1 Grantham–Lincoln; Centrebus 609 Grantham–Sleaford (both pass close Grantham ➔). **Train**: Grantham 3 miles. **Road**: 3 miles north east of Grantham on A607 Grantham–Lincoln road, easily reached and signposted from A1. **Parking**: free, 250 yards.

Finding out more: 01476 566116 or belton@nationaltrust.org.uk

Belton House		M	T	W	T	F	S	S
House								
6 Mar–14 Mar	12:30–4	·	·	·	·	·	S	S
House*								
17 Mar–31 Oct	11–5	·	·	W	T	F	S	S
Garden, park, restaurant and shop								
6 Feb–28 Feb	12–4	·	·	·	·	·	S	S
3 Mar–31 Oct	10:30–5:30	·	·	W	T	F	S	S
5 Jul–5 Sep	10:30–5:30	M	T	W	T	F	S	S
5 Nov–19 Dec	12–4	·	·	·	·	F	S	S
26 Dec–31 Dec	12–4	M	T	W	T	F	S	S
Adventure playground								
3 Mar–31 Oct	10:30–5:30	·	·	W	T	F	S	S
5 Jul–5 Sep	10:30–5:30	M	T	W	T	F	S	S

*Basement: open 11 to 12:30 (last entry 12). House conservation talks 11:30 on most days. House open for free flow from 12:30 (although guided tours may replace free flow on some days). Also open Bank Holiday Mondays. Timed ticket on busy days. Adventure playground, parkland, garden, shop and restaurant: open all week in Lincolnshire school holidays (15 March to 31 October). Bellmount Woods: open daily, access from separate car park. Bellmount Tower and boat house: open occasionally (contact property for details). House and adventure playground likely to close early in poor weather and light conditions.

Restored boat house at Belton House, Lincolnshire

Calke Abbey

Ticknall, Derby, Derbyshire DE73 7LE

Map ③ C4

1985

A country house and estate preserved in 20th-century decline. A place poised somewhere between gentle neglect and downright dereliction, telling the tale af an eccentric family who amassed a huge collection of hidden treasures. The house has been little restored, portraying a period when great country houses struggled to survive. In the walled gardens explore the orangery, the flower and kitchen gardens or walk around the fragile habitats of Calke Park National Nature Reserve. **Note**: visitors (including members) require a ticket for the house and garden or garden only.

Exploring
- Discover the stunning 18th-century silk bed.
- Walk through the servants' tunnel and explore the stable yards.
- Visit the flower garden and the unique Auricula Theatre.
- Explore Calke Park National Nature Reserve and its many walks.
- Discover veteran trees, including a 1,000-year-old oak.
- Join our new self-guided West Wing Conservation Tour.

Eating and shopping: relax in our restaurant, serving feshly prepared locally sourced produce. Browse the recently extended shop full of wonderful gift ideas. Buy local food in the new Calke Pantry. Light refreshments available from the coffee shop at peak times.

You may also enjoy: Staunton Harold Church, Kedleston Hall, Sudbury Hall and the Museum of Childhood.

Making the most of your day: self-guided West Wing conservation tours. Varied family events programme, including family activities

Calke Abbey, Derbyshire

in Squirt's Stable (weekends March to October). Dogs welcome on leads in park and stables area only.

Access for all: [icons]
Building [icons] **Grounds** [icons]

Getting here: 128:SK367226. **Bus**: Arriva 61 Derby–Swadlincote, alight Ticknall, ½ mile walk through park. **Train**: Derby 9½ miles; Burton-on-Trent 10 miles. **Road**: 10 miles south of Derby, on A514 at Ticknall between Swadlincote and Melbourne. Access from M42/A42 exit 13 and A50 Derby South. Entry via Ticknall main entrance only. **Parking**: free. 3.6-metre height restriction at Middle Lodge arch.

Finding out more: 01332 863822 or calkeabbey@nationaltrust.org.uk

Calke Abbey		M	T	W	T	F	S	S
Calke Park National Nature Reserve								
Open all year	8–8:30	M	T	W	T	F	S	S
House								
27 Feb–31 Oct	12:30–5	M	T	W	·	·	S	S
Restaurant and shop								
2 Jan–31 Dec	10:30–5	M	T	W	T	F	S	S
Garden								
27 Feb–31 Oct	11–5	M	T	W	·	·	S	S
1 Jul–3 Sep	11–5	M	T	W	T	F	S	S
West Wing conservation tour								
27 Feb–31 Oct	11–12:30	M	T	W	·	·	S	S

House open for self-guided West Wing Conservation Tours, 11 to 12:30 (by timed ticket only). Last admission 12. Admission to House by timed ticket, delays may occur at peak times. Restaurant and shop closed 1 January and 25 and 26 December and closes at 4, January, February, November and December. Calke Park closed 8:30 or dusk if earlier. House and gardens open Good Friday.

Canons Ashby

Canons Ashby House, Canons Ashby, Daventry, Northamptonshire NN11 3SD

Map ③ D7   [icons] 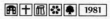 1981

Canons Ashby was first built by the Dryden family during the Elizabethan period, using stone from the Augustinian priory which previously occupied the site. The private church is all that remains of the priory. The interior is welcoming and atmospheric, with Jacobean wall paintings, plasterwork and tapestries. The house was updated in the 18th century with the south-facing rooms remodelled, and again in the 19th century, when Sir Henry Dryden's *The Antiquarian* recorded much of the history of the estate and the surrounding area. The gardens are currently being restored to their colourful designs from Sir Henry's records.

Exploring
- Enjoy the friendly house.
- Explore the medieval remains in the park.
- Watch the restoration of the gardens taking place.
- Learn about the history of the house, church and garden.
- Embark on a children's trail.
- Gain insight with the help of the morning taster tours.

Eating and shopping: browse in the shop and plant centre. Enjoy freshly prepared food in the tea-room. Relax in the tea-room garden.

You may also enjoy: Lyveden New Bield: an unfinished Elizabethan lodge set within a delightful historic landscape.

Making the most of your day: explore the medieval remains in park. Regular events throughout the year, including craft and wine fairs and summer theatre and musical performances. Dogs on leads in Home Paddock and car park only.

Access for all: [icons]
Building [icons] **Grounds** [icons]

Canons Ashby, Northamptonshire

Getting here: 152:SP577506. South of Daventry. **Foot**: on the Macmillan long-distance footpath. 3 miles on country lanes from Woodford Halse. **Cycle**: NCN70. **Bus**: to Woodford Halse, between Daventry and Banbury. **Train**: Banbury 10 miles. **Road**: easy access from either M40 exit 11, or M1 exit 16. From M1 take A45 (Daventry) and at Weedon crossroads turn left on to A5; 3 miles south turn right on to unclassified road through Litchborough and Adstone. From M40 at Banbury take A422 (Brackley) and after 2 miles turn left on to B4525; after 3 miles turn left on to unclassified road signposted to property. **Parking**: free, 200 yards.

Finding out more: 01327 860044 or canonsashby@nationaltrust.org.uk

Canons Ashby		M	T	W	T	F	S	S
House tours								
13 Feb–31 Oct	11–1	M	T	W	·	·	S	S
31 Jul–30 Aug	11–4	·	·	·	T	F	·	·
House								
13 Feb–31 Oct	1–5	M	T	W	·	·	S	S
6 Nov–19 Dec	12–4	·	·	·	·	·	S	S
Gardens, park and church								
13 Feb–19 Dec	11–5:30	M	T	W	·	·	S	S
Shop and tea-room								
13 Feb–31 Oct	11–5	M	T	W	·	·	S	S
6 Nov–19 Dec	12–4	·	·	·	·	·	S	S
Shop, tea-room, gardens, park and church								
31 Jul–1 Sep	11–5	M	T	W	T	F	S	S

Open Good Friday, 11 to 5. Closes dusk if earlier. Open all week in August. House open Thursday and Friday in August 11 to 4 (limited timed tickets only).

Clumber Park

The Estate Office, Clumber Park, Worksop, Nottinghamshire S80 3AZ

Map ③ D2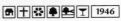

'Very good, enjoyable and fun. It is one of my favourite places.'
Charlie Parry, aged eight, Worksop

Clumber was once the country estate of the Dukes of Newcastle. Although the house no longer exists, the Walled Kitchen Garden, magnificent Gothic Revival chapel, Pleasure Ground and lake remain as clues to its past. Covering 1,537.5 hectares (3,800 acres) Clumber's mosaic of important and varied habitats are home to a world of hidden nature and a respite from the hustle and bustle of everyday life. Experience a taste of the past in our organically managed Walled Kitchen Garden, or enjoy a family day out by hiring cycles to explore or have a picnic by the lake.

Exploring
- Space for walking or relaxation, a picnic or BBQ.
- Discover 20 miles of cycle routes through spectacular scenery.
- Liven your senses in the inspiring Walled Kitchen Garden.
- New woodland play area for our younger visitors to explore.
- Get up close and personal with some amazing wildlife.
- Europe's longest avenue of double-row lime trees.

Eating and shopping: enjoy a taste of Nottinghamshire hospitality in our restaurant. Dishes use fresh seasonal produce from our Walled Kitchen Garden. Shop packed with the ideal gift, local products and souvenirs. Find inspiration for your garden at the plant sales area.

You may also enjoy: Nottinghamshire's treasures: the fascinating Mr Straw's House and The Workhouse's moving stories.

Exploring Clumber Park, Nottinghamshire

Clumber Park		M	T	W	T	F	S	S
Park								
Open all year	7 till dusk	M	T	W	T	F	S	S
Restaurant, shop, plant sales, The Clumber Story, chapel								
1 Jan–27 Mar	10–4	M	T	W	T	F	S	S
28 Mar–30 Oct	10–5	M	T	W	T	F	S	S
31 Oct–31 Dec	10–4	M	T	W	T	F	S	S
Walled Kitchen Garden								
13 Mar–27 Mar	10–4	M	T	W	T	F	S	S
28 Mar–3 Oct	10–5	M	T	W	T	F	S	S
4 Oct–31 Oct	10–4	M	T	W	T	F	S	S
Cycle hire								
2 Jan–27 Mar	10–4	·	·	·	·	·	S	S
28 Mar–30 Oct	10–5	M	T	W	T	F	S	S
31 Oct–26 Dec	10–4	·	·	·	·	·	S	S

28 March to 30 October: Saturday, Sunday and Bank Holidays all facilities open 10 to 6. Last hiring of cycles two hours before closing. Cycle hire also open midweek November to March for school holidays and booked groups. Chapel: 12 January to 28 March closed for conservation cleaning. Conservation Centre: 3 April to 26 September open Saturday, Sunday and Bank Holidays, 10:30 to 4:30. Park and all facilities closed 25 December.

Making the most of your day: packed events programme throughout the year, from open-air concerts to Christmas events. Everyone can explore, with miles of paths, family Tracker Packs and hands-on wildlife activities. Dogs welcome – on leads in Walled Kitchen Garden, Pleasure Ground and grazing areas.

Access for all: [icons]
Chapel [icons] Glasshouse [icons]
Grounds [icons]

Getting here: 120:SK629752. **Cycle**: NCN6.
Bus: Stagecoach East Midlands SA Worksop–Ollerton, alight Carburton, ¾ mile.
Train: Worksop 4½ miles; Retford 6½ miles.
Road: 4½ miles south east of Worksop, 6½ miles south west of Retford, 1 mile from A1/A57, 11 miles from M1 exit 30.
Parking: throughout park. Main parking 200 yards from visitor facilities and 250 yards from Walled Kitchen Garden.

Finding out more: 01909 544917 or clumberpark@nationaltrust.org.uk

Grantham House

Castlegate, Grantham, Lincolnshire NG31 6SS

Map ③ E4   [icons] 1944

Handsome town house, with architectural features from various eras and a riverside walled garden.

Getting here: 130:SK916362. Immediately east of St Wulfram's church in the centre of Grantham.

Finding out more: 01476 564705 or granthamhouse@nationaltrust.org.uk

Grantham House		M	T	W	T	F	S	S
1 Apr–27 May	*	·	·	W	T	·	·	·
2 Jun–24 Jun	2–5	·	·	W	T	·	·	·
30 Jun–28 Oct	*	·	·	W	T	·	·	·

*By written appointment. The property has been leased by the National Trust and the house and garden are open to visitors at various times, as advertised. The lessee is responsible for all arrangements and facilities.
Entrance via 44 Castlegate – the stable block opposite St Wulfram's Church.

Gunby Hall

Gunby, near Spilsby, Lincolnshire PE23 5SS

Map ③ G3 🏠🏡 1944

Fine red-brick house, dating from 1700, with Victorian walled gardens.

Getting here: 122:TF467668. 2½ miles north west of Burgh le Marsh, 7 miles west of Skegness on south side of A158 (access off roundabout).

Finding out more: 07870 758 876 or gunbyhall@nationaltrust.org.uk

Gunby Hall		M	T	W	T	F	S	S
House and garden								
2 Jun–25 Aug	2–5		·	·	**W**	·	·	·
Gardens only								
7 Apr–26 May	2–5		·	·	**W**	·	·	·
1 Jun–26 Aug	2–5		·	**T**	**W**	**T**	·	·
1 Sep–30 Sep	2–5		·	·	**W**	**T**	·	·

Garden also open Tuesday, Wednesday and Thursday in April and May, by written appointment only to Mrs C. Ayres (address as above).

Gunby Hall Estate: Monksthorpe Chapel

Monksthorpe, near Spilsby, Lincolnshire PE23 5PP

Map ③ G3 ✝ 2000

Remote late 17th-century Baptist chapel.

Getting here: 122:TF450654. From A158 in Candlesby, turn off main road opposite Royal Oak pub, following signs to Monksthorpe. Follow road for about 1½ miles and turn left. After 50 yards turn left at dead end sign. Parking is on the left at entrance to avenue.

Finding out more: 01526 342543 or monksthorpe@nationaltrust.org.uk

Monksthorpe Chapel		M	T	W	T	F	S	S
1 Apr–30 Sep	2–5		·	**W**	**T**	·	·	·

Chapel open and stewarded first Saturday of the month: 3 April, 1 May, 5 June, 3 July, 31 July and 4 September. Services on Saturdays at 3: 17 April, 15 May, 19 June, 17 July, 14 August, 18 September, 2 October (harvest service, 3) and 4 December (carol service, 2). Admission by key, obtained from Gunby (£10 deposit required).

Hardwick Hall

Doe Lea, Chesterfield, Derbyshire S44 5QJ

Map ③ D3

'**Our fifth visit and we learn something different every time. Wonderful.**' Mrs Bradburne, Sheffield

One of the most splendid houses in England. Built by Bess of Hardwick in the 1590s, and unaltered since: yet its huge windows and high ceilings make it feel strikingly modern. Outside, stone gleams and glass glitters in the light. Its six towers make a dramatic skyline. Climbing up through the house, from one spectacular floor to the next, is a thrilling architectural experience. Rich tapestries, plaster friezes and alabaster fireplaces colour the rooms, culminating in the hauntingly atmospheric Long Gallery. **Note**: the Old Hall is owned by the Trust and administered by English Heritage (01246 850431).

Exploring
- See a stunning collection of embroideries and tapestries.
- Try one of our new heritage tours of the stableyard.
- Relax in the fragrant herb garden, orchards and lawns.
- Learn about the stonemasonry at the Stone Centre.
- Explore the picturesque parkland on one of our circular walks.
- Family fun: garden and park children's trails and Tracker Packs.

Members may have to pay on special events days

Hardwick Hall, Derbyshire: barely altered since the 1590s, a visit is a thrilling architectural experience

Eating and shopping: buy Hardwick souvenirs at the shop. Try meat reared on the estate at our restaurant. See our lovely collection of local gifts and produce. Get a snack, drink or ice-cream at the kiosk.

You may also enjoy: Hardwick Estate: Stainsby Mill.

Making the most of your day: tours available Wednesday to Sunday at 11 (£3 donation). Family activities and events, Elizabethan costume days, circular walks. Dogs on leads and in the park and car park only.

Access for all: 🅿️ D♿ 🚻 🏢 📷 📋 🎥
🅰️ ⠿ ◉ Building 🔍 📊 🔤 Grounds ♿ ➡️

Getting here: 120:SK463638. **Foot**: Rowthorne Trail; Teversal Trail. **Bus**: Stagecoach East Midlands 'Pronto' Chesterfield–Nottingham, alight Glapwell 'Young Vanish', 1½ miles. **Train**: Chesterfield 8 miles. **Road**: 6½ miles west of Mansfield, 9½ miles south east of Chesterfield; approach from M1 (exit 29) via A6175. A a one-way traffic system operates in the park; access only via Stainsby Mill entrance (leave M1 exit 29, follow brown signs), exit only via Hardwick Inn. **Parking**: 100 yards, £2. Ponds parking, £1.50 (pay and display).

Finding out more: 01246 850430 or hardwickhall@nationaltrust.org.uk

Hardwick Hall		M	T	W	T	F	S	S
Hall								
17 Feb–31 Oct	11–4:30	·	·	**W**	**T**	**F**	**S**	**S**
4 Dec–19 Dec	11–3	·	·	·	·	·	**S**	**S**
Garden, shop, restaurant and kiosk								
17 Feb–31 Oct	11–5	·	·	**W**	**T**	**F**	**S**	**S**
4 Dec–19 Dec	11–3	·	·	·	·	·	**S**	**S**
Parkland gates								
Open all year	8:30–6	**M**	**T**	**W**	**T**	**F**	**S**	**S**
Hardwick Old Hall								
1 Apr–31 Oct	10–5	·	·	**W**	**T**	**F**	**S**	**S**

Open Bank Holiday Mondays and Good Friday: 12 to 4:30. Kiosk: open daily during main open season and between Christmas and New Year, but may close in bad weather. Tours between 11 to 12 and all day between 17 February and 14 March. Additional heritage tours also available, check on arrival at gatehouse. Hall, gardens and park close dusk during winter. Park gates close 6 during summer. Stone Centre open daily all year round. Hall: occasionally closes for 90 minutes for functions.

Hardwick Estate: Stainsby Mill

Doe Lea, Chesterfield, Derbyshire S44 5QJ

Map ③ D3   1976

Come and explore the workings of a fully operational watermill, which gives a vivid evocation of the workplace of a 19th-century miller. Flour is ground regularly and is for sale throughout the season. **Note**: nearest WC at Hardwick Hall car park.

Exploring	– Discover the secrets of a 13th-century watermill.
	– Children's trail and activity sheets available.
	– Selected days: have a go at milling your own flour.

Eating and shopping: buy Stainsby freshly milled flour. Restaurant, kiosk, shop and WCs nearby at Hardwick Hall. Buy a souvenir guide about the history of the mill.

Making the most of your day: join us to celebrate National Mills weekend in May. Dogs on leads in Hardwick Park only.

Access for all: [icons]
Building [icon] Grounds [icon]

Getting here: 120:SK455653. **Foot**: Rowthorne Trail and Teversal Trail nearby. **Bus**: Stagecoach East Midlands 'Pronto' Chesterfield–Nottingham, alight Glapwell 'Young Vanish', 1½ miles. **Train**: Chesterfield 7 miles. **Road**: from M1 exit 29 take A6175 signposted to Clay Cross, first left and left again to Stainsby Mill. **Parking**: free (not National Trust). Limited car and coach parking.

Finding out more: 01246 850430 (Hardwick Hall) or stainsbymill@nationaltrust.org.uk

Hardwick Estate: Stainsby Mill		M	T	W	T	F	S	S
17 Feb–31 Oct	10–4			**W**	**T**	**F**	**S**	**S**
4 Dec–19 Dec	11–3						**S**	**S**

Open Bank Holiday Mondays and Good Friday. Open 26 December, 11 to 3.

High Peak Estate

Edale, Peak District, Derbyshire

Map ③ B2    1936

The estate stretches from the heather-clad moors of Kinder to the gritstone tors of Derwent Edge, and from the peat bogs of Bleaklow to the limestone crags of Winnats Pass. The wild Pennine moorlands are of international importance for their populations of breeding birds and mosaic of habitats. Sites of particular interest include Mam Tor, with spectacular views, landslip and prehistoric settlement; and the famous Snake Pass. Kinder Scout, where the Mass Trespass of 1932 took place, is the highest point for 50 miles. The Trust also owns several farms and a café in the beautiful Edale Valley. **Note**: nearest WC in adjacent villages and at visitor centres at Ladybower Reservoir, Edale, Castleton.

Exploring	– Feel inspired by the wild moorland landscape and gritstone tors.
	– Wander through the oak woods of the Derwent Valley.
	– Explore the limestone caves and caverns of Winnats Pass.
	– Climb Kinder Scout, the highest point in the Peak District.
	– Discover the beautiful hay meadows in the Edale Valley.
	– Learn about wildlife and history by booking for an event.

Eating and shopping: enjoy homemade food and refreshments at Penny Pot in Edale. Stay at the remote White Edge Lodge Holiday Cottage. Camp and enjoy local food at Upper Booth Farm, Edale. Discover more about moorlands at the Visitor Centre in Edale.

You may also enjoy: our Visitor Centre and estate at Longshaw. The limestone landscape of the South Peak Estate.

Making the most of your day: 'Discover' leaflet for information on the year-round events programme. New downloadable walking trails, audio trails and podcasts from the Peak District website. Waymarked walks. Information Barns at various locations. Dogs must be on a lead at all times from March to end July.

Access for all: ♿ Penny Pot Café 🏔

Getting here: 110:SK100855. **Foot**: Pennine Way and many miles of footpaths pass through property. **Cycle**: Pennine Bridleway and many other routes pass through the property. **Bus**: frequent from surrounding areas (Sheffield, Bakewell and Manchester) to Castleton, Edale and Hope Valley. **Train**: Edale is 1½ miles from Dale Head, 2 miles from Lee Barn and 3 miles from Mam Tor; Chinley is 3 miles from Kinder Scout starting point; Hope is 3 miles from Losehill; Bamford 3 miles from Upper Derwent Valley – linked by cycle route and shuttle bus. **Road**: estate covers area north and south of A57 on Sheffield side of Snake Top, east of Hayfield and west of Castleton.

Parking: many free car parks (not National Trust). Also pay and display (not National Trust) at Edale, Castleton, Bowden Bridge, Upper Derwent Valley and Hayfield. National Trust pay and display at Mam Nick (SK123833).

Finding out more: 01433 670368 or highpeakestate@nationaltrust.org.uk. High Peak Estate Office, Edale End, Hope Valley, Derbyshire S33 6RF

High Peak Estate		M	T	W	T	F	S	S
Estate								
Open all year		M	T	W	T	F	S	S
Penny Pot Café – Edale								
2 Jan–14 Mar	10–4						S	S
17 Mar–31 Oct	10–5			W	T	F	S	S
6 Nov–26 Dec	10–4						S	S

Open and unrestricted access for walkers and other users all year to moorland, subject to occasional management closures (advertised locally). Access to farmland is via public rights of way and permitted paths. Five information shelters open all year: Lee Barn (110:SK096855) on Pennine Way near Jacob's Ladder; Dalehead (110: SK101843) in Edale; South Head Farm (SK060854) at Kinder; Edale End (SK161864) between Edale and Hope; Grindle Barns above Ladybower Reservoir (SK189895).

Walk for miles on the High Peak Estate, Derbyshire

Ilam Park and South Peak Estate

Ilam, Ashbourne, Derbyshire & Peak District

Map ③ B3  1934

Ilam Park and the South Peak Estate are situated in the spectacular setting of the Staffordshire and Derbyshire Peak District. Enjoy the Park's beautiful location beside the River Manifold. Relax in the tea-room with amazing views of Dovedale, browse in the shop or discover the newly refurbished visitor centre with changing exhibitions. You can stay on our caravan site in Ilam Park, or our Wetton Mill holiday cottages. Use it as a base to explore the other parts of the South Peak Estate, such as the rich daleside grasslands and ash woodlands in dramatic Dovedale and magnificent Manifold Valley. **Note**: Ilam Hall is let to the Youth Hostel Association.

Exploring
- Enjoy historic Ilam Park's gardens, park and walks.
- Discover the dramatic limestone dalesides of Dovedale.
- Manifold Valley – walks and cycling on the old railway line.

Eating and shopping: savour local dishes at Manifold tea-room in Ilam Park. The Ilam Park shop sells locally made ice-cream. Tea-room at Wetton Mill serves refreshments (not National Trust).

You may also enjoy: High Peak and Longshaw Estate.

Making the most of your day: varied programme of guided walks, talks and exhibitions. New downloadable walking trails, audio trails and podcasts from the Peak District website. Dogs permitted, but only on leads in areas with livestock.

Access for all: �Pⓓ 🚻 ♿ ∴ Ⓐ
Building ♿ ♿ Grounds ♿ ♿

Getting here: 119:SK132507. 4½ miles north west of Ashbourne. **Cycle**: NCN68, 2 miles. **Bus**: Bowers 442 Buxton ≋–Ashbourne, daily, alight Thorpe, 2 miles Monday–Saturday, Ilam village Sunday and Bank Holidays. **Parking**: 75 yards (pay and display). Coaches by prior arrangement only.

Finding out more: 01335 350503 or ilampark@nationaltrust.org.uk. South Peak Estate Office, Home Farm, Ilam, Ashbourne, Derbyshire DE6 2AZ

Ilam Park		M	T	W	T	F	S	S
Ilam Park, Dovedale and Manifold Valley								
Open all year	Dawn–dusk	M	T	W	T	F	S	S
Manifold tea-room, Ilam Park								
2 Jan–28 Feb	11–4	·	·	·	·	·	S	S
1 Mar–29 Jun	11–5	M	T	·	·	F	S	S
30 Jun–31 Aug	11–5	M	T	W	T	F	S	S
3 Sep–31 Oct	11–5	M	T	·	·	F	S	S
6 Nov–19 Dec	11–4	·	·	·	·	·	S	S
Ilam Park shop								
2 Jan–28 Feb	11–4	·	·	·	·	·	S	S
1 Mar–31 Oct	11–5	M	T	W	T	F	S	S
5 Nov–19 Dec	11–4	·	·	·	·	F	S	S
Ilam Park caravan site								
12 Mar–7 Nov	12 till dusk	M	T	W	T	F	S	S

Ilam Park caravan site has 20 pitches, basic facilities (electric hook up and water but no WCs). Telephone caravan site booking office 01335 350310 in season (no calls after 8) or estate office November to February. Ilam Hall is available for overnight accommodation via the YHA.

Kedleston Hall

near Quardon, Derby, Derbyshire DE22 5JH

Map ③ C4  1987

'**The view of the house as I drive over the bridge always takes my breath away.**'
Candice Oliver, Derby

Take a trip back in time to the 1760s at this spectacular Neo-classical mansion framed by historic parkland. Designed for lavish entertaining and displaying an extensive collection of paintings, sculpture and original furnishings, Kedleston is a stunning example of the work of architect Robert Adam. The Curzon family have lived here since the 12th

Kedleston Hall, Derbyshire

century and continue to live at the Hall. Lord Curzon's Eastern Museum is a treasure trove of fascinating objects acquired on his travels in Asia and while Viceroy of India (1899 to 1905). Used as a key location for *The Duchess*, the recent Hollywood blockbuster. **Note**: medieval All Saints church, containing many family monuments, is run by the Churches Conservation Trust.

Exploring
– Experience the stunning Adam interiors.
– Watch restoration in action on the state floor.
– Discover Britain's colonial connections in the Eastern Museum.
– Follow in the footsteps of *The Duchess* film using trail.
– Explore the parkland and see what wildlife you can spot.
– New: a contemporary art project supported by the Arts Council.

Eating and shopping: buy a Kedleston souvenir and local products. Peat-free plants for sale. Seasonal recipes made using local produce, including Kedleston estate lamb.

You may also enjoy: medieval Tattershall Castle, restored by Lord Curzon.

Making the most of your day: available most house open days at selected times – introductory talk, tours of fishing pavilion, great west stable or pleasure grounds, and brief talks by 18th-century housekeeper Mrs Garnett. Dogs on leads in park and pleasure grounds.

Access for all: [symbols] House – ground floor [symbols] House – state floor [symbols] Grounds [symbol]

Getting here: 128:SK312403. 5 miles north west of Derby; 12 miles south east of Ashbourne. **Cycle**: on parkland roads (not allowed on park walks and footpaths). **Bus**: Arriva 109 Derby–Ashbourne, calls at the Hall summer Saturdays only, otherwise alight the Smithy, 1 mile. **Train**: Duffield 3½ miles; Derby 5½ miles. **Road**: all traffic should aim for intersection of A52/ A38, and follow A38 (north). Take first exit (by Derby University) and continue along Kedleston Road towards Quarndon. **Parking**: 200 yards, admission fees apply.

Finding out more: 01332 842191 or kedlestonhall@nationaltrust.org.uk

Kedleston Hall		M	T	W	T	F	S	S
House								
20 Feb–3 Nov	12–5	M	T	W	·	·	S	S
Pleasure Grounds								
20 Feb–3 Nov	10–6	M	T	W	T	F	S	S
Park								
1 Jan–19 Feb	10–4	M	T	W	T	F	S	S
20 Feb–3 Nov	10–6	M	T	W	T	F	S	S
4 Nov–31 Dec	10–4	M	T	W	T	F	S	S
Restaurant and shop								
2 Jan–14 Feb	11–3	·	·	·	·	·	S	S
15 Feb–17 Feb	11–3	M	T	W	·	·	·	·
20 Feb–3 Nov	11–5	M	T	W	·	·	S	S
22 Jul–27 Aug	11–3	·	·	·	T	F	·	·
6 Nov–26 Dec	11–3	·	·	·	·	·	S	S

Last entry to house 4:15. Open Good Friday. Park occasional day closures November to February. Property closed 25 December. **20 February to 31 March: due to conservation restrictions the house will be shown by guided tour only on weekdays (places allocated on arrival). Free-flow during weekends but conservation work may be continuing.**

Longshaw Estate

Longshaw, near Sheffield, Derbyshire

Map ③ C2  1931

A wonderful place to discover spectacular views of the Peak District, ancient woods, parkland and heather moorland. Explore the unusual sites of Longshaw's past, from millstone quarries to packhorse routes. The Visitor Centre, housed in the Shooting Lodge, is the ideal starting point for Longshaw and the Peak District. **Note**: Moorland Discovery Centre is a a learning centre and not open to the public.

Exploring
- Wander through the ancient woods and hay meadows.
- Enjoy spectacular views from the gritsone edges and heather moorland.
- Discover the hidden past with the guidebook or family trail.
- New: drop in to the interpretation barn at Padley Gorge.

Eating and shopping: browse in the shop for local and wildlife-themed products. Enjoy delicious home-baked local food with wonderful views.

Making the most of your day: year-round events programme, including special family events and trails in the autumn, Christmas and Easter holidays. Circular, waymarked walks to explore the park and woodland. Dogs on estate on leads during lambing and nesting time.

Access for all: 🅿️♿♿🚾♿♿🖐️
Building ♿ Grounds ♿♿➡️

Getting here: 110/119:SK266800. **Foot**: 2 miles by footpath from Grindleford, 3 miles from Hathersage and 7 miles from Sheffield. **Cycle**: connected to Sheffield (7 miles) by Bridleway via Moss Raod and Houndkirk. **Bus**: First 272 Sheffield–Castleton (passing Hathersage ⊛), TM Travel 214 Sheffield–Matlock and 65 Sheffield–Buxton. All pass close

Sheffield ⊛. **Train**: Grindleford 2 miles (1 mile to Visitor Centre, 100 yards to Padley Gorge). **Road**: 7½ miles from Sheffield, next to A625 Sheffield–Hathersage road; Woodcroft car park is off B6055, 200 yards south of junction with A625. **Parking**: at Haywood [110/119: SK256778], Wooden Pole [110/119: SK267790] and Woodcroft [110/119: SK267802]. Only Woodcroft accessible to coaches. All pay and display.

Finding out more: 01433 637904 or longshaw@nationaltrust.org.uk. Estate Office, Longshaw Estate, Longshaw, Sheffield, Derbyshire S11 7TZ

Longshaw Estate		M	T	W	T	F	S	S
Estate								
Open all year		M	T	W	T	F	S	S
Visitor Centre								
2 Jan–7 Mar	10:30–4	·	·	·	·	·	S	S
8 Mar–31 Oct	10:30–5	M	T	W	T	F	S	S
6 Nov–26 Dec	10:30–4	·	·	·	·	·	S	S

Open Bank Holiday Mondays. Lodge is not open. Telephone for extended opening, 18 to 31 December.

Lyveden New Bield

near Oundle, Northamptonshire PE8 5AT

Map ③ E6  1922

Set in the heart of rural Northamptonshire, Lyveden is a remarkable survival of the Elizabethan age. Begun by Sir Thomas Tresham to symbolise his Catholic faith, Lyveden remains incomplete and virtually unaltered since work stopped on his death in 1605. Discover the mysterious garden lodge and explore the Elizabethan garden with spiral mounts, terracing and canals. Wander through the new orchard, containing many old varieties of apples and pears, or explore the Lyveden Way, a circular path through beautiful meadows, wooodland and villages.

Exploring
- Discover one of England's oldest surviving garden landscapes.
- Uncover the mysteries of Sir Thomas's garden lodge.

Exploring
- Relax with a picnic in the peaceful setting of Lyveden.
- Wander in Rockingham Forest or along Lyveden Way.
- Enjoy our new audio trail.

Eating and shopping: enjoy an ice-cream sitting by the moated garden. Hot and cold drinks sold in the shop. Local honey (seasonal).

You may also enjoy: another Elizabethan house and exciting garden project at Canons Ashby.

Making the most of your day: join one of the free garden tours every Sunday from June to October. Dogs on leads are welcome.

Access for all: Building Grounds

Getting here: 141:SP983853. **Bus**: Stagecoach in Northants X4 Northampton –Peterborough, alight Lower Benefield, 2 miles by bridlepath; Judges minicoaches 8 Kettering–Corby, alight Brigstock, 2½ miles. Both pass close Kettering. **Train**: Kettering 10 miles. **Road**: 4 miles south west of Oundle via A427, 3 miles east of Brigstock, leading off A6116. **Parking**: free, 100 yards.

Finding out more: 01832 205358 or lyveden@nationaltrust.org.uk

Lyveden New Bield		M	T	W	T	F	S	S
6 Feb–7 Mar	11–4	·	·	·	·	·	S	S
13 Mar–30 Jun	10:30–5	·	·	W	T	F	S	S
1 Jul–31 Aug	10:30–5	M	T	W	T	F	S	S
1 Sep–31 Oct	10:30–5	·	·	W	T	F	S	S
6 Nov–28 Nov	11–4	·	·	·	·	·	S	S

Open Bank Holiday Mondays. Open Good Friday, 10:30 to 5.

Lyveden New Bield, Northamptonshire

The Old Manor

Norbury, Ashbourne, Derbyshire DE6 2ED

Map (3) B4 1987

Medieval hall featuring a rare king post, Tudor door and 17th-century Flemish glass. Gardens include a parterre herb garden. **Note**: limited parking (cars only).

Getting here: 128:SK125424. 4 miles from Ashbourne; 9 miles from Sudbury Hall.

Finding out more: 01283 585337 or oldmanor@nationaltrust.org.uk

The Old Manor		M	T	W	T	F	S	S
2 Apr–22 Oct	11–1	·	·	·	·	F	·	·
3 Apr–23 Oct	2–4	·	·	·	·	·	S	·

Property is tenanted and visits are only available during opening hours.

Priest's House

Easton on the Hill, near Stamford, Northamptonshire PE9 3LS

Map (3) E5 1966

A delightful small 16th-century building, with interesting local architecture and a museum exploring Easton's industrial past.

Getting here: 141:TF009045. approximately 2 miles south west of Stamford off A43.

Finding out more: 01780 762619 or priestshouse2@nationaltrust.org.uk

Priest's House		M	T	W	T	F	S	S
4 Jul–29 Aug	2:30–4:30	·	·	·	·	·	·	S

Unmanned. Also open by appointment daily throughout the year. Names of keyholders on property noticeboard. Appointments for groups may be made through local representative Mr Paul Way, 39 Church St, Easton on the Hill, Stamford PE9 3LL.

Staunton Harold Church

Staunton Harold, Ashby-de-la-Zouch,
Leicestershire LE65 1RW

Map ③ C4   1954

This is one of the few churches built between
the outbreak of the English Civil War and the
Restoration period. **Note**: WCs (not National
Trust), 500 yards. Staunton Harold Estate may
ask for voluntary parking donation.

Getting here: 128:SK380209. 5 miles north
east of Ashby-de-la-Zouch, west of B587.
Access from M42/A42 exit 13, follow Ferrers
Centre brown signs – anvil symbol.

Finding out more: 01332 863822 (Calke
Abbey) or calkeabbey@nationaltrust.org.uk

Staunton Harold Church		M	T	W	T	F	S	S
3 Apr–31 Oct	1–4:30						**S**	**S**
2 Jun–27 Aug	1–4:30			**W**	**T**	**F**	**S**	**S**

Church open Bank Holidays April to October. Services:
Easter to December, second and fourth Sundays.

Mr Straw's House

5-7 Blyth Grove, Worksop,
Nottinghamshire S81 0JG

Map ③ D2   1990

'**Absolutely wondrous – great to see history
of a non-aristocratic family – the backbone
of England.**'
S. Fenton, Nottingham

Step back in time to the 1920s and find out
how a grocer's family lived in this market town.
This ordinary semi-detached house, with
original interior decorations from 1923, was
the home of the Straw family. For 60 years
the family threw little away and chose to live
without many of the modern comforts we take
for granted. Photographs, letters, Victorian
furniture and household objects spanning
100 years can still be seen exactly where their
owners left them.

Exploring
- Introductory video introduces the Straw family.
- Explore three floors of Edwardian house with informative guides.
- See annual exhibition of items not usually on display.
- Visit the garden and replica greenhouse with cacti collection.
- Children can follow a trail.
- Occasional activity days and events.

Eating and shopping: small shop area with
snacks and souvenirs.

You may also enjoy: The Workhouse.

Making the most of your day: tea and cakes,
usually on first Saturday in month in orchard
car park (provided by Friends group). 'Mr
Straw's Revealed'. Look out for the tour.

Access for all: 🖼️📷👓📷 No 5 ♿ No 7 ♿

Getting here: 120:SK592802. Private road to
north of Worksop town centre, in suburbs.
Cycle: NCN6, ¾ mile. **Bus**: Stagecoach 22
and 42 from Worksop. **Train**: Worksop ½ mile.
Road: follow signs for Bassetlaw Hospital and
Blyth Road (B6045). Blyth Grove is a small
private road off B6045, just south of Bassetlaw
Hospital A&E entrance. House signposted with
black and white sign at the entrance to Blyth
Grove. **Parking**: free, across the road.

Finding out more: 01909 482380 or
mrstrawshouse@nationaltrust.org.uk

Mr Straw's House		M	T	W	T	F	S	S
13 Mar–30 Oct	11–5		**T**	**W**	**T**	**F**	**S**	

Admission by timed ticket only for all visitors (including
members) – must be booked in advance. All bookings by
telephone or letter (with sae), not email, to Custodian. On
quiet days a same-day telephone call is often sufficient.
Last admission 4. Closed Good Friday. Due to its location
in residential area, the house is closed on Sundays as a
courtesy to neighbours.

Sudbury Hall and the National Trust Museum of Childhood

Sudbury, Ashbourne, Derbyshire DE6 5HT

Map ③ B4 🏰 🏠 ♣ 🔔 🍷 | 1967

Sudbury Hall, Derbyshire

'**Best all round family day out ever, uniting three generations, leaving us with that "glowing" feeling all day.**'
J. D. Hives, aged 16, Brixworth, Northampton

Two totally different experiences sitting side by side. The country home of the Lords Vernon, a delight of 17th-century craftsmanship, featuring exquisite plasterwork, wood carvings and classical story-based murals. Be amazed by the grandeur of the Great Staircase and Long Gallery. The Museum of Childhood is a delight for all ages with something for everyone. Explore the childhoods of times gone by, make stories, play with toys and share your childhood with others. You can be a chimney sweep, a scullion or a Victorian pupil, and be captivated by our archive film, interactives and displays.

Exploring
– Come and enjoy a morning tour of the hall.
– Stroll in the meadow by the lakeside.
– Admire our elaborate plasterwork.
– Relive your childhood by experiencing our play collections.
– Enjoy our toys, interactives and displays.
– New: the museum is open seven days a week.

Eating and shopping: step back in time in our museum shop. Buy homemade fudge to tickle your taste buds. Try our homemade cakes and scones. Indulge yourself with our Sudbury savoury herb pancakes.

You may also enjoy: Kedleston Hall and Calke Abbey.

Making the most of your day: family activities in the school holidays. Explore our treasure chests in the Hall. Join our Butler Tour. Explore our 'Have a Go' and Wicked Woodland Outdoor Adventure play areas.

Access for all: 🅿 🅳 ♿ 🚾 ♿ ♿ 📷 🖥
📺 ♿ •• 🅰 Sudbury Hall ♿ ♿
Museum of Childhood ♿ ♿ ♿ Grounds ♿ ♿

Getting here: 128:SK158322. **Cycle**: cycleway from Uttoxeter to Doveridge, then road to property. **Bus**: Arriva 1 Burton on Trent–Uttoxeter (passing Tutbury 🚉 and Hatton and close Burton on Trent 🚉). **Train**: Tutbury and Hatton 5 miles. **Road**: 6 miles east of Uttoxeter at junction of A50 Derby–Stoke and A515 Ashbourne. **Sat Nav**: enter DE6 5HT. **Parking**: free, 500 yards.

Finding out more: 01283 585305 (Infoline). 01283 585337 or sudburyhall@nationaltrust.org.uk

Sudbury Hall		M	T	W	T	F	S	S
Hall								
13 Feb–31 Oct	1–5	·	·	W	T	F	S	S
Museum, tea-room and shops								
13 Feb–28 Mar	11–5	·	·	W	T	F	S	S
29 Mar–31 Oct	11–5	M	T	W	T	F	S	S
6 Nov–19 Dec	11–5	·	·	·	·	·	S	S
Christmas event in the Museum								
4 Dec–19 Dec	11–5	·	·	·	·	·	S	S
Grounds								
13 Feb–19 Dec	10–5	M	T	W	T	F	S	S

Hall open Bank Holiday Mondays and Good Friday. Hall may have to close early if light is poor. School visits and Hall tours available 11 to 1.

Tattershall Castle

Sleaford Road, Tattershall, Lincolnshire LN4 4LR

Map ③ F3   1925

Explore the six floors of this rare red-brick medieval castle built by Ralph Cromwell, Lord Treasurer of England and one of the most powerful men in the country. Let the audio guide create a picture of what life was like at Tattershall Castle in the 15th century. Climb the 150 steps from the basement to the battlements and enjoy the magnificent views of the Lincolnshire countryside, then explore the grounds, moats, bridges and neighbouring church, also built by Ralph Cromwell.

Exploring
- Explore all six floors, from the basement to the battlements.
- Enjoy amazing views from the roof.
- Follow the audio tour.
- Picnic in the moated grounds.
- Explore the church.
- Visit the neighbouring RAF museum (weekdays only).

Eating and shopping: buy presents for all the family at our gift shop. Relax and enjoy some light refreshments.

You may also enjoy: Belton House.

Making the most of your day: major events, family activities and 'have a go' sessions.

Access for all: 🅿🚻♿🔄🎧💻👓

Building 🦽🦼♿ Grounds 🦽🦼

Getting here: 122:TF211575. **Cycle**: Hull to Harwich cycle route passes within 1 mile. **Bus**: Brylaine 5 Lincoln–Boston (passing close Lincoln ≥). **Train**: Ruskington 10 miles. **Road**: on south side of A153, 15 miles north east of Sleaford; 10 miles south west of Horncastle. **Parking**: free, 150 yards. Coaches must reverse into parking area.

Finding out more: 01526 342543 or tattershallcastle@nationaltrust.org.uk

Tattershall Castle		M	T	W	T	F	S	S
13 Feb–14 Mar	11–4	·	·	·	·	·	S	S
15 Mar–31 Mar	11–4	M	T	W	·	·	S	S
3 Apr–29 Sep	11–5	M	T	W	·	·	S	S
2 Oct–31 Oct	11–4	M	T	W	·	·	S	S
6 Nov–19 Dec	11–4	·	·	·	·	·	S	S

Open Good Friday. Last audio guide issued one hour before closing. Castle opens 1 on some Saturdays if hosting a wedding. Please telephone to confirm in advance of visit.

The medieval Tattershall Castle, Lincolnshire

Ulverscroft Nature Reserve

near Loughborough, Leicestershire

Map ③ D5   🐾 1945

Part of the ancient forest of Charnwood, Ulverscroft is especially beautiful during the spring bluebell season. Heathland and woodland habitats. **Note**: no WC. Access by permit only from Leicestershire and Rutland Wildlife Trust, 0116 272 0444.

Getting here: 129:SK493118. 6 miles south west of Loughborough.

Finding out more: 01332 863822 (Calke Abbey) or ulverscroftnaturereserve@nationaltrust.org.uk

---

Ulverscroft Nature Reserve

Access by permit only from The Secretary, Leicestershire and Rutland Wildlife Trust, Brocks Hill Environment Centre, Washbrook Lane, Oadby, Leicestershire LE2 5JJ (0116 272 0444). Please allow a week to receive permit.

Winster Market House

Main Street, Winster, Matlock,
Derbyshire DE4 2DJ

Map ③ C3   1906

This restored market house is a reminder of when fairs were prominent features of local life (now houses information room).

Getting here: 119:SK241606. 4 miles west of Matlock. Hulleys bus 172 Bakewell to Matlock.

Finding out more: 01335 350503 or winstermarkethouse@nationaltrust.org.uk. Home Farm, Ilam, Ashbourne, Derbyshire DE6 2AZ

Winster Market House		M	T	W	T	F	S	S
27 Mar–31 Oct	11–5	**M**	**T**	**W**	**T**	**F**	**S**	**S**

Woolsthorpe Manor

Water Lane, Woolsthorpe by Colsterworth, near Grantham, Lincolnshire NG33 5PD

Map ③ E4   1943

Isaac Newton was born in this modest manor house in 1642 and he made many of his most important discoveries about light and gravity here. A complex figure, Newton notched up careers as diverse as Cambridge Professor and Master of the Royal Mint, spent years studying alchemy and the Bible as well as science, and was President of the Royal Society – whose 350th anniversary it is in 2010. You can still see the famous apple tree from Isaac's bedroom window and enjoy the brand new Discovery Centre, which opened at the start of this year.

Exploring
 – New: explore the hands-on Discovery Centre.
 – Be inspired by the house where a genius grew up.

Exploring
 – Summer holidays – special exhibition 'Newton and The Royal Society'.
 – Contemplate the apple tree with a place in history.
 – See the short film about Newton as a young man.
 – Say hello to our rare breed sheep.

Eating and shopping: refuel with tea and cake in our mini café. Visit the small shop in the goat-free Goat House!

You may also enjoy: nearby Belton House, 17th-century Townend in the Lake District, and Cragside's quirky technology.

Making the most of your day: programme of events, including regular 'Tales from Woolsthorpe' and Conservation in Action. National Science Week in March and summer holiday workshops for children. Summer exhibition and Apple Day.

Access for all: 🐕♿🚻🏛️🖥️♨️👓🎧
Building 🔗♿🔓 Grounds 🔗🏔️

Getting here: 130:SK924244. 8 miles south of Grantham, ½ mile north west of Colsterworth.
Foot: 1 mile by footpath from Colsterworth; 3 miles from the Viking Way, leaving Sewstern Lane near Buckminster. **Bus**: Centrebus 608 Grantham–South Witham (passes close Grantham ≋). **Train**: Grantham 8 miles.
Road: at Woolsthorpe by Colsterworth, 8 miles south of Grantham. Leave A1 southbound at B6403 Ancaster and Easton turn, or A1 northbound at Woolsthorpe turn. From Melton follow B676 for Colsterworth and Bourne.
Sat Nav: use NG33 5PD. **Parking**: free, 50 yards. Limited coach parking (booking essential).

Finding out more: 01476 860338 or woolsthorpemanor@nationaltrust.org.uk. 23 Newton Way, Woolsthorpe by Colsterworth, near Grantham, Lincolnshire NG33 5NR

Woolsthorpe Manor		M	T	W	T	F	S	S
19 Feb–14 Mar	11–5	·	·	·	·	**F**	**S**	**S**
17 Mar–3 Oct	11–5	·	·	**W**	**T**	**F**	**S**	**S**
8 Oct–31 Oct	11–5	·	·	·	·	**F**	**S**	**S**

Open Bank Holiday Mondays and Good Friday, 11 to 5.

The Workhouse, Southwell

Upton Road, Southwell,
Nottinghamshire NG25 0PT

Map ③ D3 🏠 2002

The Workhouse, Southwell, Nottinghamshire

'We had a real insight into the lives of the Victorian poor. The real shock though, was seeing the bedsit.'
Mr and Mrs A. Rutherford, Harrogate

Discover the most complete workhouse in existence. Meet the Reverend Becher, the founder of The Workhouse, by watching the introductory film and immerse yourself in the unique atmosphere evoked by the audio guide. Based on real archive records, the guide helps bring the 19th-century inhabitants back to life. Discover how society dealt with poverty through the centuries. Explore the segregated work yards, day rooms, dormitories, master's quarters and cellars, then see the recreated working 19th-century garden and find out what food the paupers would have eaten.

Exploring
– A thought-provoking look at hidden histories of the poor.
– Share your thoughts and feelings with one of our volunteers.
– Enjoy the drama of our Living History events.
– Explore your own heritage by joining a family history class.
– Discover the challenges of conserving an 'empty' property.
– Enjoy some quiet time in the re-created vegetable garden.

Eating and shopping: browse through the many specialist publications and items on sale. Buy our fresh, seasonal garden produce to eat at home.

You may also enjoy: Back to Backs, Birmingham, and Quarry Bank Mill, Cheshire.

Making the most of your day: programme of family activities, special events, tours and exhibitions. Children's trails and games to play.

Access for all: 🅿️ 🄳 ♿ 🚾 🔆 ⌕ 📖 VT 🎦 👁 📷
Building ♿ ♿ ♿ Grounds ♿ ➡️

Getting here: 120:SK712543. **Foot**: Robin Hood Trail goes past The Workhouse. **Cycle**: National Byway (Heritage Cycle Route). **Bus**: Stagecoach East Midlands 29A Newark–Southwell–Mansfield, Premier Travel 3 Newark–Southwell–Lowdham. Both pass Newark Castle 🚉. **Train**: Fiskerton 2 miles, Newark Castle 7 miles, Newark North Gate 7½ miles. **Road**: 13 miles from Nottingham on A612 and 8 miles from Newark on A617 and A612. **Parking**: free, 200 yards.

Finding out more: 01636 817260 or theworkhouse@nationaltrust.org.uk

The Workhouse, Southwell		M	T	W	T	F	S	S
3 Mar–31 Oct	12–5			**W**	**T**	**F**	**S**	**S**

Guided tour (exterior): 3 March to 31 October, Wednesday to Sunday, 11 to 12 (numbers limited). Open Bank Holiday Mondays and Good Friday. Last admission one hour before closing. Normal house admission from 12.

West Midlands

Travel the world at Biddulph Grange Garden.
This Victorian re-creation of a Chinese
temple is just one stop on the designer's
vision of the globe's gardens

Outdoors in the West Midlands

In the West Midlands region, industry and history have shaped the countryside in our care. From the sweeping hills of Shropshire to the panoramic views from the Clent Hills – just twelve miles from the Birmingham conurbation – there are numerous paths and acres of land for a family day out or simply a relaxing walk.

Above:
the head of Carding Mill Valley on the Long Mynd in Shropshire

In the north of the region are the Staffordshire moorlands, including the lowland heath of Downs Bank, near Stone (see 'My favourite place', overleaf), where cattle have been reintroduced to graze the heathland. This has led to an increase of viviparous lizards, so if you hear a rustle in the undergrowth, look quickly and you may see one rushing to hide.

The ancient woodland at Hawksmoor Nature Reserve in the Churnet Valley is a perfect spot for visitors to see green woodpeckers, spotted flycatchers and ravens, while the wild flowers and archaeology of Gibridding Wood at Hawksmoor have attracted artists, photographers and film crews. The remote woodland is the hidden jewel of the property.

Stroll or stride, the choice is yours

Close to Birmingham are the Clent Hills – an ideal place to enjoy a gentle stroll or one of the many guided walks. If you are feeling more adventurous, then why not try your hand at geocaching? The popularity of this newly introduced outdoor treasure-hunting game is increasing fast, and it offers visitors a new and interesting twist on a walk.

Kinver Edge is not too far away, with its fascinating history and panoramic views towards Worcestershire and the Malvern Hills. At nearby Rock Houses a new tea-room provides the necessary refreshments after a relaxing walk.

Whether you like a long ramble, a brisk walk or a gentle stroll there are endless opportunities. The Long Mynd (Long Mountain) in Shropshire, a Site of Special Scientific Interest, offers excellent walking, riding and cycling opportunities. An ancient track, the Portway, extends for ten miles and is home to a wide variety of flora and fauna, as well as an increasing number of ground-nesting birds – such as snipe, skylark, curlew and red grouse.

Nearby, Wenlock Edge is another rare and special landscape. Stretching nineteen miles through Shropshire, this thickly wooded limestone escarpment offers panoramic views, historic quarries and limekilns as well as rare flowers (such as several orchids, including the bee orchid), birds and insects.

Right:
bluebells in bloom at Hawksmoor Nature Reserve, Staffordshire

Stately parkland

There is an abundance of parkland in the West Midlands region. Discover 'Capability' Brown's designs at Berrington Hall, Charlecote Park and Croome Park, or wander through George London's restored parkland at Hanbury Hall (amazingly just a few miles from Birmingham).

At Croome Park, take a gentle stroll to the outer eye-catchers, acquired and restored by the National Trust in 2009, and see James Wyatt's and Robert Adam's designs for these follies in their former 18th-century glory.

Enjoy landscaped woodlands at the Dudmaston Estate, where the modern designs of the stiles reflect the contemporary art in the house. Also in Shropshire, walk through the dappled woodland at Attingham Park near Shrewsbury, where a new bridge across the River Tern has provided more access for buggy and wheelchair users.

Below:
Dudmaston, near Bridgnorth, Shropshire

Across in Herefordshire, tuck into the award-winning local food produced on the Brockhampton Estate after enjoying a walk through this traditionally farmed land – where there are miles of orchards, woodlands and pathways to enjoy.

The parkland at Croft Castle now has a new walks leaflet which tells the story of the landscape, from the Iron Age hill fort at Croft Ambrey to the 18th-century engineering of Fish Pool Valley. Visitors can walk through 1,000 years of history in a few hours, then enjoy lunch or afternoon tea in the Carpenter's Workshop tea-room – now open all year round and at weekends in the winter.

Seize the opportunity to walk in the footsteps of William Shakespeare in the parkland at Charlecote Park; the bard was allegedly caught poaching here as a lad, caught and subsequently flogged – he then decided to travel to London to seek his fortune. The parkland is now open all year round.

There are many events and activities in our countryside, from early morning bird walks to mini-beast hunts, guided tours and foraging walks. There is definitely something for everyone.

Above: enjoying a walk along one of the trails at Brockhampton Estate, Herefordshire

My favourite place
My favourite place is the Downs Banks Brook, south of Stoke-on-Trent and north of Stone in Staffordshire. Between its source and the River Trent the brook has a short existence, but a very beautiful one.

On hot summer days it is a cool oasis, where alder trees cast shade and the slow gurgle of the stream provides gentle background music. After winter rains it has a powerful surge, which can lift the banks and change its course.

Stepping stones and bridges excite children and those who used to be children alike, while birds feed in the trees above and on the water's edge. Keep your eyes open and you may even see the fantastic blue flash of a kingfisher.

Rod Whiteman
Warden, Staffordshire Countryside

Attingham Park

Atcham, Shrewsbury, Shropshire SY4 4TP

Map ④ H4

Attingham Park was built for the 1st Lord Berwick in 1785 and was in continuous ownership by the family for more than 160 years. As their fortunes rose and fell they proved themselves to be spenders, savers and saviours. In the mansion, highlights include the atmospheric Dining Room set for an evening banquet that reflects the Regency splendour and the delicate decorative scheme in the Boudoir which has recently been revealed. The mansion is at the heart of this great estate between Shrewsbury and the River Severn and is set in beautiful parkland designed to impress. **Note**: restoration and conservation in action ongoing in various parts of the mansion.

Exploring	– Discover Attingham's story of love and neglect.
	– Find out about the Berwick family and their changing fortunes.
	– The Attingham Re-discovered Project reveals the mansion's interior restorations.
	– Walks lead you through the deer park and grounds.
	– Stroll through the walled garden as it is reinstated.
	– Choose from our range of mansion guided tours.

Eating and shopping: Shop and Carriage House Café open daily all year. Take home seasonal fresh vegetables from the walled garden. Indulge in our home-baked cakes and scones. Browse in the second-hand bookshop.

You may also enjoy: Neo-classical Berrington Hall and also Sunnycroft, an Edwardian gentleman's suburban villa.

Making the most of your day: witness developments in the mansion and walled garden as we re-discover Attingham. Family trails and activities throughout local school holidays. Events programme throughout year.

Attingham Park, Shropshire: stunning setting

Waymarked walks. Dogs welcome on leads in deer park and near the mansion.

Access for all:
Mansion Shop, bookshop and café
Grounds

Getting here: 126:SJ550099. **Foot**: from main drive walk up the park road for approximately ½ mile to Visitor Reception at stables. **Bus**: Arriva 96 Shrewsbury–Telford (passing close Shrewsbury and Telford Central). **Train**: Shrewsbury 5 miles. **Road**: 4 miles south east of Shrewsbury, on north side of B4380 in Atcham village. **Parking**: free, 25 yards.

Finding out more: 01743 708123 (Infoline). 01743 708162 or attingham@nationaltrust.org.uk

Attingham Park		M	T	W	T	F	S	S
Park, walled garden, shop, café and bookshop								
Open all year	9–6	M	T	W	T	F	S	S
Mansion								
13 Mar–7 Nov	11–5:30	M	T	·	T	F	S	S
Mansion winter tours								
9 Jan–7 Mar	11–3	·	·	·	·	·	S	S
13 Nov–28 Nov	11–3	·	·	·	·	·	S	S
Mansion tea-room								
2 Jan–7 Mar	10:30–4:30	·	·	·	·	·	S	S
13 Mar–7 Nov	10:30–5	M	T	·	T	F	S	S
13 Nov–12 Dec	10:30–4:30	·	·	·	·	·	S	S
18 Dec–31 Dec	10:30–4:30	M	T	W	T	F	S	S

Park, walled garden, shop, café and bookshop close at 5, January, February, November and December or dusk if earlier. Mansion tea-room open 13 to 21 February. **Mansion 11 to 1 tours only.** Mansion open 11 on Bank Holiday Sundays, Mondays and Good Friday. **Mansion Christmas opening: 11 and 12 December and 18 to 23 December, 11 to 4.** Whole site closed 25 December. Mansion tea-room closed 26 December.

Attingham Park Estate: Cronkhill

Atcham, Shrewsbury, Shropshire SY5 6JP

Map ④ H5 1947

Delightful Italianate villa designed by Regency architect John Nash. Stands proudly on a hillside with views across the Attingham Estate. **Note**: contents of the property belong to the tenants.

Getting here: 126:SJ535083. From Attingham Park take road to Cross Houses; Cronkhill is on the right.

Finding out more: 01743 708162 or cronkhill@nationaltrust.org.uk

Cronkhill
Open Wednesday 21 and Sunday 25 April, Wednesday 18 and Sunday 22 August and Wednesday 6 and Sunday 10 October, 11 to 4.

Baddesley Clinton

Rising Lane, Baddesley Clinton, Warwickshire B93 0DQ

Map ④ K6  1980

This atmospheric house dates from the 15th century and was the home of the Ferrers family for 500 years. The house and interiors reflect its heyday in the Elizabethan era, when it was a haven for persecuted Catholics – there are three priest's holes. There is a delightful garden with stewponds and a romantic lake and nature walk.

Exploring
– Discover the priest's hole used in 1591.
– Relax and read in the Great Hall.
– Plot to plate – discover what's fresh in the vegetable garden.

Exploring
– Murder most foul – investigate the evidence.
– Browse for bargains in the second-hand bookshop.
– Water, water everywhere – the Great Pool, fish-pools, Long Ditch.

Eating and shopping: try our homemade bread – straight from the oven. Savour seasonal food, using produce from our own vegetable garden. Our varied menu will delight all diners. Locally sourced products and plants available in the shop.

You may also enjoy: Packwood House – a mere two miles away.

Making the most of your day: set the scene with an introductory talk. Brunch lectures in the restaurant in spring and autumn. Easter trail for families. 'Hands on the Past' living history in the summer.

Access for all: ♿ WC 🅿️ 🖼️ 🔥 ⠿
Building 🔨🔨🔨 Grounds 🔨🔨➡️🔨

Getting here: 139:SP199723. **Foot**: Heart of England Way passes close by. **Train**: Lapworth, 2 miles; Birmingham International 9 miles. **Road**: ¾ miles west of A4141 Warwick–Birmingham road, at Chadwick End, 7½ miles north west of Warwick, 6 miles south of M42 exit 5; 15 miles south east of central Birmingham. **Parking**: free, 100 yards.

Finding out more: 01564 783294 or baddesleyclinton@nationaltrust.org.uk

Baddesley Clinton		M	T	W	T	F	S	S
House, grounds, shop and restaurant								
10 Feb–31 Oct	11–5	·	·	W	T	F	S	S
29 Mar–18 Apr	11–5	M	T	W	T	F	S	S
31 May–6 Jun	11–5	M	T	W	T	F	S	S
26 Jul–5 Sep	11–5	M	T	W	T	F	S	S
25 Oct–31 Oct	11–5	M	T	W	T	F	S	S
Grounds, shop and restaurant								
3 Nov–19 Dec	11–4	·	·	W	T	F	S	S
House								
1 Dec–19 Dec	11–4	·	·	W	T	F	S	S

Admission to house by timed ticket available from reception (not bookable). Open Bank Holiday Mondays.

Baddesley Clinton, Warwickshire: boasts as many as three priest's holes

Benthall Hall

Broseley, Shropshire TF12 5RX

Map ④ I5   🏠✚✿ 1958

Situated on a plateau above the gorge of the River Severn, this fine stone house has mullioned and transomed windows, a stunning interior with carved oak staircase, decorated plaster ceilings and oak panelling. There is an intimate and carefully restored plantsman's garden, old kitchen garden and interesting Restoration church. **Note**: Benthall Hall is the home of Edward and Sally Benthall.

Exploring
- Discover the hidden tile in the hall floor.
- Walk along the woodland edge.
- Relax in the gardens, which have connections with Charles Darwin.
- Find the priest's hole from the period of Charles II.

Making the most of your day: guided walks and tours of the Hall available by arrangement. Try to visit either early or late in the season to appreciate the crocus displays. Dogs allowed in the parkland and woodland.

Access for all: 🅳♿🚾••🅿
Building 🔼🔼 Grounds 🔼

Getting here: 127:SJ658025. **Bus**: Arriva 39 Telford/Wellington–Much Wenlock. **Train**: Telford Central 7½ miles. **Road**: 1 mile north west of Broseley (B4375), 4 miles north east of Much Wenlock, 1 mile south west of Ironbridge. **Parking**: free, 100 yards. Space for one coach only.

Finding out more: 01952 882159 or benthall@nationaltrust.org.uk

Benthall Hall		M	T	W	T	F	S	S
House								
6 Apr–30 Jun	2–5:30	·	T	W	·	·	·	·
4 Jul–29 Sep	2–5:30	·	T	W	·	·	·	S
Garden								
6 Apr–30 Jun	1:30–5:30	·	T	W	·	·	·	·
4 Jul–29 Sep	1:30–5:30	·	T	W	·	·	·	S

Open Bank Holiday Sundays and Mondays.
Open Easter Sunday and Easter Monday.

Berrington Hall

near Leominster, Herefordshire HR6 0DW

Map ④ H6 🏠🌣♣🏠🍷 1957

'**Exquisite interiors, furniture and settings. Very friendly, helpful stewards. Great experience, especially below stairs tour.**'
Mrs S. Sinden, Exmoor

Created as the perfect house in the perfect setting, Berrington Hall has many secrets for visitors to uncover. In this, one of Henry Holland's first houses, visitors can explore the family rooms and see how the servants moved around the house unseen by the family and guests. The interiors include Biaggio Rebecca ceilings, fine period furniture and there are some pieces on display from the Wade Collection (on loan from Snowshill Manor). The house is surrounded by Brown's final landscape. Though it has a slightly austere exterior, the house has delicate interiors and a homely, welcoming feel.

Exploring
– Experience the arrival of the new Lady Rodney in 1891.
– Touch her belongings, read her diary – discover her secret.
– See how the servants moved around the house unseen.

Exploring
– Experience the life of William Kemp, the butler.
– Walk through Brown's final landscape – explore Moreton Ride.
– Relax in the gardens, including traditional Herefordshire orchards.

Eating and shopping: browse in the shop – stocks the Heart of England range. Plant sales are inspired by the beautiful surrounding garden. Relax in the tea-room with a home-baked cake. Enjoy a light lunch inspired by the family's recipes.

You may also enjoy: learn whist or fan etiquette at Croft Castle and Parkland.

Making the most of your day: family events and activities, including signing up as servants, family trail, play area, school holiday activities. House conservation tours. Remainder of costume collection on view by appointment. Waymarked estate walks. Dogs on leads in special dog walking area.

Access for all: 🅿🚾🚻🦽📷🄫👓⠿
Building 🦽🔆 **Grounds** 🦽➡🦽

Getting here: 137:SO510637. **Bus**: Lugg Valley 492 Ludlow–Hereford (passing close Ludlow 🚆 and Leominster), alight Luston, 2 miles. **Train**: Leominster 4 miles.

Berrington Hall, Herefordshire, has many secrets for visitors to uncover

Road: 3 miles north of Leominster, 7 miles south of Ludlow on west side of A49.
Parking: free, 30 yards. Coaches: entry and exit via Luston/Eye Lane only (the B4361 off the A49). Tight turn into drive. No entry or exit for coaches directly from/to A49. Local area map on request.

Finding out more: 01568 615721 or berrington@nationaltrust.org.uk

Berrington Hall		M	T	W	T	F	S	S
Below stairs, gardens, park, tea-room and shop								
30 Jan–7 Feb	11–4	·	·	·	·	·	S	S
13 Feb–21 Feb	11–4	M	T	W	T	F	S	S
27 Feb–28 Feb	11–4	·	·	·	·	·	S	S
6 Nov–19 Dec	11–4	·	·	·	·	·	S	S
Mansion, below stairs, garden, park, tea-room and shop								
6 Mar–31 Oct	11–5	M	T	W	·	·	S	S
1 Apr–18 Apr	11–5	M	T	W	T	F	S	S
29 May–6 Jun	11–5	M	T	W	T	F	S	S
1 Jul–31 Aug	11–5	M	T	W	T	F	S	S
23 Oct–31 Oct	11–5	M	T	W	T	F	S	S

Open Good Friday. Parkland: restricted 28 February to 12 June (due to nesting birds). **House: 11 to 1 tours only. House ground floor only 4, 5, 11, 12, 18 and 19 December. Below stairs, garden, park and shop open 26 December.**

Biddulph Grange Garden

Grange Road, Biddulph, Staffordshire ST8 7SD

Map ④ J2   1988

This amazing Victorian garden was created by James Bateman for his collection of plants from around the world. A visit takes you on a global journey from Italy to the pyramids of Egypt, a Victorian vision of China and a re-creation of a Himalayan glen. The garden features collections of rhododendrons, summer bedding displays, a stunning dahlia walk in late summer and the oldest surviving golden larch in Britain, brought from China in the 1850s. The Geological Gallery shows how Bateman reconciled geology and theology. Travel through time as the gallery depicts the creation story. **Note**: many steps throughout the garden and from the car park to the entrance.

Exploring
– Tour the gardens of the world, from China to Italy.
– Exhibition and audio-visual room tell the garden's story.
– Discover the world of Victorian plant hunters.
– The unique Geological Gallery tells the story of creation.
– Explore hidden tunnels and unusual garden features.
– Join in our regular programme of events.

Eating and shopping: taste wonderful local food in our tea-room. Refresh yourself at the ice-cream and drinks kiosk. Browse in the shop for gifts. Buy plants to take home to your own garden.

You may also enjoy: Little Moreton Hall – a perfect Tudor gem.

Making the most of your day: talks, guided tours, events and children's trails throughout the year. Summer activities programme.

Access for all: 🅿️♿🔉 ▪️▪️
Building 👶 Grounds 👶

Getting here: 118:SJ895591. **Bus**: Bakers 99 from Congleton (passing Congleton ➡). **Train**: Congleton 2½ miles. **Road**: ½ mile north of Biddulph, 3½ miles south east of Congleton, 7 miles north of Stoke-on-Trent. Access from A527 (Tunstall–Congleton road). Entrance on Grange Road. **Parking**: free, 50 yards.

Finding out more: 01782 517999 or biddulphgrange@nationaltrust.org.uk

Biddulph Grange Garden		M	T	W	T	F	S	S
15 Feb–19 Feb	11–3:30	M	T	W	T	F	·	·
3 Mar–31 Mar	11–5	·	·	W	T	F	S	S
1 Apr–31 Oct	11–5	M	T	W	T	F	S	S
6 Nov–19 Dec	11–3:30	·	·	·	·	·	S	S

Open Bank Holiday Mondays. Closes dusk if earlier. Tea-room last orders 4:30; winter menu in November and December.

Birmingham Back to Backs

55-63 Hurst Street/50-54 Inge Street, Birmingham, West Midlands B5 4TE

Map ④ J5 🏠🔧🏠⏓ 2004

'**Beautifully presented, but also guided with a charm and wit which made the whole experience come to life.**'
David Johnson, West Midlands

An atmospheric glimpse into the lives of the ordinary people who helped make Birmingham an extraordinary city. On a fascinating guided tour, step back in time at Birmingham's last surviving court of back to backs; houses built literally back-to-back around a communal courtyard. Moving from the 1840s through to the 1970s, discover the lives of some of the former residents who crammed into these small houses to live and work. With fires alight in the grates, and sounds and smells from the past, experience an evocative and intimate insight into life at the Back to Backs. **Note**: visits by guided tour only (advance booking advised).

Exploring
 – The guided tour brings the houses and characters to life.
 – Make yourself at home, warm up by the fire.
 – Learn more in the thought-provoking exhibition.
 – Whose Story? events bring Birmingham's diverse heritage to life.
 – Find out about life with communal privies and wash-houses.
 – Discover stories about the people who lived and worked here.

Eating and shopping: buy mementos of your visit in our reception. Traditional 1930s sweetshop (not National Trust).

You may also enjoy: The Workhouse at Southwell.

Making the most of your day: exciting year-round events programme. Ground floor tour also available.

Access for all: 🐕♿️🅿️🔄📖📺🔊..Ⓐ
Building 🏠♿️

Getting here: 139:SP071861. **Foot**: In the centre of Birmingham next to the Hippodrome Theatre, within easy walking distance of bus and railway stations. Follow signs for Hippodrome Theatre. **Cycle**: NCN5. **Bus**: Travel West Midlands 35, 61/62/63 from Birmingham city centre (passing close Birmingham New Street 🚆). **Train**: Birmingham New Street ¼ mile. **Parking**: nearest in Arcadian Centre, Bromsgrove Street.

Finding out more: 0121 666 7671 (booking line). 0121 622 2442 or backtobacks@nationaltrust.org.uk

Birmingham Back to Backs		M	T	W	T	F	S	S
2 Feb–23 Dec	10–5	·	**T**	**W**	**T**	**F**	**S**	**S**

Admission by timed ticket and guided tour only (booking advised). Open Bank Holiday Mondays but closed on Tuesdays following Bank Holiday Mondays. Please note: during term time property will normally be closed for use by schools on Tuesday, Wednesday and Thursday mornings. Booking line open Tuesday to Friday, 10:30 to 4, and weekends, 10 to 12. Last tour times vary due to light levels, please check with the property.

The range in the living room, Back to Backs, Birmingham

Brockhampton Estate

Greenfields, Bringsty, near Bromyard,
Herefordshire WR6 5TB

Map (4) I7

At the heart of this 687-hectare (1,700-acre)
farmed estate lies Lower Brockhampton, a
romantic timber-framed manor house dating
back to the late 14th century. The house is
surrounded by a moat and is entered via a
charming timber-framed gatehouse, built
1530–40. There are miles of walks through the
park and woodland, featuring ancient trees, the
picturesque Lawn Pool, and various sculptures
depicting parts of the history of Brockhampton
and the local area. Home to a rich variety of
wildlife, along with historic farming breeds
such as Hereford cattle and Ryeland sheep.

Exploring
– Discover the charming
  medieval moated
  manor house.
– Cross the moat through the
  timber-framed gatehouse.
– Explore the orchard,
  courtyard and chapel.
– Discover our wildlife on
  camera in our nature room.
– Enjoy one of our many events
  – just ask for details!
– Pick up a walks leaflet, explore
  the woodlands and parkland.

Eating and shopping: enjoy cream teas in the
Old Apple Store tea-room. Try our delicious
local produce made by estate tenants. Browse
for something unique in our Granary shop (not
Trust). Award-winning jams and beef from the
Brockhampton Estate.

You may also enjoy: Croft Castle and Parkland
– a stunning estate, 16th-century house and
large walled garden.

Making the most of your day: year-round
family events. Living history re-enactments.
Guided tours most weekends. Woodland and
estate walks leaflet available. Picnicking.

Brockhampton Estate, Herefordshire

Nature trail with birdhide. Dogs on leads in
woods and parkland only.

Access for all:
Building 🔾 🔾 Grounds 🔾 ➡

Getting here: 149:SO682546. **Bus**: First/
Bromyard Omnibus 420 Worcester–Hereford
(passing Worcester Foregate Street ➤ and
close Hereford ➤). **Road**: 2 miles east of
Bromyard on Worcester road (A44); house
reached by a narrow road through 1½ miles of
woods and park. **Parking**: 50 yards and
1½ miles.

Finding out more: 01885 488099 (Infoline).
01885 482077 or
brockhampton@nationaltrust.org.uk

Brockhampton Estate		M	T	W	T	F	S	S
Estate								
Open all year	Dawn–dusk	M	T	W	T	F	S	S
House* and tea-room								
6 Mar–4 Apr	11–4	·	·	W	T	F	S	S
5 Apr–18 Apr	11–5	M	T	W	T	F	S	S
21 Apr–30 Jun	11–5	·	·	W	T	F	S	S
1 Jul–31 Aug	11–5	M	T	W	T	F	S	S
1 Sep–31 Oct	11–5	·	·	W	T	F	S	S
6 Nov–19 Dec	11–4	·	·	·	·	·	S	S

Open Bank Holiday Mondays. *House opens 12; courtyard,
gardens and nature trail open 11. **House and tea-room open
every day 29 May to 6 June and 23 to 31 October, 11 to 5.**
House and tea-room close 4 in March, October and
November. **Tea-room open 26 to 31 December, 11 to 4.**

Carding Mill Valley and the Shropshire Hills

Chalet Pavilion, Carding Mill Valley, Church Stretton, Shropshire SY6 6JG

Map ④ H5 🏛🎞🏊🎣🍴🍸 1965

Carding Mill Valley and the Shropshire Hills

Covering as much as 2,000 hectares (4,942 acres) of heather-covered hills with stunning views of the Shropshire Hills Area of Outstanding Natural Beauty and the Welsh hills. An important place for wildlife, geology, landscape and archaeology, with excellent visitor facilities and information in Carding Mill Valley.

Exploring
– Some of the best walking in the Marches.
– Take a picnic and sit, relax and enjoy Shropshire's food.
– Horse-riding and cycling routes across a variety of terrains.
– Join us for pond dipping, birdwatching, volunteering and much more.

Eating and shopping: Chalet Pavilion tea-room serves local food, including hot lunches. Shop next to tea-room sells maps, guides and gifts. Excellent cakes, teas, coffees, local drinks and snacks.

Making the most of your day: more than 50 walks and talks each year run by wardens. Use the shuttle bus to extend or enhance your walk. Dogs under close control (grazing livestock).

Access for all: 🅿♿🚻🍴👁🦽 Building 🏳 Grounds 🦽

Getting here: 137:SO443945. Main access from Church Stretton via Carding Mill Valley. **Foot**: many long-distance routes, including Jack Mytton Way and Shropshire Way. **Cycle**: 10 miles plus of off-road tracks and bridleways. **Bus**: Minsterley Motors 435

Shrewsbury–Ludlow, alight Church Stretton, ½ miles. Area of Outstanding Natural Beauty shuttle bus weekends and Bank Holidays (Easter–October) connects Carding Mill Valley with Church Stretton ≋ and other shuttles to Stiperstones, Discovery Centre and Bishop's Castle. **Train**: Church Stretton 1 mile. **Road**: 15 miles south of Shrewsbury, west of Church Stretton Valley and A49; approached from Church Stretton and, on west side, from Ratlinghope or Asterton. **Parking**: 50 yards (pay and display). Open daily all year. Parking £4.20 (March to October), £2.50 (January, February, November and December), up to two hours £2. Minibus £10, coach £12. Top car park closes 7 (April to October), 4:15 (January, February, March and November to end December). Opens 9.

Finding out more: 01694 723068 or cardingmill@nationaltrust.org.uk

Carding Mill Valley		M	T	W	T	F	S	S
Countryside								
Open all year		**M**	**T**	**W**	**T**	**F**	**S**	**S**
Tea-room and shop								
1 Jan–4 Jan	11–4	**M**	·	·	·	**F**	**S**	**S**
9 Jan–7 Feb	11–4	·	·	·	·	·	**S**	**S**
13 Feb–19 Mar	11–4	**M**	**T**	**W**	**T**	**F**	**S**	**S**
20 Mar–31 Oct	11–5	**M**	**T**	**W**	**T**	**F**	**S**	**S**
6 Nov–19 Dec	11–4	·	·	·	·	·	**S**	**S**
26 Dec–31 Dec	11–4	**M**	**T**	**W**	**T**	**F**	·	·

WC and information open 9 to 7 summer; 9 to 4:15 winter. Tea-room and shop closed 16 June. **Shop closed Tuesday to Thursday 23 February to 18 March and 26 December.** Shop opens 12 on weekdays, 20 March to 31 October.

Members may have to pay on special events days

Charlecote Park

Wellesbourne, Warwick,
Warwickshire CV35 9ER

Map (4) K7

Home to the Lucy family since the 15th century, whose stories are told throughout the house by their portraits, the objects they collected from around the world and the design influence they had on the house and parkland. Step into the house today and you will see how it was remodelled in Victorian times by Mary Elizabeth Lucy. The gardens include a formal parterre, sensory garden, woodland walk and the wider parkland (inspired by 'Capability' Brown) which offers miles of walks and views across the River Avon. A herd of fallow deer has been in the park since Tudor times.

Exploring
- More parkland open to explore, see deer and Jacob sheep.
- The atmospheric Victorian kitchen and scullery are brought to life.
- Enjoy walks, talks and tours of the house and parkland.
- Wander in the gardens with views of the River Avon.
- See the house festively decorated, open weekends November and December.

Eating and shopping: enjoy a range of hot meals and light snacks. We use home-grown produce where possible in the restaurant. Light refreshments available when park and gardens are open. Look out for our shops selling locally sourced produce.

You may also enjoy: Upton House and Gardens, Baddesley Clinton, Packwood House and Coughton Court.

Making the most of your day: younger children can use the play equipment in the woodland garden (from spring). Year-round programme of events. Watch conservation in action. Plenty of outdoor space for children to enjoy.

Access for all: ⬛⬛⬛⬛⬛⬛⬛⬛ ⬛⬛⬛ **Building** ⬛⬛⬛ **Grounds** ⬛⬛

Getting here: 151:SP263564. **Bus**: Stagecoach in Warwickshire 18/A Leamington Spa ▣– Stratford-upon-Avon. **Train**: Stratford-upon-Avon, 5½ miles; Warwick 6 miles; Leamington Spa 8 miles. **Road**: 1 mile west of Wellesbourne, 5 miles east of Stratford-upon-Avon, 6 miles south of Warwick on north side of B4086. **Parking**: free, 300 yards.

Finding out more: 01789 472819 (Infoline). 01789 470277 or charlecotepark@nationaltrust.org.uk

Charlecote Park		M	T	W	T	F	S	S
Park, gardens and outbuildings								
Open all year	10–5:30	M	T	W	T	F	S	S
Mansion								
1 Mar–30 Apr	12–4:30	M	T	·	·	F	S	S
1 May–28 Sep	11–5	M	T	·	·	F	S	S
1 Oct–31 Oct	12–4:30	M	T	·	·	F	S	S
6 Nov–19 Dec	12–4	·	·	·	·	·	S	S
Restaurant*								
Open all year	10:30–5	M	T	W	T	F	S	S
Shop								
6 Feb–28 Feb	11–4	·	·	·	·	·	S	S
1 Mar–31 Oct	11–5	M	T	·	·	F	S	S
6 Nov–19 Dec	11–4	·	·	·	·	·	S	S

House: open Wednesday and Thursday 31 March, 1, 7 and 8 April and every day in August (not all show rooms open). Conservation tours: 11 and 11:30, March, April and October. Ground floor only in November and December.
Park, garden, outbuildings: closes dusk if earlier.
*Restaurant: open 11 to 4, January to February and November to December (full service on house open days, light refreshments at all other times). Property closed 24 and 25 December.

Charlecote Park, Warwickshire

Coughton Court

near Alcester, Warwickshire B49 5JA

Map ④ K6  1946

Home to the Throckmorton family for 600 years, this finest of Tudor houses stands testament to a family's courage in maintaining their beliefs. From a position of high favour to one of fear and oppression post-Reformation, the Throckmortons were leaders in a dangerous age, helping to bring about Catholic emancipation in the 19th century. Explore this story of fascinating personalities through the 'family album' of portraits and Catholic treasures around the house. Coughton is still very much a family home with an intimate feel: the Throckmorton family live here, managing the stunning gardens which they have created. **Note**: charge for entrance to the walled garden, including members.

Coughton Court, Warwickshire: Tudor splendour

Exploring
- Escape into the glories of the Throckmortons' award-winning gardens.
- Marvel at the views from the Tudor tower.
- Discover the priest's hole, fascinating Catholic treasures and family portraits.
- Find out about Coughton's part in the Gunpowder Plot.
- Let our friendly guides share Coughton's secrets with you.
- Explore the bog garden, orchards, vegetable garden and lake.

Eating and shopping: sample delicious local ice-cream from the Ice-Cream Parlour. Try home-baked cakes or hot lunches in the restaurant. Treat yourself to some local honey from the shop. Take home plants from the Throckmorton plant centre.

You may also enjoy: more priest's holes and the moat at nearby Baddesley Clinton.

Making the most of your day: open-air theatre, concerts, school holiday activities. Children's play area, quizzes and house trails. Outdoor family adventure packs. 'Ten Highlights' guide. Conservation in action days. Second-hand bookshop.

Access for all: 🅿️ 🇩 🇼🇨 ♿ 🚻 📷 💻 🎵 👓
Building 🅰️🅱️🅲️ Grounds ♿➡️🅲

Getting here: 150:SP080604. **Cycle**: NCN5, ½ mile. **Bus**: First 247 Redditch–Evesham (passing Redditch ➋ and close Evesham ➋), Stagecoach in Warwickshire 26 Redditch–Stratford-upon-Avon (passing close Stratford-upon-Avon ➋). **Train**: Redditch 6 miles. **Road**: 2 miles north of Alcester on A435. **Parking**: free, 150 yards. Offsite coach parking at Alcester Rugby Club.

Finding out more: 01789 762435 (Infoline). 01789 400777 or coughtoncourt@nationaltrust.org.uk

Coughton Court		M	T	W	T	F	S	S
House								
13 Mar–28 Mar	11–5	·		·		·	**S**	**S**
1 Apr–30 Jun	11–5	·	·	**W**	**T**	**F**	**S**	**S**
1 Jul–31 Aug	11–5	·	**T**	**W**	**T**	**F**	**S**	**S**
1 Sep–30 Sep	11–5	·	·	**W**	**T**	**F**	**S**	**S**
1 Oct–7 Nov	11–5	·	·	·	**T**	**F**	**S**	**S**
4 Dec–12 Dec*	12–6	**M**	**T**	**W**	**T**	**F**	**S**	**S**
Shop, restaurant and garden**								
As house	11–5:30	·	·		·		·	
Walled garden**								
As house	11:30–4:45	·	·		·		·	

Open Bank Holiday Mondays. **Closed Good Friday and 12 June and 10 July**. Admission by timed ticket at weekends and busy days. No hot food on Tuesdays. *Garden partial opening in December. ***Coughton Christmas Fair, find out more online. **Parts of the gardens may be closed March, October to December.**

Croft Castle and Parkland

Yarpole, near Leominster,
Herefordshire HR6 9PW

Map ④ H6

'**Really excellent! I especially appreciated the 'Atmospheric Rooms'. Well done. I will certainly remember our trip to Croft Castle.**'
Sue Hall, Kendal

Home of the Croft family for nearly 1,000 years Croft Castle, a place of power, politics and pleasure, nestles in peaceful Herefordshire countryside at the heart of a 607-hectare (1,500-acre) estate of woodlands, farm and parkland. Explore the miles of woodland trails, learn about the family who have made Croft so special. See the fine Georgian interiors and family portraits. Stroll through the woods to the Iron Age hill fort at Croft Ambrey and view fourteen of the old counties. Croft has over 300 veteran trees. Enjoy the atmospheric rooms, including the 18th-century Saloon. **Note**: parts of the property may close in high winds.

Exploring
- Walk through miles of beautiful, tranquil woodland trails and glades.
- Discover the 1,000-year history of the Croft family.
- Explore the walled garden, its flowers, shrubs, apples and vines.
- Experience Georgian life, play cards or read in the Saloon.
- Enjoy the panoramic views from the Iron Age hill fort.
- Relax in the silence and solitude of the surrounding parkland.

Eating and shopping: local food and drink freshly prepared in our own kitchen. Local beers, fruit juices, ciders, delicious homemade cakes and scones. Local gifts in shop, including the Heart of England range. Plant sales, second-hand bookshop, wildlife and gardening gifts.

You may also enjoy: Brockhampton Estate and Lower Brockhampton House, a stunning 14th-century manor.

Making the most of your day: castle-inspired play area, family room, events and activities. Waymarked walks across the estate. Menu options to make the most of your day. Dogs on leads in parkland only.

Access for all: 🅿️♿🚻♿♿🎨📷

Building ♿♿♿ Grounds ♿➡️♿

Getting here: 137:SO455655. **Bus**: Lugg Valley 492 Ludlow–Hereford (passing close Ludlow ➔ and Leominster), alight Gorbett Bank, 2¼ miles. **Train**: Leominster 7 miles. **Road**: 5 miles north west of Leominster, 9 miles south west of Ludlow; approach from B4362, turning north at Cock Gate between Bircher and Mortimer's Cross; signposted from Ludlow–Leominster road (A49) and from A4110 at Mortimer's Cross. **Sat Nav**: HR6 0BL. **Parking**: 100 yards.

Finding out more: 01568 780246. 01568 780141 (Infoline) or croftcastle@nationaltrust.org.uk

Croft Castle and Parkland		M	T	W	T	F	S	S
Parkland								
Open all year	Dawn–dusk	M	T	W	T	F	S	S
Castle, garden, tea-room, shop and play area								
6 Mar–31 Oct	11–5			W	T	F	S	S
5 Apr–16 Apr	11–5	M	T	W	T	F	S	S
31 May–4 Jun	11–5	M	T	W	T	F	S	S
1 Jul–31 Aug	11–5	M	T	W	T	F	S	S
23 Oct–31 Oct	11–5	M	T	W	T	F	S	S
6 Nov–19 Dec	11–4						S	S

Open Bank Holiday Mondays. Admission to castle between 11 and 1 by tour only. **Tea-room and play area: also open 2 to 31 January weekends only; 13 to 21 February every day; 27 and 28 February, 11 to 4; 27 to 31 December, 11 to 3.** Park closes dusk if earlier.

Visit

Croome Park, Worcestershire: set in 'Capability' Brown's first complete landscape

Croome Park

near High Green, Worcester,
Worcestershire WR8 9DW

Map (4) J7    1996

'It's great seeing "Capability" Brown's first
solo effort – brilliant man, lovely landscapes.'
Mr and Mrs Page, Harlow

Croome was 'Capability' Brown's first
complete landscape, making his reputation
and establishing a new style of garden design
which became universally adopted over the
next 50 years. The outer eye-catchers, acquired
in 2009, and the elegant park buildings were
designed by Brown, Robert Adam and James
Wyatt. Croome Court, sold by the Coventry
family in 1948, is at last reunited with the
parkland, allowing visitors to appreciate the
6th Earl's vision for the estate as a whole.
The house is presented empty of contents,
giving visitors an opportunity to follow the
restoration progress over the coming years.
Note: Court owned by Croome Heritage Trust.
Park acquisition and restoration supported by
Heritage Lottery Fund.

Exploring
– Appreciate Brown's landscape
  design from within
  Croome Court.
– Relax with a stroll in the
  lakeside garden.
– Explore the wider estate with
  our walks guide.

Exploring
– Escape to the outer
  eye-catchers.
– Discover a wide array of
  plants and wildlife.
– Watch bats in their
  summer roost via our
  interactive batcam.

Eating and shopping: enjoy a meal or snack in
our 1940s-style canteen. Take home one of our
recipes. Visit our shop and plant sales area.

You may also enjoy: the fascinating story of
how The Greyfriars, in Worcester city centre,
was saved from demolition.

Making the most of your day: new children's
play area. Full programme of events
throughout the year, with plenty of family
activities in the school holidays. Dogs on leads
in garden and under close control in park.

Access for all: 🅿️♿🚻♿♿🔄👓📷🅰️
Grounds ♿➡️🚸♿

Getting here: 150:SO887452. **Bus**: Aston's
382 Worcester–Pershore, alight Ladywood
Road/Rebecca Road crossroads, 2 miles; 362
Worcester–Upton/Malvern, alight Kinnersley,
2 miles. **Train**: Pershore 7 miles. **Road**: 9 miles
south of Worcester and east of M5. Signposted
from A38 and B4084. **Parking**: free.

Finding out more: 01905 371006 or
croomepark@nationaltrust.org.uk.
National Trust Estate Office,
The Builders' Yard, High Green, Severn Stoke,
Worcestershire WR8 9JS

Croome Park		M	T	W	T	F	S	S
Park, tea-room and shop								
1 Jan–14 Feb	10–4	·	·	·	·	·	S	S
15 Feb–31 Oct	10–5:30	M	T	W	T	F	S	S
6 Nov–19 Dec	10–4	·	·	·	·	·	S	S
26 Dec–31 Dec	10–4	M	T	W	T	F	·	S
Court								
9 Jan–31 Jan	11–3:30	·	·	·	·	·	S	S
15 Feb–31 Oct	11–4:30	M	·	W	T	F	S	S
6 Nov–19 Dec	11–3:30	·	·	·	·	·	S	S

Open 1 January and Bank Holiday Mondays. St Mary Magdalene church open in association with The Churches Conservation Trust. Last admission 45 minutes before closing. Admission to the Court is free-flow. Panorama Tower is open on the second Saturday of each month (February to October).

Cwmmau Farmhouse

Brilley, Whitney-on-Wye,
Herefordshire HR3 6JP

Map (4) G7   1965

Unique early 17th-century 'black and white' timbered farmhouse with many original features, including stone-tiled roofs and vernacular barns. **Note**: open eight afternoons a year. Other times available as holiday cottage (telephone 0844 8002070).

Getting here: 148:SO267514. 4 miles south west of Kington between A4111 and A438. From Kington take Brilley road at junction opposite church, 3½ miles. Turn left at National Trust signpost. From A438 between Winforton and Whitney on Wye take Brilley road at junction opposite Stowe Farm, straight on for 2 miles. Turn right, approximately ¾ mile turn right at Trust signpost. Farmhouse is approximately ½ mile at end of 'no through road'.

Finding out more: 01981 590509 or cwmmaufarmhouse@nationaltrust.org.uk

Cwmmau Farmhouse		M	T	W	T	F	S	S
15 May–16 May	2–5	·	·	·	·	·	S	S
12 Jun–13 Jun	2–5	·	·	·	·	·	S	S
2 Oct–3 Oct	2–5	·	·	·	·	·	S	S
18 Dec–19 Dec	1–4	·	·	·	·	·	S	S

Dudmaston Estate

Quatt, near Bridgnorth, Shropshire WV15 6QN

Map (4) I5   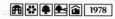 1978

Dudmaston offers something unexpected in the Shropshire countryside, a house that provides a classical setting for a collection of modern and contemporary art. The modern art galleries were assembled by diplomat Sir George Labouchere, while his wife Rachel showed off her collections of botanical drawings and watercolours. Outside, the established gardens are a stunning backdrop to art sculptures. The Big Pool is the perfect setting for a light walk with stunning views of the house. The wider estate offers miles of walking routes and can be enjoyed year-round from the new car parks.

Exploring
- Discover one family's varied art collection.
- Find out about six innovators of Dudmaston's history.
- Family activity room for creative fun for all ages.
- Children can let off steam rolling down the terraces!
- Take a romantic walk through the hidden Dingle.
- Enjoy the estate as the seasons change.

Eating and shopping: local products and hands-on art materials in the shop. Tea-room opens at 11:30 for an early lunch.

You may also enjoy: Upton House and Gardens and Nunnington Hall, Yorkshire.

Making the most of your day: open-air concerts, piano recitals in the modern art gallery, regular guided tours. Dogs on leads on footpaths only.

Access for all: 🅿️🚻♿🚻🔽🎨💻🔼:·:🅿️
Building ♿🏢🔽 **Grounds** ♿➡️♿

Getting here: 138:SO746887. **Foot**: National Trust walks from Hampton Loade car park to the property. **Ferry**: from Severn Valley Railway via river ferry and walk from Hampton Loade. **Bus**: Arriva Midlands 297 Bridgnorth–Kidderminster (passing close Kidderminster ▤). **Train**: Hampton Loade (Severn Valley Railway) 1½ miles; Kidderminster 10 miles. **Road**: 4 miles south east of Bridgnorth on A442. **Parking**: free, 100 yards, in Orchard car park and parkland. Also parking at Hampton Loade and The Holt (both pay and display).

Finding out more: 01746 780866 or dudmaston@nationaltrust.org.uk

Dudmaston Estate		M	T	W	T	F	S	S
House								
4 Apr–29 Sep	2–5:30	·	T	W	·	·	·	S
Garden								
4 Apr–29 Sep	12–6	M	T	W	·	·	·	S
Tea-room and shop*								
4 Apr–29 Sep	11:30–5:30	M	T	W	·	·	·	S

Open Easter Sunday and Bank Holiday Mondays. Booked guided tours of house: April to September, Mondays, 2 to 5. Snowdrop walks: 6, 7, 13 and 14 February. St Andrew's church, Quatt: open as house. *Shop opens at 12.

Farnborough Hall

Farnborough, near Banbury,
Oxfordshire OX17 1DU

Map ④ L7

Honey-coloured stone house with exquisite plasterwork and treasures collected during the Grand Tour, surrounded by the fine landscaped garden. **Note**: occupied and administered by the Holbech family.

Getting here: 151:SP430490. 6 miles north of Banbury, ½ mile west of A423.

Finding out more: 01295 690002 or farnboroughhall@nationaltrust.org.uk

Farnborough Hall		M	T	W	T	F	S	S
3 Apr–29 Sep	2–5:30	·	·	W	·	·	S	·
2 May–3 May	2–5:30	M	·	·	·	·	·	S

Terrace walk open as house.

The Fleece Inn

Bretforton, near Evesham,
Worcestershire WR11 7JE

Map ④ K7   1978

The Fleece Inn is a half-timbered medieval farmhouse which originally sheltered a farmer and his stock. The Inn was first licensed in 1848. Fully restored to its former glory, with witches circles and precious pewter collection, it has developed a reputation for traditional folk music, morris dancing and asparagus.

Exploring
– Annual Asparagus Auctions and Festival Day – Whit Sunday and Monday.
– Medieval thatched barn licensed for civil weddings, functions and events.
– Weekly folk session, regular gigs and other events.

Eating and shopping: mouthwatering menu using the finest local produce. Quality cask ales including landlord's own. Local ciders/wines. Special asparagus menu between 23 April and 21 June.

Making the most of your day: traditional folk music and morris dancing throughout the year. Vintage and classic car events May to September.

Access for all: ⬛⬛ Building ⬛⬛

Getting here: 150:SP093437. At the village square in the heart of Bretforton. **Bus**: Henshaws 554 from Evesham–Chipping Campden. **Train**: Evesham 2½ miles. **Road**: 4 miles east of Evesham, on B4035. **Parking**: in village square only (not National Trust).

Finding out more: 01386 831173 or fleeceinn@nationaltrust.org.uk

The Fleece Inn		M	T	W	T	F	S	S
Open all year	11–11	M	T	W	T	F	S	·
Open all year	12–10:30	·	·	·	·	·	·	S

Closed Monday to Thursday, 3 to 6, January to May and September to December.

The Greyfriars

Friar Street, Worcester,
Worcestershire WR1 2LZ

Map ④ J7 🏠❄️🔔 1966

Built in 1480, with early 17th- and 18th-century additions, this fine timber-framed house was rescued from demolition after the Second World War and has been carefully restored and refurbished. An archway leads through to a delightful walled garden.

Exploring
- Visit one of Worcester's finest buildings.
- Discover how The Greyfriars was saved from demolition.
- See the collection of interesting textiles.
- Explore the delightful walled garden.

Eating and shopping: have afternoon tea in the city garden on fine days. Buy plants grown at nearby Hanbury Hall.

Making the most of your day: family room with hands-on activities. Garden games in summer months.

Access for all: 📷🖥️📶 Building 🔍♿

Getting here: 150:SO852546. In centre of Worcester on Friar Street. **Bus**: from surrounding areas. **Train**: Worcester Foregate Street ½ miles. **Parking**: no on-site parking. Car parks at Corn Market and St Martin's Gate (pay and display).

Finding out more: 01905 23571 or greyfriars@nationaltrust.org.uk

The Greyfriars		M	T	W	T	F	S	S
3 Mar–12 Dec	1–5		·	·	W	T	F	S	S

Admission by timed ticket on Bank Holidays. Open Bank Holiday Mondays. Garden: opens 12, July and August. Closes dusk if earlier.

Hanbury Hall

School Road, Hanbury, Droitwich Spa,
Worcestershire WR9 7EA

Map ④ J6 🏠🔭❄️🌳🏠🔔🍽️ 1953

'**What a wonderful place! Stunning gardens and beautiful house interiors which you can sit and admire. I'll be back!**'
Liley Eddy, Worcester

Hanbury Hall, Worcestershire: picnic time

Hanbury Hall is a beautiful William and Mary-style house built in 1701 by Thomas Vernon, a lawyer and whig MP for Worcester. Inside a mix of interiors await to be discovered, from the restored Hercules rooms and recreated Gothic corridor, to the recently decorated parlour and stunning staircase wall-paintings by Sir James Thornhill. Surrounding the house are eight hectares (twenty acres) of recreated early 18th-century gardens and 162 hectares (400 acres) of park. Features include the intricately laid out parterre, fruit garden, grove, orangery, orchard and bowling green. Park walks enable you to explore the surrounding countryside.

Exploring
- Sit down in the house and admire the beautiful interiors.
- Discover the story of the stunning wall-paintings.
- Stroll through the gardens and enjoy a game of bowls.
- Relax and enjoy a picnic on the orangery lawn.
- Have fun in our children's play area.
- Enjoy the beautiful countryside on a park walk.

Eating and shopping: browse around our shop: spot our new extended gardening range. Buy a Hanbury-grown plant to take home. Enjoy delicious meals in our tea-room overlooking the parterre. Relax and enjoy homemade cake in our open-air café.

You may also enjoy: The Greyfriars: a 15th-century merchant's house in Worcester city centre.

Making the most of your day: year-round varied events programme, including family activity days, concerts, open-air theatre productions, art exhibitions and themed weekends. Park walks leaflet available. Dogs on leads in park on footpaths only.

Access for all: ▢▢▢▢▢▢▢▢
Building ▢▢▢ Grounds ▢▢▢▢

Getting here: 150:SO943637. **Foot**: number of public footpaths cross the park. **Bus**: First 144 Worcester–Birmingham (passing close Droitwich Spa ▣), alight Wychbold, 2½ miles. **Train**: Droitwich Spa 4 miles. **Road**: from M5 exit 5 follow A38 to Droitwich. From Droitwich 4½ miles along B4090. **Parking**: free, 150 yards.

Finding out more: 01527 821214 or hanburyhall@nationaltrust.org.uk

Hanbury Hall		M	T	W	T	F	S	S
House								
6 Feb–21 Feb	11:30–3:30	·	·	·	·	·	S	S
27 Feb–31 Oct	11–5	M	T	W	·	·	S	S
26 Jun–1 Sep	11–5	M	T	W	T	·	S	S
6 Nov–19 Dec	11:30–3:30	·	·	·	·	·	S	S
Gardens, park, shop, play area and stables café								
2 Jan–21 Feb	11–4	·	·	·	·	·	S	S
27 Feb–31 Oct	11–5	M	T	W	T	F	S	S
6 Nov–26 Dec	11–4	·	·	·	·	·	S	S
Tea-room								
27 Feb–31 Oct	11–5	M	T	W	·	·	S	S
26 Jun–1 Sep	11–5	M	T	W	T	·	S	S
6 Nov–26 Dec	11–4	·	·	·	·	·	S	S

House: 11 to 1 access by guided tours only (places limited). Admission by timed ticket on busy days. Bank holiday Mondays: free-flow visitor access, 11 to 5. Open Good Friday. Limited house opening February and November to December, access by guided tour (places limited). No house tours 4, 5, 11 and 12 December, free-flow from 11 to 3:30. Closes dusk if earlier. **Gardens, park, shop, play area and Stables café: open 1 January and 13 to 21 February, half-term and every day from 26 to 31 December.** Closed 25 December. Garden and park: close 5:30, 27 February to 31 October, or dusk if earlier.

Hawford Dovecote

Hawford, Worcestershire WR3 7SG

Map ④ J6   1973

The picturesque Hawford Dovecote survives virtually unaltered since the late 16th century and retains many of its nesting boxes. **Note**: no WC.

Getting here: 150:SO846607.

Finding out more: 01527 821214 or hawforddovecote@nationaltrust.org.uk

Hawford Dovecote		M	T	W	T	F	S	S
28 Feb–31 Oct	9–6	M	T	W	T	F	S	S

Closes dusk if earlier. Other times by appointment.

Kinver Edge and the Rock Houses

Holy Austin Rock House, Compton Road, Kinver, near Stourbridge, Staffordshire DY7 6DL

Map ④ I5   1917

Kinver's woodland sandstone ridge offers dramatic views across surrounding counties and miles of heathland walking country. The famous Holy Austin Rock Houses, which were inhabited until the 1950s, are open to visitors at selected times.

Exploring
– Miles of woodland and heathland pathways to explore.
– Rare species of plants and insects to discover.
– Explore the Rock Houses and imagine living there.
– Pick up a walks leaflet and information guide.

Eating and shopping: don't miss our Rock House tea-room.

The Holy Austin Rock Houses at Kinver Edge, Staffordshire

Access for all: ⊞ ⊞ ⊡ ⊡ ⊡ ⊡
Building 🏚 Grounds 🏚

Getting here: 138:SO836836. **Bus**: Hansons 228 🚌 Merry Hill bus station–Kinver.
Train: Stourbridge Town 5 miles.
Road: 4 miles west of Stourbridge, 4 miles north of Kidderminster. 1½ miles west of A449 – turn off and go through Kinver village.
Parking: free at Warden's lodge and on Compton Road for Rock Houses.

Finding out more: 01384 872553 or kinveredge@nationaltrust.org.uk

Kinver Edge		M	T	W	T	F	S	S
Kinver Edge								
Open all year		**M**	**T**	**W**	**T**	**F**	**S**	**S**
House grounds								
Open all year	10–4	**M**	**T**	**W**	**T**	**F**	**S**	**S**
Kinver tea-room								
4 Mar–28 Nov	11–4	·	·	·	**T**	**F**	**S**	**S**
Lower Rock Houses and upper terrace								
4 Mar–28 Nov	2–4	·	·	·	**T**	**F**	**S**	**S**

Open Bank Holiday Mondays. Lower Rock Houses open for guided weekday tours (March to November), by prior arrangement (parties of ten or over). Rock Houses closed on Kinver Fête day in May (date to be confirmed).

Kinwarton Dovecote

Kinwarton, near Alcester,
Warwickshire B49 6HB

Map ④ K7   🏠 1958

A lovely and rare 14th-century circular dovecote with metre-thick walls, hundreds of nesting holes and original rotating ladder. **Note**: no WC. Farm stock may be grazing in field.

Getting here: 150:SP106585. 1½ miles north east of Alcester, just south of B4089.

Finding out more: 01789 400777 or kinwartondovecote@nationaltrust.org.uk

Kinwarton Dovecote		M	T	W	T	F	S	S
1 Mar–31 Oct	11–6	**M**	**T**	**W**	**T**	**F**	**S**	**S**

Closes dusk if earlier. Other times by appointment.

Letocetum Roman Baths and Museum

Watling Street, Wall, near Lichfield,
Staffordshire WS14 0AW

Map ④ K5   🏠 🏛 1934

Explore the remains of this once important Roman staging post, including *mansio* (Roman inn) and bathhouse. **Note**: in the guardianship of English Heritage.

Getting here: 139:SK099067. Within the village of Wall on the north side of A5, 3 miles south of Lichfield.

Finding out more: 0121 625 6820 (English Heritage) or letocetum@nationaltrust.org.uk

Letocetum Roman Baths

Open-air site accessible at all reasonable times. Open-air site and museum manned by volunteers on the last weekend of each month and Bank Holiday Sundays and Mondays, March to October, 11 to 4.

Visit

Middle Littleton Tithe Barn

Middle Littleton, Evesham,
Worcestershire WR11 5LN

Map ④ K7   🏠 1975

One of the largest and finest 13th-century tithe barns in the country. **Note**: no WC.

Getting here: 150:SP080471.

Finding out more: 01905 371006 or middlelittleton@nationaltrust.org.uk

Middle Littleton Tithe Barn		M	T	W	T	F	S	S
1 Apr–1 Nov	2–5	**M**	**T**	**W**	**T**	**F**	**S**	**S**

Directions for access on barn door.

Morville Hall

near Bridgnorth, Shropshire WV16 5NB

Map ④ I5   🏠 ❀ 🎞 1965

Stone-built house of Elizabethan origin, enlarged and expanded around 1750, set in attractive gardens.
Note: no WC.

Getting here: 138:SO668940. 3 miles west of Bridgnorth, off A458.

Finding out more: 01746 780838 or morvillehall@nationaltrust.org.uk

Morville Hall

Admission by guided tour. By written appointment only with the tenants, Dr and Mrs C. Douglas.

Moseley Old Hall

Moseley Old Hall Lane, Fordhouses,
Wolverhampton, Staffordshire WV10 7HY

Map ④ J5   🏠 🏠 ✝ ❀ 🔔 1962

'**The whole experience at Moseley, and its great importance in our history, was the highlight of our holiday**.'
Mike Till, Sidmouth

The Brewhouse at Moseley Old Hall, Staffordshire

This atmospheric Elizabethan farmhouse conceals a priest's hole and hiding places, in one of which Charles II hid after the Battle of Worcester in 1651. The bed on which the royal fugitive slept is also on view. Follow the story of the King's dramatic escape from Cromwell's troops and find out about 17th-century domestic life in this historic home. In 2010, enjoy the 350th anniversary celebrations of the restoration of the monarchy. The garden has varieties of plants in keeping with the period and has a striking knot garden following a 17th-century design.

Exploring
- Follow in the footsteps of the King.
- Meet Charles II over the summer months.
- Take a fascinating guided tour of the house.
- Immerse yourself in 17th-century country living.

Exploring
- Sit by the log fire and soak up the atmosphere.
- Discover the delights of the walled and the knot gardens.

Eating and shopping: enjoy light lunches and homemade cakes in the tea-room. Browse in the shop for gifts and plants. Find bargains galore in the second-hand bookshop.

You may also enjoy: Baddesley Clinton, a family home and refuge, and Packwood House, a quiet country house.

Making the most of your day: events for visitors throughout the year, including demonstrations and re-creations of 17th-century life, family events and food tasting. Children's activities on family event days and Tuesdays in August. Dogs welcome on leads in the garden and grounds.

Access for all:

House **Shop and tea-room**

Grounds

Getting here: 127:SJ932044. 4 miles north of Wolverhampton City Centre. **Bus**: Travel West Midlands 533 from Wolverhampton, Arriva Midlands 7 from Cannock, both ½ mile. **Train**: Wolverhampton 4 miles. **Road**: south of M54 between A449 and A460; from north on M6 leave at exit 11, then A460; from south on M6 and M54 take exit 1; coaches must approach via A460 to avoid low bridge. **Parking**: free, 50 yards. No on-site coach parking (assigned dropping-off place only). Information available on nearby coach parking places. Narrow lanes and tight corners.

Finding out more: 01902 782808 or moseleyoldhall@nationaltrust.org.uk

Moseley Old Hall		M	T	W	T	F	S	S
6 Mar–31 Oct	12–5	·	·	**W**	·	·	**S**	**S**
5 Jul–14 Sep	12–5	**M**	**T**	**W**	·	·	**S**	**S**
7 Nov–19 Dec	12–4	·	·	·	·	·	·	**S**

Open Bank Holiday Mondays, 11 to 5, and following Tuesday (except 4 May). Entry, 12 to 1, by guided tour only (free-flow or conducted tours from 1). **Open Saturday to Wednesday during autumn half-term**. 7 November to 19 December: guided tour only. Christmas events 28 November, 5 and 12 December.

Packwood House

Packwood Lane, Lapworth,
Warwickshire B94 6AT

Map (4) K6 1941

The house is originally 16th-century, yet its interiors were extensively restored between the world wars by Graham Baron Ash to create a fascinating 20th-century evocation of domestic Tudor architecture. Packwood House contains a fine collection of 16th-century textiles and furniture, and the gardens have renowned herbaceous borders and a famous collection of yews.

Exploring
- Follow the spiral path to view the Yew Garden.
- Be inspired by the delicate stained-glass windows.
- Discover a fine collection of tapestries and furniture.
- Check your watch against the sundials.
- Experience a heady mix of fruit and flowers.
- Look out for homes for the workers – bee boles.

Eating and shopping: locally sourced products available in the shop. Garden plants for sale, many grown in our own nursery. Vending machine for soup and hot drinks.

You may also enjoy: Baddesley Clinton – two miles away.

Making the most of your day: set the scene with an introductory talk. Easter trail for families. Meet the Gardener evening tours. Open-air theatre. Dogs on leads welcome in the car park and on public footpaths across estate.

Access for all:

Building **Grounds**

Getting here: 139:SP174723. **Bus**: Johnsons of Henley X20 Birmingham–Stratford-upon-Avon, alight Hockley Heath, 1¾ miles. **Train**: Lapworth 1½ miles; Birmingham International 8 miles. **Road**: 2 miles east of Hockley Heath (on A3400), 11 miles south east of central Birmingham. **Parking**: free, 100 yards.

Finding out more: 01564 783294 or packwood@nationaltrust.org.uk

Packwood House		M	T	W	T	F	S	S
Park								
Open all year	Dawn–dusk	**M**	**T**	**W**	**T**	**F**	**S**	**S**
House, garden and shop								
10 Feb–31 Oct	11–5	·	·	**W**	**T**	**F**	**S**	**S**
29 Mar–18 Apr	11–5	**M**	**T**	**W**	**T**	**F**	**S**	**S**
31 May–6 Jun	11–5	**M**	**T**	**W**	**T**	**F**	**S**	**S**
26 Jul–5 Sep	11–5	**M**	**T**	**W**	**T**	**F**	**S**	**S**
25 Oct–31 Oct	11–5	**M**	**T**	**W**	**T**	**F**	**S**	**S**

Admission to the house by timed ticket available from reception (not bookable). Open Bank Holiday Mondays.

Rosedene

Victoria Road, Dodford, near Bromsgrove, Worcestershire B61 9BU

Map ④ J6 [🏠][❄][1997]

Cottage, organic garden and orchard illustrating the mid 19th-century Chartist movement – a time of remarkable British political change.

Getting here: 150:SO929730. Follow signs for Dodford off A448, left into Priory Road, left into Church Road, then left into Victoria Road.

Finding out more: 01527 821214 or rosedene@nationaltrust.org.uk

Rosedene

Admission by guided tours, Sundays only, 4 April to 26 September (booking essential). Limited group visits at other times by arrangement.

Rosedene, Worcestershire: Chartist cottage set in an organic garden with orchard

Shugborough Estate

Milford, near Stafford, Staffordshire ST17 0XB

Map ④ J4

The mysterious Shugborough Estate is the ancestral home of the Earls of Lichfield. With rumoured connections to the Holy Grail, the 364-hectare (900-acre) classical landscape is peppered with unusual monuments. The fine Georgian mansion house, with magnificent views over riverside garden terraces, features stunning collections of porcelain. Costumed characters work in the servants' quarters and farmstead: doing laundry, cheesemaking, milling, brewing and baking. In these areas the Staffordshire County Museum collections are held including reconstructed chemist shop, tailors' shop, Victorian schoolroom and puppet collection. In addition, the newly restored walled garden grows historic varieties of fruit and vegetables. **Note**: operated by Staffordshire County Council. Charges for servants' quarters and farm entrance, including members.

Exploring
- View the new Patrick Lichfield photographic exhibition.
- Discover our champion tree – the widest tree in Europe.
- Get stuck into dollypegging in the original Victorian laundry.
- Uncover the art of historic gardening in the walled garden.
- Meet costumed characters who bring the past to life.
- Explore the farm and servants' quarters (charges include members).

Eating and shopping: licensed tea-room serving homemade, locally sourced food. Seek out the perfect present in our gift shop. Treat yourself in the ice-cream parlour. Old-fashioned sweet shop and craft outlets selling handmade goods.

You may also enjoy: Attingham Park, Sudbury Hall and Biddulph Grange Garden.

Access for all: 🅿️🚜♿🚽👁🦮📷🛗•🅰️
Building 🔁🦽♿ Grounds 🦽➡️🚶

Getting here: 127:SJ992225. **Foot**: pedestrian access from east, from the canal/Great Haywood side of the estate. Estate walks link to towpaths along Trent & Mersey Canal and Staffordshire & Worcestershire Canal and to Cannock Chase trails. Lies on Staffordshire Way. **Bus**: Arriva 825 Stafford ➤–Lichfield (passing close Lichfield City ➤). **Train**: Rugeley Town 5 miles; Rugeley Trent Valley 5 miles; Stafford 6 miles. **Road**: signposted from M6 exit 13; 6 miles east of Stafford on A513; entrance at Milford. **Parking**: £3 (pay and display). Refunded on purchase of an all-sites ticket.

Finding out more: 01889 881388 or shugborough.promotions@staffordshire.gov.uk or www.shugborough.org.uk

Shugborough Estate		M	T	W	T	F	S	S
House, farm, servants' quarters, grounds and tea-room								
19 Mar–28 Oct	11–5		M	T	W	T	F	S	S
Shop								
19 Mar–28 Oct	11–5		M	T	W	T	F	S	S
29 Oct–23 Dec	11–4		M	T	W	T	F	S	S

Open Bank Holiday Mondays. Opening times and admission prices may vary when special events held.

Sunnycroft

200 Holyhead Road, Wellington, Telford, Shropshire TF1 2DR

Map ④ I4

This substantial red-brick villa is typical of the many thousands that were built for the prosperous middle classes in the late Victorian period. Sunnycroft is one of the very few to have survived, with a mini estate and largely unaltered contents and decoration.

Exploring
- Guided tours in the house highlight this Victorian time capsule.
- Take a peak into the Victorian medicine cupboard.

Exploring
- Discover our collection of Leek Embroidery.
- Explore the beautiful gardens and glasshouses.

Eating and shopping: delicious cakes made in Shropshire. Take afternoon tea in the main house.

Making the most of your day: our events programme reflects the heyday of the property, including traditional garden fête. Dogs on leads in grounds only.

Access for all:
Building **Grounds**

Getting here: 127:SJ652109. **Cycle**: NCN81, 1 mile. **Bus**: Arriva 66 from Telford (passing Wellington Telford West). **Train**: Wellington Telford West ½ mile. **Road**: M54 exit 7, follow B5061 towards Wellington. **Sat Nav**: enter Sunnycroft's address rather than postcode. **Parking**: free, 150 yards in orchard. Not suitable for coaches. Additional free parking (not National Trust) in Wrekin Road car park.

Finding out more: 01952 242884 or sunnycroft@nationaltrust.org.uk

Sunnycroft		M	T	W	T	F	S	S
12 Mar–31 Oct	12–5	**M**	·	·	·	**F**	**S**	**S**
17 Dec–20 Dec	12–4	**M**	·	·	·	**F**	**S**	**S**

Open Good Friday and Bank Holiday Mondays (free-flow through house). **Admission by timed ticket (not bookable) and by guided tour only**. Last admission one hour before closing.

Sunnycroft, Shropshire: Victorian middle-class villa

Town Walls Tower

Shrewsbury, Shropshire SY1 1TN

Map (4) H4 1930

This last remaining 14th-century watchtower sits on what were once the medieval fortified, defensive walls of Shrewsbury. **Note**: no WC or car parking and 40 extremely steep steps to property.

Getting here: 126:SJ492122. Close to town centre near Welsh Bridge, on south of town wall.

Finding out more: 01743 708162 or townwallstower@nationaltrust.org.uk

Town Walls Tower
Sunday 23 May and Wednesday 11 August. Tours take place at intervals between 11 and 3.

Upton House and Gardens

near Banbury, Warwickshire OX15 6HT

Map (4) L7 1948

'Excellent – love the feel of the house party and the 1930s. Well done.'
Caroline Powell, London

Join the guests of Lord and Lady Bearsted and experience the weekend house party of a 1930s millionaire. Surrounded by the internationally important art and porcelain collections, hear and discover more about family life and join in the atmosphere of the party. See the red and silver art deco bathroom and get close to art works by El Greco, Stubbs and Bosch. The stunning gardens – being returned to their 1930s heyday – consist of a sweeping lawn, giving way to a series of terraces and herbaceous borders leading to a kitchen garden, tranquil water garden and the National Collection of Asters.

The long, double herbaceous borders running down to the Mirror Pool at Upton House and Gardens, Warwickshire

Note: some areas of the gardens may be closed during bad weather.

Exploring
- Live the 1930s – listen to family stories and read papers.
- Discover works by famous artists including Guardi, Caneletto and Hogarth.
- View porcelain from Derby, Chelsea, Worcester and Sèvres factories.
- Relax in the garden, which includes a 1930s swimming pool.
- New exhibition in the 1930s squash court during winter.
- Meander through the kitchen gardens which supply the restaurant.

Eating and shopping: browse in the shop – stocks the Heart of England range. Plant sales are inspired by the surrounding beautiful garden. Enjoy homemade cakes and local produce in the restaurant. Book the restaurant or 1930s squash court for your function.

You may also enjoy: award-winning roses at nearby Coughton Court – a Tudor mansion with fascinating stories.

Making the most of your day: family events and activities. Enjoy jazz concerts, play snooker or join an art or conservation tour. Watch the introductory film. National Collection of Asters in full bloom in September.

Access for all: **Building** **Grounds**

Getting here: 151:SP371461. On the edge of the Cotswolds, between Banbury and Stratford-upon-Avon. **Foot**: footpath SM177 runs adjacent to property, Centenary Way ½ mile, Macmillan Way 1 mile. **Cycle**: NCN5, 5 miles. Oxfordshire Cycle Way 1½ miles. **Train**: Banbury 7 miles. **Road**: on A422, 7 miles north of Banbury, 12 miles south east of Stratford-upon-Avon. Signed from exit 12 of M40. **Parking**: free, 300 yards. Parking is on grass with hard-standing for coaches.

Finding out more: 01295 670266 or uptonhouse@nationaltrust.org.uk

Upton House and Gardens		M	T	W	T	F	S	S
Garden, restaurant, shop and plant centre								
13 Feb–10 Mar	11–5	**M**	**T**	**W**	·	·	**S**	**S**
13 Mar–31 Oct	11–5	**M**	**T**	**W**	·	**F**	**S**	**S**
House tours								
13 Feb–10 Mar	12–4	**M**	**T**	**W**	·	·	**S**	**S**
13 Mar–31 Oct	11–1	**M**	**T**	**W**	·	**F**	**S**	**S**
House*								
13 Mar–31 Oct	1–5	**M**	**T**	**W**	·	**F**	**S**	**S**
6 Nov–19 Dec	12–4	·	·	·	·	·	**S**	**S**
Exhibition, restaurant, winter walk and shop								
1 Nov–22 Dec	12–4	**M**	**T**	**W**	·	·	**S**	**S**
26 Dec–31 Dec	12–4	**M**	**T**	**W**	**T**	**F**	·	**S**

Winter walk, restaurant, shop and plant centre open 1 to 3 January House admission from 11 on Bank Holidays by timed ticket, but visitors may stay until 5. *Ground floor open only in house November and December.

The Weir, Herefordshire: spectacular all year round

The Weir

Swainshill, Hereford, Herefordshire HR4 7QF

Map ④ H7 1959

An unusual garden of four hectares (ten acres) with sweeping views along the River Wye and Herefordshire countryside. Managed to create a varied habitat for a wide range of wildlife, the garden is spectacular all year round – drifts of spring bulbs give way to wild flowers, followed by autumn colour. **Note**: sturdy footwear is recommended.

Exploring
– New: visit the walled garden.
– Enjoy the carpets of spring flora and fauna.
– Summer wild flowers attract a range of wildlife.
– The mature trees provide an array of autumn colour.

Eating and shopping: take a hamper to one of the riverside picnic sites.

Making the most of your day: children's days in August, with 'hands-on' activities and displays.

Access for all: ♿ Grounds 🚶♿

Getting here: 149:SO438418. **Bus**: to Hereford and then taxi. **Train**: Hereford 5 miles. **Road**: 5 miles west of Hereford on A438. **Parking**: free.

Finding out more: 01981 590509 or theweir@nationaltrust.org.uk

The Weir		M	T	W	T	F	S	S
23 Jan–31 Jan	11–4	·	·	·	·	·	S	S
3 Feb–28 Feb	11–4	·	·	W	T	F	S	S
1 Mar–3 May	11–5	M	T	W	T	F	S	S
5 May–31 Oct	11–5	·	·	W	T	F	S	S

Open Bank Holiday Mondays. Last admission 45 minutes before closing.

Wichenford Dovecote

Wichenford, Worcestershire WR6 6XY

Map ④ I7 1965

A charming 17th-century half-timbered dovecote at Wichenford Court. The building, although small, is very striking.
Note: no WC. No access to Wichenford Court (privately owned).

Getting here: 150:SO788598. 5½ miles north west of Worcester, north of B4204.

Finding out more: 01527 821214 or wichenforddovecote@nationaltrust.org.uk

Wichenford Dovecote		M	T	W	T	F	S	S
1 Mar–31 Oct	9–6	M	T	W	T	F	S	S

Open other times by appointment.

Wightwick Manor and Gardens

Wightwick Bank, Wolverhampton,
West Midlands WV6 8EE

Map (4) J5   1937

'**A fantastic house and the guides were so knowledgeable... the property is so much more than we thought.**'
Mr P. Griffin, Stafford

Mander, Mawson & Morris – a suburban paradise. A late Victorian manor house, built in the 'Old English' style by local industrialist Theodore Mander, Wightwick Manor is perhaps the best surviving example of a home furnished under the influence of the Arts & Crafts movement. The rich interiors feature many original wallpapers, fabrics and furnishings by William Morris, artwork by Rossetti and Burne-Jones, glass by Charles Kempe and ceramics by William de Morgan. The house sits in seven hectares (seventeen acres) of attractive Arts & Crafts gardens, designed by Thomas Mawson, which are Grade II listed in their own right.

Exploring
- Admire outstanding Arts & Crafts interiors and Pre-Raphaelite art.
- Impressive Arts & Crafts garden for all seasons.
- Recently reinstated kitchen garden and new Caribbean herb garden.
- Play a game of billiards and experience the year 1900.
- Nature room with activities for children.
- Stunning gardens and woodland walk to enjoy.

Eating and shopping: tea-room serving food grown in the kitchen garden. Unique William Morris and Arts & Crafts-inspired gift shop. Plant sales to tempt your green fingers. Browse the bargains in the second-hand bookshop.

You may also enjoy: Sunnycroft, a Victorian villa near Wellington, Shropshire.

Making the most of your day: guided tours of the house run every open day. Special, themed 20-minute Taster Tours run every day between 11 and 12:30. Extensive and varied calendar of events. Dogs on leads allowed in garden.

Access for all: 🅿️♿🚾🦽📷🎵🔅🅰️
Building 🦽🦼 Grounds 🦽🦼➡️

Stunning borders at Wightwick Manor and Gardens, West Midlands

Getting here: 139:SO869985. **Bus**: Travel West Midlands 543 from Wolverhampton (passing close Wolverhampton ⊠).
Train: Wolverhampton 3 miles. **Road**: 3 miles west of Wolverhampton, up Wightwick Bank (off A454 beside Mermaid Inn). **Parking**: free, 120 yards, at bottom of Wightwick Bank (please do not park in Elmsdale opposite). No coach parking.

Finding out more: 01902 761400 or wightwickmanor@nationaltrust.org.uk

Wightwick Manor and Gardens		M	T	W	T	F	S	S
House								
20 Feb–31 Oct	11–5	·	·	W	T	F	S	S
6 Nov–19 Dec	11–5	·	·	·	·	·	S	S
Garden, tea-room and shop*								
20 Feb–30 Jun	11–6	·	·	W	T	F	S	S
1 Jul–31 Aug	11–6	M	T	W	T	F	S	S
1 Sep–31 Oct	11–6	·	·	W	T	F	S	S
6 Nov–19 Dec	11–6	·	·	·	·	·	S	S

House opens 12:30. Admission by timed ticket and guided tour (only available from visitor reception on the day of visit). Taster tours: 20 February to 31 October, Wednesday to Sunday, 11 to 12:30. No guided tours on first Thursday and Saturday of the month – free-flow through house from 12:30. Property opens Bank Holiday Mondays (ground floor only). Tours vary as many of the contents are fragile, so some rooms cannot always be shown. **Gardens open seven days a week during Easter, May half-term, August and October half-term.** *Tea-room and shop close 5.

Wilderhope Manor

Longville, Much Wenlock, Shropshire TF13 6EG

Map ④ H5    1936

Beautiful Elizabethan manor house restored by John Cadbury in 1936. Surrounding farmland managed for landscape and wildlife has permissive access. **Note**: manor is a popular youth hostel, so access to some rooms may be restricted.

Getting here: 138:SO545929. 7 miles south west of Much Wenlock, 7 miles east of Church Stretton, ½ mile south of B4371.

Finding out more: 0870 770 6090 (Hostel Warden YHA) or wilderhope@nationaltrust.org.uk

Wilderhope Manor		M	T	W	T	F	S	S
3 Jan–28 Mar	2–4:30	·	·	·	·	·	·	S
4 Apr–29 Sep	2–4:30	·	·	W	·	·	·	S
3 Oct–19 Dec	2–4:30	·	·	·	·	·	·	S

Farmland at **Wilderhope Manor Farm, Shropshire**, in remote countryside on the southern slope of Wenlock Edge

North West

Soak up the atmosphere of the Industrial Revolution at Quarry Bank Mill and Styal Estate – seen here from the mill owner's 'Secret Garden'

Outdoors in the North West

Home to some of Britain's finest landscapes, amazing wildlife and fascinating industrial heritage, not to mention a haven for foodies everywhere, the North West is a region of variety and contrast.

The dramatic and internationally-renowned beauty of the Lake District to the north of our region is a magnet to those keen on physical, mental or spiritual refreshment. To the south, the urban centres of Manchester and Liverpool rely on the Trust's 'green lung', in the form of open countryside and parkland, with the Stubbins Estate and Holcombe Moor providing the same service north of Bury, Lancashire.

We look after one quarter of the Lake District National Park, including 'Britain's Favourite View' – England's highest mountain, Scafell Pike – our deepest lake, Wastwater; and 90 tenanted farms. Most of the central fell area and major valley heads are owned or leased by the Trust, together with 24 lakes and tarns, as well as one of the most important bequests the Trust has ever received.

This was courtesy of Beatrix Potter, whose love of the area is legend. When she died in 1943 she left 1,600 hectares (4,000 acres) and fourteen farms to the Trust. This great estate had already begun to be purchased piece by piece – beginning in 1902 with Brandlehow Park on the shore of Derwentwater. The Trust works with the National Park Authority and other partners on the Fix the Fells project – an upland footpath scheme which repairs dozens of footpaths on the fells which are being eroded by the sheer number of walkers. We are always delighted to welcome new volunteers to help with this worthwhile project, so why not visit **www.fixthefells.co.uk** to see what you can do?

Food glorious food

If you love local, seasonal and delicious food you are in the right place. Don't miss the Chorley cakes at Rufford Old Hall, made with fruit from their orchards. Or visit Sizergh Castle to see how they use locally grown damsons in many different and delicious ways. Sample some of the meats of the region – venison from the parks at Lyme, Dunham and Tatton or Herdwick lamb from Trust farms in Cumbria. Acorn Bank prepares gorgeous salads using home-grown herbs, as well as scrumptious cakes and fruit puddings – rhubarb is their speciality! With no less than eight main gooseberry associations in the county, Cheshire is the gooseberry capital of Britain. Try it in fools and crumbles or chutneys and tarts. Local Cheshire cheeses are also used to make unbeatable flans, quiches and sandwiches, and each property is renowned for a wonderful selection of mouthwatering cakes, scones and traybakes.

Straight from the farm

Taste Herdwick stew and other traditional Cumbrian fare at walkers' tea-rooms at our two Yew Tree Farms, in Borrowdale and Coniston, or try award-winning Kendal Crumbly cheese at Low Sizergh Barn. Many of our tenants now also supply Booths supermarkets in the region with National Trust meat, so look out for it while shopping.

Different modes of transport

Why not leave your car behind and catch the local bus, train or boat? You will find that having someone else doing the driving allows you to sit back and enjoy the view. Of course you could also take your bike, then you really will feel at one with nature. Visit the website for more details.

Stunning views and ancient woodland

In West Cheshire explore the very special Sandstone Ridge, a historic landscape offering splendid views of the Cheshire Plain and Welsh Mountains from Alderley Edge, Bickerton Hill and nearby Bulkeley Hill Wood; while Helsby Hill has views across the Mersey Estuary to Liverpool.

Both Bickerton and Helsby have Bronze Age forts at their summits, while Bulkeley, part of the Peckforton range of hills, has the Sandstone Trail running along its length and five hectares (twelve acres) of ancient woodland.

Views of the Peak District and Welsh Mountains, with wide expanses of the great Cheshire Plain stretching in between, can be seen from The Cloud, a great rocky heathland 343 metres high near Timbersbrook in Cheshire.

Ruins with history and romance

Further south lies the folly of Mow Cop; built in 1754 it is famed as the birthplace of Primitive Methodism and stands in romantic ruin. To the west of the county is the site of Lewis Carroll's birthplace near Daresbury – kindly donated to the Trust by the Lewis Carroll Birthplace Trust. Here you can find the 'footprint' of Daresbury Parsonage, in which Carroll was born in 1832, while nearby Daresbury Church has a stained glass window featuring Carroll and his Wonderland characters.

Wildlife and flowers in south Cumbria and Lancashire

Arnside Knott on the coast in Cumbria and Eaves and Waterslack Woods in Lancashire are home to a fantastic variety of wild flowers and butterflies. There are many lovely walks here and so much to spot (download a map of the area from the website to help in your hunt).

Natterjack toads, a nationally rare species, live happily at Sandscale Haws in Cumbria, and at Formby in Lancashire you can hear their extraordinary mating calls on May and June evenings. Sandscale is also home to a rich variety of birds, including shelducks, eider ducks, goldeneyes and plovers, and the high, grass-covered sand dunes are perfect for a day's exploring. Formby also has one of the last remaining red squirrel colonies in the country.

Opposite:
walkers at Wasdale, Cumbria, with the vast expanse of Wastwater in the distance
Below:
wooden camping pod on the National Trust campsite at Wasdale Head, Cumbria

Outdoors in the North West

Still waters and wild crags

In Cumbria, Coniston Water is home to many varieties of wetland plants, meadow flowers and the rare small-leaved lime. Arthur Ransome got his inspiration here, as did Donald Campbell. Walk up through the beautiful Monk Coniston grounds to the iconic landscape of Tarn Hows. Visit the website for the downloadable walk and Tree Trail.

In Borrowdale, enjoy the fascinating combination of rugged crags and dramatic fells. Fine sessile oak woodlands and colonies of internationally important lichens, mosses and insects all thrive here, as do wildfowl and waders nesting along the shores of Derwentwater.

Friar's Crag, one of the Lakes' most famous viewpoints, sits at the north end of the lake, just past the boat landings, near the handsome town of Keswick.

There is wheelchair access to Friar's Crag; also at Tarn Hows and Harrowslack, near Hawkshead, just over the ferry on Windermere.

Car parks in the Lake District

Lanthwaite Wood	NY 149 215
Buttermere	NY 172 173
Honister Pass	NY 225 135
Seatoller	NY 246 137
Rosthwaite	NY 257 148
Bowderstone	NY 254 167
Watendlath	NY 276 164
Kettlewell	NY 269 196
Great Wood	NY 272 213
Aira Force	NY 401 201
Glencoyne Bay	NY 387 188
Wasdale Head	NY 182 074
Old Dungeon Ghyll	NY 285 062
Stickle Ghyll	NY 295 064
Elterwater	NY 329 047
Tarn Hows	SD 326 995
Ash Landing	SD 388 955
Sandscale Haws	SD 199 758
Blea Tarn	NY 296 044
Harrowslack	SD 388 960
Red Nab	SD 385 995
Glen Mary	SD 321 998

Camping in the Lake District with the National Trust

Get back to nature by camping at one of our campsites, the perfect base for a holiday.

Low Wray Campsite

On the quiet western shore of Windermere, the site has spectacular lake and fell views. There is lake access for non-powered boating activities.

Set in the heart of 'Beatrix Potter' country, you can enjoy beautiful walks to Hill Top at Near Sawrey, Potter's home, as well as to the Beatrix Potter Gallery at Hawkshead and in the grounds of Wray Castle.

Great Langdale Campsite

In the heart of the Lake District mountains, this is an ideal location for climbing and fell walking.

A great base from which to climb Scafell Pike, England's highest mountain, after which you should reward yourself with a pint in one of the nearby traditional Lakeland hostelries. Just a fifteen-minute drive from Ambleside and convenient for the other Lakes' attractions.

Wasdale Campsite

This site is a mere stone's throw from beautiful Wastwater, the deepest lake in England and one with a distinctive Nordic character. The pyramidal peak of Great Gable is reflected in its waters.

Arguably, the most dramatic location in England, Scafell Pike and numerous high fell walking routes are within striking distance. This is a remote place where peace and tranquillity reign.

Camping pods

For those who prefer something a little bit more luxurious than a tent...
Telephone 015394 63862 or visit **www.ntlakescampsites.org.uk** for further information and terms and conditions.

Acorn Bank Garden and Watermill

Temple Sowerby, near Penrith,
Cumbria CA10 1SP

Map (6) E7   ⬛🔧❄🏠 1950

Best known for its collection of 250 herbs and traditional fruit orchards. Sample the tea-room menu with culinary herbs from the garden used daily in soups, salads and scones, and fruit from the orchards used in delicious puddings and cakes. Wander along the Crowdundle Beck to the partially restored watermill, spot some wildlife then enjoy the views across the Eden Valley to the Lake District from the magnificent backdrop of the sandstone house (which, although not open to the public, adds to the wonderful setting). Stay a while longer in a holiday cottage. **Note**: access to fragile grass paths in the garden may be restricted after wet weather.

Exploring
- Relax in the tranquil and sheltered walled gardens.
- Discover fascinating stories behind the plants in the herb garden.
- Find great crested newts in the garden pond.
- Spot red squirrels in Acorn Banks woodland.
- Watch the waterwheel turning at the mill (most weekend afternoons).
- Listen to bird song as you stroll beside Crowdundle Beck.

Eating and shopping: enjoy the garden's herbs and fruit in the tea-room. Plants for sale in the garden courtyard. Browse in the shop, housed in an 18th-century dovecot.

You may also enjoy: Townend, a Lakeland farmhouse at Troutbeck, or Wordsworth House at Cockermouth.

Making the most of your day: Apple Day, 17 October, is a great day out for the whole family (charge, including members). Dogs welcome on leads on the woodland walk and in the garden courtyard.

Access for all: 🅿🔢♿🚻♿📷🔭📖🔼👁🅰
Shop and admission point ♿♿ **Watermill** ♿♿♿
Grounds ♿♿♿➡♿

Getting here: 91:NY612281. **Foot**: public footpath from Temple Sowerby. **Cycle**: NCN7, 6 miles. **Bus**: Grand Prix 563 Penrith–Kirkby Stephen, to within 1 mile (passes close Penrith ≋ and Appleby ≋). **Train**: Langwathby 5 miles; Penrith 6 miles. **Road**: just north of Temple Sowerby, 6 miles east of Penrith, 1 mile from A66. **Parking**: free, 80 yards. Tight access for coaches (recommended route map available when booking).

Finding out more: 017683 61893 or acornbank@nationaltrust.org.uk

Acorn Bank Garden		M	T	W	T	F	S	S
Garden, watermill, woodland walks and shop								
27 Feb–7 Mar	10–5						S	S
13 Mar–31 Oct	10–5			W	T	F	S	S
Tea-room								
27 Feb–7 Mar	11–4:30						S	S
13 Mar–31 Oct	11–4:30			W	T	F	S	S

Open Bank Holiday Mondays, 10 to 5.

A sheltered corner of Acorn Bank Garden, Cumbria

Alderley Edge

Nether Alderley, Macclesfield, Cheshire

Map (5) D8   🏛️🔧♿ 1946

Walk the dramatic red sandstone escarpment of Alderley Edge, with views over the Cheshire Plain and to the Peak District. Explore woodland paths or walk to Hare Hill Garden. Bickerton Hill and Bulkely Hill Wood; Mow Cop, the Cloud and Helsby Hill offer a variety of landscapes with stunning views.

Exploring
– Alderley Edge is designated a SSSI for its geological interest.
– A history of copper mining since the Bronze Age.
– Derbyshire Caving Club opens the mines twice a year.
– Bickerton Hill is a SSSI, made up of lowland heath.

Eating and shopping: Wizard Country Inn, Alderley Edge (not National Trust). Wizard tea-room, Alderley Edge (not National Trust – weekends only).

Making the most of your day: series of guided walks takes place at Alderley Edge through the summer. Dogs under close control and on leads in fields (particularly during lambing/bird nesting season).

Access for all: 🅿️♿🚻♿ Grounds ♿➡️

Getting here: Alderley Edge 118:SJ860776; The Cloud 118:SJ905637; Mow Cop 118:SJ857573; Bickerton Hill 117:SJ498529; Mow Cop 118:SJ857573; Bickerton Hill 117:SJ498529; Bulkely Hill 117:SJ527553; Helsby Hill 117:SJ492754; Lewis Carroll's Birthplace 118:SJ593805; Maggoty Wood 118:SJ889702.
Parking: at some properties (roadside elsewhere); pay and display at Alderley Edge (closing time displayed at entrance).

Finding out more: 01625 584412 or alderleyedge@nationaltrust.org.uk. c/o Cheshire Countryside Office, Nether Alderley, Macclesfield, Cheshire SK10 4UB

Alderley Edge		M	T	W	T	F	S	S
Open all year	8–5:30	**M**	**T**	**W**	**T**	**F**	**S**	**S**

Closes at 6, 31 May to 26 September and closes at 5, 1 November to 31 December. Tea-room also open Bank Holidays but closed 24 and 25 December.

Alderley Edge, Cheshire: impressive views

The Beatles' Childhood Homes

Woolton and Allerton, Liverpool

Map (5) C8   🏠 2002

A combined escorted tour of Mendips and 20 Forthlin Road, the childhood homes of John Lennon and Paul McCartney, is your only opportunity to see where the Beatles met, composed and rehearsed many of their earliest songs. Imagine walking through the back door into the kitchen where John's Aunt Mimi would have cooked him his tea, or standing in the spot where Lennon and McCartney composed 'I Saw Her Standing There'. Join our custodians on a fascinating trip down memory lane, and take a moment to reflect on these incredible individuals.

Members may have to pay on special events days

Note: no WC at Mendips. Visits by National Trust minibus tour only (charge including members).

Exploring — Original memorabilia and photographs by Mike McCartney on display.
— Visit the bedroom where John Lennon did his dreaming.
— Walk in the footsteps of these music legends.
— Listen to original audio commentary by Mike and Paul McCartney.

Eating and shopping: guide books for sale at both houses and Speke Hall. Local produce served at Speke Hall's Home Farm restaurant.

You may also enjoy: nearby Speke Hall – a rare Tudor manor house, surrounded by beautiful gardens and woodland.

Making the most of your day: departures from convenient pick-up points (city centre and Speke Hall), escorted minibus tours and online booking service allow you to relax, as we take the strain out of visiting.

Access for all: ♿🅿️💻♿👁️📷 **Building** 🛗

Getting here: 108:SJ422855. No direct access by car or on foot to either house. Access is via minibus from Liverpool city centre or Speke Hall. **Parking**: nearest car park at Speke Hall.

Finding out more: 0844 800 4791 (Infoline) or mendips@nationaltrust.org.uk

The Beatles' Childhood Homes	M	T	W	T	F	S	S
27 Feb–28 Nov		*			W	T	F	S	S

Open Bank Holiday Mondays. *Admission by guided tour only, times vary, visit www.nationaltrust.org.uk/beatles for bookings. 27 February to 14 March and 3 November to 28 November: all tours depart from Liverpool city centre. 17 March to 31 October: morning tours depart from Liverpool city centre, afternoon tours depart from Speke Hall. To guarantee a place visitors are advised to book. Any photography or duplication of audio tour material is strictly prohibited. You will be asked to deposit all handbags, cameras and recording equipment at the entrance to both houses.

The Beatles' Childhood Homes, Liverpool: John Lennon's bedroom

Beatrix Potter Gallery

Main Street, Hawkshead, Cumbria LA22 0NS

Map ⑥ D8   🏠 1944

'**I have enjoyed this little pause from hectic modern life to browse a while at these beautiful mementos.**'
Mrs A. Mills, Grimsby

Step inside this charming 17th-century building to enjoy a new exhibition of Beatrix Potter's original watercolours and paintings. This gallery has an interesting history, as previously it was the office of Potter's husband, William Heelis. Many of these pictures are only displayed at this location. Learn more about Beatrix as a farmer and early supporter of the National Trust. **Note**: nearest WC 300 yards in main village car park (not National Trust). Timed ticket entry.

Beatrix Potter Gallery, Cumbria: once the office of Potter's husband William Heelis

Exploring
- New: exhibition 'Keeping House' with Mrs Tittlemouse.
- We celebrate 100 years of *The Tale of Mrs Tittlemouse*.
- Children will love the trail based on the displays.
- Let your imagination wander as you enjoy the atmospheric gallery.
- Imagine working life before computers when visiting Mr Heelis's office.
- Explore the picturesque and historic Hawkshead village.

Eating and shopping: enjoy the meals and refreshments available in Hawkshead village.

You may also enjoy: Hill Top House, Townend, 'Gondola', Wordsworth House.

Making the most of your day: visit Hill Top House to find out more about the amazing life of Beatrix Potter.

Access for all: 🅿♿🖼🎨♿👁🎧 **Building** ♿

Getting here: 96:SD352982. In Main Street, Hawkshead village, next to Red Lion pub. **Bus**: Stagecoach in Cumbria 505 Windermere ☒–Coniston. Cross Lakes Shuttle from Bowness to Hawkshead. **Train**: Windermere 6½ miles via ferry. **Road**: B5286 from Ambleside (4 miles); B5285 from Coniston (5 miles). **Parking**: 300 yards (pay and display), not National Trust.

Finding out more: 015394 36355. 015394 36471 (shop) or beatrixpottergallery@nationaltrust.org.uk

Beatrix Potter Gallery		M	T	W	T	F	S	S
Gallery								
13 Feb–25 Mar	11–3:30	M	T	W	T	·	S	S
27 Mar–20 May	11–5	M	T	W	T	·	S	S
22 May–2 Sep	10:30–5	M	T	W	T	·	S	S
4 Sep–31 Oct	11–5	M	T	W	T	·	S	S
Shop								
13 Feb–26 Mar	10–4	M	T	W	T	F	S	S
27 Mar–31 Oct	10–5	M	T	W	T	F	S	S
3 Nov–31 Dec	10–4	·	·	W	T	F	S	S

Open Good Friday (2 April) and Friday 29 October. Limited number of timed tickets available daily. Shop closes at 1 on 24 and 31 December, and is closed on 25 and 26 December.

Borrowdale

near Keswick, Cumbria

Map (6) D7  1902

Spectacular landscape around Derwentwater where the Trust cares for vast areas of the valley, including half of Derwentwater (and the main islands), the hamlet of Watendlath, the Bowder Stone, Friar's Crag, Ashness Bridge and Castlerigg Stone Circle. Visit Brandelhow Woods, the National Trust's first acquisition in the Lake District. **Note**: limited parking at Cat Bells; park at Keswick and take boat or bus.

Exploring	– Amble from Keswick to Friar's Crag for breathtaking views.
	– Float in a boat across Derwentwater to walk up Catbells.
	– Wander at Watendlath, location of Walpole's *Herries Chronicles*.
	– Explore the mined landscape of the Coledale valley.

Eating and shopping: buy souvenirs at our shop with stunning views of Derwentwater. Visit the Trust tenant cafés: Rosthwaite, Watendlath, Seathwaite, Stonethwaite. Taste local Herdwick lamb at the Flock Inn, Rosthwaite.

Making the most of your day: tours and events throughout the year. Visits to Derwent Island House five times a year. Dogs under close control only.

Access for all: ⛔ Grounds 🚶

Borrowdale, Cumbria: miles of walks

Getting here: 90:NY266228. **Cycle**: NCN71 (C2C). **Ferry**: Derwentwater launch boat service to various National Trust sites around lake, 017687 72263. **Bus**: to information centre: Stagecoach in Cumbria X4/5 Penrith ≋– Workington, 555 Lancaster–Keswick (passing close ≋ Lancaster, Kendal and Windermere). **Road**: B5289 runs south from Keswick along Borrowdale. **Parking**: car parks at Great Wood, Watendlath, Kettlewell, Bowderstone, Rosthwaite, Seatoller and Honister (pay and display). Coach parking by prior arrangement at Seatoller car park only.

Finding out more: 017687 74649 or borrowdale@nationaltrust.org.uk.
Bowe Barn, Borrowdale Road, Keswick, Cumbria CA12 5UP

Borrowdale		M	T	W	T	F	S	S
Shop and information centre								
13 Feb–31 Oct	10–5	**M**	**T**	**W**	**T**	**F**	**S**	**S**

Shop and information centre may close later on some summer evenings.

Borrowdale: Force Crag Mine

near Keswick, Cumbria

Map (6) D7 1979

Last mineral mine to be worked in the Lake District. Explore the processing mill and landscape with a guide. **Note**: charges including members. Children over ten years only.

Getting here: NY200217. 2¾ miles west of Braithwaite near Keswick.

Finding out more: 017687 74649 or borrowdale@nationaltrust.org.uk

Borrowdale: Force Crag Mine
A guided tour of the building during six open days each year. Contact National Trust Borrowdale for dates.

Bridge House

Rydal Road, Ambleside, Cumbria LA22 9AN

Map (6) D8 🏠 | 1926 |

This tiny but iconic building has 400 years of fascinating history: from an apple store to a family home.

Getting here: Bridge House Information Centre is located In Ambleside, adjacent to Rydal Road car park.

Finding out more: 015394 32617 or bridgehouse@nationaltrust.org.uk

Bridge House
Telephone for opening arrangements.

Buttermere and Ennerdale

Unit 16, Leconfield Industrial Estate, Cleator Moor, Cumbria CA25 5QB

Map (6) C7 🏛🛏🍴🏠 | 1935 |

The beautiful lakes of Buttermere, Crummock Water and Loweswater are surrounded by dramatic high fells, in some of Lakeland's most stunning scenery. Over the fells to the south lies 'Wild Ennerdale', where the National Trust and our partners are working to allow a wilder landscape to evolve. **Note**: nearest WC in Buttermere village.

Exploring
  – Walk and picnic around all the lakes.
  – Go boating: available to hire on Crummock Water and Loweswater.
  – Fishing on Crummock Water, Buttermere and Loweswater by permit.
  – Enjoy the extensive off-road cycling in Ennerdale.

Eating and shopping: pubs and cafés in Buttermere, Loweswater and Ennerdale village.

Making the most of your day: there are a wide variety of lowland and high fell walks from Buttermere and Ennerdale Water (walking guides available from shops in Keswick and Cockermouth). Dogs allowed (on leads near stock grazing).

Access for all: Grounds 🧎

Getting here: 89:NY180150. 8 miles south of Cockermouth. **Bus**: Stagecoach in Cumbria 77/77A from Keswick and Cockermouth–Buttermere; 17/22 from Whitehaven–Ennerdale, then 219F. **Parking**: at Honister Pass, Buttermere village, Lanthwaite Wood – Crummock Water (pay and display) and by Ennerdale Water (not National Trust).

Finding out more: 01946 816940 or buttermere@nationaltrust.org.uk

Buttermere and Ennerdale	M	T	W	T	F	S	S
Open all year	**M**	**T**	**W**	**T**	**F**	**S**	**S**

Loweswater, Cumbria, is surrounded by dramatic high fells

Cartmel Priory Gatehouse

The Square, Cartmel, Grange-over-Sands, Cumbria LA11 6QB

Map ⑥ D9   🏠 | 1946 |

Interesting 14th-century gatehouse of medieval priory. **Note**: mainly in private residential use. The Great Room is open several days a year.

Getting here: 96:SD378788. In the square in village centre.

Finding out more: 01524 701178 or cartpriorygatehouse@nationaltrust.org.uk

---

Cartmel Priory Gatehouse

Visit website or telephone for opening times.

Coniston and Tarn Hows

Boon Crag, Coniston, Cumbria LA21 8AQ

Map ⑥ D8    | 1930 |

Coniston covers a large area of some of the Lake District's most scenic woodland, water and fells. One of many lovely places is the iconic Tarn Hows beauty spot, with its magnificent mountain views. The readily accessible Blea Tarn in Little Langdale also has superb views and fine walking.

Exploring	– Explore the Norse settlement site at Fell Foot.
	– Visit Blea Tarn for spectacular views of the Langdale Pikes.
	– There is access to much of Coniston Water shoreline.
	– Visit the restored Monk Coniston walled garden.

Eating and shopping: ice-cream van at Tarn Hows during peak season.

Making the most of your day: superb network of paths and bridleways at Coniston. Cruise on steam-powered yacht 'Gondola', disembarking at Monk Coniston jetty for a walk through Monk Coniston grounds to Tarn Hows. Dogs on leads (stock grazing).

Access for all: �📷⬛ Grounds ♿➡

Getting here: OL7:SD325995. Tarn Hows 2 miles north east of Coniston. Blea Tarn in Little Langdale, 5 miles north of Coniston. **Bus**: Stagecoach in Cumbria 505 'Coniston Rambler' Windermere–Coniston. Cross Lakes Experience to Hawkshead. **Parking**: pay and display, at Tarn Hows, Glen Mary and Blea Tarn. Not suitable for coaches.

Finding out more: 015394 41456 or coniston@nationaltrust.org.uk

Coniston and Tarn Hows	M	T	W	T	F	S	S
Open all year	**M**	**T**	**W**	**T**	**F**	**S**	**S**

Dalton Castle

Market Place, Dalton-in-Furness, Cumbria LA15 8AX

Map ⑥ D9   🏠 | 1965 |

14th-century tower built to assert the authority of the Abbot of Furness Abbey. **Note**: opened on behalf of the National Trust by the Friends of Dalton Castle.

Getting here: 96:SD226739. In market place at top of main street of Dalton.

Finding out more: 01524 701178 or daltoncastle@nationaltrust.org.uk

---

Dalton Castle

Visit website or telephone for opening times.

Dunham Massey

Altrincham, Cheshire WA14 4SJ

Map (5) D8   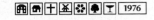 1976

'**Our expectations were high – Dunham and its staff exceeded them all**.'
Jane Metcalfe, Dursley, Gloucestershire

Set in a magnificent 121-hectare (300-acre), deer park this Georgian house tells the story of the owners and the servants who lived here. Discover the salacious scandals of the 7th Earl of Stamford, who married Catherine Cocks, a former bare-back circus rider, and the 2nd Earl of Warrington, who was so enamoured with his wife that he wrote a book anonymously on the desirability of divorce! Uncover these and other fascinating stories when you explore this treasure-packed house, then take a stroll in one of the North's great gardens, including Britain's largest Winter Garden. **Note**: visitors (including members) require a white entry ticket – available from visitor reception.

The Winter Garden at Dunham Massey, Cheshire

Exploring
– Walk among ancient trees, rest in sunny glades.
– Britain's largest winter garden awaits you.
– Experience the grim reality of life as an Edwardian servant.
– Wine coolers to potties – the Trust's greatest silver collection.
– House, park and garden tours available at no extra charge.

Eating and shopping: park to plate, much food is grown on our estate. Sample a beer from the award-winning brewery. Spring, summer, autumn or winter – our menu reflects the season. Choose a special gift from our large shop.

You may also enjoy: Europe's most powerful working waterwheel, at the awe-inspiring Quarry Bank Mill.

Making the most of your day: wide year-round events programme for all the family, including Boredom Busters during school holidays. Free children's quizzes/trails. Extensive picnic lawns. Walks leaflet. Cycling for under fives. Dogs welcome on leads in deer park and walks around the estate.

Access for all: [icons] House [icons] Restaurant [icons]
Park and garden [icons]

Getting here: 109:SJ735874. **Foot**: close to Trans-Pennine Trail and Bridgewater Canal. **Cycle**: NCN62, 1 mile. **Bus**: Warrington Coachways No 38 Altrincham Interchange ⊠–Warrington. **Train**: Altrincham 3 miles; Hale 3 miles. **Road**: 3 miles south west of Altrincham off A56: M6 exit 19; M56 exit 7.
Sat Nav: coaches please avoid Sat Nav route – low bridge. **Parking**: 200 yards approximately. March to November shuttle buggy service operates most days between car park and visitor facilities.

Finding out more: 0161 941 1025 or dunhammassey@nationaltrust.org.uk

Dunham Massey		M	T	W	T	F	S	S
House*								
27 Feb–31 Oct	11–5	M	T	W	·	·	S	S
Garden**								
1 Jan–26 Feb	11–4	M	T	W	T	F	S	S
27 Feb–31 Oct	11–5:30	M	T	W	T	F	S	S
1 Nov–31 Dec	11–4	M	T	W	T	F	S	S
Restaurant and shop								
1 Jan–26 Feb	10:30–4	M	T	W	T	F	S	S
27 Feb–31 Oct	10:30–5	M	T	W	T	F	S	S
1 Nov–31 Dec	10:30–4	M	T	W	T	F	S	S
Park*								
Open all year	9–5	M	T	W	T	F	S	S
Mill								
27 Feb–31 Oct	12–4	M	T	W	·	·	S	S
White Cottage**								
28 Mar–31 Oct	2–5	·	·	·	·	·	·	S

*11 to 12 visit to house by guided taster tour only (restricted numbers, allocated upon arrival), last admission 4:30. Open Good Friday. **Winter closure at 4 or dusk if earlier. *** March to October gates remain open until 7:30. Property closed 24 November for staff training and 25 December (including park). ****Open last Sunday of the month only – all visits must be booked on 0161 928 0075 or at dunmasswhite@nationaltrust.org.uk

Letting off steam at Fell Foot Park, Cumbria

Fell Foot Park

Newby Bridge, Windermere, Cumbria LA12 8NN

Map (6) D9   1948

The views of Lake Windermere beyond the park are breathtaking. The Victorian lawns and garden sweep away to fine picnic areas and lakeshore. Enjoy the Boathouse Café with its patio, where you can enjoy watching the boats and soaking in the atmosphere. Bring your own boat to explore the lake. **Note**: launching and slipway facilities available for a wide variety of craft.

Exploring
– Hire a rowing boat for a couple of hours.
– Stroll around the grounds and enjoy the magnificent views.
– Let the children loose on our adventure playground.

Eating and shopping: savour our hearty, warming soup, made with fresh seasonal ingredients. We use local Cumbrian produce to create great Cumbrian food. A cream tea by the lake – what could be better?

Making the most of your day: rowing boats available for hire April to October (weather permitting). Dogs on leads welcome.

Access for all: ⓟ Ⓓ ♿ ♿ 🚻 Ⓛ Grounds ♿

Getting here: 96/97:SD381869. **Ferry**: seasonal ferry links Fell Foot to Lakeside (southern terminus of main Windermere cruise ferries). **Bus**: Stagecoach Cumbria 618 Ambleside–Barrow-in-Furness (connections from Windermere ≥). **Train**: Grange-over-Sands 6 miles; Windermere 8 miles. **Road**: at the southern tip of Lake Windermere, entrance from A592. **Parking**: admission charge includes car parking. Coach access difficult (booking essential).

Finding out more: 015395 31273 or fellfootpark@nationaltrust.org.uk

Fell Foot Park		M	T	W	T	F	S	S
Park								
Open all year	9–5	M	T	W	T	F	S	S
Snack bar								
6 Mar–21 Mar	11–3	·	·	·	·	·	S	S
Boathouse Café								
27 Mar–31 Oct	10–5	M	T	W	T	F	S	S

Park closes dusk if earlier. Facilities (such as rowing boat hire): 3 April to 31 October, daily, 11 to 4 (last boat must be returned by 4:30). Weather permitting.

Formby

Victoria Road, Freshfield, Formby,
Liverpool L37 1LJ

Map ⑤ B7 ![icons] 1967

This ever-changing sandy coastline set between
the sea and Formby town offers miles of walks
through the woods and dunes. Glimpse a rare
red squirrel or see a historic landscape levelled
for asparagus. Prehistoric animal and human
footprints can sometimes be found in silt beds
on the shoreline. **Note**: WCs close at 5:30 in
summer, 4 in winter.

Exploring
   – Enjoy a bracing walk on the
     sandy beaches.
   – Explore Formby's historic
     asparagus landscape.
   – Follow the fascinating Formby
     Point audio guide trail.
   – Search for secretive red
     squirrels in the pine woods.

Eating and shopping: ice-creams, soft drinks
and coffees from mobile van.

Making the most of your day: guided walks
and awareness days. Circular walks and longer
walks linked to the Sefton Coastal Path.
Formby Point audio guide trail. Dogs on leads
(vulnerable wildlife).

Access for all: ![icons]
Accessible WC ![icon] **Grounds** ![icon]

Getting here: 108:SD275080. **Foot**: Sefton
Coastal Footpath traverses the property.
Cycle: NCN62, 3 miles. **Train**: Freshfield 1
mile. **Road**: 15 miles north of Liverpool, 2
miles west of Formby, 2 miles off A565. 6 miles
south of Southport. Follow brown signs from
roundabout at north end of Formby bypass.
Parking: cars £4.20, minibuses £10, coaches
£25 (booking essential for coaches). Dune
car park closes 5:30, April to October and 4,
November to March. Width restriction 3 yards.

Examining prehistoric footprints at Formby, Liverpool

Finding out more: 01704 878591 or
formby@nationaltrust.org.uk.
Countryside Office, Blundell Avenue,
Freshfield, Formby, Liverpool L37 1PH

Formby		M	T	W	T	F	S	S
Open all year	Dawn–dusk	**M**	**T**	**W**	**T**	**F**	**S**	**S**

Closed 25 December. Car parks may be very full in peak
season, with long queues. Groups telephone 01704 874949.

Gawthorpe Hall

Burnley Road, Padiham, near Burnley,
Lancashire BB12 8UA

Map ⑤ D6 ![icons] 1972

This imposing house, set in tranquil grounds,
resembles the great Hardwick Hall. In the
19th century Sir Charles Barry created the
opulent interiors we see today. Several rooms
display part of an international collection of
needlework, lace and costume. The wooded
park offers wonderful walks. **Note**: financed
and run in partnership with Lancashire
County Council.

Exploring
- Admire the fantastic interiors and furniture in the house.
- Enjoy displays from the nationally important textile collection.
- Observe treecreepers and woodpeckers in the woods.
- Explore the woodland and pond.

Eating and shopping: enjoy light snacks in the tea-room after your walk.

Making the most of your day: classic motorcycle show and open-air theatre. Dogs under close control in grounds only.

Access for all: ⬛⬛⬛⬛⬛⬛⬛
Building ⬛ **Grounds** ⬛

Getting here: 103:SD806340. **Foot**: pleasant walk by the River Calder from Padiham, ½ mile; on route of Bronte Way public footpath. **Bus**: frequent Transdev Lancashire United and Burnley & Pendle buses from Burnley bus station. **Train**: Rose Grove 2 miles. Also Burnley Barracks and Burnley Manchester Road stations, nearby bus links. **Road**: on east outskirts of Padiham; ¾-mile drive to house on north of A671; M65 exit 8 towards Clitheroe, then signposted from second traffic light junction to Padiham. **Parking**: 150 yards. Tight access and turning.

Finding out more: 01282 771004 or gawthorpehall@nationaltrust.org.uk

Gawthorpe Hall		M	T	W	T	F	S	S
House								
1 Apr–31 Oct	1–5	·	T	W	T	·	S	S
Grounds								
Open all year	10–6	M	T	W	T	F	S	S
Tea-room								
1 Apr–31 Oct	12:30–4:30	·	T	W	T	·	S	S

Open Bank Holidays and Good Friday. Opening times and prices are controlled by Lancashire County Council and subject to change.

'Gondola'

Coniston Pier, Lake Road, Coniston, Cumbria LA21 8AN

Map ⑥ D8 ⬛ 1980

'A ride on the "Gondola" was like going out with friends who were so proud of their boat.'
Mrs Lockwood, Nottinghamshire

The original 'Gondola', a re-built Victorian steam yacht, was first launched in 1859 and now, completely rebuilt by the National Trust, gives passengers the chance to sail in her sumptuous, upholstered saloons. This is the perfect way to view Coniston's spectacular scenery. Sail to Monk Coniston jetty at the north of the lake, then walk through the Monk Coniston garden on to Tarn Hows. Circular walk four miles. All sailings are subject to weather conditions. **Note**: charge (including members) as 'Gondola' is an enterprise. No WC.

Exploring
- Explorer cruises – hear about Coniston's famous connections!
- For a grand Victorian day out, disembark at Brantwood House.

Eating and shopping: local, freshly prepared food at the Bluebird Café, Coniston Pier. Disembark at Brantwood jetty for Jumping Jenny's tea-room. Catering provided for private hires by Wilfs. 'Gondola' souvenirs available on board.

The elegant 'Gondola' on Coniston Water

You may also enjoy: Hill Top, Beatrix Potter Gallery and Townend.

Making the most of your day: events celebrating the 150th anniversary of the 'original' 'Gondola'. Look out for cruises and guided walks, evening Campbell/Bluebird talks and more. Dogs in outside areas only.

Access for all: 🅿️ 🚻 ⊡ 📷 Gangway 🚶‍♿

Getting here: 96:SD307970. Sails from Coniston Pier (½ mile from Coniston village). **Bus**: Stagecoach in Cumbria 505 from Windermere 🚉. **Train**: Foxfield, not Sunday, 10 miles; Windermere 10 miles via vehicle ferry. **Road**: A593 from Ambleside. Pier is at end of Lake Road, turn immediately left after petrol station if travelling south from centre of Coniston village. **Parking**: 50 yards, pay and display, at Coniston Pier (not National Trust).

Finding out more: 015394 41288 or gondola@nationaltrust.org.uk

'Gondola'		M	T	W	T	F	S	S
1 Apr–31 Oct	10:30–4	**M**	**T**	**W**	**T**	**F**	**S**	**S**

Last sailing at 3:30 (April, May, September and October), 4:30 (June to August). The National Trust reserves the right to cancel sailings and special charters in the event of high winds. In the event of cancellation due to adverse weather conditions, private charters or unforeseen operational difficulties, every reasonable effort will be made to inform the public. Piers at Coniston, Monk Coniston and Brantwood (not National Trust).

Grasmere and Great Langdale

High Close, Loughrigg, Ambleside, Cumbria LA22 9HH

Map ⑥ D8  1925

The iconic Langdale Pikes stand majestic in the landscape. The Trust owns most of the valley farms, Trust campsite, the glaciated valley of Mickleden, a Victorian garden at High Close and the dramatic Dungeon Ghyll. In and around Grasmere the Trust owns the lake bed and parts of Rydal Water.

Exploring
– A wonderful opportunity to walk up to the Langdale Pikes.
– Wide range of low-level circular routes in both valleys.
– Breathtaking scenery.
– Old Dungeon Ghyll is a popular area for rock climbing.

Eating and shopping: the Old Dungeon Ghyll hotel at head of Great Langdale. Numerous cafés, restaurants and hotels in Grasmere.

Making the most of your day: annual Langdale Gala (usually held in July), and Grasmere Lakeland Sports and Show (August Bank Holiday). All non-National Trust events. Dogs under close control allowed.

Access for all: 🅿️ 🚻 Grounds ♿

Getting here: 89/90:NY290060. Great Langdale valley starts 4 miles west of Ambleside. Grasmere is 4 miles to the north of Ambleside. **Foot**: Coast to Coast footpath runs through both valleys. There is also a network of footpaths which runs through both valleys. **Cycle**: Sustrans cycle route 37, then links from Skelwith Bridge to Elterwater. Sustrans Cycle route 6 is planned to come to Grasmere. **Bus**: to Grasmere village: Stagecoach in Cumbria 555/6, 599 from Windermere 🚉. To Langdale Campsite: Stagecoach in Cumbria 516 from Ambleside. **Train**: Windermere 8 miles. **Road**: junction 36 M6. A591 to Ambleside. A591 continues to Grasmere. A593 to Skelwith Bridge, then B543 to Great Langdale. **Parking**: three National Trust car parks in the Langdale valley. Three non-National Trust car parks in Grasmere village. All pay and display.

Finding out more: 015394 37663 or grasmere@nationaltrust.org.uk

Grasmere and Great Langdale	M	T	W	T	F	S	S
Open all year	**M**	**T**	**W**	**T**	**F**	**S**	**S**

Mr Hardman's Photographic Studio

59 Rodney Street, Liverpool, Merseyside L1 9EX

Map (5) B8   2003

Step back in time to 1950 in this fascinating house – view the studio, darkroom and living quarters of the renowned portrait photographer E. Chambré Hardman and his wife Margaret. The memorabilia of post-war daily life is displayed alongside portraits of Liverpool people and landscape photographs of the surrounding countryside. **Note**: admission by guided tour (booking not required, but advised).

Exploring   – Follow photographic process from studio, to darkroom, to mounting room.
   – See how Liverpool has changed in the Hardman photographic exhibition.
   – Have your portrait photograph taken in the studio.

Mr Hardman's Photographic Studio, Liverpool

Mr Hardman's Studio		M	T	W	T	F	S	S
17 Mar–31 Oct	11–3:30		·	**W**	**T**	**F**	**S**	**S**

Open Bank Holiday Mondays. Admission by timed ticket only, including members. Visitors are advised to book in advance by telephone or email to property. Tickets on the day subject to availability.

Eating and shopping: choose from the wide range of Hardman prints and postcards.

Making the most of your day: book your place on a tour in advance. Virtual tour of the house available. Children's quiz trail.

Access for all: Building 🔾

Getting here: 108:SJ355895. Short walk north of Liverpool city centre. Rodney Street is off Hardman Street and Upper Duke Street. Follow fingerposts. **Bus**: frequent Arriva services from surrounding area. **Train**: Liverpool Lime Street ½ mile. **Parking**: No onsite parking. Offsite parking most days near Anglican Cathedral (pay and display). Slater Street NCP.

Finding out more: 0151 709 6261 or 59rodneystreet@nationaltrust.org.uk

Hare Hill

Over Alderley, Macclesfield, Cheshire SK10 4QB

Map (5) D8   1978

This tranquil woodland garden, especially spectacular in early summer, includes more than 70 varieties of rhododendrons, plus azaleas, hollies and hostas. At its heart is a delightful walled area with a pergola and wire sculptures. The surrounding parkland has an attractive permitted path to nearby Alderley Edge. **Note**: car park closes 5.

Exploring   – Walk through landscaped parkland to Alderley Edge.
   – Bring your binoculars and spot the prolific birdlife.

Access for all: Grounds 🔾🔾

Getting here: 118:SJ873763. **Train**: Alderley Edge 2½ miles; Prestbury 2½ miles.
Road: between Alderley Edge and Macclesfield (B5087). Turn off north on to Prestbury Road. Left at T junction after 200 yards, continue ¾ mile, entrance on left. From Prestbury take Chelford Road 1½ miles, entrance on right.
Parking: not suitable for coaches.

Finding out more: 01625 584412 or harehill@nationaltrust.org.uk

Hare Hill		M	T	W	T	F	S	S
2 Apr–2 May	10–5	·	·	**W**	**T**	·	**S**	**S**
3 May–30 May	10–5	**M**	**T**	**W**	**T**	**F**	**S**	**S**
2 Jun–28 Oct	10–5	·	·	**W**	**T**	·	**S**	**S**

Open Bank Holiday Mondays and Good Friday. Last admission one hour before closing.

Hawkshead and Claife

near Hawkshead, Ambleside, Cumbria

Map (6) D8 1929

Hawkshead village, home to the Beatrix Potter Gallery, is surrounded by beautiful scenery, including along Windermere lakeshore. North of the village is the Courthouse, dating from the 15th century, all that remains of the estate once held by Furness Abbey. Wray Castle offers year round access to the grounds.
Note: National Trust campsite on lakeshore at Low Wray [NY372012], visit website for opening arrangements.

Exploring
 — Some fantastic low level walks with great views.
 — Visit amazing historical buildings in countryside settings.
 — Leave the car behind and use boat, bus and boot.
 — Experience the countryside that inspired Beatrix Potter.

Eating and shopping: there are plenty of catering options available in Hawkshead.

Making the most of your day: have a day in the wonderful countryside that inspired Beatrix Potter; don't forget to visit Hawkshead and the gallery there. Dogs allowed, under close control.

Access for all: Grounds ♿

Getting here: 96/97:SD352982. Hawkshead is 6 miles south west of Ambleside. **Foot**: off-road path from Windermere ferry to Sawrey; many footpaths in the area. **Ferry**: Windermere car ferry; also passenger ferry from Bowness. **Bus**: Stagecoach in Cumbria 505 Windermere ☒–Coniston. **Train**: Windermere 6 miles via vehicle ferry. **Parking**: at Ash Landing (close to ferry) and Harrowslack (pay and display); free car park at Red Nab. All close to Lake Windermere. Car parks (not National Trust) in Hawkshead village (pay and display).

Finding out more: 015394 47997 or hawkshead@nationaltrust.org.uk. c/o Hill Top, Near Sawrey, Ambleside, Cumbria LA22 0LF

Hawkshead and Claife		M	T	W	T	F	S	S
Countryside								
Open all year		**M**	**T**	**W**	**T**	**F**	**S**	**S**
Courthouse								
27 Mar–31 Oct	11–4	**M**	**T**	**W**	**T**	**F**	**S**	**S**

Hawkshead Courthouse: access by key from the National Trust shop, The Square, Hawkshead, or the Beatrix Potter Gallery ticket office. Free admission but no parking facilities. Approx ½ mile walk from the village.

Views from Wray Castle, Cumbria

Hill Top

Near Sawrey, Hawkshead, Ambleside,
Cumbria LA22 0LF

Map (6) D8   🏠 ✼ 🍷 [1944]

Enjoy the tale of Beatrix Potter – Hill Top is a
time-capsule of this amazing woman's life. Full
of her favourite things, the house appears as if
Beatrix had just stepped out for a walk. Every
room contains a reference to a picture in a
'tale'. The lovely cottage garden is a haphazard
mix of flowers, herbs, fruit and vegetables.
Hill Top is a small house and a timed-ticket
system is in operation to avoid overcrowding
and to protect the interior. Hill Top can be very
busy and visitors may sometimes have to wait
to enter the house. **Note: tickets cannot be
booked and early sell-outs are possible**.

Exploring	– Don't miss the new children's garden trail (during holiday periods).
	– See the sights which inspired Beatrix's tales and illustrations.
	– Experience her house, just as Beatrix would have done.
	– Enjoy a traditional English country garden, all year round.
	– Leave the car behind and use boat, bus and boot.

Eating and shopping: shop specialises in
Beatrix Potter-related items. Drinks and treats
available in the shop. Sawrey House Hotel
and Tower Bank Arms serve meals
and refreshments.

You may also enjoy: the Beatrix Potter Gallery,
Townend and Wordsworth House.

Making the most of your day: leave the car
behind and come to us by boat, boot or bike;
include a visit to Hawkshead and the Beatrix
Potter Gallery.

Access for all: 🗺️ 🖼️ 🎨 ⠿ 🅰️
Building 👟 🏔️ **Grounds** 👟 ♿

Hill Top, Cumbria: Beatrix Potter's house

Getting here: 96/97:SD370955. 2 miles south
of Hawkshead, in hamlet of Near Sawrey;
3 miles from Bowness via ferry. **Foot**: off-road
path from ferry (2 miles), marked. **Bus**: Cross
Lakes Experience from Bowness Pier 3 across
Lake Windermere on to Stagecoach in Cumbria
525; also 505 from Windermere ➠ changing
at Hawkshead (April–September only, plus
weekends in October). Telephone
01539 445161 for complete ferry and bus
timetable. **Train**: Windermere 4½ miles via
vehicle ferry. **Road**: B5286 and B5285 from
Ambleside (6 miles), B5285 from Coniston
(7 miles). **Parking**: limited car parking.

Finding out more: 015394 36269 or
hilltop@nationaltrust.org.uk

Hill Top		M	T	W	T	F	S	S
House								
13 Feb–25 Mar	11–3:30	M	T	W	T	·	S	S
27 Mar–20 May	10:30–4:30	M	T	W	T	·	S	S
22 May–2 Sep	10–4:30	M	T	W	T	·	S	S
4 Sep–31 Oct	10:30–4:30	M	T	W	T	·	S	S
Shop and garden								
13 Feb–26 Mar	10:45–4	M	T	W	T	F	S	S
27 Mar–21 May	10–5	M	T	W	T	F	S	S
22 May–3 Sep	9:45–5	M	T	W	T	F	S	S
4 Sep–31 Oct	10–5	M	T	W	T	F	S	S
1 Nov–24 Dec	10–4	M	T	W	T	F	S	S

Open Good Friday, 2 April and 29 October. Limited number
of timed tickets available daily. Access to the garden and
shop is free during opening hours. Shop closes at 1
on 24 December.

Little Moreton Hall

Congleton, Cheshire CW12 4SD

Map (5) D9

Gaze at the drunkenly reeling South Range, cross the moat and marvel at the cobbled courtyard before you enter a Hall full of surprises. The skill of the craftsmen fascinates as you climb the stairs to the Long Gallery – imagine life here in Tudor times. The various delights of this unique property include some remarkable wall-paintings and a pretty Knot Garden. Colourful tales of both the Moreton family and this iconic building are revealed to you by our tour guides. Delicious home-baked local food and a visit to the shop complete your day. **Note**: South Range will be under scaffolding during late summer and early autumn.

Exploring
- Discover the fascinating history on a free guided tour.
- See elaborately carved timbers and patterned glass.
- Admire the Knot Garden and relax in the tranquil orchard.
- Experience a Tudor Yuletide during December.
- Enjoy the family trail and regular events.
- Follow the discovery trail on our short estate walk.

Eating and shopping: delicious home-cooked food in the Brewhouse Restaurant. Sample puddings, cakes and scones baked in our kitchen. Treat yourself to a souvenir from our friendly, welcoming shop. Our shop and restaurant are pleased to support local producers.

You may also enjoy: Biddulph Grange Garden – only six miles away.

Making the most of your day: regular living history and musical events bring the Hall to life. Exhibitions by local groups displaying regional arts and crafts. Open-air theatre, family activities and Yuletide celebrations.

Access for all: ⊞ 🚻 ♿ 🦯 🅿 🐕 💻 📺 🎧 ⠿
Ⓐ **Building** 🦽🦽♿♿ **Grounds** 🦽🦽➡

Getting here: 118:SJ832589. **Bus**: infrequent service. Stanways 315 Alsager ≉–Congleton (passing close Kidsgrove ≉). **Train**: Kidsgrove 3 miles; Congleton 4½ miles. **Road**: 4 miles south west of Congleton, on east side of A34. From M6 exit 17 follow signs for Congleton and join A34 Southbound (signed Newcastle) from Congleton. **Parking**: 100 yards.

Finding out more: 01260 272018 or littlemoretonhall@nationaltrust.org.uk

Little Moreton Hall		M	T	W	T	F	S	S
27 Feb–14 Mar	11–4						S	S
17 Mar–31 Oct	11–5			W	T	F	S	S
6 Nov–19 Dec	11–4						S	S

Open Bank Holiday Mondays. Closes dusk if earlier. Access during Yuletide celebrations restricted to ground floor, garden, shop and restaurant. Special openings at other times for booked groups.

Lyme Park

Disley, Stockport, Cheshire SK12 2NR

Map (5) E8

'I love to watch the gardens evolve – my childhood (late 1950s) were spent playing here!'
Mrs Angela Bostock, Stockport

On the edge of the Peak District, nestling within sweeping moorland, Lyme Park is a magnificent estate. Its wild remoteness and powerful beauty contrast with one of the most famous country-house images in England – the backdrop to where Darcy meets Elizabeth in *Pride and Prejudice*. Discover a colourful family history – from rescuing the Black Prince, sailing into exile with the Duke of Windsor, to the writing of the hit series *Upstairs Downstairs*. Enjoy hearing visitors play the piano as you discover impressive tapestries, clocks and beautifully furnished rooms, or escape to the park and feel miles from anywhere.

Lyme Park, Cheshire: powerful beauty

Note: owned and managed by the National Trust but partly financed by Stockport Metropolitan Borough Council.

Exploring
- Welcome CD to listen to as you drive to house.
- Stroll among luxurious borders and sweeping lawns.
- Take a seat in the library, view Caxton's *Missal*.
- Let off steam in the play area.
- Learn about life below stairs in the exhibition.
- Find the red and fallow deer.

Eating and shopping: grow a souvenir from the plant shop. Try Lyme Park venison. Browse in the book shop. Indulge in a cream tea.

You may also enjoy: Little Moreton Hall.

Making the most of your day: programme of events all year. School holiday and family activities. Family quizzes in house and garden. Walking leaflets available for park. Dogs under close control and in park only (on leads in some areas).

Access for all:

Building **Grounds**

Getting here: 109:SJ965825. **Foot**: northern end of Gritstone Trail; paths to Macclesfield Canal, Poynton Marina 1 mile and Peak Forest Canal 2½ miles. **Bus**: TrentBarton 199 Buxton–Manchester Airport, to park entrance. **Train**: Disley, ½ mile from park entrance. National Trust courtesy bus from park admission kiosk to house for pedestrians on days house is open. **Road**: entrance on A6, 6½ miles south east of Stockport (M60 exit 1), 12 miles north west of Buxton (house and car park 1 mile from entrance). **Parking**: coaches £18 unless bringing booked groups to house and garden.

Finding out more: 01663 762023 or lymepark@nationaltrust.org.uk

Lyme Park		M	T	W	T	F	S	S
House, restaurant and shop								
27 Feb–31 Oct	11*–5	**M**	**T**	·	·	**F**	**S**	**S**
Garden								
27 Feb–31 Oct	11–5	**M**	**T**	**W**	**T**	**F**	**S**	**S**
Park								
Open all year	8–6	**M**	**T**	**W**	**T**	**F**	**S**	**S**
Timber Yard plant sales and shop								
2 Jan–7 Mar	11–4	·	·	·	·	·	**S**	**S**
13 Mar–31 Oct	10:30–5	**M**	**T**	**W**	**T**	**F**	**S**	**S**
Timber Yard coffee shop								
Open all year	11–4	**M**	**T**	**W**	**T**	**F**	**S**	**S**

*Between 11 and 12 entry to house is by guided tour only (numbers restricted). Telephone for winter opening times of Timber Yard shop and garden. Closed 25 December.

Nether Alderley Mill

Congleton Road, Nether Alderley, Macclesfield, Cheshire SK10 4TW

Map (5) D8 1950

This charming rustic mill is one of only four virtually complete corn mills in Cheshire. **Note**: only open for booked groups. No WC.

Getting here: 118:SJ844763. 1½ miles south of Alderley Edge, on east side of A34.

Finding out more: 01625 445853 or quarrybankmill@nationaltrust.org.uk

Nether Alderley Mill
Open for group visits only by prior arrangement.

Quarry Bank Mill and Styal Estate

Styal, Wilmslow, Cheshire SK9 4LA

Map ⑤ D8  1939

Quarry Bank overflows with the atmosphere of the Industrial Revolution. A visit to the cotton mill, powered by Europe's most powerful working waterwheel, will certainly stimulate your senses. The clatter of machinery and hiss of steam engines is astonishing. Take a guided tour of the Apprentice House, which housed the pauper children who worked in the mill. Visit the stunning garden – the Greg family's picturesque valley retreat adjoining the mill. Stroll to Styal village, built by the Greg family to house the mill workers and still a thriving community, or walk through woods along the River Bollin. **Note**: no pushchairs in the Mill or the Apprentice House.

Exploring
- Experience demonstrations on how cotton was processed into cloth.
- See how water power was replaced by steam power.
- Explore the garden, its terraced paths and cave.
- See how apprentices lived and worked.
- Follow a choice of family trails.
- Enjoy a family picnic near the play area.

Eating and shopping: browse in the mill shop for gifts and mementos. Dine in the Mill Restaurant. Grab a snack from the Pantry. **New**: plants on sale in the mill yard.

You may also enjoy: Alderley Edge, Dunham Massey, Lyme Park and Tatton Park.

Making the most of your day: programme of events and guided walks throughout the year. School holiday activities for all the family. Children's play area. Picnic facilities. Trails and Tracker Packs. Cycle route. Dogs under close control on estate. On lead only in mill yard.

Quarry Bank Mill, Cheshire

Access for all: ☐☐☐☐☐☐☐☐☐☐
Building ☐☐☐ **Grounds** ☐☐☐

Getting here: 109:SJ835835. **Cycle**: NCN6, 1½ miles. RCR85 ½ mile. **Bus**: Swans Travel 200 Manchester Airport ☒–Wilmslow. **Train**: Styal ½ mile; Manchester Airport 2 miles; Wilmslow 2½ miles. **Road**: 1½ miles north of Wilmslow off B5166, 2 miles from M56, exit 5, 10 miles south of Manchester. Heritage signs from A34 and M56. **Parking**: 200 yards. Coaches £15, unless booked.

Finding out more: 01625 445896 (Infoline). 01625 527468 or quarrybankmill@nationaltrust.org.uk

Quarry Bank Mill		M	T	W	T	F	S	S
Mill and Apprentice House								
1 Jan–28 Feb	11–4	·	·	W	T	F	S	S
1 Mar–31 Oct	11–5	M	T	W	T	F	S	S
3 Nov–12 Dec	11–4	·	·	W	T	F	S	S
18 Dec–19 Dec	11–4	·	·	·	·	·	S	S
26 Dec–31 Dec	11–4	M	T	W	T	F	S	S
Garden								
1 Mar–31 Oct	11–5	M	T	W	T	F	S	S
Shop and restaurant								
1 Jan–28 Feb	11–4	·	·	W	T	F	S	S
1 Mar–31 Oct	11–5	M	T	W	T	F	S	S
3 Nov–23 Dec	11–4	·	·	W	T	F	S	S
Shop, restaurant and garden*								
26 Dec–31 Dec	11–4	M	T	W	T	F	S	S

Open Bank Holiday Mondays, Boxing Day, 1 January and 15 and 16 February. Closed 24 and 25 December. Mill: last admission one hour before closing. Apprentice House guided tours: limited availability – timed tickets only (available from Mill on early arrival. Popular school visit destination during school term time. **Restaurant, garden and shop open daily 26 to 31 December. *Garden closes 3.**

Rufford Old Hall

200 Liverpool Road, Rufford, near Ormskirk,
Lancashire L40 1SG

Map ⑤ C6 🏛️❄️🔔⊤ 1936

Step back in time at one of Lancashire's finest
16th-century Tudor buildings, where a young
Will Shakespeare once performed. His stage,
the Great Hall, is as spectacular today as when
the Bard was performing for the owner, Sir
Thomas Hesketh, and his raucous guests.
Wander around the house and marvel over the
fine collections of furniture, arms, armour and
tapestries. Then step outside and enjoy the
gardens, topiary and sculpture and a walk in
the woodlands, alongside the canal. Complete
your visit with some delicious, freshly prepared
local food in the cosy tea-room.

Exploring   – Stand behind the giant screen,
where Shakespeare made
costume changes.
– Imagine the feasts that took
place in the Great Hall.
– Live the life of the
19th-century Hesketh family.

Eating and shopping: dine in the charming
Victorian tea-room. Enjoy delicious,
homemade scones straight out of the
oven. Browse the shop and our peat-free
plant centre.

You may also enjoy: Elizabethan
Gawthorpe Hall, with its nationally
important textile collection.

Making the most of your day: circular
walks, guided tours and family events
programme. Dogs on leads in grounds
only, not formal gardens.

Access for all: 🅿️♿🚻♿🍴🔲🔲🖼️📷
Building ♿♿♿ **Grounds** ♿➡️

The 16th-century Rufford Old Hall, Lancashire

Getting here: 108:SD462161. **Foot**: adjoins
towpath of Rufford extension of Leeds–
Liverpool Canal. **Bus**: J&S 347 Southport–
Chorley, Stagecoach in Lancashire 2B Preston–
Ormskirk, Sundays only. **Train**: Rufford, not
Sunday, ½ mile; Burscough Bridge 2½ miles.
Road: 7 miles north of Ormskirk, in village
of Rufford on east side of A59. From M6 exit
27, follow signs for Parbold then Rufford.
Parking: free, 10 yards. Car park can be very
busy on summer days. Limited coach parking.

Finding out more: 01704 821254 or
ruffordoldhall@nationaltrust.org.uk

Rufford Old Hall		M	T	W	T	F	S	S
House, garden, shop and tea-room								
27 Feb–7 Mar	11–5	·	·	·	·	·	S	S
House								
13 Mar–31 Oct	11–5	M	T	W	·	·	·	S
13 Mar–30 Oct	1–5	·	·	·	·	·	S	·
Garden, shop and tea-room								
13 Mar–31 Oct	11–5	M	T	W	·	·	S	S
5 Nov–19 Dec	12–4	·	·	·	·	F	S	S

Admission to house 11 to 1 by guided tour only
(no extra charge).

Sizergh Castle and Garden

Sizergh, near Kendal, Cumbria LA8 8AE

Map ⑥ E8 🏛🏚❀♣⚓☕🏠 1950

'Truly wonderful, relaxing visit. All staff, including volunteers, were so friendly it was like being with friends.'
Mr and Mrs Taylor, Newcastle

This imposing house, at the gateway to the Lake District, stands proud in a rich and beautiful garden, which includes a pond, lake, national collection of hardy ferns and a superb limestone rock garden. Still lived in by the Strickland family, Sizergh has many tales to tell and certainly feels lived in, with centuries-old portraits and fine furniture sitting alongside modern family photographs. The exceptional wood panelling culminates in the Inlaid Chamber, returned here in 1999 from the Victoria & Albert Museum. The 647-hectare (1,600-acre) estate includes limestone pasture, orchards and ancient, semi-natural woodland.

Exploring
- Admire some of England's finest Elizabethan wood carving and panelling.
- Relax in the National Trust's largest limestone rock garden.
- See the kitchen garden, orchard and herbaceous border.
- Follow footpaths to stunning viewpoints of Morecambe Bay/Lakeland hills.
- Visit the nearby Strickland Arms pub and Low Sizergh farmshop.

Eating and shopping: savour local, seasonal food in our contemporary licensed café.
Buy a picnic to enjoy while relaxing in the garden. Plants and local products from our shop. Sample the food at the pub and farm tea-room.

You may also enjoy: Fell Foot Park, Arnside and Silverdale, as well as Townend.

Making the most of your day: varied programme of events throughout the year, including open-air theatre, adult workshops and guided walks. Explore the estate with a walks leaflet. Garden trail and house quizzes for children. Dogs in the car park and on public footpaths only.

Access for all: 🅿🄳♿🛗📷🔍📖🎦♿
⦙⦙🄰 Building ♿♿♿ Grounds ♿➡♿♿

Getting here: 97:SD498878. 3½ miles south of Kendal. **Foot**: footpaths 530002 and 530003 pass by Sizergh Castle. **Cycle**: NCN6, 1½ miles. RCR20 passes main gate. **Bus**: Stagecoach in Cumbria 555 Keswick–Kendal/Lancaster (passing close Lancaster ≋), 552 Kendal–Arnside (passing close Arnside ≋). All pass Kendal ≋. **Train**: Oxenholme 3 miles. **Road**: M6 exit 36 then A590 towards Kendal, take Barrow-in-Furness turning and follow brown signs. From Lake District take A591 south then A590 towards Barrow-in-Furness. **Sat Nav**: enter LA8 8DZ. **Parking**: 250 yards.

Finding out more: 015395 60951 or sizergh@nationaltrust.org.uk

Sizergh Castle and Garden		M	T	W	T	F	S	S
House								
14 Mar–31 Oct	12*–5	M	T	W	T	·	·	S
Garden, café and shop								
14 Mar–31 Oct	11–5	M	T	W	T	·	·	S
Café, shop								
2 Jan–13 Mar	11–4	·	·	·	·	·	S	S
15 Feb–19 Feb	11–4	M	T	W	T	F	·	·
6 Nov–26 Dec	11–4	·	·	·	·	·	S	S
27 Dec–31 Dec	11–4	M	T	W	T	F	·	·

*Access to house, 12 to 1, by guided tour only (limited places – can be booked or taken on the day, if available). Unguided access from 1. Timed ticket system may be in operation at busy times. Café and shop closed Christmas Day.

Sizergh Castle Garden, Cumbria

Speke Hall, Liverpool: rare Tudor manor house with a turbulent history

Speke Hall, Garden and Estate

The Walk, Liverpool L24 1XD

Map (5) C8  1944

A rare Tudor manor house, in a most unusual setting, surrounded by fragrant gardens protected by a collar of woodland. Constructed by a devout Catholic family, keen to impress visitors with their home's grandeur, in particular the Great Hall, this beautiful building has witnessed more than 400 years of turbulent history. Priests fleeing persecution in the 16th century were offered sanctuary, hiding in the secret priest's hole. Fascinating insights into the lives and work of the Victorian servants are revealed in the kitchen and dairy, while Tudor servants slept in the roof space. A perfect oasis from modern life. **Note**: administered and financed by the National Trust, assisted by a grant from National Museums Liverpool.

Exploring
- Join a 'Visiting the Victorians' costumed guided tour.
- Download a podcast tour of the hall.
- Enjoy a walk in the woods, discovering bugs and blooms.
- Take a walk on the bund overlooking the Mersey estuary.

Exploring
- Children can burn off energy in the adventure playground.
- Discover more with our sensory trail.

Eating and shopping: enjoy local produce served in the Home Farm restaurant. Plants for sale in our well-stocked shop.

You may also enjoy: the childhood homes of music legends John Lennon and Paul McCartney – tours from Speke Hall.

Making the most of your day: full calendar of events, including activities during school holidays, open-air theatre, festive celebrations, costumed guided tours, roof tours, waymarked woodland trails, children's play area and quiz trails. Dogs on leads in woodland and on signed estate walks.

Access for all: [icons] Building [icons] Grounds [icons]

Getting here: 108:SJ419825. **Cycle**: NCN62, 1¾ miles. **Bus**: Arriva 80A, Paradise Street Interchange–Liverpool Airport (passing Liverpool South Parkway ≋) and close Liverpool Lime Street); 500 Liverpool Lime Street ≋–Liverpool Airport. All to within 1 mile. **Train**: Liverpool South Parkway 2 miles; Hunt's Cross 2 miles. **Road**: on north bank of Mersey, 1 mile off A561 by west Liverpool Airport. Follow airport signs from M62 exit 6, A5300; M56 exit 12. **Parking**: free, 100 yards.

Finding out more: 0844 800 4799 (Infoline). 0151 427 7231 or spekehall@nationaltrust.org.uk

Speke Hall, Garden and Estate		M	T	W	T	F	S	S
House*								
27 Feb–14 Mar	11–4:30	·	·	·	·	·	S	S
17 Mar–31 Oct	11–5	·	·	W	T	F	S	S
6 Nov–12 Dec	11–4:30	·	·	·	·	·	S	S
Grounds**								
2 Jan–30 Dec	11–4:30	·	T	W	T	F	S	S
Home Farm – ticket office, restaurant and shop								
27 Feb–14 Mar	11–4:30	·	·	·	·	·	S	S
17 Mar–11 Jul	11–5	·	·	W	T	F	S	S
13 Jul–12 Sep	11–5	·	T	W	T	F	S	S
15 Sep–31 Oct	11–5	·	·	W	T	F	S	S
6 Nov–12 Dec	11–4:30	·	·	·	·	·	S	S

Open Bank Holiday Mondays. *11 to 1, entry to house by guided tour only, restricted numbers, tickets issued on first-come, first-served basis (at peak times tickets for these tours may run out). Unguided viewing of the house from 1 onwards. 27 February to 14 March, some rooms still under case covers, conservation cleaning demonstrations take place during this period. **Grounds (garden and estate) closed 1 January, 24 to 26 December and 31 December. Grounds (garden and estate) open until 5:30 16 March to 31 October.

Stagshaw Garden

Ambleside, Cumbria LA22 0HE

Map ⑥ D8   1957

A fine collection of shrubs, including rhododendrons, azaleas and camellias. Adjacent to the garden are Skelghyll Woods. **Note**: no WC.

Getting here: 90:NY380029. ½ mile south of Ambleside on A591.

Finding out more: 015394 46027 or stagshaw@nationaltrust.org.uk

Stagshaw Garden

July to end October: by appointment, send sae to Property Office, St Catherine's, Patterdale Road, Windermere LA23 1NH.

Tatton Park

Knutsford, Cheshire WA16 6QN

Map ⑤ D8

This is one of the most complete historic estates open to visitors. The early 19th-century Wyatt house sits amid a landscaped deer park and is opulently decorated, providing a fine setting for the Egerton family's collections of pictures, books, china, glass, silver and specially commissioned Gillows furniture. The theme of Victorian grandeur extends into the garden, with its Fernery, Orangery, Rose Garden, Tower Garden, Pinetum, Walled Garden with its glasshouses, Italian and Japanese gardens. Other features include a 1930s working rare breeds farm, a children's play area, speciality shops and 400-hectare (1,000-acre) deer park. **Note**: managed and financed by Cheshire East Council. RHS Show and Christmas events – supplementary charge.

Exploring
- The mansion has one of the finest Gillows furniture collections.
- A new nature trail features plants and wildlife to spot.
- The gardens contain 250 years of garden design and history.
- Explore 500 years of history at the Old Hall.
- Visit one of our 100 events held throughout the year.
- Feed rare breed animals at the 1930s working farm.

Eating and shopping: The Stables restaurant offers quality hot and cold local produce. The Housekeeper's Store sells local and estate-reared meat. Hampers are tailored to include local cheeses, wine and preserves. Visit Tatton Gifts or the garden shop for unusual presents.

You may also enjoy: Lyme Park, Quarry Bank Mill or Dunham Massey.

Making the most of your day: visit www.tattonpark.org.uk for events. Members – free admission to house and gardens only, half-price entry to farm, car entry charge. Old Hall special openings. Dogs on leads at farm and under close control in park only.

Access for all: 🅿️ 🚻 ♿ 🍴 📷 📖 🎡 ⠿ 📷

Building 🏛️ 🏛️ ♿ Grounds 🏛️ 🏛️ ➡️ 🏛️

Getting here: 109/118:SJ745815. **Cycle**: Cheshire Cycleway passes property. **Bus**: buses from Knutsford on high season Saturdays, Sundays and Bank Holidays Easter to end August; otherwise from surrounding areas to Knutsford, then 2 miles. **Train**: Knutsford 2 miles. **Road**: 2 miles north of Knutsford, 4 miles south of Altrincham, 5 miles from M6, exit 19; 3 miles from M56, exit 7, well signposted on A556; entrance on Ashley Road, 1½ miles north east of junction A5034 with A50. **Sat Nav**: follow directional signs to Tatton Park rather than using satellite navigation systems. **Parking**: charge, including members.

Finding out more: 01625 374435 (Infoline). 01625 374400 or tatton@cheshireeast.gov.uk

Tatton Park		M	T	W	T	F	S	S
Parkland								
27 Mar–3 Oct	10–7	·	T	W	T	F	S	S
Gardens								
27 Mar–3 Oct	10–6	·	T	W	T	F	S	S
Mansion								
27 Mar–3 Oct	1–5	·	T	W	T	F	S	S
Farm								
27 Mar–3 Oct	12–5	·	T	W	T	F	S	S
Shops								
27 Mar–3 Oct	10:30–5	·	T	W	T	F	S	S

Open Bank Holiday Mondays. Last admission one hour before closing. House: special opening October half-term and Christmas events in December. Guided mansion tours Tuesday to Sunday 12 by timed ticket (available from garden entrance after 10:30) on first-come, first-served basis, small charge including members. Garden tours held on alternate weeks, limited number of tickets, small charge. Old Hall special openings, call for details and prices. Closed 25 December. **1 January to 26 March and 4 October to 31 December** opening times: parkland Tuesday to Sunday, 11 to 5; gardens Tuesday to Sunday, 11 to 4; farm Saturday and Sunday, 11 to 4; shops Tuesday to Sunday, 11 to 4.

Japanese Tea Garden at Tatton Park, Cheshire

Townend

Troutbeck, Windermere, Cumbria LA23 1LB

Map (6) D8 🏠 ✼ 1948

'A hidden gem; homely and comfortable yet impressive and quirky. The stories about the family really brought it to life.'
Lucy Bradshaw-Murrow, London

The Brownes of Townend were just an ordinary farming family, but their home and belongings bring to life more than 400 years of extraordinary stories. You will understand why Beatrix Potter described Troutbeck valley as her favourite as you approach this traditional stone and slate farmhouse. Once inside, you are welcomed into the farmhouse kitchen with a real fire burning most days and a quirky collection of domestic tools. Exploring further, you can marvel at the intricately carved furniture and discover why the collection of books belonging to a farming family is of international importance.

Exploring
– Discover more about life as a Lake District farmer.
– Have a go at making a rag rug.
– Be inspired by the pretty cottage garden.
– Find out more on a guided tour in the mornings.

Eating and shopping: look through our small selection of postcards and souvenirs. Warm up with a hot drink from our vending machine. Treat yourself to a second-hand book. Buy a plant from our selection, grown in the garden.

You may also enjoy: another Cumbrian farmhouse: Hill Top, Beatrix Potter's house at Near Sawrey.

Making the most of your day: have a go at making a rag rug or enjoy our live interpretation. Our children's trail helps to bring the house to life.

Access for all: P♿ D♿ 🖼 ⬜ ⠿ ♿
Building ♿ Grounds ♿ ♿

Getting here: 90:NY407023. 3 miles south east of Ambleside at south end of Troutbeck village. **Bus**: Stagecoach in Cumbria 555, 599 from Windermere ➠, alight Troutbeck Bridge, 1½ miles. **Train**: Windermere 2½ miles. **Road**: off A591 or A592. **Parking**: free, 300 yards. Not suitable for coaches or campervans.

Finding out more: 015394 32628 or townend@nationaltrust.org.uk

Townend	M	T	W	T	F	S	S
House tours*							
13 Mar–31 Oct	11–1	·	·	**W**	**T**	**F**	**S**	**S**
House							
13 Mar–31 Oct	1–5	·	·	**W**	**T**	**F**	**S**	**S**

*11 to 1 entry by hourly guided tour only (tours at 11 and 12), 1 to 5 free-flow. Places on guided tours are limited and available on a first-come first-served basis. Open Bank Holiday Mondays. May close early due to poor light. Please note: property less busy at weekends.

Townend, Cumbria: hidden gem

Ullswater and Aira Force

near Watermillock, Penrith, Cumbria

Map ⑥ D7 ♣♿ 1906

Dramatic walks around Aira Force waterfall and picturesque pleasure grounds, renowned in Victorian times as a beauty spot. Beyond Aira Force there are four farms, beautiful woodlands and acres of wild fell. Wordsworth's famous daffodils can be found on the shores of the lake.

Exploring
— Enjoy the breathtaking waterfalls at Aira Force.
— Relax among Wordsworth's Daffodils on the shore of Ullswater.
— Enjoy the new level path around Brotherswater.
— Take in stunning views from the summit of Gowbarrow.

Eating and shopping: Aira Force tea-room (not National Trust) by car park. Walk from Glenridding to Side Farm tea-room (Trust farm).

Access for all: ♿ᵂᶜ ♿ᴵᴵ Grounds ♿ ➡

Getting here: 90:NY401203. 7 miles south of Penrith. **Cycle**: NCN71, 2 miles. **Bus**: Stagecoach in Cumbria 108 Penrith ➠–Patterdale. **Train**: Penrith 10 miles. **Parking**: two car parks at Aira Force and Glencoyne Bay (pay and display). Coaches by arrangement.

Finding out more: 017684 82067 or ullswater@nationaltrust.org.uk. Tower Buildings, Watermillock, Penrith, Cumbria CA11 0JS

Ullswater and Aira Force	M	T	W	T	F	S	S
Open all year	**M**	**T**	**W**	**T**	**F**	**S**	**S**

Wasdale, Eskdale and Duddon

The Lodge, Wasdale Hall, Wasdale, Cumbria CA20 1ET

Map (6) C8　 1929

From Scafell Pike, England's highest mountain look down on Wastwater, England's deepest lake, with its majestic screes. The National Trust owns the valley farms, campsite, lake, surrounding mountains and the nearby Nether Wasdale Estate. Walk the delightful paths of Upper Eskdale or explore the ever-changing Duddon Valley.

Exploring
- Visit Hardknott Roman Fort.
- Camp at the head of Wasdale at our Trust site.
- Admire the amazing stone walls at Wasdale Head.

Making the most of your day: explore the many paths in these spectacular valleys. Dogs under close control (stock grazing).

Access for all: Grounds 🏃

Getting here: NY152055. Wasdale–Wastwater: 5 miles east of A595 Cumbrian coast road from Barrow to Whitehaven, turning at Gosforth. Also from Santon Bridge. Eskdale [NY177013]–Boot: 6 miles east of A595, turning at Eskdale Green. Also from Santon Bridge. Duddon [NY196932]–Ulpha: 3 miles north of A595, turning at Duddon Bridge near Broughton-in-Furness. **Train**: Drigg 8 miles; Dalegarth (Ravenglass & Eskdale Railway) ¼ mile from Eskdale; Foxfield 8 miles from Duddon; Seascale 8 miles from Wasdale. **Parking**: at Wasdale Head (pay and display).

Finding out more: 019467 26064 or wasdale@nationaltrust.org.uk

Wasdale, Eskdale and Duddon	M	T	W	T	F	S	S
Open all year	**M**	**T**	**W**	**T**	**F**	**S**	**S**

Windermere and Troutbeck

St Catherine's, Patterdale Road, Windermere, Cumbria LA23 1NH

Map (6) D8　 1927

Take a footpath from Ambleside over Wansfell to the Troutbeck Valley, admire tiny Bridge House or visit the Roman Fort in Ambleside. Stroll through Cockshott Point on the lake at Bowness-on-Windermere or walk to Orrest Head, Adelaide Hill or Miller Ground, just some of our sites around Windermere. **Note**: no WC.

Exploring
- Enjoy breathtaking views from the summit of Wansfell.
- Relax by the lake on Cockshott Point.
- Visit Bridge House, Ambleside's smallest building.
- Follow in the footsteps of Romans at Galava Roman Fort.

Making the most of your day: exciting events around Windermere. Make a day of it and visit nearby Fell Foot and Townend. Dogs under close control (stock grazing).

Access for all: Bridge House 🦽

Getting here: 90:NY407023. **Bus**: Stagecoach in Cumbria 555/6, 599 from Windermere ➔, alight Troutbeck Bridge, then 1½ miles. **Train**: Windermere 2½ miles. **Road**: Troutbeck is signposted east of A591 Windermere to Ambleside road. **Sat Nav**: postcode takes Sat Nav to Property Office (not open to public). **Parking**: car parks (not National Trust).

Finding out more: 015394 46027 or windermere@nationaltrust.org.uk

Windermere and Troutbeck	M	T	W	T	F	S	S
Open all year	**M**	**T**	**W**	**T**	**F**	**S**	**S**

Wordsworth House and Garden

Main Street, Cockermouth, Cumbria CA13 9RX

Map ⑥ C7   🏠 ❀ 1938

Wordsworth House and Garden, Cumbria

'Beautiful homely surroundings: loved the hustle and bustle of the kitchen; garden a delight and knowledgeable guides full of enthusiasm.'
Mrs Gray, Rochester

Step back to the 1770s and experience life as William and his sister Dorothy might have done at this beautiful, homely property. Enjoy a warm welcome from the Wordsworths' servants and find out more about the restoration of the house and garden. William's beloved garden inspired many of his later poems and contains flowers, fruit and vegetables popular in the 18th century – all of which are used in the house. The Discovery Room has fascinating research material and touchscreens, and the property, now open on Sundays, was Small Visitor Attraction of the Year 2009, Cumbria Tourism Awards.

Exploring
- Enjoy our hands-on rooms with toys, costume and books.
- Meet the servants and enjoy a gossip.
- Come along for a talk, tour or special event.
- Listen to music from the harpsichord.
- Write with quill pen and ink, or do some baking.
- See, and sometimes sample, 18th-century Cumberland food.

Eating and shopping: browse for Wordsworth and local souvenirs in our shop. Enjoyed the garden? Buy a plant to take home. Tasty local food available from the shop.

You may also enjoy: beautiful Buttermere, or a walk along the Whitehaven coast.

Making the most of your day: costumed servants, family activities every school holiday, talks, harpsichord music, garden tours, cooking demonstrations, original Wordsworth items, Georgian tastings and games, plus craft activities. Dogs on leads in front garden only.

Access for all: 🅿️ 🚻 🚻 🅦🅒 🛗 📷 🖥️ 🎦 ♿ ⠿ 🚫
Building 🦽 ♿ 👣 Grounds 🦽

Getting here: 89:NY118307. In the centre of Cockermouth. **Foot**: close to all town car parks and bus stop. **Cycle**: NCN71 (C2C) and NCN10 (Reivers) pass door. **Bus**: Stagecoach in Cumbria X4/5 Penrith ☒–Workington; AA/Hoban/Reay's 35/6 Workington–Cockermouth. **Train**: Workington 8 miles; Maryport 6½ miles. **Road**: off A66, on Cockermouth Main Street. **Sat Nav**: enter CA13 9RX (NB entrance on Main Street not side gate on Low Sand Lane). **Parking**: nearest parking in town centre car parks. Long stay car park signposted as coach park (not National Trust), 300 yards on Wakefield Road, walk back over footbridge to house.

Finding out more: 01900 820884 (Infoline). 01900 824805 or wordsworthhouse@nationaltrust.org.uk

Wordsworth House and Garden		M	T	W	T	F	S	S
House and garden								
13 Mar–31 Oct	11–5	M	T	W	·	·	S	S
29 Mar–11 Apr	11–5	M	T	W	T	·	S	S
31 May–6 Jun	11–5	M	T	W	T	·	S	S
19 Jul–5 Sep	11–5	M	T	W	T	·	S	S
25 Oct–31 Oct	11–5	M	T	W	T	·	S	S
Shop								
4 Jan–10 Jan	10–4:30	M	T	W	T	F	S	S
13 Mar–31 Oct	10–5	M	T	W	T	F	S	S
1 Nov–24 Dec	10–4:30	M	T	W	T	F	S	S

Last entry 4. Timed tickets may operate on busy days.

Yorkshire

Graceful columns sweep up to meet the vaulted ceiling of the Cellarium at Fountains Abbey and Studley Royal Water Garden

Outdoors
in Yorkshire

Yorkshire is famed for
its acres of green fields,
drystone walls and moorland
heaths. A haven for walkers,
a home to wildlife, there
is a place where everyone
can find peace, quiet
and enjoyment.

Right:
**walkers on
Buckstones Moss
in the north of
the Marsden
Moor Estate,
West Yorkshire**

In the grand county of Yorkshire, the National Trust owns land
in the Yorkshire Dales, North York Moors, Marsden Moor and
the Yorkshire coast, including part of the Cleveland Way.
There are also hidden gems such as Brimham Rocks and
Hardcastle Crags.

Discover pepper pots and dancing bears

The Bridestones in the North York Moors is a wonderful place
to visit with views over open moorland, woodland and sheltered
grassy valleys. Three types of heather can be found here,
which create a carpet of colour throughout the summer. First
to bloom are the striking magenta flowers of the bell heather
in June, together with the pale pink cross-leaved heather on
the wetter soils, leading to the finale, the soft purple haze and
honey scent of ling.

The Bridestones themselves were formed more than 150 million
years ago, with one being affectionately named The Pepper Pot,
due to its unusual shape.

At Brimham Rocks, you'll come across more than 26 hectares
(64 acres) of fabulous rock formations, with equally imaginative
names such as The Dancing Bear, Castle Rock, The Anvil and
The Eagle. A site that is over 320 million years old, it has been
created as a result of geological movement, ice ages and the
erosive effects of the weather. For centuries, visitors have
marvelled at the Idol Rock, which, at 200 tonnes, stands on a
plinth just 12 inches across.

Meadows as far as the eye can see

In the Yorkshire Dales, centuries of farming have given us a landscape that is so familiar and yet so stunning. With drystone walls, green fields and meadows stretching as far as the eye can see, everyone should take the opportunity to discover this wonderful corner of Yorkshire.

The Malham Tarn and Upper Wharfedale estates contain some of the finest upland landscapes in the Yorkshire Dales, with limestone pavements, waterfalls and flower-rich hay meadows criss-crossed with stone walls and studded with traditional field barns. Caring for nearly 3,000 hectares (7,500 acres) in Malhamdale, the National Trust has waymarked walks and trails throughout the Dales, from Malham Cove to Fountains Fell. So go for a ramble, a circular walk or follow a trail across the ancient limestone pavements. Take a route around Malham Tarn, which with adjacent areas of raised bog, fen and woodland, is protected as a National Nature Reserve.

This special area is home to a unique community of rare plants and animals, as well as being the focal point of an outstanding region of classic upland limestone country. The limestone pavements in the Dales are a unique and irreplaceable habitat that has formed as a result of erosion by water over the centuries. Today it supports unusual and diverse plant communities. Visitors can discover more by joining one of the summer wildflower walks in Malhamdale or Upper Wharfedale hosted by the Trust.

Above:
Upper Wharfedale, North Yorkshire
Below:
Brimham Rocks

Step back into the past at Marsden Moor

If you love the outdoors and want to get out into the open countryside then take a walk on Marsden Moor. This windswept landscape appears bleak and inhospitable, but provides grazing for cattle and sheep and is home to numerous birds, such as golden plover, red grouse, curlew, snipe and the diminutive twite – in fact the estate is designated as an international Special Protection Area for birds. Footpaths across the moor sometimes follow ancient pack-horse routes, from where it is possible to glimpse evidence of the estate's industrial past.

It is easy to imagine Mesolithic hunters sitting around a campfire, or that you can hear the chink of Roman centurions' armour as they march from Chester to York, or even – from our more recent industrial past – the rattle of pack horses' harnesses and clatter of workers' clogs. Walking at Marsden is not always for the faint-hearted – so why not join one of many guided walks with our volunteers and discover stunning views, inspiring history and a rich variety of moorland?

Discover the Yorkshire coast
Explore the Yorkshire coastline, taking in the
Ravenscar Coastal Centre and Alum Works
and the Old Coastguard Station at Robin
Hood's Bay.

Nestling on the edge of the North Sea, at the
foot of Robin Hood's Bay is the Old Coastguard
Station – now an interpretive visitor centre,
with panoramic views across the bay from
Ness Point in the north to Ravenscar in the
south. Explore the hidden history of an ancient
landscape and hear how the building has been
an important focus of village life.

At Ravenscar, take in commanding views
across the bay at a height of 200 metres. The
National Trust cares for a wealth of features in
and around the village, including the remains of
a Second World War radar station, a reinstated
rocket post – once used by local coastguards –
flower-rich meadows, farmland and
bluebell woods.

Below:
**the pretty village
of Ravenscar**

My favourite hidden view
If you're taking a walk along
the Cleveland Way on the
Yorkshire coast, be sure not to
miss the Loftus Alum Quarry.

With stunning views up and
down the coastline, it's the site
of a former alum works which
is on a par with nearby (and
more well-known) Ravenscar's
alum works. You can stand
and imagine what a busy and
industrial place this once
would have been – yet today it
is peaceful and deserted, with
ruins and evidence of its past.

In the autumn, among
these industrial scars on the
landscape, masses of purple
heather burst into life – a truly
staggering sight when at
their best.

Bob Dicker
Property Manager,
North York Moors and Coast

Beningbrough Hall and Gardens

Beningbrough, York,
North Yorkshire YO30 1DD

Map (5) G4   🏰🔭❄️♣🏠🔔⛱ 1958

'**Excellent. We enjoyed the restaurant food, the portraits and interpretation.**'
Mr and Mrs Courts, York

This is a friendly house and garden. The grand 1716 Georgian mansion, with impressive baroque interior, is set in a park and gardens. There are more than 100 18th-century portraits and seven interpretation galleries in partnership with the National Portrait Gallery. There is also a fully equipped Victorian laundry, with wet and dry rooms, and a delightful working garden, which supplies the Walled Garden Restaurant. There are many family activities to enjoy and a wilderness play area.

Exploring	– Find out about Georgian life in the 18th-century mansion.
	– Discover the 'Making Faces' galleries and commission your own portrait.
	– Working walled garden supplying produce to the Walled Garden Restaurant.
	– Explore acres of gardens and wilderness play area – new activities.
	– Get Artrageous: join in with our free family art workshops.
	– Fully equipped Victorian laundry, with wet and dry rooms.

Eating and shopping: the restaurant lunches and snacks use local seasonal produce. Kiosk serves ice-cream, sandwiches, hot drinks and snacks. Shop and plant centre stocks a selection of quality goods. Special restaurant events, plus annual Food and Craft Festival.

You may also enjoy: Treasurer's House, in the centre of York. Fountains Abbey and Studley Royal, near Ripon.

Making the most of your day: specialist food events in the restaurant. Living history and family activities, including Artrageous! plus family garden interpretation. Food and Craft Festival and garden guided walks. Dogs allowed, on leads on paths in parkland only.

Access for all: 🅿️♿🚻♿♿🔎📷•• 🅰️
Georgian Mansion ♿♿♿♿ Stable block ♿♿
Grounds ♿♿➡️♿

Getting here: 105:SE516586. **Foot**: footpath from York, along River Ouse, 10 miles.
Cycle: NCN65. **Bus**: Stephensons 29 York–Easingwold, (irregular bus service). **Train**: York 8 miles. **Road**: 8 miles north west of York, 2 miles west of Shipton, 2 miles south east of Linton-on-Ouse (A19). **Parking**: free, 100 yards. Coaches must come via A19 and use coach entrance. No coach access from the west via Aldwark toll bridge.

Finding out more: 01904 472027 or beningbrough@nationaltrust.org.uk

Beningbrough Hall and Gardens		M	T	W	T	F	S	S
Grounds, shop and Walled Garden Restaurant								
2 Jan–28 Feb	11–3:30	·	·	·	·	·	S	S
1 Mar–30 Jun	11–5:30	M	T	W	·	·	S	S
1 Jul–31 Aug	11–5:30	M	T	W	T	F	S	S
1 Sep–31 Oct	11–5:30	M	T	W	·	·	S	S
6 Nov–26 Dec	11–3:30	·	·	·	·	·	S	S
House								
1 Mar–31 Oct	11–5	M	T	W	·	·	S	S
House Galleries								
2 Jan–28 Feb	11–3	·	·	·	·	·	S	S
6 Nov–26 Dec	11–3	·	·	·	·	·	S	S

Open 1 January, 13 to 17 February, Good Friday, 27 December. Closed 25 December.

Borders at Beningbrough Hall and Gardens

Braithwaite Hall

East Witton, Leyburn, North Yorkshire DL8 4SY

Map (5) E3   1941

A 17th-century tenanted farmhouse in beautiful Coverdale. The hall, sitting room and carved staircase are on show to visitors. **Note**: no WC.

Getting here: 99:SE117857. 1½ miles south west of Middleham, 2 miles west of East Witton (A6108). Narrow approach road.

Finding out more: 01969 640287 or braithwaitehall@nationaltrust.org.uk

---

Braithwaite Hall

May to September by arrangement in advance with the tenant, Mrs Duffus.

Bridestones, Crosscliff and Blakey Topping

Staindale, Dalby, Pickering, North Yorkshire YO18 7LR

Map (5) I3   1944

The Bridestones has peculiar shaped rocks, heather moorland, ancient woodland, herb-rich meadows. Blakey Topping has superb all-round views. **Note**: Dalby Forest drive – toll charges apply, including members. Nearest WC Staindale Lake car park.

Getting here: 94:SE877906. In North York Moors National Park.

Finding out more: 01723 870423 or bridestones@nationaltrust.org.uk. Peakside, Ravenscar, Scarborough, North Yorkshire YO13 0NE

Bridestones		M	T	W	T	F	S	S
Open all year	Dawn–dusk	**M**	**T**	**W**	**T**	**F**	**S**	**S**

Brimham Rocks

Summerbridge, Harrogate, North Yorkshire HG3 4DW

Map (5) F4   1970

An amazing collection of weird and wonderful rock formations which makes a great day out for families, climbers and those wanting to enjoy the simple pleasures of fresh air and magnificent views over Nidderdale. Let your imagination run wild as you explore the labyrinth of paths through this unique landscape.

Exploring
- Marvel at the fantastically shaped rock formations.
- Let children run wild in nature's theme park.
- Enjoy magnificent views over Nidderdale and beyond.
- Great for walking over moorland and through woodland.

The weird and wonderful Brimham Rocks

Eating and shopping: excellent range of Yorkshire products for sale in our shop. Great value picnic food and ice-cream at refreshment kiosk.

Making the most of your day: discover the rocks' geological and social history and how we conserve this special place in the Visitor Centre. Regular guided walks. Tracker Packs available for ages five to eleven. Dogs under control and on leads April to June (ground-nesting birds).

Access for all: ⬚⬚⬚⬚⬚⬚
Building ⬚⬚ **Grounds** ⬚

Getting here: 99:SE206650. 10 miles south west of Ripon. **Foot**: Nidderdale Way passes through. **Bus**: Harrogate & District 24 Harrogate ⬚–Pateley Bridge, alight Summerbridge, 2 miles. Sundays and Bank Holidays May to October 'Nidderdale Rambler' 825 Harrogate–Brimham Rocks circular. **Road**: 11 miles north west of Harrogate off B6165, 10 miles south west of Ripon, 4 miles east of Pateley Bridge off B6265. **Sat Nav**: only gives approximate location. **Parking**: pay and display (coins only). £4 up to four hours, then £5. Motorcycles free; minibuses £8 all day; coaches £15 all day. Coaches must book.

Finding out more: 01423 780688 or brimhamrocks@nationaltrust.org.uk

Brimham Rocks		M	T	W	T	F	S	S
Open all year		M	T	W	T	F	S	S
Visitor Centre, shop and kiosk								
12 Feb–21 Feb	11–5	M	T	W	T	F	S	S
27 Feb–28 Mar	11–5	·	·	·	·	·	S	S
2 Apr–18 Apr	11–5	M	T	W	T	F	S	S
24 Apr–30 May	11–5	·	·	·	·	·	S	S
31 May–3 Oct	11–5	M	T	W	T	F	S	S
9 Oct–24 Oct	11–5	·	·	·	·	·	S	S
25 Oct–31 Oct	11–5	M	T	W	T	F	S	S
6 Nov–26 Dec	11–dusk	·	·	·	·	·	S	S

Visitor Centre, shop and kiosk also open 1 January, 11 to dusk, and Bank Holiday 3 May. Facilities may close in bad weather.

East Riddlesden Hall

Bradford Road, Keighley, West Yorkshire BD20 5EL

Map ⑤ E5 ⬚⬚⬚⬚⬚ 1934

'**I came on Saturday and enjoyed it so much I came back on Monday to explore it further!**' Mr Burrows, Oldham

Every time that you stand in the gardens of East Riddlesden you will experience something new. The pink cherry trees, clematis, borders, daffodils and soothing lavender beds all create a sense of tranquillity far removed from the bustle of modern life. This peace is very different from the Hall's tumultuous past, which includes tales of ghosts and dastardly deeds. Going into the Hall feels like walking through someone's home; it has a cosy lived-in feel, and creates a relaxing atmosphere where visitors can feel at ease examining the exquisite embroideries and blackwork, oak furniture and pewter.

Exploring
- Spy on local birdlife in our bird-feeding station.
- Absorb the calm and tranquillity of our changing seasonal gardens.
- Go wild in our children's playground.
- Seek out the ghostly grey lady.
- Admire the exquisite embroideries and stumpwork.
- Play with the objects in the handling collection.

Eating and shopping: browse in our redesigned shop for local and gift products. Indulge in homemade soups, made using herbs from the garden. Treat yourself to our locally sourced shared platters and cakes. Get horticultural inspiration from our plant sales area.

You may also enjoy: Rufford Old Hall and Gibson Mill on the Hardcastle Crags Estate.

Making the most of your day: explore our new herb interpretation area, with fun hands-on activities for children and explanatory panels for all ages. Dogs on leads in grounds only.

Access for all: 🅿️🅿️♿🕐🔆📷🎧👁️🐕🅰️
Building 👶♿🦽 Grounds 👶

Getting here: 104:SE079421. **Bus**: Keighley & District 662 Bradford Interchange ⇌–Keighley, alight Granby Lane. **Train**: Keighley 1½ miles. **Road**: 1 mile north east of Keighley on south side of the Bradford Road in Riddlesden, close to Leeds & Liverpool Canal. A629 relief road from Shipley and Skipton signed for East Riddlesden Hall. **Parking**: free, 100 yards. Parking for one coach (no double-deckers). Narrow entrance to property.

Finding out more: 01535 607075 or eastriddlesden@nationaltrust.org.uk

East Riddlesden Hall		M	T	W	T	F	S	S
House, shop and tea-room								
27 Feb–31 Oct	11–5	**M**	**T**	**W**	·	·	**S**	**S**
Shop and tea-room								
6 Nov–19 Dec	12–4	·	·	·	·	·	**S**	**S**

At certain times, entry to the house may be by guided tour.

East Riddlesden Hall has had a tumultuous past

Fountains Abbey and Studley Royal Water Garden

Fountains, Ripon, North Yorkshire HG4 3DY

Map ⑤ F4

A World Heritage Site, set in 323 hectares (800 acres) of beautiful countryside, offers an unparalleled opportunity to appreciate the range of England's heritage. Discover the magnificent 12th-century abbey ruins and the only surviving Cistercian corn mill. Amble through the beautiful landscaped Georgian water garden of Studley Royal, complete with Neo-classical statues, follies and breathtaking views. Delight in the richly decorated Victorian St Mary's church and take time out to relax in the Reading Room in Elizabethan Fountains Hall. Complete a great day out for all the family by exploring the medieval deer park. **Note**: cared for in partnership with English Heritage.

Exploring
– Be transported to another era in the Georgian water garden.
– Let off steam in the children's play area.
– Discover the Abbey's story at the Porter's Lodge exhibition.
– Dare yourself to walk through the serpentine tunnel.
– Spot the differences between the three breeds of wild deer.
– Look for ancient graffiti at Fountains Mill.

Eating and shopping: eat and buy estate venison in the restaurant and shop. Tempt your tastebuds with our local and seasonal menu. Enjoy the lakeside view from our Victorian tea-room. Buy gifts in our shop and new plant area.

You may also enjoy: the dramatic rock formations and views at nearby Brimham Rocks.

The Temple of Piety, Studley Royal Water Garden

Making the most of your day: guided tours and wildlife walks throughout the year. Open-air theatre, Christmas entertainment, medieval re-enactments and religious services. School holiday children's trails and craft workshops. Changing exhibitions. Dogs on short leads only.

Access for all: 🅿️♿🚻👪🧺📷👓📖

Building 🏛️♿⬍ **Grounds** ♿➡️🚶♿

Getting here: 99:SE271683. **Foot**: 4 miles from Ripon via public footpaths and bridleways. **Cycle**: signed on-road cycle loop. **Bus**: Harrogate District Community Transport (Ripon Roweller 139) Ripon–Markington (connections with Harrogate and District 36 from Harrogate). **Road**: 4 miles west of Ripon off B6265 to Pateley Bridge, signposted from A1, 12 miles north of Harrogate (A61). **Parking**: at Visitor Centre car park, free, and Studley Royal deer park (pay and display). Coach parking at Visitor Centre only. Access off B6265.

Finding out more: 01765 608888 or fountainsenquiries@nationaltrust.org.uk

Fountains Abbey		M	T	W	T	F	S	S
1 Jan–31 Jan	10–4	M	T	W	T	·	S	S
1 Feb–31 Mar	10–4	M	T	W	T	F	S	S
1 Apr–30 Sep	10–5	M	T	W	T	F	S	S
1 Oct–31 Oct	10–4	M	T	W	T	F	S	S
1 Nov–31 Dec	10–4	M	T	W	T	·	S	S
St Mary's Church								
2 Apr–30 Sep	12–4	M	T	W	T	F	S	S
Deer park								
Open all year	7–9	M	T	W	T	F	S	S

Estate closes dusk if earlier. Whole estate closed 24 and 25 December. Studley Royal shop opening times vary.

Goddards Garden

27 Tadcaster Road, York,
North Yorkshire YO24 1GG

Map ⑤ H5   ✣ 1984

Visit the former gardens of Noel Goddard Terry, of the famous York chocolate-making firm. Designed by George Dillistone, the garden complements the house's Arts & Craft style. With yew-hedged garden rooms, bowling green, wilderness gardens and plants for every season, it is also an oasis for wildlife. **Note**: house not open to public (offices).

Exploring
- An excellent example of a late Arts & Crafts garden.
- Formal terraces, gardens and herbaceous borders enclosed by yew hedges.
- Explore the garden and see the newly restored greenhouse.

Making the most of your day: enjoy a picnic in this tranquil garden, surrounded by lovely scenery and the sound of one of the few British colonies of midwife toads. Dogs on leads only.

Access for all: **Grounds** ♿➡️

Getting here: 105:SE589497. **Bus**: First York 4, 12, 13; Yorkshire Coastliner 840, 842, 843, 845, X44 from York 🚉. **Train**: York 1½ miles. **Road**: follow York outer ring road (A1237/A64), turn on to A1036 Tadcaster Road, signed to York city centre, then turn right after St Edward's church, through brick gatehouse arch. **Parking**: free. Not suitable for coaches.

Finding out more: 01904 702021 or goddardsgarden@nationaltrust.org.uk

Goddards Garden		M	T	W	T	F	S	S
1 Mar–29 Oct	11–4:30	M	T	W	T	F	·	·

Closed Bank Holidays. Last admission one hour before closing.

Hardcastle Crags

Hollin Hall, Crimsworth Dean, Hebden Bridge,
West Yorkshire HX7 7AP

Map ⑤ E6   [🍴][♿][🚸][🏠][🔔][⛲][1950]

A beauty spot of the South Pennines with
more than 160 hectares (400 acres) of unspoilt
woodland. As well as being the home of the
northern hairy wood ant, there are tumbling
streams, glorious waterfalls and stacks of
millstone grit, all crisscrossed by more than
30 miles of footpaths. At its heart is Gibson
Mill, a family-oriented visitor centre, telling
the history of the valley over the past 200
years, with interactive displays, dressing up,
dancing and exhibitions. Having no link to
the national grid, the mill is unique in the UK
and is the Trust's flagship sustainable building.
Note: steep slopes throughout.

Exploring
– More than 30 miles of walking routes.
– Seasonal variations, with the autumn colours being particularly stunning.
– Spectacular springtime bluebells.
– Take a tour of Gibson Mill and learn its history.
– Enjoy the ever-changing birdsong.
– Social history and photography exhibition of the past 100 years.

Eating and shopping: food for walkers and
families. Hot and cold snacks. Savour delicious
locally baked cakes.

You may also enjoy: East Riddlesden Hall.

Making the most of your day: four circular
walks, ranging from three to seven miles. Staff
and volunteer-led themed walks and guided
tours of Gibson Mill. Christmas carols in the
mill courtyard. Dogs under control at all times.

Access for all: [P♿][D♿][♿WC][⌂♿][♿][◻][♿][:.]
Building [♿][♿] Grounds [♿]

Getting here: 103:SD988291. **Foot**: access on
foot via riverside walk from Hebden Bridge.
Pennine Bridleway passes property. **Bus**: First
593 from Hebden Bridge ➔ to within 1 mile.
Train: Hebden Bridge 2 miles. **Road**: at end
of Midgehole Road, 1½ miles north east
of Hebden Bridge off the A6033 Keighley
road. **Parking**: pay and display. Midweek
£3.50, weekend £5, weekend half day £3.50;
motorcycle £1; minibus £5. Please note: visitors
are encouraged to come on foot, by cycle or
public transport.

Finding out more: 01422 844518.
01422 846236 (weekends) or
hardcastlecrags@nationaltrust.org.uk

Hardcastle Crags		M	T	W	T	F	S	S
Open all year		M	T	W	T	F	S	S
Gibson Mill								
2 Jan–28 Feb	11–3						S	S
2 Mar–31 Oct	11–4		T	W	T		S	S
6 Nov–26 Dec	11–3						S	S
Muddy Boots Café								
2 Jan–28 Feb	11–3						S	S
2 Mar–30 Apr	11–4		T	W	T		S	S
1 May–30 Sep	11–4		T	W	T			
1 May–30 Sep	11–5						S	S
2 Oct–30 Oct	11–4		T	W	T		S	S
6 Nov–26 Dec	11–3						S	S

Gibson Mill and Muddy Boots Café open Saturday to
Thursday in all local school holidays, plus Good Friday,
Boxing Day and all Bank Holiday Mondays.

Gibson Mill at the heart of the Hardcastle Crags estate

Maister House

160 High Street, Hull, East Yorkshire HU1 1NL

Map ⑤ J6   🏠 1966

Rebuilt in 1743 after a fire, this merchant's house survives from Hull's international trading heyday. **Note**: staircase and entrance hall only on show. No WC.

Getting here: 107:TA102287. In Hull city centre.

Finding out more: 01723 870423 (North York Moors and Coast Property Office) or maisterhouse@nationaltrust.org.uk. c/o Peakside, Ravenscar, Scarborough, North Yorkshire YO13 0NE

Maister House		M	T	W	T	F	S	S
Open all year	10–4	**M**	**T**	**W**	**T**	**F**	·	·
Closed Bank Holidays.								

Malham Tarn Estate

Yorkshire Dales Estate Office, Waterhouses, Settle, North Yorkshire BD24 9PT

Map ⑤ D4    1946

This outstanding area of limestone pavements, upland hill farms and flower-rich hay meadows provides a marvellous setting for walking, cycling or just enjoying the great outdoors. The National Nature Reserve is home to a unique community of rare plants and animals – the bird hide is well worth a visit. **Note**: nearest WC at the National Park car park in Malham.

Exploring
– Excellent walking and cycling opportunities around the tarn.
– Visit the beautiful Janet's Foss waterfall.
– Awe-inspiring, far-reaching views around the estate.
– Farming exhibition at Town Head Barn in Malham.

Eating and shopping: tea-rooms and facilities in Malham village.

Making the most of your day: guided walks and events throughout the year. Dogs on leads only.

Access for all: Town Head Barn 🏞 Grounds

Getting here: 98:SD890660. Estate extends from Malham village, 19 miles north west of Skipton, north past Malham Tarn. **Foot**: 6 miles of Pennine Way and ¾ mile of Pennine Bridleway on property. **Bus**: Pennine 210 Skipton–Malham (passing Skipton ≷), limited service, 1 mile. Contact the estate office to confirm whether the Malham Tarn shuttle bus is running from Settle. **Train**: Settle 7 miles. **Parking**: in Malham village, not National Trust (pay and display). Free parking at Watersinks car park on south side of Malham Tarn.

Finding out more: 01729 830416 or malhamtarn@nationaltrust.org.uk

Malham Tarn Estate		M	T	W	T	F	S	S
Open all year		**M**	**T**	**W**	**T**	**F**	**S**	**S**
Town Head Barn								
13 Feb–31 Oct	10–4	**M**	**T**	**W**	**T**	**F**	**S**	**S**

Marsden Moor Estate

Estate Office, The Old Goods Yard, Station Road, Marsden, Huddersfield, West Yorkshire HD7 6DH

Map ⑤ E7   1955

The estate, covering nearly 2,248 hectares (5,553 acres) of unenclosed common moorland, takes in the northern part of the Peak District National Park. The landscape supports large numbers of moorland birds. The estate is an SSSI, International Special Protection Area and a candidate Special Area of Conservation. **Note**: nearest WC in Marsden village.

Exploring
- Miles of footpaths for serious walkers.
- A place to be alone with your thoughts.
- Dramatic scenery and visible industrial heritage.

Making the most of your day: Marsden Heritage Trail with defined walks of four, eight or ten miles to help you explore this dramatic countryside. Dogs on leads only.

Access for all: Exhibition 🏛️ Grounds 🏛️

Getting here: 109:SE025100. **Foot**: Kirklees Way and Pennine Way pass through the property. Huddersfield Narrow Canal towpath nearby. **Bus**: First 185 from Huddersfield. **Train**: Marsden (adjacent to estate office). **Road**: estate covers area around Marsden village, between A640 and A635. **Parking**: around the estate, free, including in Marsden village (not National Trust) and at Buckstones and Wessenden Head (National Trust).

Finding out more: 01484 847016 or marsdenmoor@nationaltrust.org.uk

Marsden Moor Estate		M	T	W	T	F	S	S
Open all year		**M**	**T**	**W**	**T**	**F**	**S**	**S**
Exhibition Centre								
Open all year	9–5	**M**	**T**	**W**	**T**	**F**	**S**	**S**

Marsden Moor Estate: dramatic scenery

Middlethorpe Hall Hotel, Restaurant and Spa

Bishopthorpe Road, York YO23 2GB

Map ⑤ H5

Built in 1699, this William and Mary house is set in eight hectares (twenty acres) of walled gardens and parkland, next to York Racecourse. Once the home of diarist Lady Mary Wortley Montagu.

The house and gardens are already accessible to the public as a hotel, and welcome guests to stay, to dine in the restaurant and to have afternoon tea (booking strongly advised). All paying guests to the hotel are welcome to walk in the garden and park.

Finding out more: 01904 641241; 01904 620176 (fax) or info@middlethorpe.com, www.middlethorpe.com

Moulton Hall

Moulton, Richmond, North Yorkshire DL10 6QH

Map ⑤ F2

Elegant 17th-century manor house with a beautiful carved staircase. **Note**: no WC.

Getting here: 99:NZ235035. 5 miles east of Richmond; turn off A1, ½ mile south of Scotch Corner.

Finding out more: 01325 377227 or moultonhall@nationaltrust.org.uk

Moulton Hall

By arrangement in advance with the tenant, Viscount Eccles. Please give as much notice as possible in order to arrange a mutually convenient time for your visit.

Mount Grace Priory

Staddle Bridge, Northallerton,
North Yorkshire DL6 3JG

Map (5) G3   ✠ 1953

England's most important Carthusian ruin. The
individual cells reflect the hermit-like isolation
of the monks. **Note**: operated by English
Heritage. National Trust members free, except
on event days.

Getting here: 99:SE449985. 6 miles north east
of Northallerton, ½ mile east of A19 and ½ mile
south of its junction with A172.

Finding out more: 01609 883494 or
mountgracepriory@nationaltrust.org.uk

Mount Grace Priory		M	T	W	T	F	S	S
2 Jan–28 Mar	10–4				T	F	S	S
1 Apr–30 Sep	10–6	M			T	F	S	S
1 Oct–31 Dec	10–4				T	F	S	S

Closed 1 January and 24 to 26 December. On summer
evening theatre dates, site will open at 12.

An elegant corner of Nostell Priory

Nostell Priory and Parkland

Doncaster Road, Nostell, near Wakefield,
West Yorkshire WF4 1QE

Map (5) G6   1954

'**Fabulous place – I could go round and
round. So much to see and the guides were
very friendly and knowedgeable**.'
V. Thompson, Norwich

Built on the site of a medieval priory, Nostell
has been the home of the Winn family for 300
years. Commissioned by Sir Rowland Winn
in 1733, James Paine built the house. Later
additions by Robert Adam created exceptional
interiors. Visitors can explore 121 hectares
(300 acres) of parkland with a range of walks
and views. Gardens include lakeside walks,
a newly planted orchard and an adventure
playground. Inside the house, see a collection
of Chippendale furniture made specially
for Nostell. Paintings by Brueghel, Hogarth
and Kauffmann. A John Harrison (*Longitude*)
longcase clock and an 18th-century dolls'
house. **Note**: stables undergoing renovation.

Exploring

- 18th-century dolls' house in
  the Museum Room.
- Look at the wooden workings
  of the John Harrison clock.
- Discover the grounds by
  following the gardens' `
  sensory trails.
- Explore the adventure
  playground in Low Wood.
- Visit the stables and see how
  important horses were.
- Take a walk through the park
  to Obelisk Lodge.

Eating and shopping: Stables tea-rooms for hot and cold food. Shop stocking wide range of interesting gifts and souvenirs. Weekend barbecue in the garden, weather permitting. Ice-cream bike around the grounds in summer.

You may also enjoy: Kedleston Hall and Clumber Park.

Making the most of your day: craft fairs, theatre, concerts and upstairs downstairs tours (booking essential). House trails. Boredom busting days in August. Guided tours 11:15, 11:45 and 12:15, Wednesday to Sunday mornings. Dogs on leads in park only.

Access for all: 🅿️🅳♿🚻🧑‍🦽🔗📷☷🔊
Building 🚶♿⬆️♿ **Grounds** ♿➡️♿

Getting here: 111:SE407172. 5 miles south of Wakefield within easy reach of A1, M1 and M62. **Foot**: via pedestrian entrance on the A638. **Cycle**: NCN67, 3 miles. **Bus**: Arriva 496 Wakefield–Doncaster; also Arriva 485, B Line 123, 223, 244 from Wakefield. **Train**: Fitzwilliam 1½ miles. **Road**: on A638 5 miles south east of Wakefield towards Doncaster. **Parking**: £2.

Finding out more: 01924 863892 or nostellpriory@nationaltrust.org.uk. Doncaster Road, Wakefield WF4 1QE

Nostell Priory and Parkland		M	T	W	T	F	S	S
Parkland								
Open all year	9–7	M	T	W	T	F	S	S
House*								
27 Feb–7 Nov	1–5	·	·	W	T	F	S	S
4 Dec–12 Dec	1–5	·	·	W	T	F	S	S
8 Dec–9 Dec	5–8	·	·	W	T	·	·	·
Gardens, shop and tea-room								
27 Feb–7 Nov	11–5:30	·	·	W	T	F	S	S
13 Nov–28 Nov	11–4:30	·	·	·	·	·	S	S
4 Dec–12 Dec	11–4:30	·	·	W	T	F	S	S
8 Dec–9 Dec	5–8	·	·	W	T	·	·	·
18 Dec–19 Dec	11–4	·	·	·	·	·	S	S
26 Dec–28 Dec	11–5	M	T	·	·	·	·	S

*House open 11 to 1 for guided tours, normal opening 1 to 5. Gardens, shop and tea-room open 8 January to 20 February, weekends, 11 to 4:30. Open local February half-term at 11:15, 11:45 and 12:15. Open Bank Holiday Mondays: house, 11 to 5; gardens, shop and tea-room, 11 to 5:30, parkland closes dusk if earlier. Rose garden may be closed on occasions for private functions.

Nunnington Hall

Nunnington, near York,
North Yorkshire YO62 5UY

Map ⑤ H4   1953

'**One of the best properties we have visited. The Carlisle Collection is stunning.**'
Mrs Twist, Scarborough

The sheltered walled garden, with spring-flowering organic meadows, orchards and flamboyant peacocks, complements this beautiful Yorkshire house, nestling on the quiet banks of the River Rye. Enjoy the atmosphere of this former family home. Explore period rooms while hearing the Hall's many tales, and then discover one of the world's finest collections of miniature rooms in the attic. The Hall also holds a series of important art and photography exhibitions during the year. Why not make a day of it? Its proximity to Rievaulx Terrace makes it an ideal double visit in one day.

Exploring   – Visit our art and photography exhibitions.
– Discover the amazing Carlisle Collection of miniature rooms.
– Enjoy a stroll in the organic walled garden.

Eating and shopping: waitress service in tea-room, serving local and seasonal produce. Special diets catered for, including gluten-free options. Lovely picnic spots and tea-garden. Look for the local ranges in the shop.

Nunnington Hall sits on the banks of the River Rye

We welcome dogs assisting visitors with disabilities

Ormesby Hall: a classic Georgian mansion

You may also enjoy: Rievaulx Terrace and Temples, Beningbrough Hall, Treasurer's House and Bridestones.

Making the most of your day: full events programme throughout the year, including temporary exhibitions, family activities, food events, concerts and many more.

Access for all: ♿ 🅿 🚾 ♿ 🎧 ⦂⦂
Building ♿ 🅰 Grounds ♿

Getting here: 100:SE670795.
Bus: Stephensons 195 Hovingham–Helmsley.
Road: in Ryedale, 4½ miles south east of Helmsley (A170) Helmsley–Pickering road; 1½ miles north of B1257 Malton–Helmsley road; 21 miles north of York, B1363. Nunnington Hall is 7½ miles south east of the National Trust Rievaulx Terrace and Temples.
Parking: free, 50 yards.

Finding out more: 01439 748283 or nunningtonhall@nationaltrust.org.uk

Nunnington Hall		M	T	W	T	F	S	S
27 Feb–31 Oct	11–5	·	**T**	**W**	**T**	**F**	**S**	**S**
6 Nov–19 Dec	11–4	·	·	·	·	·	**S**	**S**

Open Bank Holiday Mondays.

Ormesby Hall

Church Lane, Ormesby, near Middlesbrough, Redcar & Cleveland TS7 9AS

Map ⑤ G2   🏠 🏡 ♣ 🌳 🔔 🍴 1962

Home of the Pennyman family for nearly 400 years, this classic Georgian mansion, with its Victorian kitchen and laundry, attractive gardens and estate walks, provide lively resources for local schools and community groups, and a unique venue for wedding ceremonies and corporate events. Weekend visitors can experience the spirit of the intimate home of Colonel Jim Pennyman, the last of the Pennyman line, and his arts-loving wife Ruth, as well as the stylish legacy of the 18th-century character 'Wicked' Sir James Pennyman – so named due to his extravagant lifestyle and his gambling with the family fortune.

Exploring
- Enjoy beautiful gardens in an 18th-century landscape setting.
- Follow our family trails, indoors and out.
- Sit and relax a while in the Reading Room.
- Admire the working stables, home to Cleveland Mounted Police horses.
- **New**: peep into Mrs Pennyman's unrestored bathroom.

Eating and shopping: enjoy tea in the servants' hall or on the terrace. Taste scones and cakes hand-baked at the hall. Pick up a souvenir from our reception or tea-room.

You may also enjoy: a coastal contrast at Souter Lighthouse, or the intimate Jacobean feel of Washington Old Hall.

Making the most of your day: ask about our weekday programme of special-interest activities and events, including lunchtime lectures and conservation tours. Enjoy the only model railway layouts owned by the National Trust. Dogs on leads in park only.

Access for all: [icons]
Building [icons] Grounds [icons]

Getting here: 93:NZ530167. **Cycle**: NCN65, 2¼ miles. **Bus**: Arriva 5/9/63/69 from Middlesbrough (passing close Middlesbrough [icon]). **Train**: Marton 1½ miles; Middlesbrough 3 miles. **Road**: 3 miles south east of Middlesbrough, west of A171. From A19 take A174 to A172. Follow signs for Ormesby Hall. Car entrance on Ladgate Lane (B1380). **Sat Nav**: TS3 0SR. **Parking**: free, 100 yards.

Finding out more: 01642 324188 or ormesbyhall@nationaltrust.org.uk

Ormesby Hall	M	T	W	T	F	S	S
13 Mar–31 Oct	1:30–5	·	·	·	·	**S**	**S**

Open Bank Holiday Mondays and Good Friday. Closed one weekend in July for special event. Parts of the hall and grounds may occasionally be closed for private functions.

Rievaulx Terrace and Temples

Rievaulx, Helmsley, North Yorkshire YO62 5LJ

Map (5) H3   [icons]

Discover one of Ryedale's true gems – the 18th-century landscape of Rievaulx Terrace. Stroll through woods, then out on to the terrace, with its stunning views down over the Cistercian ruin of Rievaulx Abbey. In spring the bank between the temples is awash with wild flowers, in summer the lawns are the perfect spot for picnics, while in autumn the beech woods are a mass of rich hues. Rievaulx Terrace's close proximity to Nunnington Hall makes it an ideal double visit in one day. **Note**: no access to Rievaulx Abbey from terrace.

Exploring
- Take your time and enjoy the scenic walk.
- Bring a hamper and have a picnic.
- Join in the family activities.
- Find out more by joining a guided tour.
- Spot the fascinating flora and fauna.

Eating and shopping: treat yourself to an ice-cream, drinks and snacks. Don't miss the shop selling National Trust ranges.

The 18th-century Rievaulx Terrace and Temples

Roseberry Topping: distinctive and iconic landmark

You may also enjoy: Nunnington Hall, Beningbrough Hall, Treasurer's House and The Bridestones.

Making the most of your day: events programme throughout year, including family activities in school holidays and programme of guided tours. Free batricars available to book at specific times. Dogs welcome on leads.

Access for all: 🅿🄳♿🄌⠿
Building 🔼 Grounds 🔼🔼➡🦽

Getting here: 100:SE579848. **Foot**: Cleveland Way within ¾ mile. **Bus**: Moorsbus M8 from Helmsley Sunday and Bank Holidays mid March to October, daily late July to August. Discounted entry for visitors using the Moorsbus. **Road**: 2½ miles north west of Helmsley on B1257. **Parking**: free, 100 yards. Unsuitable for trailer caravans. Tight corners and no turning space beyond coach park.

Finding out more: 01439 798340 (summer). 01439 748283 (winter) or rievaulxterrace@nationaltrust.org.uk

Roseberry Topping

Newton-under-Roseberry, North Yorkshire

Map ⑤ G2 🏛🚻🍴🐕 1985

Layers of human and geological history have shaped this distinctive and iconic landmark, with its bluebell woods and heather moorland. **Note**: nearest WC at Newton-Under-Roseberry car park.

Getting here: 93:NZ575126. 1 mile from Great Ayton, next to Newton-Under-Roseberry village on A173 Great Ayton–Guisborough.

Finding out more: 01642 328901 or roseberrytopping@nationaltrust.org.uk. c/o Peakside, Ravenscar, Scarborough, North Yorkshire YO13 0NE

Roseberry Topping		M	T	W	T	F	S	S
Open all year	Dawn–dusk	**M**	**T**	**W**	**T**	**F**	**S**	**S**

Rievaulx Terrace and Temples		M	T	W	T	F	S	S
27 Feb–31 Oct	11–5	**M**	**T**	**W**	**T**	**F**	**S**	**S**

Treasurer's House

Minster Yard, York, North Yorkshire YO1 7JL

Map ⑤ H5   🏠 ❀ 🔔 🍷 1930

'**The new attic tour is superb – thanks
to the excellent guide. A gem of a house,
not to be missed.**'
Alison Coates, Leeds

Only a few metres from York Minster, this was
the first house ever given to the National Trust
complete with a collection – and it is not all
that it first seems! It has a history spanning
2,000 years, from the Roman road in the cellar
to the Edwardian servants' quarters in the
attics, and thirteen period rooms in between.
These house one man's remarkable collection
of antique furniture, ceramics, textiles and
paintings from a 300-year period. Infamous
ghost stories are another of the many quirky
attributes of this property. Outside is an
attractive formal sunken garden.

Exploring
– Take the attic tour and learn
about Edwardian servant life.
– Join the cellar tour –
hear about Roman
ghostly sightings.
– Relax in the quiet
walled garden.
– Enjoy refreshment in the
table service tea-room.
– Trails for children
available daily.
– Engaging room guides.

Eating and shopping: your favourite
National Trust photographic images are for
sale. Small selection of local artists' and craft
work for sale. Range of homemade bakes,
cakes, soups and special dietry dishes. Themed
food events, including Christmas lunches and
Edwardian breakfasts.

You may also enjoy: Beningbrough Hall
and Gardens.

Making the most of your day: attic and
cellar tours of Edwardian social history and
archaeology of Roman road. Themed tours.

Treasurer's House: 2,000 years of history

Family trails and activities every school holiday.
Vegetable plant sales. Food events. Workshops.
Dogs on leads in formal garden only.

Access for all: 📖 ♿ 🖼 📷 🎵 📱 📷
Building ♿ ♿ Grounds ♿ ➡

Getting here: 105:SE604523. In city centre
adjacent to Minster (north side, at rear).
Cycle: NCN65, ⅓ mile. Close to city cycle
routes. **Bus**: from surrounding areas.
Train: York ½ mile. **Parking**: nearest in Lord
Mayor's Walk. Park and ride service from
city outskirts.

Finding out more: 01904 624247 or
treasurershouse@nationaltrust.org.uk

Treasurer's House		M	T	W	T	F	S	S
1 Apr–31 Oct	11–4:30	M	T	W	T	·	S	S
1 Nov–30 Nov	11–3	M	T	W	T	·	S	S

1 April to 31 October: free-flow. November: entry by Ghostly
Myths guided tour to selected rooms. Herb garden openings
limited, check before visiting.

The exterior of Treasurer's House

Upper Wharfedale

North Yorkshire BD23 5JA

Map ⑤ E4 [icons] 1989

Along the Upper Wharfe Valley the characteristic drystone walls and barns of the Dales, important flower-rich hay meadows, beautiful riverside and valleyside woodland combine to create a wonderful place to relax and explore the great outdoors.

Exploring
— Spectacular scenery to explore and enjoy.
— Excellent walking and cycling opportunities.
— Beautiful picnic spots along the banks of the River Wharfe.
— Picturesque villages and hamlets to stroll around.

Eating and shopping: village tea-rooms, shops and pubs.

Making the most of your day: guided walks and events throughout the year. Dogs on leads only.

Access for all: [P&] [WC]
Town Head Barn [icon] Grounds [icon]

Getting here: 98:SD935765. Upper Wharfedale extends from Kettlewell village (12 miles north of Skipton) north to Beckermonds and Cray. **Foot**: the Dales Way runs through Upper Wharfedale following the scenic route of the River Wharfe on its way from Ilkley to Bowness in Windermere. **Cycle**: Kettlewell lies on the Yorkshire Dales Cycleway (Sustrans regional route 10) between Coverdale and Skipton. **Bus**: Pride of the Dales 72 Skipton ■-Buckden. **Train**: Skipton, 12 miles. **Road**: B6160 runs the length of Upper Wharfedale through Cray, Buckden and Kettlewell, towards Grassington (7 miles) and Ilkley in the south. **Parking**: in Kettlewell and Buckden, not National Trust (pay and display).

Finding out more: 01729 830416 or upperwharfedale@nationaltrust.org.uk. Yorkshire Dales Estate Office, Waterhouses, Settle, North Yorkshire BD24 9PT

Upper Wharfedale		M	T	W	T	F	S	S
Estate								
Open all year		M	T	W	T	F	S	S
Town Head Barn								
13 Feb–31 Oct	10–4	M	T	W	T	F	S	S

Yockenthwaite Top Farm in Langstrothdale, in the Yorkshire Dales

Yorkshire Coast

Peakside, Ravenscar, Scarborough,
North Yorkshire YO13 0NE

Map (5) I2   🏠🏚🚻♿🏛🐦🏡 1976

A diverse collection of coastal properties strung out along the Cleveland Way National Trail. Discover breathtaking views, the remains of industrial endeavours and a wildlife sanctuary. Visit the Old Coastguard Station in Robin Hood's Bay village and the Ravenscar Coastal Centre to discover more about the landscape and people.

Exploring
- See how the elements have created this stunning landscape.
- Discover more about Britain's first chemical industry.
- Spot wildlife in bluebell woods and clifftop meadows.
- Explore your very own Jurassic Park.

Eating and shopping: enjoy the shop and exhibition at the Old Coastguard Station. Explore the shop and exhibition at the Ravenscar Coastal Centre.

Making the most of your day: art exhibitions and family trails and activities at the Old Coastguard Station. Wildlife safaris and guided walks at Ravenscar, Boggle Hole and Saltburn. Boat trips from Whitby. Dogs on leads allowed.

Access for all: 🅿️📷♿📶📖
Old Coastguard Station 🚹↕
Ravenscar Coastal Centre 🚹 **Grounds** 🏔

Getting here: 94:NZ980025. **Foot**: Cleveland Way passes through property. **Cycle**: NCN1. **Bus**: Scarborough and District 115 from Scarborough Monday–Saturday. **Train**: Scarborough 10 miles from Ravenscar; Whitby 5 miles from Robin Hood's Bay/Old Coastguard Station. **Road**: Coastal Centre in Ravenscar village, signposted off A171 Scarborough–Whitby. Old Coastguard Station in Robin Hood's Bay village.

The picturesque Cowbar Nab at Staithes

Parking: 546 yards, up steep bank for Old Coastguard Station (pay and display), not National Trust, charge including members. Free roadside parking at Ravenscar.

Finding out more: 01723 870423 (Peakside office). 01947 885900 (Old Coastguard Station) or yorkshirecoast@nationaltrust.org.uk

Yorkshire Coast		M	T	W	T	F	S	S
Old Coastguard Station								
2 Jan–28 Mar	10–4	·	·	·	·	·	S	S
29 Mar–25 Jul	10–5	M	T	W	T	F	S	S
27 Jul–5 Sep	10–5	·	T	W	T	F	S	S
6 Sep–31 Oct	10–5	M	T	W	T	F	S	S
6 Nov–19 Dec	10–4	·	·	·	·	·	S	S
Coastal Centre								
6 Mar–28 Mar	10–4	·	·	·	·	·	S	S
29 Mar–18 Apr	10–4	M	T	W	T	F	S	S
24 Apr–30 May	10–4	·	·	·	·	·	S	S
31 May–2 Oct	10–4	M	T	W	T	F	S	S
3 Oct–31 Oct	10–4	·	·	·	·	·	S	S

Both centres open Bank Holiday Mondays. Old Coastguard Station also open 15 to 21 February, 20 to 23 December and 27 to 31 December daily, 10 to 4. Closed 24 to 26 December.

Members may have to pay on special events days

North East

Playing tug-of-war against the wind at Druridge Bay

by Katy Merrington,
member since 2009

Outdoors in the North East

The National Trust cares for some of the finest stretches of coast and countryside in Northumberland, Durham and Tyne & Wear. With magnificent scenery, unspoilt moorland and a dramatic coastline – this is arguably one of the finest places in Britain.

A haven for wildlife

The North East is a haven for wildlife, offering one of the few sanctuaries in England for our threatened native red squirrels. If you are out walking, keep your eyes peeled for a rare sighting. Red squirrels live in wooded areas and can be seen in the region at Allen Banks, Cragside and Wallington – the latter has a wildlife hide that is perfect for spotting these special animals.

As well as squirrels, there is an abundance of birdlife in the North East. The Farne Islands, for example, are home to more than 100,000 nesting birds and their chicks during the breeding season (May to July). Lying just off the north-east coast from Seahouses, the Farnes offer one of the most exciting wildlife experiences in the world.

Accessible only by boat, both Inner Farne and Staple Island can be landed on when the weather permits, and their inhabitants include puffins, terns, guillemots, eider ducks and a colony of grey seals.

St Cuthbert died on Inner Farne in 687, and the chapel built in his memory can be visited today.

Take a closer look at the rock pools

The National Trust cares for sixteen miles of dunes, sandy beaches and tidal rock pools along the Northumberland coast, and five miles of the Durham coast. For many years, the Durham beaches were a dumping ground for the local collieries, but this unexpectedly beautiful area of coast now has Heritage Coast status.

In the south of the region, near Horden in County Durham, a piece of coast marks the 500th mile acquired through the Trust's Neptune Coastline Campaign. Once an industrial mining hotspot, this stretch of coastline has since been dramatically restored, and while even today it may be some time before the beaches return to golden sands, the seeds have been sown for the future.

Heavenly walks and breathtaking views

Inland Northumberland offers the natural beauty and tranquillity of Allen Banks and Staward Gorge – a walking heaven with many miles of footpaths – while both Ros

My favourite view

Souter Lighthouse is a special place that has had a huge part to play in local and maritime life for many years. The first lighthouse in the world to be powered by electricity, it was a beacon on the North East coast warning ships away from the jagged rock platforms in the shallows below the cliff face.

There are some stunning views from the top of the tower, to the north, beyond the mouth of the River Tyne, up to Lynemouth, and to the south, down past Sunderland to the Durham coast. The tower overlooks The Leas, a haven for flora and fauna and a green lung on the edge of South Shields. It is a space regularly used by locals and enjoyed by visitors who are amazed by the beauty of the coast.

On a clear day, this is a breathtaking place to be, with the clifftop path giving the chance to see kittiwakes and cormorants soaring below… But I'd also recommend taking a look out to sea – you might just spot a dolphin or the occasional seal swimming by!

Nick Dolan
Property Manager,
Souter Lighthouse and The Leas

Castle and the World Heritage Site of Hadrian's Wall boast breathtaking views. There are also numerous beautiful woodland walks, including one along the banks of the River Wear at Moorhouse Woods, north of Durham City, and another beside the Derwent at Ebchester.

Above:
family birdwatching at Inner Farne on the Farne Islands in Northumberland

Opposite:
Dunstanburgh Castle, Northumberland, as seen from Greymare Rock

An island retreat

Accessible by a causeway at low tide, Holy Island is a treasure that has as its centrepiece Lindisfarne Castle. Once a Tudor fort, the castle sits on a rocky crag that can be seen for miles along the sweeping coastline. Converted into a holiday home in 1903, this enchanting place, with its small rooms full of intimate decoration and design, is totally charming. Just below the castle is the lovely walled garden planned by Gertrude Jekyll and dating back to 1922.

Be sure also to stroll along the headland and explore the village – just remember to keep an eye on the tides which cover the causeway.

Roman might and engineering

One of the most rugged stretches of countryside in the North East is home to Hadrian's Wall. Snaking across the landscape, the wall was built around AD122 when the Roman Empire was at its height. A World Heritage Site, it remains one of Britain's most impressive ruins.

The Trust protects six miles of Hadrian's Wall, including Housesteads Fort, one of the best preserved sections of the ramparts and a place which conjures an evocative picture of Roman military life.

Below:
Hadrian's Wall and Housesteads Fort, Northumberland. This northerly outpost was built at the height of the Roman Empire

Allen Banks and Staward Gorge

Estate Office, Bardon Mill, Hexham,
Northumberland NE47 7BU

Map (6) F5   1942

This extensive area of gorge and river scenery,
including the 41-hectare (101-acre) Stawardpeel
Site of Special Scientific Interest, has miles of
waymarked walks through ornamental and
ancient woods. Look out for the remains of
a medieval pele tower and a reconstructed
Victorian summerhouse. All within North
Pennines AONB.

Exploring
  – Explore miles of tranquil
    and beautiful footpaths.
  – See the views from a
    medieval pele tower.
  – Look out for wildlife,
    especially woodland
    birds and plants.

Eating and shopping: enjoy a picnic in
beautiful surroundings.

Making the most of your day: enjoy the
peaceful surroundings of Allen Banks and
Staward Gorge. Guided walks and workshops
covering a range of subjects, such as tree
identification, fungi and woodland birds.
Dogs welcome under close control.

Access for all: 🖾 Grounds 👟

Getting here: 86:NY799640. **Foot**: numerous
public and permitted rights of way give access
to walkers. **Cycle**: NCN72, 2½ miles.
Bus: Arriva/Stagecoach in Cumbria 685 Carlisle–
Newcastle upon Tyne, to within ½ miles.
Train: Bardon Mill 1½ mile. **Road**: 5½ miles east
of Haltwhistle, 3 miles west of Haydon Bridge,
½ miles south of A69, near meeting point of
Tyne and Allen rivers. **Sat Nav**: avoid using Sat
Nav. **Parking**: at Allen Bank (pay and display).
Cars £2 half day, £4 full day. Two coaches at a
time maximum (all coaches must book).
3.3 metre height restriction on approach road.
Coaches £5 half day, £10 full day.

Finding out more: 01434 344218 or
allenbanks@nationaltrust.org.uk

Allen Banks and Staward Gorge	M	T	W	T	F	S	S
Open all year	**M**	**T**	**W**	**T**	**F**	**S**	**S**

Cherryburn

Station Bank, Mickley, Stocksfield,
Northumberland NE43 7DD

Map (6) G5  1991

Cherryburn, Northumberland

'**Very interesting and friendly place – so
peaceful and tranquil with excellent events.
And our children loved the donkeys**.'
Robert Lambourn, Berwick upon Tweed

Thomas Bewick (1753–1828), Northumberland's
greatest artist, wood engraver and naturalist,
was born in the cottage here. The nearby
19th-century farmhouse, the later home
of the Bewick family, houses an exhibition
on Bewick's life and work and a small shop
selling books, gifts and prints from his
original wood engravings. Occasional printing
demonstrations take place in the adjoining
barn. There are splendid views over the Tyne
Valley. The south bank of the River Tyne, where
Bewick spent much of his childhood, is a
short walk away.

Exploring

- View the exhibition, dedicated to the work of Thomas Bewick.
- Enjoy the donkeys in the farmyard.
- Take a stroll around the Paddock Walk.
- Bring a picnic and enjoy one of our many events.

Eating and shopping: browse through the bargain books in the shop. Buy prints from the original Bewick engravings. Sample Northumbrian biscuits with your coffee. Try our fantastic picnic area.

You may also enjoy: the live interpretation at the nearby birthplace of pioneering railway engineer George Stephenson.

Making the most of your day: full events programme, with printing demonstrations most Sunday afternoons. Folk in the Farmyard first Sunday of the month, May to October.

Access for all: 🅿️ Ｄ 🦽 🚽 📶 📷 🎨 🐾 ••

Building 🏠🏠🏠 Grounds 🏠

Getting here: 88:NZ075627. Close to south bank of River Tyne. **Bus**: Arriva Northumbria 602 Newcastle–Hexham (passes Newcastle 🚉), alight Mickley Square ¼ mile. **Train**: Stocksfield 1½ miles; Prudhoe 1½ miles. **Road**: 11 miles west of Newcastle, 11 miles east of Hexham; ¼ mile north of Mickley Square

(leave A695 at Mickley Square on to Riding Terrace leading to Station Bank).
Parking: free, 100 yards.

Finding out more: 01661 843276 or cherryburn@nationaltrust.org.uk

Cherryburn		M	T	W	T	F	S	S
13 Mar–31 Oct	11–5	**M**	**T**	·	**T**	**F**	**S**	**S**

Cragside

Rothbury, Morpeth, Northumberland NE65 7PX

Map ⑥ G3   🏠 🏠 🍴 ♣ ♠ 🏠   1977

The revolutionary home of Lord Armstrong, Victorian inventor and landscape genius, was a wonder of its age. Built on a rocky crag high above the Debdon Burn, Cragside is crammed with ingenious gadgets and was the first house in the world to be lit by hydroelectricity. Surrounding the house on all sides is one of the largest rock gardens in Europe. Across the iron bridge, in the formal garden, is the Orchard House, which still produces fresh fruit. The lakeside walks, adventure play area and labyrinth are all good reasons for children to visit Cragside again and again. **Note**: challenging terrain and distances. Stout footwear essential.

Cragside, Northumberland: the first house in the world to be lit by hydroelectricity

Outstanding colourful borders at Cragside, Northumberland

Exploring
- Visit the first house to be lit by hydroelectricity.
- Marvel at the many ingenious gadgets in the house.
- Escape to the tranquillity of the woodland and lakes.
- Get lost in the labyrinth.
- See this year's carpet bedding display.
- Be awe-inspired by Armstrong's wonderful transatlantic conifer collection.

Eating and shopping: locally sourced food and drink served in our Stables restaurant. Extensive range of plants for sale in Visitor Centre courtyard. Northumbrian products and gifts in shop.

You may also enjoy: Lindisfarne Castle and Souter Lighthouse.

Making the most of your day: free mini bus shuttle service between key features. Introductory talks at front of house. Guided walks throughout the year. Family activities in school holidays. Numerous self-guided walks. Dogs welcome on estate, on leads at all times.

Access for all: [icons] House [icons] Visitor Centre [icons]
Estate [icons]

Getting here: 81:NU073022. **Bus**: Arriva 508 Newcastle–Rothbury (passes Morpeth ≷),

Sundays only, June to October. Go North East 144 Morpeth–Thropton with connections from Newcastle. **Road**: 13 miles south west of Alnwick (B6341) and 15 miles north west of Morpeth on Wooler road (A697), turn left on to B6341 at Moorhouse Crossroads, entrance 1 mile north of Rothbury. **Parking**: nine car parks throughout estate, free. Coach parking 350 yards from house, 150 yards from Visitor Centre. Coaches cannot proceed beyond the coach park or tour estate as drive is too narrow.

Finding out more: 01669 620333 or cragside@nationaltrust.org.uk

Cragside*		M	T	W	T	F	S	S
House*								
13 Mar–1 Apr	1–5	·	T	W	T	F	S	S
2 Apr–18 Apr	11–5	·	T	W	T	F	S	S
20 Apr–28 May	1–5	·	T	W	T	F	S	S
29 May–6 Jun	11–5	·	T	W	T	F	S	S
8 Jun–23 Jul	1–5	·	T	W	T	F	S	S
24 Jul–5 Sep	11–5	·	T	W	T	F	S	S
7 Sep–22 Oct	1–5	·	T	W	T	F	S	S
23 Oct–31 Oct	11–5	·	T	W	T	F	S	S
Gardens, estate, shop and restaurant								
13 Mar–31 Oct	10:30–5	·	T	W	T	F	S	S
3 Nov–19 Dec	11–4	·	·	W	T	F	S	S

*House open 11 to 5 on Saturdays, Sundays and local school holidays. Also open Bank Holiday Mondays. Open 13 to 21 February (except Mondays): house (ground floor only) 12 to 4; grounds, 11 to 4. Also open 6 to 7 March, grounds and house (ground floor only), 12 to 4. On Bank Holiday weekends the property is very crowded. Last admission to house one hour before closing. House may open late or close early if light or temperature levels are too low. Occasionally entry to house from 11 to 1 may be by guided tour only, on a first-come, first-served basis (places limited).

Dunstanburgh Castle

Craster, Alnwick, Northumberland NE66 3TT

Map (6) H3 1961

An iconic castle ruin, on one of the most beautiful stretches of Northumberland coastline. An exhilarating walk from Craster. **Note**: managed by English Heritage.

Getting here: 75:NU258220. 9 miles north east of Alnwick, approached from Craster to the south or Embleton to the north (on foot only).

Finding out more: 01665 576231 or dunstanburghcastle@nationaltrust.org.uk

Dunstanburgh Castle		M	T	W	T	F	S	S
2 Jan–29 Mar	10–4	M	·	·	T	F	S	S
1 Apr–30 Sep	10–5	M	T	W	T	F	S	S
1 Oct–31 Oct	10–4	M	T	W	T	F	S	S
1 Nov–31 Dec	10–4	M	·	·	T	F	S	S

Closed 1 January and 24 to 26 December.

Farne Islands

Northumberland

Map (6) H2 1925

Possibly the most exciting seabird colony in England with unrivalled views of 23 species – including 37,000 pairs of puffin. Large grey seal colony with more than 1,000 pups born every autumn. Strong links with Celtic Christianity and St Cuthbert. A short boat journey to a different world! **Note**: access by boat from Seahouses (charge including members). WC on Inner Farne only.

Exploring
– Opportunity to view seabirds at unbelievably close range.
– Excellent photographic opportunities.
– Chapel of St Cuthbert with fine stained-glass windows.

Exploring – Unrivalled views of the Northumberland hinterland.

Eating and shopping: visit our shop in Seahouses for beautiful local crafts. Fantastic puffin range, with fleeces, socks, mugs and coasters.

Access for all: Grounds

Getting here: 75:NU230370. 2–5 miles off the Northumberland coast, opposite Bamburgh. Trips every day from Seahouses harbour, weather permitting. **Cycle**: NCN1, ¾ mile. From Seahouses harbour. **Bus**: Arriva 501 Newcastle -Alnwick -Berwick, alight Seahouses, 1½ miles. **Train**: Chathill, not Sunday, 4 miles. **Parking**: in Seahouses opposite harbour (pay and display), not National Trust.

Finding out more: 01665 721099 (Infoline). 01665 720651 or farneislands@nationaltrust.org.uk

Farne Islands		M	T	W	T	F	S	S
Both islands								
1 Apr–30 Apr	10:30–6	M	T	W	T	F	S	S
1 Aug–31 Oct	10:30–6	M	T	W	T	F	S	S
Staple								
1 May–31 Jul	10:30–1:30	M	T	W	T	F	S	S
Inner Farne								
1 May–31 Jul	1:30–5	M	T	W	T	F	S	S
Shop								
1 Apr–30 Sep	10–5	M	T	W	T	F	S	S
1 Jan–31 Mar	11–4	·	·	W	T	F	S	S
1 Oct–24 Dec	11–4	M	T	W	T	F	S	S

Only Inner Farne and Staple Islands can be visited. Information centre and shop open half-term holidays 10 to 5.

Puffins on Inner Farne, Northumberland

George Stephenson's Birthplace

Wylam, Northumberland NE41 8BP

Map (6) G5 1949

This quaint small stone cottage was built *circa* 1760 to accommodate mining families. The furnishings reflect the year the great rail pioneer, George Stephenson was born here (1781), when his whole family lived in the one room.

Exploring
- Tread the same flagstones as young George did.
- Listen to the live interpretation.
- Learn about the pioneering steam locomotive 'Rocket'.

Eating and shopping: enjoy a light snack in the cosy Stephenson tea-room. Buy a souvenir book on the Stephenson family. Look out for the Geordie Food day in June.

Making the most of your day: extend your visit by strolling along the banks of the River Tyne.

Access for all: ⬚⬚⬚⬚⬚⬚ Building ⬚

Getting here: 88:NZ126650. **Foot**: access on foot (and cycle) through country park, ½ mile east of Wylam. **Cycle**: NCN72. Easy (flat) ride beside River Tyne (approximately 5 miles). **Bus**: Arriva 684 Newcastle–Ovington, alight Wylam, 1 mile. **Train**: Wylam ½ miles. **Road**: 8 miles west of Newcastle, 1½ miles south of A69 at Wylam. **Parking**: by war memorial in Wylam village, ½ mile, not National Trust (pay and display).

Finding out more: 01661 853457 or georgestephensons@nationaltrust.org.uk

George Stephenson's Birthplace	M	T	W	T	F	S	S
20 Mar–31 Oct	12–5			**T**	**F**	**S**	**S**

Open Bank Holiday Mondays.

Gibside

near Rowlands Gill, Burnopfield, Gateshead, Tyne & Wear NE16 6BG

Map (6) H5  1974

'**A fantastic day! Especially enjoyed the atmosphere of the beautiful chapel, and what a treat to see a red kite.**'
Anna Brunton, Sunderland

The Column of Liberty, rising above the treetops, is the first sight visitors have of this impressive landscape garden created by the Bowes family in the 18th century. Spanning 182 hectares (450 acres), Gibside is a 'grand design' of spectacular vistas, winding paths and grassy open spaces. At key points there are decorative garden buildings, including the Palladian chapel, Georgian stables, greenhouse and ruins of a bathhouse and hall. There is a wonderfully tranquil atmosphere, and visitors will feel close to nature. Much is a Site of Special Scientific Interest and wildlife, such as red kites, can be seen.

Exploring
- Walk in the 182-hectare (450-acre) landscape garden.
- Watch the skies for red kites.
- Discover hidden views and vistas.
- Visit the stunning Palladian-style Gibside chapel.
- Have fun on the family scramble trail.
- Look for wildlife along the riverside.

Eating and shopping: light lunches and cakes available in the tea-room. Make a picnic with delicious local food from Gibside Larder. Treat yourself to a hot chocolate or ice-cream. Go shopping for books, toys and items for outdoor adventures.

You may also enjoy: Cherryburn.

Enjoying a stroll at Gibside, Tyne & Wear

Making the most of your day: events, theatre and concerts. Costumed guides, tours and walks. Gibside Stables Learning and Discovery Residential Centre for school groups, Brownies, families, and corporate team-building. Dogs on leads on the walks.

Access for all: 🅿️♿🚻♿♿📷♿📷📷
Chapel ♿♿♿ Landscape Garden ♿♿➡️♿♿

Getting here: 88:NZ172583. **Foot**: ½ mile from Derwent Walk, footpath/cycle track linking Swalwell and Consett. **Cycle**: NCN14, ½ mile. **Bus**: Go North East 'The Red Kite' 45, 46/A from Newcastle (passing Newcastle ≅ and Metrocentre), alight Rowlands Gill, ½ mile. **Train**: Blaydon 5 miles; Metrocentre 5 miles. **Road**: 6 miles south west of Gateshead, 20 miles north west of Durham; entrance on B6314 between Burnopfield and Rowlands Gill; from A1 take exit north of Metrocentre and follow brown signs. **Parking**: free, 100 yards. Limited coach parking.

Finding out more: 01207 541820 or gibside@nationaltrust.org.uk

Gibside		M	T	W	T	F	S	S
Landscape garden, walks and stables								
2 Jan–7 Mar	10–4	M	T	W	T	F	S	S
8 Mar–31 Oct	10–6	M	T	W	T	F	S	S
1 Nov–31 Dec	10–4	M	T	W	T	F	S	S
Chapel								
8 Mar–31 Oct	11–4:30	M	T	W	T	F	S	S
Larder, shop and tea-room								
2 Jan–7 Mar	11–3:30	M	T	W	T	F	S	S
8 Mar–31 Oct	11–4:30	M	T	W	T	F	S	S
1 Nov–31 Dec	11–3:30	M	T	W	T	F	S	S

Closed 24 and 25 December. Larder, shop and tea-room opens 10 weekends.

Hadrian's Wall and Housesteads Fort

Bardon Mill, Hexham, Northumberland NE47 6NN

Map ⑥ F5 🏛️♿🏠 1930

Running through an often wild landscape with vast panoramic views, the wall was one of the Roman Empire's most northerly outposts. Built around AD122, it has sixteen permanent bases, of which Housesteads Fort is one of the best preserved, conjuring up an evocative picture of Roman military life. **Note**: fort is owned by the National Trust and maintained and managed by English Heritage.

Exploring
- Enjoy walking alongside the wall.
- Wander through the extensive archaeological remains.
- Take in panoramic views of Hadrian's Wall country.
- Look out for different flora and fauna.

Eating and shopping: small shop selling local and 'Roman' souvenirs. Refreshment kiosk with limited indoor seating.

Making the most of your day: limited events organised by English Heritage. Dogs welcome on leads.

Built by the Romans, Hadrian's Wall in Northumberland runs through a wild, rugged landscape

Access for all: [P] [&] [WC] [&] [••] Visitor Centre [&]
English Heritage Museum [&] Fort [&] [&]

Getting here: 87:NY790688. **Foot**: Hadrian's Wall Path and Pennine Way. **Cycle**: Sustrans Route 72. **Bus**: Stagecoach in Cumbria/Classic Coaches AD122 Hadrian's Wall service, April to November daily, Newcastle ≋–Hexham–Carlisle (passing Haltwhistle ≋). Check before journey. **Train**: Hexham or Haltwhistle connect with AD122 bus. **Road**: 6 miles north east of Haltwhistle, best access from car parks at Housesteads, Cawfields and Steel Rigg. **Parking**: Not National Trust (pay & display), charge applicable to members. Car and coach parks operated by National Park Authority at Housesteads (½ mile walk to the Fort), Steel Rigg and Cawfields.

Finding out more: 01434 344525 (Visitor Centre). 01434 344363 (EH Museum) or housesteads@nationaltrust.org.uk

Housesteads Fort		M	T	W	T	F	S	S
1 Jan–31 Mar	10–4	M	T	W	T	F	S	S
1 Apr–30 Sep	10–6	M	T	W	T	F	S	S
1 Oct–31 Dec	10–4	M	T	W	T	F	S	S

Closed 1 January and 24 to 26 December. Telephone for details or visit www.english-heritage.org.uk.

Holy Jesus Hospital

City Road, Newcastle upon Tyne,
Tyne & Wear NE1 2AS

Map (6) H5

The Holy Jesus Hospital survives amid 1960s city-centre developments, displaying features from all periods of its 700-year existence. The National Trust's Inner City Project is now based here, working to provide opportunities for inner-city dwellers to gain access to and enjoy the countryside on their doorstep. **Note**: owned by Newcastle City Council but managed by the National Trust.

Exploring
— Visit our exhibition room during the week.
— Listen to voices from the past on our interactive displays.
— Get a guided tour on first Saturday of every month.
— Don't miss the plant fair on the June open day.

Eating and shopping: tea, coffee and biscuits available on Saturday open days.

Making the most of your day: discover the site's fascinating history on a guided tour and learn about the remains of the 14th-century Augustinian friary, Tudor tower, 17th-century almshouse and Victorian soup kitchen.

Access for all: ♿ 🏠 🚻 📷 ⚡ **Building** ♿ ♿ ♿

Getting here: 88:NZ253642. In centre of Newcastle upon Tyne. **Cycle**: close to riverside routes. **Bus**: Stagecoach buses from city centre. **Train**: Newcastle ½ mile. **Underground**: Tyne and Wear Metro-Monument, ¼ mile. **Road**: close to Tyne Bridge and A167. **Parking**: nearest in city centre car parks, 30 yards (pay and display).

Finding out more: 0191 255 7610 or innercityproject@nationaltrust.org.uk

Holy Jesus Hospital		M	T	W	T	F	S	S
5 Jan–1 Jul	12–4	·	**T**	**W**	**T**	·	·	
5 Jul–27 Aug	12–4	**M**	**T**	**W**	**T**	**F**	·	
31 Aug–16 Dec	12–4	·	**T**	**W**	**T**	·	·	

Closed Bank Holiday Mondays and Good Friday. Guided tours first Saturday of every month (except January), 10 to 4.

Lindisfarne Castle

Holy Island, Berwick-upon-Tweed, Northumberland TD15 2SH

Map ⑥ G1

Dramatically perched on a rocky crag and accessible via a three-mile causeway at low tide only, the island castle presents an exciting and alluring aspect. Originally a Tudor fort, it was converted into a private house in 1903 by the young Edwin Lutyens. The small rooms are full of intimate decoration and design, with windows looking down upon the charming walled garden planned by Gertrude Jekyll. The property also has several extremely well-preserved 19th-century lime kilns. **Note**: emergency WC only.

Exploring   – Decide how old the castle is – Elizabethan or Edwardian?

Lindisfarne Castle, Northumberland, was originally a Tudor fort

Exploring
- Specialist Gertrude Jekyll garden, explore the 1911 planting plan.
- See the castle's internal wind indicator.
- Do not miss the 19th-century headland lime kilns.
- Invigorating seaside walks, with rock pools to explore.
- Search for wild flowers and spot the sea birds.

Eating and shopping: delicious honey and mustard products from Chainbridge border honey farm. Flavoursome jams and preserves from nearby Oxford Farm. Mouth-watering Heatherslaw bakery cakes and biscuits. Tasty Loopy Lisa homemade flavoured fudge.

You may also enjoy: a visit to the Farne Islands to wonder at the abundance and variety of seabirds.

Making the most of your day: children's quizzes make family visits more memorable. Specialist Gertrude Jekyll garden talks, monthly from May to August.

Access for all: ▨ ▨ ▢ ▨ ▨ ▢ ▨
Castle ▨ Shop ▨ Grounds ▨ ▨

Getting here: 75:NU136417. Tidal island off the north Northumberland coast.
Foot: approached on foot from main Holy Island village and car park, 1 mile from entrance. **Cycle**: NCN1. Coast and Castles cycle route. **Bus**: Travelsure 477 from Berwick-upon-Tweed ≊, with connecting buses at Beal to and from Newcastle. Times vary with season and tides. Some months the bus only runs twice a week on Wednesdays and Saturdays. Also private island minibus service from Holy Island car park to castle. **Train**: Berwick-upon-Tweed 10 miles from causeway. **Road**: on Holy Island, 5 miles east of A1 across a tidal causeway.
Parking: 1 mile (pay and display), not National Trust, charge including members.

Finding out more: 01289 389244 or lindisfarne@nationaltrust.org.uk

Lindisfarne Castle		M	T	W	T	F	S	S
Castle								
13 Feb–21 Feb	10–3	M	T	W	T	F	S	S
13 Mar–31 Oct	Times vary	·	T	W	T	F	S	S
27 Dec–28 Dec	10–3	M	T	·	·	·	·	·
Garden								
Open all year	10–5	·	T	W	T	F	S	S

Open some weekends in January, November and December – tide dependent, contact castle for details. Open Bank Holiday Mondays (including Scottish Bank Holidays). **Opening times vary depending on tides.** On open days the castle will open for five hours (always including 12 to 3), either 10 to 3 or 12 to 5. National Trust flag flies only when the castle is open. Castle winter opening: two weekends a month from 10 to 3, depending on tidal access. For tide tables and detailed opening times send sae to Lindisfarne Castle stating which month you wish to visit or visit www.lindisfarne.org.uk.

Souter Lighthouse and The Leas

Coast Road, Whitburn, Sunderland, Tyne & Wear SR6 7NH

Map ⑥ I5    1990

'**Stunning views, nice homemade food, great for cyclists, and something for all ages: we'd recommend Souter to anyone**.'
Lisa McGurk and Sarah Sutton, South Shields

Boldly hooped in red and white, Souter is an iconic clifftop beacon, offering a great family-friendly visit. When opened in 1871, it was a technological marvel, being the first lighthouse built to use electricity. Decommissioned in 1988, the machinery remains in working order and visitors can learn even more from our enthusiastic guides. To the north, The Leas has two and a half miles of beach, cliff and grassland with soaring seabirds and, to the south, Whitburn Coastal Park provides coastal walks and family trails. **Note**: steep stairs (ground-floor CCTV shows views from the top for those unable to climb).

Exploring
- Climb the 76 steps to the top for spectacular views.
- Clamber on 'Neptune', our open-air play area boat.

Exploring — Explore the engine room's fantastic examples of engineering and technology.
— Discover the Victorian keeper's cottage, returned to its former glory.
— Become a pirate or princess using the dressing-up box.
— Take a bracing walk along the clifftop.

Eating and shopping: relish the seasonal menu, which uses homegrown and local produce. Enjoy the tea-room catering (variety of dietary needs satisfied). Invest in our guidebook as a souvenir of your visit.

You may also enjoy: contrasting intimate homes at Washington Old Hall and Ormesby Hall, and technology at Cragside.

Making the most of your day: enjoy hands-on family activities, foghorn demonstrations, open-air play area and trails, and the picnic area. Ask about our full programme of events and activities, including rock-pool rambles. Dogs on leads in grounds only.

Access for all: 🅿️ 🄳 ♿ 🚻 🎫 📷 🖼️ 🎧
Building ♿ Grounds ♿

Getting here: 88:NZ408641. On the north-east coast south of South Shields on the River Tyne.
Foot: South Tyneside Heritage Trail; 'Walking Works Wonders' local trail. **Cycle**: NCN1, adjacent to property. **Ferry**: Shields Ferry operated by Nexus, crossing River Tyne from North Shields to South Shields, crossing time 7 minutes, runs twice hourly in season.
Bus: Stagecoach North East E1/E2/E6 Sunderland ☒–South Shields (passes Tyne & Wear Metro South Shields). **Train**: East Boldon and South Shields (Tyne & Wear Metro) both 3 miles. **Road**: 2½ miles south of South Shields and 5 miles north of Sunderland on A183 Coast Road. **Parking**: free, 100 yards. Car park barrier locked at set times in evening (see notices at entrance).

Finding out more: 0191 529 3161 or souter@nationaltrust.org.uk

Souter Lighthouse and The Leas		M	T	W	T	F	S	S
13 Feb–28 Feb	11–4	M	T	W	T	·	S	S
6 Mar–7 Mar	11–4	·	·	·	·	·	S	S
13 Mar–31 Oct	11–5	M	T	W	T	·	S	S

Open Good Friday. Telephone for details of winter opening arrangements.

The iconic Souter Lighthouse, Tyne & Wear

The west front of the impressive, yet friendly, Wallington in Northumberland

Wallington

Cambo, Morpeth, Northumberland NE61 4AR

Map G4 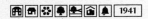 1941

Dating from 1688, Wallington was home to many generations of the Blackett and Trevelyan families, who all left their mark. The result is an impressive, yet friendly, house with a magnificent interior and fine collections. The remarkable Pre-Raphaelite central hall was decorated to look like an Italian courtyard and features a series of paintings of Northumbrian history by William Bell Scott. The formality of the house is offset by the tranquil beauty of the surrounding landscape – with lawns, lakes, parkland and woodland. The beautiful walled garden, with its varied plant collection and charming conservatory, is an enchanting must-see.

Exploring
- Relax, picnic or play in the grassy courtyard.
- Marvel at Lady Wilson's Cabinet of Curiosities.
- Look out for red squirrels at the wildlife hide.
- See our fascinating collection of dolls' houses.
- Stretch your legs with a walk on the extensive estate.
- Let off steam in the adventure playground.

Eating and shopping: browse for gifts and treats in the shop. Tuck into local produce in the Clocktower restaurant. Visit our farm shop for a tasty souvenir.

You may also enjoy: escaping to another 18th-century landscape garden at Gibside.

Making the most of your day: year-round programme of events for all ages, including open-air theatre, food and craft festival, guided walks, music, dancing and hands-on activities. Adventure playground and children's trail. Dogs on leads in grounds and walled garden only.

Access for all: [P] [D] [WC] [building icons] **Building** [icons] **Grounds** [icons]

Getting here: 81:NZ030843. **Bus**: very limited service only. Go North East 419 from Morpeth, Wednesday, Friday only (passing close Morpeth). **Road**: A1 north to Newcastle then 20 miles north west (A696, airport/Ponteland road), and turn off on B6342 to Cambo. A1 south to Morpeth (A192) then 12 miles west (B6343). **Parking**: free, 200 yards.

Finding out more: 01670 773967 (Infoline). 01670 773600 or wallington@nationaltrust.org.uk

Wallington		M	T	W	T	F	S	S
House								
1 Mar–31 Oct	11–5	·	·	·	·	·	S	S
1 Mar–31 Oct	1–5	M	·	W	T	F	·	·
Walled garden								
Open all year	10–7	M	T	W	T	F	S	S
Gift shop and restaurant								
1 Jan–12 Feb	10:30–4:30	·	·	W	T	F	S	S
13 Feb–28 May	10:30–5:30	M	·	W	T	F	S	S
29 May–26 Sep	10:30–5:30	M	T	W	T	F	S	S
27 Sep–31 Dec	10:30–4:30	M	·	W	T	F	S	S
Farm shop (outside turnstile)								
1 Jan–12 Feb	10:30–4	M	·	W	T	F	S	S
13 Feb–26 Sep	10:30–5	M	T	W	T	F	S	S
27 Sep–31 Dec	10:30–4	M	·	W	T	F	S	S

* House open daily, 11 to 5, during school holidays, except Tuesday (2 to 18 April, 29 May to 6 June, 24 July to 5 September and 23 to 31 October). Last admission one hour before closing. Booked tours available on Monday and Friday, 11 to 12:30. Garden closes 6 in March and October, and 4 from November to end December, or dusk if earlier. Gift shop and restaurant also open Tuesday during school holidays but closed Monday and Tuesday from 31 October. Farm shop also open Tuesday in December. Gift shop, restaurant and farm shop closed on certain days over Christmas.

The Drawing Room at Wallington, Northumberland

Washington Old Hall

The Avenue, Washington Village, Washington, Tyne & Wear NE38 7LE

Map ⑥ H5   1956

At the heart of historic Washington village this picturesque stone manor house and its gardens provide a tranquil oasis, reflecting gentry life following the turbulence of the English Civil War. The building incorporates parts of the original medieval home of George Washington's direct ancestors, and it is from here that the family took their surname of 'Washington'. Much-used and loved by local schools and community groups, including a hugely supportive Friends organisation, the Old Hall is also popular with couples wanting intimate wedding ceremonies and companies organising corporate events.
Note: steep steps in garden (new lift available).

Exploring
- Stroll through the Jacobean garden to the wildflower nut orchard.
- See authentic oak furniture in 17th-century room settings.
- Admire pictures showing the life and times of George Washington.
- Find out about the time when nine families lived here.
- Admire the vegetables – lovingly tended by staff, volunteers and schoolchildren.

Eating and shopping: refresh yourself in the tea-room, run by our Friends. Pick up a souvenir of your visit from our reception. Seek out bargains from our Friends' bric-a-brac display.

You may also enjoy: the intimate Pennyman family home at Ormesby Hall or a coastal contrast at Souter Lighthouse.

Washington Old Hall, Tyne & Wear, reflects gentry life following the English Civil War

Making the most of your day: picnic anywhere in the gardens, and enjoy a game of croquet. Seasonal garden trails, events and activities, including Fourth of July Independence Day ceremony. Dogs on leads in garden only.

Access for all: ⓟ🚻♿🎧📷🎁∴🅐
Building 🚶🦽♿ Grounds 🚶🦽➡️♿

Getting here: 88:NZ312566. In Washington village next to church on the hill. **Cycle**: NCN7, 1 mile. **Bus**: Go North East W2 from Washington Galleries bus station–Concord, connections from Gateshead and Newcastle. **Train**: Heworth (Tyne & Wear Metro) 4 miles; Newcastle 7 miles. **Road**: 7 miles south of Newcastle, 5 miles from The Angel of the North. From A1 exit junction 64 and follow brown signs. From A19 join A1231 and follow brown signs. From all other routes, join A1231 and follow brown signs. **Parking**: in small car park beside Old Hall, free. Unrestricted parking on The Avenue (coaches must park on The Avenue).

Finding out more: 0191 416 6879 or washingtonoldhall@nationaltrust.org.uk

Washington Old Hall		M	T	W	T	F	S	S
House								
14 Mar–31 Oct	11–5	M	T	W	·	·	·	S
Gardens								
14 Mar–31 Oct	10–5	M	T	W	·	·	·	S
Tea-room								
14 Mar–31 Oct	11–4	M	T	W	·	·	·	S

Open Good Friday and Easter Saturday.

Wales

A Georgian banqueting house, The Kymin, is still the perfect spot to enjoy a meal and fun with friends

Outdoors in Wales

With miles of rugged coastline, affording views of new-born seals or dolphins riding the waves, and some of the highest peaks in Britain, the National Trust cares for astonishingly dramatic and iconic landscapes in Wales.

A place of myth and legend

More than 60 miles of the amazingly geologically varied coastline of Pembrokeshire is looked after by the National Trust. Pembrokeshire is renowned for the many legends of Celtic saints and St David, the patron saint of Wales, was baptised at Porthclais and was inspired by this coastline.

Over the past few years there has been a major programme to restore traditional grazing by cattle, ponies and sheep on Pembrokeshire's coastal heaths and inland commons. This has resulted in spectacular improvements to the flora and fauna of these special places. Star of the Pembrokeshire coast is the chough, with more than 60 breeding pairs nesting here. In early autumn seal pups can be seen on a number of beaches, and the guillemots that nest on the cliffs at Stackpole are a sight not to be missed.

Explorers are very well catered for, with hundreds of miles of coastal and inland footpaths. Fine circular walks can be found at Stackpole (lakes and cliffs), Marloes, St David's Head, Dinas Island, near Fishguard, Little Milford and Lawrenny Woods on the secluded River Cleddau. Most areas of coast can be reached by one of the coastal shuttle buses – part of an excellent network (www. pembrokeshiregreenways.co.uk). Guides can be bought at St David's shop and most car parks.

Right: the headland at Pen Anglas on the Pembrokeshire coast

A Welsh jewel

The Llŷn Peninsula is a treasure. Multicoloured beach huts (available for hire) provide a vibrant backdrop to the long, sweeping beach at Llanbedrog.

In the sheltered bay at Porthor the sand famously whistles underfoot, due to the unique shape of the grains. The fishing village of Porthdinllaen is picture-postcard perfect. Adults can enjoy a drink at the pub on the beach, while children build sandcastles.

Mae'r wybodaeth sydd yn y llawlyfr hwn am feddiannau'r Ymddiriedolaeth Genedlaethol yng Nghymru ar gael yn Gymraeg o Swyddfa'r Ymddiriedolaeth Genedlaethol, Sgwar y Drindod, Llandudno LL30 2DE, ffôn 01492 860123.

Or for one of the best views in Wales stroll to the Coastguards' Hut on top of Mynydd Mawr, from where you can see Ireland on a clear day. Look out for the rare chough flying overhead, dolphins swimming in the bay and seals basking in the sun. A coastal path has recently been opened around the whole peninsula.

Further south, Llandanwg is not to be missed. Its beautiful, sandy beach has views across to the Llŷn Peninsula and a medieval church half buried in sand. Near Barmouth, Egryn has been continually inhabited for more than 5,000 years – footpaths around the estate take in Bronze Age and Neolithic remains. The medieval hall house and outbuildings are newly restored and are open to the public on certain days (please contact the Wales office for details).

Unbeatable majesty
In Snowdonia, a land of legend, majesty and breathtaking beauty, the National Trust cares for eleven of the peaks and many miles of footpaths. These include a wheelchair-accessible, riverside path in the village of Beddgelert, which leads to the grave of the faithful hound, Gelert, mistakenly killed by his master after saving the life of Prince Llewelyn's young baby.

At Craflwyn there are woodland walks meandering past waterfalls and streams. For the more adventurous, the Watkin path is a spectacular route from Hafod y Llan farm to the top of Snowdon. Along the route you will see where the National Trust is grazing Welsh black cattle to conserve the flora and fauna of this world-famous landscape. With the towering Tryfan, the dramatic Carneddau mountain range and the tranquil waters of Llyn Ogwen, there is always something new to explore among the peaks and valleys of Eryri.

Left:
enjoying a cycle ride at the Stackpole Estate, Pembrokeshire

Anglesey: walks and wildlife
The lagoon at Cemlyn is a haven for wildlife and nesting birds. During the winter it is a great place to come and watch the winter wildfowl, while in late spring a colony of Arctic and common terns returns to nest. The rocky sea cliffs here are among the oldest in Britain, with some being more than 1,000 million years old.

Fresh air and fossils
With its spectacular combination of sensational valleys and distinctive flat-topped summits, the Brecon Beacons is a haven to those in search of a place to unwind, relax and feast on fresh air – around 250,000 pairs of walking boots trudge along the slopes each year. Some of its most popular gems – Pen y Fan, Sugar Loaf, Skirrid and Henrhyd Falls – are looked after by the National Trust. Look out for ancient features as you explore this wonderful landscape. For example, fossils of some of the first land plants can be found on the Beacons. They appear as dark smudges in the rocks but once under a microscope the intricate cell structure can clearly be seen. These fossils are of *Gosslinga breconensis*, which emerged about 417 million years ago. During this time, the land we know now as the Brecon Beacons was being laid down in a vast shallow sea somewhere near the equator.

Waterfalls and industrial heritage

The picturesque beauty spot of Henrhyd Falls on the Nant Llech boasts the impressive title of the highest waterfall in South Wales. It is only one of a series of beautiful waterfalls produced by the narrow, steep-sided gorges at the head of the Neath and Tawe rivers.

National Nature Reserve

The Dinefwr Historic Parkland is now designated a National Nature Reserve. Why not enjoy a historic walk with stunning views towards the castle, house and along the Tywi Valley? You may even see some resident fallow deer or some of the stunning White Park cattle that have been in Dinefwr for more than a thousand years. Another view which is hard to beat is the one from Paxton's Tower. This folly was built in 1811 by Sir William Paxton as a memorial to Lord Nelson.

Of Gower's most iconic beauty spots, the largest and possibly most famous is the spectacular Rhossili. The five-mile-long, sweeping bay is on the very tip of the Gower Peninsula, and to add to the drama, the wooden ribs of the 'Helvetia' (shipwrecked in 1887) protrude from the sand at low tide. There are fabulous walks along the clifftop towards the prominent island and headland of Worm's Head and the old coastguard station. The area has a highly valued and wide range of important habitats and species. Among its gems are the black bog ant, chough, rare marsh fritillary butterfly and brown hare.

Unspoilt charm and iconic beauty

The coast of Ceredigion has an unspoilt and intimate charm, and is nationally important as a conservation resource. The gently rolling coastline, with occasional striking rocky outcrops and steep wooded river valleys which run inland, is a valuable example of man's long-term relationship with his environment. Ceredigion has been spared much of the damage caused elsewhere by agricultural intensification, and the relative lack of development in the county has preserved areas of timeless peace and beauty which would be irreplaceable should they ever be lost.

My favourite area

Mwnt is a small horseshoe-shaped bay with steep cliffs that run south from the beach. Mwnt is historically important as the site of an important 13th-century battle against the invading Flemish, which is still reflected in many place names in the area. The site was also on the route of early Celtic Christian pilgrimage, and bodies were sent from here by boat to be buried on the Island of Twenty Thousand Saints, Bardsey (or Ynys Enlli). This is probably the best place in Ceredigion for sighting a bottlenose dolphin.

A few miles north lies Penbryn – a golden beach which is a safe and popular venue for all the family. The wooded Hoffnant Valley, also known locally as Cwm Lladron (the Robber's Valley), was a well-known destination for illicit cargoes in the 18th century. Goods such as wine from Bordeaux, spirits and salt from Wicklow, tobacco and tea were brought in in considerable quantities by French and Irish vessels.

Travel north to Llangrannog for a spectacular walk to Ynys Lochtyn – a striking and conspicuous topographical feature. Experience the lofty elevation of the Iron Age fort above the towering cliffs, which jut out westward into the sea, creating an inspiring landscape. It is a popular venue with holiday strollers and serious walkers, and an important bird-nesting site.

Cwmtudu, another tiny cove famed for smuggling, is also well worth a visit. You can walk for an unbroken period of several hours in an atmosphere of semi-natural beauty and tranquillity along the coastline to New Quay. The area is rich in legend and the resonance of a distinctive Welsh cultural identity.

Paul Boland
Property Manager for Ceredigion

Aberconwy House

Castle Street, Conwy LL32 8AY

Map ④ E2 1934

This is the only medieval merchant's house in Conwy to have survived the turbulent history of the walled town over nearly six centuries. Furnished rooms and an audio-visual presentation show daily life from different periods in its history. **Note**: nearest WC 50 yards on quay.

Exploring
- Explore how people lived from Tudor to Victorian times.
- Follow the stories of centuries from room to room.
- Discover what the walls are made of.
- Let the introductory video bring old Conwy to life.

Eating and shopping: stock up on souvenirs in the shop. Conwy is full of great places to eat.

Making the most of your day: live music in the house. Ghost stories. Children's trail. Easter and Hallowe'en activities. Lace demonstrations.

Access for all: ⬚ 𝄞 Building ⬚

Getting here: 115:SH781777. At junction of Castle Street and High Street. **Cycle**: NCN5. **Bus**: from surrounding areas. **Train**: Conwy 300 yards. **Parking**: no onsite parking.

Finding out more: 01492 592246 or aberconwyhouse@nationaltrust.org.uk

Aberconwy House		M	T	W	T	F	S	S
House								
13 Feb–21 Feb	11–5	M	·	W	T	F	S	S
13 Mar–31 Oct	11–5	M	·	W	T	F	S	S
Shop								
2 Jan–12 Mar	11–5	·	·	W	T	F	S	S
13 Mar–31 Oct	10–5:30	M	T	W	T	F	S	S
3 Nov–31 Dec	11–5	M	T	W	T	F	S	S

House: open Tuesdays July and August. Shop: opens 11 on Sundays; closed 25 and 26 December.

Aberdeunant

Taliaris, Llandeilo, Carmarthenshire SA19 6DL

Map ④ E8 1996

Traditional Carmarthenshire farmhouse in an unspoilt setting. **Note**: administered on the National Trust's behalf by a resident tenant. No WC.

Getting here: 146:SN672308. Full details are sent on booking.

Finding out more: 01558 650177 (Dolaucothi Gold Mines) or aberdeunant@nationaltrust.org.uk

---

Aberdeunant

Admission by guided tour and appointment only. Tours take place April to September: first Saturday and Sunday of each month, 12 to 5. Telephone Dolaucothi Gold Mines to book. Last booking taken at 5 on Thursday prior to opening.

Aberdulais Falls

Aberdulais, near Neath,
Neath & Port Talbot SA10 8EU

Map ④ E9  1980

Set in a steep gorge, this property demonstrates the power of water and its impact on industry. Our film, *Reflections on Tin*, shows its 400-year-old history, from 1584, including a visit by the famous artist Turner. A small water-powered tin works was the last industry. Today the waters of the River Dulais are used to make Aberdulais Falls self-sufficient in environmentally friendly energy, with its waterwheel – the largest in Europe generating electricity. Lifts enable visitors to access the upper levels for excellent views of the falls. **Note**: waterwheel and turbine subject to water levels and maintenance.

Exploring
- 'The Tin Exhibition' – about adults and children who worked here.
- See *Reflections on Tin* at the Turbine House cinema.
- Watch the waterwheel generating electricity.
- Wonder at the spectacular waterfall– best when it rains!

Eating and shopping: don't miss the National Trust shop. Enjoy Welsh cakes and bara brith in the tea-room. Experience our famous welcome and lemon drizzle cake.

You may also enjoy: Dinefwr Park and Castle.

Making the most of your day: activity days, demonstrations and family quiz trails. Painting and archaeology days. Dogs on leads only.

Access for all: ♿♿♿♿♿♿♿♿♿
Stable and Tin Exhibition ♿♿♿♿
Turbine House ♿♿♿♿♿♿
Grounds ♿♿♿➡♿

Getting here: 170:SS772995. **Foot**: via Neath–Aberdulais Canal footpath. **Cycle**: NCN47 passes property. Access near B&Q Neath to Neath Canal towpath and Aberdulais Canal Basin. **Bus**: Veolia X63 Swansea–Brecon, Silverline X55 Swansea–Aberdare, First 154 from Neath, 158 Banwen and X58 from Neath bust staion. **Train**: Neath 3 miles. **Road**: on A4109, 3 miles north east of Neath. 4 miles from M4 exit 43 at Llandarcy, take A465 signposted Vale of Neath. **Sat Nav**: Follow brown signs, not Sat Nav. **Parking**: outside and on opposite side of road.

Finding out more: 01639 636674 or aberdulais@nationaltrust.org.uk

Aberdulais Falls		M	T	W	T	F	S	S
9 Jan–7 Mar	11–4						S	S
15 Feb–19 Feb	11–4	M	T	W	T	F		
13 Mar–31 Oct	10–5	M	T	W	T	F	S	S
5 Nov–19 Dec	11–4					F	S	S

Open Bank Holidays.

Bodnant Garden

Tal-y-Cafn, Colwyn Bay, Conwy LL28 5RE

Map ④ F2

Marvel at plants from all over the world grown from seed and cuttings collected over a century ago on plant-hunting expeditions. Created by five generations of one family, this 32-hectare (80-acre) garden is superbly located, with spectactular views across Snowdonia. With expansive lawns and intimate corners, grand ponds and impressive terraces, a steep wooded valley and stream, as well as awe-inspiring plant collections, there are continually changing glorious displays of colour. Paths throughout allow visitors to explore, discover and delight in the garden's beauty – enjoy the clean, fresh fragrances of nature. **Note**: garden and tea-rooms managed on behalf of National Trust by Hon. Michael McLaren.

Exploring
- Splendid displays of daffodils, magnolias and camellias in early spring.
- 180-feet long laburnum arch flowers in late May.
- Discover the magical Dell, with towering 200-year-old trees.
- See the tallest coastal redwood in the UK.
- Learn the history of our heliochronometer, and how it works.
- Superb summer colours melt into an explosion of autumnal tints.

Eating and shopping: sample the delicious home-baked cakes in the tea-rooms. Pavilion tea-room: try locally produced wine and beer. Bodnant-raised plants in the garden centre (not National Trust). Find bespoke gifts in the craft shops (not National Trust).

You may also enjoy: the Victorian walled garden at Penrhyn Castle.

Making the most of your day: varied programme of family events, open-air theatre,

Bodnant Garden, Conwy: the laburnum arch

evening plays. Family trails and Explorer Backpacks. Waymarked route for wheelchairs and pushchairs.

Access for all: 🅿️♿🚻♿📷🅰️📶
Grounds 🅰️🅰️➡️♿

Getting here: 115/116:SH801723. **Bus**: Arriva 25, from Llandudno (passing Llandudno Junction ➤). **Train**: Tal-y-Cafn unmanned station, 2 miles walk along main road, no footpath. Alternatively Llandudno Junction ➤ then bus. **Road**: 8 miles south of Llandudno and Colwyn Bay off A470, entrance 1½ miles along the Eglwysbach road. Signposted from A55, exit 19. **Parking**: 150 yards from garden entrance. Tight turning circle for coach access. Limited disabled parking.

Finding out more: 01492 650460 or bodnantgarden@nationaltrust.org.uk

Bodnant Garden			M	T	W	T	F	S	S
Garden									
20 Feb–31 Oct	10–5		M	T	W	T	F	S	S
1 Nov–21 Nov	10–4		M	T	W	T	F	S	S
Pavilion tea-room									
20 Feb–31 Oct	10–5		M	T	W	T	F	S	S
1 Nov–22 Dec	10–4		M	T	W	T	F	S	S
Magnolia tea-room									
27 Mar–31 Oct	11–4:30		M	T	W	T	F	S	S

Map ④ F2

Set in 89 hectares (220 acres) of gardens and parkland, this Grade I listed 17th-century house has spectacular views towards Conwy Castle and Snowdonia.

The house and gardens are already accessible to the public as a hotel and welcome guests to stay, to dine in the restaurants and to have afternoon tea (booking strongly advised). All paying guests to the hotel are welcome to walk in the garden and park.

Finding out more: 01492 584466; 01492 582519 (fax) or info@bodysgallen.com; www.bodysgallen.com

Chirk Castle

Chirk, Wrexham LL14 5AF

Map ④ G3 🏰❄️♣🎭🏠🔔🍽️ 1981

'**Fantastic location and magical castle. The colours in the garden were beautiful. The children loved the dungeon and dressing up.**'
Pam and Roland Thompson, Crewe

Completed in 1310, Chirk is the last Welsh castle from the reign of Edward I still lived in today. Features from its 700 years include the medieval tower and dungeon, 17th-century Long Gallery, grand 18th-century state apartments, servants' hall and historic laundry. The award-winning gardens contain clipped yews, herbaceous borders, shrub and rock gardens. A terrace with stunning views looks out over the Cheshire and Salop plains. The parkland provides a habitat for rare invertebrates, wild flowers and contains many mature trees and also some splendid wrought-iron gates, made in 1719 by the Davies brothers. **Note**: major re-servicing work underway. Some rooms may be empty and items removed from display.

Exploring	
	– Explore the stark medieval Adam Tower and dungeon.
	– Be awestruck by over 400 years of elegant family living.
	– Try on costumes and play games in our family rooms.
	– Discover 'green' technologies in the re-servicing exhibition.
	– Encounter Berkshire pigs, ancient trees and bluebells in the woods.
	– Savour peace and quiet in the award-winning gardens.

Eating and shopping: be tempted by local fresh food from the farm shop. Sample seasonal menus in the tea-room. Treat yourself to homemade cakes and delicious afternoon tea. Browse the gift shop, plant sales and second-hand books.

You may also enjoy: the magnificent architecture and gardens of Powis Castle.

Making the most of your day: snowdrop walks in the garden in February. Family activity rooms, trails and Tracker Packs. Family Thursdays in summer holidays. Living history re-enactments, craft fair. Warden-led walks. Christmas weekends. Dogs on leads and only in car park and on estate walks.

Access for all: [icons]
State rooms [icons] Adam Tower [icons]
Gardens [icons]

Getting here: 126:SJ275388. **Foot**: permitted footpaths from Chirk and Offa's Dyke Path, open April–September. Entrance and exit drives during season 1½ miles to Visitor Centre and castle. 1½ miles from Llangollen Canal–moor near Chirk Tunnel. **Bus**: Arriva 2/A Wrexham–Oswestry. **Train**: Chirk station ¼ mile to gates, 1½ miles to castle. **Road**: entrance 1 mile off A5, 2 miles west of Chirk village; 7 miles south of Wrexham, 5 miles from Llangollen, signposted off A483.

Chirk Castle, Wrexham: still lived in today

Parking: free, 50 yards to Visitor Centre, 200 yards to castle. Short, steep hill from Visitor Centre to castle and garden. One-way system on driveway, follow signs to entrance.

Finding out more: 01691 777701 or chirkcastle@nationaltrust.org.uk

Chirk Castle		M	T	W	T	F	S	S
Garden, tower, shops and tea-rooms								
6 Feb–14 Feb	10–4						S	S
17 Feb–21 Feb	10–4			W	T	F	S	S
27 Feb–28 Feb	10–4						S	S
3 Mar–27 Jun	10–5			W	T	F	S	S
1 Jul–29 Aug	10–5		T	W	T	F	S	S
1 Sep–31 Oct	10–5			W	T	F	S	S
6 Nov–19 Dec	10–4						S	S
State rooms*								
3 Mar–27 Jun	11–5			W	T	F	S	S
1 Jul–29 Aug	11–5		T	W	T	F	S	S
1 Sep–31 Oct	11–5			W	T	F	S	S

February, March and October closes 4. Open Bank Holiday Mondays. Last admission to garden and tower one hour before closing. *State rooms by guided tour only 11 to 12, free-flow 12 to closing.

Cilgerran Castle

near Cardigan, Pembrokeshire SA43 2SF

Map ④ C7 1938

This striking 13th-century ruined castle is perched overlooking the spectacular Teifi Gorge and has inspired many artists, including Turner. **Note**: in the guardianship of Cadw – Welsh Assembly Government's historic enviroment service. Dogs on leads allowed.

Getting here: 145:SN195431. On rock above left bank of the Teifi, 3 miles south east of Cardigan, 1½ miles east of A478.

Finding out more: 01443 336104 or cilgerrancastle@nationaltrust.org.uk

Cilgerran Castle		M	T	W	T	F	S	S
1 Jan–31 Mar	10–4	M	T	W	T	F	S	S
1 Apr–31 Oct	10–5	M	T	W	T	F	S	S
1 Nov–31 Dec	10–4	M	T	W	T	F	S	S

Colby Woodland Garden

near Amroth, Pembrokeshire SA67 8PP

Map ④ C8  1980

Set in a tranquil and secluded valley, this glorious, informal woodland garden with a fascinating industrial past is always bursting with colour and wildlife. Whatever the season, there's something to delight. Spring brings carpets of bluebells and an abundance of camellias, rhododendrons and azaleas. Enjoy shady woodland walks, the wildflower meadow and colourful walled garden in summer, followed by the marvellous colours of autumn. Explore the meadow with its meandering stream and abundance of dragonflies, butterflies and other insects, and discover more about the garden's wildlife and its history in the new Bothy exhibition. **Note**: house is not open.

Exploring
- Wander the woodland walks and spot the carved benches.
- Discover the tallest *Cryptomeria japonica* tree in the UK.
- Climb up to the summerhouse and glimpse the sea.
- Relax in the walled garden with its stunning gazebo.
- Explore the wider Colby Estate, with its network of footpaths.
- Walk down to the beach at Amroth (¾ mile).

Eating and shopping: buy a souvenir of your visit at the Trust shop. Visit the Bothy tea-room for a freshly prepared treat. Browse in the gallery, full of local art and crafts. Visit Summerhill Farm Shop for award-winning lamb and beef.

You may also enjoy: Tudor Merchant's House and the Stackpole Estate.

Making the most of your day: full events programme, including Easter trails, bat walks, family fun days, children's quiz, wildlife events, summer holiday activities, guided walks and lunches with the Head Gardener. Dogs on leads in woodland garden only.

Access for all: 🅿️♿🚻🏛️🔊🎧🅅🎫📷🅐
Grounds 🏔️➡️♿

Colby Woodland Garden, Pembrokeshire

Getting here: 158:SN155080. **Foot**: from beach via public footpath in Amroth (beside Amroth Arms). **Bus**: Silcox 350/1 from Tenby (passing Kilgetty ≋). **Train**: Kilgetty 2½ miles. **Road**: 1½ miles inland from Amroth beside Carmarthen Bay. Follow brown signs from A477 Tenby–Carmarthen road or off coast road at Amroth Castle caravan park. **Parking**: free, 50 yards. Contact property for route map for coaches and cars.

Finding out more: 01834 811885 or colby@nationaltrust.org.uk

Colby Woodland Garden		M	T	W	T	F	S	S
Woodland garden and shop								
13 Feb–31 Oct	10–5	M	T	W	T	F	S	S
Tea-room								
27 Mar–31 Oct	10–5	M	T	W	T	F	S	S
Walled garden and gallery								
27 Mar–31 Oct	11–5	M	T	W	T	F	S	S

Conwy Suspension Bridge

Conwy LL32 8LD

Map ④ E2   1965

See how trade and travel brought Conwy to life and discover how a husband and wife kept Thomas Telford's bridge open every day of the year, whatever the weather. **Note**: no WC.

Exploring
- Marvel at Thomas Telford's graceful bridge design.
- Enjoy the stunning views over the Conwy estuary.
- Visit the beautifully restored tiny toll house.

Eating and shopping: bring your own picnic to enjoy on the grassed area.

Making the most of your day: guided talks on Thomas Telford. Dogs allowed.

Access for all: 🅿 Building 🏔 Grounds 🅰

Getting here: 115:SH785775. 100 yards from town centre, adjacent to Conwy Castle. **Cycle**: NCN5. **Bus**: Arriva buses from surrounding areas. **Train**: Conwy ¼ mile; Llandudno Junction ½ mile. **Parking**: no onsite parking.

Finding out more: 01492 573282 or conwybridge@nationaltrust.org.uk

Conwy Suspension Bridge		M	T	W	T	F	S	S
13 Mar–31 Oct	11–5	M	T	W	T	F	S	S

Dinefwr Park and Castle

Llandeilo, Carmarthenshire SA19 6RT

Map ④ E8      1990

A magical land of power and influence for more than 2,000 years, Dinefwr Park and Castle is an iconic place in the history of Wales. Two forts are evidence of a dominant Roman presence. The powerful Lord Rhys held court at Dinefwr and influenced decisions in Wales. The visionaries, George and Cecil Rice designed the superb 18th-century landscape that you see today. The 'hands-on' Newton House gives visitors an atmospheric *circa* 1912 experience. Exhibitions on the first floor tell Dinefwr's story and inspire visitors to explore the castle and park.

Exploring
- Experience Dinefwr's magic on five walks through the park.
- Get thrilled by views from the top of the castle.
- Let off steam in the children's play area.
- Get close to the rare and historic White Park cattle.
- Help with servants' tasks in the brushing room.
- Listen to the servants chatting about their daily work.

Eating and shopping: buy local Welsh produce in the atmospheric shop. Eat our local produce in the Billiard Room tea-room. Taste local wines and beers overlooking the croquet lawn. Stay at one of our two holiday cottages.

You may also enjoy: the Roman Dolaucothi Gold Mines.

Making the most of your day: behind-the-scenes and deer park tours (charge including members). Regular school holiday and family activities. Varied programme of events. Waymarked walks around the park. Dogs on leads in outer park only.

Access for all: 🐕♿🚾👨‍👩‍👧👁️👓
Building 🪜♿⬆️👓 Grounds ♿

Getting here: 159:SN625225. **Bus**: from surrounding areas to Llandeilo, then 1 mile. **Train**: Llandeilo 1 mile. **Road**: on west outskirts of Llandeilo A40(T); from Swansea take M4 to Pont Abraham, then A48(T) to Cross Hands and A476 to Llandeilo; entrance by police station. **Sat Nav**: problems, do not use. **Parking**: 50 yards. Narrow access.

Finding out more: 01558 824512 or dinefwr@nationaltrust.org.uk

Dinefwr Park and Castle, Carmarthenshire

Dinefwr Park and Castle		M	T	W	T	F	S	S
Dinefwr Park and Castle								
14 Feb–30 Jun	11–5	M	T	W	T	F	S	S
1 Jul–31 Aug	11–6	M	T	W	T	F	S	S
1 Sep–31 Oct	11–5	M	T	W	T	F	S	S
5 Nov–19 Dec	11–4	·	·	·	·	F	S	S
Shop								
14 Feb–31 Oct	12:30–5	M	T	W	T	F	S	S
5 Nov–19 Dec	12:30–4	·	·	·	·	F	S	S
Tea-rooms								
16 Jan–30 Jun	11–5	M	T	W	T	F	S	S
1 Jul–31 Aug	11–6	M	T	W	T	F	S	S
1 Sep–31 Oct	11–5	M	T	W	T	F	S	S
1 Nov–19 Dec	11–4	M	T	W	T	F	S	S

Boardwalk and play area close 3:30 during autumn and winter, 4:30 at other times, except July and August, 5:30.

Dolaucothi Gold Mines

Pumsaint, Llanwrda, Carmarthenshire SA19 8US

Map ④ E7   🏛️🚻♿ 1941

'**Seeing the Roman pick marks left on the walls of underground adits and panning for real gold, made our day**.'
Leonie Tidd, Kent

These unique gold mines are set amid wooded hillsides overlooking the beautiful Cothi Valley. 2,000 years ago, the powerful Romans left behind a glimpse of gold-mining methods. The harsh mining environment continued in the 19th and 20th centuries, ending in 1938. Guided tours take you back to experience the conditions of the Roman, Victorian and 1930s underground workings. See and hear the 1930s mine and mine machinery. Have a go at gold panning and take the opportunity to experience the frustrations of searching for real gold. **Note**: underground tours involve steep slopes, stout footwear essential.

Exploring   — Experience the thrill of an underground guided tour.
     — Sift the panning troughs and keep what you find.
     — Get to grips with gold in the gold exhibition.

Exploring — Enjoy the walks around this beautiful upland estate.

Eating and shopping: buy rare Welsh gold jewellery in the shop. Taste local cooking in our mine tea-room.

You may also enjoy: Dinefwr Park and Castle, as well as Llanerchaeron.

Making the most of your day: frequent underground tours (charge including members, please note younger children may not be carried). Regular schools holiday and family activities. Self-guided walks around the estate. Dogs on leads only.

Access for all: 🔲🔲🔲🔲 Building 🔲🔲

Getting here: 146:SN662403. **Bus**: Morris 289 from Lampeter. **Train**: Llanwrda, 8 miles. **Road**: between Lampeter and Llanwrda on A482. **Parking**: free. Overflow car park opposite main entrance.

Finding out more: 01558 650177 or dolaucothi@nationaltrust.org.uk

Dolaucothi Gold Mines, Carmarthenshire

Dolaucothi Gold Mines		M	T	W	T	F	S	S
Dolaucothi Gold Mines, shop and tea-room								
13 Mar–30 Jun	11–5	M	T	W	T	F	S	S
1 Jul–31 Aug	10–6	M	T	W	T	F	S	S
1 Sep–31 Oct	11–5	M	T	W	T	F	S	S
Christmas shop								
3 Nov–19 Dec	11–4			W	T	F	S	S

Pumsaint Information Centre and estate walks open all year. Underground tours last one hour approximately (helmets with lights provided). Smaller children will only be allowed on tours at the discretion of staff (telephone for advice). Groups can be booked out of hours/season.

Erddig

Wrexham LL13 0YT

Map ④ H3   🔲🔲✝🔲🔲🔲🔲 1973

Widely acclaimed as one of Britain's finest historic houses, Erddig is a fascinating yet unpretentious early 18th-century country house reflecting the upstairs downstairs life of a gentry family over 250 years. The extensive downstairs area contains Erddig's unique collection of servants' portraits, while the upstairs rooms are an amazing treasure trove of fine furniture, textiles and wallpapers. Outside, an impressive range of outbuildings includes stables, smithy, joiners' shop and sawmill. The setting is a superb 18th-century formal garden and romantic landscape park – which are the starting points for walks, bicycle and carriage rides through the estate.

Exploring
- Gain a fascinating insight into life below stairs.
- Discover the unique house collection of furnishings and paintings.
- Enjoy the outstanding formal gardens and country estate.
- Look out for the themed country walking routes.
- Take a horse and carriage ride around the grounds.
- Hire a bicycle: tracks criss-cross the estate.

Eating and shopping: pick up gifts in the shop. Take home a selection of peat-free plants. Enjoy refreshments in the tea-room and restaurant. Try a bottle of our own cider.

Erddig, Wrexham: one of Britain's finest historic houses

You may also enjoy: Chirk Castle, as well as Powis Castle and Garden.

Making the most of your day: full events programme, including open-air theatre, festivals, craft fairs, Christmas markets, family fun days and exhibitions. Guided walks, tree trails and discovery tours. Dogs on leads in country park only.

Access for all: [icons]
Building [icons] Exhibition Room [icons]
Grounds [icons]

Getting here: 117:SJ326482. 2 miles from Wrexham. **Bus**: Arriva 2 from Wrexham, alight Felin Puleston, 1 mile walk through Erddig Country Park. **Train**: Wrexham Central 2½ miles, Wrexham General 3½ miles via Erddig Road and footpath. **Road**: 2 miles south of Wrexham. Signposted A525 Whitchurch road. A483 exit 3.

Parking: free, 200 yards. Accessible drop-off point. Parking for three coaches.

Finding out more: 01978 355314 or erddig@nationaltrust.org.uk

Erddig		M	T	W	T	F	S	S
House								
13 Mar–31 Oct	12–5	M	T	W	·	·	S	S
3 Jul–31 Aug	12–5	M	T	W	T	·	S	S
6 Nov–19 Dec	12–4	·	·	·	·	·	S	S
Garden, restaurant and shop								
13 Feb–7 Mar	11–4	M	T	W	T	F	S	S
13 Mar–31 Oct	11–6	M	T	W	·	·	S	S
3 Jul–31 Aug	11–6	M	T	W	T	·	S	S
6 Nov–19 Dec	11–4	·	·	·	·	·	S	S
26 Dec–31 Dec	11–4	M	T	W	T	F	S	S

6 and 7 March: guided conservation tours. 13 to 31 March and 2 to 31 October: house closes 4. 6 November to 19 December: kitchens and outbuildings of house only open. Garden, restaurant and shop: closed 22 to 26 February and 1 to 5 March. 2 to 31 October: closes 5. Guided tours of 'downstairs' at 11:30, free-flow 12 to closing. Restaurant and shop close one hour earlier 13 March–31 October. Open Good Friday. Last admission one hour before closing. July and August: access to house by guided tour only on Thursday. Tapestry and small Chinese Rooms open on Wednesday and Saturday only (by request) no electric light; for close study of pictures and textiles avoid dull days.

The Kymin

The Round House, The Kymin, Monmouth,
Monmouthshire NP25 3SF

Map ④ H8  1902

Picnic spot amongst woods and pleasure
grounds, visited by Nelson. Spectacular views
across Wales. Attractive Georgian banqueting
house and temple.

Getting here: 162:SO528125. 2 miles east of
Monmouth and signposted off A4136.

Finding out more: 01600 719241 or
kymin@nationaltrust.org.uk

The Kymin		M	T	W	T	F	S	S
Round House								
27 Mar–25 Oct	11–4	M	·	·	·	·	S	S
Grounds								
Open all year	7–9	M	T	W	T	F	S	S

Open Good Friday. Round House: last entry 3:45 (croquet
set and other games for hire when open).

Llanerchaeron

Ciliau Aeron, near Aberaeron,
Ceredigion SA48 8DG

Map ④ D6 1989

**'Relaxed, informal – gives a feel for how life
was like for gentry and the staff. When can
we move in?'**
The Long family, Vale of Glamorgan

This rare example of a self-sufficient
18th-century Welsh minor gentry estate has
survived virtually unaltered. The villa, designed
in the 1790s, is the most complete example
of the early work of John Nash. It has its own
service courtyard with dairy, laundry, brewery
and salting house, and walled kitchen gardens
(with all its produce for sale when in season).

The kitchen at Llanerchaeron, Ceredigion

The pleasure grounds and ornamental lake and
parkland provide peaceful walks. The Home
Farm complex has an impressive range of
traditional, atmospheric outbuildings and is a
working organic farm with Welsh Black cattle,
Llanwenog sheep and rare Welsh pigs.

Exploring
- Discover the main residence
  and staff quarters.
- Wander through the pleasure
  grounds and ornamental lake.
- Explore the working
  walled gardens.
- Learn about the farm – the
  buildings and inhabitants.
- Don't miss the special events
  days throughout the year.
- Experience self-sufficiency
  at its best.

Eating and shopping: catering outlet serves
light meals and cakes; picnic area. Reception
area has shop selling local beer, jams and cider.
Property farm and garden produce is on sale in
reception. Cards, gifts, books and locally made
produce available.

You may also enjoy: Dolaucothi Gold Mines
and Dinefwr Park and Castle.

Making the most of your day: seasonal
farming and gardening activities, plus family
days throughout the year. Dogs on leads in
parkland only.

Access for all: 🅿️🅳♿🅱️🛋️🎦👓∴
Building 🦽🏛️♿ Grounds ♿

Getting here: 146:SN480602. **Foot**: 2½ miles foot/cycle track from Aberaeron to property along old railway track. **Bus**: Arriva/First X40 Aberystwyth ☒–Carmarthen ☒, alight New Inn Forge, ½ mile. **Road**: 2½ miles east of Aberaeron off A482. **Parking**: free, 50 yards.

Finding out more: 01545 570200 or llanerchaeron@nationaltrust.org.uk

Llanerchaeron		M	T	W	T	F	S	S
House*, farm and garden								
15 Feb–19 Feb	11–5	M	T	W	T	F	·	·
24 Feb–18 Mar	11–5	·	·	W	T	·	·	·
24 Mar–11 Apr	11–5	M	T	W	T	F	S	S
14 Apr–18 Jul	11–5	·	·	W	T	F	S	S
20 Jul–5 Sep	11–5	·	T	W	T	F	S	S
8 Sep–31 Oct	11–5	·	·	W	T	F	S	S
Farm and garden only								
14 Jul–5 Sep	11–5	M	·	·	·	·	·	·
Christmas Fair								
4 Dec–5 Dec	11–4	·	·	·	·	·	S	S
House and shop (Christmas)								
8 Dec–12 Dec	11–3	·	·	W	T	F	S	S

*House open 11:30 to 4. Open Bank Holiday Mondays. 24 February to 11 March: Tuesday and Wednesday, specialist talk, 11:30; guided tour, 2. 31 May to 1 June: Urdd Eisteddfod (charge including members – members receive discount). **Closed Sunday 6 June**. 16 June to 7 July: open Wednesday evenings 5:30 to 8.

Penrhyn Castle

Bangor, Gwynedd LL57 4HN

Map ④ E2   🏠 ✝ ⬆T ✿ ☂ [1951]

This enormous 19th-century neo-Norman castle sits between Snowdonia and the Menai Strait. It is crammed with fascinating items, such as a one-ton slate bed made for Queen Victoria, elaborate carvings, plasterwork and mock-Norman furniture, in addition it has an outstanding collection of paintings. The restored kitchens are a delight and the stable block houses a fascinating industrial railway museum, a model railway museum and a superb dolls' museum. The 24.3 hectares (60 acres) of grounds include parkland, an exotic tree and shrub collection as well as a Victorian walled garden.

Exploring
- Wander through lavishly furnished state rooms.
- Enjoy one the finest art collections in Wales.
- Explore the warren of workrooms in the servants' area.

The enormous Penrhyn Castle, Gwynedd, is full of fascinating collections

Exploring
- Discover the castle's history in the stable-block exhibitions.
- Explore our open parkland and glorious gardens.
- Marvel at the stunning views over mountains and sea.

Eating and shopping: enjoy mouth-watering food made from local produce. Get a drink or ice-cream at the kiosk. Choose from a selection of local goods in the shop.

You may also enjoy: Plas Newydd, Aberconwy House, Conwy Suspension Bridge, Plas yn Rhiw and Ty Mawr Wybrnant.

Access for all: 🅿️♿️♿️♿️👁️📷💻🎧👁️🅰️
Building ♿️♿️♿️♿️ **Grounds** ♿️♿️

Getting here: 115:SH602720. **Cycle**: NCN5, 1¼ miles. **Bus**: Arriva 5/5X Caernarfon–Llandudno, Padarn 76 from Bangor, both to castle driveway. **Train**: Bangor 3 miles. **Road**: 1 mile east of Bangor, at Llandygai on A5122. Signposted from junction 11 of A55 and A5. **Parking**: free, 500 yards.

Finding out more: 01248 371337 (Infoline). 01248 353084 or penrhyncastle@nationaltrust.org.uk

Penrhyn Castle		M	T	W	T	F	S	S
Stable block								
13 Feb–21 Feb	11–4	M	·	W	T	F	S	S
Castle								
24 Mar–30 Jun	12–5	M	·	W	T	F	S	S
1 Jul–30 Aug	11–5	M	·	W	T	F	S	S
1 Sep–31 Oct	12–5	M	·	W	T	F	S	S
Stable block, shop and museums								
24 Mar–31 Oct	11–5	M	·	W	T	F	S	S

Grounds and tea-room: as castle but open one hour earlier. Victorian kitchen: as castle but last admission 4:45. Last audio tour 4. *Half-term opening, stable block only, adult £2.

The lamp room, Penrhyn Castle, Gwynedd

Plas Newydd Country House and Gardens

Llanfairpwll, Anglesey LL61 6DQ

Map ④ D2
 1976

Set amidst breathtakingly beautiful scenery on the Menai Strait, this elegant house was redesigned by James Wyatt in the 18th century. The 1930s restyled interior is famous for its Rex Whistler association, containing his largest painting and exhibition. A military museum contains relics of the 1st Marquess of Anglesey, who commanded the cavalry at the Battle of Waterloo. There is a fine spring garden and Australasian arboretum, with an understorey of shrubs and wild flowers, a summer terrace and massed hydrangeas, which give autumn colour. A woodland walk gives access to a marine walk beside the Menai Strait.

Exploring
- Relax in the home of Lord and Lady Anglesey.
- Study excellent portraits and landscapes in glorious state rooms.
- Discover crafted timber shelters, bird hides and Menai Boat Trips.
- Find the rhododendron garden – spectacular in May and June.
- Children: enjoy the puzzles and activities of the learning room.
- Learn about the heritage and links of the Conway Centre.

Eating and shopping: Whistlers at Plas Newydd serves food and drinks. Our gift shop includes great ideas and inspiring offers. Coffee shop in the house has a second-hand bookshop.

You may also enjoy: Penrhyn Castle, Aberconwy House, Swtan and Plas yn Rhiw.

The elegant Plas Newydd, Anglesey

Making the most of your day: take a stroll through the rhododendron garden and Marine Walk – don't miss the adventure playground! Or why not join us weekends in December for our Christmas Craft and Food fair. Dogs and picnics in the car park only.

Access for all: 🅿️ 🅳 ♿ 🚻 🍴 📷 📖 ⋯ 🅰️
Building ♿ ♿ ♿ Grounds ♿

Getting here: 114/115:SH521696. **Cycle**: NCN8, ¼ mile. **Bus**: Arriva 42 Bangor–Llangefni (passing Bangor ≋ and close Llanfairpwll ≋). **Train**: Llanfairpwll 1¾ miles. **Road**: 2 miles south west of Llanfairpwll A55 junctions 7 and 8a, or A4080 to Brynsiencyn; turn off A5 at west end of Britannia Bridge. **Parking**: free, 400 yards.

Finding out more: 01248 715272 (Infoline). 01248 714795 or plasnewydd@nationaltrust.org.uk

Plas Newydd		M	T	W	T	F	S	S
Shop, tea-room and garden								
6 Mar–14 Mar	11–5:30	·	·	·	·	·	S	S
House and garden*								
20 Mar–3 Nov	12–5	M	T	W	·	·	S	S
Shop and tea-room								
20 Mar–3 Nov	11–5:30	M	T	W	·	·	S	S
27 May–3 Sep	11–5:30	M	T	W	T	F	S	S
6 Nov–19 Dec	11–4	·	·	·	·	·	S	S

*Garden: open 11 to 5:30. Coffee shop: open Saturday to Wednesday, 11 to 5. Free special interest tour 11:15 daily (subject to availability, 12 maximum). Open Good Friday. Coffee shop and bookshop: as house but open 11:30. Rhododendron garden: open early April to early June, 11 to 5:30. Last admission 4:30. **Please note house is accessible to manual wheelchairs only.**

Plas yn Rhiw

Rhiw, Pwllheli, Gwynedd LL53 8AB

Map ④ C4   🏰 ✿ 🏖️ 🏠 │1952│

The house was rescued from neglect and lovingly restored by the three Keating sisters, who bought it in 1938. The views from the grounds and gardens across Cardigan Bay are among the most spectacular in Britain. The house is 16th-century with Georgian additions, and the garden contains many beautiful flowering trees and shrubs, with beds framed by box hedges and grass paths. It is stunning whatever the season.

Exploring
- Find out how the Keating sisters lived in the 1930s.
- Explore the meandering paths and enjoy the stunning views.
- Discover the two-seater garden privy!
- See for yourself what inspired Honora Keating's delightful landscape paintings.

Eating and shopping: enjoy a hot or cold drink from the shop. Plant sales and souvenirs from the car park shop.

You may also enjoy: on the grand scale – Penrhyn Castle, Bangor.

Making the most of your day: plant sales. Guided tours by arrangement. Easter egg hunt. Dogs on leads and only on the woodland walk below car park.

Access for all: 🅳 🚻 📷 📖 🎨 ⋯
Building ♿ ♿ Grounds ♿ ♿

Getting here: 123:SH237282. **Bus**: Arriva 17B, Pwllheli–Aberdaron (passing Pwllheli ≋) to Plas yn Rhiw driveway. **Train**: Pwllheli 10 miles. **Road**: 12 miles south west of Pwllheli. Follow signs to Plas yn Rhiw. B4413 to Aberdaron (drive gates at bottom Rhiw Hill). **Parking**: small car park, 80 yards. Not suitable for large vehicles. Narrow lanes.

Finding out more: 01758 780219 or plasynrhiw@nationaltrust.org.uk

Plas yn Rhiw		M	T	W	T	F	S	S
25 Mar–2 May	12–5	·	·	·	**T**	**F**	**S**	**S**
5 May–30 Aug	12–5	**M**	·	**W**	**T**	**F**	**S**	**S**
2 Sep–30 Sep	12–5	**M**	·	·	**T**	**F**	**S**	**S**
1 Oct–31 Oct	12–4	·	·	·	**T**	**F**	**S**	**S**

Open Bank Holidays. Garden and snowdrop wood open occasionally at weekends in January and February.

Powis Castle and Garden

Welshpool, Powys SY21 8RF

Map (4) G5 [icons] 1952

Discovering the world-famous Powis Garden, Powys

The world-famous garden, overhung with clipped yews, shelters rare and tender plants. Laid out under the influence of Italian and French styles, it retains its original lead statues and an orangery on the terraces. High on a rock above the terraces, the castle, originally built *circa* 1200, began life as a medieval fortress. Remodelled and embellished over more than 400 years, it reflects the changing needs and ambitions of the Herbert family – each generation adding to the magnificent collection of paintings, sculpture, furniture and tapestries. A superb collection of treasures from India is displayed in the Clive Museum. **Note**: visitors (including members) need a ticket from visitor reception.

Exploring
– Relax in the sumptuous 10.5-hectare (26-acre) garden.
– Delight in the grandeur of the Elizabethan long gallery.
– Be amazed by the exquisite collection of Indian treasures.
– Go behind the scenes with castle and garden tours.
– Travel back in time with our themed events.

Eating and shopping: locally sourced seasonal produce served in the restaurant. Try our bara brith, made with our own secret recipe. Take home your own Powis plant, propagated in our nursery. Gifts and products from Wales on sale in the shop.

You may also enjoy: another medieval castle, Chirk Castle in Wrexham.

Making the most of your day: children's activities during school holidays, tours and lectures about the castle and garden during autumn and winter. Weekly talks and tours about caring for the collection.

Access for all: [icons]
Building [icon] Grounds [icons]

Getting here: 126:SJ216064. **Foot**: 1-mile walk from Park Lane, off Broad Street in Welshpool. **Bus**: Tanant Valley D71 Oswestry–Welshpool; X75 Shrewsbury–Llanidloes. On both alight High Street, 1 mile. **Train**: Welshpool 1¼ miles from town on footpath. **Road**: 1 mile south of Welshpool; pedestrian access from High Street (A490); vehicle route signed from main road to Newtown (A483); enter by first drive gate on right. **Parking**: free. Telephone for advice on coach parking.

Finding out more: 01938 551944 (Infoline). 01938 551929 or powiscastle@nationaltrust.org.uk

Powis Castle and Garden		M	T	W	T	F	S	S
Castle and Clive Museum*								
1 Mar–29 Mar	1–4	M	·	·	T	F	S	S
1 Apr–30 Aug	1–5	M	·	·	T	F	S	S
2 Sep–31 Oct	1–5	M	·	·	T	F	S	S
Garden, restaurant and shop*								
1 Mar–29 Mar	11–4:30	M	·	·	T	F	S	S
1 Apr–30 Aug	11–5:30	M	·	·	T	F	S	S
2 Sep–31 Oct	11–5:30	M	·	·	T	F	S	S
6 Nov–28 Nov	11–3:30	·	·	·	·	·	S	S
Restaurant and shop								
4 Dec–19 Dec	11–3:30	·	·	·	·	·	S	S

Last admission to castle 45 minutes before closing. *Also open Wednesdays for local school holidays and throughout July and August. Earlier closing in October.

Rhossili Visitor Centre and Shop

Coastguard Cottages, Rhossili, Gower, Swansea SA3 1PR

Map (4) D9    1933

Skirting the National Nature Reserve of the South Gower Coast, overlooking Rhossili Bay, the large National Trust shop boasts a range of Trust and local gifts, as well as providing local information. It is a great place to begin touring this interesting area. The Visitor Centre above displays regular exhibitions. **Note:** nearest WC at Rhossili car park (not National Trust).

Looking down on Rhossili Bay, Swansea

Exploring — Don't miss the regularly updated exhibitions at the Visitor Centre.
— Pick up a National Trust walks leaflet and go exploring.

Eating and shopping: try our tenant farmer's salt-marsh lamb (01792 391421).

Making the most of your day: events held throughout the year. Throughout July and August take part in our 'Take It Away' campaign (ask staff how you can help).

Access for all: 🚻♿🅿📷🍴📁
Building 🚶 Grounds 🚶

Getting here: 159:SS418883. **Bus**: Veolia 118 from Swansea–South Gower. **Road**: south-west tip of Gower Peninsula, approached from Swansea via A4118 and then B4247.
Parking: 50 yards (not National Trust), charge including members.

Finding out more: 01792 390707 or rhossili.shop@nationaltrust.org.uk

Rhossili Visitor Centre		M	T	W	T	F	S	S
8 Jan–28 Feb	11–4	·	·	·	·	F	S	S
1 Mar–14 Mar	10:30–4:30	M	T	W	T	F	S	S
15 Mar–31 Oct	10:30–5	M	T	W	T	F	S	S
3 Nov–19 Dec	11–4	·	·	W	T	F	S	S

17 March to 31 October: Closes at 6 weekends during school holidays. 17 October to 2 November: closes 4:30.

St David's Visitor Centre and Shop

Captain's House, High Street, St David's, Pembrokeshire SA62 6SD

Map (4) A8   1974

Opposite The Cross in the centre of St David's, Wales's smallest historic city, the Visitor Centre and Shop is open all year. Using new interactive technology the Centre offers a complete guide to the National Trust in Pembrokeshire – its properties, beaches and walks. **Note:** no WC.

Visit

Exploring – Take a virtual tour of Pembrokeshire.
– Plan where to visit next.
– Discover more about the coast and countryside in our care.

Eating and shopping: comprehensive range of merchandise. Treat yourself to a locally made gift.

Making the most of your day: events throughout the year (ask staff for information).

Access for all: Building

Getting here: 115:SM753253. In the centre of St David's. **Foot**: Pembrokeshire Coast Path within 1 mile. **Bus**: Richards 411 from Haverfordwest ⮧. Celtic Coaster and Puffin Shuttle during main holiday season. **Parking**: no onsite parking.

Finding out more: 01437 720385 or stdavids@nationaltrust.org.uk

St David's Visitor Centre		M	T	W	T	F	S	S
2 Jan–13 Mar	10–4	**M**	**T**	**W**	**T**	**F**	**S**	·
15 Mar–31 Dec	10–5:30	**M**	**T**	**W**	**T**	**F**	**S**	**S**

Closes at 4 on Sunday. Closed 25 and 26 December.

Segontium

Caernarfon, Gwynedd

Map ④ D2

Fort built to defend the Roman Empire against rebellious tribes. **Note**: in the guardianship of Cadw – Welsh Assembly Government's historic enviroment service. Museum not National Trust.

Getting here: 115:SH485624. On Beddgelert road, A4085, on south-east outskirts of Caernarfon, 500 yards from town centre.

Finding out more: 01286 675625 or segontium@nationaltrust.org.uk

Segontium

Museum (not National Trust) open Tuesday to Sunday, 12:30 to 4:30 (open Bank Holiday Mondays). Closed end of December.

Skenfrith Castle

Skenfrith, near Abergavenny, Monmouthshire NP7 8UH

Map ④ H8

Remains of early 13th-century castle, built beside the River Monnow to command one of the main routes from England. **Note**: in the guardianship of Cadw – Welsh Assembly Government's historic enviroment service.

Getting here: 161:SO456203. 6 miles north west of Monmouth, 12 miles north east of Abergavenny, on north side of the Ross road (B4521).

Finding out more: 01874 625515 or skenfrithcastle@nationaltrust.org.uk

Skenfrith Castle		M	T	W	T	F	S	S
Open all year	Dawn–dusk	**M**	**T**	**W**	**T**	**F**	**S**	**S**

Stackpole Estate

Old Home Farm Yard, Stackpole, near Pembroke, Pembrokeshire SA71 5DQ

Map ④ B9

'**Gorgeous location – best bit was seeing an otter – fantastic.**'
S. Bishop, Liverton, Devon

Once owned by the Cawdor family, who transformed much of the natural landscape, this beautiful and varied stretch of coastline is famous for its award-winning sandy beaches, wooded valleys, dramatic cliffs and lily ponds. The Bosherston Lakes and Stackpole Warren are part of Stackpole National Nature Reserve, managed in partnership with the Countryside Council for Wales. Wildlife includes otters, herons, wintering wildfowl and dragonfly, as well as breeding seabirds and choughs.

Also on the estate is Stackpole for Outdoor Learning, a residential eco-centre for schools and families, and the Stackpole Centre, a multipurpose venue offering group accommodation.

Exploring
— Relax on excellent sandy beaches at Broadhaven South and Barafundle.
— Enjoy the spectacular clifftop scenery – look out for choughs.
— Visit Bosherston Lily Ponds, home to otters, wildfowl and dragonflies.
— Walk miles of footpaths – linking lakes, woods, cliffs and beaches.
— See where Stackpole Court once stood and admire the views.
— Coarse fishing – permits available. Conditions apply.

Eating and shopping: the Boathouse café at Stackpole Quay serves local, seasonal food. Mencap Walled Garden produces and sells plants and vegetables. Maps, books, drinks and confectionery available at Stackpole Centre. Stay in one of our holiday cottages at Stackpole Quay.

You may also enjoy: Colby Woodland Garden and Tudor Merchant's House.

Making the most of your day: theatre and music concerts at the Stackpole Centre. Guided walks. Dogs under control on the estate.

Access for all: 🅿♿🚻♿📖
Building ♿ Grounds ♿➡

Getting here: 158:SR992958. 6 miles south of Pembroke. **Foot**: via Pembrokeshire Coast Path. **Bus**: Silcox 388 Pembroke ≋–Angle. **Train**: Pembroke 5 miles. **Road**: B4319 from Pembroke to Stackpole and Bosherston (various entry points on to estate). **Parking**: at Stackpole Quay, Broadhaven South and Bosherston Lily Ponds (charge applies). Access via narrow lanes with passing places.

Finding out more: 01646 661359 or stackpole@nationaltrust.org.uk

Stackpole Estate	M	T	W	T	F	S	S
Open all year	**M**	**T**	**W**	**T**	**F**	**S**	**S**

Tudor Merchant's House

Quay Hill, Tenby, Pembrokeshire SA70 7BX

Map ④ C9   🏠 1937

Step back 500 years and discover how the Tudor merchant and his family would have lived in this fascinating three-storey house, situated close to the harbour within the historic walled town of Tenby. Features of the house include a fine 'Flemish' round chimney and the original scarfed roof trusses. **Note**: no WC.

One of the sandy beaches on the Stackpole Estate, Pembrokeshire

Wales

Exploring
- Ask the staff about how the Tudors lived.
- Don't miss the latrine tower or the Flemish chimney.
- Small herb garden open, weather permitting.

Eating and shopping: house information and Tudor replica items for sale.

Making the most of your day: children can try on Tudor costume and play with replica toys. See the staff wearing Tudor costume on Bank Holidays. Easter and Hallowe'en family events. Children's quiz.

Access for all: 🖼️🖥️🎫👓 Building 👨‍🦽

Getting here: 158:SN135004. In the centre of Tenby off Tudor Square. **Foot**: Pembrokeshire Coast Path within ¼ mile. **Bus**: from surrounding areas. **Train**: Tenby ½ mile. **Parking**: limited parking on town streets apart from July and August, when parking is in pay and display car parks only or via park and ride.

Finding out more: 01834 842279 or tudormerchantshouse@nationaltrust.org.uk

Tudor Merchant's House		M	T	W	T	F	S	S
22 Mar–31 Oct	11–5	M	T	W	T	F	·	S

Open Saturdays on Bank Holiday weekends, 11 to 5.

Tŷ Mawr Wybrnant

Penmachno, Betws-y-Coed, Conwy LL25 0HJ

Map ④ E3   🏠🖼️ 1951

Explore centuries of Welsh living in this traditional stone-built upland farmhouse. Set in the heart of the beautiful Conwy Valley, Tŷ Mawr was the birthplace of Bishop William Morgan, the first translator of the Bible into Welsh. Walks lead from the house through woodland and traditionally managed landscape.

Exploring
- View the impressive Bible collection in nearly 100 languages.

Exploring
- Discover how people survived without electricity or other creature comforts.
- New: explore the woodland animal trail.

Eating and shopping: bring your own picnic and relax by the stream.

Making the most of your day: introductory talks. Woodland walks. Exhibition room. Families will enjoy the children's art packs, family activity sheet and woodland animal trail. Dogs under close control.

Access for all: 🅿️♿🚻♿
Building 👨‍🦽👨‍🦽 Grounds 👨‍🦽

Getting here: 115:SH770524. **Bus**: Jones 64 Llanrwst–Cwm Penmachno (passing Betws-y-Coed 🚂), alight Penmachno, then 2-mile walk. **Train**: Pont-y-pant 1½ miles. **Road**: at the head of the Wybrnant Valley. From A5 3 miles south of Betws-y-Coed, take B4406 to Penmachno. House is 2½ miles north west of Penmachno by forest road. **Parking**: free, 500 yards. No access for coaches (33-seater minibuses welcome). Telephone to arrange access.

Finding out more: 01690 760213 or tymawrwybrnant@nationaltrust.org.uk

Tŷ Mawr Wybrnant		M	T	W	T	F	S	S
25 Mar–31 Oct	12–5	·	·	·	T	F	S	S

Open Bank Holiday Mondays.

Tŷ Mawr Wybrnant, Conwy: traditional cottage

Northern Ireland

How would you measure up against 'The Organ' at the Giant's Causeway? This dramatic World Heritage Site is rich in local history and legend

Outdoors
in Northern Ireland

With more than 120 miles of coastline and 40 square miles of scenic countryside in its care, the National Trust in Northern Ireland offers enticing open spaces, exhilarating challenges and serenely tranquil getaways.

The diversity of landscape, the ever-changing vistas and mild climate make it a wonderful place to explore on foot, by bicycle or even by canoe! Paddle through stunning scenery, or why not try one of our wide range of walks? There is an enormous choice for all levels, whether you are a serious rambler or someone who simply wants to take a stroll.

Be inspired by the north coast

The stunning shoreline along the North Antrim coast is dotted with some of the region's best-loved visitor attractions. Explore the iconic Giant's Causeway, discover the historic ruins of Dunseverick Castle, or stroll along the majestic sweeping arc of White Park Bay. Brave the elements and cross Carrick-a-Rede rope bridge, or marvel at the bustling seabird colonies at

Right:
building sandcastles at White Park Bay, County Antrim

Larrybane, with its views beyond to Rathlin Island and the west coast of Scotland.

There are few better places to experience this diverse coastline than the distinctive headland of Fair Head, which rises 190 metres and gives dramatic views of nearby Murlough Bay. On unspoilt Rathlin Island inspirational views across to the Scottish Islands and Mull of Kintyre can be seen from the waymarked path through Ballyconagan.

Other coastal treasures include the tiny village of Glenoe near Larne, with its spectacular waterfall, while the footpath along Skernaghan Point on the northern tip of Islandmagee leads to open headland, cliffs, coves and beautiful beaches. Along the geologically rich coastline to the north-east lies the delightful seaside village of Cushendun and the ecologically important raised blanket peat bog at Cushleake Mountain.

A haven for wildlife

The County Down coastline has much to offer the walker and naturalist, with rocky shore and heathland at Ballymacormick Point and wildfowl, wading birds and gulls at Orlock Point.

Strangford Lough, Britain's largest sea lough and one of Europe's key wildlife habitats, offers bracing coastal walks among delicate wild flowers and butterflies. There are also rock pools bursting with marine life and opportunities for spectacular birdwatching. Visitors to Ballyquintin Farm, on the Ards Peninsula, can enjoy stunning views of Strangford Lough and learn how this critical site is managed for wildlife and conservation.

Further south, the fragile 6,000-year-old sand dunes of Murlough National Nature Reserve, near Newcastle, is an extraordinarily beautiful dune landscape with a network of paths and boardwalks – perfect for walking.

Wildness and beauty

Why not escape to some of Northern Ireland's best off-the-beaten-track experiences? Within fifteen minutes of Belfast you can find yourself meandering along the Lagan river bank at Minnowburn, climbing Cregagh Glen in the Castlereagh Hills, exploring the woodland paths of Collin Glen or tramping the upland heath to the summit of Divis Mountain for spectacular views over the city.

To the west of the region, idyllic County Fermanagh boasts a kaleidoscope of tranquil landscapes to discover – including the woodland and wetlands of Crom on the serene shores of Lough Erne.

Or for a real walk on the wild side, the Trust's Mourne Mountain paths allow hikers to enjoy the dramatic scenery of Northern Ireland's highest mountain, the majestic Slieve Donard, as well as neighbouring Slieve Commedagh.

Paddle power

The National Trust has links to Northern Ireland's five new canoe trails, all offering exciting stretches of water with public access for canoeists. Each trail allows you to explore a different part of Northern Ireland's interesting countryside – from the picturesque islands in Strangford Lough to the calming countryside along the Blackwater River, and the lakeland paradise on Lough Erne. With an abundance of wildlife to see you simply have to paddle. For more information on the canoe trails visit www.canoeni.com

Below:
the wild North Antrim coastline at Murlough Bay, with Fair Head in the distance

Outdoors in Northern Ireland

Further information
Euro notes are accepted by the Trust's Northern Ireland properties.

Under the National Trust Ulster Gardens Scheme, a number of private gardens are generously opened to the public in order to provide income for Trust gardens in Northern Ireland. For the 2010 programme telephone 028 9751 0721.

To find out what is happening in Northern Ireland this year, see our 2010 *Events Guide*.

My favourite flower

Orchids have always been a particular favourite of mine, and I am not alone, for the beauty of the flowers and the variety of brilliant colours have won them numerous fans.

It can take many years for a germinated orchid seed to form a tuber and push its way above ground, and many more before it begins to flower. Coupled with a requirement for some helpful soil fungi, and in many cases very specific insect pollinators, the humble orchid needs a very stable environment in which to thrive. Luckily these conditions occur at many National Trust properties and you are rewarded with a summer of orchids, from early purple in spring to Irish lady's tresses in autumn.

It was Charles Darwin who noted how the morphological form of the orchid's flower matched the feeding apparatus of its pollinating insect. Darwin would certainly not have been disappointed had he visited some National Trust properties today, as he could expect to find frog, bee and butterfly orchids in abundance.

In early summer, White Park Bay has a fabulous flush of early purple orchids on the dunes, and with a bit of searching you may find the more inconspicuous frog orchid. In July, Portstewart dunes host an abundance of pyramidal orchids and the rarer bee orchid in a few scattered locations. Then during the latter half of the summer the common spotted orchid, which varies in colour from almost pure white to a deep lilac, can be seen at many Trust sites, including Ballyconaghan, Ballymacormick and Castle Coole.

Above:
delicate early purple orchids

Working from an office close to the wildlife-friendly managed paddock at Rowallane Garden, I have the pleasure of seeing an abundance of orchids during the summer, including the striking greater butterfly orchid in June, with its slender stem and delicate flowers.

Many of our rarer orchids are protected and need our assistance to ensure they flourish. In addition to the visual beauty, the presence of orchids can give us an idea of the general health of our environments, and the National Trust strives to manage these unique sites for all to enjoy. Come and see these beautiful wild flowers for yourself.

Maurice Turley
Biodiversity Officer
for Northern Ireland

Ardress House

64 Ardress Road, Annaghmore, Portadown,
County Armagh BT62 1SQ

Map (7) D7 ⊞ ⊡ ⊠ ⊠ | 1959 |

This charming 17th-century farmhouse,
elegantly remodelled in Georgian times, offers
fun and relaxation for all the family. Set in
40 hectares (100 acres) of countryside there
are apple orchards, charming woodland and
riverside walks. The atmosphere of a working
farmyard has been rekindled with the return
of small animals.

Exploring	– Enjoy 'The Ladies' Mile' walk through trees and shrubs.
	– Children will love feeding the chickens in the farmyard.
	– Attractive garden, with scenic woodland and riverside walks.
	– Elegant Neo-classical drawing room, with plasterwork by Michael Stapleton.

Eating and shopping: drinks and ice-cream
available. Picnic in the attractive garden and
charming woodlands.

Making the most of your day: see miniature
Shetland ponies, pygmy goats, soay sheep,
ducks and chickens. Events include Country
Capers and Ghostly Hallowe'en. Have fun
in the children's play area. Dogs on leads in
garden only.

The Argory, County Armagh: Neo-classical masterpiece

Access for all: 🚾 Building 👪👪 Grounds 👪➡️

Getting here: H418640. **Bus**: Ulsterbus 67
Portadown–Kesquin Bridge (passing close NIR
Portadown) to within ¼ mile. **Train**: Portadown
7 miles. **Parking**: free, 10 yards.

Finding out more: 028 8778 4753 or
ardress@nationaltrust.org.uk

Ardress House		M	T	W	T	F	S	S
20 Feb–21 Feb	12–4	·	·	·	·	·	S	S
13 Mar–27 Jun	1–5	·	·	·	·	·	S	S
2 Apr–11 Apr	1–5	M	T	W	T	F	S	S
3 Jul–29 Aug	1–5	·	·	·	T	F	S	S
4 Sep–26 Sep	1–5	·	·	·	·	·	S	S
28 Oct–31 Oct	12–5	·	·	·	T	F	S	S

Admission by guided tour (last admission one hour before
closing). Open Bank Holiday Mondays and all other public
holidays in Northern Ireland **including 17 March**. Grounds
('The Lady's Mile') open daily all year, dawn to dusk.

The Argory

144 Derrycaw Road, Moy, Dungannon,
County Armagh BT71 6NA

Map (7) C7 ⊞ ⊞ ⊠ ⊠ 🔔 🍷 | 1979 |

Built in the 1820s, this handsome Irish gentry
house is surrounded by its 130-hectare (320-
acre) wooded riverside estate. The former home
of the MacGeough Bond family, a tour of this
Neo-classical masterpiece reveals it is unchanged
since 1900 – the eclectic interior still evoking the
family's tastes and interests. Outside there are
sweeping vistas, superb spring bulbs, scenic
walks and fascinating courtyard displays.
A second-hand bookshop, adventure playground
and Lady Ada's award-winning tea-room provide
retreats for children and adults alike.

Exploring	– Garden, woodland and riverside walks with wonderful sweeping views.
	– Snowdrop walks and superb spring bulbs.
	– Fascinating courtyard displays and sundial in the rose garden.
	– Children's adventure playground and environmental sculpture trail.

Exploring — Mansion is a treasure trove of Victorian and Edwardian interests.
— Four generations of MacGeough Bond family lived in the mansion.

Eating and shopping: enjoy afternoon tea in Lady Ada's tea-room. Light lunches and snacks available. Browse the gift shop and second-hand bookshop.

You may also enjoy: Ardress House – a charming 17th-century farmhouse just four miles from The Argory.

Making the most of your day: lively programme of events – craft fairs, poultry fairs, musical events. The mansion is a particular delight at Christmas, when it comes alive with music. Dogs on leads and only in grounds and garden.

Access for all: 🅳♿🚻📷📶 Grounds ♿➡️

Getting here: H418640. **Cycle**: NCN95, 7 miles. **Bus**: Ulsterbus 67 Portadown–Dungannon (both pass close Portadown 🚉), alight Charlemont, 2½-mile walk. **Road**: 4 miles from Charlemont, 3 miles from M1, exit 13 or 14 (signposted). Coaches must use exit 13; weight restrictions at Bond's Bridge.
Parking: 100 yards.

Finding out more: 028 8778 4753 or argory@nationaltrust.org.uk

The Argory		M	T	W	T	F	S	S
Grounds								
1 Jan–30 Apr	10–5	M	T	W	T	F	S	S
1 May–30 Sep	10–6	M	T	W	T	F	S	S
1 Oct–31 Dec	10–5	M	T	W	T	F	S	S
House								
13 Mar–28 Jun	11–5	M	·	·	T	F	S	S
2 Apr–11 Apr	11–5	M	T	W	T	F	S	S
1 Jul–31 Aug	11–5	M	T	W	T	F	S	S
2 Sep–30 Sep	11–5	M	·	·	T	F	S	S
1 Oct–31 Oct	11–4	M	·	·	T	F	S	S

Admission to house by guided tour (last admission one hour before closing). Open Bank Holiday Mondays and all other public holidays in Northern Ireland, **including 17 March**. Tea-room, shop and second-hand bookshop open as house, but weekends only 1 September to 31 October.

Carrick-a-Rede

119a Whitepark Road, Ballintoy, County Antrim BT54 6LS

Map ⑦ D3 🏕️🏠 1967

Take the exhilarating rope bridge to Carrick-a-Rede island and enjoy a truly clifftop experience. This 30-metre deep and 20-metre wide chasm is traversed by a rope bridge traditionally erected by salmon fishermen. Visitors bold enough to cross to the rocky island are rewarded with fantastic views. **Note**: maximum of eight people on bridge at once. Suitable clothing and footwear recommended.

Exploring — Fantastic birdwatching and unrivalled coastal scenery.
— Uninterrupted views of Rathlin and the Scottish islands.
— Site of Special Scientific Interest: unique geology, flora and fauna.
— Children's discovery trail for eight to fourteen year olds.

Eating and shopping: new National Trust tea-room facilities now open. Delicious array of light lunches and snacks available.

Making the most of your day: guided tours (by prior arrangement). Breathtaking coast path experience – part of the Causeway Coast Way from Portstewart to Ballycastle and the Ulster Way. Dogs on leads (not permitted to cross bridge).

Challenge yourself at Carrick-a-Rede, County Antrim

Access for all: 🅿️♿🚻♿📷
Grounds ♿♿➡️♿

Getting here: D062450. **Foot**: on North Antrim Coastal Path and road, 7 miles from Giant's Causeway, ½ mile from Ballintoy village and 1½ miles from Ballintoy Church on Harbour Road. **Cycle**: NCN93, 5 miles. **Bus**: Ulsterbus 172, 177 from Coleraine, Ulsterbus 252 is a circular route from Belfast via the Antrim Glens. Both stop at Carrick-a-Rede. **Road**: on B15, 7 miles east of Bushmills, 5 miles west of Ballycastle. Giant's Causeway 7 miles. **Parking**: free.

Finding out more: 028 2076 9839 or carrickarede@nationaltrust.org.uk

Carrick-a-Rede		M	T	W	T	F	S	S
27 Feb–23 May	10–6	M	T	W	T	F	S	S
24 May–31 Aug	10–7	M	T	W	T	F	S	S
1 Sep–31 Oct	10–6	M	T	W	T	F	S	S
1 Nov–31 Dec	10:30–3:30	M	T	W	T	F	S	S

Last entry to rope bridge 45 minutes before closing. Car park and North Antrim Coastal Path open all year. Bridge open weather permitting.

Castle Coole

Enniskillen, County Fermanagh BT74 6JY

Map ⑦ A7  1951

'**Wonderful guided tour of basement, with stories of the people who lived and worked here, brought the house to life.**'
Clara Keenan, Belfast

Experience the stately grandeur of this stunning 18th-century mansion set in a beautiful wooded landscape park – ideal for family walks. Castle Coole is one of Ireland's finest Neo-classical houses, the sumptuous Regency interior, and the State Bedroom prepared for George IV, provides a rare treat for visitors, allowing them to glimpse what life was like in the home of the Earls of Belmore. Discover the story of the people who lived and worked below stairs as you explore the splendid suite of servants' rooms and service quarters of this magnificent property.

Exploring
– Tour one of Ireland's finest Neo-classical houses.
– Take a guided tour of the historic basement.
– Enjoy a walk in the historic landscape and woodlands.
– Explore the Grand Yard and servants' quarters.
– Discover the wildlife that live in and around Lough Coole.
– Cycle along part of the Castle to Castle Cycle Trail.

Eating and shopping: relax and unwind over lunch in the Tallow tea-room. Souvenirs and gifts can be purchased in the shop.

You may also enjoy: Castle Coole is within driving distance of Florence Court and Crom.

Making the most of your day: enjoy a walk around the recently restored Lake Walk, with breathtaking views and the opportunity to catch a glimpse of the tremendous variety of wildlife. Musical events throughout the year. Dogs on leads in grounds only.

Access for all: 🅿️🅿️🚻♿📷
Building ♿♿♿ **Grounds** ♿➡️

Getting here: H378788. **Cycle**: NCN91. **Bus**: Ulsterbus 95, Enniskillen–Clones (connections from Belfast). **Road**: 1½ miles south east of Enniskillen on Belfast–Enniskillen road (A4). **Parking**: walkers' car park. Main car park, 150 yards.

Finding out more: 028 6632 2690 or castlecoole@nationaltrust.org.uk

Castle Coole		M	T	W	T	F	S	S
Grounds								
1 Jan–28 Feb	10–4	M	T	W	T	F	S	S
1 Mar–31 Oct	10–7	M	T	W	T	F	S	S
1 Nov–31 Dec	10–4	M	T	W	T	F	S	S
House								
13 Mar–30 May	11–5	·	·	·	·	·	S	S
2 Apr–11 Apr	11–5	M	T	W	T	F	S	S
1 Jun–30 Jun	11–5	M	T	W	·	F	S	S
1 Jul–31 Aug	11–5	M	T	W	T	F	S	S
4 Sep–30 Sep	11–5	·	·	·	·	·	S	S

House: admission by guided tour (last tour one hour before closing). Open Bank Holiday Mondays and all other public holidays in Northern Ireland **including 17 March**. Tea-room and shop open as house.

Castle Ward

Strangford, Downpatrick,
County Down BT30 7LS

Map (7) F7

'One couple's discord creates
a shared heritage.'
Alexander Family, Markethill, County Armagh

Castle Ward will take you on a journey of
discovery. The 18th-century eccentric house
with two distinctly different styles, classical and
Gothic, will entice you to explore further. This
truly beautiful 332-hectare (820-acre) walled
demesne with walking trails, exotic garden,
stunning vistas and picturesque farmyard,
will unlock your imagination through family
history, leisure pursuits, events and industrial
heritage. A children's pastimes centre and
laundry are a short walk from the house in the
stableyard, alongside a gift shop, second-hand
bookshop and tea-room.

Exploring
- Challenge yourself to walking fourteen miles on atmospheric woodland trails.
- Meet 'the judge' during a living history house tour.
- Learn about Irish industrial heritage by visiting the corn mill.
- Stay in a luxury shoreside holiday cottage.
- Attempt the 'mega slide' in the adventure playground.
- Picnic in the exotic Victorian sunken garden.

Eating and shopping: shop for local produce in
the delightful gift shop. Pick up a bargain book
from the second-hand bookshop. Organic
soup, sandwiches and traybakes from the
stableyard tea-room. Stay overnight in the
caravan park for more shopping time.

You may also enjoy: discovering exotic
rhododendron species and viewing hand-fired
pottery at nearby Rowallane Garden.

Making the most of your day: extensive
programme of events throughout the year.
Pirate's Picnic, Pumpkinfest, toy trade, book
fair and Santa's house. Guided tours and
children's activity sheets. Dogs on leads in
grounds only.

Access for all: [icons]
Building [icons] Grounds [icons]

Getting here: J752494. **Foot**: on Lecale Way.
Ferry: from Portaferry. **Bus**: Ulsterbus 16E
Downpatrick–Strangford, with connections
from Belfast (passing close Belfast Great
Victoria Street ≣); bus stop at gates.
Ulsterbus Lecale Rambler (Saturday, Sunday
only) in summer. **Road**: 7 miles north east of
Downpatrick, 1½ miles west of Strangford
village on A25, on south shore of Strangford
Lough, entrance by Ballyculter Lodge.
Sat Nav: is incorrect, once on the
Strangford Road follow signs for Castle Ward
only. **Parking**: free, 250 yards.

Finding out more: 028 4488 1204 or
castleward@nationaltrust.org.uk

Castle Ward		M	T	W	T	F	S	S
Grounds								
1 Jan–31 Mar	10–4	M	T	W	T	F	S	S
1 Apr–30 Sep	10–8	M	T	W	T	F	S	S
1 Oct–31 Dec	10–4	M	T	W	T	F	S	S
House								
13 Mar–31 Oct	11–5	M	T	W	T	F	S	S

Admission by guided tour (timed tickets only). Last house
tour one hour before closing. Open Bank Holiday Mondays
and all other public holidays in Northern Ireland **including
17 March**. Corn mill operates on Sundays during open
season. Tea-room and shop open as house. Bookshop:
open daily April to September, 1 to 5. For Strangford Lough
Wildlife Centre opening times telephone 028 4488 1411.

The classical side of Castle Ward, County Down

Crom

Upper Lough Erne, Newtownbutler,
County Fermanagh BT92 8AP

Map (7) A8  1987

Escape to this breathtaking 810-hectare
(2,000-acre) demesne, set amid the romantic
and tranquil landscape of Upper Lough Erne.
One of Ireland's most important nature
conservation areas, Crom's ancient woodland
and picturesque islands are home to many rare
species. Stay for longer in our holiday cottages
or campsite. **Note**: the 19th-century castle is
private and not open to the public.

Exploring
— Hire a boat and explore
  the islands.
— Have a go at coarse angling or
  pike fishing.
— Enjoy woodland walks and
  nature trails.
— Stay at one of our holiday
  cottages or campsite.

Eating and shopping: afternoon tea available
in the Visitor Centre. Gifts and souvenirs
available to buy.

Making the most of your day: regular guided
walks by our conservation warden. Eco club
for children during the summer holidays.
Enjoy a Cot Trip on Bank Holiday Mondays.
Dogs on leads only.

Access for all:
Building [access icons] Grounds [access icons]

Getting here: H455655. **Cycle**: NCN91.
Ferry: from Derryvore church must be booked 24
hours in advance. **Bus**: Ulsterbus 95 Enniskillen–
Clones (connections from Belfast), alight
Newtownbutler, 3 miles. **Road**: 3 miles west of
Newtownbutler, on Newtownbutler–Crom road,
or follow signs from Lisnaskea (7 miles). Crom is
next to the Shannon–Erne waterway. Public jetty
at visitor centre. **Parking**: 100 yards.

Finding out more: 028 6773 8118 or
crom@nationaltrust.org.uk

Tranquillity on Lough Erne, Crom, County Fermanagh

Crom		M	T	W	T	F	S	S
Grounds								
13 Mar–31 May	10–6	M	T	W	T	F	S	S
1 Jun–31 Aug	10–7	M	T	W	T	F	S	S
1 Sep–31 Oct	10–6	M	T	W	T	F	S	S
Visitor Centre								
13 Mar–26 Sep	11–5	M	T	W	T	F	S	S

Open Bank Holiday Mondays and all other public holidays
in Northern Ireland **including 17 March**. Last admission one
hour before closing. Telephone for tea-room
opening arrangements.

The Crown Bar

46 Great Victoria Street, Belfast,
County Antrim BT2 7BA

Map (7) E6   1978

Wonderful atmospheric setting, with period
gas lighting and cosy snugs. Ornate interior of
brightly coloured tiles, carvings and glass.

Getting here: J336736. In the centre of Belfast,
on Great Victoria Street.

Finding out more: 028 9024 3187 or
info@crownbar.com

The Crown Bar		M	T	W	T	F	S	S
Open all year	11:30–11	M	T	W	T	F	S	·
Open all year	12:30–10	·	·	·	·	·	·	S

Closed 5 and 6 April, 3 May, 12 and 13 July, 25 and
26 December.

Derrymore House

Bessbrook, Newry, County Armagh BT35 7EF

Map (7) D8 1953

An elegant 18th-century thatched cottage with its peculiar gentrified vernacular style. A rich history and delightful walks. **Note**: no WC.

Getting here: J056280. On A25 off the Newry–Camlough road at Bessbrook, 1½ miles from Newry.

Finding out more: 028 8778 4753 or derrymore@nationaltrust.org.uk

Derrymore House		M	T	W	T	F	S	S
1 Jan–30 Apr	10–4	M	T	W	T	F	S	S
1 May–30 Sep	10–6	M	T	W	T	F	S	S
1 Oct–31 Dec	10–4	M	T	W	T	F	S	S

Treaty Room only open 3 and 31 May, 12 and 13 July, 30 August, 2 to 5:30.

Divis and the Black Mountain

Divis Road, Hannahstown, near Belfast, County Antrim BT17 0NG

Map (7) E6 2004

The mountains rest in the heart of the Belfast Hills, which provide the backdrop to the city's skyline. The rich, varied archaeological landscape is home to a host of wildlife. There are walking trails along a variety of terrain – through heath, on stone tracks, along boardwalks and road surface. **Note**: cattle roam freely during summer months.

Exploring
- Panoramic views across Northern Ireland, Donegal and Scotland.
- Home to a wealth of flora, fauna and archaeological remains.
- Fantastic view point for Hallowe'en firework displays.
- New six-mile trail – Divis Mountain to Lady Dixon Park.

Eating and shopping: tea and coffee machine in the Long Barn.

Making the most of your day: a haven for those seeking the wild countryside experience. Programme of guided walks to discover the wealth of biodiversity and archaeological remains. 'Changing Places' WC and accessible WCs available. Dogs welcome but please note cattle roam freely during summer.

Access for all:
Visitor Centre 👥 Mountain 👥

Getting here: J282756. 1 mile west of Belfast. **Bus**: Ulsterbus 106 – alight at Divis Road. **Road**: minor road west of A55. **Parking**: free.

Finding out more: 028 9082 5434 or divis@nationaltrust.org.uk

Divis and the Black Mountain		M	T	W	T	F	S	S
Open all year	Dawn–dusk	M	T	W	T	F	S	S

Car park open 9 to 8.

Downhill Demesne and Hezlett House

Mussenden Road, Castlerock, County Londonderry BT51 4RP

Map (7) C3 1949

'The historical artefacts of Hezlett House were beautifully counteracted by the magnificent views from Mussenden Temple, all in one afternoon.'
Natasha Burke-Manganaro, London

Visit the stunning landscape of Downhill Demesne, with its beautiful gardens and magnificent clifftop walks, affording rugged headland views across the awe-inspiring north coast. Discover the striking 18th-century mansion of the eccentric Earl Bishop that now lies in ruin, then explore Mussenden Temple, perched on the cliff edge. As an extra treat you can learn about the reality of life in the rural 17th-century cottage of Hezlett House, told through the people who once lived in one of Northern Ireland's oldest surviving buildings.

Exploring
- Enjoy a stroll around the inspiring gardens.
- Take in the panoramic views from Mussenden Temple.
- Children's Tracker Packs – includes binoculars, compass and bird identification cards.
- Downhill ounces (heraldic beasts) returned to Lion's Gate.
- Guided tours of Hezlett House offer an enthralling afternoon treat.
- Hezlett House is also home to the Downhill Marbles Collection.

Eating and shopping: tea and coffee facilities offered at reception of Hezlett House. Perfect for a picnic in the sheltered gardens.

You may also enjoy: Portstewart Strand, Giant's Causeway and Carrick-a-Rede rope bridge.

Making the most of your day: programme of events, including Easter Egg trails, Medieval Festival and music in the Temple. Combine your visit with a trip to Hezlett House. Dogs on leads only.

Access for all: ⟨P⟩⟨WC⟩ Building ⟨icon⟩ Grounds ⟨icon⟩

Getting here: C757357. **Cycle**: NCN93, borders property. **Ferry**: Magilligan–Greencastle Ferry (8 miles). **Bus**: Ulsterbus 234 Coleraine–Londonderry, alight crossroads, few minutes walk. **Train**: Castlerock ½ mile. **Road**:1 mile west of Castlerock and 5 miles west of Coleraine on Coleraine–Downhill coast road (A2). **Parking**: at Lion's Gate (pay and display). Not suitable for 50-seater coaches. Alternative parking for coaches at Bishop's Gate entrance, ½ mile from Temple.

Finding out more: 028 2073 1582 or downhilldemesne@nationaltrust.org.uk

Downhill and Hezlett		M	T	W	T	F	S	S
Downhill Demesne grounds								
Open all year	Dawn–dusk	M	T	W	T	F	S	S
Hezlett House and facilities								
27 Mar–3 Oct	10–5		M	T	W	T	F	S	S

Florence Court

Enniskillen, County Fermanagh BT92 1DB

Map ⑦ A7 ⟨icons⟩ 1954

'**Great tour, beautiful house, lovely tour guide, great gardens – we all had a lovely time at Florence Court.**'
John Rowland, Wokingham, Berkshire

There is something for all the family at this warm and welcoming 18th-century property, the former home of the Earls of Enniskillen. The house enjoys a peaceful setting in west Fermanagh, with a dramatic backdrop of mountains and forests. There are glorious walks to enjoy, as well as fine vistas and play areas. There is even a charming walled garden. Every aspect of life in this classical Irish house, with its fine interiors and exquisite decoration, are brought to life on fascinating guided tours. Outside there are numerous places to explore, including sawmill, ice house and thatched summerhouse.

Family fun at Florence Court, County Fermanagh

Exploring
- Take a guided tour of this fine 18th-century house.
- Enjoy spectacular views and discover flora and fauna.
- Visit the mother Irish yew tree.
- Visit Nelly Woolly's grave.
- Listen to the bird song in the walled garden.
- Explore the atmospheric pleasure grounds.

Eating and shopping: enjoy homemade delights in the Stables restaurant.
The Coach House shop offers a range of gifts.

You may also enjoy: Castle Coole and Crom – within easy driving distance.

Making the most of your day: range of events throughout the year. Licensed civil wedding venue, with a number of historic rooms to hire for that special occasion. Dogs on leads in garden and grounds only.

Access for all: P♿ D♿ WC♿ ♿ ♿ ▭ ∴ ⊘
Building ♿ ♿ ♿ **Grounds** ♿ ➡ ♿

Getting here: H175344. **Cycle**: NCN91. Entrance on Kingfisher Trail. **Bus**: Ulsterbus 192 Enniskillen–Swanlinbar, alight Creamery Cross, 2-mile walk. **Road**: 8 miles south west of Enniskillen via A4 Sligo road and A32 Swanlinbar road, 4 miles from Marble Arch Caves. **Parking**: 200 yards.

Finding out more: 028 6634 8249 or florencecourt@nationaltrust.org.uk

Florence Court		M	T	W	T	F	S	S
Gardens and park								
1 Jan–28 Feb	10–4	M	T	W	T	F	S	S
1 Mar–31 Oct	10–7	M	T	W	T	F	S	S
1 Nov–31 Dec	10–4	M	T	W	T	F	S	S
House								
13 Mar–25 Apr	11–5						S	S
2 Apr–11 Apr	11–5	M	T	W	T	F	S	S
1 May–30 Jun	11–5	M		W	T	F	S	S
1 Jul–31 Aug	11–5	M	T	W	T	F	S	S
1 Sep–30 Sep	11–5	M		W	T	F	S	S
2 Oct–31 Oct	11–5						S	S

House: admission by guided tour (last admission one hour before closing). Open Bank Holiday Mondays and all other public holidays in Northern Ireland, **including 17 March**. Tea-room and shop: open as house.

Giant's Causeway

44a Causeway Road, Bushmills,
County Antrim BT57 8SU

Map ⑦ D3   1962

Northern Ireland's iconic World Heritage Site and Area of Outstanding Natural Beauty is home to a wealth of local history and legend. Explore the basalt stone columns left by volcanic eruptions 60 million years ago and search for distinctive stone formations fancifully named the Camel, Harp and Organ. **Note**: construction of new Visitor Centre may cause disruption.

Exploring
- Beautiful coastal path extends 11 miles to Carrick-a-Rede.
- Geology, flora and fauna of international importance.
- Runkerry Head provides a spectacular two-mile walk.
- Some of Europe's finest cliff scenery, with fantastic birdwatching.

Eating and shopping: light lunches and snacks available in tea-room. National Trust gift shop, showcasing local products.

The spectacular Giant's Causeway, County Antrim

Making the most of your day: Finn MacCool's Causeway steeped in legend and folklore. Open for walking all year, with stunning coast and cliff paths for exploration. Guided tours for groups (fifteen plus). Dogs on leads only.

Access for all: 🅿♿♿♿♿♿
Building ♿♿ Grounds ♿♿♿➡

Getting here: C952452. **Foot**: path from Portballintrae alongside steam railway and from Dunservick Castle (4½ miles). **Cycle**: NCN93. **Bus**: Ulsterbus 172, 177 from Coleraine. Ulsterbus 252 is a circular route from Belfast via the Antrim Glens. **Train**: Coleraine 10 miles or Portrush 8 miles. Giant's Causeway and Bushmills Steam Railway, 200 yards (028 2073 2844). **Road**: on B146 Causeway–Dunseverick road 2 miles east of Bushmills. **Parking**: 100 yards (not National Trust). Charge including members. Liable to change with development of new Visitor Centre.

Finding out more: 028 2073 1582 or giantscauseway@nationaltrust.org.uk

Giant's Causeway		M	T	W	T	F	S	S
Open all year	Dawn–dusk	**M**	**T**	**W**	**T**	**F**	**S**	**S**

Telephone for shop and tea-room opening arrangements.

Gray's Printing Press

49 Main Street, Strabane,
County Tyrone BT82 8AU

Map (7) B5   1966

A treasure trove of ink, galleys and presses hidden behind an 18th-century shop front in the heart of Strabane.

Getting here: H345977. Behind a bow-windowed shop on Main Street, Strabane.

Finding out more: 028 8674 8210 or grays@nationaltrust.org.uk

Gray's Printing Press

Admission by guided tour. Last admission 45 minutes before closing. Telephone for opening dates and times.

Mount Stewart House, Garden and Temple of the Winds

Portaferry Road, Newtownards,
County Down BT22 2AD

Map (7) F6    1976

Mount Stewart is one of the most unique and unusual gardens in the National Trust's ownership. The garden reflects a rich tapestry of design and great planting artistry that was the hallmark of Edith, Lady Londonderry. The mild climate of Strangford Lough allows astonishing levels of planting experimentation. The formal areas exude a strong Mediterranean feel and resemble an Italian villa landscape; the wooded areas support a range of plants from all corners of the world, ensuring something to see whatever the season. Engaging tours of the opulent house reveal its fascinating heritage and historic world-famous artefacts and artwork.

Exploring
- Explore one of the finest gardens in Europe.
- Discover the fascinating history of Mount Stewart mansion.
- Magnificent views of Strangford Lough from Temple of the Winds.
- Follow in footsteps of Kings, Queens, Prime Ministers and poets.
- Picturesque lake surrounded by beautiful swathes of woodland.
- Dinosaurs and duck-billed platypuses jostle on Dodo Terrace.

Eating and shopping: buy the best of local craft products in our shop. Try our unique Mount Stewart ice-cream. Visit the recently opened plant centre – a haven for gardeners. Enjoy a meal in the award-winning Bay Restaurant.

Mount Stewart House, County Down

You may also enjoy: Castle Ward, famed for its stunning grounds and mansion – a fascinating mixture of architectural styles.

Making the most of your day: busy programme of events throughout the year – jazz in the garden, craft fairs, guided walks, garden tours, children's events and Santa's Grotto. Family activity packs also available. Dogs on leads in grounds and garden only.

Access for all: 🅿️ 🅳 🚻 ♿ 🪑 📷 📱 ∴
Building ♿🚶♿ **Grounds** ♿➡️♿

Getting here: J553695. **Bus**: Ulsterbus 10 Belfast–Portaferry, bus stop at gates. **Train**: Bangor 10 miles. **Road**: 15 miles south east of Belfast on Newtownards–Portaferry road, A20, 5 miles south east of Newtownards. **Parking**: free, 100 yards.

Finding out more: 028 4278 8387 or mountstewart@nationaltrust.org.uk

Mount Stewart		M	T	W	T	F	S	S
Lakeside gardens								
Open all year	10–6	M	T	W	T	F	S	S
Formal gardens								
13 Mar–31 Oct	10–6	M	T	W	T	F	S	S
House								
13 Mar–31 Oct	11–6	M	T	·	T	F	S	S
2 Apr–11 Apr	11–6	M	T	W	T	F	S	S
Temple of the Winds								
14 Mar–31 Oct	2–5	·	·	·	·	·	·	S

Open Bank Holiday Mondays and all other public holidays in Northern Ireland, **including 17 March**. House: admission by guided tour (timed tickets only); last admission one hour before closing. Lakeside gardens closed 25 and 26 December. Telephone for shop and restaurant opening times.

Murlough National Nature Reserve

Keel Point, Dundrum, County Down BT33 0NQ

Map ⑦ E8  1967

Murlough is an extraordinarily beautiful dune landscape, fringing one of Northern Ireland's most popular beaches and overlooked by the rounded peaks of the Mourne Mountains to the south.

The fragile 6,000-year-old sand dunes, Ireland's first Nature Reserve, are an excellent area for walking and wildlife. **Note**: limited WC facilities.

Exploring
– Most extensive example of dune heath within Ireland.
– Over 330 species of butterflies and moths, including marsh fritillary.
– Dune flowers, common and grey seals, wintering wildfowl and waders.
– Evidence of human habitation from neolithic times to present day.

Eating and shopping: enjoy a latte in the Beach Café. Picnics in the car park or on the beach.

Making the most of your day: network of paths and boardwalks through the dunes, woodland and heath. Self-guided nature walk, series of guided walks and volunteer events throughout the year. Dogs welcome, some restrictions apply.

Access for all: 🚻

Getting here: J410350. 2 miles north east of Newcastle, 28 miles south of Belfast. **Bus**: Ulsterbus 20 Belfast–Newcastle, alight at Lazy BJ Caravan Park after Dundrum. **Road**: follow signs on A24 between Dundrum and Newcastle. **Parking**: main car park signposted off A24. Charges when facilities open.

Finding out more: 028 4375 1467 or murlough@nationaltrust.org.uk

Murlough		M	T	W	T	F	S	S
Open all year	Dawn–dusk	M	T	W	T	F	S	S
Facilities								
13 Mar–28 Mar	10–6	·	·	·	·	·	S	S
3 Apr–30 May	10–6	·	·	·	·	·	S	S
2 Apr–11 Apr	1–6	M	T	W	T	F	S	S
1 Jun–31 Aug	10–6	M	T	W	T	F	S	S
4 Sep–26 Sep	10–6	·	·	·	·	·	S	S

Open Bank Holiday Mondays and all other public holidays in Northern Ireland, **including 17 March**.

Patterson's Spade Mill

751 Antrim Road, Templepatrick, County Antrim BT39 0AP

Map ⑦ E6  1991

Hear the hammers, smell the grit and feel the heat of traditional spade-making. Guided tours vividly capture life during the Industrial Revolution and dig up the history and culture of the humble spade. Find the origin of the phrase 'a face as long as a Lurgan spade'.

Exploring
- Last working water-driven spade mill in the British Isles.
- See red-hot billets of steel fashioned into spades.
- Listen to the thunder of massive water-powered trip hammer.
- Travel back in time to a bygone industrial era.

Eating and shopping: handcrafted spades on sale and made to specification. Tea and coffee available from drinks machine.

Making the most of your day: enjoy a 'Slippery feast' on St Patrick's Day and full steam ahead at the fascinating Stationary Engine Day. Guided tours and demonstrations for all the family with the Spade Maker. Dogs on leads only.

Access for all: 🅿️ Dg 🚻 ♿
Building ♿ 🦽 Grounds ♿

Getting here: J263856. **Bus**: Ulsterbus 110, 120 Belfast–Cookstown, bus stop at gates. **Train**: Antrim 8 miles. **Road**: 2 miles north east of Templepatrick on Antrim–Belfast road, A6; M2 exit 4. **Parking**: free, 50 yards.

Finding out more: 028 9443 3619 or pattersons@nationaltrust.org.uk

Patterson's Spade Mill		M	T	W	T	F	S	S
13 Mar–30 May	2–6	·	·	·	·	·	S	S
2 Apr–11 Apr	2–6	M	T	W	T	F	S	S
2 Jun–30 Aug	2–6	M	·	W	T	F	S	S
4 Sep–26 Sep	2–6	·	·	·	·	·	S	S

Admission by guided tour. Open Bank Holiday Mondays and all other public holidays in Northern Ireland **including 17 March**. Last admission one hour before closing.

Machinery at Patterson's Spade Mill, County Antrim

Portstewart Strand

Strand Road, Portstewart,
County Londonderry BT55 7PG

Map ⑦ €3   ☒☒☒ 1981

The magnificent two-mile strand of glistening golden sand is one of Northern Ireland's finest and most popular beaches with all ages. It is the perfect spot to spend lazy summer days and take long walks into the sand dunes, which are a haven for wild flowers and butterflies.

Portstewart Strand, County Londonderry

Exploring	– Explore the magnificent sand dunes and waymarked nature trail.
	– Many species of butterflies and moths, and colourful wild flowers.
	– Visit the newly restored Grangemore birdhide for fantastic birdwatching.
	– Enjoy lazy summer days, family picnics and sandcastles.

Eating and shopping: light refreshments available at Visitor Centre. Beach shop in the new environmentally friendly Visitor Centre.

Making the most of your day: relax and enjoy the sea and sand. Or meander through the dunes to see the wildlife – look out for the common blue butterfly, six-spot burnet moths and rare orchids. Dogs on leads only.

Access for all: ☒☒ Beach ➡

Getting here: C720360. On south side of River Bann, 1½ miles east of Castlerock and 5 miles north west of Coleraine. **Cycle**: NCN 93 runs nearby. **Bus**: Ulsterbus 140 from Coleraine (connections from Belfast route 218). **Train**: Coleraine. **Parking**: on beach.

Finding out more: 028 7083 6396 or portstewart@nationaltrust.org.uk

Portstewart Strand		M	T	W	T	F	S	S
Open all year		M	T	W	T	F	S	S
Facilities								
27 Feb–28 Mar	10–4	M	T	W	T	F	S	S
29 Mar–25 Apr	10–5	M	T	W	T	F	S	S
26 Apr–30 May	10–6	M	T	W	T	F	S	S
31 May–31 Aug	10–7	M	T	W	T	F	S	S
1 Sep–26 Sep	10–5	M	T	W	T	F	S	S
27 Sep–31 Oct	10–4	M	T	W	T	F	S	S

Rowallane Garden

Saintfield, County Down BT24 7LH

Map ⑦ E7   ☒☒ 1956

'**What makes Rowallane Garden stand out is the informality of the garden design in a natural setting – a magnificent garden!**'
Mr and Mrs Green, Craigavad, Holywood

Be inspired by this enchanting garden's dazzling array of exotic species from the four corners of the globe. Created in the mid 1860s by the Reverend John Moore, this informal plantsman's garden reflects the beautiful natural landscape of the surrounding area. There are spectacular displays of shrubs, including a large collection of rhododendron species and several areas managed as wildflower meadows. It is also home to a notable natural Rock Garden Wood with shade-loving plants. The outstanding Walled Garden includes spectacular displays of herbaceous plants, shrubs and bulbs.

The informal Rowallane Garden, County Down

Exploring

- Book a gardening tour with the Head Gardener.
- Discover exotic and rare species of rhododendron.
- Take a tranquil walk around the famous Rock Garden Wood.
- Follow the farmland trail to the summit of Trio Hill.
- Watch the master potter at work in the Secret Garden.
- Perform on the bandstand to an imaginary audience.

Eating and shopping: try delicious homemade scones from the Garden Kitchen tea-room. Pick up a bargain book from the second-hand bookshop. Purchase a unique Rowallane Garden glazed stoneware pot.

You may also enjoy: touring Castle Ward, an eccentric house with two entirely different styles of architecture.

Making the most of your day: wide range of events, such as Hot Jazz, autumn plant fair, Ghosts and Gourds and Yuletide market. Children's activity sheets available. Dogs on leads in gardens only.

Access for all: [P] [wc] [🚻] Grounds [♿] [&]

Getting here: J412581. **Foot**: ¾ mile from Saintfield village centre. **Bus**: Ulsterbus 15 Belfast–Downpatrick (passing Belfast Great Victoria Street �₧). **Road**: 11 miles south east of Belfast, 1 mile south of Saintfield, on road to Downpatrick (A7). **Sat Nav**: incorrect from Saintfeld – Rowallane Garden is one mile from Saintfield village off A7. **Parking**: free.

Finding out more: 028 9751 0131 or rowallane@nationaltrust.org.uk

Rowallane Garden		M	T	W	T	F	S	S
2 Jan–28 Feb	10–4	M	T	W	T	F	S	S
1 Mar–30 Apr	10–6	M	T	W	T	F	S	S
1 May–31 Aug	10–8	M	T	W	T	F	S	S
1 Sep–31 Oct	10–6	M	T	W	T	F	S	S
1 Nov–31 Dec	10–4	M	T	W	T	F	S	S

Closed 1 January, 25 and 26 December. Telephone for tea-room opening times.

Springhill

20 Springhill Road, Moneymore, Magherafelt, County Londonderry BT45 7NQ

Map (7) C6 [icons]  1957

'The talented young people who made the house come alive, injected some humour and involved the group throughout the tour.' Ivan Flack, Belfast

Experience the beguiling spirit of this inimitable 17th-century 'Plantation' home, with its walled gardens and parkland, full of tempting waymarked paths. Informative Sunday afternoon Living History tours breathe life into the fascinating past of this welcoming family home. There are ten generations of Lenox-Conyngham family tales to enthrall you, as well as numerous portraits and much furniture to admire – not forgetting Ireland's best-documented ghost, Olivia. The old laundry houses the celebrated Costume Collection, which features some fine 18th- to 20th-century pieces that highlight its great charm and enthralling past.

Exploring

- Fun for all the family, with new trails for children.
- Fascinating new costume exhibition every year.
- Enjoy short walks around the charming estate.
- Relax in the herb garden with a chamomile lawn.
- Admire the 1,000-year-old yew tree.

Eating and shopping: delicious cream teas in the Servants' Hall tea-room. Look for presents in our little gift shop. Select a book in our 'Well Read' bookshop. Enjoy a picnic in the garden.

You may also enjoy: Wellbrook Beetling Mill, with its water-powered mill wheel.

Making the most of your day: meet the family from long ago, enjoy the walks and then relax in the Servants' Hall tea-room with a delicious cream tea of homemade scones and raspberry jam. Dogs on leads in grounds only.

Inimitable Springhill, County Londonderry

Access for all: 🚻♿🛗📷🔊 **Building** ♿🔽

Getting here: H866828. **Foot**: from Moneymore village, 1 mile. **Cycle**: NCN94/95, 5 miles. **Bus**: Ulsterbus 210 and 110 Belfast-Cookstown, alight Moneymore village, 1 mile. **Road**: 1 mile from Moneymore on Moneymore-Coagh road, B18. **Parking**: 50 yards.

Finding out more: 028 8674 8210 or springhill@nationaltrust.org.uk

Springhill		M	T	W	T	F	S	S
Grounds								
1 Jan–30 Apr	10–4	M	T	W	T	F	S	S
1 May–30 Sep	10–6	M	T	W	T	F	S	S
1 Oct–31 Dec	10–4	M	T	W	T	F	S	S
House								
13 Mar–27 Jun	1–6	·	·	·	·	·	S	S
2 Apr–11 Apr	1–6	M	T	W	T	F	S	S
1 Jul–31 Aug	1–6	M	T	W	T	F	S	S
4 Sep–26 Sep	1–6	·	·	·	·	·	S	S

Admission by guided tour to house. Open Bank Holiday Mondays and all other public holidays in Northern Ireland, **including 17 March**. Last admission one hour before closing. Telephone property for shop and tea-room opening arrangements.

Wellbrook Beetling Mill

20 Wellbrook Road, Corkhill, Cookstown, County Tyrone BT80 9RY

Map ⑦ C6   🍴🛏♿ 1968

Nestling in an idyllic wooded glen offering lovely walks and picnic spots this, the last working water-powered linen beetling mill, offers a unique experience for all the family. Try some scutching, hackling and weaving as you take part in hands-on demonstrations, against the thundering cacophony of beetling engines.

Exploring
– Follow the head-race to the source of the power.
– Lovely walks and picnic opportunities by the Ballinderry River.
– Watch the massive water-powered wheel as it turns.
– Look out for pearl mussels in the mill race.

Eating and shopping: tea or coffee is available on request. Delicious afternoon tea on Living History days. Irish linen, for sale in the small gift shop.

Making the most of your day: tour the mill and find out about its history and linen-making processes. Experience Living History days. Walk up the head-race and then relax with a picnic on the lawn. Dogs on leads in grounds only.

Access for all: 🚻♿🛗 **Building** ♿🔽 **Grounds** ♿🔽

Getting here: H750792. **Cycle**: NCN95. **Bus**: Ulsterbus 80 from Cookstown, with connections from Belfast, ½ mile. **Road**: 4 miles west of Cookstown, ½ mile off Cookstown–Omagh road (A505): from Cookstown turn right at Kildress parish church or follow Orritor Road (A53) to avoid town centre. **Parking**: free, 10 yards.

Finding out more: 028 8675 1735 or wellbrook@nationaltrust.org.uk

Wellbrook Beetling Mill		M	T	W	T	F	S	S
13 Mar–27 Jun	2–6	·	·	·	·	·	S	S
2 Apr–6 Apr	1–6	M	T	·	·	F	S	S
1 Jul–31 Aug	2–6	M	T	W	T	·	S	S
4 Sep–26 Sep	2–6	·	·	·	·	·	S	S

Admission by guided tour. Open Bank Holiday Mondays and all other public holidays in Northern Ireland **including 17 March**. Last admission one hour before closing. Telephone for shop opening arrangements.

Heritage Lottery Fund

The Heritage Lottery Fund (HLF) enables communities to celebrate, look after and learn more about our diverse heritage. From museums and historic buildings, parks and nature reserves, to celebrating traditions, customs and history, the HLF has awarded more than £4 billion to projects that open up our nation's heritage for everyone to enjoy.

We have supported the following National Trust projects:

Attingham Park, Shropshire
Beningbrough Hall and Gardens, North Yorkshire
Biddulph Grange Garden, Staffordshire
Birmingham Back to Backs, West Midlands
Croome Park, Worcestershire
Dinefwr Park and Castle, Carmarthenshire
Divis and the Black Mountain, Belfast
Gibside, Newcastle upon Tyne
Glastonbury Tor, Somerset
Greenway, Devon
Hardcastle Crags and Gibson Mill, West Yorkshire
Hardwick Hall, Derbyshire

Holy Jesus Hospital, Newcastle
Llanerchaeron, Ceredigion
Lyme Park, Cheshire
Mr Hardman's Photographic Studio, Liverpool
Nostell Priory and Parkland, West Yorkshire
Prior Park Landscape Garden, Bath
Springhill, County Londonderry
Stowe Landscape Gardens, Buckinghamshire
Sudbury Hall and the National Trust Museum of Childhood, Derbyshire
Tyntesfield, North Somerset
Wordsworth House and Garden, Cumbria
The Workhouse, Southwell, Nottinghamshire

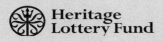

Awarding funds from
The National Lottery®

If you would like to find out more please visit **www.hlf.org.uk**

Visiting

This section of the *Handbook* provides a range of information that will help you make the most of your visits to our places. Please also see the questions and answers on page 375, as these contain important information.

Admission fees and opening arrangements

Members of the National Trust are admitted free to virtually all places (see Information about membership, page 385). Admission fees include VAT and are liable to change if the VAT rate is altered. The prices for most places include a voluntary 10 per cent donation under the Gift Aid on Entry scheme – see page 10 for full details. Current admission prices are given in full on our website **www.nationaltrust. org.uk** or are available from the Membership Department on 0844 800 1895.

Children: under-fives are free. Children aged five to sixteen usually pay half the adult price. Seventeens and over pay the adult price. Children not accompanied by an adult are admitted at the Trust's discretion. Most places offer discounted family tickets (usually covering one or two adults and up to three children, unless stated otherwise).

Concessions: as a registered charity which has to raise all its own funds, the National Trust cannot afford to offer concessions on admission fees, although we do offer free entry on Heritage Open Days (visit website for details).

Education groups: many places offer a programme of activities for education groups. Contact the place you wish to visit directly for details of sessions, fees and availability. For more information on education visits see page 373. For frequent visitors we recommend our Educational Group membership (see page 385).

Group visits: groups are always welcome at Trust places. All group visitors are required to book in advance and arrangements should be made direct with the property. Admission discounts are usually available for groups of more than fifteen people, although this can vary and needs to be confirmed when booking. The Travel Trade Office at the Trust's Central Office (see page 387) can also provide general groups information and details on special interest tours and activities for groups. For further information visit **www. nationaltrust.org.uk/groups**

National Gardens Scheme open days: each year many of the National Trust's gardens are opened in support of the National Gardens Scheme (NGS). If this is on a day when the garden is not usually open, National Trust members will have to pay for entry. All money raised is donated by the NGS to support nurses' and garden charities, including the National Trust garden careership training scheme. The Trust acknowledges with gratitude the generous and continuing support of the National Gardens Scheme Charitable Trust.

Busy days: places can be extremely popular on bank holidays and summer weekends. At some, timed tickets may be issued to smooth the flow of people entering (but not to limit the duration of a visit), and all visitors (including Trust members) are required to use these tickets. This system aims to create better viewing conditions for visitors and to minimise wear and tear on historic interiors and gardens. On very rare occasions entry may not be possible on that day. If you are planning a long journey, please telephone in advance. At a few places special considerations apply and booking is essential, for example Red House, Mr Straw's House, 2 Willow Road.

Toilets (WCs)

There is always one available, either at the place, when open, or nearby, unless the individual entry specifically indicates 'no WC'.

Guided tours

Many places now offer 'taster' tours between 11 and 1, before opening for free-flow visiting. These tours of particular rooms provide specialist insights into curatorship and conservation issues. Other places offer guided tours only for groups, so to avoid disappointment please telephone in advance or check the website.

Events

An incredible range of events takes place at National Trust places throughout the year, from springtime estate and wildflower walks, to family fun at Easter and Hallowe'en. There are live summer concerts, living history events, countryside open days and open-air theatre productions. We offer lecture lunches and 'behind-the-scenes' tours, explaining the work of our gardeners and house staff. 'Conservation in Action' events provide opportunities for you to see conservation specialists at work and talk to them about the techniques they use. Exhibitions and interactive activities may also be available to give you further insight into processes. There might also be the chance for visitors to carry out conservation work. See page 380 for details of our Working Holidays. The year ends with Christmas craft fairs and carol concerts. For details telephone 0844 800 1895 or visit **www.nationaltrust.org. uk/events**

For private and corporate events in our places, visit **www.nationaltrust.org. uk/hiring**

Enjoying the garden with the help of a mobility vehicle at Quarry Bank Mill and Styal Estate, Cheshire

Access information

Entries for each place are shown using symbols. For a key to the access symbols please see the inside front cover. More detailed information regarding the access provisions at our places can be found in the *Access Guide*, our free publication which can be requested from the Membership Department.

Our admission policy admits the essential companion, or carer, of a disabled visitor free of charge, on request, while the normal membership charge or admission fee applies to the disabled visitor. To save having to 'request' a companion's free entry, we can issue an Admit One Card in the name of the disabled person. To obtain an Admit One Card please telephone 01793 817634 or email enquiries@nationaltrust.org.uk

We are continuing to work with both local and national disability groups to improve access at our places. For example, Speke Hall in Liverpool has worked with Mencap to develop a sensory trail, Washington Old Hall worked with local groups and has installed the first garden lift in the Trust. Divis Mountain in Belfast has the Trust's first 'Changing Places' WC, and we are also working with Mencap to make volunteering opportunities more accessible.

Wherever possible, we admit users of powered wheelchairs and similar small vehicles to our buildings. This is subject to the physical limitations of the property, and any other temporary constraints which may apply on the day. Approximately 30 of our properties now have new virtual tours, some of which have British Sign Language interpretation on them.

These tours will be on the website in 2010. We always recommend that if you have a specific access requirement you contact the place direct.

The *Handbook* can only provide a brief indication of access facilities. Full detailed access information about our built places is contained in the *Access Guide*, which can be downloaded from **www.nationaltrust.org.uk** and is available free from the Membership Department: telephone 0844 800 1895 or write to FREEPOST NAT9775, Warrington WA5 7WD. This book is also available in large print and on tape.

National Trust Magazine is available free on tape to members, as are several regional newsletters. If you wish to receive these regularly, please email SoundTalking direct at admin@soundtalking.co.uk or telephone 01435 862737.

Eating and shopping

Every purchase made from National Trust shops, restaurants, tea-rooms and coffee shops makes a vital contribution to our work.

Shops: many places have shops offering a wide range of relevant merchandise, much of which is exclusive to the National Trust. These shops are indicated in relevant entries by the shop symbol and their times given in the 'Opening arrangements' table. Many are open for Christmas shopping. The Trust also operates a number of shops in towns and cities, which are open during normal trading hours (see right). We also offer many National Trust gifts for sale online at **www. nationaltrust.org.uk/shop**

Restaurants and tea-rooms: the 150 tea-rooms and cafés operated by the Trust are often located in unique buildings, such as stable blocks or hothouses. We aim to offer a sincere welcome and to showcase the best local and seasonal produce, cooking and baking. At all cafés we offer facilities for families with children, either to warm baby food or provide children's portions. There are also many autumn, winter and Christmas events. Check with your local place for full details and changing menus.

National Trust recommends: National Trust Enterprises collaborates with leading British designers and manufacturers to create inspiring collections based on the Trust's historical places, land and archives. Partners include Zoffany furnishings and wallpaper, Duresta furniture, Stevensons of Norwich plaster mouldings, Alitex greenhouses, Marshalls paving, Scotts of Thrapston summerhouses, Vale Garden Houses and Caspari stationery. For further details visit **www.nationaltrust.org. uk/werecommend**

Welcoming families

We offer various facilities to help your visit run smoothly. We also organise a wealth of activities and events to make your day with us that bit more memorable.

Facilities: on your arrival, parking is made easy, and family tickets are offered at most places. You can find baby-change and baby-feeding areas at many places – and some have purpose-designed parent and baby rooms.

Our restaurants have highchairs, children's menus, colouring sheets, and some also have play areas.

To make it easier for families to visit our historic buildings, front slings for smaller babies and hip-seat carriers or reins for toddlers are often available to borrow. There are usually arrangements for storing prams and pushchairs at the entrance, as regrettably it is not possible to take these inside. Some houses are able to admit baby back-carriers, but their use may be restricted at busy times. We regret that the restriction on back-carriers, prams and pushchairs may be inconvenient.

Activities: many National Trust places have guides, trails or quizzes for children and families, and increasingly we are trying to find ways to tell the stories of our places through activities that are more hands-on. Tracker Packs are one example – these bags are packed with activities to do as you explore together as a family. They are free to borrow, although some places will require you to leave a deposit. Handling areas and activity rooms are among other things that may be on offer.

Visit our events page and search for an event by date, location or things to do that are especially suitable for families or children: **www. nationaltrust.org.uk/events**

Look out for Trusty the hedgehog, who often appears at family friendly events or activities. You can meet him at his website **www.trusty.org.uk**

Learning and discovery – when places come to life

The National Trust is committed to placing learning at the heart of the organisation. We provide a variety of experiences, which are inspiring, stimulating and fun. We encourage everyone – local communities, young people, families – to engage with us to develop their sense of discovery and their enthusiasm for sharing it.

We welcome visitors from across the educational sector and from special interest groups. Many places have an onsite learning officer and a programme of learning activities, which provide a stimulating opportunity for learning outside the classroom. Contact the place you wish to visit for details of fees, availability and to discuss requirements. It is advisable for teachers to make a preliminary visit before

Town shops: opening times vary, so please telephone for details if you are making a special journey.

Bath Marshall Wade's House, Abbey Churchyard, BA1 1LY (01225 460249)

Cambridge 9 King's Parade, CB2 1SJ (01223 311894)

Canterbury 24 Burgate, CT1 2HA (01227 457120)

Chichester 92a East Street, PO19 1HA (01243 773125)

Conwy Aberconwy House, 2 Castle Street, LL32 8AY (01492 592246)

Dartmouth 8 The Quay, TQ6 9PS (01803 833694)

Hereford 7 Gomond Street, HR1 2DP (01432 342297)

Hexham 25/26 Market Place, NE46 3PB (01434 607654)

Kendal 16–20 Stricklandgate, LA9 4ND (01539 736190)

London Blewcoat School, 23 Caxton Street, Victoria, SW1H 0PY (020 7222 2877)

Monmouth 5 Church Street, NP25 3BX (01600 713270)

St David's Visitor Centre and Shop, Captain's House, 6 High Street, SA62 6SD (01437 720385)

Salisbury 41 High Street, SP1 2PB (01722 331884)

Seahouses Information Centre and Shop, 16 Main Street, NE68 7RQ (01665 721099)

Sidmouth Cosmopolitan House, Old Fore Street, EX10 8LS (01395 578107)

Skipton 6 Sheep Street, BD23 1JH (01756 799378)

Stratford-upon-Avon 45 Wood Street, CV37 6JG (01789 262197)

Street Clark's Village, Farm Road, BA16 0BB (01458 440578)

Swindon Heelis café and shop, Kemble Drive, SN2 2NA (shop 01793 817600; café 01793 817474)

Truro 9 River Street, TR1 2SQ (01872 241464)

Wells 16 Market Place, BA5 2RB (01749 677735)

York Shop and tea-room, 32 Goodramgate, YO1 7LG (shop 01904 659050; tea-room 01904 659282)

they bring their group. This can be arranged free of charge. Frequent visitors may want to consider educational group membership (see page 385).

Dogs allowed
We welcome assistance dogs inside our houses, gardens, restaurants and shops. Generally only assistance dogs are allowed beyond the car park, although occasionally dogs are allowed into the grounds or other specified areas. Any restrictions, such as needing to be kept on a lead, are listed at the end of the 'Making the most of your day' section.

We endeavour to provide facilities for dogs, such as water for drinking bowls, advice on suitable areas to exercise dogs and shady spaces in car parks (though dogs should not be left alone in cars). These facilities vary from place to place and according to how busy it is on a particular day. The primary responsibility for the welfare of dogs remains, of course, with their owners.

Dogs are welcome at most countryside sites, where they should be kept under close control at all times. Please observe local notices on the need to keep dogs on leads, particularly at sensitive times of year, such as during the breeding season for ground-nesting birds, at lambing time or when deer are calving. Dogs should be kept on a short lead on access land between 1 March and 31 July, and at any other time when near livestock.

In some areas we have found it necessary to introduce restrictions, usually seasonal, and particularly on beaches, due to conflicts with other users. Where access for dogs is restricted, we attempt to identify suitable alternative locations nearby.

Clear up dog mess and dispose of it responsibly. Where dog waste bins are not provided, please take the waste away with you.

Weddings and private functions
The bell and glass symbols at the top of entries in this *Handbook* indicate that the place is licensed for civil weddings (bell symbol) and/or available for private functions (glass symbol) such as wedding receptions, anniversaries, family celebrations and so on. For more information, contact the place, the Membership Department on 0844 800 1895 or visit **www.nationaltrust. org.uk/hiring**

Your safety
We aim to provide a safe and healthy environment for visitors to our places, and we take measures to ensure that the work of our staff, volunteers and contractors does not jeopardise visitors' safety or health.
You can help us by:

– observing all notices and signs during your visit;

– following any instructions and advice given by Trust staff;

– ensuring that children are properly supervised at all times;

– wearing appropriate clothing and footwear in the countryside and in gardens;

– wearing appropriate footwear in built places.

At all our places the responsibility for the safety of visitors should be seen as one that is shared between the Trust and the individual visitor. The Trust takes reasonable measures to minimise risks in ways that are compatible with our conservation objectives – but not necessarily to eliminate all risks. This is especially the case at our coastal and countryside places, where we aim to avoid measures that might restrict access or affect people's sense of freedom and adventure. As the landscape becomes more rugged and remote, the balance of responsibility between the landowner/manager and the visitor shifts. There will be fewer safety measures and warning signs, and visitors will need to rely more on their own skills, knowledge, equipment and preparation. You can help to ensure your own safety by:

– taking note of weather conditions and forecasts and being properly equipped for changes in the weather. Please note that some places (or parts of) may close in severe weather conditions. It is always advisable to check opening arrangements before setting out on your journey;

– making sure you are properly prepared, equipped and clothed for the terrain and the activity in which you are participating;

– giving notice of your intended route and estimated time of return.

Your questions answered

May I use my mobile telephone? The use of mobile telephones can interfere with the correct operation of sensitive electronic environmental monitoring equipment, and so visitors are asked to switch them off when entering houses and other buildings where such equipment is likely to be fitted.

Where can I picnic? Many places welcome picnics; some have a designated picnic area, a few cannot accommodate them. Fires and barbecues are generally not allowed. If you are planning a picnic at a National Trust place for the first time, please telephone in advance to check.

Is there somewhere to leave large or bulky bags? At historic places visitors will be asked to leave behind large items of hand luggage while they make their visit. This is to prevent accidental damage and to improve security. The restriction includes rucksacks, large handbags, carrier (including open-topped) bags, bulky shoulder bags and camera/camcorder bags. In most houses where the restriction applies (principally historic houses with vulnerable contents, fragile decorative surfaces or narrow visitor routes) it is possible to leave such items safely at the entrance; this policy reflects standard practice at museums and galleries worldwide. See the Welcoming families section on page 372 for additional information on back-carriers and pushchairs.

What types of footwear are restricted? Any heel which covers an area smaller than a postage stamp can cause irreparable damage to floors, carpets and rush matting. We regret, therefore, that sharp-heeled shoes are not permitted. Plastic slippers are provided for visitors with unsuitable or muddy footwear, or alternative footwear is available for purchase. Please remember that ridged soles trap grit and gravel, which scratch fine floors. Boot-scrapers and brushes are readily available and overshoes may be provided at properties with vulnerable floors.

Where can I sit down? Seats for visitors' use are provided at various points in all the Trust's historic houses and gardens. Distinctive seat pads may be used to identify chairs available for visitors to use; these will make it easy for you to rest, confident that you are not sitting on a fragile historic chair.

Why is it dark inside some historic rooms? To prevent deterioration of light-sensitive contents, especially textiles and watercolours, light levels are regularly monitored and carefully controlled using blinds and sun-curtains. We recommend that visitors allow time for their eyes to adapt to darker conditions in rooms where light levels are reduced to preserve vulnerable material.

Some historic houses offer special tours during the winter months, when house staff demonstrate traditional housekeeping practices. Guided tours explain why National Trust conservation policies require low light levels inside houses and closure to visitors during the winter. Events showing the process of 'Putting the House to Bed' are advertised in the local press and in regional newsletters, or details can be obtained from the Membership Department (see page 387), or **www.nationaltrust.org. uk/events**

Why is it so cold inside some houses in winter? The heating systems in National Trust houses are not designed for the levels of domestic heating that we have become used to in our own homes. Visitors are advised to dress warmly when they go to Trust houses in the winter.

Where can I take photographs? We welcome amateur photography out of doors at our places. Photography without flash is permitted indoors when houses are open at the discretion of the Property/ General Manager. The use of mobile phones with built-in cameras is similarly permitted indoors (again, no flash please). At most places special arrangements can be made for interested amateurs (as well as voluntary National Trust speakers, research students and academics) to take interior photographs by appointment outside normal opening hours. Requests to arrange a mutually convenient appointment must be made in writing to the place concerned. Not all places are able to offer this facility and those that do may make an admission charge (including National Trust members). All requests for commercial photography go through the Broadcast Media Liaison Officer (020 7799 4547).

What are the rules regarding measurements?

Area is shown in hectares (with the acre equivalent in brackets); and distances are shown in yards and miles. Heights where mentioned are shown in metres, except where a structure may have been built to achieve a very specific height in imperial measures (Leith Hill Tower in Surrey being one example).

Some of the 'boneshaker' bicycles at Snowshill Manor, Gloucestershire

Your journey

Each entry includes its OS Landranger (or OSNI) series map number and grid reference, an indicator of its location and public transport/ road access.

Car-free days out

Travelling on foot, by bike, bus, train or boat to National Trust places can be an enjoyable and environmentally friendly way of visiting. In support of car-free travel, a growing number of places offer incentives for visitors arriving without a car – from a discount on entry to a tea-room voucher. Visit **www.nationaltrust.org.uk/ carfreedaysout**

Public transport

Details of access by public transport were correct as of July 2009. No indication of service frequency is provided. You are strongly advised to check services and timetables before setting out, with **www.traveline.info** or **www.transportdirect.info** – both provide multi-modal journey planning services. The National Trust is grateful to Journey Solutions – a partnership of Britain's bus and train operators – for checking and updating the public transport information. Journey Solutions manages PLUSBUS, Britain's integrated train and bus ticketing system.

For details visit **www.plusbus.info**

Ferry: some places are best reached – or can only be reached – by boat.

Bus: unless otherwise stated, bus services pass the site entrance (although there may be a walk from the bus-stop). Many bus services connect properties with local train stations – 'passing ⊞' indicates that the bus service passes the station entrance or approach road and 'passing close ⊞' indicates that a walk is necessary.

Train/London Underground:
the distance from the place to
nearest railway stations is given.

Cycling
More than 200 National Trust
places are within 1¼ miles or
2km of the UK's 10,000-mile
National Cycle Network (NCN).
Combined with bridleways,
byways and quiet roads, this
provides many opportunities
for cycling to your favourite
places. We work closely with
Sustrans, the sustainable
transport charity, to promote
cycling as a healthy, enjoyable
and environmentally-friendly
way of reaching our places.

– *Handbook* entries give
  information on the nearest
  NCN route. For example
  NCN4, 2 miles denotes the
  property is 2 miles from
  NCN route number 4.

– Unless otherwise stated,
  most National Trust places
  have cycle parking onsite
  or nearby.

Walking
There is no better way to
appreciate the variety of
places cared for by the
National Trust than by
exploring on foot. Long-
distance walking routes,
including thirteen National
Trails, link many Trust places,
on top of a scenic web of local
paths and access land. We
have promoted the freedom to
roam over open country, coast
and woods for more than a
century and continue to work
to improve access for all today.

– Hundreds of guided walks
  take place at our places each
  year. They are a great way to
  find out more about our
  conservation work, wildlife,
  history, farming and so
  much more, while enjoying a
  healthy stroll. Many places
  also offer waymarked trails,
  leaflets and maps.

– Hundreds of walks sheets
  are available free on the
  Trust website to download,
  print and take on your
  day out.

Before setting out visit **www.
nationaltrust.org.uk/walks** for
a route map and description of
our interesting walks.

Handbook entries give
information on pedestrian
access from the nearest town
or railway station and details
of routes passing through
or nearby.

Car parks
Visitors use car parks at
National Trust places entirely
at their own risk. You are
advised to secure your car and
not to leave any valuable items
in it during your visit.

Parking in National Trust car
parks is free for members
displaying current stickers,
although a valid membership
card should always be shown
to a member of staff on
request. Individual members'
stickers cannot be used to
gain free parking for coaches.
Replacement or additional
stickers may be obtained at
our places, please ask at
visitor reception.

Further information to help plan your journey

Transport Direct: plan how to get
there by public transport or car from
any UK location or postcode using
www.transportdirect.info

Sustrans: for NCN routes and cycling
maps visit **www.sustrans.org.uk** or
telephone 0117 929 0888.

Traveline: for bus routes and times for
England, Wales and Scotland visit
www.traveline.info or telephone
0871 200 2233.

National Rail Enquiries: for train times
visit **www.nationalrail.co.uk** or
telephone 08457 484950.

Taxis from railway stations:
www.traintaxi.co.uk

**Public transport in Northern Ireland
(train and bus)**: **www.translink.co.uk**
or telephone 028 9066 6630.

National Trust Holiday Collection

The National Trust has selected a group of leading specialist travel operators to offer a range of holidays with special appeal to members and supporters. Every booking made earns important income for the Trust.

National Trust Holiday Collection

Want to holiday independently, with family and friends, or travel with like-minded people? The National Trust Holiday Collection has holidays to suit all tastes – from its own holiday cottages set in stunning locations in England, Wales and Northern Ireland, to a programme of cruises, escorted tours, activity holidays or short breaks operated by carefully selected tour operators. Enjoy one of these holidays in Britain or further afield, knowing that the Trust will benefit financially from your booking but you pay no more than normal brochure price. Or help the Trust in other ways by joining one of its own working holidays and make new friends while learning about hedge-laying or drystone-walling.

Treat yourself to an exclusive cruise on the 'MV Spirit of Adventure'

National Trust Holiday Cottages Collection

More than 360 unique properties in outstanding locations make up the National Trust's Holiday Cottages Collection. Individual and intriguing, each getaway is furnished traditionally and tastefully to complement period features. By staying with the National Trust, you can look forward to stunning locations and quality accommodation, ideal for celebrating special occasions, escaping from everyday life or simply enjoying heritage at first hand. It's a rewarding experience: whether you holiday in a fisherman's cottage or a lighthouse, a sprawling mansion or a retreat in one of the remotest corners, you'll play a part in our future. Our cottages and apartments serve as an ideal base for main holidays and short breaks – whether it's for two nights or two weeks. For a brochure call 0844 800 2072, quoting ref NTHBK. To book or check availability telephone 0844 800 2070 or visit www.nationaltrustcottages.co.uk

National Trust Cruise Collection

The National Trust Cruise Collection has been specially put together to appeal to National Trust members and supporters and is operated by Spirit of Adventure, a cruise operator known for high standards of service and excellent value for money. The Collection includes three National Trust exclusive cruises on board the intimate 'MV Spirit of Adventure', which offers small ship cruising at its best. In 2010 these unique Trust cruises will include 'Britain and Ireland's Garden Coast', with visits to some of the Trust's outstanding gardens, 'Norway's Choral Symphony' and 'Rivers and Wines of France and Iberia', a cruise organised in conjunction with Waddesdon Manor, which includes on-board wine tasting and visits to leading vineyards.

For more details of these cruises, please call 0800 092 1178, quoting reference NTHBK or visit www.saga.co.uk/nationaltrust

Saga will donate eight per cent of the purchase price of each cruise to the National Trust. This does not affect the price you pay.

National Trust Escorted Tours Collection

These tours are specially selected from Saga's own portfolio of tours to appeal to the interests of National Trust members and supporters. You can travel with like-minded people to enjoy the beauty and cultural heritage of both popular and lesser-known parts of Europe. In 2010 there will also be some unique National Trust tours focusing on art and gardens and linking up with other European heritage organisations.

For more details please telephone 0800 092 1173, quoting reference NTHBK.

Saga will donate eight per cent of the purchase price of each holiday to the National Trust. This does not affect the price you pay.

National Trust Active Holiday Collection

Discover walking and activity holidays that will invigorate, inspire and relax you – holidays where everything is taken care of. HF Holidays offers guide-yourself breaks or you can be accompanied by one of their expert guides every step of the way to stunning backdrops, hidden pathways, new friendships and a nice cup of tea. With more than 300 different holiday ideas to choose from, there is something for everyone. You can go with a partner or you can go alone; whatever you choose to do, you can be sure that you'll come away with new friends.

For a brochure telephone 0845 458 0120 or visit **www.nationaltrust.org.uk/ activeholidays**

HF Holidays will donate £10 to the National Trust for each holiday booked. This does not affect the price you pay.

National Trust Short Break Collection

An award-winning range of European short-break holidays which offer something for everyone, from city breaks to country hideaways and art exhibitions to one-off festivals. This unique collection of short breaks for the independent traveller is operated for the Trust by VFB Holidays, a leading specialist tour operator with 40-years' experience of arranging holidays. With a strong emphasis on cultural-themed breaks and a wide choice of hotels and travel arrangements, the Short Break Collection is sure to inspire you! For a brochure, please telephone 01452 715324, quoting ref: MNT or visit **www.nationaltrust.org.uk/ shortbreaks**

VFB will donate five per cent of the purchase price of each holiday to the National Trust. This does not affect the price you pay.

Lower Pentire Farm, a National Trust holiday cottage, lies at the water's edge at Loe Pool in Cornwall

National Trust European Cottages and Villas Collection

This unique collection of self-catering accommodation includes charming cottages, quaint farmhouses and villas with pools in the most beautiful rural and coastal regions of France, Corsica and the Tuscany region of Italy. The hand-picked portfolio of over 350 properties ranges from a cosy pigeonnier for two, to a chateau in the Loire sleeping sixteen. The cottages and villas in this collection are operated for the Trust by award-winning VFB Holidays, a leading specialist tour operator which first introduced the concept of gîte holidays to the UK market in 1970. For a brochure, please telephone 01452 715326, quoting ref: MNT or visit **www.nationaltrust. org.uk/frenchcottages**

VFB will donate five per cent of the purchase price of each holiday to the National Trust. This does not affect the price you pay.

National Trust Hotel Reservation Service

A reservation service offering a comprehensive range of two- to five-star hotels across Britain, operated for the Trust by leading short-break specialist Superbreak. The wide choice of locations makes it easy to get away and find hotels close to faraway Trust places you've always wanted to visit.

For a brochure telephone 0844 800 2076, quoting reference NTHBK. To book visit **www. nationaltrust.org.uk/hotels**

Superbreak will donate five per cent of the purchase price of each booking to the National Trust. This does not affect the price you pay.

National Trust Working Holidays

The National Trust Working Holidays programme provides great opportunities to make new friends, socialise and work together in a team. You can get away from the day-to-day distractions of modern living to achieve a worthwhile objective and make a significant difference to the preservation of our coast, countryside and historic houses. They are a true learning experience, with activities ranging from hedge laying or drystone walling, to archaeological digs or dragonfly identification.

For those of you who like your home comforts, premium holidays offer en-suite accommodation. Also included are Youth Discovery holidays for sixteen to eighteen year olds. Young people wanting to know more about this or other opportunities should email youth@nationaltrust.org.uk

Each holiday is run by Trust staff and trained volunteer leaders, so experience is not necessary – just plenty of energy and enthusiasm! For a brochure telephone 0844 800 3099, email working.holidays@ nationaltrust.org.uk or to book online visit www.nationaltrust. org.uk/workingholidays

Bed and Breakfast on National Trust Farms, Camping and Caravan Sites

Enjoy some of the best of our countryside and coastal areas by staying with National Trust tenant farmers or at one of our camping and caravan sites. For details visit **www.nationaltrust.org.uk/ holidays** or telephone for a B&B leaflet (0844 800 1895).

Historic House Hotels

Treat yourself to a break at Hartwell House Hotel, Restaurant and Spa near Aylesbury (page 131), Middlethorpe Hall Hotel, Restaurant and Spa in York (page 304) or Bodysgallen Hall Hotel, Restaurant and Spa in North Wales (page 335) – all donated to the Trust in 2008.

Volunteers clearing bracken on a working holiday at Bosigran Farm, Cornwall

Joining in with the Trust

As a charity we rely greatly upon additional support, beyond membership fees, to help us to protect and manage the coastline, countryside, historic buildings and gardens in our care. You can help us in several ways, such as making a donation or considering a gift to the National Trust in your Will, or by volunteering.

Volunteer with us
In the past year more than 55,000 incredible volunteers supported the Trust to achieve so much more with our limited resources. Together they contributed more than three million hours in more than 200 different roles.

We would like you to volunteer with us. There are numerous roles available, from welcoming visitors to a historic house to tackling countryside conservation tasks. Not to mention taking part in a working holiday (see page 380), joining a supporter group (see page 382) or taking part in our employee volunteering programme.

We have a number of opportunities specifically designed for young people, and we are also developing volunteering roles which families can take on together so there really is something for everyone.

By volunteering with us you can: make new friends; gain work experience; use and develop old skills in new environments; see behind the scenes of our beautiful properties and make a difference.

To find out more, contact your local place, telephone 01793 817632 or visit **www.nationaltrust.org.uk/ volunteering** or **www. nationaltrust.org.uk/youth**

Voluntary talks service
The National Trust has a group of enthusiastic and knowledgeable volunteer speakers available to give illustrated talks to groups of all sizes. Talks cover many aspects of the Trust's work, from the Neptune Coastline Campaign to garden history, conservation, individual places and regional round-ups. Talks can also be tailored to meet your group's particular interests. To find out more, contact the Talks Service Co-ordinator at your local National Trust regional or country office (see page 388).

Volunteers putting up a marquee for a fête near Lynmouth, North Devon

Join your local Trust supporter group

Do you want to see, learn and experience more with the National Trust, meet new people and help conserve our wonderful built heritage and natural environment?

As a member or volunteer you can do all of these things by joining a local supporter group.

Tens of thousands of National Trust members and volunteers are members of one of our 200 independent centres and associations. A small subscription enables you to:

– Make new friends and meet like-minded people with an interest in heritage;

– Enjoy a programme of entertaining and enlightening talks;

– Take part in social and fundraising events;

– Go on rambles, day trips, visits and holidays.

Centres and associations also act as a focus for local volunteering: whether it is managing the group as a member of a committee, organising the group's programmes, or directly working on volunteer activities at specific houses and countryside places.

You could also join one of our local Friends and advisory groups, which work in partnership with their 'adoptive' Trust built and countryside places by providing practical assistance and valuable advice.

National Trust Volunteer Groups offer great opportunities to get involved as a volunteer in a more hands-on way. These independent groups of volunteers work with places on conservation and environmental projects.

Get involved with your local supporter group today and enjoy a deeper and more rewarding experience with the National Trust.

To find out more about your local groups, telephone 01793 817636, email sglo@nationaltrust.org.uk, or visit **www. nationaltrust.org.uk/supportergroups**

Donations
You can help us protect the special places in our care by donating to appeals, such as the work to reunite Croome Landscape Garden with Croome Court, which recently came under the care of the National Trust. Or perhaps you would like to give to the ongoing work on the Lake District, or the appeal to save and protect the coastline – the Neptune campaign. All of these appeals and more you will find at **www. nationaltrust.org.uk/ donations** You could support your favourite property by giving a donation and by buying a raffle ticket when you visit.

The Trust organises several programmes to give donors the opportunity to see at first hand the work they support, such as the Benefactor, Patron and Quercus programmes. These include special behind-the-scenes events and the opportunity to talk to Trust experts. To find out more about these programmes and the unique events which come with supporting National Trust email enquiries@nationaltrust. org.uk or telephone 0844 800 1895.

Art Fund
The National Trust is grateful to the Art Fund for its continuing support in the acquisition of historic contents, and warmly welcomes Art Fund members to Trust properties.

Legacies
By making provision for the National Trust with a legacy in your Will, you would be providing a lasting gift for future generations. Every sum, whatever the size, will be put to good use and will make a positive difference to our work across England, Wales and Northern Ireland in permanently safeguarding our natural and built heritage. We guarantee never to use a single penny on administration costs or overheads. Choose too where you would like your gift to be directed – the project, place or region which means most to you.

Find out more by requesting the free colour booklet entitled *Guide to Making and Updating your Will*, available from our Membership Department, or visit us today at **www.nationaltrust.org.uk/legacies**

Your gift is as special to us as the unique places it helps to protect.

The Trust welcomes offers of chattels: works of art, furniture and other objects that may be displayed in a historical setting.

Please contact your nearest regional office with details of the objects and, if possible, with a photograph. Please be aware that many of our properties restrict their acquisitions to objects that have a historical connection to the house in question, in order to maintain the authenticity of the displays. Regrettably, therefore, we may not always be able to accept your offer, regardless of the intrinsic value and interest of the objects.

How you can support the National Trust in the US – join The Royal Oak Foundation

More than 40,000 Americans, including members and donors, belong to The Royal Oak Foundation, the National Trust's membership affiliate in the US. A not-for-profit organisation, The Royal Oak Foundation helps the National Trust, through the generous tax-deductible support of members and friends, by making grants towards its work. Member benefits include National Trust *Handbook*, three editions of *National Trust Magazine* and *The Royal Oak Newsletter*, and free admission to places of the National Trust and of the National Trust for Scotland.

The Royal Oak sponsors lectures, tours and events in the US, designed to inform Americans of the Trust's work, on topics related to UK gardens, country house interior design, art, architecture and social history.

The Royal Oak Foundation, 35 West 35th Street, Suite 1200, New York, NY 10001-2205, USA. Telephone 001 212 480 2889, fax 001 212 785 7234 email general@royal-oak.org website **www.royal-oak.org**

National Trust books, guidebooks, electronic newsletter and prints

National Trust publishes a range of books and guidebooks that promote its work and the great variety of places and collections in its care. To buy any of these books or other titles about National Trust places, please visit the National Trust Bookshop. Details of selected new titles can be found in the members' magazine or online. Visit **www.nationaltrustbooks.co.uk** or telephone 0845 672 0012.

To subscribe to the Trust's free quarterly electronic newsletter, *ABC* (Arts, Building and Conservation), email abc@nationaltrust.org.uk. Past copies of this critically acclaimed publication – full of fascinating material and news – are posted on the Trust's website.

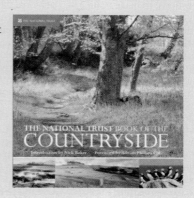

www.ntprints.com is the official decorative print sales website of the National Trust. The collection of images available to purchase vividly illustrates the rich diversity and historical range of properties and collections in the Trust's care, and includes works of fine art, sumptuous interiors and exteriors, gardens and landscapes by some of the country's leading photographers. A range of print sizes and finishes is available, including art paper and canvas, with prices starting at as little as £12.

Have your say

Governance
A guide to the Trust's governance arrangements is available on our website **www.nationaltrust.org.uk** A paper copy is also available on request from the Secretary. Copies of our Annual Report and Accounts are also available; contact our Membership Department for more information or to request a copy.

Annual General Meeting
We believe that it is a crucial part of the governance of any large organisation, such as the Trust, that once a year the members have the chance to meet the officers and senior staff of the organisation at the Annual General Meeting (AGM). It is an opportunity for you to comment and make suggestions, to make your views known to the Trustees and the staff both through questions and through putting forward and debating resolutions of real interest to the organisation.

You will receive the formal papers for our AGM – including voting papers – in the autumn magazine. We hope you will consider attending this year's AGM. However you don't need to come to the meeting to take part. You can listen to the meeting and take part in the debates on our webcast. You can also let us know your views by returning your voting papers – or voting online – ahead of the meeting.

In addition, you have the opportunity to elect members of our Council. The Council is made up of 52 members, 26 elected by you and 26 elected by organisations whose interests coincide in some way with those of the National Trust. This mix of elected and appointed members ensures that the Trust takes full account of the wider interests of the nation for whose benefit it exists. The breadth of experience and perspective which this brings also enables the Council to act as the Trust's conscience in delivering its statutory purposes.

Privacy Policy
The National Trust's Privacy Policy sets out the ways in which the National Trust processes personal data. This Privacy Policy only relates to personal data collected by the National Trust via our website, membership forms, fundraising responses, emails and telephone calls.
The full Privacy Policy is available on our website **www.nationaltrust.org.uk**

The Data Protection Act 1998
The National Trust makes every effort to comply with the principles of the Data Protection Act 1998.

Use made of personal information
Personal information provided to the National Trust via our website, membership forms, fundraising responses, emails and telephone calls will be used for the purposes outlined at the time of collection or registration in accordance with the preferences you express.

Consent
By providing personal data to the National Trust you consent to the processing of such data by the National Trust as described in the full Privacy Policy. You can alter your preferences as follows.

Verifying, updating and amending your personal information
If, at any time, you want to verify, update or amend your personal data or preferences please write to:

National Trust,
Membership Department,
PO Box 39,
Warrington WA5 7WD.

Verification, updating or amendment of personal data will take place within 28 days of receipt of your request.

If subsequently you make a data protection instruction to the National Trust which contradicts a previous instruction (or instructions), then the National Trust will follow your most recent instruction.

Subject access requests
You have the right to ask the National Trust, in writing, for a copy of all the personal data held about you (a 'subject access request') upon payment of a fee of £10. To access your personal data held by the National Trust, please apply in writing to:

The Data Controller,
National Trust,
Heelis, Kemble Drive,
Swindon SN2 2NA.

Your membership

Membership of the National Trust allows you free parking in Trust car parks and free entry to most Trust places open to the public during normal opening times and under normal opening arrangements, provided you can present a current membership card.

Remember to display your car parking sticker.

Please check that you have your card with you before you set out on your journey. Without it, we regret that you may not be admitted free of charge, nor will we subsequently be able to refund any admission charges.

Membership cards are **not transferable**.

If your card is lost or stolen, please contact the Membership Department (address on page 387), telephone 0844 800 1895.

A temporary card can be sent quickly to a holiday address.

In some instances an entry fee may apply. Additional charges may be made:

- when a special event is in progress;

- when we open specially for a National Gardens Scheme open day;

- where the management of a place is not under the National Trust's direct control, for example Tatton Park, Cheshire;

- where special attractions are additional and/or separate elements of the property, for example steam yacht 'Gondola' in Cumbria, Wimpole Hall Home Farm in Cambridgeshire, Dunster Watermill in Somerset, the model farm and museum at Shugborough in Staffordshire and the Tudor Old Hall and farm at Tatton Park in Cheshire;

- where special access conditions apply, for example The Beatles' Childhood Homes in Liverpool, where access is only by minibus from Speke Hall and Liverpool city centre, and all visitors (including Trust members) pay a fare for the minibus journey.

- The National Trust welcomes educational use of its properties. Our Educational Group membership is open to all charitable status education groups whose members are in full-time education. Membership entitles you to free entry to our places providing you book your visit in advance. For full benefits and terms and conditions telephone 0844 800 1895.

- Members wishing to change from one category of life membership to another should contact the Membership Department for the scale of charges.

- Entry to places owned by the Trust but maintained and administered by English Heritage or Cadw (Welsh Historic Monuments) is free to members of the Trust, English Heritage and Cadw.

- Members of the National Trust are also admitted free of charge to properties of the National Trust for Scotland, a separate charity with similar responsibilities. NTS properties include the famous Inverewe Garden, Bannockburn, Culloden and Robert Adam's masterpiece, Culzean Castle. Full details are contained in *The National Trust for Scotland Guide to Properties* (priced £5, including post and packaging), which can be obtained by contacting the NTS Customer Service Centre, telephone 0844 493 2100. Information is also available at **www.nts.org.uk**

- Reciprocal visiting arrangements also exist with certain overseas National Trusts, including Australia, New Zealand, Barbados, Bermuda, Canada, Italy, Jersey and Guernsey. Closer to home there is a reciprocal visiting arrangement in place with the Manx Museum and National Trust on the Isle of Man **(your current membership card is always needed).**

Application for membership

To: National Trust, FREEPOST NAT9775, Warrington WA5 7BR

Membership subscription rates for 2010/11 will be available from 1 March 2010. Please visit www.nationaltrust.org.uk or telephone the Membership Department on 0844 800 1895 for details. 2009/10 rates apply until the end of February 2010.

Twelve-month membership

☐ **Individual** One card for each member.

☐ **Two adults** One card for each member living at the same address.

☐ **Family group** Two adults, living at the same address, and their children or grandchildren under 18. Please give names and dates of birth for all children. Two cards cover the family.

☐ **Family one adult** One adult and his/her children under 18, living at the same address. Please give names and dates of birth for all children. One card covers the family.

☐ **Child** Must be under 13 at time of joining. Please give date of birth.

☐ **Young person** Must be 13 to 25 at time of joining. Please give date of birth.

☐ **Educational Group membership** See page 385. Tel. 0844 800 1895 for details.

Life membership

☐ **Individual** Please note Charities Aid Foundation payments cannot be accepted for individual life membership. One card admits the named member and a guest.

☐ **Joint** For lifetime partners. Two cards, each admitting the named member.

☐ **Family joint** Two adults, living at the same address, and their children or grandchildren under 18. Please give names and dates of birth for all children. Two cards cover the family.

Full address:					
Postcode:			Tel:		
Title	First name	Surname		Date of birth	Value £

'I would like the tax to be reclaimed on any eligible donations or membership subscriptions that I have ever made or will make to the National Trust until further notice. I confirm that I pay an amount of UK income or capital gains tax at least equal to the tax that the National Trust will reclaim.'   *gift aid it* ☐

Amount attached: £
Cheque/postal order
Delete as appropriate
Please allow up to 21 days for receipt of your membership card and new member's pack

Signature: Date:

Credit/debit card/direct debit payments can be made by telephoning 0844 800 1895 (Minicom 0844 800 4410) in office hours, seven days a week. Immediate membership can be obtained by joining at a National Trust place, shop or countryside information point, or you can join online at **www.nationaltrust.org.uk/join**

I am happy to be contacted by the National Trust by email and email newsletters about conservation, membership, fundraising and other activities. My email address is (please print)

National Trust Enterprises also works with carefully selected organisations and we may contact you by email and email newsletter with special offers from them that will benefit the National Trust. Please tick this box if you do want to receive these offers. ☐

The National Trust collects and processes personal information for the purposes of customer analysis and direct marketing so that we can contact you about our conservation, membership, fundraising and other activities. Please tick this box if you would prefer not to hear from the National Trust in this way. ☐

National Trust Enterprises also works with carefully selected organisations and we may contact you with special offers from them that will benefit the National Trust. Please tick this box if you would prefer not to receive these offers. ☐

Getting in touch

The National Trust supports the National Code of Practice for Visitor Attractions.
We are very willing to answer questions and keen to receive comments from members and visitors. Please speak to a member of staff in the first instance. Many properties provide their own comment cards and boxes. All comments will be noted, and action taken where necessary, but it is not possible to answer every comment or suggestion individually.

Enquiries by telephone, email or in writing should be made to the Trust's Membership Department (see below), open seven days a week (9 to 5:30 weekdays, 9 to 4 weekends and bank holidays). Detailed site enquiries, eg accessibility for wheelchairs, should be made to the individual place. Business callers should contact the appropriate regional or country office by telephone (0844 numbers are charged at 5p per minute from BT landlines, charges from mobiles and other operators may vary). You can also obtain information from our website **www.nationaltrust.org.uk**

Central Office
The National Trust and National Trust (Enterprises) Ltd
Heelis, Kemble Drive, Swindon, Wiltshire SN2 2NA.
Tel: 01793 817400
Fax: 01793 817401

National Trust Membership Department
PO Box 39, Warrington WA5 7WD.
Tel: 0844 800 1895
Fax: 0844 800 4642
Minicom: 0844 800 4410
Email: **enquiries@nationaltrust.org.uk** for all general enquiries, including membership and requests for information

National Trust Holiday Cottages
Tel: 0844 800 2072 for brochures
Tel: 0844 800 2070 for reservations

National Trust online

You can find information about all the places in this *Handbook* on our website at **www.nationaltrust.org.uk** Online information is updated on a daily basis. Most properties show additional information about their history and features, to help you make the most of your visit. The website includes information about volunteering and learning opportunities, hiring a venue for corporate or private functions, events and regional news. We also have a dedicated holiday cottages website at **www.nationaltrustcottages.co.uk** and an online gift shop at **www.nationaltrust.org.uk/shop**

For monthly National Trust news, events information, details of things to do and places to visit, updates on our work and suggestions of how you might get involved, sign up for your free email newsletter via **www.nationaltrust.org.uk/email**

This *Handbook* contains email addresses for those properties which can be contacted direct. General email enquiries should be sent to **enquiries@nationaltrust.org.uk**

Regional/country contacts

Devon and Cornwall
(*Devon*)
Killerton House, Broadclyst,
Exeter EX5 3LE
Tel: 01392 881691
Fax: 01392 881954
Email: dc.customerenquiries@
nationaltrust.org.uk

(*Cornwall*)
Lanhydrock, Bodmin PL30 4DE
Tel: 01208 265200
Fax: 01208 265270
Email: dc.customerenquiries@
nationaltrust.org.uk

Wessex
(*Bristol/Bath, Dorset,
Gloucestershire,
Somerset and Wiltshire*)
Eastleigh Court, Bishopstrow,
Warminster,
Wiltshire BA12 9HW
Tel: 01985 843600
Fax: 01985 843624
Email: wx.customerenquiries@
nationaltrust.org.uk

Thames and Solent
(*Berkshire, Buckinghamshire,
Hampshire, part of
Hertfordshire, Isle of Wight,
Greater London and Oxfordshire*)
Hughenden Manor,
High Wycombe,
Bucks HP14 4LA
Tel: 01494 755500
Fax: 01494 463310
Email: ts.customerenquiries@
nationaltrust.org.uk

South East
(*Kent, Surrey, East Sussex and
West Sussex*)
Polesden Lacey, Dorking,
Surrey RH5 6BD
Tel: 01372 453401
Fax: 01372 452023
Email: se.customerenquiries@
nationaltrust.org.uk

East of England
(*Bedfordshire, Cambridgeshire,
Essex, part of Hertfordshire,
Norfolk and Suffolk*)
Westley Bottom, Bury St
Edmunds, Suffolk IP33 3WD
Tel: 01284 747500.
Fax: 01284 747506
Email: ea.customerenquiries@
nationaltrust.org.uk

East Midlands
(*Derbyshire, Leicestershire,
South Lincolnshire,
Northamptonshire,
Nottinghamshire and Rutland*)
Clumber Park Stableyard,
Worksop, Notts S80 3BE
Tel: 01909 486411
Fax: 01909 486377
Email: em.customerenquiries@
nationaltrust.org.uk

West Midlands
(*Birmingham, Herefordshire,
Shropshire, Staffordshire,
Warwickshire and Worcestershire*)
Attingham Park, Shrewsbury,
Shropshire SY4 4TP
Tel: 01743 708100
Fax: 01743 708150
Email: wm.customerenquiries@
nationaltrust.org.uk

North West
(*Cumbria and Lancashire*)
The Hollens, Grasmere,
Ambleside, Cumbria LA22 9QZ
Tel: 015394 35599
Fax: 015394 35353
Email: nw.customerenquiries@
nationaltrust.org.uk

(*Cheshire, Greater Manchester
and Merseyside*)
18 High Street, Altrincham,
Cheshire WA14 1PH
Tel: 0161 928 0075
Fax: 0161 929 6819
Email: nw.customerenquiries@
nationaltrust.org.uk

Yorkshire and North East
(*Yorkshire, Teesside,
North Lincolnshire*)
Goddards, 27 Tadcaster Road,
York YO24 1GG
Tel: 01904 702021
Fax: 01904 771970
Email: yne.customerenquiries@
nationaltrust.org.uk

(*Co. Durham, Newcastle and
Tyneside, Northumberland*)
Scots' Gap, Morpeth,
Northumberland NE61 4EG
Tel: 01670 774691
Fax: 01670 774317
Email: yne.customerenquiries@
nationaltrust.org.uk

Wales
Trinity Square,
Llandudno LL30 2DE
Tel: 01492 860123
Fax: 01492 860233
Email: wa.customerenquiries@
nationaltrust.org.uk

Northern Ireland
Rowallane House, Saintfield,
Ballynahinch,
County Down BT24 7LH
Tel: 028 9751 0721
Fax: 028 9751 1242
Email: ni.customerenquiries@
nationaltrust.org.uk

National Trust for Scotland
Wemyss House,
28 Charlotte Square,
Edinburgh EH2 4ET
Tel: 0131 243 9300
 0844 493 2100 (customer
services)
Email: information@nts.org.uk

National Trust

President
HRH The Prince of Wales

Chairman
Simon Jenkins

Director-General
Dame Fiona Reynolds DBE

The National Trust is a registered charity and is independent of government

For enquiries please write to:
National Trust,
PO Box 39,
Warrington WA5 7WD
telephone 0844 800 1895
(minicom 0844 800 4410)
enquiries@nationaltrust.org.uk
Registered charity no. 205846

To contact the editor email
lucy.peel@nationaltrust.org.uk

© 2010 National Trust

Editor
Lucy Peel

Editorial assistance
Anthony Lambert
Penny Shapland
Wendy Smith

Production
Graham Prichard

Art direction
Craig Robson
Wolff Olins

Supporter relations
Alex Youel

Design
LEVEL Partnership

Database developers
Roger Shapland
Dave Buchanan

Maps
© Blacker Design,
Maps in Minutes™/
Collins Bartholomew
2007

Origination
Zebra
Printed
St Ives, Peterborough

Printed on Charisma Silk
and Cocoon Silk, both
made from 100 per cent
post-consumer waste

NT LDS stock no: 73801/10
ISBN 978-0-7078-0410-1

Index of properties by county/administrative area

Properties with no individual entries are shown in italics.
* Denotes properties shown only on maps.

Northern Ireland

Tourist areas

For information on the properties below, please visit **www.nationaltrust.org.uk** and follow links to the new website.

Isle of Wight

Bembridge and Culver Downs
Borthwood Copse
Chillerton Down
Compton Bay and Downs
Newtown National Nature Reserve
St Catherine's Down
and Knowles Farm
St Helens Duver
The Needles Headland
and Tennyson Down
Ventnor Downs

North Devon

Arlington Court and the National
Trust Carriage Museum
Bideford Bay and Hartland
Dunsland
Heddon Valley
Lundy
Morte Point
Watersmeet

The Lake District

Borrowdale
Arnside and Silverdale
Buttermere Valley
Coniston and Tarn Hows
Derwent Water
Duddon Valley
Ennerdale
Eskdale
Friar's Crag
Grasmere
Great Langdale
Hawkshead and Claife
Little Langdale
Nether Wasdale
Sizergh Castle and Garden
Ullswater and Aira Force
Wasdale
Windermere and Ambleside

Northern Ireland's North Coast

Carrick-a-Rede
Downhill Demense
and Hezlett House
Dunseverick Castle
Giant's Causeway
Murlough Bay and Fair Head
Portstewart Strand and the Bann
Estuary
Rathlin Island
Rough Fort
White Park Bay

Peak District

Derwent Valley
Dovedale National Nature Reserve
Edale Valley
Hope Valley
Ilam Park
Kinder Scout
Longshaw
Marsden Moor
Miller's Dale and Ravenstor
Stanton Moor Edge
The Manifold Valley

Suffolk Coast and Heath

Dunwich Heath: Coastal Centre
and Beach
Kyson Hill
Orford Ness National
Nature Reserve
Pin Mill
Sutton Hoo

Mid and South East Wales

Abergwesyn Common
Berthlwyd
Brecon Beacons
Clytha Park
Henryhd Falls
Lanlay Meadows
Skirrid
Sugar Loaf
The Kymin
Upper Tarell Valley

Property and general index

Properties with no individual entries are shown in italics.
* Denotes properties shown only on maps.